Security and Economy
in the Third World

SECURITY

AND ECONOMY IN

THE THIRD WORLD

·

NICOLE BALL

PRINCETON
UNIVERSITY PRESS

Copyright © 1988 by Princeton University Press

Published by Princeton University Press, 41 William Street,
Princeton, New Jersey 08540
In the United Kingdom: Princeton University Press, Guildford, Surrey

All Rights Reserved

This book has been composed in Linotron Sabon
by G&S Typesetters, Inc.

Clothbound editions of Princeton University Press books are printed on acid-free paper,
and binding materials are chosen for strength and durability. Paperbacks, although
satisfactory for personal collections, are not usually suitable for library rebinding

Printed in the United States of America by Princeton University Press,
Princeton, New Jersey

Designed by Laury A. Egan

Library of Congress Cataloging-in-Publication Data

Ball, Nicole.
Security and economy in the Third World.

Includes index.
1. Armaments—Economic aspects—Developing
countries. I. Title.
HC59.72.D4B35 1988 338.4'76234'091724 88-9875
ISBN 0−691−07782−7 (alk. paper)
ISBN 0−691−02289−5 (pbk.)

For Milton

CONTENTS

CONTENTS

LIST OF FIGURES

LIST OF TABLES

PREFACE

This volume is the result of an international collaborative project funded by the Swedish Agency for Research Cooperation in Developing Countries (SAREC), which examined the role of security expenditure in the development process. SAREC's interest in this project derived in great measure from the conviction of then-Secretary General of SAREC Karl Eric Knutsson, presently with UNICEF, that an attempt should be made to answer the question: Does expenditure in the security sector of Third World countries hinder their development, or does it, as some analysts have suggested, promote the development process?

In addition to the author, who acted as the principal researcher, nine researchers from seven countries contributed to this project. Milton Leitenberg, Visiting Research Associate, Swedish Institute of International Affairs, Stockholm, was the research director. Case studies of specific Third World countries were prepared by Carlos Portales and Augusto Varas, Facultad Latinamericana de Ciencias Sociales, Santiago (Chile); José A. Encinas del Pando, University of Lima (Peru); Mario Carranza (Argentina); Ann Schulz, Clark University, Worcester, Mass. (Iran); and J. 'Bayo Adekanye, University of Ibadan (Nigeria). A special study of the connection between security expenditure and the external orientation of Third World economies was funded by the Berghof Stiftung für Konfliktforschung and carried out by Michael Brzoska, with the collaboration of Peter Lock, both of the University of Hamburg. Portions of the case studies of Chile, Argentina, and Peru were published in *Ibero Americano* 12 (1983): 1–2 and a revised version of the Iranian study is being published by Westview Press. The results of the West German report were published in *Development and Peace 5* (Autumn 1984).

The Swedish Institute of International Affairs provided the author with research facilities for the duration of the project. The Johnson Foundation, Racine, Wisconsin, made its facilities at Wingspread available to the researchers for a preparatory meeting in September 1980. The Nordiska Samarbetskommittén provided the author with a small grant to facilitate the publication of a data compendium, an earlier product of the project. The Swedish Ministry for Foreign Affairs provided a second small grant for work on the economic effects of security expenditure, the results of which have been incorporated into the present manuscript. The late Cecilia Molander, who was for a time the project's case officer at SAREC, provided much appreciated support at crucial periods in the project's existence and was, along with Karl Eric Knutsson, one of the few people in Sweden who appreciated the value of this research.

The present volume has benefited from the comments of Milton Leitenberg, Ann Schulz, Stefan de Vylder, Peter Fraser, and Michael Brzoska. The author is particularly indebted to the latter who carefully read each chapter, made provocative but stimulating suggestions, and gave much encouragement. The manuscript was typed by Elsa Vingren. Graphics were produced by Jeremy Chatzky.

Portions of Chapter 1 were previously published in *The Military in the Development Process: A Guide to Issues* (Claremont, Calif.: Regina Books, 1982). Portions of Chapter 3 first appeared in *Third-World Security Expenditure: A Statistical Compendium* (Stockholm: National Defence Research Institute, 1984) and in "Measuring Third World Security Expenditure: A Research Note," *World Development* 12 (February 1984): 157–64. Portions of Chapter 4 were published in "Defense and Development: A Critique of the Benoit Study," *Economic Development and Cultural Change* 31 (April 1983): 507–24 (©1983 by the University of Chicago), and "Defense Expenditure and Economic Growth: A Comment," *Armed Forces and Society* 11 (Winter 1985): 291–97.

Finally, special mention must be made of the role played by the project's research director, Milton Leitenberg. The project as a whole and the writing of this book have benefited at every stage from his involvement and support, and it is to him that this volume is dedicated.

October 1987
Washington, D.C.

INTRODUCTION

The first objectives of development are to reduce poverty and ensure an adequate standard of living for all members of society. This involves meeting basic material needs such as those for food, housing, education, and health and medical care, as well as certain nonmaterial requirements such as the ability to participate in economic and political decisions affecting the course of one's life. Economic growth is a necessary but by no means sufficient condition for setting in motion the development process. In the 1950s and 1960s, however, the development process was, more often than not, thought to consist essentially of identifying and overcoming obstacles to growth: shortages of capital, inadequate supplies of foreign exchange, too little skilled manpower, low levels of technology, and a lack of management and administrative personnel. This model "had a powerful grip on the imagination of policy makers, planners and aid officials,"[1] and it strongly influenced the development policies of the industrialized countries.

By the end of the 1960s, however, it was clear that high rates of economic growth did not guarantee an end to poverty and inequality in the Third World and that development was more than just a technical problem to solve by applying the appropriate inputs. Structural changes of both an economic and political nature are necessary if development that benefits all groups in society is to be implemented. Although it is common to speak of "the third world" and there are many broad similarities among the individual economies in Asia, Latin America, Africa, and the Middle East, developing countries also differ from each other in significant respects. Thus, a factor which might constrain growth in one country may be much less important in another. Nonetheless, it is possible to enumerate those features of Third World economies and political systems that have acted as the most serious constraints on development during the post–World War II period.

Chief among the economic factors are the concentration of wealth and the related bias against rural areas and the agricultural sector in favor of

[1] Paul Streeten, "Development Ideas in Historical Perspective," p. 27, in *Toward a New Strategy for Development: A Rothko Chapel Colloquium*, Albert O. Hirschman et al., (New York: Pergamon Press, 1979). For a sampling of the literature on development written between 1950 and 1980, see Nicole Ball, *World Hunger: A Guide to the Economic and Political Dimensions* (Santa Barbara, Calif.: ABC Clio, 1981), pp. 21–40.

urban areas and the industrial sector. The Third World has generally suffered from poor policy implementation, in part derived from the low quality of management in the public sector and in part from restricted access to education. Entrepreneurship has been weak, and multinational corporations have frequently wielded considerable power within individual economies. Jobs—particularly those in the rural sector—have been characterized by low pay and low productivity.

Domestic production has been oriented toward the export market, which implies a failure to produce for local consumption. There has been considerable export concentration and substantial reliance on traditional exports of raw materials. Markets for traditional products have frequently stagnated while nontraditional goods have increasingly run afoul of protectionism in the industrialized countries. The latter have seen Third World countries as markets for, rather than sources of, manufactured goods. Indeed, developing economies retain their heavy reliance on imports from the more industrialized world. This has increased the pressure to produce for export, particularly in view of the tendency of the terms of trade between industrialized and developing countries to stagnate or even decline for large periods of time during the post–World War II period. For various reasons, some of which will be explored in this volume, Third World producers have tended to use technology ill-suited to the factor endowments of, or climatic and social conditions in, individual countries. High levels of debt have been one of the most serious outcomes of these conditions, and all the problems enumerated here have been exacerbated by this indebtedness.

The characteristics of Third World political systems that have militated against development include the absence of participatory government, political and administrative centralization, bureaucratization, and corruption. There has also tended to be an inability to resolve conflicts among groups with different ethnic or religious backgrounds. The interaction of these factors has all too often led to an unwillingness on the part of Third World governments to take politically contentious decisions in certain economically important areas such as land reform and taxation.

One constraining factor seldom mentioned by development analysts is expenditure in the security sector.[2] Security spending is widely believed to dampen or distort economic growth and development by exacerbating many of the economic and political imbalances described above. By com-

---

[2] The terms "security sector" and "security expenditure" are used in preference to the more commonly employed "military sector" and "military expenditure" to indicate the inclusion of paramilitary forces in the discussion. This usage also reflects the fact that Third World governments frequently use their armed forces to maintain themselves in power, that is, to promote regime security.

peting with rural development and social programs for scarce governmental funds, for example, security expenditure may contribute to both
urban bias and shortages of skilled manpower and administrative personnel. By purchasing weapons from abroad, the armed forces may increase
a country's debt burden and its export orientation. And in creating a domestic arms industry, tendencies toward capital-intensive production and
a reliance on imports can be strengthened. In its most detailed report on
the relationship between disarmament and development, the United Nations stated the case against security expenditure in the following terms:

> The continuing arms race will impede the world-wide prospects
> of economic growth and delay the developmental process with se-
> rious socio-economic consequences, particularly for the developing
> countries. . . .
> Economic growth and developmental processes are closely interre-
> lated as speedier economic growth can improve the developmental
> prospects. But in assessing the impact of the arms race on both it is
> helpful to maintain the distinction largely because, in simple terms,
> economic growth is described as increases in real income *per capita*
> and this implies more production, higher income and more con-
> sumption. Development, on the other hand, implies not only the
> existence of economic growth but also changes in the structure of
> demand, supply and income distribution patterns, changes in socio-
> political institutions and the improvement of material welfare. As
> some of our studies have shown, military expenditures have deleteri-
> ous effects on these macroeconomic variables and, therefore, hinder,
> to say the least, the pace of economic growth and development. . . .[3]

There are good prima facie reasons for focusing on security expenditure. Global outlays in the security sector have risen sharply in real
terms over the last three decades. The U.S. Arms Control and Disarmament Agency (ACDA) has estimated that between 1963 and 1983 security
expenditure for the Third World (measured in 1982 U.S. dollars) grew
from $53 billion to $163 billion while SIPRI data show that its share of
security expenditure tripled between 1950 and 1981 (Figures I-1 and I-2).
With a few exceptions the trend has been continuously rising. In the early
1970s, the rate of increase was quite rapid.[4] That ever larger amounts of

[3] United Nations, General Assembly, *Study on the Relationship between Disarmament
and Development, Report of the Secretary-General*, A/36/356, 5 October 1981, p. 78.

[4] It is important to remember that the industrialized countries still account for over three-
quarters of all expenditure on the armed forces. In 1984, SIPRI figures show that the United
States and the USSR alone accounted for some 52 percent of global security expenditure.
Stockholm International Peace Research Institute, *World Armaments and Disarmament,
SIPRI Yearbook, 1985* (London: Taylor & Francis, 1985).

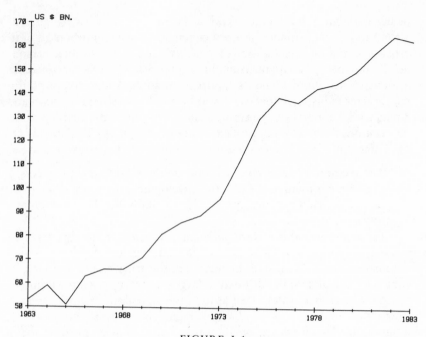

FIGURE I-1

Third World Military Expenditure, 1963–1983, U.S. $ bn., 1982 prices

Source: Calculated from various issues of U.S. Arms Control and Disarmament Agency, *World Military Expenditures and Arms Transfers* (Washington, D.C.: ACDA, 1963– 1983).

the Third World's resources are absorbed by the security sector is obvious; however, the effect of this allocation of resources on economic growth and development is unclear. The first step in understanding the relationship between these factors is to place the expenditure figures in their proper context.

First, one must ask how this expenditure is distributed within the Third World. Although the developing countries as a group have increased their share of global security expenditure, not all Third World countries have increased their expenditure at the same rate. Table I-1 shows that China, especially in the 1960s, and the Middle East, especially in the 1970s, have accounted for a disproportionately large share of the growth in Third World security spending; together they have been responsible for well over half of the expenditure of the developing countries. The remainder

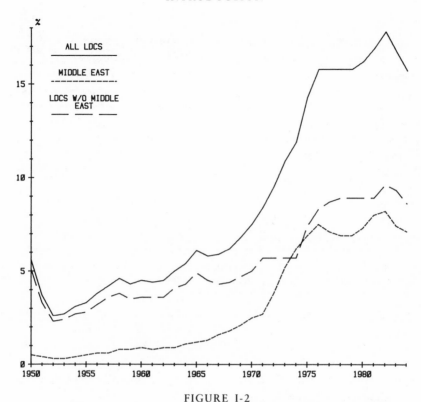

FIGURE I-2
Third World Share in Global Military Expenditure, 1950–1984

Source: Stockholm International Peace Research Institute, *World Armaments and Disarmament. SIPRI Yearbook* (Stockholm: Almqvist & Wiksell and London: Taylor & Francis, various years).

of the Third World has never accounted for more than 10 percent of global security expenditure.

The increase in security expenditure has also been distributed unequally within regions. This is particularly true for Africa, where much of the increase registered since the beginning of the 1970s can be attributed to a relatively limited number of countries. The Ghanaian political scientist, Eboe Hutchful, has commented: "Currently the continent is divided into a small group of relatively well-armed countries (South Africa, Egypt, Libya, Algeria, Morocco, Ethiopia, and Nigeria) and a much larger group of countries whose military forces and armaments levels are no more

TABLE I-1
Share of Third World in Global Security Expenditure, According to Regions, 1950–1984 (in percentages)

Region/Country	1950	1955	1960	1965	1970	1975	1980	1984
Middle East[a]	0.5	0.5	0.9	1.2	2.5	6.9	7.3	7.1
China	5.0	2.9	5.7	8.8	10.3	7.3	7.6	5.6
Far East[b]	2.0	0.8	1.3	1.6	1.8	2.1	3.0	3.1
South Asia	1.2	0.7	0.7	1.2	1.0	1.0	1.2	1.3
Africa[c]	0.1	0.1	0.2	0.7	0.9	2.3	2.5	1.7
South America	1.3	1.0	1.1	1.1	1.1	1.7	1.8	2.0
Central America	0.5	0.2	0.3	0.3	0.3	0.3	0.4	0.5
All Developing	10.6	6.2	10.2	14.9	17.9	21.6	23.8	21.3

Source: Stockholm International Peace Research Institute, *World Armaments and Disarmament sipri Yearbook, 1972, 1976, 1979, 1982, 1985* (Stockholm: Almqvist & Wiksell, 1972, 1976) and (London: Taylor & Francis, 1979, 1982, 1985).
[a] Includes Egypt.
[b] Excludes China.
[c] Excludes Egypt.

than adequate for the purposes of legitimate territorial defence (in many cases less than adequate)."[5]

Second, when evaluating the growth of security expenditure and its impact on Third World economies one must consider why outlays in this sector have increased, both in absolute terms and as a share of global expenditure. Because the determinants of security expenditure will be examined in detail in Chapter 2, it is only necessary here to point out that there are several reasons for assuming that *some* natural growth should have taken place in developing country security outlays during the last two or three decades. Approximately two-thirds of the countries now in existence became independent after 1950. Moreover, many developing countries, particularly those that did not have to fight to gain their freedom, had virtually no indigenous armed forces at independence. Finally, contributing to the rise in the Third World's share of security expenditure, although not necessarily to the growth of global outlays for security purposes, are both the decline in security assistance provided by the ma-

[5] Eboe Hutchful, "Disarmament and Development: An African View," *IDS Bulletin* 16:4 (October 1985):62. See also Robin Luckham, "Militarization in Africa," in sipri, *World Armaments and Disarmament, 1985,* p. 295.

jor powers and the shift from grant aid to loans begun in the late 1960s.

One should neither take the foregoing to suggest that Third World countries would experience no ill effects from future increases in security-related expenditure or that such expenditure has, to date, had no effect on their growth and development. Nor should one assume that simply because the Middle East and China have been responsible for a large portion of the growth of the Third World's share in security expenditure that the security-related outlays in other parts of the Third World can safely be ignored.[6] The share of the Third World in security spending is not a particularly good guide to these outlays' effect on economic growth and development for either the Third World as a whole or individual countries. The amount of its own resources each government chooses to devote to the security sector is a much better, although by no means perfect, indicator of such expenditures' impact.

The importance of identifying the appropriate level of measurement in determining how burdensome security expenditure is for particular countries is illustrated by the case of South Asia. Together, Pakistan, India, Bangladesh, and Sri Lanka accounted for just under 1 percent of global expenditures in the security sector in 1983. Compared to Sweden, Finland, Norway, and Denmark, which also accounted for just under 1 percent of global security expenditure in 1983, that figure may not appear excessive, particularly when one considers the difference in population (22 million for the Scandinavian countries; 936 million for the countries in the subcontinent) and area (1.2 million square kilometers versus 4.3 million square kilometers). In terms of assessing the economic burden of security expenditure, however, these figures indicate very little.

Somewhat more information can be derived from the share of central government expenditure (CGE) and gross domestic product (GDP) devoted to state security budgets. Since independence both the Indian and the Pakistani governments have consistently allocated a comparatively high proportion of their available resources to the security sector. In the 1951–1979 period, the security-related outlays of the Indian central government averaged 25 percent of CGE; they fell below 20 percent for the first time in 1977. Since 1963, India has spent between 3 and 5 percent of its gross product in the security sector. (It is important to note that the figures for India understate actual outlays by some unknown amount because India exchanges weapons and weapon production technology from

[6]This is, however, exactly what is implied in an article by Swadesh Rana, an Indian national who has been employed by the UN Centre for Disarmament. Swadesh Rana, "Sluta moralisera över vår upprustning!" ["Stop Moralizing About our Armament Policies!"] Rapport från SIDA no. 8 (1981):24.

the Comecon countries directly for goods produced in India without recording these transactions in its budget.) Between 1960 and 1979, the Pakistani government spent on average 29.5 percent of its CGE and 5.4 percent of its GNP in the security sector. The figures for Bangladesh have been lower, but they are still significant for a country with severe resource constraints. Only Sri Lanka gave relatively low priority to the security sector up to 1979.[7]

It is likely that a country consistently spending 25 percent of its budget, or 5 to 10 percent of its gross product, in the security sector will experience more pronounced effects—whether positive or negative—than one allocating a much smaller proportion of its resources to the armed forces. But even knowing these percentages does not give a sufficiently clear idea of the impact security-related outlays may have on the development process. To achieve that understanding it is necessary to examine in some detail the relationship between the security sector and the economy. Analysis must be directed in the first instance toward discovering whether the hypothesized effects actually exist in individual countries and then toward evaluating their overall influence. (The absence of a negative effect does not indicate the presence of a positive one and vice versa.) A country which, for example, has a very small military industrial sector may well avoid many problems anticipated from the bias toward highly sophisticated, capital-intensive technology associated with military industrialization, but it can also expect few advantages in the form of manpower training or backward linkages to the civil sector.

Finally, crucial to the correct evaluation of security-related outlays in their development context are power and politics. The more influence any societal group has over the formulation of governmental policies, the more likely it is to benefit from the implementation of those policies. The fact that power in the Third World tends to be highly concentrated has had important consequences for both the direction that development policies have taken and the outcome of the development process for the majority of the people in the Third World. Third World armed forces have increasingly become one of the main groups, sometimes essentially the only group, controlling state policy formulation. (In terms of policy *implementation,* the armed forces, like civilian politicians, must always

---

[7] Nicole Ball, *Third-World Security Expenditure: A Statistical Compendium,* C-10250-M5 (Stockholm: National Defence Research Institute, May 1984), pp. 55, 66, 84, and 101. As a result of the deterioration of the domestic political situation in Sri Lanka since 1983, security expenditure as a share of CGE, which had averaged 3.6 percent between 1975 and 1983, rose to 4.9 percent in 1984 and was estimated to have reached 5.6 percent in 1985 and 9.4 percent in 1986. See *Estimates of the Revenue and Expenditure of the Government of the Democratic Socialist Republic of Sri Lanka for the Fiscal Year, 1st January, 1986 to 31st December 1986,* Vol. I (Colombo: 1986).

share the responsibility with the civilian bureaucracy since they simply lack the manpower to staff all administrative posts.) Thus, military involvement in politics has meant less participation in government for the general public.

It is rather more difficult than one might think to categorize countries according to the degree of military involvement in the political process. Nonetheless, one can say that approximately half the countries in Asia, Africa, Latin America, and the Middle East have experienced periods of direct military rule since the end of World War II. However, the number of countries directly ruled by the military at any given time varies considerably. Latin America offers an interesting example in this respect. Since the end of the colonial period authoritarian rule based, either directly or indirectly, on the armed forces has been the norm in the region. Since 1945, only four countries (Guyana, Mexico, Costa Rica, and Belize) have not been ruled directly by the armed forces. In 1954, twelve of the twenty countries in the region were under direct military rule, but by mid-1961 only one country was governed by the armed forces. Between 1962 and 1964, there were seven coups, and by 1975 military juntas had once again taken over power in twelve countries. Ten years later, just three Latin American governments were directly controlled by the military.[8]

The influence of Third World militaries over governments cannot, however, be measured solely by the number of governments directly controlled by the armed forces as the line between "military governments" and "governments heavily dependent on and influenced by the military" is not always distinct. In many countries that have experienced military rule, and particularly those in which the military has governed for long periods of time, civilian governments may have very little room for maneuver. They are aware that if they follow policies opposed by the armed forces, they run a considerable risk of being overthrown in a military coup. In other countries, the civilian leadership is often composed of military officers who have taken off their uniforms and transformed their military governments and movements into civilian governments and parties; this change is primarily cosmetic. The same people tend to remain in power, and the armed forces continue to be important and active participants in policymaking. This pattern is frequently followed by those who wish to institutionalize a role for the armed forces in the political system. In this case, it is not even necessary for the military to intervene when problems arise. The military government can simply be reconstituted by decree.

[8] Edwin Lieuwen, *Generals vs. Presidents: Neomilitarism in Latin America* (New York: Praeger, 1964), pp. 4–5, and *Europa Year Book 1985: A World Survey,* Vols. I and II (London: Europa Publications, 1985).

Political theorists, particularly those in the Western industrialized countries, tend to assume that governments are controlled by civilians and that the influence of the armed forces is limited to their supposed area of expertise, the defense of the country. Military rule is viewed as an aberration. In many parts of the Third World, however, military rule—both direct and indirect—has been the dominant form of government for much of the postindependence period. Although the armed forces in individual countries may have more influence during one period than during another, the trend for the developing world as a whole has been one of increased political power for the military. Attempts to institutionalize military rule have been made in many countries, with varying degrees of success.

Although many Third World governments have devoted relatively large sums to the security sector, Third World armed forces have increased their participation in the political system. And although a number of theories have been proposed to describe the relationship between the security sector and economic growth and development, the role of this sector has remained curiously peripheral to the post–World War II debates on development strategy.[9] It is true that security expenditure, just one ele-

---

[9] Two excellent reviews of the most important literature on development published between the early 1950s and the mid-1970s include no discussion of the role of the security sector whatsoever. See A. F. Ewing, "Some Recent Contributions to the Literature on Economic Development," *The Journal of Modern African Studies* 4:3 (1966): 335–48, and Arthur Ewing and Gloria-Veronica Koch, "Some Recent Literature on Development," *The Journal of Modern African Studies* 15:3 (1977): 457–80. Similarly, a survey of the main themes of development thinking during the twentieth century (mostly the last three decades) by a researcher known to be interested in the role of the military sector in development also finds a good deal to say about inequalities among and within nations but nothing to say about the contribution of the security sector to these inequalities. See Björn Hettne, *Development Theory and the Third World*, SAREC Report R21:1982 (Stockholm: Swedish Agency for Research Cooperation with Developing Countries, 1982).

Although some of the more recent literature on development does include a consideration of the role of the military, it still seems to depend very much on the individual author whether the security sector will be deemed sufficiently important to be singled out for special attention. In, for example, Hirschman et al., *Toward a New Strategy*, the chapter by Minhas entitled "The Current Development Debate," pp. 75–96, includes no discussion of the role of the armed forces. The chapter by Ohlin, "Development in Retrospect," pp. 125–43, argues that "The prominence of the military in the developing countries deserves more than passing attention, not only because it is important for its own sake but also for what it reveals about the fundamental constraints within which the political process operates in the Third World" (p. 128). Reviewing three recent books about Third World development in August 1983, Carl Marcy stated: One aspect of the problems that the third world faces that does not receive significant attention in any of these books is the effect of military expenditures on development." Carl Marcy, "Future of the Third World," *The New York Times Book Review*, 21 August 1983, pp. 11, 22.

ment in the complex process of generating economic growth and development, is of only marginal importance in some countries in determining
development outcomes. In other countries, however, it is far more important. To some extent the failure to incorporate security considerations
into analyses of developmental problems reflects the general difficulty in
obtaining data about the security sector: very few countries in any part of
the world and at any stage of development are generous with security-
related information. It also, however, reflects a lack of interest on the part
of those who may be in a position to generate some data or undertake a
serious examination of various aspects of the armed forces' economic impact in the Third World.[10] Perhaps worse, it reflects a failure to use existing studies and information as a rich source of material for evaluating the
role that the security sector has played in the past and continues to play in
the development process.

This volume seeks to incorporate the security sector into the debate on
the development process in the Third World. To this end, the interaction
between security expenditure and a number of the major developmental
issues discussed since the end of World War II is examined with a view to
describing the different forms the security expenditure–growth and development relationship can be expected to take. Part I reviews some of
the basic theoretical, empirical, and methodological issues relating to security expenditure itself. Chapter 1 describes the two main schools of
thought concerning the developmental role of the security sector—the
military-as-modernizer and the military-as-promoter-of-underdevelop-
ment—and identifies their weaknesses and strengths. It shows that both
sets of theories fail to evaluate the role that the security sector plays in
promoting or hindering development in a satisfactory manner. Rather, it
is necessary to examine each country over a period of years and determine if, when, and to what extent each anticipated effect has operated,
since actual outcomes frequently differ significantly from hypothesized
consequences. Chapter 2 examines the determinants of security expenditure by focusing on several elements: the influence of external conflicts,
the requirements of internal (regime) security, domestic bureaucratic and
budgetary factors, the influence of the armed forces themselves, and the
role of the major powers. Chapter 2 also considers the extent to which
expenditures in the security sector actually protect countries against

---

[10] Between the end of the Korean War and 1983, South Korea received about half again
as much military assistance from the United States as it had received in the form of economic assistance, some $8 billion. Yet a major study of the effect of external resources on
the Korean economy, which dealt both with foreign investment and economic assistance,
did not once mention military aid. See Chapter 7.

externally and internally generated threats. Chapter 3 describes the problems associated with the measurement of security expenditure. It demonstrates that the data produced by the major sources of security expenditure are often not very reliable and that important sums of money allocated by Third World governments for security-related purposes can be and are being hidden from public scrutiny. Chapter 4 questions the applicability of macrostatistical analyses to evaluations of the relationship between security spending and development. Some of the general constraints on regression analyses are discussed, and the shortcomings of several major econometric studies of the security expenditure–growth and development relationship are explained.

Part II examines the relationship between security expenditure and economic growth and development. Chapter 5 considers the ways in which security expenditure affects the availability of resources by evaluating the hypotheses that security expenditure reduces savings and investment rates, contributes to trade imbalances, and increases indebtedness and inflation; in addition, it considers the possibility that the desire to increase outlays on state or regime security induces governments to strengthen their taxation systems. Chapter 6 looks at the role the security sector plays in promoting and hindering effective use of resources by Third World economies. This chapter covers stimulation of aggregate demand, influence over the nature of investment undertaken, and the effect on absorptive capacity.

Chapter 7 discusses security assistance which, despite its volume, has more often than not been neglected in examinations of the role played by foreign capital inflows in the development process. This chapter also evaluates the potential development-promoting effects of both military aid and the security-related portions of economic aid. Chapter 8 examines the arguments that the armed forces provide their personnel with skills transferable to the civil economy upon discharge from the services and that security expenditure increases employment opportunities in developing countries. They show that, although positive effects do exist, the claims of benefits to the civil sector have generally been overstated. Chapter 9 critically appraises the contention that the creation of military industries stimulates the industrialization process in Third World countries through purchases from domestic industry, the transfer of technology, foreign exchange savings generated by reduced weapon procurement from abroad, and manpower training. It demonstrates that Third World countries have considerable difficulty in attaining these economic objectives.

This volume does not seek to produce a general theory of the developmental role of security expenditure. Rather, its purpose is to provide a framework within which the effect of security expenditure on economic growth and development can be analyzed and to illuminate the multi-faceted nature of the security expenditure–growth and development relationship. It is also hoped the volume will help generate interest in the developmental role of the security sector within the development community.

PART I

Security Expenditure: Theoretical, Empirical, and Methodological Issues

1

THE MILITARY IN DEVELOPMENT:
THE CLASH BETWEEN THEORY
AND FACT

While mainstream development economists have tended to discount the role of the security sector in Third World development, other analysts have presented theories about the ways in which the security sector influences economic and political development, for both good and ill. As is often the case in the social sciences, however, the development of theoretical constructs has tended to take precedence over the search for facts. In some instances, the general propositions set forward—meant to apply to all countries—have been built on a very narrow empirical base. In other cases, the empirical evidence is stronger, but important gaps continue to exist. The early theorizing, which grew out of the decolonization process and the concomitant expansion of interest in the countries of Asia, Africa, Latin America, and the Middle East, was dominated by Westerners, primarily Americans. Even Soviet thinking on the political role of Third World armed forces was influenced by U.S. theorists.[1]

[1] Charles C. Petersen, *Third World Military Elites in Soviet Perspective*, Professional Paper 262 (Alexandria, Va.: Center for Naval Analyses, November 1979). Prior to the mid-1960s, the official Soviet view was that the armed forces in Third World countries were subordinate to and always reflected the political orientation of the ruling group, irrespective of whether that group were "bourgeois" or "socialist." Following the ouster of "socialist" Nkrumah in Ghana by "reactionary" military officers in 1966, the Soviet official line underwent a radical revision since it had become obvious that ideological differences could exist between the ruling group and the armed forces. Up to the late 1960s, Soviet writers argued that whereas civilians in Third World societies might fall prey to class, tribal, regional, and ideological antagonisms which would undermine the stability of the government, members of the armed forces—"'bound together by strict discipline', and the sense of belonging to a 'formally established organization'"—were more likely to be unified (p. 10). They thus "'frequently prove to be the best-organized force in public life,'" a statement which any reader of Guy Pauker, "Southeast Asia as a Problem Area in the Next Decade," *World Politics* 11 (April 1959): 325–345, would instantly recognize.

Once military officers with a more progressive orientation began to take power in the

In the first two post–World War II decades, hard data on Third World security sectors—level of expenditure, size of armed forces, and so on—were extremely limited. The first social scientists to explore the ways in which the security sector influences the development process were political theorists primarily concerned to establish the role of the armed forces in political development in the Third World, and, as such, the relative lack of expenditure data did not seriously hamper their consideration of the issue. Problematic, however, was their display of surprisingly little interest in information available on the political role of the armed forces in those Latin American, African, and Asian countries that had attained independence prior to World War II.

Beginning in 1964 with the publications of the U.S. Arms Control and Disarmament Agency (ACDA), more statistical data began to become available. The Stockholm International Peace Research Institute (SIPRI) started publishing its world military expenditure series in the late 1960s, and the IMF published its first military budget data in the mid–1970s.[2] Although important to have data on security expenditure as accurate as possible, the interactions between military, society, and economy are most vital to understanding the security sector's influence on the development process; they help us evaluate the accuracy of existing theories of the relationship between the security sector and economic growth and development. An increasing amount of information on just these interactions has become available through case studies, and in recent years Third World scholars have made a growing contribution to this literature.

The body of knowledge that can be drawn upon to test and further de-

---

Third World in the late 1960s and the early 1970s, writers expressing the official Soviet line ceased to speak of creating (civilian) vanguard parties and started to discuss the benefits of military rule more openly. One Soviet writer went so far as to call the army the "vanguard of the nation" with not only "military, political and administrative-police functions, but also important national-economic, ideological and educational functions" (p. 20). By the late 1970s, there was once again "an emphasis on the need for vanguard parties in the popular press and in other texts which may be presumed to bear the Soviet Government's imprimatur" (p. 33). Despite this, Petersen argues that the Soviet leadership accepts the fact that Third World armed forces will continue to play an important political role for some time to come. See also, Francis Fukuyama, "Gorbachev and the Third World," *Foreign Affairs* 64 (Spring 1986): 715–31.

[2] ACDA provides data from 1960, SIPRI from 1950, and the IMF from the late 1960s. The main source before ACDA and SIPRI began to collect data was the United Nations *Statistical Yearbook*. The data in this publication are rather patchy and of unknown reliability. The International Institute of Strategic Studies also began to collect military expenditure data in the 1960s. Their coverage of the Third World was initially quite limited, and their data are believed to cover only budget estimates, not actual expenditure, and are thus less reliable than ACDA, SIPRI, or IMF figures.

velop theories of the politico-economic role of Third World security sectors has thus expanded considerably over the last twenty years. That fact alone, however, has been insufficient to ensure either that all relevant experiences and data will actually be incorporated into theories or that existing theories will be revised in the light of new information. To a large extent this relative divorce between fact and theory has arisen because the theories produced to describe the political and economic roles of the security sector reflect the main ideological divisions of the last forty years.

Liberals and conservatives have judged Third World security sectors in terms of their success or failure in assisting the development of externally oriented market economies, equated with "modernization" and taken as the goal of development. Those on the political left have argued that organized force has been crucial to the development and maintenance of the world capitalist system. Because of its importance in integrating Third World areas into the capitalist economic system, the security sector is seen as a major cause of underdevelopment.

MILITARY AS MODERNIZER

The first major theory developed to explain the role of the armed forces and security expenditure in the economic and political systems of Third World countries was firmly rooted in the mainstream of 1950s and 1960s development thinking, focusing on the ways in which the military could contribute to modernization. A modernizing country sought to set in motion "urban-based industrial development, aided by foreign finance and technical know-how."[3] The assumed goal of all developing countries was to pattern their economies, as well as their political systems, after those in the industrialized West. More important, theorists hoped that the process of modernization would lead Third World governments to align themselves politically with the Western countries and stand firm against the "Communist threat."

Political theorists focused their attention on the role the security sector could play in the modernization process partly because coups d'état were occurring more and more frequently in the Third World and partly because Western governments exhibited interest in the topic.[4] Among the major powers, the United States government stood to benefit most from the growth of a body of evidence that would justify the expansion

[3] Bagicha S. Minhas, "The Current Development Debate," p. 81, in *Toward A New Strategy for Development. A Rothko Chapel Colloquium*, Albert O. Hirschman et al. contributors (New York: Pergamon Press, 1979).

[4] Ulrich Albrecht, Dieter Ernst, Peter Lock, and Herbert Wulf, "Armaments and Underdevelopment," *Bulletin of Peace Proposals*, no. 2 (1974): 179.

of military aid to the Third World. (The security-related orientation of early U.S. economic assistance programs is discussed in Chapter 7.) Although much early academic literature on the role of the military in the development process couched its arguments in terms of the benefits to be derived by developing countries from military involvement in government, it is clear that of major importance to Western governments was managing Third World social change in a manner consistent with Western strategic, economic, and political interests.

Despite a tendency when discussing the development theories current in the 1950s and 1960s to speak of *the* "mainstream" or "traditional" theory, that really is an oversimplification. Just what constitutes a successful development policy has been debated continuously over the last forty years. Paul Streeten, for example, has characterized "the early days of development economics" as "a time of intellectual pioneering, of considerable excitement, of the opening of new geographical and intellectual frontiers, of optimism and confidence." Even so, many development theorists and practitioners focused on capital formation as the crucial component in the development process and on industry as the leading sector.[5]

The availability of sufficient supplies of foreign exchange was also viewed as very important since so many goods required in the industrialization process would have to be imported. As shown in Chapter 7, inflows of foreign aid were to alleviate shortages of foreign exchange. Aid was to be focused initially on those social groups identified, by the aid donors, as most likely to use it efficiently ("modernizing élites"). These were the wealthy and powerful in the agricultural and urban-industrial sectors. Theorists argued that the economic growth generated

[5] Paul Streeten, "Development Ideas in Historical Perspective," p. 25, in Hirschman et al., *Toward a New Strategy for Development.*
David Cole and Princeton Lyman have commented:

Economists (perhaps even more noneconomists) have often lamented the lack of a universally applicable theory or model of economic growth and development. But intensive study in the past 20 years has produced substantial agreement that, even though the process is complex, some normative patterns of economic growth and structural change of developing countries do exist. Industrialization, involving rising shares of manufacturing and declining shares of agricultural output, is a universal element of growth. So, too, are urbanization and expansion of education, transport, and communication. Because these transformations all require large amounts of capital, it is essential that increased shares of the total of available resources is freed from current consumption and allocated to capital formation if growth is to be accelerated. Overall, the correlation of these variables follows a pattern.

David C. Cole and Princeton N. Lyman, *Korean Development: The Interplay of Politics and Economics* (Cambridge, Mass.: Harvard University Press, 1971), p. 2.

by these individuals' investments would "spread" or "trickle down" to the poorer groups in society, that is, the majority of the population. This strategy was buttressed by the theories of "unbalanced growth," stating that investment should be concentrated in industries with the highest combined forward and backward linkages, and of "unequal income distribution," holding that income inequality was necessary to stimulate domestic savings.[6]

The social scientists who argued in favor of the centrality of the military in the Third World were, no doubt, influenced by these theories and, simultaneously, served to entrench them further in conventional development theory. A number of politico-military and economic strands thus came together. The assessment of the military as the central actor in terms of a country's domestic unity (nation building) and economic development (modernization) as well as in terms of its external security strengthened the arguments of those policymakers in Western countries who wanted to channel more funds to Third World armed forces. It could be argued that such aid would be good economically, strategically, and politically for both the recipient and the donor.

This argument was particularly useful if one mistrusted civilians' political inclinations or capabilities. One of the earliest examples of the military-as-modernizer theory is simultaneously one of the most explicit statements of the link between focusing Western foreign assistance on the military and suppressing left-wing political movements. Writing about Southeast Asia in 1959, Guy Pauker identified "strong leadership, backed up by organizational structure and by moral authority" as the most important attributes required by governments in the area. According to Pauker, civilian nationalist leaders were "weak" and needed a decade or more to "learn" to manage the democratic form of government, while the political structures of the states in the region were too "weak" to support democracy and similarly required a decade or more to be strengthened. Pauker believed, however, that there were not decades to waste because the "Communists" were waiting to step into the "power vacuum" created by the ineffective nationalist governments.

The communists were considered a threat because they were believed to possess precisely those attributes Pauker had found lacking in the nationalist governments—organization and discipline. It was therefore of the greatest urgency to provide a countervailing power to the communist threat, one which would of necessity possess superior organization and discipline. According to Pauker, only the officer corps in Southeast Asian

---

[6] On unbalanced growth, see Albert O. Hirschman, *The Strategy of Economic Development* (New Haven: Yale University Press, 1958).

countries were sufficiently organized and disciplined to stand up to the communists, who were portrayed as acting solely in the interests of "foreign powers." Pauker argued that to "save" these countries from repressive communist governments it was necessary to eliminate, only temporarily of course, the weak democratic form of government and replace it with strong, albeit repressive, military governments characterized as more concerned with the welfare of the people in the region.[7] Most other social scientists writing at this time did not employ the same cold war rhetoric as Pauker, but their analyses were aimed in more or less the same direction.[8]

[7] Pauker, "Southeast Asia," p. 344.

According to Lucien Pye, the Western democracies had failed to offer guidance to the civilian governments in the Third World whereas "Communists" had a clearer vision of how to attain their goals. The Western democracies had thus only compounded the problems confronting Third World leaders.

> For all our commitment to democratic values, we do not know what is required for a society to move from a traditional and authoritarian basis to the establishment of democratic institutions and representative institutions. . . . We find we have little advice to give the leaders of the newly emergent countries who are struggling to realize democratic ways. We have no doctrine to offer them, no strategies for action nor criteria of priorities, no sense of appropriate programs nor sets of hypotheses for explaining the paths to representative government. At best we have been able to piece together some concepts and considerations taken from embryonic theories of economic growth and have suggested that they might serve as guiding principles. In contrast to our own bemusement, those interested in establishing other types of social and political systems—and most particularly, of course, the Communists—have a clearer sense of design and priorities to guide their efforts. More often than not we have found that instead of developmental concepts and strategic plans we can offer only statements about the nature of democratic values and our vision of end-goals of political development. By stressing ends rather than the means we have inadvertently tended to highlight the extent to which the newly emergent states have failed to realize in practice their aspirations. In doing so, we have contributed to the growing feeling of insecurity common to most of the leaders of such countries.

Lucien Pye, "Armies in the Process of Political Modernization," pp. 71–72, in *The Role of the Military in Underdeveloped Countries*, ed. John J. Johnson, (Princeton, N.J.: Princeton University Press, 1962).

Like Pauker's article, Pye's statement is closer to the realm of fantasy than it is to an analysis of actual conditions. The protection and propagation of political democracy in the Third World has not been high on the list of priorities of most Western industrialized countries over the last forty years. Rather more important has been the maintenance of certain Third World governments in power for reasons which relate to the politico-strategic and economic interests of the industrialized countries, as opposed to the welfare of the Third World countries.

[8] The main source for military-led modernization is, Marion J. Levy, Jr., "Armed Force Organizations," in his *Modernization and the Structure of Society: An International Setting* (Princeton, N.J.: Princeton University Press, 1966), vol. 2 chap. 4. Other works favorable to

The modernizing functions most frequently attributed to Third World militaries can be divided into three broad categories: (1) elements said to be inherent in the organizational structure of the armed forces, (2) activities carried out by the military in the normal course of their duties, and (3) skills and attitudes taught by military life but applicable to civilian life once a soldier is demobilized. The organizational attributes will be examined in more detail here. (The applicability of military training to civilian society will be discussed in Chapter 8.)

Modernizing Effects of the Military's Organizational Structure

Political theorists began examining the modernizing potential of Third World armed forces because, in part, by the early 1960s it had become increasingly evident to them that many civilian politicians were not only uncommitted to implementing development programs that would benefit all segments of their societies but also appeared more interested in furthering their own short-term interests than in governing. There can be no doubt that the shortcomings ascribed to civilian political leaders in many countries at that time were genuine or that they continue to afflict many civilian-led governments even today. There also can be no doubt that many civilian-led governments neither protected the democratic institutions they inherited at the time of independence nor launched self-sustaining socioeconomic development. The failure of the civilians does not, however, in any way guarantee the success of the military.[9]

Consider the situation in Ghana in the late 1960s. During the period immediately preceding the first military coup in 1966, both political and

---

the notion that the military can promote modernization include, Hans Daalder, *The Role of the Military in the Emerging Countries,* Institute of Social Studies, Minor Series 1 (The Hague: Mouton, 1962); John J. Johnson, *The Military and Society in Latin America* (Stanford, Calif.: Stanford University Press, 1964); Pye, "Armies"; Daniel Lerner and Richard Robinson, "Swords and Ploughshares: The Turkish Army as a Modernizing Force," *World Politics* 13 (January 1960): 19–44; Lucien Pye, *Military Development in New Nations* (Washington, D.C.: Smithsonian Institution, December 1961); and Morris Janowitz, *The Military in the Political Development of New Nations: An Essay in Comparative Analysis* (Chicago and London: Phoenix Books/University of Chicago Press, 1964). See also, Arturo Valenzuela, "The Military and Social Science Theory," *Third World Quarterly* 7 (January 1985): 134–36.

[9] In Chapter 8 the argument that military officers possess organizational skills, a rational and efficient approach to problems, a coherence, and a hierarchical structure making them more suited to governing than some politicians is measured against reality and found to have been wanting in many cases.

economic conditions deteriorated sharply. Real economic growth was negligible between 1960 and 1965; the foreign debt was large, and the balance of payments was strongly in deficit; unemployment was rising while real earnings were lower in 1965 than they had been in 1955. Government administration was characterized by corruption and inefficiency which led to "a high level of cynicism toward anything and everything governmental." Apart from removing Nkrumah and his Convention People's Party (CPP) from power, however, the coup of 24 February 1966 changed little.

The armed forces needed the cooperation of the civil service to govern and thus were unable (assuming they were interested) to remove public officials whose lack of cohesiveness, efficiency, and honesty had contributed in no small measure to the country's economic and political difficulties. In fact, the principal secretaries in the twenty-four governmental ministries saw their power increase for the first six months of military rule until new ministers were named. The armed forces also failed to set a good example for financial austerity: Public expenditure on industries and agriculture was cut back sharply while outlays on the military sector increased substantially. Particularly noteworthy was the large allocation of foreign exchange to the armed forces, which exceeded that to all other government ministries, departments, and agencies. To make a bad situation worse, the military allied with the police, which had both strongly advocated and implemented repressive legislation under the Nkrumah government and was considered one of the most corrupt elements in the Ghanaian government at the time.[10] None of this can be said to have nurtured modernization in Ghana.

Indeed, far from offering an alternative to chaotic and inefficient civilian rule, the first period of military rule in Ghana (1966–1969) only deepened the political and economic crisis. Robert Price has characterized the general pattern of policymaking on the part of the National Liberation Council and its outcome:

> This pattern involves the taking of policy decisions without consideration of their ramifications and repercussions, resulting in a host of unintended consequences demanding further policy decisions on the highest level. These ad hoc decisions in turn add new unintended consequences and confusion, until the policy is either ignored and left unimplemented, or nullified, and an attempt is made to deal with the problem anew.

[10] Robert M. Price, "Military Officers and Political Leadership: The Ghanaian Case," *Comparative Politics* 3 (April 1981): 361–62, 367–70.

It is not surprising, then, that the three and one-half years of military rule in Ghana were characterized by drift and stagnation. The problems which beset the country at the time of the fall of Nkrumah continued to exist, and some became worse. In the economic sphere the GNP per capita remained stagnant, inflated prices if anything grew higher, and the number of unemployed rose greatly. There was, it is true, some improvement in the trade balance and in the foreign reserve situation. These improvements, however, were produced by combining drastic cutbacks in spending on capital goods with greatly increased assistance from the United States and other Western governments, rather than by a remobilization and application of resources within Ghana. The foreign debt servicing picture was also improved, but since the solution to this involved merely a rescheduling of debts, the problem was actually left to a successor government to deal with.[11]

Ghana is by no means the only country in which the armed forces have failed completely to overcome the serious economic and political problems they inherited from a civilian government.

Another supposed strength of Third World armed forces is what Janowitz has described as a "public-service tradition." Military men were said to be able to put the concerns of society as a whole before particularistic interests, be those of family, class, ethnic group, religion, or region. Political scientists argued that this detachment made the armed forces especially well suited for leading the fight against corruption in their countries. That this battle must be fought cannot be denied: illegal payments grease the wheels in many countries and can seriously jeopardize the formulation and implementation of development programs (see Chapter 7). It is also clear that military officers are aware of the problem. A survey of twenty-nine coups d'état in sub-Saharan Africa between 1958 and 1980, for example, showed that corruption was cited as a justification for the coup in thirteen cases.[12] Two questions remain, however: How well equipped are Third World militaries to fight corruption? And how interested are they in doing so? In most cases, the answer to both questions is: not very.

It was possible for the earliest theorists to suggest that military officers were both personally honest and willing to fight governmental corruption because they restricted themselves to the experiences of the newly in-

[11] Ibid., pp. 377–78.

[12] Staffan Wiking, *Military Coups in Sub-Saharan Africa: How to Justify Illegal Assumptions of Power* (Uppsala: Scandinavian Institute of African Studies, 1983), p. 99. The most frequently cited justification was "economic failures," which appeared in fifteen cases.

dependent countries of Africa, Asia, and the Middle East and ignored the situation of older countries in the Third World such as Thailand. In the countries that had undergone decolonization after World War II, the armed forces had, for the most part, only recently been created and had no experience of involvement in government when the first theorists were writing. Simply because military officers in a country that had attained independence in the late 1950s or early 1960s had not begun to engage in any corrupt activities by 1962 or 1964 did not mean that they would never do so. Lack of corrupt behavior can never be equated with incorruptibility. As events have shown, in most cases it only meant that the military officers had never before had the opportunity to engage in corrupt activity. Indeed, when given the opportunity, many military officers showed themselves no more honest than the civilians they had displaced.

Once again Ghana offers a useful example. The instigators of the 1966 coup were, of course, aware of the extensive governmental and administrative corruption plaguing the country. They gave considerable emphasis to the economic failures of the Nkrumah government, which could at least in part be traced to corruption and inefficiency, when justifying their coup. (It is widely acknowledged that corporate grievances were the primary factors leading the Ghanaian armed forces to intervene politically.) Despite this, military officers subsequently proved just as capable as the CPP government of becoming involved in what Major-General Ocran described as "the plunder of the public treasury":[13] "The impact of military rule in Ghana on efficiency, honesty, and austerity in public life is perhaps best summed up by a popular record released in Ghana during 1968, the title of which is, "The Cars Are the Same, Only the Drivers Have Changed." Not surprisingly, the record was banned soon after its release."[14]

The situation in the Republic of Korea at the time of the 1961 coup carried out by Park Chung Hee and his associates was somewhat different. The leaders of that coup had a definite economic program they proposed to carry out. One objective was to break the power of the traditional élites, including some ranking military officers, many of whom had been engaged in the widespread corruption that had flourished under the government of Syngman Rhee. To this end, the new military government dismantled the economic mechanisms these élites had used to enrich themselves. There was, however, more to the attack on the former members of the Rhee government and their supporters than a desire to implement particular economic programs and bring efficiency to government.

[13] Major-General A. K. Ocran, *A Myth Is Broken* (London: Longmans, 1968), p. 2, cited in Price, "Military Officers," p. 365.
[14] Price, "Military Officers," p. 372.

Although the ranking military officers had been very close to the Rhee government and the traditional Korean élites, the vast majority of the armed forces had enjoyed no such connection. South Korea did not have a traditional warlord class, and a career in the military was not normally a means of attaining élite status. Individuals who had no way of gaining an entrée to the élite joined the military, forming in time a sort of counter-élite. The division that existed between the majority of the military officers and the ruling élite was reinforced by the regional origins of both groups. The traditional élites tended to come from the area around Seoul while the military officers came primarily from the rural areas: more than 70 percent of the officers who participated in the 1961 coup or became members of the military government had rural backgrounds.[15] Once in power, these officers proved rather less interested in reducing the dominant position of élites in the political and economic systems than in substituting themselves, their families, and close associates for the traditional élites. Corruption did not decline following the military take-over. It simply changed form.

The restrictive system of import quotas and the manipulation and control of scarce banking resources had together formed the backbone of a mutually corrupting and mutually profiting system of co-operation between a limited number of businessmen and government officials under the Liberal Party regime. In the reforms of 1964 and 1965, both of these systems collapsed, to the vain cries and behind-the-scenes maneuvering of those who had long lived by them. It was not the end of corruption, not even the end for most of the biggest business interests of the previous era. But it was an end to that system of corruption to which the Park administration had not been a party and which it found economically debilitating. Other forms of corruption, some of quite major proportions, grew quickly enough in its place. But they at least fitted into a different set of priorities over the next few years in which, in contrast to the Rhee regime, the independent economic growth of Korea was rated as a major objective to which older forms of corruption, as well as many previously favored interests, were sacrificed.[16]

Those who argue in favor of a modernizing role for Third World armed forces have frequently pointed to the link they believe exists between

---

[15] Cole and Lyman, *Korean Development*, pp. 14, 35–37.
[16] Ibid., pp. 93–94; see also pp. 251–53. For a review of corruption between 1948 and 1960, see Gregory Henderson, *Korea: The Politics of the Vortex* (Cambridge, Mass.: Harvard University Press, 1968), pp. 197–98.

modern weapons and industrialization. Most early promodernization theorists claimed that the possession of modern weaponry and technical training received in the military made officers aware of the extent to which their societies lagged behind the more industrialized countries; consequently, this awareness led them to promote modernization more enthusiastically than other societal groups that had not been as thoroughly exposed to modern technology and were still rooted in traditional methods. These arguments will be examined in detail in subsequent chapters. The factor that needs to be stressed here is *the commitment of the government to industrialization,* not the possession or use by the armed forces of modern military equipment.

Consider, for example, the quasi-military government of Park Chung Hee in South Korea that was particularly successful in implementing its program of industrialization. This program was almost certainly instituted both to build up the economic strength of the country and to create the base necessary for the production of weapons. The second objective was not initially stressed, however. The United States, on which the Korean government depended heavily for financial assistance (see Chapter 7), was extremely unwilling to agree to the creation of a military industry in Korea prior to 1968. The U.S. government feared that once the South Koreans had the capacity to produce a large quantity of weapons on their own, they would attack the North.[17] To avoid antagonizing the United States, the South Korean government emphasized the attainment of economic self-sufficiency in its public statements.

Under the guidance of the Park government, South Korea became one of the success stories of Third World development. Its economic strategy was based on the expansion of industry, especially for the export market, and there can be no doubt that the South Korean economy has been transformed over the course of the last two decades. At the same time, it is important to recognize that the initial successes experienced by the South Korean economy were based on the development of light industry "not dependent on a lot of modernized plant; it was mainly [based] on the smaller scale labor-intensive manufacturing." Only during the 1970s did investment in more capital-intensive, heavy industries that could form

[17] U.S. Congress, House of Representatives, Committee on International Relations, Subcommittee on International Organizations, Report: *Investigation of Korean-American Relations,* 95th Cong., 2nd Sess., 31 October 1978 (Washington, D.C.: Government Printing Office, 1978), pp. 74–76. By 1970 the United States had come to promote self-sufficiency in the production of certain weapons. This change in policy was in line with the overall U.S. objective of reducing military grant assistance. It also derived from the belief that the South Korean leadership had become sufficiently mature not to attack North Korean wantonly (p. 78).

the basis for a domestic weapon production capability become more important.[18] In addition, while the leaders of the quasi-military government defined the broad outlines of economic policy, civilian technocrats in the Economic Planning Board were (and remain) dominant in the decision-making process for long-term development strategy. "They have sweeping powers and responsibilities to establish not only overall plans for economic development but also for national budgeting, mobilization of resources and investment, and coordination with other ministries related to national economy and finance."[19]

The Divorce between Theory and Reality

⌊The argument that the possession and operation of modern weapons have spin-off effects in terms of modernization for Third World economies may have been attractive to those who wanted to provide Third World governments with military assistance because they could argue that such aid would strengthen both the recipient's ability to defend itself and its economy. An examination of the extent to which such spin-off has occurred indicates, however, that the link is tenuous. The same can be said of the other organizational attributes identified by adherents of the military-as-modernizer school.⌋

In part this problem arose given insufficient understanding of the development process. Most military-as-modernizers were political theorists, and it is thus perhaps not surprising that they failed to evaluate critically the economic development policies they promoted. Nevertheless, the negative effects of these policies cannot be denied. The emphasis on industrialization, for example, was in line with the prevailing development theory of the 1960s, but it is increasingly recognized that focusing on industry encouraged or enabled governments to neglect investment in agri-

[18] U.S. Congress, House of Representatives, Committee on International Relations, Subcommittee on International Organizations, Hearings: *Investigation of Korean-American Relations,* Part 6, 95th Cong., 2nd Sess., 19 July and 2 August 1978 (Washington, D.C.: Government Printing Office, 1978), p. 51 (statement by David Cole).

[19] Changsoo Lee, "Civil-Military Relations and the Emergence of 'Civiltary' Bureaucrats in Korea," p. 98, in *Modernization of Korea and the Impact of the West,* ed. Changsoo Lee (Los Angeles: East Asian Studies Center, University of Southern California, 1981). Between 1961 and 1963 when the military government ruled South Korea, the armed forces relied much more on their own resources to formulate and implement economic policy. As Chapter 8 discusses, this was not entirely successful, and recourse to professional economists was clearly indicated. After the installation of the quasi-civilian government, civilian economists were given considerable power. In 1964, the deputy prime minister who headed the Economic Planning Board "was practically given *carte blanche* in shaping and directing economic policies over the next few years. . . ." Cole and Lyman, *Korean Development,* p. 46.

15

culture, particularly in the smallholder sector, and more or less ignore landless laborers. This, in turn, prevented the development of the necessary links between agricultural and industrial growth and has undermined the ability of many Third World countries to feed themselves, often with disastrous consequences. At the same time, the inability to see far enough into the future and predict the economic imbalances that would result from the implementation of, for example, an industrialization-first policy did not afflict only the military-as-modernizers. Although the best way of achieving development has been under continual debate over the last forty years, the policies favored by the military-as-modernizers were those that formed the mainstream of Western development thinking in the 1960s and were widely applied in the Third World. Where the modernizers can be faulted more directly is in the fact that their interpretations of how Third World armed forces would act frequently did not accord with reality. This gap between theory and reality arose because the military modernizers were not particularly interested in empirical evidence.

All the modernizers' theories are built upon a slender body of facts. Generalizing on the basis of only a few examples is always a dangerous enterprise, and the role of the security sector in the development process has proven to be no exception. Given the wide variety of conditions shaping both armed forces and societies in the Third World, it has always been possible to find a few examples to fit whatever theoretical construct one might choose to devise. These theories were, however, developed at a time when relatively few militaries in Africa, Asia, or the Middle East had been in power, or sometimes even in existence, for any length of time. The one developing area where militaries had a long history of political involvement and which presumably would have yielded a good deal of empirical evidence was Latin America. The experience of Latin America was rejected, however, because the militaries there were of the old, traditional variety and provided an image of "administrative incompetence, inaction, and authoritarian, if not reactionary, values." In contrast, the armed forces of Asia, Africa, and the Middle East provided less hard data but were favored by the theorists because they were said to possess a "dynamic and self-sacrificing military leadership committed to progress and the task of modernizing traditional societies that have been subverted by the 'corrupt practices' of the politicians."[20]

---

[20] Pye, "Armies," p. 69. One Asian country, Thailand, did have a thirty-year history of military rule at the time that Pye was writing, but it is unlikely that he would have wanted to examine the Thai experience too closely either. As Chapter 6 explains, the Thai military has helped to institutionalize a system of corruption that is one of the factors distorting the development process in that country.

As soon as researchers actually began to examine the activities of militaries—particularly those holding political power—in some detail, it became evident that a wealth of counterexamples could be used to demonstrate that the nation-building and modernizing characteristics ascribed to the military frequently lacked substance. In other instances, the modernizing attributes can be shown to have existed in particular countries at specific points in time, but they cannot be assumed to exist in all countries continuously. To propagate a theory unsupportable by the facts is both dishonest and dangerous.

One cannot help but admire these creative extrapolations, built upon a rather slim empirical basis by the power of logic, the force of intellect, and the gift of intuition. But one wishes that those who venture to serve as guides to what is still recognized as *terra incognita* with respect to systematic research would tread more tentatively. Conjectural charts, especially when impressionistically drawn with bold and assertive strokes, can too easily be mistaken by the unwary for precisely plotted maps. Admittedly, an exploration of a relatively uncharted realm of knowledge must begin with one or a set of assumptions. These are frequently derived analogically from knowledge gained in a familiar context. These assumptions then serve as a starting point around which to organize preliminary investigations of the units of observation in the unfamiliar universe to ascertain whether they are similarly relevant as the basis for further working hypotheses. But when analogically derived assumptions are transferred *in toto* to become the scaffolding upon which to erect a skyscraper of deduction devoid of empirical bricks and mortar, and when what are no more than further assumptions are treated as data, this is dangerous. What may well have originally been intended as suggestive hypotheses emerge by some alchemy as substantive conclusions. That way lies the new scholasticism.[21]

It might be thought that because so many of those who believed most strongly that the military has a modernizing role to play wrote in the late 1950s and early 1960s and because considerable evidence has since been gathered to demonstrate the weakness of many of their theories that the

---

[21] Ann Ruth Willner, "The Underdeveloped Study of Political Development," *World Politics* 16 (April 1964): 479. Another useful article by Willner which offers more detailed criticisms of the military-as-modernizer theories is Ann Ruth Willner, "Perspectives on Military Elites as Rulers and Wielders of Power," *Journal of Comparative Administration* 2 (November 1970): 261–76. Robin Luckham speaks of theories that "are not adequate to the facts," A. R. Luckham, "A Comparative Typology of Civil-Military Relations," *Government and Opposition* 6 (Winter 1971): 5–8.

influence of these writers is now negligible. That is unfortunately not true. At the end of the 1970s, one could still find serious researchers quoting, for example, vague generalizations by Pye written in 1962 and concluding that "in many cases, the military is the most progressive sector of an LDC economy, in terms of organisational structure, technology and ideology. It therefore possesses an immanent desire for modernization." [22]

ARMAMENT AS A CAUSE OF UNDERDEVELOPMENT

While promodernizers have concentrated on the positive contribution Third World militaries can make, radical analysis of the developmental role played by Third World armed forces has focused on the negative aspects. Those who adopt this approach have argued that organized force prevents the kinds of structural changes necessary for fostering self-sustaining socioeconomic development and thus leads to underdevelopment by ensuring that Third World countries remain subservient members of the international capitalist system. It is pointed out that not only were colonies acquired and maintained by force, but also the production of commodities desired by colonial powers was organized and ensured by force. State violence during the postcolonial period is both a continuation of previous behavior and a necessity to prevent a serious realignment of economic and political power.

> Whatever stage we consider in trading relations and the growth of dependency between the metropolitan countries and the periphery, we find that the exchange relationship has always been one of force and that the threat or use of armed force has been a determining factor in the history of the world-wide spread of the capitalistic form of production. . . .

[22] David K. Whynes, *The Economics of Third World Military Expenditure* (London: MacMillan, 1979), p. 113. Whynes almost certainly did not reach this conclusion out of ignorance of the literature. His bibliography includes, for example, both Samuel Finer, *The Man on Horseback: The Role of the Military in Politics* (London: Pall Mall Press, 1962), and Eric A. Nordlinger, "Soldiers in Mufti," *American Political Science Review* 64 (December 1970): 1131–48. Finer's study includes many facts which argue against the universality of the modernizing role for the armed forces in the Third World. Nordlinger provides a short summary of the arguments of some of the main "modernizers"—Pye, Johnson, Shils, Pauker, and Halpern, among others—and notes that these authors, "have presented remarkably little evidence for their arguments, while failing to analyse—as opposed to simply stating—the supposed connections between the officers' technical orientations and social backgrounds and their hypothesized modernizing activities and motivations" (p. 1133).

Similarly, in the early 1970s Emile Benoit had given considerable weight to modernizing arguments in his analysis of the effect of security expenditure on economic growth. These arguments have also been repeated uncritically in recent years. See Chapter 5.

In the colonial era, the accumulation of capital in Europe and its dwindling in the periphery were already based on the threat or use of force. . . .

One of the chief bases for all colonial conquests was the military superiority of the European powers. It was by military means, that following the seizure of peripheral territories, the forcible destruction of their existing social and production structures, and social order, was undertaken. . . .

With the progressive industrialization of the peripheral countries—even though this was only partial, mainly confined to import-substitution industries—and in the face of the open challenge represented by independence movements, the military were given new tasks. The protection of raw material concessions, important during the earlier colonial era, became a secondary consideration: the vital thing now was to back up the growing penetration of capital, breaking down the resistance of the developing industrial labour force and ensuring that decolonization would be gradual, that is to say, preventing any abrupt or violent transition from domination by the metropolitan country to political independence. In many cases, colonial armies were completely transformed into instruments of repression at the service of the local ruling classes.[23]

The importation of weapons from industrialized countries and the domestic production of arms by Third World countries play an important role in this schema because these activities are seen as ensuring the continuous channelling of resources from the largely agricultural poor to élites in both industrialized capitalist and developing countries. The acquisition of weapons from abroad is also said to have served to entrench the export-oriented development strategy in the Third World. The import of weapons, weapon-related services, military technology, spare parts, and the like from abroad requires (in the absence of military grants) the expenditure of foreign exchange, generally acquired by expanding exports or by obtaining foreign loans.

Spending on arms has a number of significant implications for the patterns of national development—or underdevelopment—which prevail in the Third World. Armies do not on the whole create the

[23] Ulrich Albrecht, Dieter Ernst, Peter Lock, and Herbert Wulf, "Arming the Developing Countries," *International Social Science Journal* 28:2 (1976): 335–36. A similar argument is made in their "Armaments and Underdevelopment," pp. 173–85. Both articles summarize the discussion contained in their *Rüstung und Unterentwicklung. Iran, Indien, Griechenland/Türkei: Die verschärfte Militarisierung, (Armament and Underdevelopment. Iran, India, Greece/Turkey: Intensified Militarization* (Reinbek: Rowohlt, 1976).

surplus value which sustains their own expansion. The resources have to be provided from taxation or by subsidies from international patrons and suppliers of arms. In the first place this puts the military in a special position relative to the remainder of the state machinery through which the necessary resources have to be raised internally or negotiated externally. Second, it implies a degree of integration with the international economy from which internationally negotiable purchasing power has to be obtained in order to acquire military hardware.[24]

In addition, countries which import military technology, in both the forms of hardware and production capacity, from capitalist countries are said to be inevitably influenced by the latters' military organization, social and economic structures, and conflict patterns.[25] Mary Kaldor has argued that the transfer of military equipment defines "rather precisely" the way in which soldiers must be organized; this, in turn, affects the political orientation of the soldiers and the structure of the social system. The structure of society is shaped partly by the need for an industrial base to service and produce weapons and partly by the tendency of Third World armed forces to support governments that attempt to create a society which mirrors that in the metropolitan countries.[26]

As much of the discussion in subsequent chapters will demonstrate, the armament-underdevelopment approach corresponds more closely to present realities in most of the Third World than does the theory which posits that the military is a force for modernization. What is more, it focuses on relationships which, for the most part, have not been satisfactorily addressed by either those who study Third World militaries or development analysts.

Linkages between militarism and international dependence are hardly dealt with at all in the existing literature on the military in developing countries. This largely concentrates on epiphenomena such as

[24] Robin Luckham, "Militarism and International Dependence: A Framework for Analysis," pp. 155–56, in *Transnational Capitalism and National Development: New Perspectives on Dependence,* ed. José J. Villamil (Hassocks, England: Harvester Press, 1979).

[25] The armament-underdevelopment theorists thus share one assumption with the military-as-modernizer school: The transfer of weapon technology implies the simultaneous transfer of military organization and social and economic structures. The two groups draw quite different conclusions about the effects of these transfers, however. For the latter, such transfers are beneficial since for them the goal of development is to make Third World countries as much like the industrialized countries of the West as possible. For the former, they imply a strengthening of inequitable socioeconomic relations and are therefore damaging.

[26] Mary Kaldor, "Military Technology and Social Structure," *Bulletin of Atomic Scientists* 33 (June 1977): 52.

coups, military regimes, the ideology of soldiers, spending on arms and its relation to GNP growth rates; and thus tends to leave aside more fundamental questions about the role of military force in the state and international relations, in the accumulation of flow of economic surpluses, and in the determination of patterns of development and underdevelopment.[27]

The armed forces in many Third World countries have supported governments that have shown little or no inclination to share economic and political power with the majority of their own population but have instead shown considerable enthusiasm for expanding their own economic and political power and entering into close relationships with Western governments and corporations. Where civilian governments have sought to move leftward, or at least have given the appearance of doing so, the military has often intervened directly by taking over the government. In the process, it has seemingly sought to protect the interests of domestic élites, foreign governments, and multinational corporations. One need only to think of Guatemala in 1954, Brazil in 1964, the Dominican Republic in 1965, Uganda in 1971, or Chile in 1973.

In a few cases where serious social strife has seemed likely because power has remained in the hands of a landed oligarchy with no interest in economic or political liberalization, the military has intervened to increase the opportunities for participation available to the second tier of the socioeconomic élite, the urban middle class. Here one might include Egypt in 1952 and Peru in 1968. Even in these cases, however, the armed forces have been careful not to produce too open a political system, excluding workers and peasants from the decision-making process.

In Peru, for example, official pronouncements by the Velasco government, particularly in its early years, strongly favored the economically disadvantaged groups: peasants, urban workers, shop employees, and other low-paid individuals. Yet, in reality, the Velasco government's strong opposition to the creation of grassroots organizations by peasants and workers probably stemmed from the military's dislike of communism and its fear that such spontaneously organized groups could be used by communist activists to further their own ends. Instead, the military decided to establish a government agency that would be charged with directing "social mobilization." SINAMOS (National System for Support of Social Mobilization) came into being in April 1972. Although many of those who worked with SINAMOS were genuinely concerned to increase popular participation in decision making, the armed forces were unwilling to allow

[27] Luckham, "Militarism," p. 146.

21

other groups to gain any significant measure of power, and SINAMOS became more conservative from about 1974. Where SINAMOS did actually improve the conditions for political participation, as with the National Agrarian Confederation (CNA), the government was ultimately unable to deal with such a strong, popularly based organization and had to assert its own power.

By progressive criteria, some SINAMOS activities were successful. Perhaps the organization's most important success was its work with the National Agrarian Confederation. Despite the unfortunate consequences of its structure and concerns for commitment to the Velasco government among established cooperative members, the CNA was the first organization in Peru to bring thousands of peasants into national politics. SINAMOS worked with the CNA, but did not co-opt it; indeed, as the CNA became increasingly radical and powerful, the only way the Morales Bermúdez government saw to deter the confederation was to decapitate it—which it did in June 1978.[28]

The main beneficiaries of military rule in Peru during the 1970s were local industrialists and bankers, the public sector, and foreign firms. Although the replacement of Velasco by Morales Bermúdez caused government policies to become more conservative, even the reforms instigated by the Velasco government failed to benefit large numbers of the poorest Peruvians. Cynthia McClintock has reported that "By 1973, it was evident that the government's [land] reforms had benefited primarily families in the upper two or three deciles of the income distribution."[29]

For the most part, therefore, it can be said that militaries in the Third World have acted as guarantors of a status quo which favors the interests of local and international capital, even when more progressive elements in the armed forces have been in control. It would, nonetheless, be incorrect to view all military involvement in politics or the economy solely in terms of the protection or promotion of capitalism. Like any other bureaucratic organization, the military is not a monolithic entity, and its segments may have quite different ways of viewing the world. The Peruvian military, for example, was composed in 1968 of three major political groups: conservatives, institutionalists, and reformists. The conservative group "placed particular emphasis on traditionalism, order and authority" and included "a recalcitrant fascist-inclined wing." The institution-

[28] Cynthia McClintock, "Velasco, Officers, and Citizens: The Politics of Stealth," p. 303, in *The Peruvian Experiment Reconsidered*, ed. Cynthia McClintock and Abraham F. Lowenthal (Princeton, N.J.: Princeton University Press, 1983). See also, Luis Pásara, "When the Military Dreams," pp. 309–43, in the same volume.

[29] McClintock, "Velasco," pp. 289–90.

alists "defended the professional character and political impartiality of the Armed Forces as an institution." The reformists "favored structural changes in order to obtain a faster socio-economic development, conceived as a basic element of national security." The reformists were further subdivided into "developmentalists" and "revolutionaries." Immediately after the 1968 coup, the government enjoyed broadly based support within the military. Rather soon, however, all but the reformists were eliminated. At first the revolutionary reformists held the upper hand, but eventually the developmental reformists gained control. Instrumental in deciding which group of reformists should control the policy-making process was a fourth group of military officers, the "friends of President Velasco." With the ouster of Velasco by Morales Burmúdez in 1975, the reformists lost power to a combination of conservative and institutionalist officers.[30]

Cleavages within the military reflect cleavages within society as a whole, and it is not always possible to predict which civilian group the military will support. In fact, it is generally incorrect to speak of "the military" as a unit supporting "the ruling class" as a whole. As the Peruvian experience demonstrates, different groups within the armed forces ally themselves with different groups of civilians. Moreover, these alliances can shift over time.

In general, militaries rarely ally themselves with nonélite groups, and the support of members of the armed forces can be important in determining which élite group holds power at any given time. Still, to say that factions within the armed forces ally themselves with civilians and play an active role in politics *solely* to protect the economic interests of civilian élites is a considerable oversimplification. More accurately, the personal and class interests of civilians interact with the personal, corporate, and class interests of members of the armed forces, and this interplay of interests influences the way in which a country is governed and to whose benefit the government functions.

There may be broad agreement among the members of a ruling élite that a country should operate within the general capitalist framework, but that will not prevent different factions within the élite from competing with each other for power. In a country such as Thailand where cliques are the basic building blocks of all political activity, different military groups ally with different civilian groups, and each major coalition

---

[30] José Encinas del Pando, "Economic, Military and Socio-Political Variables in Argentina, Chile and Peru (1950–1980)" (Lima: University of Lima, 1983, mimeographed), p. 135. See also Edwin Lieuwen, *Arms and Politics in Latin America* rev. ed. (New York: Praeger, 1961), p. 81.

attempts to gain as much power and wealth as possible for itself; but this all occurs within the same economic system. Since 1932, Thailand has experienced at least six successful coups d'état, many unsuccessful ones, and several elections of varying degrees of fairness. Yet none of this has produced any serious alteration in the Thai élite.

A central objective of the 1932 coup was to increase the power of the nonroyal members of the élite group at the expense of its royal members. The absolute monarchy was replaced by a constitutional monarchy, and power passed into the hands of a coalition of military and civilian bureaucrats. Although the civilians initially dominated this coalition, by 1933 the military had gained control. In the 1930s and 1940s, the military-dominated government did attempt both to break the not inconsiderable economic power of the ethnic Chinese community and to strengthen the state sector and the ethnic Thai middle class. By the 1950s, however, the economic power of the ethnic Chinese businessmen clearly remained strong, and Thai military and civilian élites began to ally themselves with the businessmen by joining the boards of Chinese-owned companies. This produced a pattern of relations that endures to this day.

The following characterization of the Thai political system, written in the early 1960s, essentially still applies.

> Regardless of which leader is nominally in control, government goes on, and on much the same path. The fact that the ruling class is small and largely overlaps the bureaucracy is at the root of this situation. The ruling class, consequently, is responsible to a political public whose interests it shares to a large extent. Its political concerns have been narrow, where not actually personal, and conflicts have revolved largely around the basic question of political status—how shall the rewards of goods, prestige, and power be distributed within the ruling class?[31]

This system has survived for several reasons. First, Thailand's social structure has prevented political parties and other social organizations from becoming strong, effective entities. Then, attempts to exclude the dominant elements of the business community—the ethnic Chinese—from the political process has led this group to employ their personal connections for influencing the government. Finally, the peasantry has for the most part been "politically inarticulate."[32]

---

[31] David A. Wilson, "The Military in Thai Politics," pp. 253–54, in *The Role,* ed. Johnson. See also, David Elliott, *Thailand: Origins of Military Rule* (London: Zed Press, 1978), especially Chapter 3, "Monarchism to Militarism: Seizure of the Rice Economy," pp. 85–113.

[32] Wilson, "The Military," p. 254.

The coexistence of several political orientations within Third World officer corps is further illustrated by the fact that the armed forces of a country can intervene against governments with rather different economic and political outlooks within the space of a few years. In Ghana, for example, Nkrumah's attempt to institute "African socialism," characterized as "forced industrialization through import substitution, government controls and public enterprises," was largely discredited by 1966. The military government that overthrew Nkrumah and held power from 1966 to 1969 followed essentially market-economy policies, although, as discussed above, it failed to follow any policy consistently. When elections were held in 1969, the military's dominant faction, led by General Afrifa, backed the Progressive party, led by Kofi Busia, which supported private enterprise and minimal state control over the economy. By 1972, however, the military, now led by Colonel Acheampong, had overthrown the Busia government and replaced the reliance on the free-market economic system with a more self-reliant posture.

The Ghanaian armed forces can thus be said to have intervened once in favor of capitalism and once against; however, these interventions should not be seen strictly in terms of economic policies. Corporate grievances strongly influenced the decisions to intervene, and ethnic politics were not unimportant in determining which military officers allied themselves with particular political parties. For example, both Afrifa and Busia, were Ashanti. In addition, governments—both civilian and military— have tended to rise and fall in Ghana along with the price of cocoa on the international market.[33]

Integration into the world capitalist system can occur without the armed forces necessarily playing a dominant role in the political system as the case of Mexico demonstrates. Foreign investment and credits were important in helping build up Mexico's rail system and its mining sector prior to the 1910 revolution, but only during World War II did the Mexican economy become increasingly open to foreign capital. In the Aleman administration (1946–1952) the integration of the Mexican economy into the world capitalist system was intensified as foreign, primarily U.S., transnational corporations became active in both manufacturing and agricultural sectors. During the 1950s and 1960s, direct foreign investment grew sharply, from $566 million in 1950 to $1 billion in 1960 and to $2.8 billion in 1970, as Japanese and West European companies joined U.S. firms in the Mexican market. The importance of foreign credit is underlined by the huge debt incurred by the Mexican government during the 1970s and 1980s.

[33] Björn Hettne, "Soldiers and Politics: The Case of Ghana," *Journal of Peace Proposals* 17:2 (1980): 173–93.

To be sure, the Mexican armed forces have been used to suppress rural discontent and were used against the students in 1968. Yet the armed forces have not overthrown any government since 1920, and civilians have sought to instill in military officers a belief in civilian rule. In fact, Mexico's economy became more open long after the military had been depoliticized. In part depoliticization has been effected by buying off the officer corps.

> It became government policy to corrupt the Army. Senior officers were encouraged to enrich themselves with assorted business opportunities, sinecures and favors, and even illicit activities, such as contraband, drug trafficking and prostitution, were tolerated. Corruption also helped maintain tensions between the Army and the Presidential Military Staff: promotions were more rapid in the Army, but the opportunities for contraband, influence peddling and other rackets were greater on the Staff. At the same time, the government protected the armed forces from media criticism, and even when files on the rackets of several top generals were presented to the De la Madrid administration, no action was taken.[34]

There is absolutely no comparison between the political influence exerted by the Mexican armed forces and that enjoyed by the Chilean, Brazilian, or Argentinian security forces.

When assessing the political and economic functions of Third World armed forces, the corporate interests of the officer corps should never be underrated. To consider but one example, prior to 1945, politics in Venezuela were dominated by senior army officers who, it has been claimed, "ran the government as their personal domain." Lower-ranking officers, resentful of the economic and political advantages enjoyed by their senior officers, were also particularly angry at the slowness with which promotions were awarded. These lower-ranking officers eventually allied with the main civilian opposition party, Acción Democrática, and in 1945 this coalition overthrew the senior officer-dominated system.

Under Acción Democrática leadership, reforms favoring the middle classes and labor were introduced, a new democratic constitution was promulgated, and elections were held in 1947. By 1948, however, the constitutionally elected government of Gallegos had been overthrown by its former military supporters. While the armed forces claimed that the Acción Democrática government had "attempted to incite the people to conduct a general strike of a political nature," clearly the main disagree-

---

[34] Alan Riding, *Distant Neighbors. A Portrait of the Mexicans* (New York: Alfred A. Knopf, 1985), p. 91. See also pp. 92–93, 134–56.

ment between the party and the military was the issue of civilian control of the military.[35] Without taking into account the corporate interests of the military, it would be possible to view the situation as one in which younger military officers began a period of reform (the 1945 coup) they subsequently felt was becoming too radical (the 1948 coup). In fact, in both cases the interveners had as their primary goal the protection and enhancement of their own interests.

The armament-underdevelopment school correctly identifies the importance of force in preventing structural change in the Third World. In focusing on the way in which force is used to integrate Third World countries into the global capitalist system, however, two important facts tend to be either ignored or at least vastly underrated. First, the use of force did not originate with the rise of capitalism; the history of the world is the history of larger and stronger groups attempting to dominate smaller and weaker ones, generally by violent methods. Second, in the modern world, Western capitalist countries are not alone in promoting the use of force in developing countries.

It is true that security assistance from socialist countries has been instrumental to the success of some national liberation movements, for example those in Vietnam, Angola, and Mozambique. More often than not, however, the policies of socialist countries toward such movements have been strongly influenced by power politics.[36] Although the main recipients of Soviet and Chinese economic and security assistance have been movements or governments sharing the donors' commitment to the creation of a socialized economy, socialist support has also been extended to regimes as repressive and antisocialist as any backed by Western govern-

---

[35] Lieuwen, *Arms and Politics,* pp. 84–87.

In Guatemala in the mid-1940s, the armed forces were divided between those who wanted a continued military dictatorship under the control of senior officers and a group of younger officers who supported social change. In 1944, the younger officers gained control, set up a civilian-military junta, and inaugurated a period of reform. For the civilian members of the government, one element of these reforms was to reduce the political power of the military. The coup of 1954 was not so much a reaction against reform in general as it was a move against those groups that threatened what some military officers perceived as the "traditional" military right to control the Guatemalan political system. The 1963 coup was carried out to prevent the labor-left from regaining power, both because the armed forces had come to oppose social reform in principle and, even more important, because the armed forces believed they had to protect themselves from revenge on the part of left-wing civilians. Ibid., pp. 91–94, and Edwin Lieuwen, *Generals vs. Presidents: Neo-Militarism in Latin America* (New York: Praeger, 1964), pp. 42–43.

[36] Stockholm International Peace Research Institute, *The Arms Trade with the Third World* (Stockholm: Almqvist & Wiksell, 1971), pp. 198–214, and Roger E. Kanet, "Soviet Military Assistance to the Third World," pp. 51–54, in *Communist Nations' Military Assistance,* ed. John F. Copper and Daniel Papp (Boulder, Colo.: Westview Press, 1983).

ments. Uganda under the Amin regime, for example, received considerable Soviet support.[37]

Even governments which profess to share the same ideological goals as the Soviet Union—the Dergue in Ethiopia, for example—are perfectly capable of repressing their own citizens. Strong Soviet support for the Dergue's attempt to eradicate the groups that have been fighting for more than twenty years for an independent Eritrea is perhaps not of the same magnitude as the French and U.S. involvement in Indochina, but its intent is the same. More on a par with Western attempts to control southeast Asia is the Soviet invasion of Afghanistan in the name of socialist brotherhood. The Vietnamese communists, having gained complete control of their country in the late 1970s, have succeeded in virtually colonizing both Kampuchea and Laos. The tendency of countries to make the most of every opportunity to dominate other countries unfortunately respects no ideological boundaries.

It has been suggested that arms sold by the socialist countries may not produce the same negative effects on Third World economies as Western arms sales and assistance because recipient countries are not required to pay in hard currency for the former.[38] Prior to about the mid-1970s, the Soviet Union generally accepted payment in the form of commodities or local currency. Since the mid-1970s, the USSR has increasingly requested payment in hard currency. The exact percentage of arms deals carrying this stipulation is not known, but it was estimated that in 1977 the Soviet Union may have earned as much as $1.5 billion in hard currency through the sale of weapons.[39]

Even if all East-bloc arms transfers involved barter agreements, it is not clear that there is a significant difference between producing commodities to sell on the international market in order to obtain hard currency to purchase weapons from capitalist countries and producing commodities to exchange with socialist countries for weapons. In both cases the orientation of the economy is at least in part determined by the needs and interests of an external power. In addition, as Chapter 7 shows, the terms of trade between socialist and Third World countries can be as unequal as those between Western and Third World countries.[40] For those countries

[37] Luckham, "Militarism," pp. 159–64.

[38] Ibid.

[39] United States, Congress, Joint Economic Committee, Compendium: *Soviet Economy in a Time of Change*, vol. 2, 96th Cong., 1st Sess., 10 October 1979 (Washington, D.C.: Government Printing Office, 1979), pp. 212, 214. See also Chapter 3, n. 29.

[40] Luckham, "Militarism," p. 159. See also David Chaffetz, "Afghanistan in Turmoil," *International Affairs* 56 (January 1980): 18–19, for a brief account of how the USSR set the terms of trade for nonmilitary exchanges to its advantage in Afghanistan during the

of which the Soviet Union demands payment in hard currency, the problems they face in paying for Soviet weapons are the same as if they had purchased arms from Western sources.

Also to be reckoned with is the cost of maintaining the imported weapons. Arms imports from Western countries are recognized to have various costs attached to them beyond the original price tag. Money must be found to pay for spare parts and often, in the case of the more sophisticated equipment, for foreign technicians to service and sometimes even operate the weapons. A country heavily dependent on one arms supplier can find itself under strong pressure to accede to that supplier's demands on any number of issues. There is no reason why the same additional costs should not be attached to weapons imported from socialist countries. Indeed, Egypt was reportedly paying in hard currency for the services of the approximately 15,000 Soviet troops and advisers in that country in 1971. Reportedly, Somalia also came under considerable pressure to make political concessions favorable to the USSR in exchange for supplies of spare parts for Soviet-produced weapons.[41]

Another troubling aspect of the armament-underdevelopment theory is its focus on the transfer of weapons and technology. As Chapter 3 shows, much Third World security expenditure takes the form of operating costs, particularly personnel costs. In the 1950s and 1960s, many developing

---

Daoud period. See also Alain Cass, "Moscow Aid Woos the Third World," *Financial Times,* 4 March 1980, which discusses Soviet economic aid to the Third World, and K. K. Sharma, "India Re-assesses Comecon Trade Links," *Financial Times,* 15 March 1983, which discusses problems caused by fluctuations in Comecon purchases and reported resale of Indian commodities for hard currency.

Although barter trade can also produce economic distortions, some governments—notably the Indian government—are happy to continue to barter commodities for weapons with the Soviet Union. This may be because the USSR and Eastern European countries will accept goods of poorer quality than could be sold for hard currency on the international market. It may also be because the terms of trade are actually favorable to the developing countries. Deepak Nayyar, "India's Trade with the Socialist Countries," pp. 105–42, in *Economic Relations Between Socialist Countries and the Third World,* ed. Deepak Nayyar (London: MacMillan, 1977), suggests that "The terms of trade under bilateral agreements were, on balance, probably favourable to India and, at any rate, no worse than those obtained from other countries" (p. 136). The benefits accruing to Third World countries from nonmilitary barter agreements with Soviet-bloc countries are described in Deepak Nayyar, "Economic Relations Between Socialist Countries and the Third World: An Introduction," p. 5, in the same volume.

[41] Regarding Egypt, see Seymour M. Hersh, *The Price of Power: Kissinger in the Nixon White House* (New York: Summit Books, 1983), pp. 208–9. On Somalia, see United States, Senate, Committee on Foreign Relations, Report: *Prospects for Multilateral Arms Export Restraint,* 96th Cong., 1st Sess. (Washington, D.C.: Government Printing Office, April 1979).

country armed forces made do with rather few and relatively unsophisticated weapons, U.S. military assistance notwithstanding. Even in the 1970s, arms purchases were concentrated in a fairly small number of countries (see Table 3–5). This means that many Third World countries have probably been more influenced in terms of technology transfer by activities in the civil sector than by the purchase of weapons from abroad.

The belief that the transfer of weapons from Western countries implies a transfer of military organization, social and economic structure, and conflict patterns is also problematic. If this is true, then the transfer of weapons from Soviet-bloc countries should influence Third World countries in the direction of socialism. Yet it is difficult, if not actually impossible, to imagine in what way the effect of transferring a MIG-19, for example, might differ from that of transferring an F-5E. There is nothing in the construction or possible mission of either aircraft that distinguishes one as the product of a capitalist system and the other as the product of a socialist system. Indeed, since Soviet-bloc weapons are primarily designed with NATO countries in mind and vice versa, the weapons possessed by each of the two blocs are quite similar. When sold to third parties, therefore, they should have similar secondary effects, whatever those might be. Yet the secondary effects of Soviet-bloc weapons are not discussed in the armament-underdevelopment literature.

It is evident, then, that the armament-underdevelopment theory fails to incorporate some rather important kinds of information. Most serious is the tendency to ignore or downplay the use of force to influence economic and politico-strategic relations between socialist countries and the Third World and to consider the transfer of weapons from socialist countries as more benign than those from Western industrialized ones. This theory also understates the extent to which military intervention is important in helping to decide which élites will benefit from *whatever* economic system is in place as well as the degree to which the armed forces become involved in politics for *noneconomic* reasons. At the same time, this approach to the relationship between the armed forces and development illuminates an issue that tends to be ignored in more conventional examinations: the importance of military force in shaping socioeconomic and sociopolitical relations within and between states.

COMPLEX ISSUES DEMAND COMPLEX ANALYSIS

One fact clearly emerging from the foregoing discussion is that Third World security sectors play a complex role in the development process. To obtain a complete picture of the importance of the armed forces in shaping the future of developing countries, it is necessary to include as many different kinds of information as possible. Differences occur not only from country to country but also over time within the same country. Neither of the two major approaches used during the last thirty years for analyzing the role played by the armed forces have succeeded in integrating all the different kinds of information necessary to produce a comprehensive image of the military in development.

In part, the problem can be traced to both the relative lack of detailed case studies in the literature prior to the 1970s and the corresponding lack of interest in producing such studies. Development literature proper contains many case studies, of course, but it is rare to find a discussion of the role played by the military in developing countries in the literature on socioeconomic development; countries ruled by the armed forces for many years are exceptions. It is always easier to take one or two facts and weave them into a theoretical artifice than to take hundreds of facts and mold them into an all-embracing model. Case studies are not, however, the answer to all the problems confronting research to date on the military in development.

As the discussion of these two approaches demonstrates, one primary problem has been the inability of many people who have written on this topic to remove their ideological blinders. The following chapters show quite clearly, however, that if one wants to evaluate the role that the military sector plays in promoting or hindering development, it is necessary to look at each country over a period of years and determine *if, when* and *to what extent* each anticipated effect has operated. It is also necessary to identify those groups—foreign and domestic—that stand to gain in some way from the involvement of the military in the political and economic systems of a country and to clarify what each group expects to obtain from the military's participation. Finally, it is necessary to accept the fact that generalizations will be difficult to make.

2

. . . .

THE DETERMINANTS OF

SECURITY EXPENDITURE

In the industrialized countries, security issues are viewed primarily from the perspective of potential external conflicts, and the role of the armed forces is to protect governments and citizens alike against external threats. In the Third World, internal security considerations often tend to outweigh those of external security, and the foremost task of many armed forces is to protect governments and élite groups against the mass of the population. Irrespective of whether internal or external security objectives dominate, the level of security expenditure should, in theory, be determined by an assessment of the likely security threats confronting a country and the most effective means of meeting them, within the overall framework of resource availability.

In reality, this simple formula is complicated by additional considerations unrelated to the security environment itself. For example, the tendency of bureaucracies to attempt to reproduce themselves endlessly knows no political or ideological boundaries. Security bureaucracies are just as likely to try to increase their share of governmental resources as are civilian portions of the state administration. In addition, it is not always easy to reach an agreement on what does and does not constitute a threat to a country's security. Within any political system, even the most authoritarian, unanimity of purpose is rare, and the allocation of resources for security purposes requires bargaining and negotiation. Different groups within either society as a whole or the ruling élite will have divergent notions of what constitutes security as well as the importance of security vis-à-vis other goals. More security expenditure often means the allocation of fewer resources to other sectors; the advisability of making such trade-offs and in which sectors may be open to debate. For some developing countries, the actions of the major powers can add a further dimension to the security equation, for example by exacerbating regional or domestic conflicts.

For the purposes of this discussion, the major focus that condition the level of security expenditure in developing countries are divided into five broad groups: the influence of external conflicts, the requirements of internal (regime) security, domestic bureaucratic and budgetary factors, the influence of the armed forces themselves, and the role of the major powers. These groupings have been made in order better to organize the discussion and facilitate thinking about the determinants of security expenditure; however, they should not be seen as entirely independent of each other. In any country, one or two factors may be dominant when decisions are made concerning the allocation of resources to the security sector. That does not mean the other factors exert no influence. Furthermore, the relative importance of individual determinants will vary over time. For example, the break-up of Pakistan in 1971 reduced the potential threat to India from one of its major regional adversaries while the reunification of Vietnam in 1975, along with Hanoi's foreign policy, caused considerable unease among several of its neighbors.

THE INFLUENCE OF EXTERNAL CONFLICTS

Protection against external aggression provides the *raison d'être* for all armed forces, and external security considerations are most often used to justify increases in security expenditure. Many Third World countries are involved in unresolved conflicts with neighboring states which, with greater or lesser frequency, flare into active combat. All interstate wars since the end of World War II have taken place in the Third World, although there have been industrialized country participants in some of these conflicts. Yet the vast majority of Third World countries face few, if any, serious threats from abroad.

The noncommunist countries of Southeast Asia are typical of many developing countries in this respect. Despite fears of Vietnamese aggression following Vietnam's reunification in 1975, political and military élites in Thailand, the Philippines, Malaysia, Indonesia, and Singapore have not considered their countries to be in any danger of direct external aggression since the late 1970s. Instead, concern tends to be directed toward what can be described as indirect aggression from abroad, but even here the level of concern has not been very high. "Indirect external threats were of three kinds: outside support to insurgent movements that drain government resources; a sharp increase in Soviet military power in the region which, if unbalanced by a continued U.S. presence, might prove psychologically unsettling and politically constraining; and other forms of subversion."[1]

---

[1] Franklin B. Weinstein, "The Meaning of National Security in Southeast Asia," *The Bulletin of the Atomic Scientists* (November 1978), p. 21.
Other commentators have described the external-security concerns of ASEAN countries:

Although the external security threats facing most Third World countries are minimal, leaders do not hesitate to invoke the actions of other countries to justify either an increase in the armed forces' share of state expenditures or the purchase of a new weapon system. For example, tensions between Argentina and Chile in the mid- to late-1970s over the Beagle Channel were reflected in increased aircraft purchases on the part of the Chilean Air Force.[2] In a similar vein, Third World leaders argue that security and economic development are intimately related. A growing economy is said to be necessary to fund defense requirements, although without adequate security from external attack the benefits of economic development can all too easily be forfeited. The fact that conflicts can often be resolved more effectively through negotiation and compromise rather than by the threat or actual use of force is frequently lost sight of.

When external threats can clearly be seen to have declined, it may become difficult for proponents of increased security expenditure to invoke external threat as a reason for more spending on the security sector. This was one effect of the United States-dominated system of hemispheric defense in Latin America during the 1950s and much of the 1960s. With the United States guaranteeing the security of the region, rivalry among Latin American countries was temporarily reduced, and one of the main arguments in favor of higher security spending was undercut.[3] Although these countries allocated not inconsiderable portions of their national resources to the security sector between 1950 and 1980, their share in global security outlays has increased at a much slower rate than that of other developing countries (Tables 2-1 and 2-2).

The subsequent development of security relations in Latin America shows that once an arms race mentality has been adopted, it can be extremely difficult to overcome. One goal of U.S. arms transfer policy to-

---

No ASEAN country expects to be invaded by land or by sea. The only "external" threats which worry them is the threat of foreign cultures which could uproot and replace the indigenous ethnic values with an alien system, the threat of economic penetration by foreigners, and the threat posed by technology transfer—all of which have political and economic implications—and above all the premature evolution of rising expectations within the population which the government cannot cope with.

"ASEAN Foreign Policies and Threat Perceptions," *Military Technology* 9 : 12 (1985) : 37. See also Weinstein, "The Meaning," p. 23, regarding economic and social threats from external sources.

[2] Carlos Portales and Augusto Varas, "The Role of Military Expenditure in the Development Process: Chile 1952–1973 and 1973–1980: Two Contrasting Cases," *Ibero Americana* 12 : 1–2 (1983) : 42.

[3] Ibid., pp. 23–24.

TABLE 2-1

Security Expenditure of Selected South American Countries,
Actual Outlays, 1950–1980 (in percentages)

Year	Argentina		Chile		Colombia		Peru	
	GDP	CGE	GDP	CGE	GDP	CGE	GDP	CGE
1950	2.8	13.9	2.7	—	1.1	20.7	3.9	35.4
1955	2.5	16.8	2.2	—	1.9	20.0	3.7	37.0
1960	2.2	16.7	3.2	14.7	1.3	18.2	3.4	35.5
1965	1.6	15.0	2.8	13.3	1.4	15.0	4.8	27.3
1970	1.9	14.2	4.5	21.0	1.6	11.7	5.3	27.9
1975	2.0	9.6	5.7	19.3	1.0[c]	—	6.0	14.2
1980	2.6[a]	16.7[a]	5.6[b]	16.4[b]	0.9[c]	—	3.1[b]	17.9[b]

Sources: All data except Colombia 1975 and 1980: Nicole Ball, Third-World Security Expenditure: A Statistical Compendium, C-10250-M5 (Stockholm: National Defense Research Institute, 1984). Colombia 1975 and 1980: Stockholm International Peace Research Institute, World Armaments and Disarmament, SIPRI Yearbook 1983 (London: Taylor & Francis, 1983), p. 174.
[a] Based on estimated expenditure.
[b] Data from 1979.
[c] Expenditure category unknown. These data may not be comparable to the others.

TABLE 2-2

Growth of Regional Shares in Global Security Expenditure,
1950–1984 (in percentages)

Region	1950–1955	1955–1960	1960–1965	1965–1970	1970–1975	1975–1980	1980–1984
South and Central America	−33.3	16.7	0	0	42.9	15.0	8.7
South America only	−30.8	22.2	0	0	54.5	5.9	11.1
All LDCs[a]	−41.1	36.4	35.6	11.5	90.7	13.3	−3.1
LDCs minus Middle East	−45.1	28.6	36.1	−4.1	48.0	20.3	−3.4

Source: Derived from Stockholm International Peace Research Institute, World Armaments and Disarmament, SIPRI Yearbook (Stockholm: Almqvist & Wiksell, 1972, 1974) and (London: Taylor & Francis, 1979, 1985).
[a] The category "All LDCs" excludes the People's Republic of China.

ward Latin America in the 1960s was to prevent the introduction of sophisticated aircraft into the region and thereby avoid lifting local arms races to new technology and cost levels. As long as the hemispheric security system remained in place and the United States was the main supplier of weapons to Latin America, this policy could be upheld. It did not, however, eradicate old rivalries among Latin American countries: Argentina and Brazil monitor each others' acquisitions very closely; Chile tends to react to Argentinian purchases and Peru to Chilean.

The Peruvian introduction of supersonic aircraft into Latin America, which the United States had tried to prevent, originated in a U.S. sale of F-4 aircraft to Argentina. The Argentinian purchase was used to justify the Chilean acquisition of British Hawker Hunters,[4] and Peru responded by procuring the supersonic Mirage-5 fighter aircraft from France in 1968. As soon as Peru broke ranks and acquired a supersonic plane, several other Latin American countries felt obliged to follow suit. The Mirage-5 sale provided the justification for purchases by Brazil, Colombia, and Argentina of Mirage aircraft in the early 1970s. The Chilean Air Force took delivery of the first of its American-supplied supersonic F-5Es in 1975, and it has been reported that the Peruvian Mirage purchase caused the Chilean military to feel weak and potentially threatened.[5] This perception must be set against the fact that the two countries had not engaged in serious conflict for nearly one hundred years.

The procurement of weapons does not account for the major portion of most developing countries' security budgets. (Chapter 3 discusses the composition of security expenditure in detail.) Nonetheless, weapons purchases can and do make noticeable bumps in these budgets. In Chile in 1975, for example, real outlays declined for all sections of the security forces except the Air Force, which was beginning to pay for its F-5E aircraft.[6] Furthermore, the purchase price is far from the only economic cost attached to weapons. Because weapons must be maintained and repaired regularly if they are to operate efficiently and effectively, technicians must be trained and paid, equipment purchased, workshops constructed, and so on. As weapons have become more technologically advanced, the costs of repair and maintenance have climbed accordingly. For example, the

[4] Stockholm International Peace Research Institute (SIPRI), *The Arms Trade with the Third World* (Stockholm: Almqvist & Wiksell, 1971), p. 701. The thinking behind the United States's hemispheric defense system, based on bilateral agreements, is discussed on pages 702–22. See pages 716–20 for more details of the introduction of supersonic aircraft into Latin America. None of the parties was really concerned with vital strategic issues.

[5] Portales and Varas, "The Role," pp. 24, 42.

[6] Ibid.

helicopters operated by Iran during its war with Iraq have required eleven hours of maintenance for each hour they have been in the air.[7]

Reactive arms procurement policies are clearly not likely to lower security budgets; in fact, some believe they are a major contributing factor to war. Areas in which local arms races flourish—for example the Middle East, the Korean peninsula, and the Indian subcontinent—have been major scenes of armed conflict during the last thirty years or more. It is nonetheless much more likely that arms races are the symptoms of unresolved conflicts than the causes of them. Wars result from political decisions, not from either the simple accumulation of weaponry or high levels of expenditure on the security sector in general. Some countries build up their armed forces and procure various weapons because they believe that at some point they might become involved in a conflict with a neighboring state which has, in all likelihood, undertaken a similar build-up. (In addition, weapons are sometimes acquired because of interservice rivalries unrelated to external security environments.) Reactive arms procurement does not, however, necessarily lead to war. South America in the 1970s offers a good example of how the tensions surrounding an arms race can be defused.

Regional military élites believed that a series of wars might break out in South America during the 1970s. Chile and Peru underwent particularly large build-ups, with Peru importing a considerable amount of weaponry from the USSR. Yet no wars occurred. The reason peace was maintained had nothing to do with the level of armament in the region; rather, it was entirely dependent on political factors. The left-leaning military government of Velasco in Peru had felt threatened by the extreme right-wing coup d'état in Chile in 1973. The Chilean military government in turn believed itself threatened by the Velasco regime. The removal of Velasco by the more right-wing Morales Bermúdez and the reversal of many of the previous government's policies reduced the tension between Chile and Peru and ended the most recent round of war scares involving the two countries.[8]

Weapons and soldiers are committed to war as a result of political decisions. Wars do not occur *simply* because the men and the weaponry to carry out an attack exist. Some evidence suggests, however, that governments controlling large military establishments may be more likely to at-

[7] Ann Schulz, "Military Expenditures and Economic Performance in Iran, 1950–1980" (Worcester, Mass.: Clark University, 1980, mimeograph), p. 27.

[8] José Encinas del Pando, "The Role of Military Expenditure in the Development Process. Peru: A Case Study, 1950–1980," *Ibero Americana* 12:1–2 (1983):78.

tempt to resolve conflicts through force, rather than through negotiations aimed at resolving underlying political or economic problems. It may also be true that governments controlled by military officers will be more likely to see threats in military terms. In the Third World, of course, political and military leaders are often one and the same.

One distinction is clear. Countries engaged in armed conflict or involved in unresolved disputes that periodically flare into violence are among the Third World heaviest spenders on the security sector. While many developing countries consistently spend 2 percent or less of their gross domestic product on security-related activities, 5 percent of gross product is a minimum estimate for most Middle Eastern countries during the last two decades. Others have spent considerably larger amounts. North and South Korea are technically still at war. In those few years during the 1970s for which estimates are available for the former, the Pyongyang government is shown to have devoted between 9 and 10 percent of its gross product to the security sector annually; South Korea is estimated to have spent between 4 and 7 percent of its gross domestic product on the armed forces since the late 1950s.[9] Heavy inflows of U.S. military and security-supporting assistance in the late 1950s and throughout the 1960s enabled the South Korean government to build up one of the world's largest military establishments with a relatively modest— 4 percent of GDP— outlay of domestic resources. The reduction in U.S. grant aid since the early 1970s has led to a corresponding increase in the proportion of South Korea's own resources allocated to the security sector.

India and Pakistan, which have gone to war with each other three times since independence in 1947, spend sizable portions of their central government budgets and their national products on the security sector. Since the early 1960s, India has allocated on average nearly 4 percent of its gross product and nearly 25 percent of its central government budget to the security forces; the corresponding figures for Pakistan are 5 percent and 30 percent. When considering these figures recall that state (provincial) governments in India have responsibility for some expenditure which in Pakistan is the responsibility of the central government; thus, the two

[9] Stockholm International Peace Research Institute, *World Armaments and Disarmament. SIPRI Yearbook, 1979* (London: Taylor and Francis, 1979), pp. 42–43, 46–47; and *SIPRI Yearbook 1983*, p. 172. Gavin Kennedy surveyed forty-one countries during the 1960s and concluded: "The annual average defense allocation out of state budgets in the 1960s shows a strong relationship between military hostilities and the size of the allocation." Gavin Kennedy, *The Military in the Third World* (London: Duckworth, 1974), p. 158. Kennedy used data from the United Nations *Statistical Yearbook* which, as explained in Chapter 3, are not particularly reliable. The SIPRI figures cited here indicate that other, more reliable data confirms this relationship.

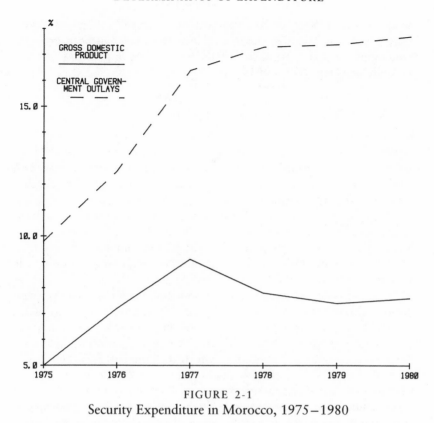

FIGURE 2-1

Security Expenditure in Morocco, 1975–1980

Source: Nicole Ball, *Third World Security Expenditure: A Statistical Compendium,*
    C-10250-M5 (Stockholm: National Defence Research Institute, 1984), p. 146.
Note: These proportions are based on credits appropriated. It is possible that actual expen-
    diture data would present a somewhat different picture. The data presented here are,
    however, broadly in agreement with data produced by other sources in terms of expen-
    diture trend.

central government proportions are not strictly comparable. India's 1962
war with China and the 1965 and 1971 wars with Pakistan stimulated
higher levels of security spending. The 1962 war ended a ten-year downward trend in the proportion of Indian central government expenditures
devoted to the security forces, begun in 1951, causing the proportion of
gross product devoted to security to double between 1961 and 1963.
This higher level of security spending in gross product has essentially
been maintained since that time.

  In the same way, Morocco's security expenditure has been affected by the conflict in the Spanish Sahara, which began in 1975 (Figure 2-1). Security expenditure as a proportion of gross product had been growing throughout the early part of the 1970s, but the rate of growth increased markedly between 1975 and 1977.[10]

INTERNAL SECURITY

Although external security considerations can play an important part in determining the level of expenditure on the armed forces, some Third World countries, which have not engaged in conflict for many years and which are under no obvious external threat, still allocate considerable portions of state and national resources to the security sector. In addition, countries for which external threats have diminished substantially have nonetheless continued to allocate substantial sums to the armed forces largely because preserving internal security is an important function of most armed forces in the Third World today. In fact, in some countries, it is the primary function.

The term *internal security* is actually something of a misnomer since its purpose is rarely to make all citizens equally secure. Rather, in many countries, the point is to enable the ruling élite—whether civilian, military, or most likely some combination—to remain in power and to sustain a socioeconomic system under which the élite enriches itself at the expense of the vast majority of the population. In these cases, it is more accurate to speak of regime security.

The predominantly internal role of the armed forces is particularly clear in Latin America where interstate conflicts have occurred very infrequently over the last century but military establishments nonetheless flourish. The concept of national security, which assigns to the armed forces a central role not only in guaranteeing external security but also in defining and protecting internal security, is a Latin American invention. Similar doctrines exist in Asian countries such as Burma, Indonesia, and Bangladesh. African militaries have not produced formal policies analagous to the Latin American and Asian ones. Nonetheless it is clear that internal security (that is, élite protection) is of much greater importance for most African armed forces than external security functions.[11]

[10] Nicole Ball, *Third-World Security Expenditure: A Statistical Compendium*, C-10250-M5 (Stockholm: National Defence Research Institute, 1984), pp. 145–46.

[11] There was at least one attempt to institutionalize the Nigerian military's influence over the political system. In 1972, a former politician, Nnamdi Azikiwe, proposed the creation of a joint civilian-military administration which would rule Nigeria for at least the first five years after the military relinquished total control of the government. Known as "dyarchy," this proposal created considerable political controversy in Nigeria and indirectly contrib-

The Latin American doctrine of national security has been most influential in Argentina, Chile, Brazil, and Peru; its details vary from country to country, but the broad outlines are essentially the same. National security is believed to depend not only on the defense of a country from external attack but also on the existence of a strong economy and a unified society. Since development strengthens both the economy and society, it is a vital component of national security. A total development strategy is of first importance, and this, in turn, requires a strong government and an efficient planning apparatus. The executive branch of government in particular must be powerful, and considerable emphasis is placed on social control and the need to respect hierarchical authority. Pluralism is seen merely as a factor dividing the nation. In a similar vein, theorists claim justice can exist in the absence of political freedom. The military officers in Argentina, Peru, Chile, and Brazil eventually came to believe that civilians could not produce the developed and ordered society they deemed necessary for the preservation of national security. From there it was but a short step to deciding that the economic and political aspects of national security should be under the direct control of the armed forces, as well as the purely military ones.

The roots of the Latin American national security doctrine and the military's arrogation to itself of the central role in implementing that doctrine can be traced to the economic crises Latin American countries experienced in the 1930s, 1950s, and 1960s, to the underdeveloped state of Latin American economies and societies, and to the unwillingness of the ruling élites to share their power with the broad mass of the population.

---

uted to Gowon's fall after he retracted, in late 1974, his pledge to return Nigeria to civilian rule by 1976. See J. 'Bayo Adekson, *Nigeria in Search of a Stable Civil-Military System* (Boulder, Colo.: Westview Press, 1981), pp. 13–16, and J. 'Bayo Adekanye, "The Role of Military Expenditure in Nigerian Development" (Ibadan: Ibadan University, 1982, mimeograph) Part 3, pp. 20–22.

For a view of African armed forces as primarily concerned with internal security and control, see Seth Singleton, "Supplementary Military Forces in Sub-Saharan Africa: The Congo, Kenya, Tanzania, Uganda and Zaire," pp. 201, 205–6, in *Supplementary Military Forces, Reserves, Militias, Auxiliaries,* ed. Louis A. Zurcher and Gwyn Harries-Jenkins (Beverly Hills and London: Sage, 1978). Interviews with Asian élites most commonly elicit the response that "external threats are nonexistent or limited, but that 'the real threats are internal—and more economic than military.'" Weinstein, "The Meaning," p. 23. See also Harold W. Maynard, "Views of the Indonesian and Philippine Military Elites," pp. 148–50, in *The Military and Security in the Third World: Domestic and International Impacts,* ed. Sheldon W. Simon (Boulder, Colo.: Westview Press, 1978). Both the internal and external components of security threats faced by fourteen major Third World countries are discussed in Edward A. Kolodziej and Robert E. Harkavy, ed., *Security Policies of Developing Countries* (Lexington, Mass.: Lexington Books, 1982).

The disturbances resulting from these economic and political conditions were not answered by negotiations and accommodation but with force. The growing involvement of Latin American militaries in counterinsurgency during the 1960s played an important role in shaping the national security doctrine. As military officers studied counterinsurgency tactics, they also learned about the conditions that facilitated the growth of guerrilla movements. The training received from the U.S. military, which emphasized civic action programs to undercut the strength of revolutionary movements, was not without importance, but it did not play a central role in the development of the national security doctrine.

Probably the single most important factor in this respect was the outcome of the Cuban revolution. Not only did a small revolutionary group win the allegience of the population and succeed in overthrowing the extremely corrupt, inefficient civilian government headed by Batista, the new revolutionary armed forces executed many officers from the army who had served Batista's government. Other Latin American militaries absorbed this lesson and became determined never to allow opposition forces in their own countries to grow sufficiently strong to overthrow the established order—and with it, the regular armed forces.[12]

The Latin American national security doctrine not only provides the military with a useful justification for assuming control over the state, for discrediting the civilian leadership, and for preventing serious change in the existing power structure; but it also ensures a central role for the armed forces in a situation where their traditional, external security-oriented role is being eroded. The military, an organic part of the state bureaucracy, is just as concerned to maintain, and preferably expand, the share of national resources it controls as are the civilian portions of the bureaucracy. The national security doctrine has two distinct benefits in this regard. First, it justifies continued expenditure on the military in the absence of serious external threats. Second, if the military controls the government or holds a veto over it, serious reductions in security expenditure become more difficult to achieve. Even military-dominated governments are subject to the overall spending restraints necessitated by declining state reve-

---

[12] This discussion of the Latin American national security doctrine has been drawn primarily from Alfred Stepan, *The Military in Politics: Changing Patterns in Brazil* (Princeton, N.J.: Princeton University Press, 1971), pp. 172–83; Alfred Stepan, "The New Professionalism of Internal Warfare and Military Role Expansion," pp. 47–53, in *Authoritarian Brazil*, ed. Alfred Stepan (New Haven: Yale University Press, 1973); and José Encinas del Pando, "Economic, Military and Socio-Political Variables in Argentina, Chile and Peru (1950–1980), A Regional Analysis" (Lima: University of Lima, 1983, mimeograph), pp. 222–24. A summary of U.S. counterinsurgency and civic action programs can be found in SIPRI, *The Arms Trade*, pp. 707–15.

nues in times of economic crises (see the following discussions of Chile and Nigeria).

Burma and Indonesia have developed their own versions of the Latin American national security doctrine, and Bangladesh is in the process of formulating one as well. The Burmese "National Ideology of the Defence Services," which actually developed about the same time as its Latin American counterpart, similarly equates national security both with defense against external enemies and maintenance of the integrity of the country and with implementation of successful development programs. In this case, the accent has been on socialist-oriented development. The attempt of the civilian government led by U Nu to reach an accommodation with separatist ethnic movements and the economic problems confronting the civilian regime were two of the more important reasons the Burmese military decided in 1962 to assume total control over the government.

The Indonesian armed forces (ABRI) have developed a doctrine called *dwi fungsi* (dual function). This doctrine evolved over a period of years, but it was most clearly enunciated after the armed forces overthrew Sukarno. According to ABRI itself, "The army does not have an exclusively military duty but is concerned with all fields of social life." Essentially this means that the army has reserved for itself the permanent right to intervene in the "ideological, political, social, economic, cultural, and religious fields." In Bangladesh, the late General Zia developed a concept called "total national defense." According to the current military ruler of Bangladesh, General Ershad, this "calls for combining the role of nation-building and conflict defence into one concept." Like "national security" in Latin America, each of these Asian doctrines is motivated by the desire to justify a central role in society for the armed forces, both now and in the future.[13]

The use of the armed forces in an internal security role is not limited to those countries facing relatively low levels of external threat. Pakistan has fought two wars with India since both gained independence from Britain in 1947. Pakistani leaders have also traditionally feared the Soviet Union which is a close, although not actually contiguous, neighbor. The Soviet invasion of Afghanistan in 1979 gave that threat somewhat more sub-

[13] On Burma, see Moshe Lissak, "Military Roles in Modernization: Thailand and Burma," pp. 455–62, in *The Political Influence of the Military. A Comparative Reader*, eds. Amos Perlmutter and Valerie Plave Bennett (New Haven and London: Yale University Press, 1980). On Indonesia, see Harold Crouch, "Generals and Business in Indonesia," *Pacific Affairs* 48 (Winter 1975–1976):519–20. On Bangladesh, see S. Kamaluddin, "An Army is Forged in a Decade of Friction," *Far Eastern Economic Review* 1983), p. 28.

43

stance than it had held previously. At the same time, throughout the last thirty-five years, Pakistan's armed forces have been very much involved in controlling the government and preventing changes to the country's socioeconomic and political power structures.

> There are armies that defend their nation's borders; there are armies that are concerned with protecting their own position in society; and there are armies that defend a cause or an idea. The Pakistan Army does all three. From the day Pakistan was created, it has been active in helping to establish internal order and in protecting Pakistan's permeable and often ill-defined borders. During this period it has used its power and special position within Pakistan to ensure that it received adequate weapons, resources, and manpower.[14]

The same can be said, to varying degrees, about many other national militaries. The armed forces in the Middle East, for example, have often been engaged in interstate conflict, yet they are also important elements in the power structure of states such as Iraq, Syria, and Egypt. Although the military government which came to power in Egypt in 1952 has since adopted a parliamentary veneer, the armed forces are still very much a part of the power élite. Because Egyptian policymakers frequently appear to equate threats to the regime with threats to the nation, the priority accorded the Egyptian armed forces in terms of resource allocation is not solely determined by its role as defender of Egypt's sovereignty. A similar situation exists in Syria and Iraq where regime security is a basic function of the armed forces.[15]

The ways in which considerations of regime and external defense can interact was illustrated by Mohammad Reza Pahlavi's Iran. Iran under

[14] Stephen Philip Cohen, "Pakistan," p. 108, in *Security Policies*, ed. Kolodziej and Harkavy. There have been rumors that one consequence of the Soviet intervention in Afghanistan has been the virtual annexation of a portion of Afghan territory by the USSR which would give Pakistan and the USSR a common border.

[15] See for example the chapters on Egypt, Iraq, and Syria in *Security Policies*, ed. Kolodziej and Harkavy, especially pp. 195–98, 235–38, and 267–70. The importance of security expenditure in retaining the loyalty of the Egyptian armed forces in the early 1980s is discussed in Charles Richards, "Higher Spending Aims to Keep Armed Forces Happy," *Financial Times* (4 October 1983), Egypt V.

With regard to Southeast Asia, it has been argued that "The central analytic problem is to distinguish between threats to the security of the nation and threats to the security of certain ruling groups. To be sure, the ruling elites see their national responsibilities in broader terms than the preservation of their own privileges. Egalitarian ideologies have become part of the everyday rhetoric of political discourse in Southeast Asia. But when these leaders are forced to make hard decisions, they tend to interpret any threat to their leadership as a challenge to national security." Weinstein, "The Meaning," p. 20.

the shah embodied the curious phenomenon of a militarized regime in which the military establishment itself had surprisingly little power. This pattern can be observed in a number of semifeudal states—such as Iran, Jordan, Morocco, Saudi Arabia—that appear to be militarized but have relatively weak military establishments. Iranian rulers have traditionally relied on the support of the armed forces to help them gain and retain power. In the case of the shah, this desire to ensure the continuation of his rule was so great that he not only used the military to protect himself domestically, but he also took numerous precautions designed to prevent the armed forces from becoming too strong in their own right and presenting themselves as an alternative source of power. A number of his actions, meant to protect his regime, were counterproductive in terms of external security.

As another precaution against a military coup against the monarchy, the shah ordered restrictions on the type of training that the army undertook. Exercises were limited to daylight hours, and tended to be parade ground maneuvers rather than simulations of possible operations. Armored batallions were not allowed to travel more than 200 kilometers within one year.

Also to prevent top military officers from acting independently of the throne, the shah structured military authority and communication along vertical lines. The commanders of provinical military units had no direct contact with one another. The shah's permission was required for them to meet or for them to travel to Teheran.[16]

A good deal of the shah's fear of the Soviet Union and Iraq derived not only from the possibility of direct invasion of Iran but also from the support these countries gave to left-leaning guerrilla forces in the region. The Iranian intervention in Oman should be seen primarily in this light. The shah considered the Omani operation, in which U.S. advisers helped coordinate the activities of non-Omani forces (those from Iran, Jordan, and Pakistan), as a sort of training exercise whose purpose was to teach Iranian troops to fight effectively against guerrillas. This particular element of the shah's regime security policy has been adopted by the Khomeini government as well, since it is equally concerned to prevent the growth of left-wing guerrilla movements in Iran.[17]

The central role accorded the Iranian armed forces by the shah in protecting regime security was reflected by the priority they were given in terms of budgetary allocations. Even before the shah's arms purchasing

---

[16] Schulz, "Military Expenditures," pp. 20–21.
[17] Ibid., chap. 1, passim.

spree began in the early 1970s, the armed forces received a large share of governmental and national resources. Much Iranian military expenditure has always been used to pay the salaries of military officers and thus buy their loyalty to the regime of the day; conscripts, technicians, and non-commissioned officers have fared much less well in this respect. The rapid influx of weapons during the 1970s caused security expenditures to absorb even larger amounts of Iranian resources. The high point in terms of budgetary outlays between 1950 and 1980 was reached in 1976 with about 35 percent and in terms of gross product in 1975 with nearly 17 percent of GDP.[18]

As suggested by the Iranian experience, the armed forces can be both an important source of power for many Third World governments and a potential rival. Keeping the officer corps well paid and supplied with amenities and equipment is seen by some governments as a way of preventing coups d'état. One associates this kind of reasoning most often with civilian governments. In Uganda after the 1964 army mutiny—when the army demanded more rapid Africanization of the officer corps and higher rates of pay—the Obote government sought to avoid further confrontations with the military by meeting many of the army's demands. As a result, even the average soldier was quite well paid in terms of what he could expect to earn in the civilian economy at that time. It has been estimated that the ordinary soldier earned between fifteen and thirty times as much as the average civilian.[19] In the event, Obote's strategy failed since the army, under the leadership of Lieutenant General Idi Amin, took control of the government in January 1971.

[18] Ball, *Third-World*, p. 69.

[19] Michael F. Lofchie, "The Uganda Coup—Class Action by the Military," *Journal of Modern African Studies* 10 (March 1972):19–35.

In addition, the Ugandan government proved to be powerless when confronted with massive overexpenditure on the part of the armed forces.

In December 1970 the quiet voice of Gasparo Oda, member of Parliament for Arua, and the Chairman of the Public Accounts Committee, was raised in a series of questions about the flagrant over-expenditure by eleven of the Ministries, most particularly by the Ministry of Defence. The total overspending amounted to £2.4 million according to the 1970 report by the Auditor General, rather more than half this amount being attributed to the Ministry of Defence. These sums referred to unauthorized expenditure, to what the Auditor-General drew attention in his preface as "a disturbing increase in the number of instances of abuse of public funds". In addition, the Ministry of Defence had overspent its budget by £1.5 million on military equipment, salaries and maintenance. The "abuses" turned out to be personal ones, and to cover sums of money allegedly banked but in fact retained by the bearer and used for entertainments, illicit mileage, and the settlement of officers' accounts.

Hugh Dinwiddy, "The Ugandan Army and Makerere under Obote 1962–71," *African Affairs* 82:326 (January 1983):58.

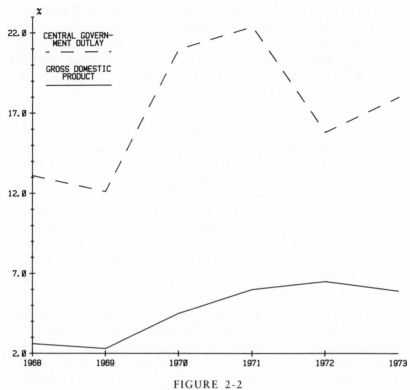

FIGURE 2-2

Growth of Security Expenditure in Chile, 1968–1973, Actual Outlays

Source: Nicole Ball, *Third-World Security Expenditure: A Statistical Compendium,* C-10250-M5 (Stockholm: National Defence Research Institute, 1984), p. 198.

In Chile, security spending rose rapidly in terms of both central government outlays and gross domestic product during 1970, the last year of the Frei administration, and 1971, Allende's first year in power (Figure 2-2). Although concern over an apparent Peruvian military build-up (the purchase of the Mirage-5s, for example) motivated some of the increased expenditure, the Allende administration was also interested in keeping the armed forces out of the political arena. Ironically, Peruvian President Fernando Belaúnde Terry is said to have authorized the Peruvian Mirage-5 purchase in order not to jeopardize further his already strained relations with Peru's armed forces.[20] However, civilian governments are not alone

[20] On Chile, see Portales and Varas, "The Role," p. 27. On Peru, see SIPRI, *The Arms Trade,* p. 692. Both attempts, of course, ultimately failed.

in their use of the security budget to placate the armed forces. Military-dominated governments are no less concerned to guarantee the loyalty of the armed forces to their comrades turned politicians. In Indonesia, for example, the Suharto government has been able to remain in power for twenty years because Suharto, controlling the patronage system, was able to pay off both his supporters and his potential critics.

After 1966, General Suharto gradually tightened his hold on the armed forces. The expansion of his authority was backed by his growing capacity to use coercion against resisting groups; but the main means was through the distribution of patronage. In full control of the government administration, he was able to reward loyal supporters and win over dissident and potentially dissident officers with appointments to civilian posts that offered prospects of material gain. Other officers were encouraged to go into business, with a promise of help from the administration whenever they needed licenses, credit, or contracts. Control over the machinery of patronage was thus the key factor that enabled Suharto to win and maintain the support of the armed forces for his leadership.[21]

The internal security role of Third World armed forces has been portrayed here as essentially negative. Nonetheless, the involvement of the armed forces in internal security, including control of the government, can at times be genuinely popular. This, in turn, can be reflected in a lack of public criticism for the allocation of a relatively large proportion of state and national resources to the security sector. The Nigerian civil war offers a good example of this phenomenon.

The Civil War created a new socio-psychological climate initially supportive of the military establishment and its claims on the country's resources. This was reflected in the observation that while most Nigerians disagreed on "how much of defence spending is enough," only a few initially would contest the point that enough defence was the amount required to safeguard the country's integrity and interests. By the same token, since fewer Nigerians than before were now willing to gamble with national defences, as government officials often put it, defence experts particularly from the army could and began in fact to claim that . . . what they had allocated to them in terms of money and material, if not also men, were not enough; and the general public, including the educated élites, could not be bothered initially about questioning this judgment. In short, that they

---

[21] Harold Crouch, "Patrimonialism and Military Rule in Indonesia," *World Politics* 31 (July 1979): 576–77.

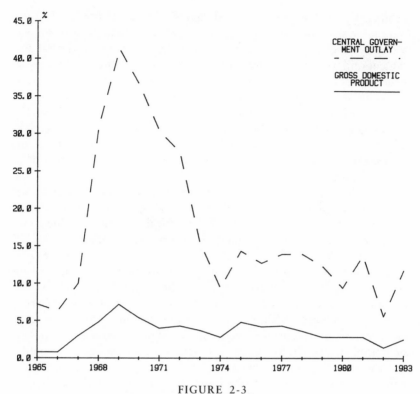

FIGURE 2-3

Growth of Security Expenditure in Nigeria, 1965–1983

Source: Nicole Ball, *Third-World Security Expenditure: A Statistical Compendium,* C10250-M5 (Stockholm: National Defence Research Agency, 1985), p. 150, and U.S. Arms Control and Disarmament Agency, *World Military Expenditures and Arms Transfers, 1985,* Publication 123 (Washington, D.C.: ACDA, August 1985), p. 75.

Note: The security expenditure data for 1965–1980 are based primarily on actual outlays. For 1968, 1969, 1973–1975, a small amount of capital spending is estimated outlays. The data for 1982 are estimates. The classification of security expenditure as a percentage of gross domestic product for 1978–1981 and 1983 and for percentage of central government expenditure in 1981 and 1983 is unknown. The figures for security expenditure as a percentage of gross domestic product for 1978–1983 are not entirely comparable to those for earlier years.

emerged or were seen from their Civil War role as "saviours of society" very much served the military's vested interests, in addition to the needs of national identity and cohesion.[22]

---

[22] Adekanye, "The Role," Part 2, pp. 9–10. These sentiments were expressed in the Second and Third Plans in the following ways. Second: "Although the defence and security

49

During the civil war itself, the federal armed forces naturally absorbed a very large share of state and national resources. The high point came in 1969 when the security sector was allocated 41.3 percent of central government outlays and 7.2 percent of GDP (Figure 2-3). In addition, the size of the armed forces increased substantially, from about 10,000 in 1966 before the first coup d'état headed by General Aguiyi Ironsi to some 250,000 in January 1970 at the time of the Biafran surrender. The military sought to avoid demobilizing a large portion of these troops in the early 1970s, which meant that the security sector's demand for funds did not decrease as radically when the war was over as it had increased when the war began.

Although the proportion of the national budget devoted to security expenditure had fallen to roughly its prewar level by 1974, that was more a reflection of the increased wealth of the central government (due to the rise in oil prices) than to a genuine return to the situation of the early 1960s. Security expenditure continued to command a much larger share of gross domestic product than it had prior to the Ironsi coup and the civil war.[23] In the late 1970s, the size of the armed forces was reduced substantially, and the need to implement austerity measures forced the civilian government which took power from the military in 1979 to reduce somewhat allocations to the security sector. Because of the massive corruption engaged in by civilian politicians during the second republic, which was overthrown 31 December 1983, rule by the armed forces continues to be preferable to civilian government for many Nigerians, although individual military officers may be more popular than others.

BUDGETARY CAUSES AND CONSTRAINTS

Resource Availability

[The outer limits of all public expenditure are ultimately determined by] the availability of resources, and security expenditure is no exception. There is no agreement, however, about the relative importance of this factor. Some econometric work surveying many Third World countries sug-

---

sector can be regarded as largely unproductive from an economic stand-point, recent experience shows that its effective performance is very crucial to the very existence of the nation." Third: "Although Defence cannot be considered as productive in the economic sense, it is realized that strong and efficient Armed Forces, which are strong to guarantee national peace and security, as indispensable for the normal economic progress of any country," Ibid., Part 3, p. 4.

[23] Ibid., Part 2, pp. 9–10, 14.

gests that the level of security expenditure is relatively independent of the rate of economic growth. A macroeconomic analysis of thirty-three African countries between the years 1960 and 1973 found a significant negative relationship between per capita gross national product and the rate of growth of military expenditure and a similar negative relationship between the level of GNP and military expenditure as a proportion of GNP. This led the study's author to conclude that "military expenditure in Africa is determined not so much by the level of development as by the geo-political context in which a régime is situated. African governments apparently perceive the necessity for a certain level of military expenditure . . . and this weighs more heavily on those states with lower G.N.P." In contrast, two studies of Latin America emphasize the importance of resource availability. In the first study, where sixteen countries were surveyed for the period from 1948 to 1968, changes in resources were named as one of the two most important factors conditioning levels of security spending. (The second factor, prior levels of expenditure, will be discussed later in this chapter.) The second study, which examined nineteen countries for the period from 1945 to 1970, reached even stronger conclusions: resource availability (size of the gross domestic product) was termed the most important factor in determining the level of a country's security outlays.[24]

These different conclusions are not entirely contradictory. No government controls the entire national product, and the government expenditure/gross product ratio can vary considerably from country to country as well as within the same country over time. Many Third World countries have increased this ratio since becoming independent; this explains why the security sector's share in central government expenditure can fall at the same time as the security budget absorbs a larger proportion of

---

[24]The African study is John Ravenhill, "Comparing Regime Performance in Africa: The Limitations of Cross-National Aggregate Analysis," *The Journal of Modern African Studies* 18 (March 1980): 99–126; the quotation is from page 117. The two Latin American studies are by Barry Ames and Ed Goff, "Education and Defense Expenditures in Latin America: 1948–1968," pp. 186, 193, in *Comparative Public Policy: Issues, Theories and Methods,* ed. Craig Liske, William Loehr, and John McCamant (New York: Halstead Press/John Wiley, 1975), and Philippe Schmitter, "Foreign Military Assistance, National Military Spending and Military Rule in Latin America," pp. 132, 180, 183, in *Military Rule in Latin America. Function, Consequences and Perspectives,* ed. Philippe C. Schmitter, Vol. III, Sage Research Progress Series on War, Revolution and Peacekeeping (Beverly Hills, Calif.: Sage, 1973). See also Saadet Deger, "The Development Effect of Military Expenditure in LDCs," pp. 94–109, in *Armament—Development—Human Rights—Disarmament,* ed. G. Fischer (Brussels: Establissements Bruylant pour la Faculté de Droit, Paris V, 1985), and Saadet Deger, *Military Expenditure in Third World Countries. The Economic Effects* (London and Boston: Routledge & Kegan Paul, 1986).

gross product. An increase in gross product not translated into a higher government expenditure/gross product ration cannot be considered to have increased resource availability; the exception to this occurs in countries such as Indonesia where security expenditure is derived in part from extrabudgetary sources (see Chapter 3).

The oil producing countries of the Middle East provide the classic example of increased resource availability leading to larger security-related outlays by governments. To some extent, other OPEC countries such as Mexico and Nigeria also took advantage of the oil bonanza in this way. Greater resource availability did not cause higher levels of security expenditure: it simply enabled certain governments wanting to spend more on their security sectors to do so. For a number of years, it enabled them to do so without jeopardizing other categories of public spending. By the end of the 1970s, countries such as Iran and Nigeria were once again facing budgetary squeezes as oil income declined.

With regard to Nigeria, it has been suggested that the post–civil war honeymoon enjoyed by the armed forces may have been more important in determining the level of security expenditure than the additional income provided by the rise in oil prices. Nonetheless, the growth of public revenues and expenditure that occurred as a result of the higher oil prices clearly played an important role in 1975 in reversing the downward trend in the proportion of state and national resources allocated to the security sector (see Figure 2-3).[25] Similarly, the oil glut of the late 1970s and overambitious development plans contributed to a decline in the amount of state and national resources devoted to the armed forces.

The OPEC countries are not the only ones to show a correspondence between resource availability and levels of security expenditure. In Zaire in the late 1970s a sharp decline in economic activity clearly caused a drop in security spending. In both Brazil and Gabon there is some indication of a positive association between income from agricultural exports and security expenditure. In Colombia during the 1950s, a doubling of security outlays can be traced to rapid economic growth and a corresponding increase in state revenues.[26]

[25] Adekanye, "The Role," Part 2, p. 9. In real terms, the armed forces continued to receive approximately the same amount of funds between 1970 and 1974. See subsection in text, "Corporate interest and personal gain."

[26] Regarding Colombia, see Gertrude E. Heare, *Trends in Latin American Military Expenditures, 1940–1970. Argentina, Brazil, Chile, Colombia, Peru and Venezuela,* Department of State Publication 8610 (Washington, D.C.: Office of External Research, Bureau of Intelligence and Research, Department of State, December 1971), p. 6. Regarding Brazil, Zaire, and Gabon, see, Michael Brzoska, "External Trade, Indebtedness, Foreign Direct Investment and the Military Sector in LDCs. A Study on the Effects of Militarization on External Economic Relations" (Hamburg: IFSH, Arbeitsgruppe Rüstung und Unterentwicklung, November 1982, mimeograph), chap. 6.

TABLE 2-3
Growth of Public Expenditure, Security Spending,
and Gross National Product in Chile,
1973–1979 (1973 = 100)

	1973	1974	1975	1976	1977	1978	1979
Public expenditure	100	69	46	47	57	67	76
Security expenditure	100	136	108	108	139	156	170
GNP	100	106	94	98	106	112	—

Source: Derived from Carlos Portales and Augusto Varas, "The Role of Military Expenditure in the Development Process. Chile 1952–1973 and 1973–1980: Two Contrasting Cases," *Ibero Americana* 12: 1–2 (1983): pp. 46 and 48, Tables XIX and XXI.

Even governments that give high priority to security expenditure at the expense of other public-sector outlays cannot entirely ignore economic conditions. For ideological reasons the military junta which overthrew Allende in 1973 chose to reduce the size of the public sector at the same time it increased the budget of the security forces (Table 2-3). Even so, the Pinochet government was forced to make substantial cuts in the security budget during the two depression years of 1975 and 1976. As economic conditions improved in 1977, however, the security budget grew much more rapidly than either total public expenditure or national product.

For some countries, security assistance has provided an important supplement to domestic security expenditure, effectively increasing the recipient's resource base. (Security assistance is discussed in detail in Chapter 7.) Military grants were probably particularly important during the 1950s and 1960s in enabling newly independent countries to build up their armed forces to levels that they could not have supported relying solely on domestic resources but that were consistent with the ambitions of the ruling élite. Here one should think not only of U.S. aid to countries such as South Korea, the Philippines, Taiwan, or Pakistan, but also of the assistance provided by the French and the British to excolonies in Africa and Asia. The total assistance provided by the latter may have been much less than the sums transferred by the United States, but for many of the smaller African countries in particular the training and equipment received was extremely important for establishing the armed forces.

For most countries security assistance has not provided a permanent solution to problems of resource availability. For one thing, political alliances have shifted over time. For another, the industrialized countries have generally proved less willing to supply aid in the 1970s and 1980s than they were during the cold war period. Beginning in the late 1960s, the grant component of security assistance declined sharply. (This trend was reversed for the United States by the Reagan administration in the early 1980s.) But the reduction in security-related grants did not necessarily imply a corresponding reduction in the size of security-related outlays. Some countries—particularly those for whom security-related loans were available—increased the share of domestic resources devoted to the armed forces. In the Republic of Korea, for example, the security budget absorbed on average 4 percent of gross product before 1975 when U.S. military grants were still available in sizable amounts. Since 1975, it has absorbed about 6 percent of GDP.[27]

Politics and Inertia
in the Budget-Making Process

The two macroeconomic studies of Latin America mentioned above not only stressed the importance of resource availability in determining the size of a country's security budget, but they also suggested that prior expenditure levels were extremely important in predicting the amount of future expenditure. In one of these studies, researchers found that in twelve of the sixteen countries surveyed between 60 and 95 percent of the variance in security expenditure for any given year could be explained by the level of security expenditure in the previous year. The current expenditure portion of the security budget was found to be particularly well correlated with prior spending.[28]

Intuitively, a close relationship between prior and current expenditure levels makes sense. Large portions of Third World security budgets are composed of operating costs, not capital costs (weapon procurement and construction). Operating costs can be expected to increase in an incremental way through pay or pension rises or normal price increases for recurrent items such as fuel, food, electricity, and medical, education and office supplies. Personnel costs often account for a large share of Third World security spending, and these typically increase one year, remain constant for a number of years, increase once again, remain constant for several more years, and so on. Thus, barring rapid changes in the size of the security establishment, a large portion of security budgets will be predetermined each year as troops are paid, fed, clothed, and housed and

---

[27] SIPRI, *World Armaments and Disarmament, 1979*, p. 45, and *World Armaments and Disarmament, 1986* (London: Oxford University Press, 1986), p. 244.

[28] Ames and Goff, "Education," pp. 181–84. See also Schmitter, "Foreign Military Assistance," pp. 159–63.

certain basic requirements of the command and administrative apparatus are met.

Appendix 1 shows the evolution of noncapital costs as a proportion of total security budgets in twenty developing countries during those years between 1950 and 1980 for which data were available. For ten of these countries it has been possible to estimate the proportion allocated to personnel costs. Although their weight varies both over time within individual countries and from country to country, personnel costs have tended to account for between 50 and 70 percent of all security expenditures. The significant exception is India, where personnel costs have exhibited a more developed-country profile, ranging between 25 and 45 percent of total security outlays. Total operating costs—personnel plus operations and maintenance costs—show greater variability, but they have tended to absorb a very large share of the security budgets in the twenty countries surveyed. The one exception is Iran during the 1970s where, just as one would expect, capital costs were dominant. For several countries, particularly the Philippines and Colombia, the consistently very high ratios of operating costs to total security expenditure reflect inflows of U.S. security-related assistance. Between 1949 and 1974, for example, the Philippines received on average $35 million a year in security-related grants from the United States. Much of this probably was used to purchase equipment and, unlike security-related loans, would not have appeared in the Philippine budget. Colombia received less from the United States—some $9.3 million a year between 1961 and 1970—but the effect was probably much the same. Both countries could concentrate domestic security outlays on operating costs.

In view of the figures presented in Appendix 1, it is not at all surprising that there seems to be considerable inertia in security budgets. Political decisions, often made by a rather small number of individuals, concerning force size and structure and weapon procurement will therefore have important long-term consequences on expenditure levels. The more isolated those individuals who ultimately determine the scale of security expenditure are from other members of the bureaucracy and the executive as well as from elected representatives and the general public, the less likely it is that there will be a serious evaluation of funding priorities.

In Iran prior to 1979, a handful of individuals controlled the military budget formulation process: the shah, the chief of weapons procurement General Hassan Toufanian, and a few other military officers known to be particularly loyal to the shah. The military portion of the budget was exempted from the audit procedures to which the expenditure proposals of civilian ministries and agencies were subject. Essentially the shah decided what weapons would be procured, and security-related loans were automatically approved by members of the shah's cabinet without receiving any details about them.[29]

In India, the responsibility for budget formulation has been wider. Nonetheless, the prime minister and the ministers of finance and defence have been especially important in determining the level of funds allocated to the security sector. Because of the dominance of the Congress party throughout most of the postindependence period, parliamentary consideration of security issues has not been significant and has not deviated from official Congress party policy. Parliamentary oversight of the security sector has been limited to ensuring that funds appropriated for the armed forces have not been misused. Attempts to create committees to examine defence proposals before funds are actually allocated have failed, largely because the Congress party has opposed such activity. As a result, most members of the Indian Parliament, the Lok Sabha, have been rather ill-informed concerning security issues.

Prior to the 1962 Sino-Indian War, Indian defence ministers were very weak and/or very closely associated with Nehru (especially Krishna Menon). The ministers of finance tended to be occupied with nonmilitary issues. Nehru's belief that development should have priority over defense thus became the single most important general criterion in deciding levels of security expenditure. In terms of gross domestic product, Indian security spending before 1962 was rather low, about 2 percent. In addition, the armed forces often did not use all the funds allocated to them, and "savings" were frequently reported. After the 1962 war, the poor showing of the Indian armed forces led to a reversal of priorities; defense became progressively more important. Under the new guidelines the Ministries of Defence and Finance came to play the leading roles in determining the size of Indian security outlays.

It is primarily the Defence Ministry which proposes and the Ministry of Finance which decides how to allocate resources among competing (civilian versus military) requirements. The approval of the finance minister is particularly important for any project involving the use of foreign exchange. The finance minister also plays a leading part in cabinet decisions on allocation of funds among different segments of the bureaucracy. Whereas in a properly functioning parliamentary system, parliamentary debates would provide an input to allocation decisions, the general abdication of interest on the part of most members of the Lok Sabha concerning matters of security policy and funding means that the bureaucracy—including, of course, representatives of the three military services—and the

---

[29] Schulz, "Military Expenditures," pp. 33–40.

for the last decade for costs to rise substantially. In the late 1950s, many developing countries made do with World War II–type weapons, often provided by the major powers under security assistance programs. Since they had paid very little or nothing at all for these weapons and the cost of all weapons has increased many times over during the last thirty or forty years, the simple replacement of the older models has involved much greater financial outlays for many Third World countries. Upgrading weaponry because a neighbor has done so or to gain the advantage over a neighbor (as occurred in Latin America with supersonic aircraft in the late 1960s and early 1970s) is another matter.

Influence of the Military

Corporate interest and personal gain

It is often assumed that the military is the single most important actor in government decisions concerning security expenditure. Military officers are seen to have strong corporate and personal reasons for promoting large security budgets. The military as an organization will be concerned to see that the armed forces maintain their share of government allocations, that their members (at least the officer corps) are as well paid as other comparable societal groups, and that they are well equipped (in terms of both potential opponents and arms available in the market). In addition, the regular armed forces will be concerned to ensure that they are not at a disadvantage in terms of pay and equipment to paramilitary forces, and the different services within the armed forces may compete with each other for allocations, thereby driving up total security outlays.[36]

As individuals, military officers will seek to enhance their own status and wealth. One way this can be done is to ensure that budgeted salaries are high and that the military provides health and education services and other prerequisites not only to its members but also to officers' families. Another means of improving personal wealth and status is to either take rake-offs from arms import contracts or be in a position to funnel other kinds of military procurement and construction contracts to firms with which the officer in question or his family has close ties and which therefore will provide the officer with some form of remuneration in exchange.

The post–civil war Nigerian armed forces offers a good example of the way in which corporate concerns help increase security outlays. Recall

---

[36] SIPRI, *The Arms Trade*, pp. 694, 696, discusses interservice rivalry in several Latin American countries.

that during the civil war (1967–1970) the Nigerian armed forces expanded enormously in size, from just over 10,000 men to 250,000, and that no immediate postwar demobilization occurred. The armed forces, unwilling to reduce their manpower, took advangage of the postwar goodwill on the part of large portions of the Nigerian population and growing national income from oil revenues to keep security expenditure at a level considerably higher than it had been prior to the civil war. In the late 1970s, the Nigerian armed forces continued to command some 4 percent of gross domestic product whereas they had received no more than 0.8 percent of GDP before the Ironsi coup in 1966 which had precipitated the civil war (Figure 2-3).

In real terms the budget of the armed forces stagnated between 1970 and 1974. In 1975 it grew by about 50 percent. This increase is also reflected in the proportion of GDP and central government expenditures allotted to the security sector. Since then, Nigerian security expenditure has tended to decline. By 1979 it was estimated that real security outlays were lower than they had been in 1973; they nonetheless remained considerably larger than pre–civil war security outlays.[37]

The 1975 increase, of course, derived largely from the military's share of the pay awards granted in April of that year. Not only were military wages increased more than those of most other groups, but the armed forces were also approximately twice what some Nigerian officers believed to be their optimum size. Furthermore, once it had become clear that the military would remain close to its civil war size for some years to come and that oil income was providing sufficient state revenues, the Third National Plan (1975–1980) budgeted large capital outlays for military purposes. Of the revised plan estimates for military-related capital expenditure, approximately one-quarter was designated for barracks-building programs to house the troops. Total construction outlays accounted for about 40 percent of all military-related capital costs, including training schools, hospitals, workshops, hangars, runways, and port facilities in addition to the barracks. The barracks program was not only alloted the lion's share of military-related construction under the revised plan estimates, but also its true cost was seriously underestimated. By the end of 1979, only 16 percent of the barracks program had been completed, but the cost overrun was already approaching 45 percent.[38]

By the late 1970s it was clear that, despite what many officers wanted, the armed forces would have to be significantly reduced in size. The econ-

[37] SIPRI, *World Armaments and Disarmament, 1979,* p. 49, and *World Armaments and Disarmament, 1983,* p. 165.
[38] Adekanye, "The Role," Part 2, pp. 23–29.

omy could not maintain and equip a 250,000-man force indefinitely, and the security implications of the large force were, ironically, said to be negative. In 1978, for example, it was reported that "Nigeria has an army of 250,000, the largest in black Africa. But according to some military attachés, the force is badly equipped and trained. One observer called it 'the largest outdoor welfare organization in the world.' Many units have not been on training maneuvers for more than five years and the few crack units are said to be required at home to protect against coups or civil unrest."[39]

By 1979, a serious demobilization was underway. Although it was said at that time that the armed forces would ultimately stabilize at about 100,000 to 120,000 men, in 1985 their strength was reported to have fallen to about 94,000 regular troops.[40] Although weapons procurement under the Third Plan (1975–1980) was placed at 1.6 billion nairas, this must be set against the expenditure of 1.3 billion nairas on 16,000 housing units (out of the projected 100,000 units) over the same period. In terms of total security spending between 1975 and 1980, weapons procurement accounted for approximately 25 percent.[41] While Nigeria was one of the major arms purchasers of sub-Saharan Africa during the late 1970s, over 70 percent of its security outlays had been used to cover recurrent costs and construct 16,000 units of military housing. This pattern of expenditure was a direct outgrowth of many military officers' desire to bolster the political power of the armed forces, and perhaps their own power as well, by keeping large numbers of men under arms.

The existence of a military-industrial complex is frequently cited as a major reason for rising security expenditures in the industrialized countries of the West. Arms producers and military officers are said to work together to induce governments to procure increasingly costly weapons to their mutual benefit. This sort of relationship can only be rather limited in Third World countries since so few of them have an arms industry of any size and so much of their arms production capacity is government owned. In some countries—for example, Brazil and South Korea—private and often foreign capital is allowed to participate in military-related enterprises; in others, it is not, for varying reasons. In Iran, the shah was unwilling to allow private companies to produce any military-related equipment. He feared this equipment could fall into the hands of opponents to

[39] Michael T. Kaufman, "In Africa, When Lagos Speaks, Everybody Else Listens," *New York Times*, 2 July 1978.

[40] "Cutbacks Continue," *Financial Times* (10 October 1979), special section on Nigeria, VIII; Alain Boebion, "Nigeria Trims its Military Machine," *Times*, 7 January 1980; and "Nigeria", *Military Technology* 9:13 (1985):226.

[41] Adekanye, "The Role," Part 2, pp. 29, 31, and Ball, *Third-World*, pp. 150–51.

his regime if the state sector did not control production. In India it has been government policy to avoid the creation of private armaments firms. While this has sometimes been justified on the basis of the inability of the private sector to produce items of sufficiently high quality, the real reason may be ideological. Congress party policy has always been to promote a socialized economy and basic industries in India are owned by the government. Some production of weapons components has been allowed in the private sector, but the majority of Indian domestic arms production occurs by law in the public sector; there is no reason to anticipate any change in the near future.[42]

If the Western pattern of military-industrial relations is still rather rare in the Third World, there is nonetheless a very definite pattern of military-business relations in evidence in many developing countries. In these cases the businesses most often do not produce weapons, and the armed forces do not benefit from the procurement of new equipment. Rather, military officers derive personal benefits from these relationships. The classic examples are found in Thailand and Indonesia, but the business community and the officer corps are closely linked in many other countries as well.

The implications for socioeconomic development of the reliance of the Thai political system on corrupt relationships between military, civilian,

[42] On Iran, see Schulz, "Military Expenditures," pp. 80–81; on India, see Thomas, *The Defence of India,* pp. 114–25.

In India

The industrial policy enunciated by the new Government in 1948 "envisaged a mixed economy with an overall responsibility of the government for planned development of industries and their regulation in the national interest", and set the country on the path of rapid industrial development. . . . A large number of industries became the exclusive preserve of the State—Schedule A—while those in Schedule B were to be progressively state-owned.

. . . .

Schedule A Industries are: Arms and ammunition and allied items of Defence equipment; atomic energy; iron and steel; heavy castings and forgings of iron and steel; heavy plant and machinery required for iron and steel production, for mining, for machine tool manufacture and for such other basic industries as may be specified by the Central Government, heavy electrical plants including hydraulic and steam turbines; coal and lignite; mineral oils, mining or iron ore, manganese ore, chrome ore, gypsum, sulphur, gold, diamonds; mining and processing of copper, lead, zinc, molybdenum, and wolfram; minerals specified in the Schedule to the Atomic Energy (Control of Production and Use Order 1953); aircraft; air transport; railway transport; ship building; telephones and telephone cables; telegraph and wireless apparatus (excluding radio receiving sets); generation and distribution of electricity.

Lt. Col. Gautam Sharma, "Defence Production in India," *IDSA Journal* 10:4 (1978):322, 344–45.

bureaucratic, business, and political élites are discussed in Chapter 6. These same relationships can also influence the level of security-related spending. Officers in a position to purchase any item for the armed forces are also able to ensure that firms with which they have personal ties will receive the contract. They, in turn, will receive some sort of remuneration, either in cash or in kind, for seeing that the deal is approved. To cover the costs of pay-offs, the firm will charge a somewhat higher price to the Defense Ministry. In a system such as that in Thailand, where business is conducted in this way more often than not, the resultant increment to the budgets of all government ministries must be substantial.

Higher security outlays can also be used to buy the loyalty of fellow officers. Even relatively uncorrupt Thai officers—for example, General Kriangsak Chamanan who was head of government from October 1977 to February 1980—have been required to play this game if they are to remain in power.

> At the beginning of the year [1978] there were several factions in the military which could be divided loosely into two circles. The first was composed of officers who were widely respected for their professional abilities, had few business involvements, and were generally sympathetic to a return to some form of democratic government. . . . They included Kriangsak. . . .
>
> The second circle was composed of more conservative officers. Several had extensive business involvements which detracted from their professionalism, and they were not eager for a return to electoral politics, or for reforms which might threaten their interests. . . .
>
> Prime Minister Kriangsak succeeded in strengthening his own position during the year and weakening some of the conservative factions. . . .
>
> In orchestrating the promotions Prime Minister Kriangsak was careful to mollify at least some of the factions in the more conservative circle. General Yot continued as Deputy Defense Minister, and his in-law and protégé Lieutenant General Thep Kranloet was promoted to command the First Army. As further reassurance to conservative factions, Kriangsak approved a 15.8% increase in military spending in 1979 and emphasized that government spending would give first priority to military security.[43]

The Indonesian political system is similar to its Thai counterpart: it depends on institutionalized corruption and kickbacks and pay-offs to keep

[43] Ansil Ramsay, "Thailand 1978: Kriangsak—The Thai Who Binds," *Asian Survey* 19 (February 1979): 105–6.

the economy functioning. The Indonesian military leadership, simultaneously the political leadership, is just as concerned as the Thai military leadership to keep the armed forces happy, but the actual mechanism employed is somewhat different. During the Sukarno period, the Indonesian armed forces began running their own businesses to supplement government security outlays. Their involvement in commerce and industry expanded considerably once they assumed power in the 1965–1966 period. In addition, private sector companies have found it prudent to have military officers on their company boards.

Access to these off-budget funds enables the Indonesian government to claim that it spends modest amounts on the armed forces and simultaneously to compensate military officers for what are said to be rather low salaries (compared with those in the private sector) and to buy enough equipment to satisfy the armed forces. In terms of the Suharto government's stability, this policy of allowing off-budget security expenditure has clearly been positive; in terms of the amount of national resources absorbed by the security sector, it is almost certainly wasteful. If the various military-run enterprises were brought under government control and the armed forces were forced to rely solely on official budget allocations for their funding, it seems quite likely that the government would find itself with additional revenue to apply to expenditures in the civil sector. The income from the military enterprises would almost certainly exceed the extra outlays on security which would be necessitated by raising salaries for the armed forces and by increasing official, on-budget purchases of equipment. These economic benefits would, however, be heavily outweighed by the destruction of military unity, and no one in Indonesia thinks the government would attempt such a reform.[44]

Military Coups and Regimes

Although all military establishments may have similar reasons for promoting high levels of security spending, the armed forces have a greater chance of influencing the budgetary process in countries where they themselves control the government. Nonetheless, military coups d'état and direct rule by the armed forces do not guarantee that security expenditure will rise. Military-dominated governments cannot avoid the necessity of having to choose between alternative ways of allocating state resources.

---

[44] David Jenkins, "The Military in Business," *Far Eastern Economic Review* 99 (13 January 1978), p. 24. See also J. A. C. Mackie, "Indonesia's Government Estates and their Masters," *Pacific Affairs* 34 (Winter 1961–1962): 337–60, and Crouch, "Patrimonialism."

Nor, as the discussion on resource availability showed, can they completely exempt the security sector from reductions in public expenditure in times of economic crisis. Before assuming that a coup in a given country will result in an immediate rise in security outlays and that an attempt will be made subsequently to retain security expenditure at the new, higher level, one must at a minimum know something about the military government's proposed economic policies and the relative strength of the country's economy.

In Latin America it is definitely more likely that a coup d'état will cause an immediate rise in security expenditure than a decline, but that initial rise will not necessarily be translated into a permanent upward trend.[45] In Brazil, the 1964 coup against the civilian government led by Goulart did produce a temporary increase in security spending in terms of both central government expenditure and gross domestic product. Since the late 1960s, however, this trend has been reversed. To some extent, the fact that security spending has absorbed progressively less of state and national resources reflects the relative moderation the Brazilian armed forces have shown in their budgetary demands. It also, however, reflects the expansion of the state sector during the period of military rule and the rapid rate at which the Brazilian economy grew up to the late 1970s.

In Chile during the 1970s the trend was just the opposite. In 1970, security spending nearly doubled as the civilian government led by Allende attempted to ensure the loyalty of the Chilean officer corps (Figure 2-2). In 1971, the security sector absorbed an even larger portion of national resources, rising by about one-third to 6 percent of GDP. The security budget remained at roughly this level until the September 1973 coup d'état. In 1974, the first year of military government, security expenditure rose again, reaching its highest point in terms of GDP in more than forty years—6.8 percent. Because of the 1975—1976 recession, the military government was unable to expand the security budget as rapidly as it would have liked; nonetheless, as soon as economic conditions began to improve, it allocated a larger amount of resources to the security sector. Table 2-3 shows that despite the contraction in the size of the state sector between 1973 and 1979, security expenditure continued to grow. By 1979 it was 70 percent larger than its 1973 level while total public expenditure was 24 percent lower than its 1973 level. These divergent trends were possible partly because state outlays on certain social services— health and housing—had been cut back sharply under military rule and

---

[45] These conclusions are based on surveys of seventeen coups d'état in fifteen Latin American countries between 1950 and 1980. See the data in Ball, *Third-World*, pp. 181–248.

partly because the junta had transferred primary responsibility for investment from the public to the private sector.[46]

After studying the security budgets of six Latin American countries between 1940 and 1970, Gertrude Heare argued that increases in security expenditure apparently linked to periods of military rule could be better explained by the need to compensate the military for salary rises or equipment purchases deferred for a number of years, by favorable economic conditions expanding state resources, or by the existence of conflict situations.[47] The possibility still remains that many military governments are particularly sensitive to requests from within their own ranks for higher wages and new equipment, if only to minimize threats to their rule from disgruntled segments of the officer corps. As such, military governments may be more willing to take advantage of economic upswings to meet the demands of the security forces than civilian governments which might choose to use additional revenue for other purposes.

The security expenditure of countries in Africa, the Middle East, and Asia during periods of military rule show similar variations. The leaders of the 1980 Liberian coup came to power ostensibly eager to redress many of the economic imbalances characteristic of all previous Liberian governments; yet, as explained above, one of their earliest acts was to double the pay rates of the armed forces.

The 1966 coup against Kwame Nkrumah in Ghana was largely a protest against what the armed forces felt was discrimination in terms of resource allocation and other corporate matters. During the first two years of military rule, security spending aborbed larger amounts of state and national resources than ever before (Figure 2-4). As explained in Chapter 1, the armed forces, unable to resolve Ghana's economic problems, were rather quickly forced to reduce allocations to the security sector. Under the civilian government led by Kofi Busia, this downward trend continued. Dissatisfaction on the part of the Ghanian armed forces with the expenditure cuts proposed by the Busia government in its 1971 austerity budget was instrumental in influencing the decision to take over the government once again. In this case, it seems personal reasons were stronger than corporate ones for the officers, since Busia had proposed to

[46] Portales and Varas, "The Role," pp. 48–49. The percentage shares of security expenditure are from Ball, *Third-World*, p. 198. The way in which Argentinian security expenditure has fared under civilian and military regimes is described in Mario Esteban Carranza, "The Role of Military Expenditure in the Development Process: The Argentina Case 1946–1980," *Ibero Americana* 12:1–2 (1983):128–29. Argentinian trends are portrayed graphically in Ball, *Third-World*, p. 186.
[47] Heare, *Trends*, p. 8.

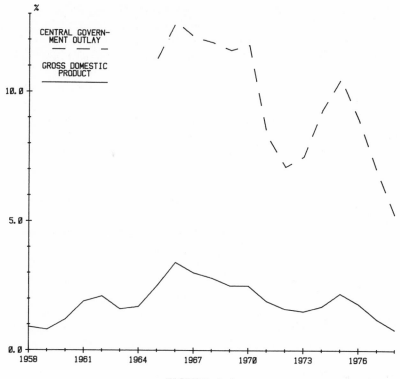

FIGURE 2-4
Security Expenditure in Ghana, 1958–1978

Source: Nicole Ball, *Third-World Security Expenditure: A Statistical Compendium,*
C10250-M5 (Stockholm: National Defence Research Agency, 1984), p. 126.
Note: Based on a combination of actual outlays and estimated expenditure.

cut salaries and other perquisites significantly. Following the 1972 coup, security expenditure did absorb more of both state and national resources, but by 1975 the economic problems facing Ghana were so severe that these increases could not be sustained.[48]

[48] The reasons behind the 1966 coup are discussed in Björn Hettne, "Soldiers and Politics: The Case of Ghana," *Journal of Peace Research* 17:2 (1980): 178. The 1972 coup is discussed on pages 181–82, and also in Valerie Plave Bennett, "The Motivation for Military Intervention: The Case of Ghana," *The Western Political Quarterly* 27 (1974): 659–74.

In the Philippines, the security budget absorbed progressively smaller amounts of state and national resources from the early 1950s to the mid-1960s. Around 1965 the downward trend was reversed, but the imposition of martial law in 1972 caused the steepest increases in security spending, especially in terms of GDP. The Philippines has nonetheless not been immune to the general slowdown that has afflicted the world economy in the last decade, and during the late 1970s its security outlays declined in real terms. In Indonesia it is impossible to determine the true effect of military rule on security spending because large portions of Indonesian security expenditure are not reported publicly. In South Korea, the level of U.S. economic and military aid has been more important in determining the level of security expenditure than regime type. Large inflows of U.S. grant aid in the 1960s enabled the Park government to maintain a very large military force with a relatively modest domestic input.

Clearly then the relationship between coup d'état and regime type, on the one hand, and levels of security expenditure, on the other, is not straightforward. In many cases, a military coup does mean increased expenditure on the armed forces, at least temporarily. Although it is likely that, all things being equal, militaries in power would prefer not to reduce security expenditure, they often cannot avoid such an outcome. As the discussion throughout this chapter has shown, there are many factors in addition to regime type and the corporate and personal interests of the armed forces which must be taken into account when expenditure levels are set and which militate against a straightforward relationship between security expenditure and control of the political system by the armed forces.

THE ROLE OF EXTERNAL POWERS

External powers often play an important role in the creation and exacerbation of conflicts in the Third World. As a result of this involvement, security expenditures rise. There are essentially five main ways in which external powers have contributed to the growth of conflict in the Third World: as colonial powers, as interventionary forces, as promoters of coups d'état, as providers of military assistance, and as arms salesmen. Although the traditional European powers plus the United States have involved themselves most actively in this respect, Third World countries have increasingly adopted some of these roles as well. Brazil has emerged as a major exporter of weapons while the post-1973 oil price rises were important in enabling countries such as Libya, Saudi Arabia, Kuwait, Algeria, Iran, Iraq, and the United Arab Emirates to fund expeditionary forces in Third World countries or to help friendly governments purchase weapons and hire technicians and other specialists to operate and maintain these weapons. The larger the number of countries involved in these kinds of activities, the more difficult it becomes for conflicts to be settled peacefully.

Colonialism

The term *colonialism* is associated in the minds of most people with the period beginning in the fifteenth century and ending essentially in the 1960s when a number of European countries controlled large areas in the Americas, Africa, the Middle East, and Asia. Throughout the history of the world, however, states have sought to exert their hegemony over others to enhance their own political and economic power. The Roman empire controlled large areas of Europe, the Middle East, West Asia, and North Africa for about four hundred years at the beginning of the Christian era while the Ottoman empire held sway in a somewhat less extensive area in Eastern Europe, Southwest Asia, the Middle East, and North Africa for approximately six hundred years from the beginning of the fourteenth century. In West Africa, Ghana controlled a sizable area between the Niger River in the south and the Sahara in the north from about 300 to 1100 A.D. In the twelfth century Ghana's dominance was replaced by that of Mali, and in the fourteenth century the Songhay empire became the principal political entity in the region, eventually absorbing both Ghana and Mali before declining in turn at the end of the sixteenth century. Similar political groupings have developed in other parts of the world throughout historical times.

For the purposes of this discussion, however, colonialism will refer only to control established by European powers, the United States, and Japan in areas now described as the Third World prior to World War II. It might be argued that Vietnam has now semicolonized Kampuchea and Laos and that the Soviet Union colonized Eastern Europe after World War II and has attempted to colonize Afghanistan; these issues will not, however, be taken up here. The colonial powers frequently followed policies which set different ethnic, religious, or socioeconomic groups against each other. The ensuing resentments and conflicts, which sometimes predated the coming of the colonial power, frequently carried over into the postindependence period and caused serious domestic unrest. In some countries, for example Nigeria, the political system inherited at independence intensified these divisions. Colonial powers also tended to draw boundaries somewhat arbitrarily, ignoring the territorial claims of vari-

ous indigenous ethnic or religious groups. Once these colonial boundaries were transformed into national borders, disputes inevitably arose between sovereign states.[49]

Recognizing the threat to peace implied in the dissatisfaction felt by
many African governments with the borders inherited at independence,
the Organization of African Unity (OAU) adopted the position that its
members should not seek to adjust their boundaries. This has not, however, been sufficient to end all territorial disputes. Although most such
conflicts have tended to be kept at a rather low level, some have been
long-lived and have periodically flared into open conflict. Somalia, for example, has never renounced its irredentist claims to large portions of
Kenya and Ethiopia. Despite a resolution by the OAU council in May
1973 stating that Somali claims to Ethiopian territory contravene the
OAU charter, the Somali government has continued to support separatist
guerrillas in the Ogaden region of Ethiopia. Since 1977, there have been
periods of active fighting between Cuban-supported Ethiopian troops
and Somali-backed guerrillas.[50]

In Asia, too, colonial policies lie at the root of many conflicts. With
regard to Southeast Asia, it has been argued that "Many security problems . . . stem from internal conflicts which are aftereffects of colonialism. The unwillingness of minority ethnic groups to accept the hegemony
of the dominant group is a major source of conflict; this problem is directly attributable to the relatively arbitrary way in which national boundaries were defined in colonial times."[51]

---

[49] Eboe Hutchful, "Disarmament and Development: An African View," *IDS Bulletin* 16
(October 1985): 63. On Nigeria, see Ruth First, *The Barrel of a Gun* (Harmondsworth,
England: Penguin, 1970), pp. 144–69.

[50] "A World at War—1983," *The Defense Monitor* 12:1 (1983): 17. These conflicts have
their domestic political uses. For example, Malien President Moussa Traoré has used the
border conflict with Upper Volta as a means of keeping potential opponents to his domestic
policies within the armed forces away from the capital.

Colin Legum has reported that

> In the reforms of the early 1980s, army officers played only a minor role. Traoré delib-
> erately kept them away from the capital by rotating them in hinterland posts. He also
> used the border conflict with Upper Volta and tension with Niger to deploy the bulk of
> the armed forces along Mali's eastern frontier. And to reconcile Col. Fifiling Sissoko
> and Col. Youssouf Traoré to their less prominent positions in the government, he
> raised their rank to brigadier-general at the same time as he promoted himself to that
> of full general.

Colin Legum, ed., *Africa Contemporary Record: Annual Survey and Documents, 1982–
1983*, (New York and London: Africana Publishing Company, 1984), p. B 501. See also
pp. B 503–B 509.

[51] Weinstein, "The Meaning," p. 20.

A similar problem is evident in other parts of Asia. India, for example, had had to contend with many separatist and regional movements based on caste, ethnic, and religious distinctions since it became independent in 1947. Directly related to British colonial policies has been the occasional violence between Assamese and Bengalis in the Indian state of Assam.

The turmoil over immigration which has torn the East Indian state of Assam for the past three years [since 1980] has been brewing since the turn of the century. The seeds were sown during British rule in India, which was primarily responsible for starting the mass influx of immigrants into Assam 80 years ago.

Eager to consolidate their rule over this lush but backward province, British officials flooded Assam with clerks from Bengal, tribals from the surrounding hill regions to work in their tea gardens, and Muslim peasants from East Bengal to cultivate vast tracts of fallow land which the easy-going Assamese farmers had not bothered to plough. . . .

By 1931 not only had the land owned by Assamese peasants reduced drastically but the census that year revealed that the Assamese-speaking people constituted only 31.5 percent of the state's population—just 5 percent more than the Bengalis. . . .

A series of clashes between the Assamese and the Bengalis soon followed. Although the two communities are fairly close culturally and linguistically, the locals were naturally resentful of Bengali dominance—they were, by this time, virtually running the state.[52]

After independence, the Assamese population made a concerted effort to reassert their dominance within the state; this caused additional tensions between the two groups. What provoked bloodshed in the early 1980s was, ironically, another by-product of British colonialism—the Pakistani civil war of 1970, which occurred because the East Bengalis resented the political and economic domination of their province by West Pakistanis from Punjab and Sind. As the result of the civil war, many Bengali Muslims emigrated to Assam. This influx of refugees both increased the number of non-Assamese in the population and reawakened the nationalism of those Bengali Muslims whose families had come to Assam during the colonial period. Fears that the Assamese would once again be dominated by Bengalis and the discovery that some 45,000 Bangladeshi refugees had been illegally included on the electoral rolls in the late 1970s culminated in widespread communal violence in 1983.

In addition to drawing arbitrary boundaries and following policies

---

[52] Ajoy Bose, "Blend that didn't work in Assam," *Guardian*, 17 February 1983.

which encouraged disunity among colonial populations, the colonial powers frequently at independence turned over the government to groups whose primary concern was gaining control of state resources to guarantee their own economic well-being rather than to promote the development of the economy in a manner beneficial to the population as a whole. "For those who led the independence struggles and their successors, equality with the former colonialists—including the consumption of 'luxury' items taken for granted in the industrialized nations—is an important part of what independence means to them as individuals."[53] As a result, income disparities have remained wide, and in some cases they have grown larger, producing considerable discontent. This is one reason why the internal security role of Third World armed forces is so important today. Repression has been necessary to maintain in power regimes that, in the words of the Palme Commission, have lost or never had the national consensus to enable them to govern.[54]

Direct Intervention

Some of the conflicts in which the traditional powers have intervened are well known: the USSR, China, and the United States in Korea; France, the United States, the USSR and China in Indochina; France and Britain in the Suez crisis; the USSR in Afghanistan. The United States succeeded in obtaining the participation of South Korean, Thai, Australian, Filipino, and New Zealand troops in Indochina while France and Britain acted together with Israel in the Suez dispute. In terms of direct intervention in conflicts, however, these more widely known vents are just the tip of the iceberg. In addition to Indochina and Korea, United States troops have intervened in countries such as Lebanon, the Dominican Republic, and Granada. U.S. military advisers have assisted local troops in countries such as Oman and El Salvador. United States–sponsored invasions have occurred in Cuba, Guatemala, and Nicaragua. Soviet forces have in turn played active combat roles in Sudan, Iraq, Egypt, Syria, Yemen, and Ethiopia. French troops have intervened extensively in Africa, for example in Cameroon, Gabon, Congo-Brazzaville, Tunisia, Chad, Somalia, the Central African Republic, Djibouti, Mauritania, and Zaire. British intervention has been heavily, but not exclusively, oriented toward the Middle East (Jordan, Lebanon, Kuwait, Aden, and Oman) and has also occurred in Libya, Malaysia, and Mauritius.[55]

---

[53] Weinstein, "The Meaning," p. 20.

[54] Altaf Gauhar, "The Military Necessity," *South* no. 22 (August 1982): 15.

[55] A useful summary of over 300 conflicts which have occurred in the post–World War II period is found in Robert Lyle Butterworth with Margaret E. Scranton, *Managing Inter-*

The direct intervention of Third World countries in conflicts in other Third World countries is a phenomenon that has expanded significantly over the last decade. The main Third World interventionary powers are Libya, Cuba, Israel, Vietnam, South Africa, Pakistan, and North Korea. Despite the publicity surrounding Cuban involvement in countries such as Ethiopia and Angola, Libya has been the most active of all the newer interventionary powers in the past decade. The post-1973 oil price rises undoubtedly assisted Qaddafi in pursuing his predilection for involving himself in the affairs of other countries. Cuba's extraterritorial involvements are, of necessity, financed by the Soviet Union, but Cuban officials insist that they in no way contradict Cuban foreign policy goals. The Pakistanis are primarily interested in earning money, and Pakistani forces have been involved mainly in the Middle East and in Libya.

Many other Third World countries have intervened on a lesser scale outside their own borders in recent years. For instance, Moroccan troops served in Syria in 1973, transported there by the Soviet Union, and in Zaire in 1977 and 1978, fighting along with French troops. Egyptian troops have fought in Sudan, Nigeria (on the same side as Israeli troops), and Yemen. Syria currently occupies a large portion of Lebanon.[56]

The participation of external powers in intra- and interstate conflict in the Third World is likely both to exacerbate these conflicts and to prevent them from reaching a rapid conclusion. The apparently greater willingness of an ever-growing number of countries to intervene in the affairs of others thus suggests the difficulty to reduce security-related expenditures both in the countries party to the conflict and in those that intervene.

Coups d'État

Coups d'état offer additional fertile ground for foreign intervention in Third World countries, although the involvement of outside powers can be difficult to substantiate. Often the assistance provided is passive. The foreign power takes no steps to overthrow the sitting government, but it makes clear to the leaders of the coup that a government led by them will receive recognition or aid once established. Active involvement can follow two main paths: support can be given directly to the members of the armed forces who are planning the coup; alternatively, economic and po-

---

state Conflict, 1945–74: Data with Synopses (Pittsburgh, Pa.: University Center for International Studies, University of Pittsburgh, 1976). For a survey of some of the major actors, see Milton Leitenberg, "The Impact of the Worldwide Confrontation of the Great Powers: Aspects of Military Intervention and the Projection of Military Power," pp. 406–59, in Fischer, ed., Armament.

[56] Leitenberg, "The Impact," pp. 445–54.

litical support can be withdrawn from the government that is the target of the coup. The objective of the latter is to weaken the domestic position of the sitting government and make the coup acceptable to at least some segments of domestic and international opinion.

Both forms of active involvement were employed by the Nixon administration in the United States against Chile following Allende's election in 1970. U.S. intelligence officers were allegedly directly involved in the coup against Prince Sihanouk of Cambodia in 1970. The Soviet Union is supposed to have tried to convince Afghani leader Amin to resign in 1979 and to have been involved in his death when he refused to be set aside. The British and Israeli intelligence services have long been suspected of complicity in Amin's coup in Uganda in 1971. Among Third World countries, Libya has once again been most active in supporting or instigating coups against leaders who Qaddafi opposes; for example, Libya has reportedly been involved in attempted coups against Barre in Somalia, Nimieri in Sudan, Sadat in Egypt, and Hassan in Morocco.[57]

To the extent that direct control of the government by the armed forces or civil unrest as a result of a coup causes security expenditure to rise, actions on the part of foreign governments that encourage the armed forces to overthrow the sitting government contribute to larger defense budgets. Actions prior to the coup—such as the Nixon administration's destabilization policy against the Allende government—may even contribute to rising security expenditure before the coup takes place. By reducing the Allende government's access to foreign capital, the Nixon administration helped to bring about a deterioration in the Chilean economy. This produced growing dissatisfaction among the government's opponents which, in turn, strengthened the determination of segments of the armed forces to overthrow the government. Partly in an attempt to forestall a coup, Allende significantly increased the amount of national resources devoted to the armed forces during his tenure. In the decade preceding Allende's election, military budgets absorbed on average 2.8 percent of GDP; between 1970 and 1973, they averaged 5.7 percent of gross product.[58]

[57] Regarding Chile, see U.S. Congress, Senate, Intelligence Committee, Report: *Covert Action in Chile, 1963–73* (Washington, D.C.: Government Printing Office, 18 December 1975), and Report: *Alleged Assassination Plots Involving Foreign Leaders* (Washington, D.C.: Government Printing Office, 20 November 1975), pp. 225–54. Additional information on the Nixon administration's anti-Allende policy and a useful summary of its activities in Chile, particularly prior to Allende's assumption of power, appear in Seymour M. Hersch, *The Price of Power: Kissinger in the Nixon White House* (New York: Summit Books, 1983), pp. 258–96. Hersh discusses the alleged U.S. involvement in the Sihanouk coup on pp. 175–83. Regarding Libyan-backed coup attempts, see Leitenberg, "The Impact," pp. 447–48.

[58] Data from Ball, *Third-World*, p. 198. See also, Portales and Varas, "The Role," p. 25.

Security Assistance

Security assistance can be another source of rising expenditure on the armed forces (see detailed discussion in Chapter 7). When a military is able to procure a certain type of weapon, it naturally wishes eventually to procure a newer generation of the same weapon. Military grant aid allowed many Third World countries to procure equipment during the 1950s and 1960s that they would not otherwise have been able to afford. Since the early 1970s, however, many donors of security assistance have hardened their terms, and many countries are no longer eligible for grant aid. Thus, militaries seeking to replace equipment obtained under concessional terms in earlier years frequently find themselves faced with the choice of either not replacing older weapons or allocating more of their own resources to purchase military equipment and services.

Where security-related loans are offered in the place of grant aid, countries may be encouraged to purchase weapons that they can neither really afford nor would have bought if they had had to rely solely on their own resources or to raise commercial loans. While the terms of the traditional donors of security assistance (the United States, the USSR, Great Britain, and France) hardened during the 1970s, some Third World governments have been able to substitute aid from OPEC countries, primarily Saudi Arabia, Kuwait, Libya, Algeria, the United Arab Emirates, and Iraq (the latter being up to the beginning of its war with Iran in 1980). Although the terms of assistance offered by OPEC countries are not well known, some aid has taken the form of grants and some the form of loans at concessional rates. With the decline in the price of oil experienced in the mid-1980s, it is likely that the generosity of this group of donors has decreased accordingly.

Like domestic security expenditure, security assistance in and of itself does not create conflicts or wars. For those to occur, political decisions are necessary. Nonetheless, it seems likely that military assistance does not encourage countries or warring factions within countries to solve their disputes by peaceful means. With regard to the Iran–Iraq arms race, for example, one analyst has concluded, "The ever-increasing willingness of some powers to supply and finance arms exports to their clients has led to new arms races in the region. This development has particularly exacerbated the previously low-level conflicts in the Persian Gulf."[59] Along

---

[59] Farid Abolfathi, "Defense Expenditures in the Persian Gulf: Internal, Inter-state, and International Factors in the Iraqi-Iranian Arms Race (1950–1969)," in *Exploring Competitive Arms Processes*, ed. W. Ladd Hollist (New York: Marcel Dekker, 1978). For a description of how U.S. military assistance programs in the 1960s influenced the shah of Iran's view of domestic security and ultimately raised Iranian security expenditures, see Schulz, *Military Expenditures*, pp. 50–51.

with the heightened perception of threat came increased security expenditures and, eventually in 1980, war between the two countries. Security assistance and arms have been supplied to one or both parties by Western, Soviet-bloc, and OPEC-member governments as well as China.

Arms Sales

One of the most widespread images of external involvement in Third World security affairs is that of the arms seller. Arms sales increased significantly in volume and value during the 1970s. The archtypical arms salesman is a Western corporation—Lockheed, Grumman, Dassault, Hawker-Siddley, Krupp—but this picture must be modified in two important respects. In the first place, the Soviet Union is a major exporter of weapons. While the terms under which it sold weapons prior to the mid-1970s were probably more favorable to the buyer than the terms offered by Western governments or firms, the fact remains that the USSR expected to be paid for many of the weapons it has transferred to the Third World. The second modification involves the new producers who are increasingly entering the export market; notable among these are Brazil and Israel.

In the public mind, the arms salesman presses his wares on a reluctant client who is overwhelmed by "hard sell" techniques. It is true that Western arms companies promote their products. Sometimes promotion is undertaken by employees of private corporations; other times, it is undertaken by an employee of a government bureau whose function it is to find markets for weapons produced by national industries (for example, the Délégation Générale pour l'Armement in France). But the client is rarely reluctant; indeed, he is often quite eager. Anyone who doubts that the arms business is a two-way street need only look at the record of the capital-surplus oil-producing states in the Middle East in the mid- to late 1970s. Most countries do not have the means to indulge themselves to the same extent as the shah of Iran or the Saudi monarchy. This is one reason why security assistance, even in the form of loans, is necessary and eagerly sought by many Third World governments.

Few military officers, however, need to be convinced about the desirability of purchasing weapons. The 1985 SIPRI Yearbook, for example, listed eighty-five Third World countries that took delivery of some sort of major weapon between 1978 and 1985; the vast majority of these deliveries occurred between 1982 and 1984. They ranged from the acquisition of one transport aircraft by Nepal to the purchase of a wide variety of aircraft, armored vehicles, naval craft, and missiles by countries such as Libya, Saudi Arabia, Egypt, and India.[60]

WHATEVER form it may take, the intervention in Third World conflicts by countries not party to the original dispute does nothing to promote the peaceful resolution of these conflicts. There are now so many potential interveners that the involvement of any one in a dispute increasingly means that the other external powers will be drawn in as well. Once antagonistic pairs of interventionary powers become involved on either side of a conflict—particularly if these are the United States and the USSR or obvious proxies for the superpowers—that conflict takes on a new dimension and, in all likelihood, gains new momentum. Patrons may compete with each other to provide more weapons, more money to buy weapons or other forms of assistance to the disputing parties. The fact that technicians and military specialists (for example, pilots) can be hired from third countries to service and operate sophisticated equipment means that countries can be encouraged to purchase weapons not only beyond the capacity of their armed forces to use effectively, but also really beyond their capacity to finance.

Countries have sometimes intervened in disputes in a positive way, for example by placing embargoes on warring parties as in the 1965 Indo-Pakistani war or by making known their opposition to coups d'état before they are carried out as the Carter administration did with regard to El Salvador in the late 1970s. For the most part, however, external intervention implies an exacerbation of the original dispute and necessitates higher levels of expenditure in the security sectors of all participants.

SECURITY EXPENDITURE
AND THE PROMOTION OF SECURITY

It is clear from the foregoing discussion that the reasons Third World countries allocate resources to their security forces are varied and subject to change over time, depending partly on economic conditions, partly on bureaucratic considerations, and partly on the political orientation of governments. The ways in which these various factors interact can be seen by examining individual countries over a period of years, as the case of Chile demonstrates.

[60] SIPRI, *World Armaments and Disarmament, 1985*, pp. 389–423. For summaries of the policies and interests of arms producers and purchasers see SIPRI, *The Arms Trade*, and M. Brzoska and T. Ohlson, *Arms Transfers to the Third World 1971–85* (Oxford, 1987).

In the 1950s and for much of the 1960s, the American-dominated system of interhemispheric defense helped keep the perception of external threat within Latin America at a relatively low level. Furthermore, between 1956 and 1959 and again between 1962 and 1964, the Chilean economy was not sufficiently strong to support a constantly expanding security sector. During these periods the rate of growth of security spending either stagnated or declined. Throughout most of the 1930s and 1940s, the Chilean military had also been kept rather short of funds due to poor economic conditions.

By the 1950s and 1960s, a considerable pent-up demand for salary and pension rises and equipment modernization had been created. In addition, there was a perception among the officer corps during the 1950s that, after two decades of austerity, the Chilean armed forces were less well equipped than those of neighboring countries, particularly Argentina. Despite the lack of any real external threat, there was pressure to bring the level of armament possessed by the Chilean armed forces nearer to that of the Argentinian military; recall that the Chilean armed forces have traditionally followed the armament acquisitions of Argentina quite closely. To the extent that economic conditions allowed, the various demands of the armed forces were met.

The disturbances in the armed forces during 1968 and 1969 centered around corporate issues—salary levels, equipment modernization, and the composition of the Army High Command. Nonetheless, the armed forces had become increasingly unhappy with the domestic political situation, a problem clear to both the outgoing Frei and the incoming Allende administrations: expenditure on the security sector increased sharply after the tacnazo in 1969. A coup d'état was nonetheless carried out in September 1973. The socioeconomic policies followed by the junta have necessitated increased expenditure on the two forces used for internal repression—the Carabineros and the Bureau of Investigation. Fears of conflicts with Argentina and Peru, whether realistic or not, have been used to justify increasing expenditure on the regular armed forces—the Army, Navy, and Air Force. Serious economic difficulties in 1975–1976 and in the early 1980s caused cutbacks in real security outlays. Nonetheless, according to SIPRI data, real security expenditure in 1981 was approximately 100 percent higher than it had been in 1973, the last year of constitutional government in Chile.[61]

Other developing countries will show similar shifting patterns of factors influencing the level and content of their security expenditure. Prob-

[61] This discussion on Chilean security expenditure has been derived from Heare, *Trends*, pp. 7–8; Portales and Varas, "The Role," pp. 25–27, 37–42; and SIPRI, *World Armaments and Disarmament, 1983*, p. 166.

ably the most important among these are the existence of external conflicts, the requirements of internal security, bureaucratic inertia, resource availability, and pressures from the military (both corporate and personal). Whatever the specific combination in individual countries, one question remains: Do these expenditures help countries meet their security needs? There is reason to question how cost effective these outlays have been, in terms of both external and internal security.

External Security

Some analysts believe that the weapons produced by the industrialized countries primarily for use in conflicts with each other are not suited to the conditions under which Third World militaries must operate. Essentially, these weapons are seen as too sophisticated for Third World armed forces to operate. The oversophistication of the weapons produced by industrialized countries compared to the capabilities—and pocketbooks—of Third World armed forces is one reason behind the relatively rapid growth of the export market for weapons from some of the newer arms producers, such as Israel and Brazil. Third World militaries tend to lack sufficient numbers of qualified technicians to maintain and repair the equipment, forcing them to rely on foreign experts to fulfill these functions. They also tend to depend on external sources of supply for spare parts, fuel, and ammunition for their weapons. If money is lacking to pay for these materials and services or if the relationship between supplier and recipient breaks down for some reason, the operational value of sophisticated weapons can decrease drastically. The experiences of some developing countries confirm the existence of such problems.

Soviet supplies of aircraft and naval vessels to the Indonesian armed forces during Sukarno's rule made Indonesia the most powerful military force in Asia by the early 1960s in terms of the quality of its weaponry. Indeed, Indonesian acquisitions of Soviet arms—for example, submarines—were used by India to justify requests of similar equipment from Western suppliers. By 1965, however, at the time of the coup d'état against Sukarno, it became evident that the Indonesian armed forces could not operate most of this equipment. The Indonesian threat to countries such as India was nonexistent, despite the accumulation of arms.[62]

In the case of Iran, members of the U.S. Military Assistance Advisory Group (MAAG) believed that Iranian weapons purchases were made without any consideration of the country's long-term strategic needs. Probably more serious, MAAG advisers found that weapons purchases were not

[62] Thomas, *The Defence of India*, pp. 210–12.

synchronized with training and construction schedules; thus, the amount of security Iran was buying in the 1970s was much less than if the same weapons had been purchased by, say, France. Once Iran found itself at war with Iraq in 1980, an infantry-based defense, not a reliance on so-phisticated weapons, was primarily responsible for repelling the initial Iraqi invasion.[63]

The problems facing Third World militaries in operating sophisticated equipment they have increasingly been buying from the industrialized countries are not the only ones they confront in terms of external security. Despite the significant expansion of the arms trade during the 1970s, so-phisticated equipment is still spread unevenly around the Third World. Most developing countries continue to spend rather small amounts of their security outlays on weapons. Operating costs predominate, espe-cially personnel costs. This means that governments can spend large sums of money on the security sector and do little more than pay, clothe, feed, and house their troops; soldiers often have neither the training nor the equipment to engage in large-scale, extended combat.

The refusal of the Nigerian armed forces to demobilize large portions of its army for nearly a decade following the civil war has already been described; it led to operating costs and military housing projects absorb-ing more than 70 percent of the Nigerian security budget even at the end of the 1970s. Because of this, the Nigerian armed forces entered the 1980s with relatively few weapons, despite devoting some 4 percent of gross do-mestic product to the security sector throughout the 1970s. The army was said to be a poor match for "a well-armed and determined foe." Similarly, the Nigerian naval forces were small, and the Nigerian air force was "equipped to act only in limited air-support and interdiction roles." The external security implications of this situation depend to some extent on the anticipated opponent. If Nigeria envisions itself fighting only against its immediate neighbors, then extensive up-grading of equipment is probably not necessary, although the quality of training received by the ground forces must be raised. If, however, it envisions itself in conflict

---

[63] Schulz, "Military Expenditures," p. 200. More recently, Iran has begun to use con-verted speed-boats supplied by the Swedish company, Boghammer Marin, to attack neutral vessels in the Persian Gulf. Armed with machine guns, hand-fired rockets, and 106 mm. recoilless cannons capable of piercing the hulls of oil tankers, these boats were exported as a nonmilitary item from Sweden whose government maintains that it sells no weapons to ei-ther Iran or Iraq. American officials have alleged that these boats have been involved in at-tacks against seventeen noncombattant vessels in the Gulf since February 1987. See David B. Ottaway, "New Iranian Naval Weapon: High-Speed Patrol Boats," *Washington Post*, 26 July 1987, p. A25.

with South Africa, as Lagos often claims may one day be the case, then the Nigerian armed forces are at a distinct disadvantage in all respects.[64]

SIPRI data shows that Nigerial ordered a sizable number of major weapons in the early 1980s. These, combined with the cutback in troop levels and a presumed emphasis on training for the remaining soldiers, should increase Nigeria's capacity to defend itself against a serious external attack. Increased imports of more modern weapons will, however, cause the Nigerian armed forces to run up against the maintenance/repair problem, and there is some reason to suspect that this problem will seriously impair the effectiveness of the new weaponry. It was pointed out in the early 1980s, for example, that the Nigerian air force was unable to maintain adequately its small force of MIG-17s and MIG-21s. Newer weapons will only bring with them more complicated maintaince problems.[65]

Another aspect of the external security issue infrequently discussed in the literature is the effect that an internal security role has on the warfighting capabilities of Third World armed forces. Because many militaries in the Third World have not been required to fight against an external enemy for many years, indeed may not have had a serious external engagement since gaining independence, and have been restricted to fighting usually poorly trained and equipped domestic opposition groups, there has been little or no opportunity to judge their ability to stand up to full-scale external attack. As Third World military establishments have become increasingly involved in running governments in addition to maintaining domestic order, the need to examine the external-internal security relationship has correspondingly grown. The experience of the Argentinian army and navy in the Falklands/Malvinas war with Great Britain in 1982 leads one to suspect that when the militaries assume political roles they can severely damage their ability to provide external defense.

> This experience has confirmed that a political army loses its ability to provide defence, and that one cannot at the same time carry out the functions of a party and of a military machine. In fact, for non-operational reasons, there were three Falklands wars, conducted without coordination by each of the three branches of the armed forces. The way in which the three forces tried to outbid each other prevented even the government from grasping possibilities of avoiding confrontation by diplomatic means. But in the eyes of the public it is the incompetence of numerous army officers, their corruption,

[64] John M. Ostheimer and Gary J. Buckley, "Nigeria," p. 292, in Kolodziej and Harkavy, ed., *Security Policies.*
[65] Ibid., p. 293, and SIPRI, *World Armaments and Disarmament, 1983,* p. 326.

which caused the most indignation, for they put at risk the lives of the conscripts. From ex-servicemen who fought in the Falklands, military chaplains, and journalists have come numerous reports which bring out the incompetence, even the cowardice, of certain senior officers—in contrast with the heroism of the air force—and the lack of preparedness of soldiers who were ill-equipped or ill-nourished as a result of the trafficking in equipment or rations.[66]

Internal Security

The doubtful capacity of many Third World militaries to defend their countries against external attack many in the end have little relevance for the security of these countries since the main threats confronting most governments are of an internal, not external, nature. Many analysts, when considering the ability of Third World armed forces to fulfill internal security roles, focus on the inappropriateness of procuring sophisticated weapons.

First, are the LDCs buying the right kind of equipment to meet their needs? Over the past decade, [1970s] . . . LDC imports of highly sophisticated weaponry have been growing. Yet most conflicts in LDCs over the past several decades have involved internal security disturbances or limited border disputes. Advanced weapons are seldom very useful in such conflicts. Supersonic combat aircraft (often the most expensive item in a country's arsenal) or missile systems seldom play a decisive role in resisting a coup attempt or eliminating an insurgency movement.[67]

To the extent that countries facing primarily internal security threats are importing (or in a few cases producing) sophisticated military equipment, this judgment is valid. Despite the periodic war scares among Latin American countries, one can really question why countries such as Chile, Peru, Colombia, Argentina, and Brazil need supersonic aircraft.[68] Although the Nicaraguan National Guard under the Somoza government was equipped only with the A-37B, a small single-seat counterinsurgency

---

[66] Alain Rouquié, "Argentina: The Departure of the Military—End of a Political Cycle or Just Another Episode?," *International Affairs* (U.K.) 59:4 (Autumn 1983):580.

[67] Carol Lancaster and Anthony Lake, "Trends in LDC Military Expenditures" (Paper prepared for the Independent Commission on Disarmament and Security Issues, August 1981, mimeograph), pp. 15–16.

[68] Chief among the reasons behind the weapons procurement policies of major Latin American countries during the 1950s and 1960s was, according to SIPRI, their value in intra-élite power struggles. SIPRI, *The Arms Trade*, pp. 691–702.

aircraft, it had no serious trouble establishing air superiority over the Sandinista forces which had no aircraft and a minimal air defense. The Burmese armed forces, which have been fighting ethnically-based insurgencies throughout Burma for over thirty years, have relied to date very heavily on infantry weapons and the ability of their soldiers to fight effectively in the mountainous jungle terrain in which the guerrillas operate.[69]

Although sophisticated weapons clearly have a limited role to play in internal security conflicts, one should not automatically assume that the security situation of the Third World countries would be enhanced if they were to import only counterinsurgency-type weapons.[70] In most cases, threats to Third World governments arise out of decades or even centuries of exploitation of one group by another. In Burma, for example, non-Burmese ethnic groups—Shan, Karen, Kachin, and Karenni—are fighting against absorption into a political unit dominated by ethnic Burmese. In Nicaragua, a large portion of the population ultimately became involved in opposing the domination of the country by the Somoza family and its associates who controlled most of the country's wealth and its political system. In Zimbabwe, the black population reasserted its right to control the country after a century of white rule. In South Africa, where the white population is larger than Zimbabwe's (about 18 percent of the total) and has been settled in the area for some three hundred years, it is nonetheless likely that the same process will occur.

These examples, along with the many others that could be named, underline a vital fact almost always ignored by governments: What is inappropriate in dealing with internal disputes is not the use of sophisticated military equipment but the decision to rely on force at all. In most cases, internal security measures are required because the ruling élites are unwilling to make significant alterations in exploitative socioeconomic and political systems. As long as basic inequalities persist, some sort of domestic unrest will continue to exist as well. The purchase of weapons designed specifically for counterinsurgency will not cause these inequities to disappear; only a transformation of political and economic structures can produce that outcome.

[69] Rodney Tasker, "A Rag-Tag Armed Force Which Gets the Job Done," *Far Eastern Economic Review* 121 (7 July 1983): 32–33.
[70] This is the implication of the argument on pages 157–58 of Kennedy, *The Military in the Third World.*

3

. . . .

THE MEASUREMENT OF

SECURITY EXPENDITURE

Not all societies place equal importance on the collection and dissemination of data. Third World countries are generally less well equipped for these activities than Western industrialized ones. In addition, the collection of data is frequently not accorded the same priority in the Third World as in the West. Some developing countries have also opted for what might be termed the East-bloc pattern of data dissemination: the fewer data published, the better. Thus, there are serious problems of validity with much of the data measuring economic and social conditions in Third World countries.[1] Even at the beginning of the 1980s a World Bank official had to admit: "We [international agencies] all use each other's figures and no one really knows how good they are." While the measurement of gross product is far from troublefree, a good deal more attention has been directed toward the quantification of this indicator than toward less traditional ones such as income distribution, labor utilization, or agricultural productivity. As soon as one tries to broaden one's analysis with these less traditional indicators, it is immediately apparent that one is in relatively uncharted waters.[2]

[1] According to Gurr, "A measure is *valid* if it is an adequate measure of what it is supposed to represent. . . . A particular measurement procedure or indicator is *reliable* to the extent that it yields results that are consistent in successive measurements of the same case, and comparable among cases." Ted Gurr, *Politimetrics* (New York: Prentice-Hall, 1972), pp. 43, 49.

[2] An extremely useful examination of the problems associated with measuring the less traditional indicators is found in William Paul McGreevy, ed., *Third-World Poverty: New Strategies for Measuring Development Progress* (Lexington, Mass., and Toronto: Lexington Books, 1980). The issues surrounding the measurement of gross product are discussed in: F. Thomas Juster, "On The Measurement of Economic and Social Performance," *National Bureau of Economic Research 50th Annual Report* (1970): 3–24; Simon Kuznets, "National Income and Industrial Structure," and "National Income and Economic Welfare," in his *Economic Change* (New York: W. W. Norton, 1953), chaps. 6 and 7; and Dudley Seers,

There are also serious problems of validity regarding the security expenditure of developing countries.[3] The question of how much of its resources a country devotes to security-related activities is often considered sensitive and subject to secrecy on the part of governments. A restrictive policy concerning the provision of security expenditure data is one means of reducing the information available to other governments, which may be considered either potential or actual opponents. At the same time, another objective of such a policy is almost certainly to prevent the general public from learning too much about their own security sector. Researchers examining the relationship between the allocation of resources to the security sector and development in the Third World are thus confronted with a number of obstacles when collecting security expenditure data. Many governments' desires to make public as little information as possible hamper efforts to collect data, and many figures available are of dubious accuracy. In addition, although some governments do publish reasonably detailed security budgets, it can be difficult for individuals outside those countries to obtain the relevant documents. As a result, publications providing statistical information on the security-related outlays of many Third World countries are widely used in the research community.

A number of sources provide information concerning only the military-related component of government expenditure for 80 to 110 developing countries. The best known of these are the United States Arms Control and Disarmament Agency (ACDA) (*World Military Expenditures and Arms Transfers*), the Stockholm International Peace Research Institute (SIPRI) (*World Armaments and Disarmament, SIPRI Yearbook*), and the International Institute of Strategic Studies (IISS) (*The Military Balance*). Other groups provide functional breakdowns of government expenditure; for the most part, these include security outlays. Chief among these are the International Monetary Fund (IMF) (*Government Finance Statistics Yearbook*) and the United Nations (*Statistical Yearbook*).

ACDA and SIPRI rely on the NATO definition of military expenditure, although in estimating the security spending of Third World countries they

---

"The Political Economy of National Accounting," pp. 193–209, in *Employment, Income Distribution and Development Strategy: Problems of the Developing Countries,* ed. Alec Cairncross and Mohinder Puri (New York: Holmes & Meier, 1976).

[3] Based on Gurr's definition of "valid" and "reliable" measures, there are also serious problems of reliability insofar as security spending is concerned. As will be discussed in more detail below, different countries include different items in the defense category, and even within the same country what is included and excluded can vary over time. The standard sources are, for the most part, unable to deal with this problem.

do little more than reproduce data provided in one form or another by governments.[4] The UN *Statistical Yearbook* and the IISS have no general definition to begin with and accept whatever figure national sources provide for security outlays. The IMF has its own definition, similar to the NATO definition, and IMF members are supposed to use it as a guideline when supplying data on government expenditure. (See Appendix 2 for the definitions employed by the IMF, ACDA, and SIPRI.)

This means that, with the exception of the IMF, the major sources of security expenditure rely on the widely varying domestic definitions of military expenditure for most countries they survey. This is unsatisfactory both because countries include different items under the heading of "Defense" or "Armed Forces" and because security-related expenditure can be moved from one category to another in the same country over a period of time. In Iran, expenditure on the paramilitary force, Gendarmerie, has been included under the Ministry of Defense during some years and under the Ministry of the Interior during others. The same has been true of the paramilitary Garde Républicaine in the Central African Republic. Any source which simply takes the expenditure listed under the Ministry of Defense for these two countries, presumably all sources except the IMF, will produce an expenditure series which, over the years, will have serious internal inconsistencies. In some countries, expenditure listed under "Ministry of Defense" or "Armed Forces" may include civilian-type activities, such as civil aviation; this is the case in both Pakistan and Saudi Arabia. In other countries, important military-related categories may be excluded. Items such as military pensions, debt incurred through the procurement of weapons, and construction for the armed forces often appear as subheadings in ministries other than the Ministry of Defense.

Since the IMF security expenditure data are supposed to include all items listed in the IMF definition, how a country chooses to arrange its budget is, in theory, irrelevant for those who use IMF statistics. Iran and the Central African Republic should always report their paramilitary expenditures, irrespective of where in their budgets these items are placed. Saudi Arabia and Pakistan should never report the portion of their "Ministry of Defense" budget spent on civilian aviation. (Whether or not countries follow these guidelines will be discussed below.) IMF data are supposed to be comparable, both over time and among countries, and the

---

[4] Additional information on ACDA is found in Edward T. Fei, "Understanding Arms Transfers and Military Expenditures: Data Problems," pp. 40, 43, in *Arms Transfers in the Modern World*, ed. Sephanie G. Neuman and Robert E. Harkavy (New York: Praeger, 1979).

IMF is a much-used source for both ACDA and SIPRI. In reality, therefore, the situation regarding security expenditure is much the same as it is for economic and social indicators: The major sources frequently quote each other, but just how good any of these data are is open to question.

THE RELIABILITY ISSUE

The public perception, shared by many researchers, is that the data collected by groups such as the IMF, ACDA, SIPRI, or the IISS are more reliable than those produced by national governments.[5] Two points, however, are not fully appreciated by those who hold this opinion. First, the ultimate source of the security expenditure data published by these groups is national governments. Second, for most developing countries very little adjustment is made by ACDA, SIPRI, the IISS, or the UN *Statistical Yearbook* to the single figure published by national governments in budgetary documents under headings such as "National Defense," "Armed Forces," or "Ministry of Defense."

Part of the problem can be traced to data availability. It is difficult to collect all the documents necessary if security expenditure figures based on a common definition are to be produced on a regular basis for the large number of countries that SIPRI, the IISS, and ACDA survey each year. Because ACDA is an agency of the U.S. government and therefore has some possibility of obtaining information from U.S. intelligence agencies such as the CIA or the DIA (Defense Intelligence Agency), people tend to assume that ACDA data always come from intelligence sources and that they are, therefore, rather reliable.[6]

ACDA does use CIA figures for estimates of Soviet security expenditure. For most countries in the Third World, however, ACDA has relied on unclassified sources. Until recently, ACDA simply adopted the estimates produced by the U.S. Agency for International Development (USAID). USAID

[5] Michael Brzoska, "The Reporting of Military Expenditures," *Journal of Peace Research* 18:3 (1981):261. This article summarizes portions of the findings of Michael Brzoska, P. Lock, F. Peters, M. Reichel, and H. Wulf, "An Assessment of Sources and Statistics of Military Expenditure and Arms Transfer Data: A Report Written as a Contribution to the United Nations Study on the Relationship between Disarmament and Development" (Hamburg: IFSH—Study Group on Armaments and Underdevelopment, 1980, mimeograph).

[6] Brzoska et al., "An Assessment." The main exception here regarding reliability would be figures for the Soviet Union where, it is argued, the CIA's method of valuing the components of security expenditure overestimates outlays on the Soviet security sector. In a work aimed at the general public, two researchers who should have a good grasp of the problems surrounding military expenditure data have incorrectly stated that ACDA "makes considerable use of data produced by the Central Intelligence Agency." See Dan Smith and Ron Smith, *The Economics of Militarism* (London: Pluto Press, 1983), p. 19.

used some primary, national budgetary documents in preparing its estimates, but it relied quite heavily on IMF data. A few estimates were also taken from SIPRI and IISS publications. USAID has reduced its collection of security expenditure data since the mid-1980s, and ACDA now relies heavily on IMF statistics and "the publications and files of other US government agencies,"[7] some of which may be intelligence sources. In addition, it continues to make some use of SIPRI and IISS data. It is somewhat surprising that ACDA does not make more use of budgetary documents it could obtain on a regular basis from U.S. embassies and consulates. That SIPRI and the IISS rely on secondary sources is less surprising, since they are not as well placed as ACDA in terms of collecting budgetary documents. Nonetheless, it seems fair to state that neither SIPRI nor the IISS has made full use of the primary data obtainable without too much difficulty.

Another reason why there is relatively little checking of national government data by SIPRI, ACDA, and the IISS is quite simply lack of manpower. SIPRI has had one or two researchers working on military expenditures over the years, often only part time. The USAID office on which ACDA relied for so much of its military expenditure data up to the mid-1980s had only one researcher compiling these figures. ACDA itself has now assigned one staff member to this task. The IISS had for many years one person who spent no more than half time compiling data on security outlays. Therefore, it is hardly surprising that these researchers do not undertake the detailed examination of national budgets necessary for the compilation of comparable and reasonably reliable security expenditure figures.

Of the major sources considered here, the IISS is generally thought the least reliable by careful researchers although it is a widely used source, especially by the media. It is easy to understand why nonexperts in particular might be attracted to *The Military Balance;* it is a compact publication, and information on the size of the armed forces, their weaponry, and annual defense expenditures is summarized concisely in each issue. But what makes the IISS data especially attractive is the belief that the IISS receives information from official sources, for example, from foreign military attachés in London. This lends an air of authority to IISS publications which they do not, in reality, deserve. It is assumed that data provided by official (intelligence) sources are more accurate than data com-

[7] U.S. Arms Control and Disarmament Agency, *World Military Expenditures and Arms Transfers,* 1985 (WMEAT), Publication 123 (Washington, D.C. ACDA: August 1985), p. 140. ACDA actually uses IMF data that are updated by the World Bank. For certain countries where the expenditure data are judged to be particularly weak, ACDA does attempt to readjust the IMF/World Bank figures, as discussed below.

piled from open sources, such as those used by SIPRI. This need not be true; intelligence-based data can be purposefully misleading for any number of reasons. Furthermore, the IISS's use of intelligence sources is exaggerated. Many IISS security expenditure data are gathered from open sources such as newspapers and military journals.

There are other problems with IISS data as well. The Third World has never been an IISS strong point, although coverage of the areas outside Europe and North America has been increasing in recent years.[8] Anyone seeking to compile a historical series of military expenditure in local currencies using IISS data will experience difficulties. First, IISS data for many Third World countries do not extend very far into the past. Then, because the data expressed in local currency units are "the latest available budget figures,"[9] these data are first, or at best, revised budget estimates. Actual outlays very often differ significantly from estimates, and IISS data are likely to be rather unreliable insofar as the local currency figures are concerned.

Expenditure is also given in U.S. dollars in a summary table at the back of each issue of *The Military Balance*. These U.S.-dollar figures do appear to be updated, and an increasing number of Third World countries are represented in the summary table. In the 1984–85 issue of *The Military Balance*, this table compared fifty-seven countries. Anyone using this expenditure series, however, should be aware of all the problems surrounding the conversion of many national currencies into a common currency.[10] Moreover, since the IISS does not provide any updated figures in local currencies, it is impossible to compare the IISS's basic data with those of other major sources and to determine how reliable IISS data really are.

In view of these problems, anyone interested in security expenditure statistics would do well to consult sources other than *The Military Balance*. Unfortunately, many users of *The Military Balance* are unaware of its shortcomings and use IISS figures indiscriminately; this is true even of some researchers who should be alert to such problems. For example,

[8] Brzoska, "The Reporting," pp. 266–68, 272. See also Chapter 8 in Ulrich Albrecht, Asbjørn Eide, Mary Kaldor, Milton Leitenberg and Julian Perry Robinson, *A Short Research Guide on Arms and Armed Forces* (London: Croom Helm, 1978), pp. 49–61.

[9] International Institute of Strategic Studies, *The Military Balance, 1982–1983* (London: IISS, 1982), p. vi.

[10] Brief discussions of these problems are found in Fei, "Understanding Arms Transfers," pp. 44–46; Brzoska, "The Reporting," pp. 268–73; and Stockholm International Peace Research Institute, *World Armaments and Disarmament, SIPRI Yearbook 1980* (London: Taylor & Francis, 1980), pp. 12–14. Some of the major problems involved in such conversions are discussed in Nicole Ball, *Third-World Security Expenditure: A Statistical Compendium*, C-10250-M5 (Stockholm: National Defence Research Institute, May 1984), pp. 30–34.

David Whynes used data from both the IISS and SIPRI in his study, *The Economics of Third World Military Expenditure*. He justified this decision in the following way:

> The two principal sources for military data are the International Peace Research Institute in Stockholm (SIPRI) and the International Institute for Strategic Studies, London (IISS). Throughout the present text, use will be made of data from both these sources, although it must be pointed out that each of these organisations employs its own measurement convention. Estimates, therefore, might not be mutually consistent in all aspects, *although the general trends will be common.*[11]

But such a conclusion is not warranted as a general rule. A comparison of SIPRI's security expenditure as a proportion of gross product with corresponding IISS figures shows considerable areas of disagreement for many countries, particularly over the shorter term. When these two sets of figures are compared with the trends shown by ACDA figures and those collected by this author based on national budgetary sources, most frequently the IISS percentages go against the trend.[12] One would be ill-advised, therefore, to mix IISS figures with those from any other source.

Prior to the 1984 issue of *World Military Expenditures and Arms Transfers* (WMEAT), which covered the years from 1972 to 1982, ACDA stated that it published only actual expenditure data, but the ordinary user of the WMEAT series had no means of assessing the accuracy of this statement since the military expenditure figures that appear in WMEAT volumes are given only in U.S. dollars. The local currency data prepared by USAID that formed the basis for most of ACDA's Third World military expenditure figures up to the 1985 volume of WMEAT are not widely available. In most years, they have appeared only in an annual report to the U.S. Congress, a volume not sold by the U.S. Government Printing Office.[13] It has, nonetheless, been possible to obtain some of these reports

[11] David Whynes, *The Economics of Third World Military Expenditure* (London: MacMillan, 1979), p. 10; emphasis added. Gavin Kennedy, *Defense Economics* (London: Duckworth, 1983), also mixes his sources. See Tables 3.5 and 3.6, pp. 64–66.

[12] Ball, *Third-World*. See, for example, pp. 70, 85, 194, 205, and 248.

[13] U.S. Agency for International Development, International Development Cooperation Agency, *Implementation of Section 620(s) of the Foreign Assistance Act of 1961, As Amended. A Report to Congress* (Washington, D.C.: AID, various years). Hereafter, *Section 620(s)*. Although section 620(s) remains part of the Foreign Assistance Act, AID librarians were unable to produce any reports for the mid-1980s when a request was made in December 1987. The 1980 report was published by Congress in a form that makes it available for purchase and contains data for the years 1974 to 1978. U.S. Congress, House, Committee on Foreign Affairs, Report: *Economic Development versus Military Expen-*

and to assess whether or not ACDA was publishing only "actual expenditures, not budgets or appropriations" estimates as claimed prior to the 1984 WMEAT.[14]

A comparison between USAID/ACDA data and figures published in national budgetary documents suggests that USAID/ACDA data may not always have been as reliable as claimed. It is easiest to compare countries for which security expenditure is concentrated under the Ministry of Defense heading. While actual expenditure figures are available for a number of countries, many of them distribute their security expenditure among various ministries, making it easier to produce different estimates. One country for which actual expenditure figures are available and where security spending is concentrated in a single ministry is Guyana. In Table 3-1, data from Guyanese final expenditure accounts are divided into two force groups—military forces and police/paramilitary forces—according to operating costs (personnel and operations and maintenance) and capital costs (weapon procurement and construction).[15] The USAID/ACDA fig-

---

ditures in Countries Receiving US Aid: Priorities and the Competition for Resources, 96th Cong., 2nd Sess. (Washington, D.C.: Government Printing Office, 1980).

[14] Fei, "Understanding Arms Transfers, p. 46. ACDA's policy of publishing military expenditure data in U.S. dollars complicates not only the reliability issue, but also its practice of changing the base year for its constant-dollar series from volume to volume of WMEAT renders the construction of a constant-dollar series longer than ten years a complicated process. Only recently has ACDA explained how this conversion could be carried out. A long time series for current dollars is also difficult to construct because ACDA produces the current-dollar figures by reinflating the constant-dollar data.

> In addition to a constant-dollar series which shows the real trend in defense expenditure, it may be desirable to know the value of a state's military expenditure in that year's prices. ACDA produces this series by applying the US rate of inflation to the constant-dollar series to "reinflate" the constant dollars. However, because the current-dollar series is derived from the constant-dollar series, the current-dollar values do not always remain the same from one edition of WMEAT to the next. . . . This problem occurs because, when the base year for constant dollars is advanced for a new edition of WMEAT, the process of deflating local currency values with the new base year price index, converting to constant dollars at the next exchange rate, and then reinflating to current dollars using the new base year US price index, does not necessarily produce the same result given by the price indexes and change rate for the preceeding year (p. 45).

See also, U.S. Arms Control and Disarmament Agency, *WMEAT, 1970–1979,* p. 38.

[15] Definitions for force groups, operating, and capital costs follow the United Nations definitions presented in United Nations, Centre for Disarmament, *Reduction of Military Budgets: International Reporting of Military Expenditures,* Study Series 4, Sales no. E.81.I.9 (New York: United Nations, 1981), pp. 32–41. The definition for operating costs and capital costs differ from those used by the IMF which defines weapon procurement as recurrent expenditure.

ures for 1972–1975 are exactly the same as the figures provided by the Guyanese government for the operating costs of military forces (rounded to the nearest million as is USAID practice). The figures for 1972–1975 do indeed report actual outlays, but only part of them as capital costs are omitted. The AID figures for 1976–1979 are clearly taken from IMF sources. Those for 1976 and 1977 correspond more closely to Guyanese government figures for total security expenditure than the ACDA figures for earlier years. Unlike IMF data, however, ACDA expenditure figures are meant to *exclude* outlays on police and paramilitary forces. The USAID figures for 1978 and 1979 correspond to the Guyanese government's figure for total expenditure on military forces, but here it must be noted that the latter's figure reflects estimated outlays. Thus, the AID figure does not reflect actual expenditure. It is possible, of course, that the data for 1978 and 1979 will be revised in subsequent issues of WMEAT. One must conclude, however, that ACDA data do not always report actual expenditures and exhibit serious internal inconsistencies.

At the same time ACDA reduced its reliance on USAID-generated data and increased its use of the IMF as a source, it sought to deal with a problem widely recognized among compilers of security expenditure statistics: the failure of many governments to report accurately military-related capital expenditure, particularly outlays on weapon procurement. In order to obtain what ACDA believed to be a more valid estimate of expenditure for some of these countries, ACDA began adding the value of arms imported in a given year to the reported security expenditure for that year. The use of such a methodology raises additional questions, a fact of which ACDA itself is aware: "It must be cautioned, however, that this method may over- or underestimate the actual expenditures in a given year due to the fact that payment for arms may not coincide in time with deliveries. . . . Also in some cases, arms acquisitions may be financed by other countries." [16]

Like the IISS, SIPRI publishes very recent data, although it provides much longer time series in each volume of the *SIPRI Yearbook* than the IISS does in *The Military Balance*. SIPRI data are, therefore, subject to updating, and the first figures published for a country are often changed in subsequent issues of the *SIPRI Yearbook*. Thus, a 1979 security expenditure figure from the 1983 *SIPRI Yearbook* is likely to be more reliable than one published in the 1980 *SIPRI Yearbook*. Furthermore, it is often not known what category many expenditure figures fall under, particularly for the earlier years. Without access to primary documents, it is, of

[16] U.S. Arms Control and Disarmament Agency, *WMEAT, 1985*, p. 140. Because of these problems, ACDA will probably discontinue this practice in the near future.

TABLE 3-1

Comparison of USAID/ACDA, IMF, and Guyanese Security Expenditure Data, 1967–1979
(in million Guyanese dollars)

Year	USAID/ACDA	IMF	Total Security Guyana			Military Forces Guyana			Paramilitary Guyana		
			Total	Op	Cap	Total	Op	Cap	Total	Op	Cap
1967	—	4.1	11.2	9.6	1.6	4.3	3.1	1.2	6.9	6.5	0.4
1968	—	4.0	11.1	10.2	0.9	4.1	3.4	0.7	7.0	6.8	0.2
1969	—	4.5	12.8	12.5	0.3	4.7	4.5	0.2	8.1	8.0	0.1
1970	—	6.7	15.5	15.2	0.4	6.7	6.5	0.2	8.8	8.6	0.2
1971	—	6.2	15.3	14.7	0.6	6.1	6.0	0.1	9.2	8.7	0.5
1972	7.0	7.5	17.4	17.0	0.4	7.1	7.0	0.1	10.3	10.0	0.3
1973	9.0	10.6	22.7	21.0	1.7	10.1	8.8	1.3	12.6	12.3	0.3
1974	16.0	24.8	32.9	30.0	2.9	17.9	15.9	2.0	15.0	14.1	0.9
1975	25.0	76.4	49.6	40.3	9.3	32.7	24.5	8.2	16.9	15.8	1.1
1976	87.0	86.7	99.9	76.3	23.6	70.0	48.3	21.7	29.9	28.0	1.9
1977	61.0	61.9	67.0	58.0	9.0	47.5	38.7	8.8	19.5	19.3	0.2
1978[a]	44.0	44.2	67.0	65.8	1.2	43.8	42.8	1.0	23.2	23.0	0.2
1979[b]	44.0	43.8	67.1	65.4	1.7	40.7	39.7	1.0	26.4	25.7	0.7

Sources: USAID, International Development Cooperation Agency, *Implementation of Section 620(s) of the Foreign Assistance Act of 1961, as Amended, A Report to Congress* (Washington, D.C.: USAID, various years); World Bank, *World Tables, 1976* (Baltimore: Johns Hopkins University Press, 1976), p. 322; International Monetary Fund, *Government Finance Statistics Yearbook*, Vol. 5 (Washington, D.C.: IMF, 1981), p. 336, and Vol. 9 (Washington, D.C.: IMF, 1985), p. 335; Guyana, *Estimates, Current and Capital of Guyana as Passed by the National Assembly*, various years.

[a] The figures provided by the Guyanese government are for revised estimates.
[b] The figures provided by the Guyanese government are for first estimates.

course, impossible to ascertain whether one is dealing with estimates, appropriations, or actual expenditure.

SIPRI data have an important advantage over those produced by ACDA and the IISS. In addition to publishing its security expenditure data in constant dollars, SIPRI also provides a current local currency expenditure series that is updated from time to time. As explained above, the IISS publishes security expenditure in local currency for only the most recent year or two in each issue of *The Military Balance,* and these figures do not appear to be updated. Until recently, ACDA's current local currency series for Third World countries could be found in USAID's annual *Section 620 (s)* report to the U.S. Congress, although that report was difficult to obtain. Now that USAID has downgraded its collection of security expenditure data, there is no single local currency source for the figures ACDA publishes in U.S. dollars in *World Military Expenditures and Arms Transfers.* In most cases, however, it can be assumed that ACDA has simply adopted the figure provided in World Bank-updated IMF tapes. SIPRI has correctly taken the position that original data should be published so that researchers can use it in whatever way suits their purposes—in current local currency, converted into another currency, and/or in constant values. Access to a local currency series is also an important first step in evaluating both the validity and the reliability of estimates produced by the standard sources.

The IMF supplies only current local currency figures for security expenditure. These data are widely used by ACDA and SIPRI, given the common definition of security expenditure to which all countries are supposed to adhere when reporting to the IMF; however, there is no means of verifying that they do in fact follow that definition when supplying information on security expenditure. The IMF requests information on a broad range of expenditure from member countries, defining closely what each category should contain. Member countries provide the IMF with a single figure for each category and, without further checking on the part of the IMF, these statistics are reproduced in IMF publications.

The IMF staff members who work with these data state that many governments would be considerably less forthcoming with data if they knew that the information provided were subjected to independent verification procedures by the IMF. They nonetheless feel reasonably confident that the budgetary information they publish for Third World security sectors is fairly accurate, particularly the portions dealing with personnel and other operating costs. The problem arises with those items funded through "special accounts," a frequent occurrence in Latin America, or financed off-budget; IMF staff believe the items funded in this way tend to be weapons. The amount of weaponry a country procures is thus important in determining the accuracy of the information provided to the IMF. The larger the percentage of total security expenditure attributable to operating costs, the more accurate the IMF's figures are likely to be.

Tables 3-1 and 3-2 suggest that some governments may omit more than weapon procurement from the figures they provide to the IMF. Between 1967 and 1973 and in 1978 and 1979, the figures shown in the IMF column in Table 3-2 are quite close to those published by the Guyanese government as its total outlays on military forces. The small differences in the first period might be explained by one of the two sources using provisional actual expenditure and the other using actual expenditure. What is significant, however, is that the IMF definition of security spending includes outlays on paramilitary forces (see Appendix 2). According to the *Area Handbook for Guyana* published by the U.S. government, the Guyanese Police Force "is an armed, semi-military unit charged with the prevention and detection of crime, the repression of internal disturbance, protection against external aggression, and other duties as required by the government." [17] A very large proportion, if not all, of the expenditure on the Police Force (shown in Table 3-1 as "Paramilitary Guyana") should have been included in the IMF's figures; however, it is clear that for the years 1967–1973, 1978, and 1979 all expenditure on the Police Force has been excluded despite the explicit IMF definition.

The data presented by the IMF for 1974 to 1977 are somewhat confusing when compared with Guyanese government figures. With the exception of 1977, they are not particularly close to any of the actual expenditure figures found in Guyanese sources. Either the publicly available official Guyanese statistics were completely unreliable during those four years, or, with the possible exception of 1975, the IMF was given some form of estimated expenditure for total security outlays. The very large discrepancy between the figure published by the Guyanese government for total security outlays in 1975 and that reported to the IMF could have arisen if the IMF figure included expenditure on the National Service, administered by the Ministry of Defence. But this does not seem to be a satisfactory explanation because no other figure reported by the IMF *appears* to include costs associated with the National Service. Since the IMF publishes only a single figure, it is impossible to state with any certainty how the discrepancies in the data for 1974 to 1977 arose.

In the case of Sri Lanka, Table 3-2 indicates that not only is expenditure on the police force omitted from the figures submitted to the IMF, but expenditure on the minister of defence also appears to be excluded. While arguments might be presented justifying the omission of police expenditures, it is harder to understand why the Sri Lankan government has

---

[17] William B. Mitchell et al., *Area Handbook for Guyana* (Washington, D.C.: Government Printing Office, November 1969), pp. 338–39.

TABLE 3-2

Comparison of IMF and Sri Lankan Security Expenditure Data,[a]
1975–1983 (in million rupees)

Year	IMF	Total Security Sri Lanka[b]	Total Military Sri Lanka[c]	Army, Navy, Air Force Sri Lanka
1975	192	324.2	197.9	196.0
1976	179	335.1	177.7[d]	177.7
1977	224	402.2	223.5[e]	223.5
1978	308	547.3	314.5	307.6
1979	393	690.0	430.9	392.4
1980	458	913.2	563.3	476.7
1981	479	1,029.9	641.8	520.4
1982	486	1,112.6	700.8	543.1
1983	979	1,748.9	1,235.6	998.8

Source: International Monetary Fund, *Government Finance Statistics Yearbook 1985*
(Washington, D.C.: IMF, 1985); and *Estimates of the Revenue and Expenditure of the
Government of the Democratic Socialist Republic of Sri Lanka for the Financial Year,
1st January 1986 to 31st December 1986,* Volume One (Columbo: 1986).
[a] Actual outlays.
[b] Includes expenditure on the police.
[c] Includes Army, Navy, Air Force, and minister of defence.
[d] Data for minister of defence unavailable.
[e] Minister of defence expenditure recorded as nil.

chosen not to report outlays for the defence minister. In the mid-1970s the discrepancies are not too large, but by the end of the decade and in the early 1980s they become significant. In 1983, for example, the security expenditure figure reported in the *Government Finance Statistics Yearbook* is just over 20 percent lower than that reported in Sri Lankan government documents for outlays on the defence minister, the Army, the Navy, and the Air Force.

There is clearly considerable scope for examining the different security expenditure estimates, particularly those produced by SIPRI and the IMF, and comparing them with the final expenditure data produced by governments. Although the IMF estimates may in fact be the most reliable ones available, their validity should not be taken as given. The comparison of Guyanese government data with USAID/ACDA and IMF estimates demonstrates that it is of utmost importance to have access to disaggregated expenditure data in order to assess correctly and improve the quality of security expenditure data. In addition, it is preferable to have disaggregated data when determining the economic effects of expenditure in the security sector. Disaggregated data may also help in ascertaining whether or not a country's stated security expenditure actually accords with the size and quality of its armed forces.

The United Nations's
Unified Reporting System

In 1975, the United Nations began to develop a unified reporting system for security expenditure which required data to be presented in a disaggregated form. This effort grew out of a resolution proposed by the Soviet Union in December 1973 which called for a 10 percent reduction in the military expenditure of the major powers and the transfer of 10 percent of the money saved in this way to international development programs.[18] The expert group mandated by the UN Secretary-General to prepare a report on the issues surrounding this resolution concluded that "a prerequisite for negotiating the reduction of military expenditures was agreement on the scope and content of such expenditures."[19]

Unfortunately, many governments resist giving information on the "scope and content" of their security expenditure, and the Soviet government has been foremost among them. In 1978, the UN Expert Group on the Relationship between Disarmament and Development, established at the UN Special Session on Disarmament in June of that year, recommended to the Secretary-General that UN member governments provide information on their security spending broken down "in terms of personnel, administration, procurement, research and development, capital investment."[20] Senior Soviet administrators in the UN Department of Political and Security Council Affairs were able to prevent action upon this recommendation. The Secretary-General confined his request to data pertaining to the "present-day utilization of resources for military purposes."[21]

Work nonetheless continued within the United Nations on the unified reporting system. The first practical test of that system was carried out by

---

[18] United Nations, Resolution 3093 B (XXVIII), 7 December 1973.

[19] United Nations, *Reduction of Military Budgets*, p. 1. A brief history of the development of the UN's international reporting system is contained on pages 1–5 of this document.

[20] Note transmitted to the Secretary-General from the Group of Governmental Experts on the Relationship between Disarmament and Development, Geneva, 26 January 1979, see Annex, p. 1.

[21] Secretary General of the United Nations, PO 131/2 (4-1), 28 February 1979.

the Ad Hoc Panel on Military Budgeting during 1979 and 1980. Yielding substantive responses from fourteen countries, it was deemed sufficiently successful to warrant repetition. Table 3-3 indicates which countries have participated in the first six reporting exercises. If viewed solely as an attempt to collect comparable military expenditure data, these exercises have clearly been less than fully successful. Only thirty-five countries participated at any point during the first six years, and only three of them participated for all six years. Just one member of the Warsaw Treaty Organization supplied data. Fifteen developing countries reported to the UN at one time or another, but none participated for the entire 1980–1985 period.[22]

If one examines the *quality* of the information supplied, the situation is not much brighter. Table 3-4 analyses the responses of the sixteen participants in the 1981 reporting exercise. Nine of them left more than half the matrix blank. Of the remaining seven countries, three (Canada, the Netherlands, and Sudan) indicated that over 60 percent of the matrix was "not applicable" to them. One country (the United States) claimed that for over 50 percent of the matrix categories expenditure did occur but the exact figures were "not available." In subsequent years, many of the reporting countries stated that information was unavailable for many of the expenditure categories or left categories blank. Detailed data on weapon procurement costs are particularly scarce. Perhaps the only encouraging point is that most countries have said that they were reporting actual expenditure, rather than budget estimates.

The quality of the replies from the developing countries has been variable. Table 3-3 shows that Cyprus and the Seychelles participated in the UN exercise for the first time in 1982, but they provided only very limited information. Similarly, Turkey (1981–1985), Chile (1984–1985), and Togo (1983) have not been very forthcoming. Table 3-4 shows that in

---

[22] Although a member of NATO, Turkey is classified here as a developing country. The thirty-five countries referred to in this paragraph do not include countries which responded to the UN request for information by explaining that they could not provide data. In 1985, for example, the government of Lesotho informed the UN that "Lesotho has no army, but a paramilitary force, and for security reasons the Government of Lesotho is unable to provide the data requested." United Nations, General Assembly, "Reduction of Military Budgets: Military Expenditures in Standardized Form as Reported by States. Report by the Secretary-General," A/40/313, mimeograph, 20 May 1985. A number of other countries have replied in the same vein.

The failure of the Soviet Union to participate and the loss of interest in the exercise by several NATO members such as the United States and the Federal Republic of Germany, directly attributable to the Soviet attitude, are two major problems that may jeopardize the future of the reporting system. As Table 3-2 shows, far fewer countries supplied information to the United Nations in 1985 than in any of the previous years.

TABLE 3-3
Countries Participating in UN Military Expenditure Reporting Exercises, 1980–1985

Country	1980	1981	1982	1983	1984	1985
Argentina						x
Australia	x		x	x	x	
Austria	x	x	x	x	x	x
Belgium	x	x	x	x	x	
Canada	x	x	x	x	x	
Chile[a]					x	x
Colombia				x		
Cyprus[a]			x			
Denmark		x	x	x	x	
Finland		x	x	x	x	
France	x		x	x		x
Germany, Federal Republic	x	x	x	x	x	
Indonesia	x	x	x			
Ireland			x	x		
Italy	x	x	x	x	x	
Ivory Coast				x		
Japan			x	x	x	
Luxembourg				x		
Mexico	x	x	x			
Netherlands	x	x	x	x	x	x
New Zealand	x	x	x	x		
Niger					x	
Norway	x	x	x	x	x	
Portugal				x	x	
Romania						x
Senegal			x			
Seychelles[a]			x			
Sudan		x			x	
Suriname					x	
Sweden	x	x	x	x	x	x
Thailand				x	x	
Togo[a]				x		
Turkey[a]		x	x	x	x	x
United Kingdom			x	x	x	x
United States	x	x	x	x	x	

Sources: United Nations, Group of Experts on the Comparison of Military Budgets, "Conference Room Paper no. 2," 8 March 1982; United Nations, General Assembly, *Reduction of Military Budgets: Military Expenditures in Standardized Form Reported by States*, A/38/434 (2 November 1983), A/39/521 (16 October 1984), and A/40/313 (20 May 1985).

[a] Very limited information provided.

TABLE 3-4

Amount and Type of Information on Security Expenditures
Reported to United Nations, 1981 (in percentages)

Country	Figures	Not Available	Not Applicable	Nil or Negligible	Blanks
Austria	9.7	0.0	0.0	0.0	90.3
Belgium	23.0	17.0	5.4	5.6	49.0
Canada	28.7	0.2	60.0	1.7	9.4
Denmark	6.6	0.0	0.0	0.0	93.4
Finland	14.8	4.1	0.0	3.4	77.7
Germany, Federal Republic	32.7	9.3	0.0	6.0	52.0
Indonesia	23.8	15.5	28.6	25.0	7.1
Italy	21.8	0.0	0.0	0.0	78.2
Mexico	3.6	0.0	14.3	0.0	82.1
Netherlands	24.5	0.0	73.6	0.0	1.9
New Zealand	21.6	0.0	0.0	0.0	78.4
Norway	23.1	2.4	5.1	8.2	61.2
Sudan	12.9	6.8	65.5	0.0	14.8
Sweden	35.0	1.7	37.1	26.2	0.0
Turkey	0.7	0.0	0.0	0.0	99.3
United States	17.2	57.8	4.4	17.0	3.6

Source: United Nations, General Assembly, "Reduction of Military Budgets," A/S-12/7, 6 May 1982, p. 55.
Note: Percentages are based on the 588-item matrix prepared by the United Nations.

1981 the Turkish government left over 99 percent of the matrix entirely blank, a practice it continued in subsequent years. With regard to Mexico, one can note a clear decline in the amount of information provided. Although Mexico left fewer categories entirely blank in 1981 than in 1980 by indicating in 1981 that certain categories were "not applicable," a comment not made in 1980, it provided over 50 percent fewer expenditure figures (twenty-one compared with forty-eight in 1980). In 1982, Mexico provided its own 25-item matrix (rather than using the UN's 588-item matrix) and supplied nineteen expenditure figures within that framework. Since 1983, Mexico has provided no information at all. Indonesia supplied the most detailed accounting of any developing countries for the three years in which it reported, but, as will be explained below, there is reason to believe that these figures grossly understate the true value of Indonesian security outlays.

When the United Nations first began developing its unified security expenditure reporting system, there were suggestions that the proposed matrix might be too complex for the accounting systems of many UN member states and that developing countries in particular might not be able to participate in the expenditure reporting exercises. Considerable information is required to complete the entire 588-item matrix; however, this cannot be considered a sufficient reason for the failure of any country to present the UN with at least some of the requested data. For the first test of the reporting system, the UN requested member governments to provide information at whatever level of aggregation the government itself desired. The hope was, of course, that information would be provided down to the subsubcategory level, but, should that prove impossible for any reason, governments were urged "not to refrain from participating in the test but to present their figures on the level of aggregation that they find appropriate."[23] Even to have *accurate* security expenditure data at the first level of disaggregation—operating costs, procurement and construction, research and development—would be a great step forward for most countries. It is precisely this degree of information that the Turkish government, for example, has provided.

Likewise, it is important to stress that many governments withhold information. There is reason to believe that most countries could provide at least as much information as Turkey has, and probably a good deal more. Of the fourteen countries taking part in the preliminary test of the matrix carried out by the Ad Hoc Panel on Military Budgeting only one—France—provided no information at all at the third, subsubcategory level of disaggregation. The two participating developing countries, Mexico and Indonesia, presented very detailed breakdowns of their security expenditures. It might be argued that the statistical offices of Mexico and Indonesia are more competent than those of some other developing countries, and there is surely some truth in that contention. Nonetheless, an examination of the data provided by more than fifty developing countries in the budgetary documents they themselves publish demonstrates quite clearly that a large number of Third World countries could very easily provide information at the first level of disaggregation and that for many

[23] United Nations, *Reduction of Military Budgets*, p. 35.

of these the second and third levels would pose no very great difficulty either.[24]

As is so often the case when dealing with security-related issues, the real obstacle is political. Governments do not want to provide information or undertake meaningful negotiations to reduce military expenditure. They would be quite happy to see their neighbors disarm, but they are unwilling to follow suit regarding their own armament policies. The reply from the government of India to the Ad Hoc Panel on Military Budgeting explaining why India could *not* participate in the preliminary test of the security expenditure matrix in 1979–1980 is instructive in this regard. Claiming that it wanted to apportion correctly the "blame" for the high levels of world military expenditure, the government of India avoided any discussion of reductions in its own security outlays, which are not inconsiderable.

> Considering the basic fact that six States account for more than 80 percent of the total global military expenditure, India has consistently taken the position that the question of reduction of military budgets is primarily a political matter, which can be resolved through parallel actions based on a policy of mutual example by the States concerned. Further, keeping in view the essential link between armament and development, India has also stressed that the funds released by reductions in military expenditures should be used for providing additional assistance to developing countries over and above what they were already receiving.[25]

It is true that the members of NATO and the WTO account for a large proportion of total world military expenditure. That fact, however, does not give the Indian government or other Third World governments any reason to avoid reporting domestic security expenditure. The unwillingness of the Indian government in particular to provide these data can in no way be seen as the result of an inability to collect or process statistical information. India has one of the best developed statistical services in the

[24] Data for forty-eight of these countries published in Ball, *Third-World.*

[25] United Nations, *Reduction of Military Budgets*, p. 122.

Although the Indian government claims to be concerned about the link between disarmament and development, it nevertheless reduced the proportion of its gross product devoted to development outlays from 3.3 percent in 1961–1962 to 2.6 percent in 1970–1971 while it simultaneously increased the proportion of GNP devoted to the armed forces from just under 2 percent to 3.1 percent. Ved P. Gandhi, "India's Self-Inflicted Defence Burden," *Economic and Political Weekly* 9 (31 August 1974): 1285–94. Gandhi also points out that during the 1960s development expenditure as a percentage of total central and provincial government outlays fell from 62.5 percent to 55.3 percent.

Third World and regularly publishes a wealth of information about its expenditures, including those in the security sector.[26] Nonetheless, when it came to reporting exactly the same security expenditure within the framework of the United Nations exercise, the Indian government declined to do so.

As explained in the Introduction, relatively few countries have accounted for the rather rapid rise in total Third World security expenditures since the mid-1960s. This does not mean, however, as the Indian government would like to have one believe, that the issue of Third World security expenditure can safely be ignored. There have been too many inter- and intrastate conflicts, too many coups d'état, and too little development in the Third World to warrant such a position. It may appear unjust to the reader to focus on the Indian government when, in fact, most developing countries would prefer to talk about the security expenditures of the industrialized states rather than their own security-related outlays. India is, however, somewhat of a special case. Despite the persistence of serious economic, political, and social inequities, it remains the most populous multiparty state in the world. Although the military is not without political influence, India has never experienced a coup d'état. In these two respects, it stands in stark contrast to most Third World countries. If the Indian government chooses to follow a policy of noncompliance with regard to the reporting of security expenditure data, it is hard to imagine very many other Third World governments will be encouraged to disclose such information.

Yet the disclosure of disaggregated security expenditure data is the first step, albeit a small one, in dismantling the wall of secrecy behind which so much security-related information is hidden. Access to accurate security expenditure data is an important prerequisite for negotiating agreements on the reduction of defense budgets. The availability of disaggregated expenditure data might help to determine the accuracy of the figures provided by governments; for example, they might enable a rough check on the procurement portion of budgets. It is difficult to determine whether a country is accurately reporting its procurement costs since, even when the quantity of imported weapons and services are known,

---

[26] Each year the government of India publishes the *Defence Services Estimates* which provide an extremely detailed breakdown of central government outlays for the armed forces. Not all Indian security-related expenditure is listed under "defence services," but the major categories of Army, Navy, Air Force, Pensions, and Capital Outlays on Defence Services are covered. Other budget documents provide sufficiently disaggregated data on the components of security expenditure not listed under "defence services" to make it clear that the Indian government would have no trouble completing the UN matrix down to the third level of disaggregation.

their real cost to the importer tends to be in doubt. Security assistance complicates the calculation further. Most Third World countries have received some form of security assistance over the last thirty-five or forty years, and the terms under which it has been granted have varied from country to country.

Nonetheless, it may be possible to estimate whether countries are reporting expenditure on armaments more or less accurately by comparing procurement outlays, weapon stocks, and military assistance inflows. For example, the figures published by the government of Nicaragua during the late 1970s would appear greatly to underestimate Nicaraguan security outlays. The weapons and ammunition known to have been purchased for use by the National Guard during the civil war with the Sandinista forces simply do not appear in the budget.[27] If one had only a single figure for Nicaraguan expenditure on the armed forces during those years, it would be impossible to question its completeness.

Although many governments publish detailed budgets, their contents are not widely available, and other countries publish only a single figure for their security-related outlays. The lack of disaggregated data has meant, among other things, that military expenditure reduction proposals such as the one set forward by the Soviet Union in 1973 have been little more than propaganda exercises: Governments have been able to make such proposals safe in the knowledge that they will never be implemented.[28] The unwillingness of governments suggesting reductions in military spending to make public even a few details about their own defense budgets makes it difficult to believe that these governments can be serious about any arms limitation or arms reduction proposals they present. In this respect the refusal of the Soviet Union to participate in the United Nations military expenditure reporting system and the decision of the United States to cease providing information do not bode well for the future, not only because of the potential implication for East-West relations but also for the message these attitudes on the part of the superpowers send to other UN members.

Had the Soviet Union provided even a small amount of the information sought by the United Nations and had the United States therefore chosen to continue to report as well, other countries would have taken the UN reporting system more seriously. Although it could only have been expected that the number of countries reporting disaggregated data to the

[27] Ball, *Third-World*, pp. 229–30. See also Appendix 1 in this volume.

[28] On the need for reliable security expenditure data acceptable to all parties to disarmament negotiations, see Hans-Christian Cars, "Reduction of Military Expenditures as a Disarmament Concept," *Bulletin of Peace Proposals* 14:4 (1983):345–50.

United Nations would have grown slowly, it could nonetheless have been hoped that the reporting of these data would have progressively become routine for an increasing number of countries, making it more and more difficult for governments to avoid providing information to the United Nations. As it stands now, it is clear that the UN reporting system is not being taken seriously. In 1985, only nine countries reported, and three Western countries that had participated in each of the five preceding exercises (the United States, West Germany, and Canada) failed to respond.[29]

Disaggregated security expenditure data are important not only as input to arms control negotiations, but they are also helpful when assessing the economic effects of security expenditure in individual countries and knowing in as much detail as possible what the armed forces are buying with their money. "What the armed forces are buying" can be divided into salaries, purchases of operating material, weapons procurement, construction, and research and development (R&D) costs. Each of these categories of expenditure can variously effect a country's economy. The payment of salaries might, for example, increase the demand for locally produced goods, or, because of training received in the armed services, it might expand the available pool of skilled workers or competent managers available to the civil sector, both of which could promote growth. If, on the other hand, military personnel were trained at the expense of civil-

---

[29] In part the USSR's reluctance to participate in the military expenditure reporting exercises has stemmed from weaknesses in its own accounting system. High Soviet officials have begun stating that they have instituted a new cost accounting system which will enable them to generate military expenditure figures comparable to those produced by NATO countries within a few years. In an interview with the *New York Times* in October 1987, the chief of the Soviet General Staff, Marshal Sergei Akhromeyev stated,

> Although, as we know, attempts were made in the past to compare military spending, they proved unproductive due to fundamental differences between the Warsaw Pact and NATO regarding arms production costs and price setting mechanisms. For instance, the defense budget that we make public (to the tune of 20.2 billion rubles) serves to reflect the Soviet ministry of defense spending on military personnel, logistics, combat training, pensions, and several other items. Funds for arms procurement are appropriated under other items of the Soviet Union's state budget.
>
> Currently, we are preparing a radical reform of the price-setting mechanism. Its completion would enable us to compare, in objective terms, military spending in the Soviet Union and Western countries. If we are persistent enough, we should be able, within the next two or three years, to compare figures that would truly reflect military spending on both sides.

General Secretary Gorbachev has made similar remarks in *Pravda* and *Izvestiya*. See "Excerpts of Interview with Soviet Armed Forces Chief of Staff," *New York Times*, 30 October 1987.

sector employees or the training received were not transferable to the civil sector, economic growth might be hindered.

Similarly the domestic procurement of weapons and construction materials might cause an increase in investment and expand the industrial capacity of the economy as a whole. Alternatively, military-related investment might occur at the expense of more productive civil-sector investment or encourage an overly heavy emphasis on capital-intensive techniques of production and ultimately reduce the growth potential of the economy. A government might promote backward linkages between military industries and supplier industries in the civil economy, or it might encourage the defense industry to produce its own components as much as possible, reducing the multiplier effects of defense-related industrialization. Procurement of weapons or construction materials from abroad can impose an intolerable burden on an economy short of foreign exchange, but it may be an acceptable burden for an economy not faced with such shortages.[30] The more detailed the information available on security expenditure, the more accurately the economic effects of security expenditure in individual countries can be evaluated.

THE COMPOSITION OF SECURITY EXPENDITURE

Although there is clearly a need for disaggregated data, none of the major sources of security expenditure have ever attempted to provide more than a single figure. Even in the World Bank publication *World Tables, 1976,* where all other governmental expenditure is divided into its recurrent and

---

[30] In assessing the economic effects of arms imports for oil-importing countries, Lance Taylor has commented that,

> a current account deficit (or the World Bank's related concept of a "resource gap" . . .) in principle benefits a country. Purchasing more than one produces means that resources are flowing in—these can be transformed into investment, productivity increases, and better economic performance . . . if an increase in the resource gap is translated completely into increased investment, the economic payoff may be large. On the other hand, if the larger gap takes the form of more arms imports, domestic economic performance may be penalized. In addition, using and maintaining sophisticated weapons may occupy a large proportion of scarce material and technical talent that could otherwise be assigned to capital formation. The implication is that the efficiency with which investment projects are translated into real productive capacity will fall. Arms purchases may not only reduce investment for financial reasons. In the development economists' jargon, they can push the economy up to its 'absorptive capacity' constraint as well.

Lance Taylor, "International Adjustment to the Oil Shocks and the Arms Trade" (Paper prepered for the Independent Commission on Disarmament and Security Issues, Cambridge, Mass.: MIT, November 1981, mimeograph), p. 3.

capital portions, defense expenditure remains aggregated. Some break-downs according to recurrent and capital expenditure are to be found in the *Europa Yearbooks* and in confidential IMF reports. There is, however, no means of discovering whether what is listed in these sources as capital expenditure comprises solely arms procurement and construction outlays or whether it includes the purchase of items such as office machinery, spare parts, tools for maintenance and repair, or even office furniture—all of which some countries classify as capital costs, presumably because they are financed out of the capital budget, but which under the UN system of classification are considered operations and maintenance costs. Indeed, since the IMF itself classifies most defense expenditure as recurrent expenditure, it is possible that the figures for capital outlays in IMF country studies exclude arms procurement. Only the United Nations, with its unified reporting system, has attempted to collect comparable disaggregated security expenditure data for a large number of countries and, as seen in the previous section, its progress to date has been slow.

In the public mind, security expenditure in the Third World is firmly linked with the arms trade. It is commonly assumed that a large portion of all developing countries' security outlays are used to purchase weapons and related services from abroad. This popular conception extends even to researchers and government civil servants.[31] In view of the well-publicized rise in the volume and value of arms transfers during the 1970s, it is perhaps natural that security expenditure is so frequently presumed interchangeable with arms procurement. Most developing countries do not, however, conform to this pattern. Operating costs have always absorbed a large portion of their security expenditure. Personnel-related costs alone have often absorbed 50 percent or more of total security outlays.

Appendix 1 shows the evolution of operating costs as a percentage of total security expenditure for twenty Third World countries in the post–World War II period. As discussed in Chapter 2, operating costs clearly dominate the budgets of these countries, with the one exception of Iran in

---

[31] This author, for example, was told in no uncertain terms by a staff member of a U.S. Senate Foreign Relations subcommittee in 1981 that it was a waste of time to collect national security expenditure data: All that was necessary was to look at U.S. arms-trade statistics. Similarly, a paper entitled "Trends in LDC Military Expenditures" prepared for the Palme Commission focused heavily on arms transfers as did an academic monograph entitled "Military Expenditures and the Level of Economic Development." See Carol Lancaster and Anthony Lake, "Trends in LDC Military Expenditures" (Paper prepared for the Independence Commission on Disarmament and Security Issues, CD 031, August 1981, mimeograph) and Hossein Askari and Michael C. Glover, *Military Expenditure and the Level of Economic Development* (Austin: Bureau of Business Research, University of Texas, 1977).

the 1970s. Almost all the countries in Asia, Africa, and the Middle East obtained their political independence in the post–World War II period, and it can be expected that newly independent countries beginning to build up their armed forces would devote a large amount of their resources to operating costs, particularly personnel costs. The weapons procured by such forces would initially be relatively unsophisticated and inexpensive and might even be purchased from the departing colonial power at a reduced rate. Similarly, base facilities for the armed forces might have been taken over from the former colonial power.[32] In addition, outright grants of military equipment were more common in the 1950s and early 1960s when many countries became independent than is now the case. In Chapter 2, it was shown that for several countries at least some of the predominant operating costs could be explained by in-

---

[32] Gertrude Heare has explained why Latin American countries might have rather high operating costs/total security expenditure ratios.

All South American forces have experienced conflicting pressures for budget appropriations, with sometimes acute conflicts between various requirements. When a choice has to be made between personnel requirements on one hand and operating, maintenance, and capital requirements on the other hand, the former may be preferred. For example, the Argentine navy in 1945 had a 50–50 budget ratio between personnel and other costs, according to official statements. In the late 1960s—naval appropriations having remained near the 1945 level in constant prices—it was estimated that personnel costs were absorbing three-quarters of these appropriations, with one-quarter remaining for maintenance, operations, and replacement costs.

Were such data available on other South American military services over a 20–30 year period, the pattern would probably show an early buildup in the proportion of operating, maintenance, and capital costs, which would reach a peak and tend to level off when the forces became "mature". Subsequently, the pressures of personnel costs—pay increases, pension systems, fringe benefits—would become increasingly strong. As a result of such trends, only during exceptional periods of prosperity are the professionalized forces apt to find themselves able to finance equipment maintenance or replacement and operations costs without infringing on benefits to military personnel.

Gertrude Heare, *Trends in Latin American Military Expenditures, 1940–1970: Argentina, Brazil, Chile, Colombia, Peru & Venezuela,* Department of State Publication 8618 (Washington, D.C.: Government Printing Office, December 1971), p. 7.

Another factor which has certainly contributed to the low capital expenditures by Latin American armed forces is the absence of serious external conflicts.

The four Latin American countries listed in Appendix 1 for which personnel costs could be estimated (Guyana, Brazil, Venezuela, and Trinidad & Tobago) tend to have personnel costs:total security expenditure ratios that are higher than those for Asian and African countries. The number of countries compared in Appendix 1 is, however, rather small, and it would not be advisable to draw any hard-and-fast conclusions on the basis of such a small sample.

flows of security assistance, a large portion of which was probably used for equipment purchases.

Over time, however, one would expect the proportions between operating and capital costs to change somewhat. This has happened, although to a greater extent in some countries than in others. In Iran, the capital portion of the security budget began to exceed operating costs in the early 1970s, just as one would have anticipated given the rate at which Iran purchased weapons during that period. If it were possible to obtain disaggregated data for some of the other major arms importers—Iraq, Saudi Arabia, Libya, and Syria, for example—it seems likely that a similar trend would be observed. Some Third World countries have consistently increased their capital costs relative to total security expenditure, but less dramatically than Iran. The Philippines and India fall into this category. Other countries show considerable annual variations in the proportion of security outlays devoted to procurement and other capital costs, for example Argentina, Ghana, Sri Lanka, and Morocco. One would expect to find this latter pattern for most Third World countries not importing large amounts of weapons on a regular basis.

According to the U.S. Arms Control and Disarmament Agency, annual world arms transfers (measured in 1982 U.S. dollars) grew from $21.6 billion in 1972, the year before the first increase in the price of petroleum, to $37.3 billion in 1983. ACDA arms transfer data do not, however, reflect the true value of arms transfers since, in addition to what may inadvertently be excluded, ACDA omits the cost of military-related construction, training, and technical services. It has been estimated that these omissions may be equivalent to some 15 percent of total arms transfers.[33] ACDA figures, like those from SIPRI, can, however, be used to indicate trend.

A majority of the trade in weapons with the Third World is concentrated in a relatively few countries. According to ACDA data, the ten largest importers of weapons in the years from 1973 to 1983 accounted for slightly more than 55 percent of all Third World arms imports. Twenty countries accounted for 70 percent of developing country arms imports (Table 3-5). The effects of the rise in petroleum prices and the continuation of the various conflicts in the Middle East/Persian Gulf regions on the export of arms to the Third World can be seen quite clearly from this table. Eight of the ten major Third World importers of weapons are found in those two regions and/or derive a substantial proportion of their in-

[33] See United Nations, "Study on the Relationship Between Disarmament and Development, Report of the Secretary-General," A/36/356 (New York: 5 October 1981, mimeograph), pp. 63–64.

TABLE 3-5
Major Third World Arms Importers, 1973–1983

Country	Value 1982 $ m.	% Developing Country	Cumulative %
Iraq	27,713	10.4	10.4
Libya	21,065	7.9	18.3
Iran	20,446	7.7	26.0
Syria	19,416	7.3	33.3
Saudi Arabia	17,925	6.7	40.0
Israel	11,930	4.5	44.5
Egypt	9,587	3.6	48.1
India	8,188	3.1	51.2
Vietnam	7,186	2.7	53.9
Algeria	6,362	2.4	56.3
South Korea	4,947	1.9	58.2
Cuba	4,557	1.7	59.9
Jordan	4,507	1.7	61.6
Taiwan	4,338	1.6	63.2
Morocco	3,483	1.3	64.5
Pakistan	3,462	1.3	65.8
Peru	3,241	1.2	67.0
Ethiopia	3,044	1.1	68.1
Yemen (Sanaa)	2,849	1.1	69.2
Afghanistan	2,679	1.0	70.2
Total Third World	266,509		

Source: U.S. Arms Control and Disarmament Agency, *World Military Expenditures and Arms Transfers, 1985,* Publication 123 (Washington, D.C.: ACDA, August 1985), Table II.

Note: ACDA data have been used here in preference to SIPRI data because they are more inclusive. SIPRI data, which measure transfers of major weapons only, show a similar degree of concentration.

come from exports of petroleum: Iraq, Libya, Iran, Syria, Saudi Arabia, Israel, Egypt, and Algeria. Together they accounted for just over half of all arms imported by Third World countries between 1973 and 1983.

This means that approximately ninety Third World countries imported fewer weapons (in terms of value) during the 1970s than the first four countries listed in Table 3-5. It is thus not surprising that weapon procurement does not form a major part of the security budgets of most developing countries. The concentration of the arms trade does not, however, signify an absence of sophisticated equipment in the armed forces of the minor importers. Nor does it mean that the economic effects of importing weapons are never serious for these countries. The point is simply that, for most of the Third World, the arms trade and security expenditure are not synonymous: Operating costs, particularly personnel-related outlays, form a large and permanent portion of most developing countries' security budgets.

Unidentified Expenditure

The popular impression that security expenditure data published by national governments are not reliable is, to a large extent, accurate. There is growing evidence that important amounts of security spending do not enter the budgets of many Third World countries. What is more, budgets are arranged by some countries in such a way as to make the identification of security-related outlays by ministries other than the Ministry of Defense very difficult or impossible. Even governments which publish copious amounts of security expenditure data, such as India, or provide the United Nations with detailed information about their security outlays, such as Indonesia, can understate the amount they spend on the security sector.

It is extremely difficult to determine which countries have understated their security expenditure or during which periods and to what degree this has occurred. In part this is because of the secrecy surrounding the security sector and in part because researchers have not focused on this issue in the past. Nonetheless, it can be said that for many developing countries, even the most accurate data available may seriously understate the security expenditures of governments. In the following discussion, the five most frequently mentioned mechanisms used to obscure security expenditures will be described and illustrated wherever possible with specific examples. These include double bookkeeping, the use of off-budget financing, highly aggregated budget categories, security assistance, and governmental manipulation of foreign exchange.

Double Bookkeeping

It has been alleged that some Third World governments keep two sets of budget accounts: one is used as the basis of published accounts, and the other is intended for purely internal government consumption; the latter is supposedly more accurate. One member of the U.S. intelligence community who was responsible for the collection of developing country security expenditure data in his agency went so far in the early 1980s as to claim in private conversation that the security expenditure of many, if not all, developing countries as reported either in their publicly available documents or in international sources such as the IMF is inaccurate. Such an allegation is extremely difficult to substantiate; moreover, it gives no idea of the magnitude of the problem. It could mean that all or very many of the reported security expenditure figures are understated by some small, relatively unimportant amount, perhaps no more than 10 percent. Alternatively, most of the values reported could be relatively accurate while a small portion were grossly understated. There are, of course, even more possibilities.

The vagueness of this allegation should not cause it to be dismissed out of hand. Independent corroboration of the existence of double bookkeeping has been obtained in one specific case from private conversations with an official of the U.S. Department of State. This case involves a developing country with modestly sized armed forces and no large imports of sophisticated weapons. It was stated that this country keeps (or kept in the past) two separate sets of accounts for the military sector. The discrepancies between the two accounts were said to be significant by a U.S. official who had seen both. The figures produced for internal, governmental use were *several times* larger than those presented to agencies such as the IMF. Just how many developing countries engage in this sort practice cannot be estimated.

Off-Budget Financing

This mechanism involves the creation within a country of funding sources independent of the national budget. The classic example of this sort of activity is found in Indonesia where off-budget outlays are financed by a special military fund fed by the earnings of Indonesia's many military-linked enterprises. Harold Crouch has described how this system developed.

> The involvement of the military in economic affairs suddenly expanded after the introduction of martial law in 1957. Martial law put military men in positions of considerable power, especially in the Outer Islands where countervailing civilian forces were relatively weak. . . . However, it was not until the end of 1957, when nationalist demonstrators began to take over Dutch enterprises (following an adverse vote on West Irian in the United Nations) that vast new economic opportunities presented themselves. The army immediately

responded by using its martial law powers to place all Dutch enterprises under military supervision. Later, after the nationalisation of these enterprises, army officers continued to participate in the management of the new state corporations which had inherited the dominant position of the Dutch in mining, plantations, banking and trade. During the 1960s further expansions of the army's role in the economy took place when British enterprises were placed under military supervision in 1965. In addition an army-sponsored oil corporation, *Pertamina,* which had been set up in 1957, continued to expand its activities, and at the regional level, individual military units established their own business concerns, usually in association with Chinese partners.

The army's participation in the economy was, in part, in implementation of the concept that army officers should play a role in civilian activities. . . . However, it appears that the most important aim was to utilise many of the new state corporations, as well as military-connected business concerns, as sources of funds for the army. Officers involved in economic management were entrusted with the task of siphoning off funds which were transferred directly to the army, rather than to the government, so that the army's dependence on allocations from the central government budget was reduced. As the Dutch had previously owned some of the nation's most profitable concerns, the resources coming under the control of army officers were substantial, although some enterprises soon fell into financial difficulties as a result of mismanagement and the excessive diversion of funds.[34]

This system continued to develop during the 1970s. At the beginning of that decade, Alexis Rieffel and Aninda Wirjasuputra reported that "It is common knowledge that the state budget only provides a fraction of the resources required to support the military establishment of Indonesia. Estimates of the proportion of total resources generated by military enterprises range from 30 percent to 60 percent."[35] By the mid-1970s, Harold Crouch stated that the importance of off-budget sources of income for the Indonesian armed forces (ABRI) had declined as the government had been able to increase its share of openly appropriated national resources through improved tax collection. The post-1973 rise in oil prices was re-

[34] Harold Crouch, "Generals and Business in Indonesia," *Pacific Affairs* 48 (Winter 1975–1976): 520–21.

[35] Alexis Rieffel and Aninda S. Wirjasuputra, "Military Enterprises," *Bulletin of Indonesian Economic Studies* (July 1972), p. 106.

CHAPTER 3

portedly especially important in expanding the government's revenue base. No figures were provided by Crouch for the proportion of security expenditure accounted for by budgetary allocations. If such a decline in reliance on off-budget sources did occur, it seems to have been reversed by the end of the decade. In 1980, David Jenkins reported that "many experts now believe that funds set aside for ABRI in the state budget cover only 40–50% of the military's real needs." Any type of expenditure can be financed by the off-budget accounts; the most visible use is for the purchase of weapons. Jenkins has reported that purchases of A-4 and Hercules transport aircraft and LST landing craft in 1979 never appeared in the budget.[36] By the end of the 1970s, ABRI's business activities were extensive.

Each of the nation's 16 regional military commands stands at the centre of an interlocking web of business operations, many of which are highly profitable. The four separate forces (army, navy, air force and national police) also have their own companies as do elite units such as Kostrad, the army strategic reserve. For example Inkopad, the army cooperative, is involved in shipping, forestry, fishing, hotels, a cold storage company and a small bank. The navy cooperative, Inkopal, is active in banking, logging, fishing and air transport while the air force cooperative, Inkopau, specialises in such things as air charter and cargo services as well as the inevitable logging interests.
P. T. Tri Usaha Bhakti, a holding company sponsored by the defence ministry, holds shares in at least 38 companies, the majority in partnership with regional military commands or foreign investors, 14 of them in the forestry sector. The business interests of the Kostrad "foundation" include the Bank Windu Kencana, which is said to be run by the prominent Chinese businessman Liem Sioe Liong, and a car import agency.[37]

It is not inconceivable that similar mechanisms are employed in other countries where the armed forces play an active role in the economy. This

[36] David Jenkins, "The Military's Secret Cache," *Far Eastern Economic Review* 107 (8 February 1980):70. See also, David Jenkins, "The Military in Business," *Far Eastern Economic Review* 99 (13 January 1978):24, and David Jenkins, "The Defence Budget Gives Little Away," *Far Eastern Economic Review* 121 (15 September 1983):46.
[37] Jenkins, "The Military's Secret Cache," p. 71. Jenkins also reported (p. 72) that Pertamina's role in financing the Indonesian armed forces may have declined significantly in recent years. See also Richard Robison, "Toward a Class Analysis of the Indonesian Military Bureaucratic State," *Indonesia*, no. 25 (April 1978):17–39, for a discussion of the way in which the military and particularly high-ranking military officers and their families have come to hold important positions in the Indonesian economy.

possibility must at the very least be considered when evaluating the reliability of security expenditure data from such countries.

Highly Aggregated Budget Categories

Some developing countries publish no more than a single figure for their expenditure on the armed forces in their national budgets. This practice is followed by, for example, Pakistan (from 1966), Bangladesh, and even Botswana. Other governments, such as Saudi Arabia and Sudan up to the early 1970s, provide very little detail about their security expenditure.[38] For countries such as these, it would pose no problem to insert figures into the budget which represent no more than a fraction of the actual expenditure on the security forces.

Some governments publish not very detailed data because they wish to obscure the true extent of their security expenditures. In other countries, data collection systems are not especially well developed, in part because the need to collect precise figures is not recognized. Members of the U.S. Military Assistance Advisory Group (MAAG) in Iran, for example, constantly pressured the Iranian bureaucracy during the 1960s to improve its budgeting practices. Although some changes were made in budget categories (so that they came to resemble more closely U.S. budget categories familiar to the MAAG teams), Iranian bureaucrats apparently never came to share their American advisers' concern with data. An official at the U.S. embassy in Teheran in late 1977 is reported to have stated that, "The Iranian budget tends to be notional and caution is suggested in use of the data. There are large basket items and some unusual placement of activities."[39]

[38] See Ball, *Third-World*, pp. 54–83, 112, 157–58, 177.

[39] U.S. Embassy official cited in Stephanie Neuman, "Security, Military Expenditures and Socioeconomic Development: Reflections on Iran," *Orbis* 22 (Fall 1978):275.

The value of generating false data was not unappreciated in Teheran, as will be discussed below. On the attempts of MAAG advisers to improve the quality of Iranian data, see Ann Schulz, "Military Expenditures and Economic Performance in Iran, 1950–1980" (Worcester, Mass.: Clark University, 1981, mimeograph), pp. 40–41, 43, and personal communication from Ann Schulz, Clark University, 2 June 1983. The problem of properly accounting for all Iranian security expenditure was further complicated in 1969 when the Majles passed a bill which " . . . authorized the government to reallocate funds from other departments to the military at its own discretion and without prior parliamentary approval"; Schulz, "Military Expenditures," p. 93. In addition, the budgets of Iranian military enterprises were virtually nonexistent. Schulz reports that the budget of the Military Industries Organization (MIO), under the control of the shah's arms procurement agent, General Hassan Toufanian,

was a skeletal profit and loss statement. The figure for MIO's total expenditures that appeared in the final state budget was not broken down by activity and appeared to

In other countries, the quality of statistical services has steadily improved over the years. Varas and Portales have reported, for example, that the Chilean accounting system has steadily developed over the last thirty-five years. In 1950, it was able to provide security expenditure data only in a highly aggregated form. By the early 1980s, the data provided were more detailed.[40]

In those countries where security expenditure is highly aggregated, for whatever reason, it would be easy not only to provide false figures in categories correctly identified as security-related but also, assuming that the entire budget is no more detailed than the armed forces' portion, to conceal security-related expenditure in categories supposedly entirely civilian in nature. In the case of Saudi Arabia, where progressively less information about government expenditure has been made available over the last decade, it is believed that significant portions of security-related outlays are hidden from public scrutiny in this manner. For example, expenditure on the King Khalid Military City and other kinds of military-related capital outlays are believed to be classified as "Other" expenditure in the budget category "Projects"; similarly, the Security Forces and the Frontier Forces are believed to be included under the heading "Interior" while the paramilitary National Guard is thought to be funded through the "Council of Ministers & Foreign Aid" category. On the other hand, as much as 30 percent of the "Defense & Aviation" category is thought to be composed of civil aviation expenditures. Anyone looking at the budget estimates provided by the Saudi Arabian Monetary Agency in its *Annual Report* would, however, only be able to identify as security-related the outlays listed under "Defense & Aviation," a gross understatement of total Saudi security spending.

Even budgets that itemize outlays fairly thoroughly can conceal portions of state security expenditure. The budget documents published by the Nigerian government are quite detailed, for example. Nonetheless, a

---

be inaccurate. The costs of in-country production and service contracts, for example, were higher than the total MIO budget during several years after 1974, although theoretically some of them should have been included in that budget.

The finances of individual military enterprises were equally obscure. The IEI [Iran Electronics Industry] reportedly had no operating budget at all, just "internal working documents". Its projects were initiated without cost estimates with the understanding that they would be underwritten by the PBO [Plan and Budget Organization]. The management of the IEI was unclear whether or not its expenditures were subsumed under the MIO budget. (p. 82)

[40] Carlos Portales and Augusto Varas, "The Role of Military Expenditure in the Development Process, Chile 1952–1973 and 1973–1980: Two Contrasting Cases" (Santiago: FLACSO, 1981, mimeograph), Methodological Appendix.

Nigerian researcher contends that "we know as a matter of fact that a good portion of the estimates during this period [the 1970s] covering 'general administration' and under such expenditure heads as 'State House (or Dodan Barracks)', and 'Cabinet Office', tended to contain (hidden) components of military expenditure."[41] The amount of expenditure concealed in this manner is probably much less important, however, than the sums for repayment of military-related debts which very often cannot be identified in budgets. It is rare for military-related debt repayment to be included in the specifically military portions of budgets—categories such as "Ministry of Defense" and "Armed Forces." Most countries for which it has been possible to survey annual budget documents do not provide sufficiently detailed breakdowns of loan repayment to identify debt incurred in the security sector. As the global arms trade has grown and military credit financing become more frequent since the early 1970s, it can be expected that the repayment of military-related debts is now and will continue to be for many years an important portion of the security outlays of a fair number of Third World countries. To the extent that security-related debt repayments are concealed in a country's total debt repayment, the difficulties in measuring accurately the security expenditure of countries are increased.[42]

Security Assistance

The repayment of military-related debt is, of course, intimately related to security assistance, which will be discussed in detail in Chapter 7. Prior to the 1970s, a large proportion of Western security assistance took the form of grants. This was particularly true of the major supplier, the United States. Since the beginning of the 1970s, Western security assistance has mainly consisted of credits which must be repaid with interest, just like any loan for commercial or economic development purposes. East-bloc, essentially Soviet, security assistance tended to be based on long-term, low-interest credits which were frequently repayable by commodity exports, although the grant element in these loans may have been substantial for at least some countries. During the 1970s it began to be reported more and more frequently that Soviet weapon transfers were to be paid for in hard currency and that the terms on which weapons were sold had hardened. The budgetary implications of this for Third World countries

[41] J. 'Bayo Adekson, *Nigerian in Search of a Stable Civil-Military System* (Boulder, Colo.: Westview Press, 1981), p. 56.

[42] IMF staff members have suggested to this author that military-related debt could be approximated by examining each importer's balance-of-payments statistics. The problem is that the publicly available figures are often not sufficiently detailed to permit such estimates.

should be the same as for the shift to credit financing by the Western countries.[43]

Over the last fifteen years or so, the importance of aid for military purposes from a number of oil-producing Third World states to other developing country governments has grown. Regular contributions to other Arab states, such as Jordan, Syria, and Egypt, as well as to the PLO have been made by Saudi Arabia, Kuwait, the United Arab Emirates, Qatar, Bahrain, Algeria, Libya, and, perhaps, Iraq (prior to its war with Iran). Although these payments may not have been made specifically to the defense budgets of recipient countries, the intent has often been to reduce the burden of security expenditure for the recipients. As such, these subsidies, assumed to be grants, are similar to economic aid provided by the United States under the Economic Support Fund (formerly Security Supporting Assistance) which is considered to be security-related assistance. In addition, the oil-producing donors have provided specifically military-related assistance to developing countries, some of which has been in the form of grants, some in the form of loans.

GRANTS

Military equipment, training, services, or financial aid provided free-of-charge should properly appear in the accounts of the donor country. This means, for example, that Saudi security assistance to Egypt—estimated at perhaps $4 billion between 1973 and 1979—should be listed in the Saudi budget. It is believed that a sizable contribution for purchasing weapons for other countries, training foreign troops, and maintaining troops in third countries is in fact included in the Saudi budget under the heading "Council of Ministers & Foreign Aid." Like the Saudi budget, the Kuwaiti budget is highly aggregated and, in addition to expenditure listed under "Ministry of Defense and National Guards," security-related outlays are thought to be located under the heading "Ministry of Finance—General A/C Department" as "Unclassified Expenses and Transferable Payments." It is presumably from this category that subsidies for other countries' military budgets would come. Although it has not been

[43] Over the last ten to fifteen years, arms exports have been an increasingly important source of hard currency for the Soviet Union. In the 1970s, Soviet arms sales reportedly accounted for some 3 percent of the country's hard currency income. By the early 1980s, that figure had risen to 10 to 15 percent. It has been estimated that between 25 and 30 percent of all hard currency earnings in the late 1980s derives from arms sales. See Wayne Limberg, "Soviet Support for Third World Marxist Regimes: Military Assistance" (Paper presented at the Kennan Institute, September 1986, revised Summer 1987). Although some of this increase may be accounted for by a decline in the value and/or volume of other Soviet exports, for example petroleum, it is not likely that this would entirely explain the growth in export share of arms exports.

possible to review the budgets of the other oil-producers who are believed to provide such subsidies, it seems unlikely that their public versions are any more detailed than the Kuwaiti budget.

Thus, it is difficult for any outside analyst to make more than a rough guess at the amount of security-related assistance disbursed by these governments each year. This seriously complicates the matter of estimating the security outlays of the oil-producing aid donors whose governments are extremely reticent about revealing the extent of their security spending.

LOANS

The repayment of military credits should appear in the accounts of the recipient countries. As discussed above, it is extremely difficult to obtain detailed information about the debt repayment of Third World countries from their budgets and, as will be discussed below, it is fairly easy for trade statistics to be falsified, which complicates attempts to track down imports for the security sector. In countries such as Iran, where most of the government was given very little information on expenditure in the security sector during the shah's reign, including security-related loans, it is impossible to unravel the obligations taken on in the government's name by a very small group of individuals and thus to have an accurate accounting of security expenditure. In Indonesia, not only is perhaps 50 percent of all expenditure on the armed forces derived from off-budget sources, but there is no functional or departmental breakdown of debt repayment in the Indonesian budget; it is therefore impossible to determine how much of the official security-related debt is repaid in any given year.[44]

Manipulation of Foreign Exchange and Trade Statistics

The fifth and final major mechanism for obscuring security expenditure that will be examined here involves the manipulation of foreign exchange and trade statistics by governments. With regard to foreign exchange, it has been suggested that some portion of the hard currency earned by the sale of products (often, but not exclusively, raw materials) abroad is not entered into any government accounting system and is not repatriated. Rather, these funds are used for off-budget purchases of all kinds, including weapons. Concerning the trade statistics, it has been alleged that imports of weapons are disguised as imports for the civil sector or are lumped

---

[44] On Iran, see Schulz, "Military Expenditures," pp. 35–37. On Indonesia see Jenkins, "The Military's Secret Cache," p. 71.

together for accounting purposes with civil-sector imports in broad categories, for example "capital goods," which can include a wide variety of different items.

In India, purchases of Soviet arms are sometimes paid for by exporting unspecified "special goods" which may not be entered into official Indian trade statistics[45] or which, if they are entered, are reported in ways that obscure their military nature. Some Indian analysts have maintained that the value of Soviet weapons purchased off-budget is recorded in Indian trade statistics but in such a way as to conceal the nature of the imported goods. The goods exported in payment for the weapons are also recorded, but their export in exchange for arms is obscured by virtue of the original classification of the imports. Support for the theory that at least some transactions are not recorded in the trade statistics has been supplied by Deepak Nayyar who discovered a gap of some $486 million between the figure supplied by India for its imports from socialist countries between 1966–1967 and 1972–1973 and the value these countries assigned to their exports to India. According to Nayyar,

> the gap of $486 million can be explained largely in terms of imports of defence and military equipment. For political reasons, the Indian government probably did not want to reveal the magnitude of these imports, which were consequently left out of the trade statistics. Admittedly, this is pure conjecture, but available evidence suggests that our estimate of defence imports is quite plausible. Firstly, the USSR, Czechoslovakia and Yugoslavia, which were the principal suppliers of military equipment, accounted for 75 per cent of the unrecorded imports. Secondly, defence imports in the Third Plan period are estimated in the range of $158–210 million, so that a figure of $486 million is not unreasonable for a seven-year period that witnessed two wars.[46]

Iranian officials are known to have tampered with the trade statistics during the shah's reign. Weapons purchases were sometimes listed as nonmilitary imports, including food, and custom forms were not filled in for these transactions. It is thus impossible to trace any particular ship-

[45] In May 1983, the Indian Commerce Minister V. P. Singh reportedly stated in Parliament that Soviet arms were paid for by exporting "special goods" that were not entered into official Indian trade statistics. See "To Buy or Not to Buy," *Far Eastern Economic Review* 120 (2 June 1983): 30.

[46] Deepak Nayyar, "India's Trade with the Socialist Countries," p. 113, in *Economic Relations between Socialist Countries and the Third World,* ed. Deepak Nayyar (London: Macmillan, 1977). Nayyar points out that "Under the *note pass* system, government departments can clear shipments without going through customs" (p. 138).

ment dealt with in this manner. Some evidence that Iran may have paid for these weapons by manipulating its oil income has been provided by U.S. government figures. The U.S. Department of State estimated in 1977 that Iran's oil income was $2 billion higher than recorded in Iranian statistics, and U.S. officials calculated that Iranian military expenditure was $11 billion while official Iranian figures placed it at $9 billion.[47]

The budgetary implications of these kinds of transactions are unknown for either India or Iran. It does seem unlikely, however, that governments that go to such lengths to conceal weapon imports would mention the same imports in budget documents. Staff members of the IMF, however, have suggested that Latin American countries which engage in these practices would record the purchases in extrabudgetary accounts which should then be reported to the IMF. It is extremely difficult to obtain detailed information on such accounts, and it has not been possible to verify this contention. Irrespective of how these transactions are recorded, it is widely believed that a number of Latin American countries do retain a certain percentage of their foreign earnings abroad and use these to finance military procurement. One frequently heard allegation is that Chile has used income from its copper exports in this manner. It has also been suggested that in Ecuador income from petroleum exports is divided among the various ministries with the armed forces reportedly obtaining some 15 percent of these revenues each year. These funds are over and above what each ministry receives in the budget, and it certainly is not impossible that they would be recorded in extrabudgetary accounts.

Other countries allegedly diverting export income include Pakistan (jute) and Ethiopia. In the latter case, it has been said that Haile Selassie began the secret fund derived primarily from coffee revenues which was maintained by the Dergue at least up to the early 1980s, and possibly longer. Under Haile Selassie, the export revenue earmarked for this special fund was repatriated and put at the disposal of the emperor; no one knows with any certainty how this money was spent. Under the Dergue, it has been suggested that the money remains outside the country. It has also been suggested that the Dergue barters commodities directly for arms, on the Indian pattern. The commodities used to pay for the weapons do not appear in any Ethiopian trade statistics.

Any country in which the state plays a central role in producing through nationalized industries or marketing through state marketing boards goods must be considered a possible candidate for such extrabudgetary funding. It is not known, however, how many countries actually supple-

[47]Schulz, "Military Expenditures," pp. 40–41, 43.

121

ment their security budgets by manipulating foreign exchange receipts or trade statistics or how many have done so in the past.

THE NEED FOR ACCURACY

It is clear from the foregoing discussion that the data produced by the major sources of security expenditure may not be very reliable and that important sums of money allocated by Third World governments for security-related purposes can be and are being hidden from public scrutiny. Although military security can contribute to the political and economic development of countries, the diversion of a large share of state and national resources to the armed forces may not buy all that much security and may actually undermine socioeconomic and political development by reducing the resources available for productive investment and manpower development and by helping to maintain an inequitable distribution of wealth.

An important first step in assessing the impact of security expenditure on development is knowing how much is actually spent on the security sector. If, for example, the opportunity costs of security spending in Indonesia were to be calculated using figures provided by the Indonesian government, the results of that calculation would be highly misleading since the amount spent on the armed forces would have been underestimated by 50 percent or more. Indeed, one reason suggested why the Indonesian government continues with its off-budget financing practices is to give the impression that the military burden carried by Indonesia is not very heavy.[48] Unfortunately for the general public in developing countries such as Indonesia, the real effect of security spending depends on the actual outlays in the security sector, however accurately or inaccurately they are reported, and on the degree of military influence over the economy and society; the effect does not depend on some counterfeit figure produced for public consumption at home and abroad.

[48] Jenkins, "The Military's Secret Cache."

4

. . . .

SUBSTITUTING THE COMPUTER

FOR ANALYSIS

The methods researchers adopt to study a problem can have an important bearing on the outcome of their investigations.[1] This is particularly true when the relationship under consideration is as complex and requires the evaluation of as many different kinds of information as the one between security expenditure and economic growth in the Third World. To understand the role played by security spending in promoting or impeding economic growth in one country, an in-depth case study is the most satisfactory approach. It is clear, however, that a general theory cannot be built on one case study alone and that to produce the number of case studies necessary to provide a basis for such a theory would involve many researcher-years of work. In addition, a researcher could easily be overwhelmed by the variety of facts presented in these case studies and fail to identify important patterns of relationships.

Another problem confronting researchers who wish to undertake case studies is that of data availability. In the previous chapter, the problems associated with collecting reliable statistics on security expenditure were examined in detail. Even outside the security sector developing countries do not always share the concern of OECD countries to generate data, but

---

[1] Speaking of the causes of coups d'état, Ruth First pointed out that

> The search for an overall classification system has been punctuated by quantitative studies probing for the role of the isolated common factor: stage of economic development; types of political organization; length of independence period; size of army. The computer as a substitute for social analyses has produced arid or trivial conclusions—such that the chances of military involvement increase year by year after independence.

Ruth First, *The Barrel of a Gun: Political Power in Africa and the Coup d'Etat* (Harmondsworth, England: Penguin, 1970), p. 14.

Although it might be argued that the relationship between economic growth and expenditure on the armed forces is more amenable to quantitative methods of analysis, it is unfortunately the case, as will be shown below, that the computer is frequently used as a substitute for economic analysis as well.

most Third World statistical services have become more efficient over the years. Multilateral organizations such as the World Bank, the United Nations, and the IMF have also helped to expand the available supply of statistical information. More data are thus now available for a larger group of countries than was the case in the early 1950s and 1960s, although the reliability of these data may be open to question. The difficulties connected with data collection in that earlier period were exemplified by the experience of Emile Benoit, the researcher who carried out the first major survey of the effects of military expenditure on economic growth in Third World countries. Begun in the late 1960s, this study was originally intended to be based on case studies but "it proved much more difficult than anticipated to obtain the required information in sufficient depth, and we were able to prepare a substantial study only of India. Our brief surveys of Argentina, Israel, South Korea, Mexico, and the UAR are quite superficial."[2] While this study may have exaggerated some of the difficulties in obtaining satisfactory information, it remains true that even today the available database for very many Third World countries is rather weak.

In the absence of adequate case study material, Benoit decided to employ aggregate, cross-section analysis. Many political scientists and economists have been attracted to this methodology, based on the use of statistical techniques to analyze a relatively small number of variables for a large number of countries and to identify associations between these variables. The application of cross-section techniques to economic and political systems became popular in the United States in the early 1960s as social scientists began to make use of computer technology for the first time. Longitudinal analysis, which examines yearly variations in relationships between variables in one or a small number of countries, has been used much less frequently than cross-sectional analysis, particularly by political scientists. The preference for cross-sectional analysis has derived from several factors. Longitudinal studies require the researcher to collect annual data over a long period of time—a sometimes difficult task in developing countries. Longitudinal analysis is also more difficult since considerable knowledge of the country is necessary to determine which factors are relevant over the long term, and it is likely that different measures will need to be employed at different points in time. In addition, it is harder to account for changes in longitudinal studies whereas with cross-section analysis, changes, if they occur, emerge clearly. Finally, like case studies, longitudinal analyses of a few countries cannot be used as a basis for a general theory.

[2] Emile Benoit, *Defense and Economic Growth in Developing Countries* (Lexington, Mass.: Lexington Books, 1973), p. 5.

The desire to produce general economic and political theories has perhaps been the most important factor leading analysts to adopt cross-sectional methods. These techniques offer a way of ordering the large amount of information that would inevitably result from the comparative analysis of more than a handful of countries and of rapidly identifying patterns in the relationships among variables. According to Robert Burrowes, the popularity of cross-sectional analysis

> can be traced largely to the postwar coincidence of a remarkable increase in the number of independent states and the twin calls for an empirical general theory and a truly comparative study of politics. Confronted with the prospect of a universe of national actors sufficiently numerous for statistical analysis, students of comparative and international politics were led almost irresistibly to the conclusion that they had but to adapt to their purposes the techniques applied so successfully to a universe of individual human actors. The cross-sectional analysis of nation-level aggregate data seemed a practical and appropriate research strategy to many students who were committed to empirical general theory and frustrated by the problem of empirical verification in comparative and international politics. It held out the tantalizing promise of a tailor-made means to generate and test theories of modernization, political development, foreign policy decision-making, and so on.[3]

Unfortunately there is no such thing as a "quick-fix" when it comes to economic and political analysis. Many factors can affect the rate of growth of an economy. As far as the strictly economic factors are concerned, development economists have not yet reached complete agreement among themselves as to which are the most important determinants of growth. Furthermore, a significant relationship in one country may be relatively inconsequential in another. Perhaps most important, because they cannot be reduced to a number, political variables such as policy decisions cannot be included in statistical analyses at all. Such policy decisions are, however, extremely important in explaining the developmental successes

---

[3] Robert Burrowes, "Multiple Time-Series Analysis of Nation-Level Data," *Comparative Political Studies* 2 (January 1970): 467–68. Regarding statistical analysis in general, Kenneth Boulding has pointed out that, "It is not surprising . . . that faced with large, complex, and partly inaccessible systems the researcher turns to numbers, that is, to data which can be expressed in quantitative form, and to the statistical analysis of these numbers, which have the delightful property that they can be added and subtracted, multiplied and divided, and hence they are much easier to manipulate and analyze than sentences." Kenneth Boulding, "'Thirsting for the Testable,'" p. 8, in *Comparative Public Policy. Issues, Theories, and Methods,* ed. Craig Liske, William Loehr, and John McCamant (New York: Halsted Press/John Wiley & Sons, 1975).

and failures of individual countries. It is very doubtful that a general theory of the relationship between security expenditures and economic growth applicable to all Third World countries at all times can ever be devised. This does not mean that macrostatistical techniques are of no value at all, but it does suggest that their usefulness is somewhat more limited than initially thought.

Empirical analysis of the links between military expenditure and growth faces inevitable difficulties. While there are a multitude of ways by which the military and military expenditures may influence growth, any formal model is only able to provide a limited representation of the possible channels of influence. In addition, there is much greater structural variation in the social and economic roles of the military in LDCs than in the case among OECD countries, which may reduce the likelihood of any stable empirical relations being observed in cross-section. A further problem is that the economic structure itself may influence the need or pressure for military expenditure, making identification of causation more difficult. Nonetheless, if these qualifications are kept in mind, it seems useful to examine what conclusions can be drawn from the empirical evidence.[4]

REGRESSION ANALYSIS: SOME CONSTRAINTS

For whatever purpose regression analyses are employed, a number of constraints inevitably face all researchers using these techniques, and these confines can affect the result obtained and the conclusions drawn from these results. Careful researchers take note of the problems raised by these constraints and, insofar as is possible, test for specification uncertainty, modifying their conclusions where these are shown to be overly sensitive to factors such as data source or variables employed. Five of the constraints with which regression analysts must deal most frequently are: the quality of available data, the choice and definition of variables, sample size, the need to treat all countries equally, and the attribution of causality.

DATA

Data quality is an important consideration for any study irrespective of the methodology employed. It is of particular importance to statistical analyses, however, since nonquantifiable phenomena cannot be included in macrostatistical models. Chenery and Syrquin have stressed this point: "The value of a large-scale statistical analysis of development patterns de-

[4]Saadet Deger and Ron Smith, "Military Expenditure and Growth in Less Developed Countries," *The Journal of Conflict Resolution* 27 (June 1983): 340.

pends heavily on the quality and comparability of the data on which it is based."[5] But case studies are not forced to rely solely on material which can be reduced to numbers and can take into account nonquantifiable factors such as policy decisions, quality of available manpower, and type of investment undertaken—all important determinants of growth and development.

On the issue of data alone, macrostatistical analyses of the relationship between security expenditure and economic growth run into considerable problems. As Chapter 3 explained in detail, the quality and comparability of the security expenditure data currently available are uncertain. Problems with data are not limited to security expenditure, but there are so many questions surrounding the accuracy of these data and so many variations among sources that one is justified in questioning whether these data should be used in macrostatistical analyses. Deger and Smith have demonstrated the effect of sensitivity to data source by running a simple regression of growth on military expenditure using first SIPRI and then ACDA data. For eighteen African countries, the regression produced a negative coefficient for both data sets; in neither case was the coefficient significantly different from zero. "But in absolute value the ACDA coefficient of −0.39 is over four times the size of the SIPRI coefficient of −0.09." For twelve Latin American countries, the correlation coefficient was negative for ACDA figures (−0.125) but positive using SIPRI data (0.088).[6] As with the African sample, neither coefficient is significantly different from zero, but one is left with a somewhat different notion of what the relation between these two variables might be depending on whether one looks at the ACDA results or the SIPRI results. Deger and Smith explain that they believe the SIPRI series to be more consistent; but, as was shown in Chapter 3, the basic data sources for ACDA and SIPRI Third World security expenditure data are quite similar, and it is difficult which might be more accurate and consistent.

Another case in which data from different sources produced contradictory results was reported by a team of West German researchers. They reran a linear regression analysis carried out by David Whynes using data from the U.S. Arms Control and Disarmament Agency. Whynes's results

---

[5] Hollis Chenery and Moises Syrquin with Hazel Elkington, *Patterns of Development, 1950–1970* (New York: Oxford University Press, 1975), p. 4, n. 2. Concerning the quality of data as a source of error in econometric analyses, see also, Jacques Fontanel, "Formalized Studies and Econometric Analyses of the Relationship Between Military Expenditure and Economic Development. The Examples of a Developed Country, France, and an Underdeveloped Country, Morocco," Report submitted to the UN Special Experts Group on Disarmament and Development (Grenoble: Centre for Security and Defence Studies, March 1980), pp. 130–31.

[6] Deger and Smith, "Military Expenditure," pp. 347–48.

were based on data from the International Institute of Strategic Studies (IISS), the least reliable of all major data sources. The West German team concluded: "While the IISS data give a correlation coefficient of .224, the ACDA data yield a coefficient of .128. Whynes' conclusions that there is statistical evidence ascertaining 'that defense spending can play an enhancing role in the development process' is clearly dependent on the statistical data material used."[7]

It has been suggested that longitudinal studies are less prone to the problem of unreliable data than cross-sectional analysis because statistics from a large number of countries are not required. Researchers employing longitudinal methods can concentrate on countries where the data are known to be relatively plentiful and reliable. Although this might lead to an overemphasis on particular countries, researchers could also spend time developing more reliable data from hitherto untapped national sources than are available in the international literature. By concentrating on a relatively small number of countries, researchers are also better able to evaluate their results and to use nonquantifiable information to assess whether statistical associations are meaningful or not.[8]

Even if a researcher develops his or her own data series, the problem of unidentified security expenditure must be faced irrespective of statistical technique employed. In Chapter 3 it was explained that the most accurate estimates may still understate the security outlays of many Third World countries. Under these conditions, the reliability of results produced by statistical analyses must be questioned. Regardless of whether longitudinal or cross-sectional analysis was used, a researcher examining the effect of security expenditure on economic growth in Indonesia would have to know that the Indonesian government regularly understates its security budget by as much as 50 percent. Anyone familiar with this fact could increase all reported values by an appropriate amount. But how does one take into account the unspecified exports from India to the Soviet Union and other East European countries to pay for unspecified amounts of imported weaponry? Or the exchange of Ethiopian coffee for Soviet arms? Or Chilean copper and Pakistani jute for weapons from other countries? Not to mention all the as-yet-unknown hidden funds, unrecorded exports, and other methods employed to make security budgets appear smaller and more benign than they really are.

Burrowes had commented that "the development of concept and the-

[7]Michael Brzoska, P. Lock, F. Peters, M. Reichel, and H. Wulf, "An Assessment of Sources and Statistics of Military Expenditure and Arms Transfer Data. A Report Written as a Contribution to the United Nations Study on the Relationship between Disarmament and Development (Hamburg: IFSH-Arbeitsgruppe Rüstung und Unterentwicklung, 1980, mimeograph), p. 1.

[8]Burrowes, "Multiple Time-Series Analysis," pp. 474–75.

ory has often far out-distanced attempts to push back existing data constraints."[9] Nowhere is this problem more evident than in assessing the effects of the security sector on economic growth and development. Few researchers have shown much interest in improving the security expenditure data base despite its well-known weaknesses. Researchers who have decided to employ macrostatistical techniques almost ritualistically remark upon the deficiencies of the data and then proceed with their analyses as if the data were perfectly reliable. More serious attention must be given by researchers to the constraints imposed by existing security expenditure data.

THE CHOICE AND DEFINITION OF VARIABLES

The decisions about the choice and definition of variables are crucial for both cross-sectional and longitudinal analyses. In view of the relatively limited number of variables which can be tested at any one time, it is extremely important that those included in a model "actually measure the theoretical constructs they claim to measure."[10] There are, however, at least two ways in which researchers can be frustrated in their attempts to find the most appropriate variables.

In the first place, researchers may disagree about which variables most accurately measure a particular phenomenon. Given the disagreement among development economists concerning which factors are most important in determining rates of growth in Third World countries, two researchers from different theoretical backgrounds might well model the relationship between economic growth and security expenditure in different ways and produce different results. Deger and Smith, for example, examined the relationship between security expenditures and economic growth for fifty countries in the 1965–1973 period. Their model "was derived from a production function together with assumptions regarding the determinants of productivity growth and structural change. However, other theoretical specifications are possible. In particular, the concept of export-led growth may be relevant for LDCs, as has been suggested by many developmental theorists."[11] When the share of exports in national

---

[9] Ibid., p. 470. Burrowes was speaking solely of cross-section analysis, but in view of the special problems confronting the measurement of security expenditure, his comments would seem to be applicable to longitudinal analysis as well.

[10] Ibid., p. 468.

[11] Deger and Smith, "Military Expenditure," pp. 349–50. One can also expect results to vary according to whether military burden is measured as military (security) expenditure as a share of gross national product or as a proportion of central government expenditure. As Appendix 3 indicates, the most frequently used measure is military expenditure as a share of gross product.

income was added to the original Deger-Smith model, the negative effect of defense on growth produced by the original model was increased.

Part of the definition of variables involves deciding on the most appropriate time frame for comparison. Some researchers prefer to compare variables in the same time frame (growth of x versus growth of y, or level of x versus level of y) while others will mix time frames. Researchers at MIT examined the effect of security expenditure on economic growth for sixty-nine developing countries in the 1952–1970 period by measuring all variables in terms of growth rates. Their finding that security expenditure has a negative effect on economic growth directly contradicted Emile Benoit who had either examined the same relationship for forty-four developing countries between 1950 and 1965. The MIT researchers attributed this difference to three factors, one of which was that Benoit compared the *rate of growth* of the economy with the *level* of the defense burden.[12] (There is good reason to believe that Benoit's data did not actually show the positive relationship between security expenditure and economic growth that he claimed they did; some shortcomings of the Benoit analysis will be discussed in greater detail in the following section.)

Both longitudinal and cross-sectional analyses require well-defined, appropriate variables. Researchers using cross-sectional techniques are likely to have greater difficulty in choosing variables, however, since data for the most appropriate variable may not be available for all countries in the sample. Burrowes reports that researchers are often faced "with the Hobson's choice of using highly questionable data or not engaging in national-level cross-sectional research at all. The analyst who chooses to proceed under these circumstances is forced to accept bad data on valid indicators or to include indicators of tenuous theoretical relevance but on which good data are available."[13]

Whichever choice is made, the outcome of the research will be affected to some degree. Researchers should discuss the alternatives faced in choosing variables and report the results of tests to determine the sensitivity of the model employed to choice of variables. This makes it easier for others to evaluate the results of the analyses for themselves. Unfortunately many researchers fail to discuss the shortcomings of their chosen variables,

[12] Riccardo Faini, Patricia Arnez, and Lance Taylor, "Defense Spending, Economic Structure & Growth: Evidence Among Countries and Over Time," Contribution to the UN Special Experts Group on the Relationship Between Disarmament and Development (Cambridge: MIT, October 1980, mimeograph), p. 17, n. 4. The findings of this study have been published as Riccardo Faini, Patricia Arnez, and Lance Taylor, "Defense Spending, Economic Structure, and Growth: Evidence Among Countries and Over Time," *Economic Development and Cultural Change* 32:3 (1984): 487–98.
[13] Burrowes, "Multiple Time-Series Analysis," p. 469.

which can all too easily lead to confusing tentative findings with firm results.

SAMPLE-SIZE AND EQUALITY AMONG COUNTRIES

Two constraints that apply solely to cross-sectional analysis are the need for data from a large number of countries and the necessity of treating all countries in a sample alike. When a sample includes only a small number of countries, the statistical significance of the results will not be very high because any observed associations between variables from a small sample could be the result of chance. With a large sample, the role played by chance is considerably reduced but not entirely eliminated. It is not always possible, however, to expand a sample so that a statistically significant number of observations is involved. A researcher may want to study only countries in a particular region or within a certain income range. Such a sample may include no more than fifteen or twenty countries, too few to produce reliable results.[14]

Ironically, having a sufficiently large number of observations to produce statistically significant results can create its own problems. When many countries are compared, no uniform pattern of associations may easily emerge for the sample as a whole. Given the political and economic diversity of Third World countries, such a result should not come as a surprise. In specific countries, however, the variables in question might in fact be closely associated. For them, the null results obtained from the cross-section are actually misleading. In the same vein, even when a particular association is observed between variables, individual countries can diverge from the norm. Researchers at the University of London who examined the relationship between economic growth and security expenditure in OECD member countries and in fifty Third World states concluded that

---

[14] A 1969 Rand Corporation report which examined the effect of military expenditure on economic growth in nineteen Latin American countries pointed out, for example, that "the number of countries involved (only twenty or so) is so small that high degrees of statistical significance usually cannot be obtained. That is to say, most patterns which appear in the data may be explained away as mere chance without unduly stretching credulity." Despite this and other compelling constraints on the use of statistical analyses mentioned by the author, he concluded that, "it still seems worthwhile to look at what data are available, fuzzy and conflicting though they may be, in attempting to determine the effects of military programs in Latin America. After all, decisions must be made even in the absence of absolute scientific proof that this or that policy will have the desired effect." Thomas A. Brown, *Statistical Indications of the Effect of Military Programs on Latin America, 1950–1965,* P-4144 (Santa Monica, Calif.: Rand Corporation, July 1969), pp. 2, 3.

It is also important to recognize that the selection of the sample—irrespective of its size—is crucial and influences the results obtained.

There can be little doubt that military expenditure in OECD countries is not beneficial to the growth rate. While it might in principle have an important positive effect through "spin-off" the allocation of investment resources to military purposes reduced growth, and ultimately it is the negative effect which dominates. In LDCs the situation is less clear and no systematic relation is obvious. There are two constraints on the growth process—one structural, and the other resource-based. The military's social role may contribute to structural changes which stimulate growth, but military expenditure allocates scarce resources away from productive civil investment, fails to mobilise substantial savings by itself and appears to depress the rate of saving. The extent to which the military has a positive structural effect and whether or not this dominates the negative effect on resource allocation are questions best answered by studies of individual countries within an historical perspective. Given large differences in socio-economic structures among the LDCs in our sample and the important role of influences specific to individual countries, it pays to treat cross-section results with great caution.[15]

The need for a significantly large sample can affect results in a second way. Researchers can be led to define variables so broadly that the comparative value is lost. When it comes to determining the relationship between security expenditure and economic growth, it is important to remember that not all countries are equally endowed with such determinants of growth as skilled manpower, raw materials, capital, infrastructure, and access to technology. To assume that security expenditure, or indeed any form of public expenditure, will have the same effect in countries as structurally different as Argentina and Sri Lanka or Venezuela and Sudan is unwise. Yet this is precisely what cross-sectional analyses do.[16]

[15] Dan Smith and Ron Smith, "Military Expenditure, Resources and Development," Contribution to the United Nations Study on the Relationship between Disarmament and Development (London: Department of Economics, Birkbeck College, University of London, April 1980, mimeograph), pp. 17–18.

[16] On this point see Morris Janowitz, *Military Conflict. Essays in the Institutional Analysis of War and Peace* (Beverly Hills: Sage Publications, 1975), p. 107, and Burrowes, "Multiple Time-Series Analysis," p. 469.

The fifty countries comprising the sample in both Smith and Smith, "Military Expenditure," and Deger and Smith, "Military Expenditure," are: Algeria, Argentina, Brazil, Burma, Chad, Chile, Colombia, Costa Rica, Dominican Republic, Ecuador, Egypt, El Salvador, Ethiopia, Gabon, Ghana, Greece, Guatemala, Guinea, Honduras, India, Indonesia, Iran, Iraq, Israel, Jordan, Kenya, Libya, Malaysia, Mexico, Morocco, Nigeria, Pakistan, Peru, Philippines, Saudi Arabia, Singapore, Somalia, South Africa, South Korea, South Vietnam, Spain, Sri Lanka, Sudan, Syria, Tanzania, Thailand, Tunisia, Turkey, Uganda, Venezuela. The countries comprising the sample in Faini, Arnez, and Taylor, "Defense Spending" (1980), are listed in Figure 5-1.

CAUSALITY

There is widespread agreement among statisticians that it is impossible to test for causality. Causality is embodied in the theoretical model employed. If variables do not show the appropriate associations, then the hypothesized model must be rejected. It does not follow, however, that if variables are closely correlated with each other then the causal agent can be identified. Even if the hypothesis that variables A and B are associated is confirmed and competing hypotheses do not give better statistical results, it is not possible to determine through statistical analysis that some other unanalyzed factor is not in fact responsible for the observed association between variables.

It has been suggested that longitudinal analysis can eliminate some of the uncertainties surrounding the attribution of causality.

As Michael Hass points out, "longitudinal research can be designed to ascertain the directionality of relationships between variables . . . one can observe whether trends in postulated independent variables consistently precede those in the hypothesized dependent variables. . . ." The determination of directionality can appreciably reduce the number of possible causal paths in a complex multivariate model. Hopefully, it can also lessen somewhat the task of separating real and spurious relationships.[17]

Most statistical work on the relationship between security expenditure and economic growth in the Third World has been based on cross-sectional analysis because researchers have been interested in discovering general patterns of relationships applicable to a broad spectrum of Third World countries. They have been much less interested in determining what relationships look like for individual countries and how these relationships do or do not change over time. However, even if statistical analysis of the security expenditure growth relationship had been oriented toward longitudinal studies, the problem of causality would still be far from resolved.

A researcher may, for example, build a model based on the hypothesis that a given change in variable A will produce a particular change in variable B. Using longitudinal methods it may be possible to show not only that the variables move in the anticipated directions but also that variable

---

[17] Burrowes, "Multiple Time-Series Analysis," p. 472. The Haas quotation is from Michael Haas, "Aggregate Analysis," *World Politics* 19 (October 1966): 118. See also, Philippe C. Schmitter, "Foreign Military Assistance, National Military Spending and Military Rule in Latin America," pp. 149–51, in *Military Rule in Latin America: Function, Consequences and Perspectives,* P. C. Schmitter, ed. (Beverley Hills and London: Sage, 1973).

A consistently precedes variable *B* in time. Although this cannot prove
that *A* causes *B* to behave in a certain way, the possibility that *A* acts on
B does at least exist, which it would not if it were shown that *B* consistently preceded *A*. This is somewhat closer to causality than one can get
using cross-sectional techniques, but it is not necessarily very close. The
possibility that some variable not included in the model has caused the
observed relationship cannot be ruled out. Furthermore, as with cross-
sectional analysis, longitudinal techniques cannot model policy decisions,
yet an accurate understanding of such decisions is vital to assessing causality. Two variables may be strongly correlated; one may consistently precede the other in time; nonetheless the variables may appear to interact
because of decisions taken by the government on matters unrelated to the
first variable.

THE MISUSE OF STATISTICAL ANALYSIS

Macroeconomic statistics must be handled with care, can often be
misleading and unreliable, and do not automatically reveal relationships between variables. . . . [There do exist] econometric and statistical methods which can be deployed precisely to allow for weaknesses, unreliability and possible inconsistency in data. Moreover,
the sensible researcher applying such techniques specifies the theoretical models in which the data are deployed, and notes explicitly
the problems so that results may be presented with due caution.[18]

Unfortunately, not all users of these techniques proceed with the necessary caution. One of the conceptually and methodologically weakest of
all statistical examinations of the security expenditure–growth relationship was the study commissioned by the U.S. Arms Control and Disarmament Agency from Emile Benoit. Despite its shortcomings, discussed at
some length in several critiques, it remains the major empirical source for
those who argue in favor of a positive role for Third World militaries.
Others who do not necessarily wish to argue that security expenditure
promotes economic growth have nonetheless been impressed by the apparent complexity of Benoit's analysis and have failed to evaluate his
work critically. Still other researchers, seemingly unaware of the study's
shortcomings, have adopted its concepts and data, deficiencies and all,
into their own statistical analyses. All this has only served to confuse the
debate on the economic effects of security expenditure.[19]

[18] Dan Smith and Ron Smith, "Reflections on Neuman," *Orbis* 23 (Summer 1973): 471.
[19] Benoit, *Defense and Economic Growth.* Gavin Kennedy has praised Benoit's honesty
for publishing results (more defense expenditure may produce higher rates of economic
growth) which were at variance with his original thesis (defense expenditure and economic
growth are negatively related). Gavin Kennedy, *Defense Economics* (London: Duckworth,

Many of Benoit's problems centered around his definition of foreign assistance and the way in which he interpreted the relationship between foreign assistance, economic growth, and security expenditure. For his study, Benoit had been able to obtain what he considered satisfactory data for thirty-six countries for periods of eleven to sixteen years between 1950 and 1965 and for an additional eight countries covering all years between 1960 and 1965. Two series were constructed, each containing forty-four countries: the first, called the A series, included all available data for each country between 1960 and 1965; the second, the B series, included only data for the 1960–1965 period. Simple regression analysis involving the defense burden and the rate of economic growth resulted in the discovery of a positive relationship between the two variables for both the A and the B series instead of the negative one Benoit had anticipated.

Benoit was not alone in anticipating a negative relationship between economic growth and defense burden. ACDA had become interested in this subject because evidence was beginning to accumulate suggesting that high rates of expenditure in the security sector were inversely correlated with growth in industrialized countries. It was thought that the Benoit study would demonstrate a similar relationship for developing countries. Benoit was unable to find evidence of any systematic bias in the data which would account for the unexpected positive relationship. He then hypothesized that the defense burden might merely be acting as a

---

1983), pp. 194–97, and personal communication, 6 December 1983. Kennedy fails to understand that Benoit's work is seriously flawed and that Benoit did everything possible to avoid acknowledging that the observed correlation between defense burden and economic growth was spurious. On this subject Kennedy's own conclusions are that: "in deciding on the net contribution of military structures to growth and development in the Third World we have to take each case on its merits. However, nothing in this view suggests that the military is a preferred road to growth and development or that it is a necessary one. Discussion of the role of the military must consider the circumstances, including the security environment, in which the military emerges as a dominant factor in the developing country" (p. 201).

Since 1982, two researchers at the Naval Postgraduate School have published several papers in which they sought to extend the "seminal work by Emile Benoit." Using his data and many of his concepts, they showed that there was a negative relation between security expenditure and economic growth in the poorer developing countries and a positive relation between the two variables in richer developing countries. Their work will be discussed in greater detail below. See P. C. Frederiksen and Robert E. Looney, "Defense Expenditures and Economic Growth in Developing Countries," *Armed Forces and Society* 9 (Summer 1983): 633–45, and Peter C. Fredericksen and Robert E. Looney, "Defense Expenditures and Economic Growth in Developing Countries: Some Further Empirical Evidence," *Journal of Economic Development* 7:1 (July 1982): 113–25.

Portions of the following discussion of the Benoit study were first published in Nicole Ball, "Defense and Development: A Critique of the Benoit Study," *Economic Development and Cultural Change* 31 (April 1983): 507–24.

proxy for some other variable in reality more closely linked with rising growth rates. In technical terms, this would mean that the positive relationship identified between defense burden and economic growth was spurious. The variable Benoit decided to investigate in this respect was the inflow of external resources, specifically bilateral economic aid. It would, however, have been more correct for Benoit to have adopted a more inclusive definition of external resources. By using only bilateral economic aid, Benoit biased the outcome of his statistical analyses of the relation between defense burden, the inflow of external resources, and economic growth in favor of the military component.

Benoit divided the foreign financial flows into four main categories. First, economic aid included "official grants and loans whether these be bilateral (government to government) or multilateral (from international agencies) not directly tied to the transfer of military goods or services." Second, long-term private investment was composed of "direct investment (with reinvested earnings), net portfolio and other long term private investment, and guaranteed export credits." Third, military aid (given the American acronym MAP) included "the transfer of military equipment or other military supplies or military services (particularly training) at no charge or at concessionary prices or terms of payment." Fourth, military transfer payments were "overseas military expenditures" of foreign governments (primarily the United States because of data restrictions) in the country under study.[20]

Using these concepts, Benoit prepared four different estimates of foreign resource inflow. Bilateral economic aid (coded R_2) was considered the most satisfactory quantity to use in multiple regression analysis to test whether or not the defense burden had acted as a proxy for external resource inflow in the simple regression analysis.

> Our analysis was directed toward understanding the extent to which external resources might be enabling recipients to carry heavier than normal defense burdens without correspondingly reducing their civilian investment and hampering their growth. On reflection, total R appeared somewhat excessive for this purpose. First, the military assistance it included comprised mostly transfers of military equipment. Most of much equipment did not truly substitute for domestic resources that might otherwise have flowed into domestic investment and raised growth rates. The recipients would for the most part not have been able to use their domestic resources for manufacturing comparable defense equipment, or would lack foreign exchange to buy such equipment as commercial imports. Second, military trans-

---

[20] Benoit, *Defense and Economic Growth*, p. 126.

action receipts, which in some respects are more like a gift than an export, did nevertheless require some sacrifice of domestic resources in the form of additional imports required to provide the services. . . . Moreover, they did to some extent absorb scarce and valuable domestic resources (e.g., materials, skilled labor, tools and machinery for construction work) including new housing and improvements on existing housing for the foreign troops. For these reasons it appeared that military receipts should either be omitted or included only in part as possible offsets to domestic resources that might otherwise have been absorbed by defense.[21]

Benoit appears to have switched purposes in midanalysis, for surely the point of doing the multiple regression analysis was to discover which variable—the defense burden or the inflow of foreign resources—was more closely associated with economic growth. To ignore foreign private investment, multilateral aid, and military assistance was to stack the deck in favor of the defense burden. It was particularly misleading to ignore the inflow of military aid, since for many of the fastest growing countries in Benoit's sample, military assistance accounted for, on average, 50 percent of their foreign financial inflows.

In view of the way in which both Third World security expenditure has been increasing since the mid-1960s and the arms trade has been flourishing even in the face of cutbacks in security assistance from the major donors, it seems somewhat divorced from reality to estimate as Benoit did that the equipment would be unavailable or unobtainable for the major recipients of security assistance. In general terms, Benoit's evaluation might have been more correct in the 1950s than it has been since then, but the assertion would have to be investigated on a country-by-country basis. During the 1950s and 1960s, the Soviet Union tended to trade weapons for commodities, obviating the need for foreign exchange. The major donor of security assistance, the United States, did begin to reduce the amount of grant aid offered to Third World countries during the 1960s, but instead it provided sizable loans for the purchase of military equipment. These have enabled recipients to overcome, at least in the short run, cash-flow problems and to purchase considerable amounts of weaponry and related services. Furthermore, some particularly favored recipients, for example in the U.S. client South Korea, have had a large portion of operations and maintenance costs covered by security assistance.

Benoit argued that multilateral aid and foreign private investment

---

[21] Ibid., pp. 35–36. Total R = total economic aid + long-term private investment + military aid + military transfer payments. See also Benoit's Table 3-12, which divides the net inflow of external resources into its economic and military components.

should not be included in the foreign resource variable since, unlike much bilateral economic aid, they were not "in intention or in fact, related to the level of the recipient's defense program." Indeed, Benoit suggested that these two types of inflows were, "if anything, *discouraged* by too high a defense burden."[22] To substantiate this generalization, only a single example was offered, the "reversal of the IBRD on financing the Aswan Dam in the fifties, which was related more or less explicitly to Egypt's diversion of potential exports to pay for large military imports from Czechoslovakia." Benoit, however, directly contradicted his own argument by pointing out that, "the IBRD was responding to a US government decision not to supply another key segment in the total financing, *rather than directly to Egypt's military decision.*"[23] The decisions of both the U.S. government and the IBRD are most appropriately viewed in terms of East-West politics, a factor conspicuous in Benoit's study by its absence. The "Czech" arms deal was concluded only after the Egyptian government had failed to obtain an equally large arms package from the United States. The "Czech" weapons were actually provided by the Soviet Union. The Eisenhower administration had offered to conclude a smaller arms deal, but the size of the arms package proposed by the U.S. government was not related to the belief that the cost of the weapons would harm Egypt development efforts in any way. Had Egypt in fact imported arms from the United States, or from Britain or France, *signifying a friendly rather than an antagonistic relationship with the West,* it is highly likely that no sanction would have been imposed, either by the U.S. government or by the IBRD.

The issue here should not be why foreign financial resources are provided to Third World economies, but how much is given and to what extent these resources enable governments to maintain investment ratios favorable to economic growth. From the preceding discussion clearly there is good reason to suspect that the multiple regression analysis which used only bilateral economic aid to evaluate the relative importance of the defense burden and foreign financial resources in accounting for changes in economic growth was biased in favor of the defense burden. Just as important, however, as Benoit's underestimation of foreign inflows was his manipulation of the results of the multiple regression analysis. A proper interpretation of these results would have led Benoit to conclude that the association was between growth and external resources and that the defense burden had acted as a proxy for external resources, *even when defined solely as bilateral economic aid,* and that the observed positive relationship between defense burden and economic growth was spu-

[22] Ibid., p. 135; emphasis in original.
[23] Ibid., p. 320, n. 40; emphasis added.

rious. Instead, he concluded that "even if the correlation between defense burdens and growth rates may be regarded as technically spurious in a narrowly statistical and non-causal sense, we doubt that this truly eliminates the possibility of defense burdens exerting a significant positive cause and effect influence on growth rates in developing countries."[24] Benoit reached this conclusion in the following way.

He ran two multiple regression analyses—one using the longer A series data for 1950–1965, the other using the B series data for 1960–1965. In the A series, the defense burden seemed to be acting as a proxy for bilateral economic aid; in the B series, it did not. One possible explanation of this statistical disagreement was that the findings from the A series were unreliable because that series did not include data for the same years for all countries. Benoit was able to show statistically that the results from the A series were reliable. The extreme shortness—six years—of the B series strengthened the argument in favor of using the results of the longer series.

At this point one might have expected Benoit to conclude that the effect of the defense burden on the rate of growth of developing economies was negligible. Benoit, however, announced himself "skeptical" that this was in fact the case. His doubts on this score derived "from complications introduced into the interpretation of the results by the considerable degree of intercorrelation of the variables and the relatively large amount of R square that cannot be specifically attributed to any particular variable."[25] A close examination of Benoit's explanation of the "intercorrelation of the variables" demonstrates that the "complications" were primarily of his own making.

In the longer time series Benoit found that investment and bilateral economic aid accounted for some 59 percent of the variance in the growth rate. When the defense burden was added in, the three variables together accounted for just over 60 percent of the variance. From the point of view of a "purely predictive model," Benoit argued, it is clear that the defense burden "can be rejected as a redundant, insignificant, useless addition to the model." Benoit declared himself, however, interested in more than prediction. He wanted to understand "cause and effect relations." As explained earlier in this chapter, the attribution of causality based on regression analysis is an operation considered suspect by many statisticians. Benoit was aware of this but proceeded to explain why he believed that the "line of influence between Defense, Investment, Foreign Aid, and Growth [can be seen] as partly reciprocal."

Regarding investment, Benoit argued that, although multiple regres-

[24] Ibid., p. 22.
[25] Ibid., p. 77.

sion analysis with the defense burden as the dependent variable showed the rate of investment to have no influence on the size of the defense burden, it might be the case that defense-related construction "could readily increase the amount of gross capital formation in the national accounts." Benoit therefore felt justified in "attributing to B [defense burden] a substantial part of the overlap in the contributions of I [investment] and B to the variance of G prime [rate of growth of civilian GDP]." In fact, an examination of the contents of security expenditure of forty-eight countries between 1950 and 1980 indicates that the capital portion of defense budgets—procurement and construction—tends to be extremely small, especially in the early part of this period, which coincides with the time frame of Benoit's study.[26] Although this does not mean that the influence of defense-related investment on economic growth was nonexistent, it seems unlikely that it was as strong as Benoit postulated.

Benoit believed that the relationship between the defense burden and bilateral economic aid was much closer than the one between defense burden and investment. He characterized that relationship and its effect on economic growth:

> In interpreting this relationship, there is no reason to doubt the commonsense impression that foreign aid enables the recipient to maintain larger defense programs than would otherwise be possible. In a good number of cases, indeed, this has been the obvious intention of the donor.
>
> Yet even here the line of causation has not run all in one direction. The fact that certain LDCs maintain exceptionally large defense programs and are willing to increase them when this appears to suit the interests of certain allies has certainly been instrumental in their obtaining far more bilateral foreign aid than other countries. One thinks of China (Taiwan), S. Korea, Greece, Turkey, Jordan, Israel, Vietnam, and the UAR [Egypt] as examples. The aid was often enough to cover a substantial part of even the country's normal defense expenditures, and by so doing contributed substantially to its economy. Where the aid was effectively enough utilized and there was not too much military destruction or waste associated with the large defense programs the net effect for growth may have been highly favorable. Several of the countries listed above have in fact been in the top quartile of growth rates in our sample.[27]

[26] Nicole Ball, *Third-World Security Expenditure: A Statistical Compendium*, C 10250-M5 (Stockholm: National Defence Research Institute, 1984).

[27] Benoit, *Defense and Economic Growth*. This last quotation is from pages 80–81. The entire discussion of Benoit's attempt to attribute causality is drawn from pages 79–81.

It is clear that even if a country's willingness to adopt a particular defense posture does guarantee that it receives much more economic aid than it might have under other circumstances and if these additional resources allow the country to raise its economic growth rate, this can in no way be interpreted as an indication that defense expenditure per se leads to higher rates of economic growth. There is by no means complete agreement among development economists about the effect of aid on economic growth. There are those who argue that even if some of these resources are used to finance consumption rather than investment, they promote growth; others have argued the opposite.[28]

To the extent it can be shown that economic aid allows a country to maintain an investment rate sufficient to promote a high level of economic growth, the fact remains that the economic aid has been growth inducing. To argue that by attracting economic aid the defense burden causes growth is to substitute arbitrarily one cause for another and be willfully misleading. Yet Benoit used precisely this disingenuous argument to ignore the findings of his own statistical analyses which suggested that the level of the defense burden did not explain the rate of growth of the civilian economy particularly well. It freed him to state that if the relationship between security expenditure and economic growth had not been proved, neither had it been disproved.[29] This assertion's doubtfulness is portrayed graphically in Figure 4-1. The matrix is based on one

[28] For examples of the first opinion, see Hollis B. Chenery and N. G. Carter, "Foreign Assistance and Development Performance," *American Economic Review* 63 (May 1973): 459–68, and Gustav F. Papanek, "The Effect of Aid and Other Resource Transfers on Savings and Growth in Less Developed Countries," *Economic Journal* 82 (September 1972): 934–50. The second viewpoint is set forward in Keith B. Griffin and J. L. Enos, "Foreign Assistance: Objectives and Consequences," *Economic Development and Cultural Change* 18 (April 1970): 313–27, and Thomas E. Weisskopf, "The Impact of Foreign Capital Inflow on Domestic Savings in Underdeveloped Countries," *Journal of International Economics* 2 (February 1972): 25–38.

[29] Having convinced himself that the findings of his original simple regression analyses did not have to be rejected, Benoit proceeded to "prove" that causality did not run from growth to defense burden, that is that countries did not spend more on the security sector simply because they had rapid rates of economic growth. This being the case, he argued, the positive relationship between defense burden and rate of economic growth in the simple regression analyses must have derived from the influence of expenditure in the defense sector on the economy and he posited a number of channels through which this influence might occur. Benoit, *Defense and Economic Growth*, pp. 81–90.

Had he not manipulated the findings of his multiple regression analyses, Benoit could never, of course, have gotten to this point. In addition, it can be shown that many of the ways in which Benoit suggested that defense expenditure would promote growth were much less important in the actual experiences of individual countries than he believed them to be. See, for example, the discussion of military manpower in Chapter 8 of this volume, and Ball, "Defense and Development," pp. 515–19.

DEFENSE BURDEN

		LOW	HIGH	
RATE OF GROWTH OF GNP	**LOW**	Mexico Zambia Venezuela Philippines Sudan Tunisia* Brazil [6]	Spain Greece* Iraq Israel* UAR* Yugoslavia Taiwan* South Vietnam* [7]	Jordan* Peru Thailand Turkey* Burma Syria South Korea
	HIGH	Costa Rica Ecuador Kenya Uganda Nigeria Sri Lanka Guatemala Honduras Ghana* Tanzania South Africa Indonesia El Salvador Argentina Colombia [14]	Malaysia* Iran Chile India Pakistan Morocco Dominican Republic [6]	

FIGURE 4-1

Defense Burden, Rate of Growth, and Foreign Aid, 44 Third World
Countries, 1950–1965

Source: Kenneth Boulding, "Defense Spending: Burden or Boon?" War/Peace Report,
8 November 1974, p. 20.

Note: Figures in brackets show the number in each quadrant that remain once the recipients
of substantial foreign aid are eliminated; those countries that are eliminated are indicated
by an asterisk.

prepared by Kenneth Boulding to substantiate his argument that the observed relationship between higher defense burdens and higher rates of
economic growth disappear when those countries which received substantial amounts of foreign aid are eliminated from Benoit's sample.
What remains is a negative relationship between the two variables in the
low-growth countries.

Although the Benoit study is frequently cited as showing that security
expenditure does not have a negative effect on economic growth in developing countries, Benoit's actual conclusions are somewhat less precise:
"we have been unable to establish whether the net growth effects of de-

fense expenditures have been positive or not. On the basis of all the evidence we suspect that it has been positive, for the countries in our sample and at past levels of defense burden, but we have not been able to prove this." [30] The thrust of the discussion here has been that a careful reading of Benoit's study suggests he should have concluded there was no association at all between growth rates and defense burden. More recent statistical studies have concluded that there is a negative relationship between defense burden and economic growth in Third World countries: that is, countries with higher rates of defense expenditure have lower rates of economic growth. Strictly speaking, these results are not entirely comparable to those produced by Benoit's analyses since the studies cover different countries and time periods and use different data sources and estimation methods. (Eight statistical studies of the relationship between economic growth and security expenditure are compared in Appendix 3 in terms of time period covered, countries surveyed, main hypotheses, variables, and conclusions.) Thus, although several of these studies, particularly those carried out by groups at MIT and the University of London, are methodologically sounder than Benoit's work, they do not absolutely disprove his findings.

It was therefore of some interest when two researchers at the Naval Postgraduate School, Peter Frederiksen and Robert Looney, chose to employ Benoit's data in "an extension of [his] seminal work" to evaluate the effect of resource constraints on the defense burden-economic growth relationship. Specifically, Frederiksen and Looney hypothesized "that relatively poor countries tend to cut back high-growth development expenditures in favor of maintaining defense programs, while relatively rich countries are much less likely to abandon development expenditures given a constant level of defense preparedness. Thus, we should expect a negative relationship between defense and growth in the poorer countries but a positive relationship in the richer countries." [31] They divided Benoit's initial sample of forty-four countries into four groups of which the first two—resource-abundant and resource-constrained—were of most interest. The resource-abundant group included twenty-four countries; the resource-constrained group included nine countries. When linear regression analyses were conducted for these two groups, it was concluded that the hypothesized relationships could be confirmed. [32]

[30] Benoit, *Defense and Economic Growth*, p. 4.

[31] Frederiksen and Looney, "Defense Expenditures," p. 633.

[32] In their second paper, "Defense Expenditures: Some Further Empirical Evidence," Fredericksen and Looney examined the relationship between growth and expenditure in the security sector for ninety developing countries during the years from 1970 to 1978. "Defense spending was found to be positively associated and statistically significant for those

It is legitimate to question whether such small samples—particularly the one containing only nine countries—produce results that can be generalized for such a heterogenous group as the Third World. Equally serious, Frederiksen and Looney failed entirely to take into account any of the numerous shortcomings of the original Benoit study.[33] Benoit's definition of and data on foreign assistance, bilateral economic aid, were accepted without question. Thus, in their regression equations the effect of foreign resources on economic growth is underrated, just as it was in the original Benoit analysis. In the Frederiksen-Looney resource-abundant group, at least ten countries received sizable contributions of military assistance from the United States during the 1950–1965 period: Greece, Spain, Taiwan, Thailand, South Korea, Iran, Yugoslavia, Chile, Colombia, and Turkey. Egypt received considerable security assistance from the

---

countries classified as resource rich. The effect of defense on growth in the poor countries appear to be neutral." In this paper, the resources abundant group consisted of twenty-two countries and the resource constrained group of fifty-one countries.

[33] This is not the only problem evident in the Frederiksen-Looney work. According to them, Benoit concluded that the initial positive relationship between the defense burden and the rate of economic growth was spurious. As the foregoing discussion on the Benoit study explained, Benoit *should* have reached such a conclusion but went to great lengths to avoid doing so. As far as this author is aware, Frederiksen and Looney are the only individuals ever to have read Benoit in this way.

In defense of their interpretation, the authors cite part of a paragraph from an article published by Benoit in 1978. They seem, however, to have stopped reading that article just at the point where their quotation ends, for had they continued one sentence further, they would have seen that Benoit rejected the findings of his own data and argued for a positive association between defense burden and the rate of economic growth. There can be little doubt of Benoit's meaning either, since he went on in that article to explain briefly why he doubted that the relationship between defense burden and growth in the 1950–1965 series was spurious. He concluded: "Thus there seemed a good probability that the correlation between defense burdens and growth rates in LDCs was not only positive but strongly positive enough to make one a significant determinant of the other and to reveal the existence of direct interaction between them." Emile Benoit, "Growth and Defense in Developing Countries," *Economic Development and Cultural Change* 26 (January 1978):275. See also p. 274, for the complete quotation; Frederiksen and Looney, "Defense Expenditures," p. 634 for the partial quotation; and Nicole Ball, "Defense Expenditure and Growth: A Comment," *Armed Forces and Society* 11 (Winter 1985):291–97, for a critique of the Frederiksen and Looney argument.

One very curious aspect of Frederiksen and Looney's work is that they seem to change their interpretation of the purpose of the Benoit study to suit their readership. In *Armed Forces and Society,* they refer to Benoit's "examination of the effect defense spending has on economic growth." In the *Journal of Economic Development,* they claim that "while Benoit's primary purpose was to examine the effect of economic aid on the growth of Gross Domestic Product, he also calculated some simple correlation coefficients between defense spending as a percent of GDP and GDP growth" (p. 114).

Soviet Union. Had the full weight of external resources been taken into account for the resource-abundant group, it seems likely that the strength of the defense coefficient would have been reduced and that of the aid coefficient increased.

But even without the full complement of external resources, clearly the high defense burden-high economic growth relationship may only be illusory (see Figure 4-1). Boulding's review of the Benoit study from which this figure is derived, tends to be overlooked. It is, therefore, worth quoting here at some length because the Frederiksen and Looney study, having adopted Benoit's methodology and data, is open to precisely the same criticisms:

> I have one complaint to make about both the methodology and the presentation of the work, which might make some difference in the results. All the relationships explored are linear, yet it is clear from quite casual inspection that significant nonlinear relationships may be involved. The failure to perceive these perhaps arises because no diagrams are presented, neither scatter diagrams nor even quartile tables. This is perhaps one of the external diseconomies of the computer. In the days when I learned statistics from Henry Schultz and we beat out our calculations hour after hour on old hand calculators, he consoled us by saying that at least we were getting thoroughly familiar with the data. Now, of course, the computer gets familiar with the data but the investigator does not, unless he takes very special precautions. To illustrate this . . . [one can divide] the countries into four groups corresponding to the quartiles: high, medium-high, medium-low, and low for two variables, the defense burden and the rate of growth. . . . The nonlinear character of the relationship is immediately apparent. For low and medium-low rates of growth, we see a negative relationship between the rate of growth and the defense burden. . . . In the upper part of the figure, however, the positive relationship between defense burden and rate of growth becomes very clear. *If we eliminate those countries with high foreign aid . . . we see that the positive relationship between the rate of growth and the defense burden in the upper half of the diagram disappears.* There is really no relationship at all, as there are virtually equal numbers of countries in each of the boxes. There is still a negative relationship in the lower half of the figure, that is, in the low growth countries.[34]

[34] Kenneth E. Boulding, "Defense Spending: Burden or Boon?" *War/Peace Report*, 8 November 1974, pp. 19–20; emphasis added.

Additional support for the notion that linear regression analysis is not sufficiently sophis-

Not only does the Frederiksen-Looney study ignore the problems surrounding Benoit's foreign assistance variable, it also fails to provide any clear indication of the multiplicity of factors involved in the functioning of all economies, any number of which might have had as serious an effect on the development of Third World economies as security expenditure. Two broad categories of factors must be considered: those that can be incorporated into statistical analyses and those that cannot.

As far as the nonquantifiable factors are concerned, Frederiksen and Looney disregard them almost entirely. They give passing mention to "positive aspects (education, linkages with industry, etc.)" that "may play an important and positive role in increasing growth." Here they are simply following Benoit in assuming, first of all, that these factors exist in the countries in their sample and, then, that their effects will always be positive. They provide no evidence to substantiate this assertion. It is far from certain, however, that such positive effects are very widespread. Indeed, strong evidence points in the opposite direction. (These alleged positive effects will be analyzed in depth in the chapters on manpower and military-led industrialization.) In the case of military-led industrialization, for example, even today only a handful of developing countries have invested heavily enough in domestic arms industries to have reasonable expectations of positive spinoffs. In the period under consideration by Frederiksen and Looney, military industries in the Third World were much less developed, and the opportunities for spinoff were smaller still. What is more, the potential negative impact of security expenditure in this and other areas is never even mentioned by Frederiksen and Looney. One possible negative effect of military-led industrialization would, for example, be the orientation of a country's industrial sector toward capital-intensive

---

ticated to capture the complexity of the defense burden–economic growth relationship comes from work undertaken by Deger and Smith at the University of London. They examined fifty developing countries (Benoit's forty-four plus six others) between 1965 and 1973; see note 16 above. They divided the countries into high-, middle-, and low-income groups. (High income is per capita income over $375, middle income is per capita income between $201 and $375, and low income is per capita income of $200 or less.) Their results were:

A simple specification where growth is allowed to depend on *only* military expenditure is shown initially. For the high income countries the effect of military expenditure on growth is significantly positive, for middle income countries the effect is negative and significant at the 10% level and for low income countries it is negative but not significantly different from zero.

However, this simple regression does not allow for feedbacks, simultaneity or other influences on growth. When the complete system given by equations (11), (12) and (13) is estimated separately for the three groups of countries, the total multiplier is negative in each case. (p. 349)

production processes and products not most urgently required by the large majority of the country's population.

With regard to the quantifiable factors, a comparison of the model produced by Frederiksen and Looney with that employed by Deger and Smith shows clearly that the former is considerably less sophisticated and takes into account far fewer variables than the latter. Frederiksen and Looney rely on linear regression analysis involving civilian economic growth as the dependent variable and the investment rate, bilateral aid, and average annual defense expenditure as the independent variables. Deger and Smith employ a "three-question simultaneous system," where economic growth rate, national savings ratios, and share of military expenditure in GDP are the three dependent variables. Each of these appears as independent variables as well, along with external capital flows, population growth, per capita income, growth of agricultural product, price changes, total population, and two dummy variables (one for the oil-exporting countries and one for countries with war economies).[35] Although even more complex models, such as those employed by Deger and Smith or the MIT team, do not and cannot include all influences on economic growth, they at least reflect more of the complexity of the growth–defense burden relationship than the models used by Benoit and by Frederiksen and Looney.

---

[35] The Deger and Smith model is:

$$g = -(\alpha_0\delta - \alpha_4) + \alpha_0 v_1 s + \alpha_0 v_2 a + \alpha_1 p + \alpha_2 m - \alpha_3 y + \alpha_5 r$$
$$s = (1 - \beta_0) + \beta_1 g + \beta_2 yg - (1 - \beta_3)m - \beta_4 a + \beta_5 p$$
$$m = \gamma_0 + \gamma_1 y + \gamma_2(q - y) + \gamma_3 N + \gamma_4 D_1 + \gamma_5 D_2$$

g = average annual growth rate of real GDP
s = national savings ratio
a = net external capital flows as a percentage of GDP
m = share of military expenditure in GDP
p = rate of growth of population
y = 1970 per capita income at official exchange rates
r = average annual growth rate of agricultural product
p = rate of change of aggregate price level per annum
q = 1970 per capita income at purchasing power parity
N = total population
D2 = dummy for Israel, Jordan, South Vietnam, Egypt, Syria, India, Pakistan (war economies)
D1 = dummy for Iran, Iraq, Libya, Saudi Arabia (oil-exporting countries)
Deger and Smith, "Military Expenditure," pp. 340–45.

Similarly, the model produced by the MIT research team was more complex than the Frederiksen-Looney model. The MIT model included growth rate of GDP as the dependent variable and growth rate of exports, growth rate of population, change in share of arms spending in GDP, change in capital inflows from abroad, growth rate of capital stock, and GDP per capita as independent variables.
Faini, Arnez, and Taylor, "Defense Spending" (1980), pp. 3–6.

CHAPTER 4

Frederiksen and Looney described the main findings of their study:

Defense expenditures in countries that are relatively resource constrained compete less for scarce resources. As a result of their other
positive aspects (education, linkages with industry, etc.), defense expenditures may play an important and positive role in increasing
growth. Countries suffering from a relative lack of foreign exchange
and government revenues, on the other hand, experience the reverse.
For these countries, defense expenditures apparently siphon funds
away from more productive investments with a subsequent detrimental effect on growth.[36]

In assuming that more defense expenditure means less productive investment and thus less growth for resource constrained countries, these
researchers have simplified the growth–investment–military expenditures relationship to an unrealistic extent. There can be no doubt that in
some cases more security expenditure means less investment. (The relationship between savings and investment, on the one hand, and security
expenditure, on the other hand, is also discussed in Chapter 5.) Additional support for this argument comes from Lance Taylor and his associates at MIT in the early 1980s; this econometric study demonstrated a
negative association between defense burden and investment as a share of
gross domestic product for forty-six developing countries between 1952
and 1970 (see Appendix 3 and the discussion below). Table 4-1, however,
which compares the share of gross domestic investment (GDI) and security expenditure (milex) in gross domestic product (GDP) between 1955
and 1977 for twenty-six countries, demonstrates that the relationship between these two variables is far from uniform. In some cases, a declining
trend in the GDI/GDP ratio is associated with a rising trend in the milex/
GDP ratio (for example, Iraq, 1955–1970). In others, a decline in the
milex/GDP ratio is associated with a rise in GDI/GDP (Venezuela, 1960–
1977). Not infrequently, however, the two indicators move in the same
direction (Syria, 1965–1977).

Several countries in Table 4-1 are included in the Frederiksen and Looney sample, and it is interesting to compare the information in this table
with the results of their work. In a number of the resource-unconstrained
countries (marked with a U in the table), the GDI/GDP ratio increases at
the same time as a large portion of GDP is devoted to the security sector
(Iran, 1960–1977, and Malaysia, 1960–1977). In some of the resource-
constrained countries (marked with a C), the two variables move in oppo-

[36] Frederiksen and Looney, "Defense Expenditures," p. 643.

site directions (Philippines, 1955–1965). These patterns of association are predicted by the Frederiksen-Looney model. But in other cases, resource-constrained countries are able to increase the shares of *both* security expenditure *and* gross domestic investment in GDP (India, 1955–1965, and Sudan, 1955–1970), just the opposite of the predicted relationship.

The importance of unquantifiable factors in determining investment levels is illustrated by Burkina Faso, a country not included in Frederiksen and Looney's sample but without a doubt resource-constrained. According to the World Bank, Burkina Faso's per capita income in 1982 was $210 and had grown by about 1 percent annually between 1970 and 1982. Agriculture, which employed some 85 percent of the population at the end of the 1970s, grew by nearly 1.5 percent each year between 1970 and 1982. Burkina Faso's population, however, grew by 2 percent annually, which meant that per capita agricultural output actually declined. Over the same period, the armed forces absorbed an increasingly large portion of state resources. In the early 1970s, about 10 percent of the budget was allocated to the military. Since 1975, that proportion has risen significantly to on average 20 percent.[37] It would be wrong, however, to attribute Burkina Faso's economic crisis solely to this rise in security spending.

Three élite groups—the army, the patrons of the political parties, and the members of the public employee unions—have absorbed a very large portion of the country's limited resources. Almost nothing has been left either for the majority of the population or for investment purposes. In 1979, more than three-quarters of the budget was allocated to personnel costs.[38] To make matters worse, the government of Burkina Faso has controlled a rather small amount of gross domestic product, even in comparison with other poor West African countries. In 1977, for example, Burkina Faso's public expenditure: gross domestic product (at market prices) ratio was 15.4 percent. In Sierra Leone that ratio was 24.2 percent; in Senegal, 20.4 percent; in Mali, 20.1 percent; and in Togo, 33 percent. The amount of gross domestic investment (GDI) financed by gross national savings (GNS) during the 1960s and 1970s was no more than 27 percent. Again, even among poor West African countries, that is a rather low proportion. Togo, Sierra Leone, and Senegal, for example, all had

---

[37] World Bank, *World Development Report 1984* (New York: Oxford University Press, 1984), pp. 218, 330, 254, and U.S. Arms Control and Disarmament Agency, *World Military Expenditures and Arms Transfers, 1972–1982*, Publication 117 (Washington, D.C.: ACDA, April 1984), p. 49.

[38] Howard Schissel, "Six Months into Sankara's Revolution," *Africa Report*, March–April 1984, pp. 16–19.

TABLE 4-1
Gross Domestic Investment and Security Expenditure,
1955–1977 (in percentage GDP)

Country	1955	1960	1965	1970	1977
AFRICA					
Bénin					
GDI	—	15.0	11.5	15.2	20.2
Milex	—	1.3[a]	2.2	2.1	1.8
Burundi					
GDI	—	6.3	5.8	6.3	12.3
Milex	—	—	1.4	1.5	2.5
Cameroon					
GDI	—	10.6	15.1	14.9	21.7
Milex	—	—	2.3	1.9	1.5
Central African Republic					
GDI	—	19.6	21.4	18.9	22.5
Milex	—	0.7[a]	1.3	2.4	—
Ethiopia					
GDI	—	11.5	13.3	11.5	8.9
Milex	—	1.7	3.2	1.9	4.0
Ivory Coast					
GDI	—	14.6	19.0	22.1	27.3
Milex	—	0.6[a]	1.3	1.2	0.8
Kenya					
GDI	—	—	14.4	24.4	21.2
Milex	—	—	1.0	1.1	3.3
Mauritania					
GDI	—	37.4	16.3	20.5	51.8
Milex	—	2.3[a]	1.4	1.4	11.6
Nigeria (U)					
GDI	—	13.2	18.3	14.9	31.1
Milex	—	0.5	0.8	5.7	4.0
Sudan (C)					
GDI	3.8	8.6	9.1	10.3	15.3
Milex	1.0[b]	1.6	3.0	4.4	2.6
Upper Volta					
GDI	—	9.5	9.7	11.4	25.1
Milex	—	0.7	1.5	1.3	2.9
Zambia					
GDI	25.3	23.9	24.7	27.1	25.9
Milex	—	1.1	1.8	1.8	10.0

(TABLE 4-1 CONT.)

Country	1955	1960	1965	1970	1977
MIDDLE EAST					
Iran (U)					
GDI	11.0	17.4	17.3	18.9	33.4
Milex	—	4.2	4.7	6.3	10.5
Iraq					
GDI	19.4	20.0	15.7	15.8	—
Milex	4.1	7.1	8.8	11.2	10.4
Syria					
GDI	—	—	10.5	15.4	39.3
Milex	—	—	7.9	11.9	15.3
ASIA					
Burma					
GDI	14.2	12.0	18.7	14.2	14.1
Milex	5.9	6.0	6.6	5.7	4.0
India (C)					
GDI	13.7	17.2	18.4	18.6	21.3
Milex	1.7	1.9	3.6	3.0	2.7
Malaysia (U)					
GDI	9.9	14.1	18.2	19.9	23.3
Milex	3.2	2.2	2.9	4.1	4.7
Pakistan					
GDI	—	11.6	21.5	15.8	18.8
Milex	3.1	2.8	4.0	3.8	5.4
Philippines (C)					
GDI	14.6	16.0	20.8	21.2	28.8
Milex	1.8	1.5	1.1	1.2	3.2
LATIN AMERICA					
Argentina (C)					
GDI	17.7	21.5	19.2	20.4	19.1
Milex	2.2	2.3	1.8	1.9	2.4
Bolivia					
GDI	—	13.8	15.8	16.9	22.1
Milex	—	1.1	2.5	1.6	2.1
Brazil					
GDI[c]	14.9	22.1	18.4	22.3	21.9
Milex	2.3	2.0	2.5	1.9	1.1
Colombia (U)					
GDI	18.0	20.5	17.7	22.0	20.5
Milex	2.1	1.2	2.0	1.4	0.8

(TABLE 4-1 CONT.)

Country	1955	1960	1965	1970	1977
LATIN AMERICA					
Guatemala (U)					
GDI	11.6	10.3	13.3	12.8	20.9
Milex	1.0	0.9	1.1	1.5	1.4
Mexico (C)					
GDI	18.1	19.7	21.7	22.4	20.5
Milex	0.6	0.7	0.7	0.7	0.5
Paraguay					
GDI	11.6	16.9	15.1	14.7	24.7
Milex	—	1.8 [a]	1.7	2.0	1.6
Venezuela (U)					
GDI	29.1	20.6	23.6	27.9	39.6
Milex	1.9	2.1	2.0	1.7	1.6

Sources: GDI: World Bank, *World Tables* 2d ed. (New York: Oxford University Press, 1980), pp. 384, 386. Military expenditure: Stockholm International Peace Research Institute, *World Armament and Disarmament, SIPRI Yearbook 1976, 1978* and *1983* (Stockholm: Almqvist & Wiksell, 1976 and 1978) (London: Taylor & Francis, 1983).

Resource classification: P. C. Frederiksen and Robert E. Looney, "Defense Expenditures and Economic Growth in Developing Countries," *Armed Forces and Society* 9 (Summer 1983): 633–45.

Note: Figures for those countries marked (C) indicate resource-constrained, according to Frederiksen and Looney, and those marked (U) indicate resource-unconstrained.

[a] Data from 1961.

[b] Data from 1956.

[c] Gross Domestic Fixed Investment.

GNS/GDI ratios during these two decades which ranged between 50 and 80 percent.[39]

Undoubtedly, the armed forces absorb a large portion of state resources

[39] Richard Vengroff, "Soldiers and Civilians in the Third Republic," *Africa Report,* January–February 1980, pp. 6–8; World Bank, *World Tables,* 2d ed. (Baltimore, Md.: Johns Hopkins University Press, 1980), pp. 133, 171, 173, 197, 207; and International Monetary Fund, *Government Finance Statistics Yearbook,* vol. 4 (Washington, D.C.: IMF, 1980): 350, 472, 480, 559.

In August 1983, Captain Thomas Sankara led a coup which had as one of its goals the emasculation of Burkina Faso's traditional elites. The Sankara government did pursue an anticorruption campaign under which some 100 former officials had been tried, and in some cases acquitted, by 1985. What the developmental and political legacy of the Sankara government will be is unclear, however, since it was overthrown in October 1987. It seems possible that Sankara's efforts to replace the former ruling groups provided at least some of the impetus for his overthrow.

in Burkina Faso, and this factor impedes economic growth and development in that country; however, it is not the only impediment. The Burkinan élites' lack of commitment to serious development planning and their concern to guarantee their own economic security has been of greater importance in determining the country's growth record than the level or rate of growth of security expenditure. Given the political situation in the country, increased expenditure on the armed forces has occurred not so much at the expense of investment as at the expense of recurrent expenditures while *all* recurrent spending competes with investment.

All this indicates that researchers should anticipate considerable variation from one country to the next and that domestic political structures are extremely important in explaining how different variables interact with each other. Cross-national aggregate analyses are designed to minimize variations and pick out similarities and cannot incorporate political variables. It is thus open to question just how much can be learned from studies employing this methodology.

BOTH the Benoit and the Frederiksen-Looney studies demonstrate particularly well the care with which statistical techniques must be applied to Third World economic systems, the dangers inherent in overgeneralization, and the degree to which the results of such analyses can be manipulated to suit the purposes of the investigator. Boulding has pointed out that

> all knowledge, and even perception, is gained by the orderly loss of information, and that the abstractions which are involved in quantification are often necessary in the reduction of information to manageable proportions.
>
> The fact that quantification does involve large reductions of information, however, should never be forgotten. Quantification should never be regarded as an end in itself. Statistical significance is a mere milestone on the road to epistemological significance, which is something much more fundamental. The critical question is, "When we have a number do we know any more than we did before we had it?" and the answer is often, "Yes, but not very much." . . . There is always a danger . . . particularly with well-trained social scientists, that the training is in the rituals of the craft and that epistemological significance may sometimes be submerged in the sheer delight of statistical numerology.[40]

Statistical analyses can suggest the types of relationships that should be investigated in more detail in case studies, but they can never be a sub-

---

[40]Boulding, "'Thirsting for the Testable,'" pp. 8–9.

CHAPTER 4

stitute for a thorough-going historical examination of the economic and political systems of individual countries.[41] Ideally, macrostatistical studies—both cross-sectional and longitudinal—should be combined with case studies to determine the extent to which models derived from statistical analysis reflect reality. Having adopted this approach, however, a researcher must be willing to accept information from the case studies which apparently contradicts the findings of the statistical analyses as well as the fact the more case studies undertaken, the greater the likelihood that diversity, rather than conformity, of experience will be the rule of the day. If a researcher cannot do either of these things, the value of the case studies is entirely lost.

Benoit, for example, supplemented his statistical analyses with a half-dozen case studies. The one on India, the most detailed, was considered particularly important as it suggested or confirmed many of the hypotheses Benoit tested in the course of his macrostatistical analyses. Of special interest was the fact that two years of sharp rises in defense expenditure (1961–1963), which resulted from deteriorating relations with China, and the Sino-Indian border war were associated—with a one-year lag—with two years of significant increases in civilian GDP (1962–1964). To Benoit, this apparent correlation exemplified the connection seemingly revealed in the initial simple regression analysis: Higher levels of defense expenditure were linked to higher rates of economic growth.

Benoit was thus able to incorporate information from the case studies which supported his contention that military expenditure had a positive effect on economic growth. He was less successful in incorporating results contradictory to his main thesis. In the case study of Mexico, Benoit concluded that a very low level of military expenditure had contributed to Mexican economic growth primarily because the military program had *not* siphoned off considerable industrial-type resources and foreign exchange from the civilian sector and because the military had contributed to "maintaining public order . . . with the minimum use of scarce resources." Interestingly for someone who had spent some 200 pages explaining why there was a positive association between high defense burdens and high rates of economic growth, Benoit stated, "This does not imply, however, that if the defense program had been larger, it would have been still more favorable to growth. On the contrary, the main reason it appears to have had a net favorable effect is that it has been so small and economical in its use of resources."[42]

[41] Even extremely detailed macrostatistical studies of individual countries must be tested against historical realities. The most detailed macroeconomic study of the effect of military expenditure on the economy of a developing country is Fontanel, "Formalized Studies."
[42] Benoit, "Defense and Economic Growth," p. 230.

154

The importance of foreign aid as an autonomous factor in the security expenditure–economic growth equation was given additional support by the case studies on India, Israel, South Korea, and Mexico. In the case of India, aid valued at about three and one-half times the amount of additional money expended on the armed forces was received in the 1962–1965 period due to the conflict with China. For South Korea, "Militarily motivated aid has . . . been a key element in the Korean success story. It explains how South Korea could combine a very high level of defense expenditure despite a very low average income, a little higher than that of India, and with natural resources far poorer than India's— yet end up with a growth rate of civilian output almost double that of India (6.23 compared to 3.20)."[43]

Israel, Benoit pointed out, received external resources worth 14 percent of its GDP between 1950 and 1965. Since the defense sector absorbed on average some 6 percent of GDP during the same period, security expenditure was more than offset by the inflow of foreign resources. The Mexican case was exactly the reverse. Mexico was never a recipient of a large amount of aid, and Benoit concluded that an increase in military expenditure would probably not be matched by "a large increase in foreign aid to offset the real cost of a rise in defense expenditures, as did India. . . . Thus, Mexico would probably not have *the important external resources offset to an enlarged defense expenditure which has been characteristically associated with the combination of high defense burdens and rapid growth rates in other countries.*"[44]

Benoit also had difficulty in accepting the variety of experiences recorded by the different case studies.

That there is an extraordinary diversity not only in the surrounding circumstances but—as we shall see—in the dynamic interaction between defense and development in LDCs is the chief single conclusion of our country studies. This conclusion tends to support the need for statistical analysis of a wider sample such as we have presented in earlier chapters, since the bewildering variety of situations encountered in individual cases will not readily lead to clear-out uniform conclusions on the basis of what happened in particular cases.[45]

To some extent Benoit's problem was not the lack of "clear-out uniform conclusions" since, as has just been shown, the importance of foreign as-

[43] Ibid., p. 250. Regarding India, see p. 178.

[44] Ibid., p. 231; emphasis added. In this regard it is interesting to note that Benoit remarked a bit further on in this discussion that "All the other countries in the top-growth quartile, except Mexico, benefited from really large inflows of external resources (measured in relation to GNP)" (p. 231). On Israel, see p. 255.

[45] Ibid., p. 222.

CHAPTER 4

sistance as an autonomous factor was evident from several of the case studies. His problem was rather that he wanted to prove that defense expenditures were growth-inducing in developing countries, and he went to considerable lengths in his statistical analyses to downgrade the importance of foreign aid and expand the influence of the defense burden.

At the same time it is necessary to ask to what degree "clear-out conclusions" can be expected to emerge from analyses of countries which exhibit "extraordinary diversity . . . in the dynamic interaction between defense and development." As Boulding rightly pointed out, some information must be eliminated when comparisons are made. Every available piece of information about a country cannot be incorporated into cross-national analyses whatever methodology may be employed. In addition, certain similarities *do* exist among developing countries. Most are, for example, highly sensitive to changes in the international environment. High rates of un- and underemployment are common. Many Third World economies depend on a very small number of commodities for a large portion of their foreign exchange earnings, and so on. It is not unreasonable to think that Third World economies might be affected in a similar manner by certain factors, such as security expenditure.

Yet, to anyone who has any understanding of how the development process functions, clearly it is both extremely difficult to reduce this process to a few equations and extremely unlikely that very many "clear-out conclusions" *should* be anticipated. The use of econometric techniques to examine the relationship between economic growth and security expenditures has been popular because it enables researchers to survey simultaneously many countries. Even the more sophisticated of these studies, however, such as those carried out by Deger and Smith, assign physical capital a central role in explanations of growth. In part this derives from the fact that problems such as efficient use of resources can be addressed only if the resources are available in the first place and that countries in the Third World tend to operate under severe financial constraints.

Perhaps more important, however, is the fact that macrostatistical models can only incorporate quantifiable variables. Factors amenable to quantification such as rate of growth of gross product, savings, inflow of foreign capital, investment rate, and inflation can thus be included. Non-quantifiable factors such as the nature of expenditure on the civilian portion of the public sector, the type (not simply volume) of investment undertaken, the quality and availability of trained manpower, the interest of the political leadership in promoting development, and the influence of corruption on political and economic systems may be crucial in determining how efficiently and effectively available physical capital is employed. It is, however, impossible to measure these factors in such a way that they can be included in econometric analyses.

Some researchers, for example Deger and Smith, recognize that these unquantifiable variables are of considerable importance in explaining whether and how growth occurs and if and how growth is translated into development. Yet they and all econometricians are required to rely on the quantifiable variables in their analyses.[46] Statistical analyses can, therefore, suggest what associations might be important, but they can never offer a definitive explanation of developmental successes and failures.

[46] Deger and Smith, "Military Expenditure," pp. 339, 344. Deger and Smith did attempt to include in their model not only the influence of the availability of capital on growth but also the effect of labor inputs and factor productivity. Because of data constraints, it was necessary for them to accept data which approximated the indicators chosen rather than measured them directly. Although this is more than most macrostatistical analyses of the security expenditure–growth relationship attempt to do, it is highly doubtful that adequate weight has been given to those difficult-to-quantify variables.

PART II

Security Expenditure and Development

5

....

SECURITY SPENDING

AND THE AVAILABILITY

OF RESOURCES

Prior to the Korean War, it was widely believed that high levels of expenditure on the armed forces were not compatible with high rates of economic growth. Rather, it was argued that the sustained allocation of a larger share of a country's resources to the security sector could produce "declining civilian consumption, lost economic growth, runaway inflation, and the necessity of onerous controls."[1] At the beginning of 1950, a debate began within the United States government about the need to rearm to counter an international situation which some members of the Truman administration believed threatened the United States. Although the debate focused primarily on strategic considerations, it did include a discussion of the effects that a substantial increase in military expenditure would have on the U.S. economy.

On one side of the debate were those who argued that World War II had demonstrated that "the American economy, when it operates at a level approaching full efficiency, can provide enormous resources for purposes other than civilian consumption while simultaneously providing a high standard of living." Given the recessionary tendencies characterizing the U.S. economy in 1950, it was argued that military expenditure could stimulate the economy by increasing capacity utilization without necessitating a reduction in living standards because the increases in gross product generated by military spending might more than offset the higher expenditure on the armed forces. On the other side of the debate were those who argued that, although the U.S. economy might have been able to sustain a high level of security expenditure for a relatively short period of time during World War II without serious long-term effects on the

[1]Hugh G. Mosley, *The Arms Race: Economic and Social Consequences* (Lexington, Mass.: Lexington Books, 1985), p. 5.

economy, it was far less certain that it could do so for a much longer period. Among the anticipated negative effects were lower rates of investment and reductions in public outlays for social and economic development of great importance for the continued strength of the economy.[2]

As it happened, the outbreak of the Korean War in June 1950 and the intervention of the Chinese government in that conflict enabled the advocates of higher military expenditure to prevail, ushering in the era of what has been termed "military Keynesianism." It became the conventional wisdom that expenditure in the security sector would promote economic prosperity. Some Marxist economists have gone so far as to claim that military expenditure is necessary for the successful functioning of advanced, capitalist economies.[3] Other analysts have maintained that, while not necessary for the survival of these economies, spending in the security sector creates well-paying jobs, increases demand for a wide variety of services and manufactured goods, and promotes technological progress.

Today the existence of a positive relationship between security expenditure and economic growth in the industrialized countries is once again being questioned. All security expenditure has an opportunity cost: Once money is allocated to the armed forces, it cannot be spent for any other purpose. Research carried out during the 1970s suggests that rapid economic growth, investment, employment, and productivity growth are inversely related to high levels of military expenditure in the OECD countries.[4] It has taken longer to disprove the belief in the net positive effects

[2] See *Foreign Relations of the United States, 1950, Volume 1* (Washington, D.C.: Government Printing Office, 1977), pp. 258, 286, 304–5; quotation from p. 286. This debate is described in Mosley, *The Arms Race*, pp. 7–12.

[3] Examples of the Marxist literature on the defense expenditure–economic growth connection in the United States are: M. Reich, "Does the US Economy Require Military Spending?" *American Economic Review* 62 (May 1972): 296–303, and R. B. DuBoff, "Converting Military Spending to Social Welfare: The Real Obstacles," *The Quarterly Review of Economic and Business* 12 (Spring 1972): 7–22. In general, articles of this nature fail to prove their contentions.

[4] The negative consequences of security expenditure for the economies of industrialized countries are discussed in Robert W. DeGrasse, Jr., *Military Expansion, Economic Decline* (New York: Council on Economic Priorities, 1983), esp. chap. 2; Ron P. Smith, "Military Expenditure and Capitalism," *Cambridge Journal of Economics* (March 1977): 61–76; Kurt W. Rothschild, "Military Expenditures, Exports and Growth," *Kyklos* 26 (1973): 804–15; Michael Boretsky, "Trends in US Technology: A Political Economist's View," *American Scientist* 63 (January–February 1975): 70–82; and Seymour Melman, *The Permanent War Economy* (New York: Touchstone, Simon & Schuster, 1974). A useful summary of the recent debate is found in Steve Chan, "The Impact of Defense Spending on Economic Performance: A Survey of Evidence and Problems," *Orbis* 29 (Summer 1985): 403–34.

It is important to understand that the results of studies based on cross-sectional techniques have sometimes been contradicted by those based on longitudinal techniques.

of security expenditure in developing countries. In fact, it has been easier for many people to accept that the military and civil sectors compete for material, financial, and human resources in the industrialized countries of East and West than in the developing countries. The latter typically experience shortages of growth-promoting resources such as foreign exchange, capital, skilled labor, and technology. If security expenditure were to increase the supply of such resources to the economy, it would by definition be considered to have increased the growth potential of the economy. The question of whether these resources might be more productively or efficiently used in the civil sector is important, but it is not the only one. Perhaps in the absence of expenditure in the security sector, these resources would be consumed wastefully, remain idle, or be invested abroad, none of which would promote growth in the domestic economy.[5]

Recent econometric research suggests that security expenditure has a negative effect on economic growth in developing countries, either because security spending competes with investment (the state being an important source of investment funds in many Third World countries) or because it dampens the savings rate (which in turn affects investment). As explained in Chapter 4, this offers a starting point for evaluating the economic effect of security expenditure, but it does not describe the relationship in specific countries. Deviations from the norm are to be expected. Indeed, this was one of the more significant findings in the UN study on the relationship between disarmament and development: "An important respect in which the reports commissioned by the Group go farther than

---

International comparisons seem to support the notion that high defense spending retards productivity growth. Advanced industrial nations that have experienced relatively high growth since 1950, such as Japan and Germany, have devoted a smaller share of their output to defense than have nations that have experienced relatively slow rates of productivity growth, such as the United States and the United Kingdom. Time series data on productivity, however, do not support this hypothesis. Productivity growth in the United States and other industrialized countries has slowed while defense had commanded a shrinking share of resources.

United States Congress, Congressional Budget Office, *Defense Spending and the Economy* (Washington, D.C.: Government Printing Office, February 1983), pp. 38–39.

In this regard, the importance of governmental priorities should not be underrated. Japanese governments have not only chosen to devote a much smaller share of Japan's gross national product to the security sector than the United States, but they have also followed policies which specifically promote civil-sector investment and research and development. In addition to spending a much larger portion of the national product in the security sector, U.S. economic tradition allows for considerably less governmental involvement and guidance, except of course in the defense-industrial sector.

[5] See, for example, the discussion on pages 198–204 in Gavin Kennedy, *Defense Economics* (London: Duckworth, 1983).

many already available on the subject is the emphasis placed on the individual character of the experience of different developing countries in calculating the opportunity costs of military spending and identifying any causal linkages or definitive relationships between their military expenditure on the one hand and socio-economic problems on the other."[6]

Another important point must be taken into account when the results of these macrostatistical analyses are evaluated. Expenditure in the security sector can affect growth rates in two broad ways: its effect on the availability of resources and its influence on the efficiency with which resources are used. It was shown in Chapter 4 that econometric analyses of the security expenditure—economic growth relationship in the Third World of necessity concentrate on the allocation of financial resources, specifically on the association between security-related outlays on the one hand and savings and investment rates and the availability of foreign exchange on the other hand. Many other factors must, however, be taken into account when analysing the effect security expenditure has on economic growth. This is illustrated by the following exposition of the major determinants of the rapid growth experienced by South Korea since the mid-1960s.

> The main constraints on growth are savings and foreign exchange. The factors that foster rapid growth are those that sustain and complement heavy investment demand, those that increase the requisite supply of savings, those that earn the foreign exchange needed when the level of effective demand is high, and, finally those that foster efficient resource allocation, evidenced by a very low incremental capital-output ratio. . . .
>
> In addition to these factors, which in varying degrees influence the growth of most developing countries, there are some that are peculiar to Korea . . . [which have] contributed to a favorable environment for investors and helped sustain brisk investment demand. For example, the work force in Korea is highly educated. . . .
>
> South Korea also has an abundant supply of entrepreneurial and managerial expertise. . . .
>
> Another advantage favoring Korea's economic development was the political stability that prevailed during the period of most rapid growth. Park Chung Hee has made economic development the symbol of his government's legitimacy. His efforts have been aided by Korea's cultural homogeneity. . . .

[6]United Nations, General Assembly, "Study on the Relationship Between Disarmament and Development, Report of the Secretary-General," A/36/356, 5 October 1981, mimeograph, p. 91. (Hereafter, cited as A/36/356.)

South Korean development has also benefited from the weakness of the labor movement. . . . Because the labor force is docile and unaccustomed to collective bargaining, upward pressure on wages is negligible except when manpower is scarce. Stable real wage rates helped to keep profits high and to stimulate investment demand.

Finally, ties with Japan encouraged growth. . . . The Koreans adopted the technology, the approach to labor relations, the expansionary psychology, and many of the government policies that had worked so well for the Japanese. As a result, the emphasis on export promotion, the system of trade and foreign exchange controls, and the close cooperation between the public and private sectors that are reputed to be characteristic of Japan alone are typical of South Korea as well.[7]

This chapter will examine how security expenditure might increase or decrease the financial resources available to the civil sector of the economy. The influence of security expenditure on resource availability will be evaluated by considering its effect on savings and investment, inflation, taxation, and the balance of payments. In Chapter 6, some insights into the relationship between security expenditure and the efficient use of resources will be provided through an examination of the interaction between security spending and aggregate demand, absorptive capacity, and the nature of investment.

RESOURCE AVAILABILITY

In countries where the public sector plays a central role in the economy—that is, in very many Third World countries—the potential of state expenditure to influence growth and development is correspondingly large. In common with other forms of public expenditure, outlays in the security sector can both promote and hinder economic growth. They will tend to encourage economic growth, for example, if they use resources that were previously idle or if the balance between resources consumed and resources invested is altered in favor of investment. To the extent that expenditure in the security sector contributes to inflation-promoting budget deficits or reduces the rate of saving, it will hinder economic growth.

The dominant development strategy anticipates that Third World economies will evolve in essentially the same way that the industrialized econo-

[7]Charles R. Frank, Jr., Kwang Suk Kim, and Larry E. Westphal, *South Korea* (New York: National Bureau of Economic Research, 1975), pp. 225–27. See also David C. Cole and Princeton N. Lyman, *Korean Development: The Interplay of Politics and Economics* (Cambridge, Mass.: Harvard University Press, 1971), pp. 198–202.

mies of the West are believed to have developed. Capital-intensive investment, particularly (indeed almost exclusively) in the urban-industrial sector, is said to spur economic growth by raising the productivity of Third World labor. Foreign exchange must be available in sufficiently large quantities to enable the developing countries to purchase the necessary intermediate and capital goods from abroad. It was originally believed that foreign exchange gaps would be filled by foreign assistance but, as will be discussed in more detail in Chapter 7, this expectation has not been fulfilled. As a result, commercial borrowing has become more and more important. The three most commonly cited "main barriers to growth" are "investment, saving and foreign exchange constraints."[8]

Savings and Investment

In view of the centrality accorded savings and investment in development strategies during the last four decades, it is not surprising that they have received considerable attention in evaluations of the relationship between security expenditure and economic growth. Most analysts agree that if security expenditure reduces the resources available for savings and investment, the effect on economic growth is likely to be negative. Although investment is far from being the sole, or even the most important, source of increased labor productivity and hence economic growth, investment is necessary for growth to occur. In many developing countries, the government is an important source of investment financing because of the weakness of domestic private capital. Government outlays on noninvestment items in these countries may thus compete with total national investment to a greater degree than they would in countries where the role of the private sector is relatively greater.

In most developing countries, a large portion of total investment is financed out of national savings; if it can be shown that security expenditure hinders saving then it is possible that security spending will also inhibit growth. Security expenditure may also compete to some extent with investment goods for scarce foreign exchange as will be explained in the following section. With regard to savings, researchers at the University of London have found that higher rates of security expenditure were associated with lower rates of saving (total saving/GDP) for fifty developing countries in the 1965–1973 period. Similarly, researchers at MIT discovered a negative association between the amount of GDP devoted to the security sector and the amount of GDP devoted to investment for a sample

[8] Cole and Lyman, *Korean Development*, p. 198.

of forty-six developing countries between 1952 and 1970.[9] Both studies identified a negative relationship between rate of economic growth and share of defense in GDP, concluding that this relationship was determined at least in part by the negative relationships between security expenditure and savings, on the one hand, and investment, on the other hand.

The problem with these studies, as with all macrostatistical analyses, is that their findings do not actually apply to each country in the sample. In the MIT study, seven of the forty-six countries surveyed showed a significant negative relationship between the two variables and another seven showed a marginally significant negative relationship. Three countries showed a significant positive relationship (that is, higher defense burdens were associated with higher rates of investment), and one country showed a marginally significant positive relationship. Of the remaining twenty-eight countries, twelve had nonsignificant relationships, and sixteen had nonsignificant positive relationships. The MIT researchers commented that, "For specific countries, the cross-sectional results carry over as strongly as might be expected in this type of regression"[10] (Figure 5-1).

It is true that the MIT data show that more countries tend to experience lower investment rates as they spend more on the security sector, but some do not. Furthermore, for the majority of countries in the sample, no strong relationship is evident. This agrees with the data shown in Table 4-1. Variation must be anticipated from one country to another and over time within the same country. The MIT researchers themselves point out that "Cross-country results of the type described here . . . cannot isolate the specific mechanisms via which shifts in defense spending (or any other variable) affect the economic structure in a particular country."[11] Nor can these results be taken to indicate causality.

Consider the example of Peru where, according to the MIT study, higher defense burdens were associated with lower rates of investment between 1952 and 1970. As Figure 5-2 shows, security expenditure rose for much

[9]Saadet Deger and Ron Smith, "Military Expenditure and Growth in Less Developed Countries," *The Journal of Conflict Resolution* 27 (June 1983): 344–46; Saadet Deger, *Investment, Defence and Growth in Less Developed Countries,* Birkbeck College Discussion Paper no. 105 (London: Department of Economics, Birkbeck College, October 1981); Riccardo Faini, Patricia Arnez, and Lance Taylor, "Defense Spending, Economic Structure & Growth: Evidence Among Countries and Over Time" (Cambridge, Mass.: MIT, October 1980, mimeograph), p. 13, and Faini, Arnez, and Taylor, "Defense Spending, Economic Structure and Growth: Evidence Among Countries and Over Time," *Economic Development and Cultural Change* 32:3 (1984): 494–95.

[10]Faini, Arnez, and Taylor, "Defense Spending" (1980), p. 13, and personal communication from Lance Taylor, 23 March 1984.

[11]Faini, Arnez, and Taylor, "Defense Spending" (1980), pp. 15–16.

NEGATIVE		POSITIVE
South Korea		Bolivia
Nigeria		Ecuador
Peru		Guatemala
Philippines	**Significant**	
Tunisia		
Egypt		
Venezuela		
[7]		[3]
Colombia		Dominican Republic
Haiti		
Jordan	**Marginally**	
El Salvador	**Significant**	
Mexico		
Thailand		
Uruguay		
[7]		[1]
Argentina		Chile
Brazil		Taiwan
Cambodia		India
Sri Lanka		Indonesia
Costa Rica		Iran
Ethiopia	**Non-significant**	Jamaica
Honduras		Kenya
Ivory Coast		Libya
Nicaragua		Malaysia
Pakistan		Morocco
Panama		Paraguay
Uganda		Saudi Arabia
		Sierra Leone
		Syria
		Tanzania
		Turkey
[12]		[16]

FIGURE 5-1

Correlation between Security Expenditure as a Share of GDP and Share
of Investment in GDP

Source: Riccardo Faini, Patricia Arnez, and Lance Taylor, "Defense Spending, Economic
Structure and Growth: Evidence Among Countries and Over Time" (Cambridge, Mass.:
MIT, October 1980, mimeograph), p. 13, and personal communication from Lance Tay-
lor, 23 March 1984.

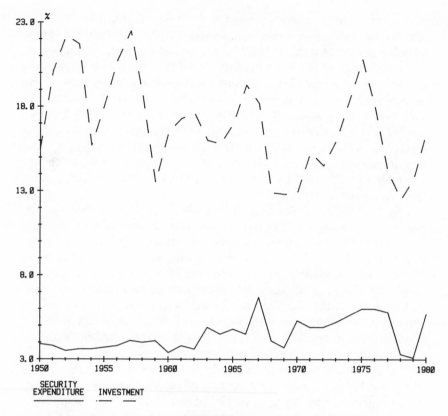

FIGURE 5-2
Peru: Shares of Investment and Security Expenditure in GDP,
1950–1980

Source: Investment/GDP: José A.Encinas del Pando, "Peru: A Case Study, 1950–1980"
(Lima: University of Peru, October 1981, mimeograph), Table 2.7.7. These are Peruvian
data and vary somewhat from World Bank data, although the trends are similar.
Security Expenditure/GDP: Nicole Ball, *Third-World Security Expenditure: A Statistical
Compendium,* C10250-M5 (Stockholm: National Defence Research Agency, 1984),
p. 239, for 1950–1979; Stockholm International Peace Research Institute, *World Armaments and Disarmament, SIPRI Yearbook 1985* (London: Taylor & Francis, 1985),
p. 284, for 1980.

of the period while the average rates of investment declined for each decade. For the 1950s, investment/GDP averaged 18.9 percent; for the 1960s, 16.3 percent; and for the 1970s, 15.7 percent. More interesting, however, is the variability of the investment/GDP ratio compared with the security expenditure/GDP ratio. The MIT study concluded that "an increase of one percentage point in the defense burden is associated with a reduction of 0.23 percentage points in the share of investment GDP." Looking at Figure 5-2 it is immediately apparent that, while changes in security expenditure may have accounted for some small portion of the variation in the investment/GDP ratio, it could scarcely have accounted for the entire variation unless the multiplier were an order of magnitude or more greater than 0.23 percent.

This is all the more true when it is recalled that prior to 1968 the private sector, including direct foreign investment, accounted for more than 70 percent of gross domestic investment (GDI) annually, with the exception of 1955 (Figure 5-3). It frequently accounted for 80 percent or more of total GDI. A small portion of the sharp drop in the public investment/GDP ratio in 1958 and 1959 could perhaps be attributed to previous increases in the share of GDP devoted to security expenditure. The primary cause, however, was the international recession, which produced a contraction in Peru's foreign trade. This in turn resulted in decreased state revenues and necessitated reduced public expenditure, particularly public investment. Similarly, the nearly 30 percent drop in GDI between 1967 and 1968 was related to a period of recession which saw a sharp drop in private-sector investment. The advent of the Revolutionary Military Government (RMG) in 1968 reinforced the disinclination of the private sector to invest, and the latter's share of GDI stagnated at a low level throughout the 1970s.[12]

It has often been suggested that the policies of the RMG under Velasco scared off private investment, but the situation was more complex than that. Even before 1968 private investment had been shifting from industry to more immediately profitable areas such as real estate.

In the 1960s, the state had already begun to increase its infrastructure provision and development loans on an insufficient savings base, leading to inflationary budget deficits and considerable foreign borrowing. After 1968 this imbalance assumed far more significance because the state became the center of accumulation—accounting for two thirds of productive investment by the 1974–1976 period—

[12] José Encinas del Pando, "Peru: A Case Study, 1960–1980" (Lima: University of Lima, October 1981, mimeograph), pp. 101–12. The quotation from the MIT study appears in Faini, Arnez, and Taylor, "Defense Spending" (1984), p. 494.

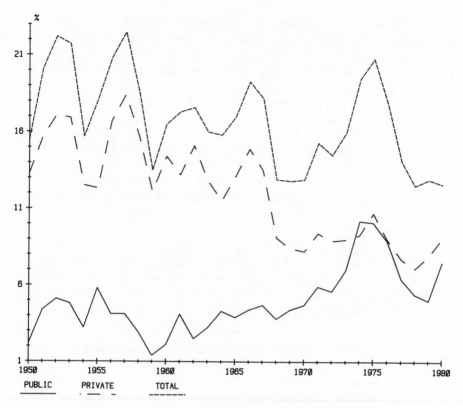

FIGURE 5-3

Peru: Public and Private Sector Shares in Gross Domestic Investment,
1950–1980

Source: Derived from José A. Encinas del Pando, "Economic, Military and Socio-Political
Variables in Argentina, Chile and Peru (1950–1980). A Regional Analysis" (Lima: University of Lima, 1983, mimeograph), Tables 2.54 and 2.56, pp. 322, 324.

while the private sector (apart from foreign oil and mining ventures
in conjunction with the state) was investing only enough to cover replacement requirements. The state failed to acquire a significant proportion of the profits previously earned by the private sector, however, although private profits and private domestic savings continued
to *rise* as a proportion of national income, dividend distribution increased and capital flight worsened, while the rate of private investment fell. . . .

The military regime wanted "independent" industrialists to invest, and considerable fiscal incentives were offered under the General Industrial Law—against which the Industrial Community was hardly an insurmountable obstacle. . . . But this the independents did not do. The reason, in retrospect, was not just that they lacked confidence in the future but also that the structure of ownership in industry determined that the two groups badly hit by other reforms—the oligarchy and the multinationals—were in fact responsible for most industrial assets. The major multisectoral ownership groups were in organizational disarray by the 1960s and were effectively dismembered by the post-1968 forms, while the nonmining multinationals clearly regarded government policy in general—and the enforcement of Andean Pact provisions in particular—as inimicable to their interests.

Throughout the 1968–1979 period, private domestic investment net of replacements and housing was almost negligible. Foreign investment was confined to mining and oil; only two special projects of any size were undertaken in other sectors (the Bayer chemical plant for the Andean Common Market and the Lima Sheraton to use up blocked compensation funds).[13]

Increased security expenditure during the 1970s, particularly the large purchases of weapons from the Soviet Union, must have contributed to some extent to the inability of the Peruvian public sector to finance investment adequately and without recourse to deficit financing and a growing international debt. Inflation, which in part derived from high levels of security expenditure in the early 1970s (see Chapter 6), contributed to the private sector's tendency to consume rather than reinvest profits. As shall be seen in the following section, however, arms procurement was not the sole cause of the country's budgetary imbalances or its general economic crisis. These derive primarily from the policies followed by Peruvian governments, the structure of the Peruvian economy, and changes in the international economy. If Peruvian governments had reduced, rather than increased, the share of gross product allocated to the security sector

[13] E. V. K. FitzGerald, "State Capitalism in Peru: A Model of Economic Development and its Limitations," pp. 72–76, in Cynthia McClintock and Abraham Lowenthal, ed., *The Peruvian Experiment Reconsidered* (Princeton, N.J.: Princeton University Press, 1983), emphasis in the original. Schydlowsky and Wicht have commented that "After 1971, Peru's foreign debt policy was to borrow to the hilt. The Peruvian government clearly was ready to borrow to finance all projects for which someone was willing to lend. The justification was often the importance, not the quality, of the investment projects." Daniel M. Schydlowsky and Juan Wicht, "The Anatomy of an Economic Failure," in McClintock and Lowenthal, *The Peruvian Experiment, ibid.,* p. 117.

during the 1960s and 1970s, a small amount of additional resources would have been available for productive investment. Yet even assuming that these resources would have been invested in their entirety, Peru's economic situation would not have been significantly better than it is today if one does not at the same time posit different global economic conditions and different domestic policies.

In assessing the effect that security expenditure has on investment, it is important to know individual countries' ratios of public expenditure consumed to that invested. Indian analyst K. Subrahmanyam has argued that security expenditure cannot be held responsible for insufficient investment in India because public, including security expenditure, and private consumption have together absorbed between 80 and 90 percent of Indian GDP since 1950. Therefore, it is wrong, according to Subrahmanyam, to claim that the major constraint on growth and investment is security expenditure. Transferring 1 or 2 percent of GDP from security expenditure in fiscal year 1971/1972 (when it stood at 3.8 percent of GDP) would have increased investment from only 12 percent to 13 or 14 percent. Subrahmanyam has suggested that much larger increases could have been produced by reducing consumption of the Indian élite. In addition, without any change in the consumption/investment ratio, it is unlikely that the full amount of reductions in security expenditure would be applied to investment; rather, large portions would almost certainly be used for nondefense consumption.

Raju Thomas has concurred that "a major inhibiting factor to self-sustaining capital formation and economic growth" in India is the very high rate of consumption. He also has agreed that, given current patterns of consumption and investment, reductions in security expenditure are more likely to be consumed than invested. At the same time, he has pointed out that, in view of the low rate of investment in the Indian economy, even a small increase in investment would not be insignificant. For example, a transfer of 1 percent of GDP from the security sector to industrial investment in 1971 to 1972 would have implied an 8.5 percent increase in the investment rate.[14] Security expenditure may not be the major constraint on investment in India, but it nonetheless is a constraint.

There are countries in which security expenditure clearly competes with the civil sector for investment funds, for example Iran during the 1970s. In just one year, 1977, the official military budget was nearly equivalent to the total funds allocated by the state for industrial investment during the entire Fifth Plan period (1973–1978). Investment in the

[14] Raju G. C. Thomas, *The Defence of India: A Budgetary Perspective of Strategy and Politics* (Delhi: Macmillan Company of India, 1978), pp. 130, 134.

industrial sector during the shah's rule was considerable, but this does not mean that all needs were met. Rather, as Ann Schultz has concluded, "Although industrialization was a declared objective to the monarchy, the regime's financial decisions showed it to have lower priority than the military sector."[15] In plastics, metal products, and communications, for example, the domestic sector was unable to meet the demand generated by large military-related programs, and a large proportion of the inputs for these projects had to be imported. These industries were thus doubly burdened. Not only did the original expenditure on military-related projects reduce the funds available for civil investment in these sectors, but the need to import inputs absorbed foreign exchange which might have instead been used to increase the capacity of the domestic industry.[16]

Balance of Payments: Trade and Indebtedness

Foreign exchange is often in short supply in developing countries, and that which is available frequently must be apportioned among competing requirements. Over the last decade, the non-oil exporting developing countries have faced an increasingly difficult external payments situation. Trade deficits increased more than elevenfold between 1970 and 1982 for these countries as a group. For most of them the largest increases occurred following the oil price rises of 1973 and 1979 (Table 5-1). Third World indebtedness grew rapidly during the 1970s and early 1980s, and the debt-servicing burden has accordingly grown more onerous for a greater proportion of the developing countries over the last decade. This combination of negative trade balances and heavy debt-servicing charges has produced a serious external payments crisis that has affected the growth potential of many developing economies.

These negative trade balances reflect in part the difficulty Third World countries have had in diversifying their exports and the considerable fluctuations in the prices obtained for many traditional Third World exports. Raw materials continue to account for a sizable share of developing country sales abroad. The prices of these commodities have shown substantial variability over the last forty years, but in general they have failed to hold their own against the prices of goods imported from the industrial countries. Although there have been periods in which commodity prices—at least some of them—have boomed, there have also been periods in which commodity prices have fallen precipitously.

[15] Ann Schulz, "Military Expenditures and Economic Performance in Iran, 1950–1980" (Worcester, Mass.: Clark University, 1982, mimeograph), p. 146.
[16] Ibid., pp. 73–76.

IMF figures show that the terms of trade generally declined for the oil-importing developing countries between 1955 and 1982, with a particularly sharp and prolonged drop after 1977 (Figure 5-4). Not surprisingly, they improved markedly for the oil-exporting countries after 1974. According to UNCTAD, the higher prices for manufactures in the 1974–1975 period contributed to Third World deficits to approximately the same degree as higher oil prices.[17]

Of the nearly 115 developing countries for which UNCTAD has information on export commodity dependence at the beginning of the 1980s, 49 were dependent on just one item for over 50 percent of their export income. Another 26 were dependent on two commodities to the same degree (Table 5-3). The influence of the oil price boom is evident; 24 countries earned 50 percent or more of their export income from crude or processed petroleum. These proportions would likely be higher if information were available for all countries categorized as "least developed" or "low income." Only 22 of the 36 least-developed countries and 19 of the 35 Third World states designated as low-income by the World Bank are included in Table 5-2.

In order to overcome this obstacle to their development, Third World countries have been advised to reduce their dependence on just a few "traditional" exports and to attempt to increase their export of manufactured goods. There are at least two problems here: First, the industrialized countries have generally been unwilling to open their domestic markets to large amounts of Third World manufactured goods. Second, even the more industrialized of the Third World countries, such as Korea and Brazil, have not been immune to the general downward trend of the developing countries' terms of trade (Figure 5-5).

As the terms of trade increasingly turned against Third World coun-

---

[17] UNCTAD, *International Financial Cooperation for Development,* TD/188, TD/188 Supp. 1, Add. 1, May 1976.

Desirable as it is for developing countries to improve their export income, it must be recognized that commodity price stabilization would have different effects for different countries and that while Third World countries might benefit from price stabilization *as exporters,* they might not benefit *as importers.* Petroleum offers the most obvious example. A World Bank study carried out at the end of the 1970s concluded that as exporters Third World countries would benefit from price stabilization for cocoa, coffee, wood, jute, cotton, and sugar; as importers, however, they would benefit only from more stable wheat prices. See Ezriel M. Brook, Enzo R. Grilli, and Jean Waelbroeck, *Commodity Price Stabilization and the Developing Countries: The Problem of Choice,* Working Paper 262 (Washington, D.C.: World Bank, July 1977). See also Alberto Valdés and Barbara Huddleston, *Potential of Agricultural Exports to Finance Increased Food Imports in Selected Developing Countries,* Occasional Paper 2 (Washington, D.C.: International Food Policy Research Institute, August 1977).

TABLE 5-1

Third World Balance of Payments (in $U.S. billion)

Region	1970	1971	1972	1973	1974	1975	1976	1977	1978	1979	1980	1981	1982	1983	1984
AFRICA															
Trade balance	0.2	-1.0	1.2	3.2	8.9	-1.5	1.9	3.2	-1.1	10.3	17.7	-3.5	-4.2	2.7	7.7
Current account balance	-2.4	-3.4	-1.6	-1.5	2.2	-8.8	-7.4	-8.3	-12.3	-3.4	-1.4	-21.8	-21.1	-11.7	-5.2
Capital account	2.1	2.4	2.4	2.4	3.3	6.7	6.0	5.9	9.5	6.8	4.8	11.1	10.7	5.7	1.5
Reserves, etc.	0.3	0.9	-0.8	-0.9	-5.5	2.1	1.4	2.4	2.8	-3.4	10.7	10.7	10.4	6.0	3.7
ASIA															
Trade balance	-4.0	-3.8	-1.9	-1.4	-8.0	-8.5	-1.8	-0.5	-8.5	-12.6	-19.9	-21.1	-19.6	-16.8	-3.4
Current account balance	-2.9	-2.6	-0.3	-0.1	-5.3	-8.2	-1.5	1.1	-6.6	-12.1	-19.6	-21.1	-16.8	-14.2	-4.5
Capital account	3.8	4.3	3.3	3.5	6.6	6.5	7.7	4.5	10.4	17.3	23.0	24.9	20.2	19.6	13.4
Reserves, etc.	-0.9	-1.7	-2.9	-3.5	-1.4	-1.8	-6.2	-5.5	-3.7	-5.2	-3.3	-3.9	-3.4	-5.4	-8.8
MIDDLE EAST															
Trade balance	3.9	6.1	6.2	10.8	59.9	40.0	48.7	48.8	35.8	79.0	121.0	89.6	41.6	16.6	16.4
Current account balance	-0.9	1.3	3.7	5.6	53.3	28.9	34.2	29.3	8.8	52.4	88.8	43.5	-6.3	-18.4	-22.1
Capital account	0.8	1.0	0.3	-2.4	-26.3	-23.2	-26.6	-17.5	-12.5	-35.2	-63.4	-55.0	-13.5	10.9	15.9
Reserves, etc.	0.1	-2.3	-4.0	-3.2	-27.0	-5.7	-7.7	-11.8	3.7	-17.3	-25.4	11.5	19.8	7.5	6.2

(TABLE 5-1 CONT.)

Region	1970	1971	1972	1973	1974	1975	1976	1977	1978	1979	1980	1981	1982	1983	1984	1985
AMERICAS																
Trade balance	0.2	-0.8	-0.4	1.5	-0.3	-5.8	-2.2	-0.5	-3.7	-0.2	-1.8	-2.6	7.4	29.9	37.4	33.4
Current account balance	-3.6	-4.9	-4.4	-3.7	-7.5	-13.9	-11.1	-11.6	-18.1	-19.4	-27.5	-39.9	-41.5	-8.2	-0.9	-4.3
Capital account	4.3	5.1	6.9	7.7	11.1	13.7	15.6	16.9	25.5	28.1	27.4	35.8	7.8	-16.0	-11.8	-10.8
Reserves, etc.	-0.7	-0.2	-2.5	-4.0	-5.4	-7.4	-8.8	0.1	4.0	33.7	24.2	4.0	33.7	24.2	12.7	15.1
OIL EXPORTERS																
Trade balance	7.1	10.1	10.6	19.2	83.8	54.4	62.9	62.1	44.0	108.2	168.1	124.0	62.4	44.3	52.8	56.1
Current account balance	-0.1	1.3	3.3	6.4	67.3	32.6	35.0	24.5	-2.9	56.2	103.4	45.5	-19.7	-19.5	-12.7	-2.5
Capital account	0.7	0.9	0.9	-2.1	-28.4	-24.0	-23.3	-11.6	-4.3	-30.2	-67.7	-63.1	-18.1	10.9	10.7	12.7
Reserves, etc.	0.4	-2.2	-4.2	-38.9	-8.6	-11.7	-12.8	7.1	-26.0	-35.6	17.6	17.6	37.8	8.5	2.0	-10.2
NON-OIL THIRD WORLD																
Trade balance	-9.9	-13.5	-8.7	-9.9	-33.9	-41.1	-26.7	-25.0	-35.2	-50.5	-73.0	-79.7	-50.1	-21.5	-2.6	-9.0
Current account balance	-9.7	-11.7	-5.3	-5.3	-28.8	-39.2	-25.4	-21.7	-31.6	-48.5	-75.2	-94.5	-72.0	-36.5	-21.9	-24.7
Capital Account	11.4	13.3	13.7	14.6	26.1	29.1	28.8	26.8	42.9	54.5	70.6	87.4	47.6	12.7	10.6	3.7
Reserves, etc.	-1.7	-1.6	-8.3	-9.3	2.7	10.2	-3.4	-5.1	-11.3	-6.1	4.6	7.1	24.4	23.8	11.3	21.0

Source: International Monetary Fund, *International Financial Statistics Yearbook, 1986* (Washington, D.C.: IMF, 1986) pp. 132–43.
Note: Reserves, etc. means figures shown for reserves, exceptional financing, and liabilities constituting foreign authorities' reserves.

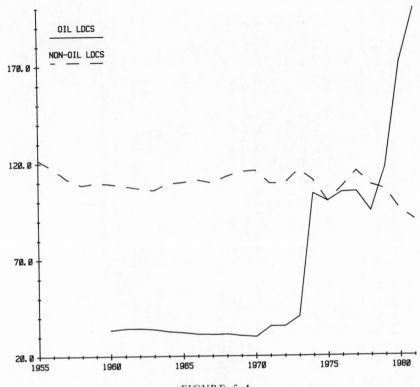

FIGURE 5-4
Terms of Trade, Developing Market Economies, 1955–1981
(1975 = 100)

Source: International Monetary Fund, *International Finance Statistics, Supplement on Trade Statistics,* Supplement Series no. 4 (Washington, D.C.: IMF, 1982), pp. 158–59.

tries, the 1974–1975 recession in the industrialized countries reduced the volume of Third World exports as well. Many governments sought to cover these shortfalls through foreign borrowing. As debts mounted, the U.S. dollar grew stronger, interest rates climbed, and the recession of 1980–1982 made itself felt, more and more fresh capital was needed to service existing debts and to keep Third World economies functioning. Even before the near default of Mexico in 1982 inaugurated "the debt crisis," it was evident that the round of lending that had begun in the mid-1970s could not continue indefinitely. By the time, however, that borrowers and lenders began to question seriously "the future magni-

TABLE 5-2
Export Commodity Dependence, 1981

Countries dependent on one commodity for over 50% of export earnings	Percentage	Commodity
Libya	99.6	petroleum
Iraq	99.2	petroleum
Nigeria	96.9	petroleum
Saudi Arabia	96.9	petroleum
Uganda [a, b]	94.6	coffee
Oman	93.0	petroleum
Venezuela	92.7	petroleum
Qatar	92.1	petroleum
United Arab Emirates	91.5	petroleum
Algeria	91.1	petroleum
Bahrain	90.5	petroleum
Yemen, Democratic [a]	90.0	petroleum
Trinidad & Tobago	87.2	petroleum
Gabon	86.5	petroleum
Mauritania	83.2	iron ore
Iran	82.7	petroleum
Syria	81.6	petroleum
Kuwait	80.9	petroleum
Tuvalu	80.6	oil seeds
Zambia	80.5	copper
Maldives [a]	80.3	fish
Niger [a, b]	79.4	uranium
Burundi [a, b]	79.3	coffee
Chad [a, b]	78.4	cotton
Fiji	77.6	sugar
Vanuatu	76.4	oil seeds
Angola	75.1	petroleum
Rwanda [a, b]	74.7	coffee
Congo	72.0	petroleum
Somalia [a, b]	70.4	live animals
Mauritius	69.8	sugar
Mexico	68.7	petroleum
Egypt	64.4	petroleum
Liberia	62.1	iron ore
Seychelles	62.0	oil seeds
Ecuador	61.9	petroleum
Indonesia	61.6	petroleum
Suriname	61.0	alumina
Jamaica	60.4	alumina
Brunei	60.0	petroleum
Ethiopia [a, b]	60.0	coffee
Cuba	59.0	sugar
El Salvador	57.5	coffee
Cape Verde [a]	54.3	fish
Dominican Republic	54.3	sugar

(TABLE 5-2 CONT.)

Countries dependent on one commodity for over 50% of export earnings	Percentage	Commodity
Tunisia	54.0	petroleum
Ghana[b]	53.5	cocoa
Mali[a, b]	52.2	cotton
Togo[a, b]	50.5	crude fertilizers

Countries dependent on two commodities for over 50% of export earnings	Percentage	Commodity
Gambia[a]	74.7	oil seeds (43.1), vegetable oil (31.6)
Grenada	73.7	fruit/nuts (37.1), cocoa (36.6)
Guyana	70.8	bauxite (41.9), sugar (28.9)
Guinea-Bissau[a]	69.9	oil seeds (44.7), fish (25.2)
Belize	68.5	sugar (48.3), fruit/nuts (20.2)
Malawi[a, b]	68.3	tobacco (42.2), sugar (26.1)
Papua-New Guinea	65.8	copper (48.9), coffee (16.9)
Central African Republic[a, b]	64.9	precious stones (38.4), coffee (26.5)
Comoros[a]	64.1	spices (49.9), non-ferrous, base metal ore (14.2)
Kiribati	63.9	oil seeds (43.4), wood (20.5)
Paraguay	63.1	cotton (44.3), oil seeds (18.8)
Sierra Leone[a, b]	61.4	precious stones (38.7), natural abrasives (22.7)
Tonga	60.3	oil seeds (39.0), fruit/nuts (21.3)
Bolivia	59.3	tin (31.9), gas (27.4)
Madagascar[b]	59.3	spices (29.7), coffee (29.6)
Burkina Faso[a, b]	58.2	cotton (40.7), live animals (17.5)
Bénin[a, b]	57.1	cocoa (34.1), vegetable oil (23.0)
Cameroon	55.6	petroleum (36.5), coffee (19.1)
Nicaragua	54.7	coffee (29.7), cotton (26.0)
Honduras	54.2	fruit/nuts (30.2), coffee (24.0)
Burma[b]	53.8	rice (28.3), wood (25.5)
Colombia	53.8	coffee (49.5), fruit/nuts (4.3)
Afghanistan[a, b]	53.5	gas (35.4), fruit/nuts (18.1)
Sudan[a, b]	53.5	oil seeds (29.6), cotton (23.9)
Chile	53.2	copper (42.2), nonferrous base metal (11.0)
Ivory Coast	53.0	cocoa (33.8), coffee (19.2)

Source: United Nations Conference on Trade and Development, *Handbook of International Trade and Development Statistics, Supplement 1984* (Geneva: United Nations, 1984), Table 4.3 (D).

[a] Least-developed country.

[b] Low-income country as defined by the World Bank.

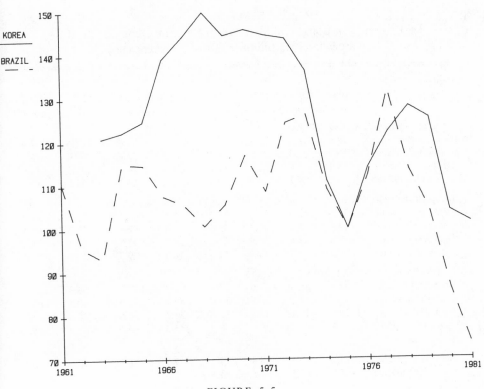

FIGURE 5-5

Terms of Trade, South Korea and Brazil, 1961–1981 (1975 = 100)

Source: International Monetary Fund, *International Finance Statistics. Supplement on Trade Statistics,* Supplement Series No. 4 (Washington, D.C.: IMF, 1982), pp. 158–59.

tudes and terms of international lending, the role of such lending in the future development of the borrowing countries, and the effects of the debt situation on these countries' growth prospects," the total debt incurred by the Third World was in the neighborhood of $800 billion, and servicing it was becoming increasingly onerous for many governments.[18]

The debt problem is not, however, shared equally among all Third

[18] International Monetary Fund, *World Economic Outlook,* Occasional Paper 27 (Washington, D.C.: IMF, 1984), p. 59. A useful early article which both described the situation in many Third World countries in the mid-1970s and predicted with reasonable accuracy the likely outcome of increased indebtedness for them is Emma Rothschild, "Why the Banks Should be Scared," *The New York Review of Books,* 27 May 1976, pp. 16–22.

TABLE 5-3

Debt Service on Long- and Short-Term External Debt, 1977–1984
(values in U.S.$ billions; ratios in percentages)

Group of Countries	1977	1978	1979	1980	1981	1982	1983	1984
ALL DEVELOPING COUNTRIES								
Debt service values	40.3	54.5	71.2	87.9	113.7	124.0	114.6	122.6
of which interest	15.1	21.4	31.5	46.6	63.9	71.6	67.4	75.0
Debt service ratio	15.3	18.0	17.9	17.1	21.0	24.3	22.5	21.9
of which interest	5.7	7.1	7.9	9.1	11.8	14.1	13.2	13.4
MAJOR BORROWERS								
Debt service values	32.0	42.9	57.6	71.0	93.6	102.1	93.4	99.8
of which interest	12.1	17.3	26.2	39.5	55.3	62.4	58.2	65.1
Debt service ratio	19.1	22.5	22.9	21.5	27.3	32.3	29.9	29.2
of which interest	7.2	9.1	10.4	11.9	16.1	19.7	18.6	19.0
ALL NON-OIL DEVELOPING COUNTRIES								
Debt service values	32.8	47.5	61.0	73.4	97.2	107.7	96.6	103.4
of which interest	12.7	18.1	25.9	39.0	54.7	63.0	59.2	63.7
Debt service ratio	14.8	18.1	18.1	17.2	21.3	24.5	21.6	21.1
of which interest	9.1	11.2	10.4	8.0	9.3	10.2	8.4	8.1
ASIA								
Debt service ratio	7.9	10.1	8.4	8.4	9.9	11.5	10.8	10.5
of which interest	3.1	3.5	3.6	4.4	5.6	6.3	5.9	5.6
AFRICA								
Debt service ratio	11.9	15.5	16.6	17.4	19.7	23.7	25.1	24.3
of which interest	5.0	6.7	7.3	8.1	9.2	11.0	10.8	11.9
MIDDLE EAST								
Debt service ratio	13.3	12.9	13.9	12.1	16.3	16.7	21.0	21.9
of which interest	5.4	6.0	5.7	5.7	7.0	7.6	9.1	9.8
WESTERN HEMISPHERE								
Debt service ratio	28.2	36.5	38.0	34.1	44.1	54.1	44.0	42.7
of which interest	10.0	12.9	15.6	18.9	25.6	34.2	32.2	31.1

Source: International Monetary Fund, *World Economic Outlook,* Occasional Paper 27 (Washington, D.C.: IMF, 1984), Table 38, pp. 209–10.

World countries. In 1983, twenty-five major borrowers were responsible for 79 percent of all Third World debt. The ten largest debtors alone held over half the outstanding debt at the end of 1983, and the five largest held more than one-third. Most of the very poorest countries have remained dependent on noncommercial sources of foreign credit and several countries, notably China and India, have consciously limited their dependence on commercial borrowing.[19]

Not only the size of a country's debt determines how much of a burden indebtedness is, but also the ease with which a country can repay the money it has borrowed depends in large part on its ability to generate foreign exchange. Table 5-3 shows that, as a group, the major borrowers have consistently had to devote a larger share of their export earnings to debt-servicing than the Third World as a whole. Asian countries have tended to have the lowest debt service ratios, and Latin American countries the highest.

The expansion of commercial credit to the Third World was precipitated largely by the increased liquidity in the international financial system following the 1973 oil price rise. Prior to the early 1970s, very little business was done between U.S. banks and developing country governments. Innumerable stories have been told about the way in which bankers eagerly offered loans to governments and private industry in the developing countries in the early and mid-1970s.[20] It is also true, however, that many Third World governments sought these loans just as eagerly. Low or even negative real interest rates made foreign borrowing attractive,

---

[19] A few low-income countries, as well as some in the middle-income bracket, whose ability—or inability—to repay rests heavily on the level of commodity prices were able to obtain commercial loans in the 1970s. The subsequent fall in commodity prices reduced their credit-worthiness, and banks stopped lending to them. World Bank, *World Development Report 1985* (New York: Oxford University Press, 1985), p. 45, and IMF, *World Economic Outlook*, p. 60.

[20] It was reported, for example, in "The Debt Bomb Threat," *Time*, 10 January 1983, p. 45, that

> Based largely in London, the networks of leading US, West European and, later, Japanese, Arab and Latin American banks arranged syndicates of hundreds of smaller banks to put together billion-dollar deals in days. . . . Profits were large, because the typical developing country, a higher-risk borrower, paid a higher interest rate than a domestic blue-chip corporation. . . . So attractive was the business that smaller US regional and West European banks rushed to open representative offices in London. Between 1975 and 1982 more than 60 banks entered the game each year.

> Not surprisingly, the young gunslingers, the loan-marketing officers working for such syndicate leaders as Citicorp, France's Société Générale, and Switzerland's Crédit Suisse, often paid little attention to whether the borrower could repay. The fact that Mexico sat on an ocean of oil, that Zaire had mountains of copper was thought to be collateral enough. Annual bonuses and career prospects were at stake; if one bank did not get the business, another would. "They had to meet specific profit targets, sometimes even monthly targets," recalls a senior British financier in discussing US banks in particular. "Money was just a raw material to be fed into the sausage machine. They did not want to hear about the risks. By the time the country couldn't repay, the people who had made the loan were off and away to some other bank." (p. 45)

See also, Rothschild, "Why the Banks."

and the boom experienced by some commodity prices in the 1970s encouraged governments and lending institutions to believe that these loans could easily be repaid. It was also often easier for Third World governments to obtain loans from abroad than to raise domestic savings or carry out other domestic reforms.[21]

Not only were many loans made without adequate calculations of the borrower's ability to repay, but additional burdens were also created by the rise of interest rates to unprecedented heights and by the large appreciation of the U.S. dollar in the first half of the 1980s. These latter two factors have greatly increased the cost of servicing debts. The World Bank has calculated, for example, that "Brazil's net interest payments in 1981 were 60 percent larger than they would have been if real rates had remained constant, and in 1982, 80 percent larger. These increases were equivalent to 15 percent and 25 percent of actual exports in those years.[22] As Table 5-3 indicates, the interest component of debt service costs climbed from about 37 percent to just over 60 percent between 1977 and 1984 for the developing countries as a whole. For the major borrowers, the increase was even greater.

Although the debt problem has been particularly severe in Latin America, the economies of sub-Saharan Africa are in the most precarious position. G. K. Helleiner has summarized their situation in the early 1980s:

> The "import strangulation" associated with terms of trade deteriorations of twenty-five percent and more in recent years has created substantial underutilisation and depreciation in existing capacity. Without crucial imported inputs and spare parts, much of the capital stock—in transport, industry, agriculture and, even social infrastructure such as schools and hospitals—cannot function adequately. This results frequently in long-term physical deterioration, often accelerated in tropical conditions. In some instances, the unavailability of fuel, inputs, and spare parts has severely reduced the capacity to move potential foreign exchange earning export products to the ports. Thus, the vicious cycle is reinforced.[23]

It has been estimated, for example, that industry in Mozambique was operating at 15 to 20 percent of capacity in early 1984, and Tanzanian industry at about 20 percent of capacity.

---

[21] Rothschild, "Why the Banks," and, World Bank, *World Development Report 1985*, pp. 45, 58, 60.

[22] World Bank, *World Development Report 1985*, p. 55. See also p. 32 for an explanation of the problems caused by the appreciation of the dollar for commodity exporters.

[23] G. K. Helleiner, "The IMF and Africa in the 1980s," *Canadian Journal of African Studies* 17:1 (1983): 20.

While the low-income countries in Africa are among those most seriously affected by the economic conditions of the last decade, underutilized industrial capacity is not a problem unique to them. Most Third World economies have been forced to cut back on vital imports. In Vietnam, for example, industry was estimated to be operating at 50 percent of capacity in 1983. In Peru, capacity utilization stood at approximately 30 percent in 1985. Even in the most industrially advanced countries in Latin America, Mexico and Brazil, industrial output, employment, and capacity utilization have declined substantially since the beginning of the 1980s. Just what these figures imply for financial stability in individual countries is illustrated by the International Labour Office's (ILO) analysis of the state of the Tanzanian economy in the early 1980s: "if industry was operating at a normal level of capacity utilization instead of its present low level, sales and excise tax revenues would be doubled, which would not only eliminate the current fiscal deficit, but also make a sizable contribution to the capital account."[24]

In view of the rise in the security expenditure of developing countries over the last two decades, especially the sharp increases in arms imports for some of them, and the decline in security-related grants to help pay for weapons, it is sensible to ask whether there might not be some link between outlays on the security sector and the external payments problems in specific countries. Ethiopia, for example, one of the poorest countries in the world, ranks 125th out of 126 countries in terms of per capita GNP by the World Bank and has a current account balance more often in deficit than not. Yet, in 1977 and 1978, Ethiopia imported some $1.5 billion in weapons from the Soviet Union and its allies. It has been suggested that this debt is being repaid by shipments of coffee to the USSR. In all likelihood, this use of a commodity which has accounted for approximately 60 percent of all Ethiopian exports since the mid-1960s (with the exception of 1972–1975) has contributed to Ethiopian current account deficits. Similarly, Raju Thomas believes that the biggest constraint imposed by India's defense spending, particularly for modern weapons and the development of an indigenous defense industry, on the civil sector is the reduced availability of foreign exchange.[25] Unfortunately, it is diffi-

[24] Ajit Singh, "The Interrupted Industrial Revolution of the Third World: Prospects and Policies for Resumption," *Industry and Development* no. 12 (1984): 48. The ILO report referred to by Singh is JASPA/ILO, *Tanzania: Basic Needs in Danger* (Addis Ababa: ILO, 1982). On Mozambique, see Michael Holman, "Why Machel is Wooing the West," *Financial Times*, 24 April 1984. On Vietnam, see Nils Öström, *Vietnam. En landbeskrivning* (*Vietnam. Country Description*) (Stockholm: SIDA, 1984), pp. 42, 45. On Peru, see Johnny Lundström, "Landsbygden toppar APRAS reformlista" ("Rural Areas Head APRA's List of Reforms"), *Dagens Nyheter*, 3 May 1985.

[25] Thomas, *The Defence of India*, pp. 124–35. The foreign exchange requirements of

cult, although not impossible, to address this question in an entirely satis-factory manner because of shortcomings in the existing data.

For example, it is not clear if arms transfers are included in inter-national trade statistics. Although it is known that some countries falsify imports records in order to hide arms transfers (see Chapter 3), how widespread this practice is and how many countries may simply remove military equipment from their import statistics is not known. Further-more, it is difficult to obtain arms transfer statistics which accurately re-flect the price of weapons to the purchaser. The U.S. Arms Control and Disarmament Agency cautions readers of its *World Military Expendi-tures and Arms Transfers* series:

> The statistics published here are estimates of the value of goods actually delivered during the reference year, in contrast both to the value of programs, agreements, contracts or orders which may result in future deliveries, and to payments made during the period. . . .
>
> Close comparisons between the estimated values shown for arms transfers and for GNP and military expenditures are not warranted. Frequently, weapons prices do not reflect true production costs. The relative economic value of arms to supplier and to recipient may dif-fer considerably. Furthermore, much of the international arms trade involves barter arrangements, multiyear loans, discounted prices, third-party payments, and partial debt forgiveness. Acquisition of armaments thus may not impose the burden on an economy, in the same or in other years, that is implied by the estimated equivalent US dollar value of the shipment. *Therefore the value of arms imports should not be related in detail to other categories of data.*[26]

The same disclaimer applies to arms transfer figures produced by SIPRI.

TRADE BALANCE

Increased military expenditure and arms procurement can be reflected in a country's trade balance in a variety of ways. On the import side, an increase in imports for the security sector could

(1) reduce civil-sector imports but allow the overall import level to re-main stable;

(2) reduce civil-sector imports but cause the overall import level to rise; or

---

Nigerian security expenditure are discussed in J. 'Bayo Adekanye, "The Role of Military Expenditure in the Development Process: Nigeria" (Ibadan: University of Ibadan, 1983, mimeograph).

[26] U.S. Arms Control and Disarmament Agency, *World Military Expenditure and Arms Transfers, 1971–1980,* Publication 115 (Washington, D.C.: ACDA, March 1983), pp. 127–28; emphasis added.

(3) stimulate civil-sector imports and cause even larger increases in the overall import level.

In the first case, all other things being equal, the short-term effect on the trade balance would be nil. The long-term consequences, however, might be a reduction in growth capacity if imports for the security sector displaced goods that would have increased the productivity of either the industrial or the agricultural sector.

Where security-related imports—weapons and related services, construction, materials or services, spare parts, fuel, for example—cause the total level of imports to rise, the trade balance will be negatively affected unless additional capital can be raised, by either expanding exports or importing foreign capital. If, in addition, security-sector imports cause reductions in civil imports, growth rates may suffer over the long term. If, on the other hand, security-related imports stimulate domestic production and lead to increased civil-sector imports, the longer-term growth effect may be positive. It is important to bear in mind, however, that a reduction in civil-sector imports does not automatically imply a reduction in growth rates since it may mean that fewer consumer goods are imported. To evaluate the effect of rising security-sector imports on economic growth, it is important to know what kinds of goods are not imported when demand from the armed forces increases.

It is also important to be able to disaggregate imports in order to determine the relative weight of security-related purchases. Table 5-4 shows the evolution of Peruvian imports over three decades. Arms imports are included in the category "Adjustments." This category increased its share of total imports over the thirty-year period, and it can be assumed that the growth of arms imports after 1973 at least in part produced the rise in the 1970s. There were, however, other reasons why imports grew from about 10 percent of GDP in the early 1970s to about 16 percent of GDP in the late 1970s.

Various government policies had brought on a balance of payments crisis. The overvaluation of the currency sharply stimulated imports and consumption, despite high international prices, while at the same moment exports were stagnating. Second, increasing government subsidies for food and fuel imports weighed more and more heavily on the balance of payments and discouraged agrarian production. Third, the public enterprises were obliged to continue both subsidies to private capital and sale prices below the cost of production, leaving them underfinanced and adding a burden to the state budget. As if all this were not enough, from the end of 1973, because of military fears of war with Chile . . . the GRFA [Revolutionary

TABLE 5-4
Peru: Classification of Imports

Category	1950s	1960s	1970s
Consumer Goods			
U.S.$m	578.7	967.9	1,721.9
% Imports	20.8	16.4	9.3
Raw Materials and Intermediate Goods			
U.S.$m	912.9	2,250.3	8,343.2
% Imports	32.9	38.2	45.3
Capital Goods			
U.S.$m	968.5	1,881.8	5,492.3
% Imports	34.9	31.9	29.8
Other			
U.S.$m	21.8	15.3	69.9
% Imports	0.8	0.3	0.4
Adjustments			
U.S.$m	294.8	780.7	2,800.0
% Imports	10.6	13.2	15.2
Total Imports			
U.S.$m	2,776.7	5,896.0	18,427.3

Source: José A. Encinas del Pando, "Economic, Military and Socio-Political Variables in Argentina, Chile and Peru (1950–1980). A Regional Analysis" (Lima: University of Lima, 1983, mimeograph), p. 302.

Government of the Armed Forces] began a frantic arms purchasing campaign.[27]

It is difficult to disentangle the effects of rises in security-related imports from general economic trends which affect the capacity of developing countries to import. Economic downturns in industrialized countries, for example, frequently necessitate reductions in imports on the part of developing countries as important markets for their exports contract. Falling commodity prices can have a similar effect. Sharp rises in the prices of goods imported by the developing countries can also cause these

[27] Julio Cotler, "Democracy and National Integration in Peru," p. 26, in McClintock and Lowenthal, ed., *The Peruvian Experiment.*

countries to import smaller quantities of particular goods.[28] The rise in the price of petroleum and derivative products which has taken place since 1973 is recognized to have effectively reduced the import capacity of many developing countries. Arms imports grew rapidly for a number of countries during the 1970s as well, and it can be expected that these too reduced the ability of countries to import other goods. The problem is determining how much each of these items has constrained the import capacity of individual countries.

Since it is impossible to use the arms transfer figures produced by ACDA and SIPRI to evaluate the economic burden of weapons imports, Table 5-5 compares the share of petroleum in total imports (c.i.f.) in six countries with the security-related capital expenditure/total imports ratio. It is unlikely that all security-related capital expenditure requires outlays of foreign exchange: for one thing, it includes construction costs which often involve expenditure on domestic materials; for another, some countries have significant domestic arms production capacity. Nonetheless, it is known that a number of countries—India, for example—do not report all arms imported in their national accounts or state budgets. Also, countries producing a large amount of their own weapons—Brazil and India in Table 5-5—will have security-related imports for industries such as aircraft, machinery, and electronics which cannot be distinguished from civil-sector imports for the same industries. The capital expenditure portion of state security budgets may, therefore, provide a rough approximation of the value of security-related imports.

For all countries in Table 5-5 with the exception of India and of Morocco in 1976–1978, petroleum has consistently accounted for a larger portion of the import bill than security-related capital expenditure. In India, the importance of oil grew significantly after 1973. According to ACDA figures, India was the eighth largest Third World importer of arms between 1973 and 1983 and Morocco was the fifteenth. (Table 3-4 showed that the top twenty Third World arms importers accounted for 70 percent of all weapon imports during that ten-year period.) It is important to remember, however, that both Morocco and the Philippines have received considerable amounts of security assistance over the years.

It has been suggested that imports of weapons are most likely to crowd out imports of similar goods in the civil sector: primarily machinery and transport equipment. Even if no change were recorded in total imports as

[28] "A Survey of International Trade Developments Since 1950," *International Financial Statistics, Supplement on Trade Statistics,* Supplement Series, no. 4 (Washington, D.C.: IMF 1982), pp. xiv–xxii.

TABLE 5-5

Oil Imports and Security-Related Capital Expenditure as Percent Imports (c.i.f.), 1960–1980

Year	Brazil		India		Malaysia		Philippines		Morocco		Madagascar	
	Oil	CapEx	Oil	CapEx	Oil	CapEx	Oil	CapEx	Oil	CapEx[a]	Oil	CapEx
1960	17.5	—	2.1	3.4	—	—	2.9	0.1	—	1.9	—	—
1961	16.8	—	2.7	3.1	—	—	3.0	b	—	1.6	—	0.3
1962	16.5	—	3.5	5.0	—	—	6.8	b	—	1.3	—	0.2
1963	16.3	—	3.1	10.1	5.4	1.8	7.4	0.1	—	1.1	—	0.2
1964	17.7	—	2.4	10.7	5.4	2.5	7.4	b	—	—	—	0.2
1965	18.2	—	2.3	11.5	5.6	2.2	6.7	b	—	—	—	0.3
1966	14.4	—	1.9	7.8	6.3	4.0	6.6	b	3.3	0.7	—	0.2
1967	13.7	—	2.8	7.4	7.1	3.7	6.6	0.2	3.1	0.8	3.2	0.6
1968	13.6	—	2.9	7.6	7.5	3.1	7.2	0.2	3.8	0.9	3.9	0.5
1969	12.1	—	5.2	9.5	7.1	3.4	7.4	0.2	3.6	0.1	4.1	0.3
1970	11.4	—	6.4	10.9	8.8	3.9	8.3	0.2	3.3	0.5	5.1	b

											b
1971	12.6	4.8	7.7	11.2	9.4	3.5	9.5	0.2	4.1	—	4.1	0.2
1972	12.0	2.9	8.5	13.8	3.9	4.6	9.9	0.5	4.8	—	6.0	0.4
1973	14.1	2.7	9.6	9.3	2.9	1.9	9.2	0.5	4.8	4.5	7.4	0.5
1974	22.8	1.4	22.7	5.5	5.0	2.5	16.4	0.5	11.9	—	16.0	0.2
1975	24.3	1.4	18.1	4.0	6.6	2.6	18.9	0.8	8.6	5.0	18.7	
1976	29.7	1.7	18.7	5.0	7.4	4.3	20.3	0.9	9.1	10.5	18.2	2.4
1977	31.7	2.2	26.4	5.5	7.8	4.1	20.1	—	8.6	13.5	12.7	0.6
1978	30.7	2.1	25.8	4.5	6.8	—	17.6	—	10.1	12.2	11.3	1.0
1979	34.9	1.3	31.2	3.9	7.3	—	16.9	—	17.0	10.5	6.5	2.2
1980	41.4	—	40.6	—	8.0	—	22.4	—	14.1	9.0	4.7	—

Sources: International Monetary Fund, *International Financial Statistics Yearbook, 1984* (Washington, D.C.: 1984), pp. 192, 193, 328, 329, 398, 399, 406, 407, 428, 429, 484, 485. Nicole Ball, *Third-World Security Expenditure: A Compendium*, C10250-M5 (Stockholm: National Defense Research Institute, 1984), pp. 65, 76, 91, 134, 145, 193.

[a] The capital expenditure data on which these estimates are based are highly tentative.
[b] < 0.1%.

CHAPTER 5

security expenditure and arms imports increased or decreased it might be
the case that more arms imports implied fewer purchases of goods in the
SITC-7 category from abroad. (Section 7 of the Standard International
Trade Classification [SITC] includes machinery and transport equipment.)
A study of twenty-eight developing countries found that this relationship
held in the short term for arms imports but only weakly for military expenditure. Over the longer term, higher levels of both security expenditure and arms imports were weakly associated with higher levels of
SITC-7 imports.[29] It is somewhat difficult to interpret the importance of
these findings since, for some countries, the value of weapons imported
might be included in the figures for SITC-7 imports. In addition, given the
relatively large portion of Third World security expenditure devoted to
personnel and other operating costs, increased security outlays do not
necessarily mean that more weapons are procured.

Growing security expenditure can result in rising levels of SITC-7 imports if a country attempts to produce weapons before domestic supplier
industries are capable of meeting the demand for inputs. This occurred in
Iran during the 1970s. Had not a shortage of funds curtailed ambitious
plans by the Turkish government to invest in military industries, a similar
situation would, in all likelihood, have arisen there as well. The industrial
sectors that would have provided the basis for domestic arms manufacturing were already heavily dependent on imports, and it has been argued
that the creation of a domestic arms industry would only have exacerbated this dependence.[30]

There are two main ways in which security expenditure and arms imports might interact with a country's exports. The most frequently mentioned relationship is that increased arms imports could cause an increase
in exports since money must be earned to pay for the weapons. A second
possibility is that export capacity could be reduced by previous arms imports or security expenditures which drew resources from civil-sector
investment.

Most attention has been focused on the first relationship. There is some

[29] Michael Brzoska, "External Trade, Indebtedness, Foreign Direct Investment and the
Military Sector in LDCs: A Study of the Effects of Militarization on External Economic Relations" (Hamburg: Working Group on Armament and Underdevelopment, IFSH, November
1982, mimeograph), pp. 77–78 and 98–100.

In this regard, it is interesting to note in Table 5-4 that as the share of capital goods in
total Peruvian imports declined by about 5 percentage points between the 1950s and the
1970s, adjustments (the category including arms imports) increased its share by approximately the same amount.

[30] Ron Ayres, "Arms Production as a Form of Import-Substituting Industrialization: The
Turkish Case," World Development 11:9 (1983): 817–18. See also Chapter 8 for more
details.

evidence that higher levels of both security expenditure and arms imports are associated with increased exports over the long term. This is particularly true for the 1970s. Since so many Third World countries rely on agricultural commodities for a large share of their export earnings, it has been hypothesized that arms imports will be paid for by increasing exports of agricultural goods. There is, however, no evidence that increased outlays for weapon procurement or for the security sector in general produce a rise in agricultural exports either as a proportion of total exports or as a proportion of agricultural production, nor do they seem to affect manufacturing exports as a proportion of total manufacturing production.[31]

These findings underline the difficulty experienced in attempting to disentangle the effects of security expenditure from those of general economic conditions. For example, over the last two decades, the share of agricultural products in total exports has fallen for many countries as manufactures and fuels, minerals and metals have come to account for a larger share of exports. The general rise in Third World security expenditure and arms imports has not altered this fact. In addition, the growth of Third World exports depends heavily on conditions in the industrialized countries. If the latter reduce their imports of goods from the Third World, then the export earnings of developing countries are likely to decline, unless there are sharp increases in the prices of these goods. Similarly, commodity prices are well known for their variability, and the export earnings of developing countries fluctuate accordingly.[32]

As with imports, it is likely that these general economic trends tend to be more influential in determining the volume and value of Third World exports than either security expenditure in general or arms imports. Nonetheless, for particular countries at specific moments in time, a direct link can be shown between expenditures in the security sector and export policy. In Iran under the shah, for example, "The regime's industrial objectives were closely attuned to its military policies. When the emphasis in foreign economic policy after the Third Plan, for example, shifted from import substitution to export promotion, the rising costs of arms imports were partly responsible. Economic planners in the country ascribed the export promotion policy directly to Iran's rising arms bills."[33]

Because military grant aid has been reduced by all major donors since the late 1960s, it is reasonable to assume that the need to export to pay for weapons and other security-related imports has increased over the last

[31] Brzoska, "External Trade," pp. 73–76 and 94–98.
[32] "A Survey," *International Financial Statistics.*
[33] Schulz, "Military Expenditures," p. 138.

decade or so. Interestingly, the export of weapons has become a means of improving the trade balance for a number of Third World countries. Since the late 1970s, Brazil has actively supported the export of domestically produced weapons, but, in view of Brazil's foreign exchange requirements for purchases of fuel and industrial inputs as well as for debt servicing, it is difficult to argue that this export drive was strongly influenced by the need to support imports for the security sector. It was, however, probably important for the profitability of the Brazilian defense-industrial sector; see the discussion in Chapter 9. Indeed, the importance of the fuel bill can be deduced from the "arms for oil" agreements that Brazil has concluded.[34]

INDEBTEDNESS

The most commonly discussed causes of the sharp rise in the debt burden carried by Third World countries since the late 1970s have been declining terms of trade resulting in negative trade balances and deficits on current account, stagnation of official development assistance, rising interest rates, the strength of the U.S. dollar, and harder terms for new loans contracted to service old debts. Despite the growth of the arms trade with the Third World, which, as we have just seen, can contribute to negative trade balances, and the decline in security-related grants, which parallels the decline in official development assistance, during the 1970s, no detailed analysis has been made of the contribution by the security sector to the debt problems facing Third World countries today. Although World Bank debt figures are said to include loans acquired for security purposes, the bank has thus far proved unwilling to make public any information on the proportion of Third World debt acquired for military purposes. SIPRI estimated in 1985 that "at least one-fifth of new borrowing [between 1972 and 1982] was directly or indirectly for weap-

---

[34] Peter Lock, "Brazil: Arms for Export," p. 97, in *Arms Production in the Third World*, ed. M. Brzoska and T. Ohlson (London: Taylor & Francis, 1986), states that "The government was forced to seek new directions as the impact of oil prices increased." For Alexandro Barros, "Brazil," pp. 79–80, in *Arms Production in Developing Countries*, ed. James Katz (Lexington, Mass.: Lexington, 1984): "Brazilian arms exports are relatively small in balance-of-payments terms. The importance of arms exports rests much more in the role they play in relation to the Brazilian foreign policy. . . . An important part of [Brazil's desire for independence in foreign policy from the United States] is the attempt to develop and supplement relations with the countries in the Third World, expecially those which may constitute markets for Brazil." Brazilian weapons, by virtue of their relative simplicity and low cost, have proven attractive to many Third World governments.

On the relative importance of imports of petroleum products and of capital goods, see Pedro S. Malan and Regis Bonelli, "The Brazilian Economy in the Seventies: Old and New Developments," *World Development* 5 : 1–2 (January–February 1977): 26–27.

onry."[35] In the absence of reliable information on security-related loans, it is difficult to determine how accurate these estimates are.

Knowing the proportion of total Third World debt that derives from security-related purchases is less important than being able to ascertain the military-related debt burden of individual countries. With the exception of credits extended under the U.S. Foreign Military Sales (FMS) financing program, it is extremely difficult to trace the security-related portion of the debt incurred by specific Third World countries. In its annual presentation of security assistance programs to the Congress, the U.S. government provides a repayment schedule for credits extended to individual countries under the FMS program; each schedule shows estimated payments of interest and principal over a ten-year period. As with the security expenditure data produced by the IMF and SIPRI, these figures are updated, and, if one wants to know what a country will be obligated to pay in, say, fiscal year 1985, it is better to consult the congressional presentation for FY 1985 or FY 1986 than one from FY 1982 or FY 1983.[36]

---

[35] Stockholm International Peace Research Institute (SIPRI), *World Armaments and Disarmament, SIPRI Yearbook 1985* (London: Taylor & Francis, 1985), p. 448. World Bank estimates of military-related indebtedness are incomplete. The Bank refuses to divulge the proportion of each country's debt accumulated for military purposes for fear of antagonizing member governments. The OECD has reportedly decided not to include any military-related debts in their figures because they feel the data are too uncertain.

A study carried out for the Ford Foundation in 1983 estimated that "approximately 9 percent of total average yearly debt service" between 1962 and 1982 derived from military purchases. See Walter F. Kitchenman, *Arms Transfers and the Indebtedness of Less Developed Countries,* N-2020-FF (Santa Monica, Calif.: Rand, December 1983), p. 14. See also Michael Brzoska, "The Accumulation of Military Debt" (Working Papers 7, Hamburg: IPW, Centre for the Study of Wars, Armaments, and Development, 1987).

[36] Harry J. Shaw, "US Security Assistance: Debts & Dependency," *Foreign Policy* no. 50 (Spring 1983): 115, reported:

> The fiscal 1983 congressional presentation document estimated that Turkey's payments on principal and interest due on FMS loans will total $135 million in fiscal year 1983—growing to $259 million by 1986. But these estimates only include payments due on loan agreements signed before October 1, 1981. They do not include payments that will be due on loans included in the $343 million in new 1982 assistance, in the $465 million in 1983 assistance, the $525 million in 1984 assistance, and in the undetermined amounts of assistance in 1985 and 1986. If the effects of new loans are taken into account, Turkey's total FMS repayments will very likely reach $320 million in 1986. As grace periods for payments on principal expire, Turkey's annual payments could exceed $500 million by the end of the decade if current levels of FMS financing continue.

In fact, the congressional presentation for FY 1986 estimated that Turkey's total FMS repayments in FY 1986 would be $405 million. *Congressional Presentation: Security Assistance Programs,* FY 1986 (Washington, D.C., 1985), p. 229.

Statistics on military-related commercial loans and on credits extended by other major arms exporters—the Soviet Union, France, Great Britain, the Federal Republic of Germany, and Italy—[37] and by the oil rich countries in North Africa and the Middle East are not plentiful. In fact, accurate information on the true cost of military-related purchases to the importing country and on the terms of financing are often impossible to obtain. Prices, interest rates, and repayment periods frequently vary according to the political relationship between client and supplier government. For example, up to the early or mid-1970s, Soviet arms transfers are reported to have contained a considerable grant element, especially those used to establish relationships with certain African countries. Although Soviet terms have hardened over the last decade, concessional rates are still available for certain countries; for example, Ethiopia is said to have received military equipment from the USSR at a 50-percent discount since the late 1970s.

The emergence of several oil wealthy countries as major donors of security assistance after 1973 has complicated the picture even further since very little accurate information is publicly available about the value or terms of their assistance. To take just one example, in the latter half of the 1970s, both security expenditure and arms imports as a percentage of total imports increased sharply in Morocco (Figure 5-6 and Figure 2-1). The rise in security-related imports resulted primarily from the Moroccan government's attempt to take over the western Sahara and the ensuing conflict with the Polisaro guerrillas. Since the procurement portion of the Moroccan security budget increased substantially after 1975, it seems clear that Morocco has paid for some of these weapons itself. At the same time, the U.S. Agency for International Development has reported that "A substantial portion of the increased Moroccan defense expenditures was financed by Middle Eastern countries."[38] The terms of this financing are unknown, but some may have taken the form of grants and others soft loans. Without information on interest rates, repayment periods, and the grant component of these transfers, the economic effect of Morocco's arms imports cannot be calculated.

[37] Along with the United States, these five countries accounted for over 80 percent of the arms trade with the Third World between 1973 and 1983 and over 90 percent of the trade in major weapons between 1980 and 1984. Michael Brzoska and Thomas Ohlson, "The Trade in Major Conventional Weapons," p. 346, in SIPRI, World Armaments and Disarmament, 1985, and U.S. Arms Control and Disarmament Agency, World Military Expenditures and Arms Transfers, 1985, Publication 123 (Washington, D.C.: ACDA, August 1985), Table II.

[38] U.S. Agency for International Development, Implementation of Section 620(s) of the Foreign Assistance Act of 1961, as Amended. A Report to Congress (Washington, D.C.: AID, 1980), p. 6.

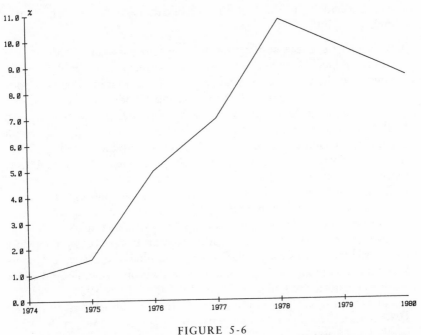

FIGURE 5-6

Morocco: Military Imports as Percentage of Total Imports, 1974–1980

Source: U.S. Agency for International Development, *Implementation of Section 620(s) of the Foreign Assistance Act of 1961, as Amended. A Report to Congress* (Washington, D.C.: USAID, 1980, 1981, 1982).

Under the Reagan administration, the U.S. government has sought to reverse the trend toward credit financing at market rates which had characterized its security assistance program during the 1970s, arguing that such a shift had become necessary in view of the increasingly heavy debt burden carried by a number of its Third World arms clients.

It was immediately obvious when this Administration took office that the trend away from grants and toward Treasury rate credits had contributed to a growing debt service burden for many of our key friends and allies. The Administration, therefore, supported and encouraged by Congress, sought greater concessionality for our military assistance programs in conjunction with strengthened economic assistance programs (a policy supported by the Carlucci Commission in its final report of November 1983). Obviously, it does little good for us to strengthen the self-defense capabilities of key third-world friends if, in the process, we contribute to the weakening of their economies.[39]

To a large extent, the administration's concern has been shaped by the economic difficulties experienced by just one recipient—Israel—and by the desire to channel a substantial amount of weaponry to two very poor Central American countries, El Salvador and Honduras. The unwillingness of Congress to appropriate as much military grant aid as requested by the administration has presumably also played a role in the expansion of concessional loans offered by the U.S. government since the early 1980s. Also of importance has been what might be termed the spread effect: Once Israel received certain concessional rates, it became necessary to make the same terms available to Egypt. Once Israel and Egypt received concessional rates, it became difficult to avoid making them available to certain other important recipients of U.S. security assistance.[40]

There is no doubt that U.S. security assistance was costing recipients less by the mid-1980s than it had at the beginning of the decade. Under-Secretary of State for Security Assistance, Science and Technology William Schneider reported to Congress in late 1985 that "In FY 1981, 84 percent of our FMS program was in the form of Treasury rate credits. In our FY 1986 request, the figure had dropped to 34 percent. MAP, on the other hand, has increased from 5.2 percent of total military assistance to 14.2 percent over the same period."[41] Not only has the direct grant element been increased, if at a slower rate than that requested by the admin-

[39] "Statement of William Schneider, Jr., Under-Secretary of State for Security Assistance, Science and Technology, before the Senate Foreign Relations Committee," 26 September 1985, mimeograph, pp. 6–7.

[40] A U.S. State Department official commented to this author that for the purposes of allocating foreign aid, there is a single country called "Israel-Egypt."

According to the State Department, the FY 1986 request for military grant aid under the Military Assistance Program was $950 million, but by the time the foreign aid appropriations bill left the House Appropriations Committee it had been cut by just over 20 percent to $740 million. Ibid., p. 8.

[41] Ibid., p. 1. The Military Assistance Program (MAP) is the conduit through which security-related grant assistance for equipment and related services has been channeled. In a 1985 study, the GAO found that "The data show FMS market rate loans declined from 68 to 29 percent in fiscal year 1985 as a percentage of the total military aid, whereas grants, including loans with repayments forgiven, increased from 32 to 59 percent of the total military aid. Grants and concessional interest rate loans increased from 32 percent to 71 percent of military aid in fiscal year 1985." U.S. General Accounting Office, *Military Loans: Repayment Problems Mounts As Debt Increases,* NSIAD-86-10 (Washington, D.C.: GAO, October 1985), p. 27. This report provides information on military-related debt to the U.S. government for some forty Third World governments; see pages 55–56. It also provides short profiles of three of the major recipients of U.S. military assistance: Israel, Egypt, and Turkey; see pages 29–32.

istration in some years, but the use of two types of concessional loans has become more common, and recipients of MAP have been allowed, since 1980, to use these grants to make payments on weapons procured through the FMS program—the so-called MAP-merger program.[42]

The first form of concessional loans involves extended repayment terms. Instead of the twelve years normally allowed for the repayment of FMS credits, a few countries have been granted a ten-year grace period followed by a twenty-year repayment period. Within the U.S. Department of State, these are known as "Israeli rates" since they were first granted to Israel around 1980; it immediately became necessary to make the same rates available to Egypt, and by 1985 they had been extended to six other countries—Portugal, Greece, Turkey, the Philippines, the Republic of Korea, and Thailand. The second form of concessional loan, introduced only in FY 1985, has been portrayed by the Reagan administration as a "direct result of our concern, and that of the Congress, that FMS credits at Treasury rates of interest would only continue to add to the debt service burdens of many countries." Interest rates for these loans are half the market rate prevailing at the time the agreement is signed, but not less than 5 percent. This is considerably lower than the 12 to 14 percent that had been charged during the first half of the 1980s. Fifteen countries were slated to conclude agreements at the lower rates in FY 1986, with the main recipients being Turkey, Jordan, the Philippines, Thailand, Portugal, Indonesia, and Tunisia.[43]

One form of concessionality that has not spread very far beyond Israel and Egypt is the decision by the U.S. government to waive repayment on a portion of the loans made to Israel, Egypt, and Sudan. Between FY 1974 and FY 1984, repayment was waived on nearly 40 percent of the FMS credits received by Israel. Some 20 percent of the FMS credits made available to Egypt were forgiven between FY 1979 and FY 1984 while about one-third of the FMS credits received by Sudan between FY 1980 and FY 1982 were cancelled. This has proved insufficient as debt relief, and since FY 1985 all FMS credits extended to both Israel and Egypt have been forgiven. In FY 1985, these two countries were allocated 50 percent of all U.S. FMS financing. In the administration's proposed FY 1986 budget,

---

[42] In a report to the U.S. Congress, the Congressional Research Service described the MAP-merger program as "in effect, a subsidy for military sales. . . ." Library of Congress, Congressional Research Service, Report: *US Military Sales and Assistance Programs: Laws, Regulations, and Procedures,* prepared for Subcommittee on Arms Control, International Security and Science of the Committee on Foreign Affairs, U.S. House of Representatives, 99th Cong., 1st Sess. (Washington, D.C.: Government Printing Office, 23 July 1985), p. 57.

[43] Ibid., pp. 50, 53; "Statement of William Schneider, Jr.," pp. 8–9; and *Congressional Presentation,* pp. 15–18.

CHAPTER 5

they were allocated 55 percent.[44] When these figures are added to those
for MAP grants and concessional loans, it is clear that a large portion of
the U.S. security assistance program is now provided on concessional
terms. In FY 1985 and in the initial FY 1986 request to Congress, some
70 percent of U.S. military assistance consisted of MAP, concessional
loans, and forgiven credits. The FY 1987 budget authority devoted just
over 70 percent of military aid to these categories.[45]

Although the U.S. government is eager to claim credit for not increasing the debt burden of a number of its more important arms clients
in the Third World, it is also careful to stress that past FMS loans have not
been a major contributing factor to the debt problems confronting these
countries.

In only a handful of countries do we find high debt service ratios *with* a significant portion of that debt service attributable to
FMS. . . .
Of our major military recipients, Israel and Egypt have the highest
total debt service ratios at 28 and 34 percent respectively. For Israel,
20 percent of its debt service is attributable to past FMS loans, and
for Egypt the comparable figure is 18 percent. . . .
There are only a few other FMS recipients whose FMS payments
constitute a significant percentage of a sizeable debt service burden.
They include Pakistan with a 22 percent overall debt service ratio, of
which 8 percent is FMS related; Greece—28 percent debt service
ratio, 11 percent FMS related; and Turkey—29 percent debt service
ratio, 11 percent FMS related.[46]

This says nothing, of course, about the debt that recipients of FMS financing may have incurred with other supplier countries or with commercial
banks.
Although the increase in concessionality is meant to limit the debt

---

[44]U.S. Department of State, *International Security and Development Cooperation Program*, Special Report no. 116 (Washington, D.C.: Department of State, April 1984), p. 8;
Congressional Presentation, pp. 15–16; and U.S. Department of Defense Security Assistance Agency, *Foreign Military Sales, Foreign Military Construction Sales and Military Assistance Facts as of September 30, 1984* (Washington, D.C.: Department of Defense, 1984),
pp. 24–25, 30–31.
[45]United States Department of State, Bureau of Public Affairs, *Foreign Assistance Program: FY 1986 Budget and 1985 Supplemental Request*, Special Report no. 128 (Washington, D.C.: Department of State, May 1985), p. 3, and *Congressional Presentation Security
Assistance Programs, FY 1987*, Vol. 1 (Washington, D.C., 1986), pp. 5–7.
[46]"Statement of William Schneider, Jr.," pp. 11–12. Emphasis in the original. The debt
service ratios have been derived by the Department of State from the World Bank's *World
Debt Tables, 1984–1985*.

problems of recipients of U.S. military assistance, one can legitimately ask if, in fact, it does not run the risk of increasing indebtedness. Under-Secretary of State Schneider explained to the Senate Foreign Relations Committee in September 1985 that the decision to introduce lower rates of interest on FMS loans for certain U.S. clients was based in part on the recognition that "the economic conditions in many of these countries were such that they could afford to repay loans if they received a more favorable interest rate."[47] This implies that at market rates these countries would find it difficult to repay FMS credits. It is not impossible that in the absence of the new, cheaper loans at least some of the governments involved might have chosen to procure less under the FMS program than they are now able, given the drop in interest rates. The direct effects for growth and development in such a situation would depend on the policies followed by the governments concerned. One fact is evident, however: security-related debt would have grown less rapidly.

According to Schneider, "Israeli rates" were designed for "those countries who require externally financed military purchases to meet their security needs but who wish to defer repayment of principal in order to devote more local resources to economically productive activities. Such investments are designed to stimulate greater economic growth which, in turn, would make principal repayment easier after expiration of the grace period."[48] The U.S. General Accounting Office has pointed out, however, that such loans made at market rates will accumulate interest payments that exceed the face value of the original loan *before* the expiration of the grace period.[49] It is not clear whether "Israeli rates" will be combined with the lower interest rates; if they were, this would only mitigate, not remove, the problem. Countries would still be accumulating relatively large interest payments that would add to the debt burden. There would be no guarantee that countries would increase their foreign exchange earnings sufficiently rapidly during the grace period to meet these payments as they came due. What might appear as a solution to the debt problem in the short-term could produce a significant problem ten or twenty years later.

Although security-related purchases clearly do engender increased borrowing on the part of Third World governments, there are many other reasons why these countries have contracted the debts they currently hold. Peru, for example, imported an estimated $1 billion worth of arms between 1974 and 1978 ($650 million of which came from the USSR).

[47] "Statement of William Schneider, Jr.," p. 9.
[48] Ibid.
[49] Shaw, "U.S. Security Assistance," p. 114.

TABLE 5-6
Peru: Public Foreign Debt According to Use, 1968–1980
(in percentages)

Year	Investment	Food	Petroleum	Refinancing	Other[a]
1968	44.7	0.0	0.0	53.2	2.1
1969	26.4	7.0	0.0	0.0	66.6
1970	39.8	9.5	0.0	21.9	28.8
1971	65.1	20.2	0.0	1.4	13.3
1972	58.3	14.6	0.0	22.9	4.2
1973	40.9	5.4	0.0	28.6	25.1
1974	73.1	4.0	0.0	10.5	12.4
1975	42.2	6.9	11.6	16.2	23.1
1976	41.9	5.6	0.0	1.1	51.4
1977	50.1	8.8	2.6	0.0	38.4
1978	47.4	25.2	0.0	13.8	13.6
1979	50.3	7.5	0.0	23.4	18.8
1980	62.9	8.9	0.0	0.0	28.2
Average	49.5	9.5	1.1	14.8	25.1

Source: Derived from Table 2.43 in José A. Encinas del Pando, "Economic, Military and Socio-Political Variables in Argentina, Chile and Peru (1950–1980). A Regional Analysis" (Lima: University of Lima, 1983, mimeograph).
[a] Includes debt related to military procurement.

The effect of these purchases on the distribution of Peruvian public-sector borrowing can be seen from Table 5-6 where the category "Other," which includes debt related to weapon procurement, increased substantially in the mid-1970s. Nonetheless, for the period shown in Table 5-6, nearly half the debt incurred by the Peruvian government was used for investment purposes.

Iran provides another interesting example of the relationship between the use of foreign exchange by Third World armed forces and indebtedness. The Iranian government had a tradition of borrowing to obtain foreign exchange, long predating the shah's forceful entry into the weapon market during the early 1970s. The state regularly used its revenue from foreign trade as collateral for foreign loans. It continued this policy when oil revenues skyrocketed in the early to mid-1970s even though it had sufficient income from its sale of petroleum to cover the foreign exchange requirements of both civil-sector investment and military-related purchases. By 1977–1978, as oil income fell, borrowing became necessary to maintain the level of investment and arms purchases desired by the shah.

The rise in public debt was a result of the multiplicity of objectives that the shah's regime tried to pursue simultaneously. This included military modernization as well as establishing major industries and creating industrial infrastructure. While most loans were contracted to pay for civilian projects, loans that were explicitly military were among the largest and the earliest. They helped to commit the Iranian military to imported arms and make it a significant consumer of foreign exchange.[50]

It stands to reason that as the terms for weapon sales become harder, the more weapons a country buys, the more it has to finance out of its own pocket. If export earnings are not sufficient to cover the cost of both military and civil-sector imports and if grants are unavailable or limited in amount, then arms purchases will necessitate increased borrowing and will burden the economy with additional debt service requirements. Access to loans at concessional rates will enable debt to be accumulated at a slower rate, but it will not alter this basic equation. The growth of military-related debt as one legacy of the 1970s is clear, even if detailed data are not available. At the same time, arms imports are not the sole, or often even the major, source of indebtedness in the Third World. Security-related borrowing has come to play an increasingly important role in the debt profile of many Third World countries, but it cannot be blamed for the entire debt crisis which emerged at the beginning of the 1980s. Indeed, in the two most heavily indebted countries—Mexico and Brazil—only a small amount of the debts incurred during the 1970s and 1980s can be traced to imports destined for the security sector.

Inflation

High levels of inflation can reduce the resources available for the development effort in a number of ways—for example, by discouraging savings and by reducing exports, which means decreased inflow of foreign exchange and lower government revenues from taxes on the export trade. Although the relationship between security expenditure and inflation is the subject of continual debate, it is generally agreed that such expenditure can contribute to inflationary pressures in an economy. There are essentially three channels through which the inflationary tendency of security spending can make itself felt. To the extent that security outlays are used to make purchases from the domestic economy, they may combine with civil-sector demand to create shortages of particular industrial inputs, thus, the costs of production are raised and, with them, the general

[50] Schulz, "Military Expenditures," p. 115. See also pp. 88–98.

level of prices. If wages and salaries paid in the security sector tend to be higher than those in the civil sector, they may also contribute to inflationary pressures by helping to push up wages in the latter faster than increases in productivity would warrant. Finally, it has been suggested that security expenditures have historically contributed to inflation by leading to a growth in the money supply without a corresponding increase in output.[51]

Security expenditure is, of course, not the only portion of the state budget with inflationary effects. Governmental outlays in the civil sector that cause bottlenecks in manufacturing industries, allow wages to rise faster than productivity, and result in uncompensated budget deficits that can contribute to inflation as well. Various corrective measures can be taken to mitigate the inflationary effects of any portion of the budget, for example reductions in expenditure in other sectors of the economy, but these are not always applied or, when applied, are not always successful.[52]

Some analysts have suggested that mild inflation can induce growth, and therefore they argue that, although security expenditure may increase inflation, it is not necessarily a bad thing. Emile Benoit discovered that after the "hyperinflationary" countries (those with inflation rates in excess of 25 percent annually), were removed from his sample,

> there was a statistically significant positive simple correlation between the rate of price increase and the rate of growth of real GDP. The countries maintaining a rate of wholesale price increase between 5% and 14% per annum averaged a substantially faster real growth than those with under 5% inflation. Moreover, we also found a significant positive simple correlation between the degree of inflation and the defense burden.[53]

---

[51] United Nations, General Assembly, A/36/356, pp. 84–85. In the latter case, the chain of causation is: security expenditure contributes to budget deficits; budget deficits financed by means other than borrowing from the nonbank public expand the money supply; the expansion of the money supply without a corresponding increase in output contributes to inflation.

[52] For example, see Schulz, "Military Expenditures," pp. 109–11, for an explanation of how the shah's government failed to control inflation in the early and mid-1970s which was exacerbated, if not caused, by the high level of arms imports during the 1970s. Miles Wolpin has pointed out that inflation induced by security spending can be reduced by raising taxes but that this will negatively affect consumption and employment and thus be unacceptable to some governments. Miles Wolpin, *Comparative Perspectives on Militarization, Repression and Social Welfare,* PRIO Report 4/93 (Oslo: International Peace Research Institute, 1983), p. 4.

[53] Emile Benoit, *Defense and Economic Growth in Developing Countries* (Lexington, Mass.: Lexington, 1973), p. 19.

Other cross-section studies have not produce such definite results, and it has been suggested that although inflation may have growth-inducing effects it might equally well have growth-inhibiting effects, necessitating a case-by-case examination of developing countries.[54]

When one examines the experiences of individual countries, it is frequently possible to conclude that both security-related expenditure contributes to inflation and it is only one of several inflation-inducing factors. It is often difficult to determine with precision which element or elements have been the most influential in this respect. The relationship between inflation and economic growth depends, in turn, on other factors such as the rate of inflation or the existence of demand constraints on growth.

Benoit used India to illustrate his argument that inflation induced by security expenditure could promote economic growth. Prior to the war with China in 1962, the Indian economy had been characterized by a relatively low defense burden (security expenditure as a proportion of gross product) and minimal inflation. The Sino-Indian conflict caused security expenditure to rise considerably, and in a year or two the rate of inflation did not further dampen the already rather slow rate of growth. Instead, real GDP grew faster for a few years (until the poor harvests in 1965 and 1966) than it had before. Benoit thus concluded that security expenditure can stimulate inflation and that moderate inflation can stimulate economic growth.[55]

Other sources offer support for at least portions of this line of reasoning. Computer simulations of the Indian economy between 1951 and 1973 indicate that public expenditure—of which security spending was an important component—promoted both growth and inflation between 1962 and 1967. It contributed to inflation by raising the budget deficit and by encouraging other public-sector employees to demand wages commensurate with those received by defense-sector employees.[56] However,

---

[54] Deger and Smith, "Military Expenditures," p. 338, state that "Cross-sectional studies reported by Thirwell reveal no strong bias in either direction." See, A. P. Thirwell, *Inflation, Saving and Growth in Developing Economies* (New York: Macmillan, 1974). Deger and Smith identify both potentially positive and potentially negative effects of inflation on economic growth in developing countries as do Lancaster and Lake. The latter argue that because—in their view—it is frequently a shortage of inputs such as skilled labor and capital which cause underutilized capacity and low investment in industry rather than a lack of demand, "military expenditures are unlikely to stimulate anything but price increases." Carol Lancaster and Anthony Lake, "Trends in LDC Military Expenditures." (Paper prepared for the Independent Commission on Disarmament and Security Issues, CD 031, August 1981, mimeograph), p. 12.

[55] Benoit, *Defense and Economic Growth*, pp. 18–19.

[56] The computer simulation results are reported in I. Ahluwalia, "An Analysis of Price

Raju Thomas has pointed out that although "between 1962 and 1965 the growth rate was accelerated by higher defense outlays, and the moderate price inflation perhaps aided the short period of economic prosperity," security expenditure was not the only factor contributing to inflation during this period. Thomas cites "agricultural failures, monetary expansion, deficit financing, general shortfall in industrial production, structural imbalances and distribution bottlenecks, and population growth" as "other more important factors" contributing to inflation in India during the mid-1960s.[57]

Similarly, the effects of inflation on the Indian economy during this period are still in some dispute. Most analysts agree that in the short-run, inflation promoted growth to some degree. Thomas, however, has argued that whatever adverse effects occur cannot be laid at the door of security expenditure because it was but one and indeed a minor cause of inflation. Terhal, on the other hand, has taken the position that inflation "eroded the public budget to the point that net public savings got severely restricted" which harmed the long-term growth potential of the economy. Terhal believes that even if security expenditure was only one cause of this inflation, it was a contributing factor and cannot be ignored.[58]

Peru is another country in which security expenditure has contributed to inflation, although it is difficult to determine with exactitude the extent to which inflation is security-related. A rather large number of factors, both domestic and foreign, have been identified as stimulating inflationary pressures in Peru. These can be grouped into four categories:

(a) long term endogenous causes, such as the savings gap, the supply inelasticity of the agricultural sector, monopolistic and oligopolistic markets and others;

(b) long term exogenous causes, such as the foreign trade gap, adverse terms of trade, the unequal allocation of foreign trade gains and others;

(c) short term endogenous causes, such as high government deficit spending, a national demand that outpaced national supply, mounting bureaucratic and military expenditures, including

---

and Output Behaviour in the Indian Economy: 1951–1973," *Journal of Development Economics* 6 (1979). These results and the inflation-promoting aspects of security expenditure are discussed in P. Terhal, "Guns or Grain: Macro-Economic Costs of Indian Defence, 1960–1970," *Economic and Political Weekly* 16 (5 December 1981): 1998, 2001.

[57] Thomas, *The Defence of India*, p. 138.

[58] Ibid., pp. 137–38, and Terhal, "Guns or Grain," pp. 1998, 2001.

high-level procurement abroad, the short-term economic costs
of the reforms undertaken; and
(d) short-term foreign causes, such as international and stubborn
stagflation, which was imported by the country, thus fueling
domestic inflation and the financial crisis.[59]

Prior to 1975, Peru enjoyed comparatively low rates of inflation, particularly in Latin American terms. After 1975, however, the country was
plagued by "spiraling inflation." When the military took power in 1968,
"inflation was at an all-time high of 19 percent per annum"; ten years
later, in 1978, it was estimated to have reached 73 percent.[60] Insofar as it
has been possible to rank the above-cited contributing factors, domestic
causes—especially heavy deficit spending by the government—are considered to have been the most important. The rapid increases in security
expenditure between 1971 and 1975 played a central role in expanding
government outlays. Nonetheless, the domestic causes of inflation were
not the only ones, and there were reasons other than military spending
behind the strong rise in government budgets during the early 1970s. It is
thus difficult to determine to what degree security expenditure contributed to inflation.[61]

Resource Mobilization

When thinking of the relationship between security expenditure, on the
one hand, and savings, investment, the balance of trade, indebtedness,
and inflation, on the other hand, it tends to be the negative, resource-
constraining aspects that come to mind first, although as we have just
seen there can be positive aspects as well. One way in which security expenditure might primarily act to increase the resources available for
growth and development is by encouraging governments to strengthen
their tax systems. Third World governments, often relying heavily on
the taxation of foreign trade for revenue, are slow to find new methods
of raising income. Many resist altering tax structures which favor the
wealthy at the expense of those with earned incomes since they wish to

---

[59] José A. Encinas del Pando, "Economic, Military and Socio-Political Variables in Argentina, Chile and Peru (1950–1980): A Regional Analysis" (Lima: University of Lima, 1983,
mimeograph), pp. 115–16.

[60] Schydlowsky and Wicht, "The Anatomy," pp. 95, 107.

[61] Encinas del Pando, "Economic, Military and Socio-Political Variables," pp. 109,
115–16, and Encinas del Pando, "Peru," pp. 113–22.

avoid alienating those groups that form the basis of their political power. The need to finance extra expenditure in the security sector may, however, encourage some governments to raise additional revenue by improving the collection of existing taxes, raising tax rates, broadening the tax base, or creating new taxes.

It has been suggested that during periods of crisis people are more disposed to accept changes in the tax system to supplement the armed forces' budget and that governments can take advantage of this situation to raise additional revenue to finance outlays in the civil sector. Both long-term and short-term effects can be anticipated. The long-term effect occurs when a government that has raised its level of taxation in one way or another does not return to the precrisis level when the emergency has ended and security expenditure can decline or at least level off. The short-term effect involves the ability of the government to take some of the extra revenue collected for the military effort and apply it productively in the civil sector during the crisis.[62] In this case, some economic benefit would be derived even if the tax system eventually returned to its precrisis state.

It is difficult to evaluate the extent to which governments respond in these ways. It has been claimed that Ghana, India, Nigeria, and Guatemala, all of "which have experienced rapid rises and falls in defence spending," have been able to raise taxation levels and apply some of the additional taxes to social programs.[63] The data behind this assertion are weak. More detailed study of India demonstrates that the anticipated benefits of crisis-related taxation increases have not materialized.

The Indian analyst Ved Gandhi has shown that while taxation rates have been raised by the Indian government during war periods (1962–1964, 1965–1966, and 1971–1972), the effect on growth and development has been minimal. The long-term fiscal effect did not apply in the Indian case because India's "revenue effort slackened substantially after every war." Nor did the short-term effect seem to operate because "a very large part of the increased revenue effort during the war years, and surprisingly even in later years, was always absorbed by defence."[64] Other countries may, of course, have followed different policies with more positive growth and development outcomes. But the Indian case demonstrates that there is nothing automatic in the relationship between crisis-induced

[62] Ved P. Gandhi, "India's Self-Inflicted Defence Burden," *Economic and Political Weekly*, 31 August 1974, pp. 1491, 1493.

[63] David K. Whynes, *The Economics of Third World Military Expenditure* (London: Macmillan, 1979), p. 40.

[64] Gandhi, "India's Self-Inflicted Defence Burden," p. 1493.

taxation increases and economic growth. The higher tax rate may be only temporary, and the extra revenue raised may be spent in the defense sector or on some other nonproductive form of expenditure.

A country need not be engaged in open warfare for the demands of the security sector to cause a government to increase taxes. There is a clear relationship between the South Korean government's tax policies and decreased availability of both military assistance and counterpart aid from the United States which had been used to finance a large share of the defense budget during the 1950s. (See the discussion in Chapter 7.) Cole and Lyman have described this interaction in the following way.

> Military assistance and the counterpart funds generated by economic assistance have declined very markedly from about 25 percent of GDP in 1958 to 7 percent in 1967–1968. This decline in the relative role of external resources for government has been offset mainly by reducing the share of government in the economy, but also to a degree by better domestic revenue mobilization.
>
> Declining levels of counterpart aid after the peak year of 1957 seemed initially to stimulate a stronger tax collection effort, so that current government revenues went up from 10 percent of GDP in 1958 to 13.8 percent in 1960. Then the devaluation of early 1961 raised the flow of counterpart from a given amount of assistance and revenue growth stopped. Subsequent inflation shrank the real value of both revenues and counterpart even more, with a consequent decline in the total budget. Finally, from 1965 on, as the relative importance of counterpart became quite limited, the pressures to raise the real size of the budget and increase the government's command over resources by noninflationary means forced a new attack on revenue problems. . . .
>
> The main feature of the Korean tax system is the degree of administrative discretion allowed in assessing most types of taxes. . . . Bargaining, compromise, and payoff were common features of the assessment process. These conditions meant that the way to increase tax collections was not to raise tax rates but simply to raise assessments. . . .
>
> To further strengthen the administrative apparatus, the government in 1966 set up a new Office of National Taxation and the president took a strong, personal interest in its effectiveness. He appointed one of his trusted subordinates (a member of the original coup group) to head the office and apparently supported him against the political and economic pressures brought by persons who sought relief from the higher taxes. . . .

Because of a growing feeling that the limits of increased revenue through stronger tax enforcement were being reached, some new tax legislation was pushed through the National Assembly in late 1967. The new laws broadened the tax base, raised tax rates, and introduced a number of equity and incentive features into the tax system.[65]

Since the share of fixed investment financed by the government in gross national product increased substantially between the mid-1960s and the early 1980s, it is likely that some of the extra revenue generated by the tax reforms inaugurated in 1965 was used to finance growth.[66]

SUMMARY

State security expenditure—like any other form of public spending—can affect economies in various ways; it can both increase and decrease the resources available for investment in productive undertakings. What the discussion here has attempted to demonstrate is that the existence of a potential influence, either positive or negative, should never be confused with an actual effect. The intensity and manner in which security expenditure acts upon economies vary from country to country and over time, and they depend on a large number of economic, political, and social variables. It can be quite difficult to disentangle the effects of security spending from general economic trends at both the national and the international levels. Nonetheless, an attempt should be made. Finally, the data on which such evaluations must be based tend to be weak. At a mini-

[65] David C. Cole and Princeton N. Lyman, *Korean Development: The Interplay of Politics and Economics* (Cambridge, Mass.: Harvard University Press, 1971), pp. 173, 176–77. See also, David Cole, "Fiscal and Financial Development," pp. 314–26, in *The Economic and Social Modernization of the Republic of Korea*, Edward S. Mason, Mahn Je Kim, Dwight H. Perkins, Kwang Suk Kim, David C. Cole with Leroy Jones, Il Sakong, Donald R. Snodgrass, and Noel F. McGinn, (Cambridge, Mass.: Harvard University Press for Council on East Asian Studies, Harvard University, 1980).

[66] Cole, "Fiscal," p. 325, has argued that

In sum, the Korean fiscal system has imposed taxes most heavily on urban consumption and has used the proceeds to invest in the infrastructure of economic development while maintaining adequate defence forces (with the help of military assistance) and minimal public expenditure on social services. In comparison with other countries at comparable stages of development, government revenues are close to the norm (based on Chenery-Syrquin predictions), but government consumption is below the norm. This is the case despite relatively large defense expenditures, which further emphasizes the very low level of other current government expenditures. Government investment spending, on the other hand, has been high, especially over the past decade [the 1970s]."

mum, more information is needed on what the security sector buys with its money and how much foreign exchange is absorbed by security-related purchases. Despite these problems, it is possible, as many of the studies cited in this chapter indicate, to go a long way toward understanding the effect that security spending has on the availability of resources in individual Third World countries.

6

. . . .

THE SECURITY SECTOR

AND THE EFFECTIVE USE

OF RESOURCES

Without access to adequate amounts of capital and in the absence of sufficient investment, economic growth will be sluggish or nonexistent. It has become increasingly clear, however, that there is a need to look beyond the availability of financial resources when evaluating the success individual countries have had in strengthening their economies. In discussing Western theories of development, Keith Griffin has pointed to some of the problems associated with assigning investment a central role in determining the rate of growth.

> The key to faster growth was believed to be a rising capital-labour ratio. No matter that empirical studies show that capital formation could account for only a fraction of the rise in labour productivity, or that the effectiveness of investment (as measured by the incremental capital-output ratio) varied enormously from one country to another, if only a country could reduce consumption and raise saving and investment, growth would accelerate and all would be well. In practice, this view gave governments the excuse to squeeze the consumption of the poor and redistribute income in favour of the "saving classes," i.e. the rich.[1]

While external economic conditions over which Third World countries have little, if any, control frequently handicap development efforts, many governments have failed to manage their economies as best they could under existing conditions. It is increasingly common to read that a country's economic difficulties are "due, among other factors, to a serious

---

[1] Keith Griffin, "Economic Development in a Changing World," *World Development* 9 (March 1982): 224.

'misallocation of resources' and to corruption" or that "financial mis-management, corruption and overspending by ministries have worsened the country's debt problems. . . ."[2] Such evaluations are not limited to the more conservative critics from the industrialized countries; also made by analysts from the Third World, they are increasingly heard within official circles. In 1985, for example, the Organization of African Unity (OAU) announced that a large number of countries in Africa were approaching "economic collapse" due to a combination of "an unjust and inequitable economic system," natural disasters, and "domestic policy shortcomings."[3]

Since many governments spend a not-inconsiderable amount of their available resources in the security sector and the armed forces control or strongly influence the government in many developing countries, it is reasonable to assume that the security sector has affected the efficiency with which resources are employed in many parts of the Third World. In this chapter, the discussion will focus on the way in which the security sector might affect aggregate demand and absorptive capacity and influence the nature of investment, thereby enhancing or diminishing a country's development prospects.

AGGREGATE DEMAND

In economies operating at less than full capacity, increased demand from any sector should provide beneficial stimulation. Many analysts have recognized that security expenditure has the potential to increase growth in Third World countries in this way.

> A military twist on the basic Keynesian model is the most cogent argument in support of a positive impact of increased arms spending on growth. In an economy with excess production capacity, increased aggregate demand from the military or any other source will drive up output, capacity utilization, and (under plausible assump-

[2] The first quotation is from Roy Stevens, "Momoh takes over in time of trouble," *Africa Now,* October 1985, p. 61. The second quotation is from Richard Everett, "Liberian economy faces dollar showdown," *African Business,* January 1986, p. 11.

[3] Edward Gargan, "Rise in Africa Debt," *New York Times,* 26 August 1985. Describing the critical situation facing Africa in the mid-1980s, the Ghanaian Marxist Eboe Hutchful has commented that "Much of the responsibility for this crisis must be located within the continent itself, in adverse natural and ecological conditions, and perhaps even more in colossal waste and mismanagement by African leaders. Nevertheless, it is equally clear that this crisis is part of the generalised crisis of capitalism." Eboe Hutchful, "Disarmament and Development: An African View," *IDS Bulletin* 16:4 (October 1985): 64.

tions) profit rates. Investment may respond to higher profits, increasing to put the economy on a faster long-term growth path.[4]

What is not clear is the extent to which Third World countries suffer from inadequate demand compared with shortage of capital and other resources.

According to Lance Taylor,

> At the macroeconomic level, there are two reasons why decreasing returns [on security expenditure] may not hold. First, there may be excess capacity in the system; and second, military spending may add to productivity growth even if resources are fully employed. Where there is excess capacity, it is clear enough that spending on arms and military personnel will add to aggregate demand. In most poor countries, where there is little sophisticated industry, the demand injection from spending on military equipment would leak to suppliers abroad. However, both construction workers on military bases and newly employed soldiers and sailors spend their wages, and this spending could give other people jobs.
>
> How seriously one should take this argument is not clear. . . . On *a priori* grounds, however, it can be stated immediately that straightforward demand expansion arguments look weak, for the simple reason that one scarce resource or another (land, physical capital, foreign exchange or skilled labor) seems to restrict total output in an underdeveloped economy. Without excess capacity, the military demand injection can have no effect on output, and will reduce civilian consumption spending, or else capital formation and growth.[5]

Some evidence suggests that demand constraints do exist in the Third World and that security expenditure can help to overcome them.

Econometric studies of India and Morocco indicate that, all things being equal, military expenditure—just like any other item of public

---

[4] Riccardo Faini, Patricia Arnez, and Lance Taylor, "Defense Spending, Economic Structure & Growth: Evidence Among Countries and Over Time" (Cambridge, Mass.: MIT, October 1980, mimeograph), p. 2.

[5] Lance Taylor, "Military Economics in the Third World" (Paper prepared for the Independent Commission on Disarmament and Security Issues, Cambridge, Mass.: MIT, October 1981, mimeograph), pp. 2–3. Speaking essentially of industrialized countries, Smith and Smith point out that the aggregate demand-stimulating effects of security expenditure on output and employment are dependent "on a very large number of factors. But as long as there was spare capacity to begin with, and as long as taxes are not increased by more than is needed to finance the extra military spending, output and employment should both increase," at least over the short term. See Dan Smith and Ron Smith, *The Economics of Militarism* (London: Pluto Press, 1983), pp. 85–86.

spending—can stimulate growth.[6] With regard to India, Emile Benoit believed that restrictive monetary and fiscal policies followed by the government between 1950 and 1961 contributed to the slow rate of growth experienced during that period. The war with China in 1962 was said to have stimulated the Indian government to raise its level of taxation and carry a larger budgetary deficit. The increased demand from the public sector engendered by these policies stimulated the economy to grow at a faster rate according to Benoit. Additional support for this line of reasoning has been provided by computer simulations based on a macroeconomic model of the Indian economy for the years 1951 to 1973 which demonstrated that public expenditure, including the defense budget, had a positive effect on economic growth between 1962 and 1967.[7]

Indian economists have suggested that limited domestic demand has contributed to the relatively slow rate of growth experienced by the Indian economy over the last twenty years: "paradoxical as it may appear, the major constricting factor in the development of the Indian economy along the path that it has been taking so far is the limitation of the domestic market."[8] When this assessment was made in the late 1970s, India's estimated population was 650 million, a large proportion of whom lived in conditions of extreme poverty.

Although output has increased, poverty and inequalities of a staggering nature still continue. On the basis of the basic nutritional norm, 48 percent of the people in rural areas and 41 percent in urban areas,

---

[6]The Moroccan case is discussed in Jacques Fontanel, "Formalized Studies and Econometric Analyses of the Relationship Between Military Expenditure and Economic Development: The Examples of a Developed Country, France, and an Underdeveloped Country, Morocco" (Study prepared for the UN Special Expert Group on Disarmament and Development, Grenoble: Grenoble Centre for Security and Defence Studies, 1980, mimeograph). Fontanel concludes that "it is possible to say that in the absence of any other action, increased military expenditure may lead to a slight increase in gross domestic product, but public action would be better justified, at the strictly economic level, if it were aimed at other items of public expenditure (education, health, etc.)" (pp. 31–32).

[7]Emile Benoit, *Defense and Economic Growth in Developing Countries* (Lexington, Mass.: Lexington 1973), pp. 18–19, and Peter Terhal, "Guns or Grain: Macro-Economic Costs of Indian Defence, 1960–1970," *Economic and Political Weekly* 16 (5 December 1981): 2001.

[8]C. T. Kurien, "The New Development Strategy: An Appraisal," *Economic and Political Weekly* 31:31–33 (Special Number 1978): 1264. In Iran, where half the population lived in rural areas in the 1960s and 1970s, low rural incomes "prevented the development of internal markets that would support domestic industries." Iran thus had to turn to the export market to sell its manufactured products. Ann Schulz, "Military Expenditures and Economic Performance in Iran, 1950–1980" (Worcester, Mass.: Clark University, 1982, mimeograph), p. 138.

together constituting a massive 290 million are reckoned to be below the poverty line in 1977–78. Also, the analysis of consumption expenditure shows that in 1973–74 the lowest 20 percent accounted for 9.5 percent of total consumption in rural areas while the highest 20 percent accounted for 38 percent. For urban areas the corresponding figures were 9.2 percent and 40 percent. Similarly, it is now documented that the bottom 20 percent of rural households each having less than Rs 1,000 of assets account for less than 1 percent of rural assets, while the top 4 percent with asset-values of Rs 50,000 or more own over 30 percent.[9]

The importance of domestic demand stands out most clearly in periods of global recession when export markets for Third World products shrink due to the contraction of industrialized economies. Under such conditions, excess capacity is more likely to exist and the possibility that expenditure in the security sector will stimulate demand and contribute to growth increases. As explained in Chapter 5, the recession of 1980–1982 did produce considerable excess capacity, but, since much of this was generated by the inability to import vital components and raw materials, it is not clear what effect increased demand from the security sector would have in any particular country.

The composition of security expenditure is central to an evaluation of the relationship between the defense budget and aggregate demand. As Taylor rightly pointed out, some portions of security spending have the potential to stimulate aggregate demand (salaries, procurement from the

[9] Kurien, "The New Development Strategy," p. 1258. According to Ajit Singh, "The 'Basic Needs' Approach to Development vs the New International Economic Order: The Significance of Third World Industrialization," *World Development* 7 (June 1979): 598, it was "clearly the lack of demand which is holding back industrial expansion" from about 1978 onward. It is not entirely certain, however, what has caused the general deceleration in the growth of industrial output in India since 1965. According to Singh, *one* of the explanations of this phenomenon has also centered around insufficient demand from the domestic market.

It has been contended that in the 1950s and early 1960s industrial demand expanded fast because of import substitution, but that once this process was completed there was insufficient internal demand, because of unequal income distribution and other institutional rigidities. (In a country of India's size, although exports can aid growth, internal demand must play the leading role.) . . .

However, whether any of these theories can help to explain deceleration—and a great deal of research is needed in this area—a "basic needs" strategy, leading to a more equal income distribution or more public expenditure on meeting the requirements of the poor (e.g. provision of water supply or electricity in the villages, etc.), should greatly help industrial development at this stage. (p. 599)

local economy), and some do not (procurement from abroad). Chapter 3 showed that many countries devote a large proportion of their security budgets to salaries and wages. Personnel-related items such as food, clothing, and medical care also frequently account for a sizable share of the nonsalary portion of operating costs. These as well as other operating costs (office supplies, repair and maintenance equipment, for example) and even some capital costs (construction material) should theoretically be available for purchase from the domestic economy. In practice, however, the situation may be somewhat more complex.

In some countries, the armed forces produce a portion of the food they consume on military farms (see Chapter 8). Although this means that the armed forces in food-deficit countries do not compete with the civilian population as much as they might, it also means that demand is lower than it would be if all food were purchased from civilians. Some governments have diverted food aid from its intended recipients to the armed forces. In both these cases, the effect of security expenditure on the civil economy is reduced.[10]

Although most salaries and wages paid in the security sector are likely to be used to consume locally produced goods, some will leak abroad. In Iran during the 1970s, for example, foreign technical personnel tended to command high salaries and consume imported products. The same patterns of consumption might be expected for domestic military élites in many developing countries. For Iranian conscripts, however, the pay received in the security sector was superior to what many of them could have earned in the civil sector—particularly in agriculture—which presumably increased their demand for locally produced items.

Military-related construction can also be expected to have both positive and negative effects on aggregate demand. In Iran during the 1970s, when facilities for the troops were built, local materials and construction skills were employed. In contrast, the construction of major bases and installations was contracted out to foreign companies, and many necessary materials and skills had to be imported. In Nigeria, large-scale military construction in the 1970s stimulated both investment in a domestic cement industry and massive imports of cement. In South Korea, military-related construction, first for domestic facilities and then in South Vietnam, laid the basis for what subsequently became a profitable construc-

---

[10] The diversion of food aid has been best documented for Bangladesh. See, for example, Donald F. McHenry and Kai Bird, "Food Bungle in Bangladesh," *Foreign Policy* no. 27 (Summer 1977): 72–88, and Betsy Hartmann and Jim Boyce, *Bangladesh: Aid to the Needy?*, International Policy Report (Washington, D.C.: Center for International Policy, 1978). See also, "Bangladeshi Aid: The New Ruling Class," *South*, March 1982, pp. 46–47.

tion industry and, for some years at least, an important earner of foreign exchange.[11]

Security expenditure clearly has the potential for stimulating aggregate demand, and its growth-inducing effects may have been underrated by analysts who have seen factors other than insufficient demand as the most important constraints on economic growth in the Third World. At the same time, the various components of security spending will affect domestic demand in different ways, and it is important to know what the armed forces spend their money on in order to evaluate the interaction between security spending and aggregate demand in individual countries.

THE NATURE OF INVESTMENT

It is not enough to ask how much investment occurs in an economy when evaluating its growth potential; it is also important to know what form investment takes. There are two very broad areas of choice: agriculture versus industry and capital-intensive versus labor-intensive processes. It is often argued that a stagnant agricultural sector results in a stagnant national economy and that development must therefore proceed simultaneously in both industry and agriculture.

> The growth of industry without a parallel growth of agriculture limits the market for industrial products and tends therefore not only to bring industrialisation to a halt but also to stimulate the demand for imports, and thus lead to balance-of-payments difficulties. As already shown, the inputs of agriculture are the outputs of some key industries: iron and steel, machinery, and chemicals, which are also among the main motive forces for the growth of the whole economy. Furthermore, though part of the process of development is high productivity in the rural sector, the fact remains that this sector (agriculture and the infrastructure of the countryside) is capable of absorbing significant quantities of unemployed or under-employed labour.[12]

[11] On Iran, see Schulz, "Military Expenditures," pp. 78–79, 125–26, 138. On Nigeria, see J. 'Bayo Adekanye, "The Role of Military Expenditure in the Development Process: Nigeria" (Ibadan: University of Ibadan, 1982, mimeograph). On South Korea, see David Cole, "Foreign Assistance and Korean Development," pp. 183–84, in *The Economic and Social Modernization of the Republic of Korea*, Edward S. Mason et al. (Cambridge, Mass.: Harvard University Press, 1980).

[12] A. F. Ewing, "Some Recent Contributions to the Literature on Economic Development," *Journal of Modern African Studies* 4: 3 (1966): 342–43. References to a number of relevant studies are listed on page 343. For additional references, see Nicole Ball, *World Hunger: A Guide to the Economic and Political Dimensions* (Santa Barbara, Calif.: ABC-Clio, 1981), pp. 76–81.

Despite this, development strategies devised throughout the post–World War II period have tended to emphasize industrialization as the most efficient means of promoting economic growth and modernization in the Third World. As a result, development planners, from both developing countries and from international banks and aid agencies, have frequently neglected the agricultural sector.

This does not mean that there was a complete absence of investment in agriculture. A much larger proportion of investment has, however, tended to occur in the industrial sector. Furthermore, the main beneficiaries of agricultural investment have in very many cases (although not exclusively) been the wealthier domestic farmers and transnational corporations, particularly if they produce crops for export. In 1973, for example, Robert McNamara, then president of the World Bank, admitted that "In our more than a quarter century of operations, less than $1 billion out of our $25 billion lending has been devoted directly to" increasing "the productivity of subsistence agriculture."[13] More than a decade later and despite an attempt on the part of several major donors—notably the World Bank and the U.S. Agency for International Development—to channel a larger proportion of their development assistance to small farmers, a sizable proportion of the world's population remains extremely poor and dependent for its livelihood on subsistence agriculture.[14]

[13] Robert S. McNamara, "Address to the Board of Governors, Nairobi" (Washington, D.C.: World Bank, 1973), p. 44.

[14] To a large extent, this is due to the fact that

In the vast majority of the Bank's rural development projects the principal beneficiaries were to be small-scale farmers who owned and operated their own properties. Virtually none of the projects were designed to reach the rural landless at all, nor were they principally oriented toward tenant farmers, sharecroppers, or squatters. This focus on small owner-operators as the principal target group meant that the projects were not likely to assist the "poorest of the poor". The small owner-operators, while poor, were still comparatively better off.

Robert L. Ayres. *Banking on the Poor: The World Bank and World Poverty* (Cambridge, Mass.: MIT Press, 1984), p. 102.

According to another source, some of the "small farmers" had access to fairly large plots of land. In addition, large landowners continued to benefit from aid projects.

The Bank's claims that it had a new "poverty orientation" were based largely on its lending for projects in rural areas, where, according to new rhetoric, the "poorest of the poor" were to be found. It is nevertheless probably a near-universal phenomenon of Bank rural development projects that their benefits are appropriated by the better-off peasants and landowners. Thus, according to Cheryl Payer,

In Guatemala the Bank solved the problem of reaching "small farmers" by defining them as anyone with less that 45 hectares of land (108 acres)—a category which encompasses 97 per cent of all Guatemalan farmers. Half of the funds

A clear example of what happens when the agricultural sector receives only a small share of available investment funds is provided by the experience of Nigeria since the early 1970s. The prourban, antirural bias which has characterized government policy since the colonial period intensified following the oil price rise of 1973. Sufficient financial resources were available to cover production shortfalls in the domestic agricultural sector with imports. The government, led by the armed forces until late 1979, gave priority during the 1970s to heavy industry (metallurgy and allied engineering), construction (road network), and technical education. The Third Plan proposed allocating 7 percent of total (federal and state government) capital expenditure to agriculture, irrigation, livestock, forestry, and fisheries. By contrast, manufacturing and crafts, with the accent on heavy manufacturing, were to be given 12.7 percent of total capital outlays; transport, 22.3 percent; and defense and security, 10 percent.[15]

Although it was realized as early as 1971 that the food crop sector was experiencing difficulty in keeping up with the country's rather high rates of population growth, the measures adopted in the 1970s to deal with the problem were ad hoc in nature and did little, if anything, to ameliorate it. Many of the government's programs in the agricultural sector were directed toward the production of export crops, and larger farmers, including transnational corporations, reaped most of the benefits. In addition to the preference for white-collar jobs, the construction boom generated by the oil bonanza meant that higher wages could be obtained in the urban areas, and migration from the rural areas was substantial. The government was not unaware of the problems facing agriculture in Nigeria, as is evident from the following constraints on agricultural production identified by (civilian) President Shagari's special adviser on agriculture in 1983, but it was unable to address them seriously.

(a) inadequate use of land and water resources;
(b) migration of young hands from rural to urban centres in search of white-collar employment;

---

would go to "small farmers" thus defined, while the other half would go to "medium" and "larger" farms in the top 3 per cent. "I don't care what country you take", an agricultural specialist with wide experience in Latin America told me, "if you follow World Bank money down through the distributing institutions, it's all going to the wrong people".

Teresa Hayter and Catharine Watson, *Aid: Rhetoric and Reality* (London: Pluto Press, 1985), p. 152. The citation from Payer is found in Cheryl Payer, *The World Bank* (New York: Monthly Review Press, 1982), p. 236.

[15] Adekanye, "The Role," Part 3, pp. 54–68, 98–115.

(c) Nigeria's level of horsepower—0.05% is lower than the minimum 0.5% on the farm to support the rate of national development;

(d) chaotic state of research institutes;

(e) inadequate funding of research work on agricultural production;

(f) incompetence of extension workers and researchers on the production of many food crops except cocoa and rubber;

(g) ineffective and inefficient opening of new land areas;

(h) farmers' lack of resources and capital to improve food production;

(i) inadequate investment on agricultural production;

(j) disintegration of the time-honoured extension services;

(k) the negative role of middle men;

(l) rice importation.[16]

The Nigerian reliance on imported food grew rapidly during the 1970s. Between 1971 and 1981, the value of Nigerian food imports, measured in 1980 nairas, grew from some 193 million to 1.7 billion nairas (equivalent to approximately $335 million and $3.1 billion respectively). As long as income from the oil sector continued to expand, these purchases could be sustained. The collapse of oil prices which began in 1981 meant, among other things, that large food imports were increasingly difficult to finance.[17]

The developmental priorities of many Third World governments—preference accorded to urban areas, the industrial sector, and the larger landowners in the agricultural sector—have worked against the interests of the majority of Third World farmers, smallholders or landless peasants, and have worsened, rather than improved, their situation.[18] By failing to eradicate rural poverty, it has also weakened the long-term pros-

[16] Toyin Falola and Julius Ihonvbere, *The Rise and Fall of Nigeria's Second Republic, 1979–84* (London: Zed Press, 1985), p. 141. See also pp. 122–45 and Otto Sano, *The Political Economy of Food in Nigeria 1960–1982*, Research Report no. 65 (Uppsala: Scandinavian Institute of African Studies, 1983), esp. Part I.

[17] Falola and Ihonvbere, *The Rise and Fall*, p. 133. Deflator and exchange rates from International Monetary Fund, *International Financial Statistics, 1984 Yearbook* (Washington, D.C.: IMF, 1984).

[18] See, for example, Susan George, *How the Other Half Dies* (Harmondsworth, England: Penguin, 1976); E. G. Vallianatos, *Fear in the Countryside: The Control of Agricultural Resources in the Poor Countries by Nonpeasant Elites* (Cambridge, Mass.: Ballinger, 1976); International Labour Office, *Poverty and Landlessness in Rural Asia* (Geneva: ILO, 1977); Milton Esman, *Landless and Near-Landless in Developing Countries*, LNL no. 1 (Ithaca, N.Y.: Cornell University, Rural Development Committee, September 1978); and Barbara Dinham and Colin Hines, *Agribusiness in Africa* (London: Earth Resources Research, 1983).

pects of attaining self-sustaining growth in the Third World since, as discussed in the preceding section, the constraints placed on domestic demand when large segments of the population live in extreme poverty can inhibit economic growth. In a country with a limited domestic market, firms must succeed in the export market.[19] When the world market is in recession, as was the case in the mid-1970s and early 1980s, they are all too often faced with inadequate demand at both the national and the international levels.

The smallholder versus larger farmer dichotomy is, in a way, replicated in the industrial sector by the need to choose between production processes that are relatively more or less labor- or capital-intensive. Third World economies are typically characterized by an abundance of labor, much of it unskilled, and a shortage of capital. Under such conditions, it is sensible to invest the scarce capital in production processes that use as much labor as possible. The purpose of this strategy is to maximize employment per unit of investment and better enable domestic demand to sustain local industries, assuming that these industries are producing essential goods for domestic consumption and not simply items for export.

An initial emphasis on labor-intensive processes neither excludes all capital-intensive methods of production nor contradicts the extremely important goal for many Third World development planners of setting up producer-good industries, as the Chinese experience indicates. According to Ajit Singh, the Chinese economy had undergone a significant structural change by the mid-1970s: industry had been the "main engine of growth"; industry's share in output "increased dramatically," and productivity in industry grew more rapidly than in agriculture; heavy industry's share in total industrial output "has more than doubled since the early 1950s and is now very much larger than that of consumer goods."[20]

[19] UNCTAD has taken the position that, "There is no correlation between the size of population and the degree of industrialization, either in developing countries or in developed market economy countries. Small and medium sized countries can achieve a high degree of industrialization through industrial specialization and trade." UNCTAD, *Restructuring of World Industry: New Dimensions for Trade Cooperation* (New York: United Nations, 1978), quoted in Singh, "The 'Basic Needs' Approach," p. 595.

[20] Singh, "The 'Basic Needs' Approach," pp. 589–90.

Whether heavy industry, at 56 percent of total industrial output in 1976, is "very much larger" than consumer goods industry, at 44 percent of total industrial output in 1976, is a matter of definition. It is interesting to note, however, that its share was considered too large by the mid-1980s when the Chinese government argued that the composition of industrial products did not correspond adequately to the needs of society as a whole. According to the director of the State Statistical Bureau of China, there was a "serious disproportion between various economic sectors" by the end of the 1970s.

Agriculture and light industry became weaker than before and heavy industry grew at a disharmonious, fast pace. . . .

TABLE 6-1
China: Structure of Economy, 1949–1976

Year	(1) Agriculture % Gross Product	(2) Industry % Gross Product	Heavy Industry[a] (3) Total Industrial Product	(4) % Gross Product	Light Industry[a] (5) Total Industrial Product	(6) % Gross Product
1949			27		73	
1950			30		70	
1951			32		68	
1952	46	27[b]	36		64	
1953			37		63	
1954			38		62	
1955			42		58	
1956			46		54	
1957	43	33[b]	48		52	
1958–1965	—	—	—	—	—	—
1966	30	53	51	27	49	26
1967	33	50	47	23	53	26
1968	35	49	46	22	54	26
1969	30	52	50	26	50	26
1970	28	55	54	29	46	25
1971	26	57	57	32	43	24
1972	26	57	57	33	43	25
1973	26	57	57	32	43	27
1974	26	56	56	31	44	25
1975	25	58	56	32	44	26
1976	25	58	56	32	44	26

Sources: Columns 1 and 2, 1952 and 1957: Dwight H. Perkins, "Estimating China's Gross Domestic Product," Current Scene 15: 3 (1976): 16, cited in T. G. Rawski, Industrialization, Technology and Employment in the People's Republic of China, Working Paper no. 291 (Washington, D.C.: World Bank, 1978), p. 2.

Columns 3 and 4, 1949–1957: State Statistical Bureau (China), Ten Great Years (Peking: 1960), cited in R. M. Field, "Civilian Industrial Production in the People's Republic of China: 1949–74," p. 168, in Compendium: China—A Reassessment of the Economy, U.S. Congress (Washington, D.C.: 10 July 1975).

All other data: "Comprehensive Statistics for the National Economy," Beijing Review 27 (19 March 1984): 27.

[a] In Ten Great Years, industrial production is divided into "producer goods" and "consumer goods."

[b] Transport included here. For 1966–1976, transport accounted for approximately 3% of gross product annually.

Table 6-1, based primarily on data released by the Chinese government, confirms Singh's assessments.

According to Singh, the Chinese government effected these structural changes by simultaneously using labor- and capital-intensive production techniques and developing small- and large-scale manufacturing enterprises. Important amounts of some producer goods have been manufactured in rural and other small-scale industries using relatively labor-intensive methods in the absence of more capital-intensive techniques. Such industries were estimated, for example, to have produced half of China's total output of fertilizer and cement in 1972. The importation of large-scale fertilizer plants in the late 1970s means that small-scale producers of fertilizer will account for a progressively smaller proportion of total output in the 1980s.[21]

It can be difficult, especially for smaller developing countries, to shift to large-scale, capital-intensive production of producer goods. Local markets may be even less able to absorb a sufficient amount of the output of producer-goods industries to make them profitable than they are to absorb the products of the consumer goods industries. The ability to export is thus important, and the state of the global economy, essentially the industrialized country economies, is crucial to the success of these industries in the smaller Third World countries. As more and more developing countries expand into producer goods industries, they run greater risks of competing with production in the industrialized countries and of running into protectionist barriers in the latter. The development of an indigenous technological capacity is also difficult since the multinational corporations responsible for the transfer of production processes to the Third World prefer to retain control over their technology.[22] Nonetheless, it re-

---

Commodity transport and circulation slowed down and transport became a very weak link in the national economy.

The irrational structure of the national economy is seen most clearly in the figures for major industrial and agricultural products. The average annual output of grain increased only 3 per cent and cotton cloth, just 1.9 per cent. Production of cotton and oil-bearing crops dropped. Manufacture of the means of production, especially of machines, went up rapidly. But most of the increased products of heavy industry were made to serve the industry itself and gave no boost to the production of consumer goods. The slow growth of consumer goods, in turn, hindered the development of the means of production.

Li Chengrui, "Are the 1967–76 Statistics on China's Economy Reliable?," *Beijing Review* 27 (19 March 1984): 25.

[21] Singh, "The 'Basic Needs' Approach," p. 592.

[22] A brief description of some of the problems confronting Third World countries in their attempts to import technology is found in Ahmad Sakr, "How Unfair Contracts Shackle the South," *South*, March 1982, p. 43. See also Chapter 9 below.

EFFECTIVE USE OF RESOURCES

mains true that a country with a weak industrial base will not be able to absorb the more sophisticated processes successfully even if they are available.

The well-known trio of Asian countries—Taiwan, Singapore, and South Korea—which, along with Hong Kong, have experienced extremely rapid economic growth over the last two decades or so began by investing in labor-intensive consumer goods industries. Now attempting to move beyond this initial stage into more capital-intensive and technologically advanced processes for producer goods, they are meeting with varying degrees of success. Because their domestic economies are small, they must depend on the export market to a large degree. The global economic recession that began in 1980 was felt the least in Taiwan and the most in South Korea. In mid-1980, for example, it was reported of South Korea that, "Past spending has not been so wise. The dramatic surge into heavy and chemical industries has saddled the nation with a heavy debt and returns from some of the industries will be slow to materialise. Over-capacity is colossal in shipbuilding, heavy electrical, steel fabrication and motor industries and in some chemical and engineering industries."[23] Nonetheless, it is difficult to believe that any of these countries would have been better able to succeed in establishing intermediate and capital-goods industries if they had begun their postindependence industrialization efforts by concentrating heavily on capital-intensive techniques.[24]

[23] Philip Bowring, "Overconfidence and Bad Luck Led to a Fall," *Financial Times*, 9 June 1980.

[24] It should be pointed out that to an important degree the success of the labor-intensive, export-led strategy followed by Taiwan, Singapore, and South Korea has depended on the ability of governments to enforce low wages. Thus, the benefits of economic growth have not been shared as equitably as they could have been, particularly in South Korea. Comparing Taiwan and South Korea to Japan, Bruce Cumings has commented that, in the first two countries, "there is no permanent employment, working hours are much longer (52 hours per week in the big firms, longer in small firms), and wages are much lower in relation to living cost." Bruce Cumings, "The Origins and Development of the Northeast Asian Political Economy: Industrial Sectors, Product Cycles, and Political Consequences," *International Organization* 38 (Winter 1984): 30–31.

What is more

Exploitation of labor, particularly females, is so marked that it is foolish to deny it (even though many American specialists continue to do so). In both the Kachsiung [Taiwan] and the Masan [South Korea] FEZs [Free Export Zones] 80 percent of the workforce is female, and teenage girls are about 60 percent of that total. Most of the work is unskilled assembly, done by girls recruited from peasant families. Their wage rates are at the bottom of the heat in world scales—one-third of Japan's level, one-fifth to one-tenth of the US level, even one-half of the level in Hong Kong where similar practices prevail. (ibid., pp. 31–32)

CHAPTER 6

The security sector affects the kind of investment that occurs and the production techniques chosen both through the goods and services it purchases from the domestic economy and through the policies followed by

---

Interestingly, in 1979 the Singapore government inaugurated a policy of raising wage levels in order to force industry to move into more technologically advanced industries with higher value-added. Some initial successes were recorded, but shrinkage in the U.S. market during the first half of the 1980s produced problems, particularly in the electronics and computer industries. See Kathryn Davies, "Manufacturing Sector Hit by Recession in The West," *Financial Times*, 22 November 1982, Singapore VIII, and "The Air Goes Out of Asia's Business Balloon," *US News & World Report*, 16 December 1985, p. 48.

Another similarity shared by Singapore, Taiwan, and South Korea is the authoritarian character of their governments. It is frequently suggested that the export-led policy requires authoritarianism to enforce the necessary restraints on labor. But this is not entirely true, as evidenced by Japan which has based its industrial development on a low-wage policy without resorting to political authoritarianism. It might be argued that to some extent Japan's low-wage, procapital policies have been mitigated by higher levels of social expenditure than have occurred in Taiwan or South Korea while the latter have preferred to build up their repressive forces. Cumings has pointed out, for example,

> In 1973, expenditures on social insurance, public health, public assistance, welfare, and veterans' relief represented 0.97 percent of GNP in the ROK, 1.2 percent in Taiwan; this compares with 3 percent in Malaysia and 5.3 percent in Japan. Such figures capture the tradeoff between Japan and Korea and Taiwan: the latter two spend 4 to 10 percent of GNP on defense, and Japan can hold defense expenditures under one percent; but Japan, by virtue of its "New Deal" during the Occupation and its democratic systems, must spend 5 percent on social programs (still low by world standards). In any case both the ROK and Japan until recently escaped with spending about 6 percent of GNP on defense and welfare combined. Korean and Taiwanese workers pay the cost in the periphery.

Cumings, "The Origins," p. 31.

If Japanese defense expenditure were calculated according to the NATO definition, it would, in fact, exceed 1 percent. But the point that should be made here is that the form of government and level of security expenditure of each of these countries reflects certain politico-strategic, as well as internal economic, considerations. In South Korea, the as yet unresolved conflict with North Korea has contributed to the military's interest in controlling the government. The late President Park Chung Hee's promulgation of the authoritarian Yushin Constitution in 1972 owed much to his personal desire to remain in power. In Taiwan, the immigrants from the mainland who have controlled the government since 1949 long nourished dreams of using Taiwan as a springboard for the invasion of China. Particularly in the early years, control of Taiwan's government, its economy and society were elements of KMT plans to regain control over the mainland. While the existence of authoritarian government undeniably facilitated the exploitation of labor, there were other reasons—at least in Taiwan and South Korea—for them to have come into being.

Some of the problems faced by South Korea, Taiwan, and Singapore in their attempts to deepen their industrialization processes are discussed in the following articles. On Singapore see: "Rapid Growth Continues as Economy is Restructured," *Financial Times*, 17 November 1981, and Davies, "Manufacturing Sector." On Taiwan see, David Housego, "How Taiwan Gains from S. Korea's Turmoil," *Financial Times*, 2 December 1980; on South Korea see, Cumings, "The Origins," pp. 35–37, and Bowring, "Overconfidence."

226

governments that are controlled or heavily dependent upon the armed forces. The military's influence over the industrialization process and some of the likely technical and economic effects of military-led industrialization are discussed in detail in Chapter 9. A few comments are nonetheless in order here. In general, Third World armed forces tend to promote industrialization, both to enhance economic independence and to lay the basis for the domestic production of weapons. This may contribute to a bias in favor of the urban-industrial sector and to a relative neglect of agriculture. The production of weapons will enhance any tendency to employ capital- rather than labor-intensive processes and will result in large investments in industries that produce goods and industrial inputs too specialized for the general market.

It is also true, however, that demand from the armed forces might encourage the establishment or improve the profitability of certain basic industries, both producer (Argentinian iron and steel) and consumer (South Korean textile). In addition, it is often difficult to say that governments led by civilians and those led by the armed forces follow radically different policies. In Nigeria, both military and civilian governments chose to spend the bulk of their oil revenue outside the agricultural sector, despite clear signs that that sector was heading for a crisis. If a military government is now showing more interest in rural areas, it is because Nigeria quite simply lacks the foreign exchange necessary for large-scale food imports.

Absorptive Capacity

An economy is said to have reached the limits of its absorptive capacity when the growth rate is "constrained by factors *other* than either 'savings' or 'foreign exchange', in other words, by factors such as the supply of skilled labour, administrative capacity, entrepreneurship, social change etc. . . ." [25] While many development analysts would agree with the statement that "Absorptive capacity is . . . only marginally relevant to most

---

[25] Robin Marris, "Can We Measure the Need for Development Assistance?" *Economic Journal,* September 1970, p. 652. Marris also comments,

> Absorptive capacity is restrained by the residual factors in economic growth, and to attempt to measure it, therefore, is akin to attempting to estimate a dynamic form of macro-economic production function. On the stylised assumption of an unlimited supply of unskilled labour, we would say that if we attempt to accumulate capital too fast its marginal productivity will be permanently reduced because time is required to build up the required stock of co-operating factors, such as skilled labour and management: by definition the process cannot be accelerated by more rapid accumulation of capital itself (although ambiguities arise, for example, over educational plant). (pp. 652–53)

less-industrialized countries where the limitations on financial resources typically are severe," [26] there can be no doubt that factors such as the lack of skilled labor, inefficient bureaucracies, shortages of industrial managers, corruption, and the persistence of inequitable social systems do hamper efforts to use available capital resources in a way effectively promoting economic growth and development.

The failure of many Third World governments to set their countries on the path of self-sustaining, self-reliant economic development is in part a legacy of the colonial era, particularly in Asia and Africa. Control over many colonies was not only gained by the use of force but was also maintained by military officers and quasi-military administrative systems. Writing of Africa, Ruth First commented:

> Colonialism in its different variations was more like than unlike in the form of rule it imposed. This was, whether conscious or not, military in conception and organization. More than anything else, colonial administrations resembled armies. The chain of authority from the top downwards was untouched by any principle of representation or consultation. For long periods in some territories, indeed, the colonial administrations not only resembled armies in their para-military formation and method; they were, as in the Sudan, the instruments of military men. [27]

Although democratic institutions were transferred to the colonies prior to independence, they were exported from the metropolis with little con-

[26] Schulz, "Military Expenditures," p. 201.

[27] Ruth First, *The Barrel of a Gun: Political Power in Africa and the Coup d'Etat* (Harmondsworth, England: Penguin, 1970), p. 31. Specifically on the Sudan, see Robert Collins and Francis Deng, ed., *The British in Sudan, 1898–1956* (London: MacMillan, 1984). See also, William Gutteridge, "Military and Police Forces in Colonial Africa," p. 286, in *Colonialism in Africa, 1870–1960, Volume 2: The History and Politics of Colonialism 1914–1960*, ed. L. H. Gann and Peter Duignan (Cambridge: Cambridge University Press, 1970).

J. C. Hurewitz, *Middle East Politics: The Military Dimension* (London: Pall Mall Press, 1969), p. 15, has described the situation in the Middle East:

Islamic political systems, before the advent of European imperialism, could almost uniformly be classified as varieties of military authoritarianism, commonly with the strict alternative of autocracy under a strong monarch and praetorianism or tribal supremacy under a weak one. Military authoritarianism persisted in most Muslim lands under European rule, although it was often disguised or cushioned by an imperial bureaucracy made up of technicians or by native bureaucracies used to administer the dependencies. In either case it was military rule. What is remarkable, in the circumstances, is not that the military in the first two postwar decades seized power in eight Middle East states, but that a larger number of civilian regimes did not vanish in these years.

cern, for how, or indeed if, they could be assimilated by other cultures. Furthermore, in many colonies, particularly in Africa, they were in place for only a short period of time before independence was granted, and the way in which these institutions functioned in the period prior to independence was often more bureaucratic than democratic in nature.

> As late as 1950, in Uganda, when only eight of thirty-two members [of the Legislative Council] were African, and only five were elected and those indirectly, Governor Hall said: "All I ask of all African members of the Council is that they will take the pains to acquaint themselves with the facts and will make it their business to pass on the facts in simple terms to as many as possible of their fellow Africans outside the Council chamber." . . . It was clear that the function of the legislative council was not at all to represent the people to the government, still less to make the government responsible to the people, but instead to act as a spokesman for the administration to the people. . . . In Uganda, changes in policy were made public before they were announced—much less debated—in the legislative council.[28]

An additional problem was that in most of the colonial world, governments were turned over to the members of the privileged classes—the large landowners or the bourgeoisie—who did not so much object to the prevailing economic system as to the fact that they were not receiving what they believed to be their fair share of its benefits.[29] As a result, these leaders most often followed development strategies that kept their coun-

---

[28] B. B. Schaffer, "The Concept of Preparation: Some Questions about the Transfer of Systems of Government," World Politics 18 (October 1965): 53–54.

[29] For example, Martin Kilson, Political Change in a West African State: A Study of the Modernization Process in Sierra Leone (Cambridge, Mass.: Harvard University Press, 1966), pp. 285–86, has described the "common interests" that the middle-class élite in Sierra Leone and the British colonial government had "in facilitating constitutional change: The élite required such change to advance their own socio-economic standing; the colonial masters obtained greater efficiency through the advancement of the new élite. The colonial oligarchy also expected greater stability in local society as the new élite, abetted by constitutional changes (including ultimately the mass franchise), spread their political influence and leadership into rural society." At independence the government was turned over to these middle-class élites, and throughout most of Africa relations between the colonial authorities and the new élites took a similar form. Nowhere in the Third World did the less privileged classes assume power (including Latin America in the 1800s) although in some countries the élites who controlled the newly independent governments chose to follow policies quite different from those of the colonial powers. On the whole, the economic record of the latter has not been markedly better than that of the countries which remained more closely linked to the industrialized capitalist countries.

tries closely tied to the economies of the more developed states. Policies promoting the more equitable distribution of wealth were not implemented not only because Western aid agencies convinced Third World governments during the 1950s and 1960s that growth must precede redistribution or that the latter would be the logical consequence of the former. But Third World leaders have themselves also been unwilling to antagonize important political allies, never the poor and the powerless, and to undertake significant social and economic reforms necessary to set in motion a more independent form of development.

An increasing number of people in the Third World have recognized that "the real solution of the development problem lies primarily in the capacity of each of the developing countries to mobilize its resources and energies."[30] Third World societies have greater autonomy than they are often credited with: Their leaders are not merely passive spectators at the mercy of the great powers, the multinational corporations, the foreign banks, and the aid agencies; they have the capacity to influence their environment in addition to being influenced by it.[31] Probably the central obstacle to far-reaching change is the domestic power structure. Those who control the political system would all too often jeopardize their own position of economic privilege and that of their closest supporters were they to implement the reforms necessary to produce more equitable, self-reliant development. "The fact remains that the two most effective meth-

[30] "Towards a New International Order: An Appraisal of Prospects," Report on the Joint Meeting of the Club of Rome and of the International Ocean Institute, Algiers, October 25–28, 1976 (Algiers, 1977), p. 21, cited in Geoffrey Barraclough, "The Struggle for the Third World," *New York Review of Books,* 9 November 1978, p. 53.

[31] See for example J. D. Y. Peel, *Ijeshas and Nigerians: The Incorporation of a Yoruba Kingdom, 1880s–1970s* (Cambridge: Cambridge University Press, 1984), in which it is argued that theories of African social change which focus nearly exclusively on external, global factors as determinants of change ignore both the variation within Africa and the independent internal dynamics of African societies.

Discussing the link between militarization of society in Latin America and the capitalist economic system which many Marxist theorists have identified, Mario Carranza has argued that

> It would . . . be inadequate to analyse the emergence of a new type of "permanent" military government in Latin America after the 1964 Brazilian coup and of the "national security doctrine" by which it has been legitimised, solely as a response to the imperatives of capitalist development in the centre. Such an approach would overlook internal factors and the "relative autonomy" of such regimes, and it would have difficulty explaining the "Brazilian miracle" which took place before the oil shock of 1973–74.

Mario Carranza, "Disarmament and World Development from a Latin American Perspective," *IDS Bulletin,* p. 69.

ods of mobilizing internal resources—viz. the systematic improvement of agricultural conditions and a high level of saving—require reforms which, almost certainly, could only take place at the expense of privileged, wealthy minorities." [32]

Nearly a decade ago, Paul Streeten listed a number of "neglected obstacles" to development which have been ignored, "treated in separate compartments as 'exogenous' variables, not integrated into development analysis and policy, or dismissed as biased partisan views." According to Streeten, these obstacles should be given serious attention because they are "closely linked" to the success or failure of development policies. The list, as relevant today as when it was drawn up in the late 1970s, includes:

(1) The unwillingness of governments to grasp firmly the political nettles: land reform; taxation, especially of large landowners; excessive protectionism; labor mobilization.
(2) Linked with the first, nepotism and corruption.
(3) Behind these, again, various forms of oligopoly and monopoly power: the power of large landowners; of big industrialists; and of the transnational enterprises. [33]

The continued survival of élite-dominated economic and political systems has depended in large part on the armed forces. The latter have both supported civilian governments intent on maintaining the status quo and intervened directly in the political process to prevent significant change from occurring. Regimes primarily concerned with ensuring their own survival and the well-being of political insiders and their friends and relations are likely to follow policies that will hamper rather than promote development. Considering the situation in Africa, Richard Sandbrook has commented that many governments "lack the capacity to establish the crucial conditions for capital accumulation and, additionally, act in economically irrational ways. This nondevelopmental or even antidevelopmental thrust is manifest in the mismanagement, inefficiency, and pervasive corruption of the public sector as well as political instability and the inability to prevent widespread evasion of laws and regulations. [34]

As suggested above, various factors can affect the absorptive capacity

[32] Barraclough, "The Struggle," p. 53.

[33] Paul Streeten, "Development Ideas in Historical Perspective," p. 45, in *Toward a New Strategy for Development. A Rothko Chapel Colloquium*, Albert O. Hirschman et al. (New York: Pergamon Press, 1979).

[34] Richard Sandbrook, "The State and Economic Stagnation in Tropical Africa," *World Development* 14: 3 (1986): 321. This problem is, of course, not limited to Africa.

of an economy. The discussion in the remainder of this section will focus on the way in which the security sector can contribute to just one of these—systematized corruption. (The argument that the security sector provides the civilian economy with trained technical and administrative manpower is discussed in detail in Chapter 8; on corruption, see also Chapter 1.) As Paul Streeten has pointed out, corruption presents a serious obstacle to growth and development but is rarely accorded the attention it deserves in analyses of the development process. It has been accepted as a fact of developing country life—albeit an unpleasant one—and little, if any, systematic effort has been made to eradicate it.

Developing countries are often perceived as more corrupt than industrialized ones. James Scott has suggested that, although corruption is an integral part of most political systems, Third World countries appear more corrupt because they tend to have larger public sectors than many Western industrialized countries, and public-sector corruption is more visible than private-sector corruption.[35] However Third World corruption compares with corruption elsewhere, Scott's study of politics in Asia and Africa illustrates the degree to which it saps the economies of many developing countries.

Although some Third World corruption does have its roots in traditional patterns of social behavior such as gift-giving and kinship ties, Scott has suggested that nontraditional forms of corruption with structural underpinnings are, in fact, more important. First, the public sector in the Third World is an important source of scarce commodities such as jobs, goods, and services; many people will resort to corrupt activities in order to obtain a share of these items. Second, another legacy of the colonial period is that the bureaucracies in many Third World countries are relatively stronger than other institutions, such as political parties, the domestic business community, and trade unions.[36] The military, which some view as an armed branch of the bureaucracy, is also in a strong position. According to Scott, the opportunities for influencing the decision making of military governments is frequently extremely low and in some cases nonexistent. This would increase the likelihood that individuals will resort to corrupt activities.

> No extrabureaucratic institution is strong enough to enforce either passive obedience to the political rulers or a service orientation toward the citizenry. In the absence of agencies that could enforce performance standards, bureaucratic factions blossom luxuriantly and

[35] James C. Scott, *Comparative Political Corruption* (Englewood Cliffs, N.J.: Prentice Hall, 1972), p. 9.
[36] Ibid., p. 26.

each division of the apparatus becomes a virtual feudal domain that may parasitically exploit its clientele or the portion of the economy over which it wields power. Such chaotic patterns of corruption are often the hallmark of unchecked bureaucratic politics. . . .[37]

Finally, civil servants are often considerably better educated than ordinary citizens. The latter, rather than seeing the bureaucracy as enforcing legal rights, may tend to feel that civil servants dispense favors and that it is necessary to win the approval of officials by offering a gift of some sort.

That Third World corruption can have an important bearing on development efforts is amply demonstrated by even a brief examination of the political system in Thailand. The Thai example is of particular interest here because Thailand has been governed for most of the post-1932 period by a coalition of military officers and bureaucrats. According to James Scott, the political system in Thailand is characterized by three factors. First, political competition is restricted to a very small élite that exhibits a high degree of shared values. Second, differences among groups of élites are based on struggles between various cliques, or factions, for power, wealth, and status; they are not based on policy issues or ideological concerns. And third, wealthy Chinese businessmen have been formally excluded from influencing the political system, thus, they have had to buy their way in through the "back door." The government is the main source of patronage, and the main political activity in the country is government administration. It is therefore not surprising that the Thai administration is entirely caught up in politics and that the technical competence of administrators and government officials is of less importance than an individual's ability to control a clique. The structure of cliques in Thailand (vertical ties, dependence on subleaders) causes them to be extremely vulnerable to fragmentation. The cement is material rewards. Once a leader at any level of the clique loses the capacity to provide subordinates with payoffs, he is rapidly deserted by his followers.

The way that all this affects development is quite simple. The money for the pay-offs must come from somewhere. Since the government is the main source of patronage, cliques compete to control the government and, therefore, governmental revenues. According to Scott, "The process of budget allocation is a political test of each clique's ability to extend its empire at the expense of its competitors. Development programs or government enterprises are calculated more to augment the funds and patronage of a clique than to raise national productivity."[38] The growth of

[37] Ibid., p. 15.
[38] Ibid., p. 62.

public enterprises during the 1950s, in part designed to break the economic power of the ethnic Chinese, also fit the requirements of the Thai political system. Scott asserts that "There is every indication . . . that the growth of public ventures under [Prime Minister] Phibun was explicitly seen as a way of adding to the legal financial opportunities of clique supporters."[39]

The extent to which clique politics has taken precedence over development can be seen in the manipulation of the National Economic Development Corporation (NEDCOL). NEDCOL, established in 1954, was administratively subordinate to the Ministry of Finance. The Ministry of Finance was closely affiliated with General Phao, the man Phibun had appointed director-general of the police. After a coup d'état ousted Phibun in 1957, it was discovered that less than half of the funds allocated to NEDCOL had actually been used for investment purposes; the remainder had disappeared. The implication is that these funds were used to keep Phao's clique together.[40] This sort of activity has been repeated innumerable times since the 1950s.

Corruption in Thailand is not limited to such spectacular events as the diversion of NEDCOL funds. Petty corruption is extremely common among lower-ranking officials. It takes essentially two forms: payments to *speed up* a decision and payments to *alter* a decision. While the amount of money changing hands for each individual bribe may be relatively small, taken together such payments represent very large sums of money. According to Scott, lower-level officials participate in this system mainly because there is no one to prevent them from doing so. They are encouraged to solicit bribes because they know it will increase their personal prestige and authority and because Thai bureaucrats have suffered a decline in real wages since World War II.[41]

There is little reason to anticipate that the disappearance of the military from the political system would end corrupt activity. It might reduce the degree to which corruption is practiced since corruption is essential for cementing alliances within and between the different military cliques that determine who rules Thailand. A shift to genuine parliamentary democracy might reduce the necessity of buying political allies, but the transformation of the current Thai political system into a genuine parlia-

[39] Ibid., p. 71.

[40] Ibid. For a description of the way in which NEDCOL operated, see David Elliott, *Thailand: Origins of Military Rule* (London: Zed Press, 1978), pp. 116–17, and Chakrit Noranitipadungkorn, "Thailand's National Economic Development Corporation Limited: An Evaluation with Special Emphasis on the Political Implications," *Thai Journal of Development Administration* 9 (October 1969): 732–45.

[41] Scott, *Comparative Political Corruption*, pp. 66–68.

mentary democracy can only be expected to occur over a very long period of time, if ever.

Corruption is well-embedded in the civil bureaucracy and the business community, both of which would surely subvert any attempt on the part of politicians to eradicate it. Only if civilian politicians were backed by the armed forces does it seem likely that corruption in Thailand could be ended one day. Since military officers are among the largest beneficiaries of the current system, it is unlikely that the military as an organization would support such moves on the part of civilian politicians. The possibility that a "Young Turk" movement might arise within the armed forces—in which junior officers or even noncommissioned officers would carry out a coup to remove the most corrupt of the senior officers and seriously implement an anticorruption program—seems highly unlikely in the Thai case. The South Korean example, where lower-ranking officers removed corrupt senior officers and ended the latter's system of corruption only to substitute a system of corruption from which they as the new leaders could benefit, is not one which should be emulated. Furthermore, civilian politicians are unlikely to attempt any such housecleaning operations because they, too, are heavily involved with corrupt activities, and many of the more important ones have close ties with ethnic Chinese businessmen, just as the military officers do.

Thailand may be one of those countries in which corruption has been most highly institutionalized. It is not unique, however, in the extent to which corruption occurs. Scarcely any government is immune from its occurrence: Civilian and military governments in market-oriented and centrally planned systems are equally likely to fall prey to corruption. The notion prevalent in the 1950s and early 1960s that military-led governments were less likely to engage in corrupt practices was shown in Chapter 1 to have no basis in fact.

No estimate has yet been made of what corruption means in terms of revenue foregone for the developing countries as a whole, but it must be a considerable sum. A study of India's "black economy"—the use of unreported income as payoffs to obtain government services—carried out in the mid-1980s estimated that corruption involved $30 billion, a sum equivalent to 20 percent of the Indian GNP.[42] Furthermore, to the extent that corruption conditions the form development takes, as with the

---

[42] Steven R. Weisman, "India's Underground Economy is Said to Reach Epidemic Level," *International Herald Tribune*, 12 February 1986, p. 5. This study, carried out by the National Institute of Public Finance and Policy, a semiautonomous agency within the Ministry of Finance, is the only official report on Third World corruption of which this author is aware. Case studies of corruption in other Third World countries have, however, been carried out by academic researchers. See, for example, David J. Gould, *Bureaucratic Corrup-*

buildup of the state-enterprise sector in Thailand during the 1950s, the task of formulating and implementing a coherent development strategy that will promote self-sustained economic growth and development becomes ever more complicated.[43]

---

tion and Underdevelopment in the Third World. The Case of Zaire (New York: Pergamon Press, 1980).

The theme of Gould's work is that "The ruling class in Zaire has effectively 'privatized' the public bureaucracy and converted it into an instrument for self-enrichment. Out of greed and fear for their own survival, those at the top institutionalize corruption and lock their subordinates into these practices in a systematic, normative way" (xiii).

According to a 1985 article in *Forbes*, "A high government post [in Zaire] is not simply political patronage . . . it's more like a license to steal. There are 47 corporations in the government portfolio and the top jobs work on a revolving-door basis, allowing the occupant enough time to make his fortune until someone else can be shifted in." Hesh Kestin, "God and Man in Zaire," *Forbes*, 18 November 1985, p. 105. According to Gould, Mobutu went so far in a public speech in 1976 to explain to his followers: "If you want to steal, steal a little cleverly, in a nice way. Only if you steal so much as to become rich overnight, you will be caught" (xiii).

[43] Peter Bell has pointed out with regard to Thailand in the late 1960s that the ruling élites were "increasingly insulated from the rest of society through their dependence on US aid funds, and thus ignored the need for more rational policies. As a result the planning mechanism which had been carefully constructed by the World Bank fell into neglect. Decision-making was centralized in the junta, but implementation was left to a range of unco-ordinated agencies. . . ." Peter F. Bell, " 'Cycles' of Class Struggle in Thailand," p. 67, in *Thailand: Roots of Conflict*, eds. Andrew Turton, Jonathan Fast, and Malcolm Caldwell (Nottingham, England: Spokesman, 1978).

7

. . . .

CAPITAL, GROWTH, AND

SECURITY ASSISTANCE

Despite the amount of money made available to developing countries in the form of security-related grants and loans since the end of World War II, security assistance has remained peripheral to discussions of the role played by foreign capital inflows in the development process. On the one hand, economic assistance provided specifically to enable recipient governments to support larger security establishments than they could by using only their own resources tends not to be distinguished from other forms of economic aid in the literature on economic assistance. Included in this category would be items such as general budgetary support to strategically important client-states granted by, for example, the governments of the United States and of several oil-exporting countries of the Middle East as well as certain transfers of U.S. food aid under the PL-480 program. On the other hand, security assistance that takes the form of transferring military equipment and related services either free-of-charge or under donor-government credit programs is rarely included in evaluations of the relationship between external capital flows and development.

For example, South Korea received approximately $8 billion in military assistance and $5.5 billion in economic aid from the United States between the end of the Korean War and 1983. Yet a major study of the influence of external resources, foreign investment and economic assistance, on the growth of the Korean economy omitted all discussion of security assistance; nor did it explain that approximately 40 percent of the economic assistance provided by the U.S. government during the same period took the form of security-supporting assistance designed to compensate the South Korean government for expenditure on its armed forces. Another 25 percent of U.S. economic aid, provided under Title I of the Food for Peace (PL-480) program, generated counterpart funds primarily intended to support the security sector. Given that some 60 percent of the economic assistance provided to South Korea by its major aid donor was intended to sustain the South Korean security establishment, one might well ask why security assistance was not examined. According to the study's author, "it was not part of my assignment" to take into account the security-related aspects of the foreign aid received by South Korea.[1]

Some development specialists have suggested that it is not possible to evaluate the economic effects of security-related assistance since, in its absence, a country might have purchased fewer or less-expensive weapons and related services from abroad.[2] Although this assertion is difficult to prove, it is likely that the Third World procurement bill would have been lower in the absence of aid to the security sector. There can be no doubt, for example, that the South Korean economy could not by itself have supported a security sector of the size that U.S. assistance enabled it to build up and maintain during the 1950s and 1960s. This fact does not, however, allow security assistance to be entirely discounted. What might have occurred in the absence of security aid will not explain the state of the economy or the balance of political forces within a country that has received such transfers.

The three most important ways in which security assistance can affect the development prospects of recipient countries are as a source of additional capital resources, as a source of manpower training, and as a source of political support for the armed forces. This chapter will discuss security assistance as a source of capital. The influence of security assistance on the supply of skilled manpower will be considered in Chapter 8.

[1] Anne O. Krueger, personal communication to Nicole Ball, 18 August 1983. The study on Korea is Anne O. Krueger, *The Development Role of the Foreign Sector and Aid* (Cambridge, Mass. and London: Harvard University Press, 1979). Information on U.S. military assistance from United States, Department of Defense Security Assistance Agency, *Foreign Military Sales, Foreign Military Construction Sales and Military Assistance Facts as of September 30, 1984* (Washington, D.C.: Department of Defense, 1984). Information on U.S. economic assistance from United States, Agency for International Development, Office of Planning and Budgeting, *US Overseas Loans and Grants and Assistance from International Organizations: Obligations and Loan Authorizations July 1, 1945—September 30, 1983* (Washington, D.C.: AID 1983), p. 74.

[2] Anne Krueger, for example, has stated that the economic role of security assistance "depends heavily on what is assumed about the level of military expenditures in the absence of foreign assistance." Personal communication to Nicole Ball, 18 August 1983. Emile Benoit made a similar argument in his controversial study of the effect of military expenditure on economic growth in developing countries: "a considerable amount of the equipment and services obtained under MAP [U.S. Military Assistance Program] would simply not be obtainable at all in the absence of MAP, and MAP recipients would simply get along with simpler or less equipment, etc., and often be relieved of costly maintenance as well." Emile Benoit, *Defense and Economic Growth in Developing Countries* (Lexington, Mass.: Lexington, 1973), p. 142. Although this might have been true for some countries in the 1950s, it was probably less likely to be true in the 1960s and 1970s. To the extent that either of these statements is true, neither presents any argument for ignoring inflows of specifically security-oriented assistance.

ECONOMIC ASSISTANCE, THE SECURITY SECTOR, AND DEVELOPMENT

Development economics as we know it today is a creation of the post–World War II period. Prior to the war, mainstream Western economists did not concern themselves with economic conditions in Latin America, Asia, Africa, and the Middle East. To a large extent, of course, the post–World War II decolonization process generated interest in the areas that have come to be known as the Third World. In addition, many individuals involved with postwar planning believed that, once the war ended, relations among nations would be characterized by greater interdependence.[3] This belief was reflected, for example, in Article 55 of the Charter of the United Nations which declared that economic development was important for all countries.

In the immediate postwar years, however, the attention of the major source of financial and technical assistance—the United States—was focused on Europe. With the exception of the Philippines, South Korea, Japan, and China, the developing regions received very little economic and technical assistance before 1948.

The need for a change in this policy became apparent as soon as production was restored in Europe. Further European recovery and economic development elsewhere were then seen to be closely connected. European manufactured goods essential to developmental projects could be exchanged for raw materials from underdeveloped areas. When rearmament began in the West, the demand for raw materials greatly increased, making the mutual dependence between the developed and underdeveloped areas even more evident.[4]

Once economic development in the nonindustrialized areas became a subject in its own right, the main obstacles to its attainment were seen to inadequate capital resources (both real capital, that is, physical goods, and money capital), an insufficient supply of skilled manpower, and a lack of modern technology. Although there was considerable discussion in academic circles about the ways in which economic development might best be promoted, the attention of policymakers and aid officials

[3] For a discussion of the pre-1945 period, see H. W. Arndt, "Development Economics Before 1945," pp. 13–29, in *Development and Planning. Essays in Honor of Paul Rosenstein Rodan,* ed. Jagdish Bhagwati and Richard S. Eckaus (London: Allen & Unwin, 1972). Arndt points out that while "Almost wholly ignored by the mainstream of Western economics during the inter-war period, the economic problems of underdeveloped and developing countries were at the same time the subject of quite a large specialist literature . . ." (p. 19).

[4] William Adams Brown, Jr., and Redvers Opie, *American Foreign Assistance* (Washington, D.C.: Brookings Institution, 1953), pp. 383–84.

focused for a decade or more on reducing the perceived shortage of capital resources. Capital was believed to be in short supply for two reasons: first, the developing countries were said to be too poor to save a sufficiently high proportion of their national income to support a satisfactory rate of investment (savings gap); second, they were also thought to be unable to generate adequate export income to pay for necessary imports (foreign exchange gap). The role of the industrialized countries was to provide the missing capital resources.[5]

Shortages of foreign exchange were considered particularly serious because Third World development was believed to depend on industrialization and the success of industrialization on large-scale imports of machinery and other inputs. David Wall has described the importance ascribed by the United Nations Conference on Trade and Development (UNCTAD) to the growth of import capacity, and thus the availability of foreign exchange, for economic growth and development.

> The outcome of a less-developed country's attempts to accelerate its rate of economic growth depends on the rate of investment in fixed capital which it manages to achieve. On the assumption that most less-developed countries are unable to produce most of the machinery and equipment required by the investment process, the success of a growth programme is dependent upon the import of such goods. The ability to import such goods is obviously subject to the constraint of the availability of adequate supplies of foreign exchange. If domestic saving falls short of investment requirements, this only increases the potential constraining role of a shortage of foreign exchange, and foreign investment in the form of either a balance-of-payments deficit or aid becomes more important. Second, whatever the level of domestic saving, foreign exchange shortages can always frustrate the achievement of the optimum composition of investment. Thus UNCTAD argued that foreign exchange plays a dominant role in the growth process.[6]

[5] See, for example, Paul Streeten, "Development Ideas in Historical Perspective," pp. 26, 36–39, in Towards a New Strategy for Development. A Rothko Chapel Colloquium, Albert D. Hirschman et al. (New York: Pergamon Press, 1979). Streeten reported that "In the early literature, capital was regarded as the key to development and lack of it an essential—or the main, or even the only—constraint" (p. 37). See also Brown and Opie, American Foreign Assistance, pp. 384–86.

[6] David Wall, "Import Capacity, Imports and Economic Growth," Economia, May 1968, p. 157. Wall concluded that "there is no evidence of a 'close' association between imports of investment goods and growth. . . . UNCTAD over-emphasizes the position of foreign exchange shortages as a constraint in the growth process" (p. 168).

Mechanisms for Obtaining Foreign Capital

The four sources of external capital upon which attention focused were export earnings, direct foreign investment, commercial loans, and foreign aid.

EXPORT INCOME

From the very beginning of its involvement in Third World development, the World Bank sought to strengthen the export sectors of developing countries in order to increase the availability of foreign exchange.[7] Table 5-2 demonstrated that a large proportion of all Third World countries derived more than half of their export income from one or two commodities in the early 1980s. In the years following World War II, Third World economies were even less diversified, and exports were even more likely to consist of raw materials than they do today. At the same time, it is now accepted that the variability in demand for and in prices of commodities produces considerable instability in export earnings and makes commodities an unreliable source of development financing.

It is not entirely surprising, however, that considerable faith was placed on export income in the immediate postwar period. Throughout the war and up to 1951, demand for Third World commodities had generally been high, and the terms of trade for the developing countries as a group had improved. The Korean War boom of 1950–1951 caused a sharp improvement in Third World terms of trade, but this unfortunately disappeared nearly as quickly as it had arisen. Between 1952 and 1962, the trend in the terms of trade for the developing countries as a whole was essentially downward (Figure 5-3).

Even when raw material prices are generally high, however, all producers do not benefit equally. In the early 1950s, Ragnar Nurkse commented:

> The great advantage of this potential source of capital formation is that it gives rise neither to a foreign debt burden nor to the various frictions that may arise from inter-governmental loans and grants. That it is very uneven and haphazard in its incidence must be counted among its disadvantages. From the raw-material boom of 1950–51, India, for instance, derived no net improvement for her terms of trade, whereas Malaya benefited a great deal. The distribution of this

[7] J. H. Adler, "The World Bank's Concept of Development—An In-House *Dogmengeschichte*," p. 40, in *Development and Planning*, ed. Bhagwati and Eckaus.

possible source of capital is in accordance not with needs, but rather with ability to supply goods in special demand on the world market.[8]

It was thus clear from the beginning that export income could not be exclusively relied upon to fuel Third World development.

DIRECT INVESTMENT

Prior to World War II, foreign capital had aided some countries in developing their productive capacity by investing in communications, power generation, and plantation agriculture (for export); it was hoped that the postwar period would see large-scale industrial investments in the developing areas. The United States government was a particularly strong supporter of this form of capital transfer. Despite the fact that U.S. private investment in the developing areas was virtually nonexistent at the end of the war, the U.S. government expected development to occur on the basis of private investment. One exception was that infrastructure would be financed through the World Bank and the Export-Import Bank of the United States. The 1950 Act for International Development included the requirement that the United States' economic development policy seek to improve "the climate for foreign private investment" at the same time as it inaugurated a small technical assistance program.[9]

Although U.S. investment in Latin America did increase sharply around 1950, direct investment did not expand as rapidly for the Third World as a whole as some analysts had hoped. In the early 1950s analysts argued that American investors were slow to increase their activities in the developing countries because many Third World governments preferred public ownership, given the "generally prevailing views in underdeveloped countries on the 'exploitative' nature of foreign capital."[10] Moreover, the already industrialized countries of Europe were seen as considerably more profitable sites for investment than the Third World. The foreign investment that took place outside the industrial countries in the immediate postwar period tended to be oriented toward the export market, in part because demand from domestic markets was considered too weak to support large investments, and to be in the extractive industries. With time, investment in the industrial and service sectors increased, and the Third World's share in total direct investment grew, reaching 27 percent in the 1980–1983 period according to the World Bank. However, "about three-quarters of foreign direct investment has gone to industrial countries on

[8] Ragnar Nurkse, *Problems of Capital Formation in Underdeveloped Countries* (Oxford: Basil Blackwell, 1953), p. 98.
[9] Brown and Opie, *American Foreign Assistance*, pp. 391–96.
[10] Ibid., p. 419.

average since 1965. The remainder has been concentrated for the most part in a few developing countries, predominantly the higher-income countries of Asia and Latin America" (Brazil, Mexico, Hong Kong, Malaysia, Philippines, and Singapore).[11] For many countries in the Third World, therefore, direct foreign investment has not been a major source of foreign capital.

COMMERCIAL LOANS

In the course of World War II discussions on the structure of the postwar world, it was stated that "international lending has been one of the most powerful engines of economic progress throughout the world, and . . . an immense task remains for it to do."[12] In particular, countries such as Japan and Australia were said to have benefited from government investment in public services and infrastructure financed by loans from abroad.[13] Although the United States had shown itself willing to aid in the reconstruction of Europe following the war by lending large sums to European governments, it was clearly less enthusiastic about promoting Third World development in the same way. Only relatively small sums were made available through the Export-Import Bank to non-European governments in Latin America and Asia. The loans that were made to Latin America up to 1951 have been described as "facilitating American foreign trade, directly by financing specific export and import transactions, and indirectly by assisting in the development of resources of foreign countries in order that they might become better markets and suppliers for the United States."[14]

In the late 1940s, the U.S. Congress had been unwilling to increase the lending authority of the Export-Import Bank so that it could finance economic development projects in the developing countries. With the onset of the Korean War, however, the procurement of strategic materials became more important, and Congress approved a $1 billion increase in the Ex-Im Bank's lending authority, about half of which was earmarked for the development of new sources of strategic materials, primarily in the

---

[11] Nurkse, *Problems*, pp. 82–88; Charles Wolf, Jr., and Sidney C. Sufrin, *Capital Formation & Foreign Investment in Underdeveloped Areas*, Maxwell School Series—1 (Syracuse, N.Y.: Syracuse University Press, 1955), p. 54; and World Bank, *World Development Report 1985* (New York: Oxford University Press, 1985), pp. 125–36; quotation from p. 126.

[12] Arndt, "Development Economics Before 1945," p. 27.

[13] Nurkse has stated that "Past experience suggests that governmental investment financed by foreign loans can be a suitable method of laying the foundations of a country's economic development in the form of public services and social overhead capital." Nurkse, *Problems*, p. 91.

[14] Brown and Opie, *American Foreign Assistance*, p. 415.

developing areas.[15] For the most part, however, the United States held fast to its policy that foreign private investment should provide the bulk of the capital resources required by the developing economies.

The World Bank, formally known as the International Bank for Reconstruction and Development, thus became an important source of capital for the developing world. The initial role of the World Bank had been to provide funds to assist postwar reconstruction in Europe. By the early 1950s, however, it had shifted its activities to the Third World and was lending money at commercial rates to governments in the developing areas for public-sector undertakings. To provide money for the private sector in the Third World, the Bank established a subsidiary called the International Finance Corporation (IFC) in 1956. The IFC has three tasks: providing risk capital to private enterprise in developing countries; developing Third World capital markets; and stimulating private investment in developing countries.[16]

Economists have argued that loans are preferable to grants because loans are less likely to be used to increase consumption and more likely to be used for investment purposes since they must eventually be repaid. Grants, on the other hand, "can be used directly or indirectly for consumption without any subsequent inconvenience."[17] It rapidly became evident, however, that many developing countries lacked the capacity to earn sufficient income from exports to repay loans obtained on commercial terms. By the early 1950s, the need for both loans on concessional terms and grants was recognized by many national and international officials concerned with the economic development of the Third World.

ECONOMIC AID

The purpose of economic aid is to enable developing countries to overcome resource constraints which may, in themselves, be relatively small but can lead to the underutilization of other resources and cause slower growth. Aid is thus a facilitator rather than a major determinant of economic growth.

> A country setting out to transform its economy without external assistance must provide for all of the requirements of accelerated growth from its own resources or from imports paid by exports. . . .

[15] Ibid., pp. 414–17.

[16] David Wall, *The Charity of Nations: The Political Economy of Foreign Aid* (New York: Basic Books, 1973), p. 138. The IFC also provides capital on commercial terms.

[17] Nurkse, *Problems*, p. 92. Nurkse recognized, of course, that loans could also be used to increase consumption and that the receipt of loans could lead to a slowing of the domestic rate of saving.

When growth is limited . . . by a few bottlenecks, there is likely to be underutilization of other factors such as labor, natural resources, and specific types of productive capacity.

By relieving these constraints, foreign assistance can make possible fuller use of domestic resources and hence accelerate growth. Some of the potential bottlenecks—of skills, savings, or foreign exchange—can be temporarily relaxed by adding external resources for which current payment is not required. More efficient use can then be made of other resources, so that the growth of total output may be substantially higher than would be permitted by the rate of increase of the most restrictive domestic factor.

While this alternative sequence recognizes the existence of a given set of requisites for continued growth, it makes the timing of their appearance much more flexible. The full set of requirements need only become available from domestic sources as the inflow of foreign resources is reduced. To achieve this result, the additional resources produced through more rapid growth must be used to make good the deficiencies which are temporarily being supplied from outside assistance.[18]

The Organisation for Economic Cooperation and Development (OECD) distinguishes three types of foreign flows from industrialized to developing countries: official development assistance (ODA), other official flows,

---

[18] Hollis B. Chenery and Alan M. Strout, "Foreign Assistance and Economic Development," *The American Economic Review* 56: 4—Pt. 1 (September 1966): 480–81. They conclude that "Over the whole period of the transition to self-sustaining growth, the use that is made of the successive increments in GNP is likely to be more important than the efficiency with which external assistance was utilized in the first instance. . . . The critical elements in the development sequence are getting the initial increase in the rate of growth, channeling the increments of income into increased saving, and allocating investment so as to avoid balance-of-payments bottlenecks" (p. 724).

Chenery and Carter have summarized the "analytical and philosophical basis for the aid and development programs" of the 1960s as follows:

(a) external resources can be used by underdeveloped countries as a basis for a significant acceleration of investment and growth;
(b) the maintenance of higher growth rates requires substantial changes in the structure of production and trade;
(c) external capital can perform a critical role in both resource mobilization and structural transformation; and
(d) the need for concessionary aid declines once these structural changes are well under way (although further capital inflow may be productive).

See Hollis B. Chenery and Nicholas G. Carter, "Foreign Assistance and Development Performance, 1960–1970," *American Economic Review* 63 (May 1973): 459.

and private capital flows. Of these, only ODA contains a concessional element. According to the OECD,

> Official development assistance is defined as all flows to less-developed countries and multilateral institutions provided by official agencies, including state and local governments, or by their executive agencies, which meet the following tests:
> (a) they are administered with the promotion of the economic development and welfare of developing countries as their main objective; and
> (b) their financial terms are intended to be concessional in character.[19]

During the first two decades of the postwar period, the United States was the main donor of economic assistance to the Third World. It was only in 1969 that the United States contributed less than half of the ODA recorded by the OECD (Table 7-1). The vast majority of U.S. assistance has been bilateral. In the early 1950s, the authors of a major review of U.S. foreign assistance policy since the beginning of World War II stated that the United States was providing assistance to Third World countries because of "a humanitarian impulse to aid the less fortunate, a desire to promote sound and expanding world trade, the necessity of increasing supplies of raw materials, and the firm determination to forestall the spread of communism."[20] It is interesting to note that the promotion of development was not offered as a justification of these early programs. Indeed, a review of U.S. economic assistance written in 1957 described the granting of aid to promote development as "a continuing *though minor* strand" of U.S. aid policies.[21] During the 1950s, the fourth factor listed above—forestalling the spread of communism—was clearly dominant. Ensuring the supply of raw materials, particularly those consumed by the U.S. defense sector, was also important but it was essentially a corollary of the preoccupation with the Soviet Union and the People's Republic of China. The foreign assistance programs of the United States grew out of assistance provided to a handful of Asian countries—the Republic of China, the Republic of Korea, and the Philippines—in the late

[19] Organisation for Economic Cooperation and Development (OECD), *Resources for the Developing World: The Flow of Financial Resources to Less-Developed Countries 1962–1968* (Paris: OECD, 1969), p. 323.

[20] Brown and Opie, *American Foreign Assistance*, p. 387.

[21] Center for International Studies, MIT, "The Objectives of United States Economic Assistance Programs," p. 1, in *Foreign Aid Program. Compilation of Studies and Surveys*, U.S. Congress, Senate, Special Committee to Study the Foreign Aid Program, 85th Cong., 1st Sess. (Washington, D.C.: Government Printing Office, July 1957); emphasis added.

1940s. Economic and security assistance to these countries was strongly intertwined. These early aid programs were primarily motivated by security concerns, and the failure of Chiang Kai-Shek's forces to retain control of mainland China and the invasion of South Korea by the North Koreans only intensified the security orientation of U.S. "economic aid" programs.[22]

Thus, a very large portion of the economic aid allocated to the developing areas in the first decade and a half following World War II went to countries on the borders of the Soviet Union and China. More than two-thirds of these transfers were intended to support the security sector in recipient countries (Table 7-2). Not until the late 1950s did the United States begin to make a clear distinction between "economic development aid" and "stability assistance." The latter had "the primary purpose of helping a recipient maintain security against external and internal threats," went hand-in-hand with military assistance, and took two forms, defense support and the sale of PL-480 surplus agricultural commodities.[23]

To some extent, the amount of defense support was exaggerated. In 1955 and 1956, *all* economic assistance to countries receiving U.S. military assistance was classified as defense support. In 1956, a number of Latin American countries, not even recipients of U.S. military aid, had their economic aid classified as defense support. Beginning in 1956, a series of U.S. government reports and studies argued that military and economic aid should be appropriated separately, with military assistance being brought under the budget of the Department of Defense, but this never occurred. Defense support, renamed "security-supporting assistance" in 1961, subsequently included only aid "specifically designed to sustain and increase military effort." In the early 1960s, the main objectives of stability assistance were: to provide budget support to enable

---

[22] An excellent survey of U.S. foreign aid policies is found in Brown and Opie, *American Foreign Assistance*. On the relative priority accorded security concerns in the U.S. foreign assistance program from 1950, see especially pages 553–55, and Harold A. Hovey, *United States Military Assistance. A Study of Policies and Practices* (New York: Praeger, 1965), p. 256. The aid programs for both the Philippines and South Korea in the immediate post–World War II period required their governments to adopt various economic reforms that American officials believed would improve the economic situation in the two countries. A considerably shorter summary of the history of U.S. aid programs is found in U.S. Congress, Congressional Budget Office, *Bilateral Development Assistance. Background and Options*, Budget Issue Paper (Washington, D.C.: Congressional Budget Office, February 1977), pp. 3–8.

[23] Amos A. Jordan, Jr., *Foreign Aid and the Defense of Southeast Asia* (New York: Praeger, 1962), pp. 7–9. Most defense support took the form of "financing the import of commodities not tied to specific projects but intended for distribution or resale in the recipient economy" as a means of generating additional government revenue (p. 9).

TABLE 7-1

Net Official Development Assistance Disbursed by Major Western Donors to Developing Countries
and Multilateral Agencies, 1956–1982 (in U.S. $ million)

Year	Total ODA $m	United States		United Kingdom		France		West Germany		Japan	
		$m	%	$m	%	$m	%	$m	%	$m	%
1956	3,312	2,006	60.6	205	6.2	647	19.5	161	4.9	—	—
1957	3,859	2,091	54.2	234	6.1	819	21.2	297	7.7	—	—
1958	4,419	2,410	54.5	276	6.2	884	20.0	278	6.3	—	—
1959	4,398	2,322	52.8	377	8.6	835	19.0	325	7.4	—	—
1960	4,718	2,702	57.3	407	8.6	847	18.0	237	5.0	105	2.2
1961	5,217	2,943	56.3	457	8.8	943	18.1	330	6.3	108	2.1
1962	5,539	3,232	58.3	421	7.6	976	17.6	398	7.2	85	1.5
1963	5,468	3,395	62.1	356	6.5	794	14.5	368	6.7	132	2.4
1964	5,723	3,525	61.6	425	7.4	802	14.0	427	7.5	107	1.9
1965	5,613	3,330	59.3	398	7.1	718	12.8	413	7.4	232	4.1
1966	5,666	3,245	57.3	408	7.2	709	12.5	371	6.5	267	4.7
1967	6,189	3,333	53.9	410	6.6	796	12.9	461	7.4	360	5.8
1968	5,924	3,106	52.4	351	5.9	816	13.8	482	8.1	322	5.4
1969	6,214	2,928	47.1	373	6.0	916	14.7	508	8.2	394	6.3

1970	6,379	2,869	45.0	390	6.1	927	14.5	518	8.1	408	6.4
1971	7,237	3,092	42.7	496	6.9	1,026	14.2	655	9.1	458	6.3
1972	8,088	3,106	38.4	539	6.7	1,257	15.5	723	8.9	538	6.7
1973	8,729	2,712	31.1	518	5.9	1,430	16.4	982	11.2	915	10.5
1974	11,302	3,437	30.4	717	6.3	1,616	14.3	1,433	12.7	1,126	10.0
1975	13,587	4,007	29.5	863	6.4	2,093	15.4	1,689	12.4	1,148	8.4
1976	13,665	4,334	31.7	835	6.1	2,146	15.7	1,384	10.1	1,105	8.1
1977	14,696	4,159	28.3	914	6.2	2,267	15.4	1,386	9.4	1,424	9.7
1978	19,992	5,664	28.3	1,465	7.3	2,705	13.5	2,347	11.7	2,215	11.1
1979	22,820	4,684	20.5	2,157	9.5	3,449	15.1	3,393	14.9	2,685	11.8
1980	27,267	7,138	26.2	1,854	6.8	4,162	15.3	3,567	13.1	3,353	12.3
1981	25,540	5,782	22.3	2,192	8.6	4,177	16.4	3,181	12.5	3,171	12.4
1982	27,731	8,202	29.6	1,800	6.5	4,034	14.5	3,152	11.4	3,023	10.9
1983	27,560	8,081	29.3	1,610	5.8	3,815	13.8	3,176	11.5	3,761	13.6
1984	28,686	8,711	30.4	1,418	4.9	3,788	13.2	2,782	9.7	4,319	15.0

Source: Organisation for Economic Co-operation and Development, *Development Assistance Efforts and Policies, 1966 Review, Development Co-operation, 1969 Review, Development Co-operation, 1974 Review, Development Co-operation, 1978 Review, Development Co-operation, 1984 Review, Development Co-operation, 1985 Review,* (Paris: OECD, 1966, 1969, 1974, 1978, 1984, 1985), pp. 148, 298, 207, 191, 212, and 295, respectively.

Note: Data for 1956–1959 are for gross official flows and thus are not strictly comparable with those for 1960–1984.

TABLE 7-2
U.S. Security-Related Economic Aid, 1953–1961,
Selected Countries and Regions, Authorized Expenditure
(in U.S. $ million)

Country/Region	Economic Aid (1)	Defense Support[a] (2)	(2) as % of (1)
TOTAL UNITED STATES	24,053.0	8,853.0	36.8
EUROPE	4,486.1	1,210.5	27.0
CANADA	11.5	0.0	0.0
ALL OTHER REGIONS	19,555.5	7,642.5	39.2
EAR EAST AND SOUTH ASIA	7,596.4	1,741.9	22.9
Greece	476.0	264.8	55.6
Iran	548.1	166.0	30.3
Pakistan	1,418.7	586.6	41.3
Turkey	1,093.0	724.5	66.3
LATIN AMERICA	1,552.2	176.7	11.4
Bolivia	192.5	114.7	59.6
EAST ASIA	7,509.4	5,629.1	75.6
Kampuchea	219.9	203.6	92.6
South Korea	2,579.0	1,861.9	72.2
Laos	267.1	256.9	95.2
Philippines	286.0	154.3	54.0
Thailand	264.2	190.9	72.3
South Vietnam	1,548.2	1,394.3	90.1
Taiwan	978.8	743.5	76.0
12 Country Total	9,871.5	6,662.0	67.5

Source: United States Agency for International Development, Office of Planning and Budgeting, *US Overseas Loans and Grants and Assistance from International Organizations, Obligations and Loan Authorizations July 1, 1945–September 30, 1981* (Washington, D.C.: USAID, 1981).

[a] Column 2 includes only expenditure listed as defense support. It does not include sales of U.S. surplus food under the PL-480 program which were intended to generate counterpart funds that recipient governments could use as budgetary support. The true proportion of security-related economic aid is thus somewhat higher than the figures here suggest.

governments to maintain a certain level of security spending without resorting to deficit spending, cutting back on other public outlays, or being required to implement politically unpalatable tax reforms; to fill resource gaps; to combat inflation; and to promote economic development.[24] By far the most important of these was to support the security sector in recipient countries.

In the mid-1970s, security-supporting assistance became the "Economic Support Fund" Program (ESF). The purpose of ESF is

> to promote economic or political stability in areas where the United States has special security interests and it is determined that economic assistance can be useful in helping to secure peace or to avert major economic or political crises.

> Funds are made available on a loan or grant basis and can be used for a variety of purposes, including balance of payments support, financing infrastructure and other capital projects, and support for development projects which benefit the poor. Although a substantial amount of the ESF goes for balance of payments type aid, it also provides for programs aimed at primary needs in health, education, agriculture, and family planning.[25]

Since 1977, over half of each year's ESF allocation has been directed to Israel and Egypt in the form of grants, primarily as balance-of-payment support.

Despite their use in the security sector, ESF and its various predecessors have been listed as components of economic aid in the U.S. accounting system. The same has been true of the sales of surplus agricultural commodities under the PL-480 program although in many cases the counterpart funds generated by the latter have been used to support Third World security sectors. What is more, the OECD has accepted this categorization, even though it is clear from OECD documents that the aid is *not* intended to promote development.

> Military assistance and expenditures directly linked to specific defense efforts are excluded, although where assistance has some military association, but is in effect for development purposes, it is included.

. . . .

[24] Ibid., pp. 79, 86–97, and Hovey, *United States Military Assistance,* pp. 257–66.
[25] United States General Accounting Office, *US Security and Military Assistance: Programs and Related Activities,* GAO/ID-82-40 (Washington, D.C.: General Accounting Office, 1 June 1982), p. 18. Some details about the ESF program for each recipient are found in the annual report, *Congressional Presentation. Security Assistance Programs* (Washington, D.C.).

Supporting Assistance

This part of the AID programme, although providing economic and not military assistance, is nonetheless closely linked to security considerations. It is extended to countries whose political and economic security is threatened and where military and political considerations are very important.

Supporting assistance is extended mainly in the form of grant aid. . . . Typically, it consists of commodity assistance furnished by a United States exporter who is reimbursed by AID in dollars while the importer in the recipient country pays his government in local currency. The "counterpart" funds thus generated are used by the recipient government for programmes agreed upon by it and AID; *these are most frequently joint defense programmes.*[26]

Table 7-2 demonstrates that nearly 40 percent of the "economic aid" provided by the United States to the developing areas between 1953 and 1961 was intended for defense support. For the twelve largest recipients of U.S. economic aid during this period—together receiving half of all U.S. economic aid to developing countries—the fraction was two-thirds. If budget support generated by sales of agricultural commodities under the PL-480 program were included, the figures would be higher. Although the figures presented here may be somewhat inflated due to the classification of all economic aid as defense support for recipients of U.S. military assistance in 1955 and 1956, it is nonetheless clear that a large part of U.S. economic aid during the 1950s was meant for other than developmental purposes. In the 1960s and 1970s, the relative importance of defense support declined, although it was an important source of U.S. funds for South Vietnam during the 1960s and early 1970s and for Egypt and Israel since the mid-1970s. Beginning in the early 1960s, developmental concerns became progressively more important in granting economic aid.[27]

Like the United States, the other major aid donors—France, Great Britain, Japan, and the Federal Republic of Germany—have in most years chosen to channel 90 percent or more of their assistance bilaterally.[28] However, for the most part their objectives in providing aid have been politico-economic rather than politico-strategic. While the United States has concentrated its aid on countries deemed to be "in the forefront of the

---

[26] OECD, *Resources.* The first quotation is from page 318, the second from page 205; emphasis has been added. Regarding the uses of supporting assistance and PL-480 transfers, see Hovey, *United States Military Assistance,* pp. 117–20.

[27] OECD, *Resources,* p. 205, and USAID, *US Overseas Loans and Grants.*

[28] OECD, *Resources,* pp. 70, 88, 178.

fight against communism," the other major donors have primarily sought to maintain their political and economic position in former colonial areas (Britain, France, and Japan) or build up their economic influence in the Third World (Germany).

For the first seven or eight years following World War II, the Soviet Union and its East European allies concentrated on restoring and, in the case of Eastern Europe, restructuring their own economies. Not until 1953, after the death of Stalin, did the Soviet Union begin to contribute to multilateral aid organizations and extend credits to noncommunist Third World countries. Whereas in the case of the United States it has sometimes been difficult to distinguish between economic aid and certain forms of security assistance, for the USSR

> it was not possible to draw a clear distinction between aid and trade, since the USSR almost never offered outright grants but only low interest loans to cover the purchase of Soviet machinery and services for the projects to be built with Soviet assistance. Similarly, much of the debt repayment could be made through the shipment of traditional exports. Thus there has always been an automatic conversion of what has been loosely termed "aid" (both by the Soviets and Westerners) into trade flows.[29]

The economic aid provided by the Soviet Union and other members of COMECON (Council for Mutual Economic Assistance) to noncommunist countries has had both political and economic objectives. Political objectives dominated in the 1953–1964 period when the USSR sought to weaken and displace the influence of the West in particular Third World countries. The focus was on radical, anti-Western governments, and by 1964 some 80 percent of Soviet economic aid to non-COMECON members was channeled to eight countries, six of which were considered to belong to the "progressive" camp (Egypt, Ghana, Iraq, Syria, Algeria, and Indonesia).[30] Economic objectives became more important during the next ten years as the USSR and Eastern European countries began to conclude agreements with developing countries, calling for the credits provided to be repaid with raw materials in short supply in the Soviet-bloc countries or with manufactured goods that could be produced more cheaply by the aid recipients. Although political considerations remained important, "States with a moderate pro-Western outlook that could boast a solvent or dynamic economy as well as a sizable domestic market were no longer

---

[29] Elizabeth Kridl Valkenier, *The Soviet Union and the Third World: An Economic Bind* (New York: Praeger, 1983), p. 3.

[30] Ibid., pp. 3–11. The other two countries were India and Afghanistan.

scorned as the pliant objects of imperialist machinations. Both on the diplomatic and the economic fronts, Moscow began to pursue a more even-handed policy wherein state-to-state relations were based more on the obvious needs and capabilities of the two partners than on revolutionary calculations."[31]

Soviet data on economic assistance are scanty, and analysts tend to rely on Western estimates. Table 7-3 reports the value of Soviet, Eastern European, and Chinese economic grants and credits to non-COMECON developing countries between 1954 and 1981 as estimated by the U.S. Central Intelligence Agency. One point that emerges clearly from this table, and upon which analysts of Soviet economic assistance are agreed, is the considerable gap between funds committed and the sums disbursed. Somewhat less than half the Soviet aid committed between 1954 and 1981 is believed to have been disbursed; for Eastern European countries the proportion is about one-third. This ratio holds even for some of the Soviet Union's more important client states, such as Afghanistan and Angola. For Ethiopia and Mozambique, the percentages are reportedly 25 and 10 respectively. The low rates of disbursement are said to be "partly due to the fact that the assistance is geared almost exclusively to projects and partly to the USSR's refusal to finance local costs, which are often beyond the means of recipient countries. For the last few years, non-CMEA [COMECON] countries, other than Laos, Afghanistan and Cambodia, have in fact paid back to the USSR more than they received, the negative figures amounting to $35 million in 1981 and $108 million in 1982."[32] The primary recipients of Soviet aid among the non-COMECON countries in recent years have been Laos, Kampuchea, Afghanistan, Angola, Mozambique, Ethiopia, the People's Democratic Republic of Yemen, and Nicaragua.

The major recipients of Soviet economic aid have, however, been the three developing country members of COMECON: Cuba, Vietnam, and Mongolia. It has been estimated, for example, that in 1981 and 1982 these three countries received 95 percent of the credits and grants disbursed by the USSR to the Third World. With about $5.5 billion reportedly disbursed to Cuba, Vietnam, and Mongolia[33] and some $715 million

[31] Ibid., p. 35. See also Francis Fukuyama, *Moscow's Post-Brezhnev Reassessment of the Third World*, R-3337-USDP (Santa Monica, Calif.: Rand, February 1986).

[32] United Kingdom, Foreign and Commonwealth Office, "Soviet Aid to Special Friends," Background Brief, London, January 1984 (revised), p. 1.

[33] Ibid., pp. 1–3. It is important to remember that while Mongolia is technically an independent state, the Soviet Union is responsible for its defense. Approximately six Soviet divisions are stationed permanently in Mongolia, there are two Soviet airbases, and Soviet medium-range nuclear ballistic missiles are deployed on Mongolian territory.

TABLE 7-3

Soviet, Eastern European, and Chinese Economic Credits and Grants
to Non-Comecon Developing Countries, 1954–1981
(in $U.S. million)

Year	Committed				Disbursed			
	Total	USSR	E. Eur.	China	Total	USSR	E. Eur.	China
1954–1968	9,491	6,081	2,385	1,025	4,185	2,870	800	515
1969	895	476	403	16	535	355	105	70
1970	1,175	200	195	780	605	390	145	70
1971	2,190	1,125	485	585	795	420	190	190
1972	2,185	655	925	605	865	430	175	260
1973	1,945	715	630	600	970	500	230	240
1974	1,935	815	840	280	1,190	700	235	255
1975	2,865	1,955	545	365	955	500	270	185
1976	2,015	1,030	835	150	1,180	475	385	320
1977	1,085	430	460	195	1,265	550	480	235
1978	4,795	3,000	1,575	220	1,125	480	405	240
1979	4,125	3,345	645	135	1,025	575	290	160
1980	3,400	2,070	1,330	—	1,065	810	255	—
1981	1,115	450	665	—	1,040	715	325	—
Total	39,216	22,347	11,918	4,956	16,800	9,770	4,290	2,740

Sources: United States Central Intelligence Agency, *Communist Aid Activities in Non-Communist Less Developed Countries, 1978* and *1979 and 1954–79,* ER 79-10412 U and ER 80-10318 U (Washington, D.C.: September 1979 and October 1980), pp. 11 and 17, respectively; and United States, Department of State, *Soviet and East European Aid to the Third World, 1981* (Washington, D.C.: Department of State, February 1983), p. 16.
Note: Because of rounding, components may not add up to totals.

disbursed to non-COMECON developing countries (Table 7-3) in 1981, that proportion would seem reasonably accurate. The ratio between economic aid to COMECON developing countries and the other Third World recipients of Soviet aid in earlier years is not known, but it is likely that Cuba, Vietnam, and Mongolia also received a large share prior to 1981. The main forms of Soviet economic assistance to Cuba at the beginning of the 1980s were commodity subsidies (primarily for sugar but also for nickel) and commodity aid (oil, priced by the USSR not only below the world rate but also lower than the rate charged to the Eastern European members of COMECON). Project aid comprised less than 15 percent of Soviet economic assistance. For Vietnam and Mongolia, project aid accounted for a larger share of Soviet economic aid. Although these two countries have also received petroleum at subsidized prices, but probably not as low as those offered to Cuba, Soviet oil subsidies to Cuba have been much larger, both in absolute terms and as a share of Soviet economic aid. In 1982, Cuba reportedly received an oil subsidy worth some $950 million or about 25 percent of Soviet aid; Vietnam, $7 million or about 1 percent; Mongolia, $10 million or about 2 percent.[34]

It is difficult to ascertain what proportion of Soviet economic assistance takes the form of grants. Some countries, notably Cuba and Vietnam, are said to have received considerable grant aid, and some disaster assistance has been provided free-of-charge. Beyond that, Soviet credits were calculated at the beginning of the 1980s to contain a grant element of approximately 38 percent.[35] COMECON aid to nonmembers has tended to take the form of credits enabling the aid recipient to purchase Soviet or Eastern European goods and services and which are to be repaid in kind.[36] According to the OECD, up to 1965 the majority of these credits carried low interest rates (2.5 to 3 percent) and were repayable over eight to twelve years. Since 1965, in line with the growing importance of economic objectives to COMECON aid donors, the terms under which credits are extended have hardened. In the late 1960s, interest rates of 3 to 3.5 percent and repayment periods of three to ten years became more common.[37] In

---

[34] Ibid., pp. 2–3.

[35] Quintin V. S. Bach, "A Note on Soviet Statistics on Their Economic Aid," *Soviet Studies* 37: 2 (April 1985): 269. According to Bach, Western aid is calculated to contain a 90 percent grant element.

[36] Interestingly,

diversification is beginning to take place in Soviet cooperation with some of the more advanced of its major LDC partners. Several contracts were signed by India and the USSR in 1977 for supplying Indian equipment to steel projects built with Soviet assistance in Egypt, Turkey, Bulgaria and Cuba. Plans for expanding the steel mills put up in India with Soviet aid envisage production of equipment to be supplied to third countries, especially other LDC's, and India has prepared a report on its ability to participate in Soviet-aided metallurgical projects in Algeria, Libya, and Nigeria. Indeed, these proposals have been incorporated into the long-term economic cooperation agreement signed by the USSR and India in March 1979, and to judge from comments in the Indian press, cooperation in third countries will not be limited to Soviet-aided projects.

Elizabeth Kridl Valkenier, "The USSR, the Third World, and the Global Economy," *Problems of Communism* 28: 4 (July–August 1979): 30.

[37] OECD, *Resources*, "Annex II: Communist Countries' Economic Aid to Developing Countries," pp. 293–315.

the 1970s, a new pattern began to emerge in COMECON aid/trade relations with the Third World: the "joint production scheme." "Under this
pay-back arrangement, Soviet credits for extracting or processing of raw
materials, or for the manufacture of a finished product, were repaid by
shipments of the project's output."[38]

Although economic aid from the COMECON countries is less concessional and smaller in volume than Western economic aid, it has not supported the security sector in most recipient countries as *directly* as some
economic aid from the West, notably the United States, or from the OPEC
countries. With the exception of commodity aid and subsidies to the developing country members of COMECON, no equivalent to budget support
provided by the United States and OPEC countries appears designed to enable recipients to maintain a larger security sector than they could using
only their own resources.

Shortcomings of Economic Aid

There are shortcomings associated with each form of capital transfer discussed above. Export income depends heavily on demand in the industrialized countries, and the prices paid for raw materials, which remain the
major export of many developing countries, have varied sharply over
time. When there is recession in the industrialized countries, when the
costs of Third World imports rise or when commodity prices decline, the
export sector is less able to finance economic development. Private investment may fail to generate growth in developing countries for several reasons: it is too limited; the goods produced are exported; imported inputs
are prefered to domestic ones; capital-intensive methods of production
are employed; or too few of the profits earned are reinvested in the domestic economy of the host country. The main shortcoming of commercial borrowing is, of course, the ease with which a heavy debt burden can
be accumulated.

In this section, three problems associated with economic aid will be
discussed in some detail: donor self-interest, the degree to which aid is
used to increase consumption rather than investment, and the suggestion
that aid depresses domestic savings rates.

DONOR SELF-INTEREST

One of the main criticisms of economic aid has been that donors provide it to fulfill certain economic, political, and strategic interests of their

---

[38] Valkenier, *The Soviet Union*, p. 17. The primary consideration is thus which materials
are required by the COMECON economies, not by the economy of the aid recipient.

own, not first and foremost to promote economic development in recipient countries. The failure of aid donors to give top priority to development in their economic assistance programs does not, however, guarantee
that economic aid will fail to promote growth and development, at least
in theory. Gustav Papenek has argued that "Clearly, most aid is allocated
in large part on the basis of political considerations. But among countries
who have a claim for political reasons it tends to go disproportionately to
those who need foreign resources more, and any one country is likely to
receive more than its average allocation during its periods of greatest
need." [39] To the extent that these foreign resources are used to create or
maintain productive capacity or strengthen a country's infrastructure, it
might be argued that development is promoted. When, however, projects
are, in the words of the World Bank, "selected either on the basis of political prestige or on the basis of inadequate regard for their likely economic and financial rate of return," [40] development will not be served.
Nor, in the long run, will it be aided by budgetary support enabling excessively large security and civilian bureaucratic sectors to be maintained.

It was demonstrated above that a significant portion of the economic
assistance provided by the United States to the Third World since the end
of World War II has been used to support the security sector of recipient
countries. Although one can argue that some degree of security is neces-

[39] Gustav Papanek, "The Effect of Aid and Other Resource Transfers on Savings and
Growth in Less Developed Countries," *Economic Journal* 82 (September 1972): 941. Papanek's description could, of course, easily cover the large U.S. grants to Israel since 1974.
With a per capita income in 1982 estimated by the World Bank to be U.S. $5,000, Israel can
hardly be defined as a "poor" country. Its military, political, and economic policies for the
last thirty years, however, have created a situation in which Israel has suffered a severe
shortage of foreign exchange and therefore experiences a "need" for external sources of
capital.

Between 1972 and 1983, Israel received $6.7 billion in economic aid from the United
States; of this, $5.4 billion were outright grants. Of the $1.3 billion in loans extended to
Israel during this period, $800 million were subsequently written off as grants. That means
that the total economic grant aid received was $6.2 billion, or nearly 93 percent of total
economic aid transfers from the U.S. government to Israel during those years. (Another
$13.5 billion in military assistance was made available between 1974 and 1982.) These
sums might be compared with the assistance offered by the U.S. to Africa. Between 1946
and 1981, nearly fifty African countries, excluding Egypt, shared about $11 billion in eco-
nomic assistance from the United States, of which some $7.7 billion (70 percent) took the
form of grants. On U.S. aid to Israel, see United States General Accounting Office, *US Assistance to the State of Israel*, GAO/ID-83-51 (Washington, D.C.: General Accounting Office,
24 June 1983), p. 30. For U.S. aid to Africa, see USAID, *US Overseas Loans and Grants*,
p. 85. Data on Israel are for assistance disbursed; for Africa, they are for aid committed.

[40] World Bank, *Toward Sustained Development in Sub-Saharan Africa. A Joint Program
of Action* (Washington, D.C.: AID, September 1984), p. 24.

sary for countries to develop and that the security sector can promote development in other ways as well (manpower training, for example), any developmental benefits that might result from channeling budgetary support to the security sector are minimal compared to the benefits that would have accrued had resources been invested directly in productive undertakings. In a similar vein, much French economic aid to former colonies in sub-Saharan Africa has taken the form of budget subsidies necessary for the continued functioning of the governments in these countries. Again it might be argued that only if the government is operating can development plans be formulated and implemented. While this is true, it is also the case that in many of these countries the bureaucracy is primarily concerned with administering its own salaries, not promoting development.

Even investment in productive sectors can be of doubtful value developmentally if projects do not meet the needs of the domestic economy and are mainly designed to benefit the industrialized world. Economic aid projects financed by Western countries and the World Bank frequently run up against this criticism, and for good reason.[41] What is perhaps less

---

[41] Teresa Hayter and Catharine Watson, *Aid: Rhetoric and Reality* (London: Pluto Press, 1985), pp. 240–42, for example, argue that, although there are often political rationales behind Western aid policies,

economic considerations provide an even more compelling justification for the existence of aid. As the Brandt report correctly points out, not only is the "South" dependent on the "North," but the North is dependent on the South. . . . Having built up a system under which the Third World provides it with cheap and abundant raw materials and primary commodities, markets for its manufactured goods and super-profits for some of its major firms and banks, the West would find it difficult to adjust to the loss of these advantages. Some raw materials crucial to Western industries are to be found only or mainly in the Third World. A large part of the proven reserves of oil are in the Third World. . . . Western consumers would suffer from any diminution in the willingness of Third World countries to turn over their land to export crops in their desperate attempts to satisfy the requirements of their urban élites for Western manufactured goods. If more land was devoted to food crops for local consumption, there could be shortages of tea, coffee, bananas and other tropical crops and their prices could go up, feeding inflation. . . .

Between a quarter and a third of the exports of developed countries and nearly 40 per cent of us exports go to the Third World. . . . Economic policies in the Third World directed primarily at meeting the needs of the poor might reduce the need for imports and would certainly mean that different types of manufactured goods were imported. . . . The profits made by multinational companies are higher in the Third World than they are at home and in other developed countries, mainly because wages are much lower; some of the major multinational companies make most of their profits and in some cases most of their sales in the Third World. Left-wing governments might be more interested in a debtors' cartel, which would threaten major banks.

CHAPTER 7

well appreciated is that the economic aid programs of the USSR and Eastern Europe are also often designed with the needs of the donor's economy in mind. The increasing tendency of COMECON aid to be directed toward the development of natural resources and the creation of manufacturing capacity for certain goods either in short supply in the USSR or Eastern Europe or produced more cheaply in the Third World than by the donor countries is a clear indication that East-bloc countries perceive economic advantages can be derived from economic "aid."

A crucial element in this equation are the prices set by the COMECON countries for the goods imported from Third World aid recipients as repayment for development credits. These prices are often, although not uniformly, below world prices and are lower than the cost of domestic production by COMECON countries. For example, Soviet aid to Iran in the late 1960s was to be repaid in natural gas for a period of fifteen years, from 1970 to 1985. This gas was valued by the USSR at about $6 per thousand cubic meters, reportedly less than the cost of production in the Soviet Union. Similarly, 95 percent of Afghanistan's natural gas production is imported by the USSR at prices below those prevailing on the world market. Guinea concluded an agreement with the Soviet Union in 1969 for the exploitation of bauxite deposits in Kindia. Beginning in 1971, Guinea was to repay the Soviet costs associated with this project by shipping most of the high-grade ore produced by this mine to the USSR for a period of thirty years; it has been reported that the value assigned by the USSR to this ore was "well below the ruling world prices."[42]

Very special client states, notably Cuba, have received extremely advantageous prices for their raw material exports to the Soviet Union. The price of Cuban sugar is apparently indexed to the price of goods imported from the USSR. The USSR is reportedly paying Cuba three to four times the world price for sugar, but this must be seen as a unique case.[43] India has also received favorable terms from the Soviet Union. A study of ten Indian exports to the USSR and Eastern Europe between 1960 and 1973 found that "except for jute manufactures, cashew kernels and tobacco,

[42] Bach, "A Note," p. 275. See also, United Kingdom, Foreign and Commonwealth Office, "Soviet Aid," p. 3; Leo Tansky, "Soviet Foreign Aid: Scope, Direction and Trends," pp. 772–74, in Compendium: *Soviet Economic Prospects for the Seventies*, U.S. Congress, Joint Economic Committee, 93rd Cong., 1st Sess. (Washington, D.C.: Government Printing Office, 27 June 1973); and Valkenier, *The Soviet Union*, pp. 16–18.

[43] United Kingdom, Foreign and Commonwealth Office, "Soviet Aid," p. 2. Mozambique, for example, has made strenuous efforts to be granted special status and gain the sort of economic privileges accorded Cuba, Vietnam, and Mongolia, but it has failed to engender a substantial Soviet commitment. See, Francis Fukuyama, "Gorbachev and the Third World," *Foreign Affairs* 64 (Spring 1986): 723.

the Eastern Bloc countries paid consistently higher prices than the con-vertible currency countries." For two of these commodities, manganese and iron ores, the prices paid by the members of COMECON were as much as 70 to 90 percent higher in some years.[44]

COMECON countries are also said to benefit financially from their eco-nomic aid agreements with the Third World by reselling some of the goods imported from aid recipients. It is extremely difficult to obtain reliable information on this point; however, it has been reported that the Soviet Union has resold olives, honey, raisins, and nuts obtained from Afghani-stan in Eastern Europe at a profit. Estimates of the amount of India's total exports to East-bloc that are resold vary from 3.5 to 10 percent.[45]

In addition to supporting projects useful to their own economies, most aid donors have sought to derive financial advantage from their economic assistance by tying aid to purchases of goods and services from their own economies. (This is obviously very difficult for the OPEC countries.) Tying has often reduced the value of aid, not only because recipients have been unable to seek out the least expensive supplier but also because suppliers have often charged inflated prices for materials purchased under aid con-tracts. An estimate produced in the late 1960s claimed that goods pur-chased from OECD countries under aid contracts have frequently been overpriced by as much as 20 to 50 percent of the value of the aid. Ac-cording to the OECD, 30 percent of all ODA supplied by its members in 1982–1983 was tied and another 7 percent was partially tied. Of the five major donors, 21 percent of German ODA was tied, 46 percent of French ODA, 32 percent of U.S. ODA, 41 percent of British ODA, and 17 percent of Japanese ODA. If partially tied ODA is included, the figures increase for each of these countries except for West Germany; for Japan, the propor-tion nearly doubles. If tied and partially tied aid are taken as a share of bilateral ODA, the figures become higher still (Table 7-4).[46]

Nearly all COMECON aid is tied to the purchase of goods and services

[44]Deepak Nayyar, "India's Trade with the Socialist Countries," pp. 132–33, in *Eco-nomic Relations Between Socialist Countries and the Third World,* ed. Deepak Nayyar (London: MacMillan, 1977). For jute manufactures and tobacco, Nayyar suggests that the lower prices paid by East-bloc countries can be attributed to the fact that they were of lower quality than the goods imported by Western countries.

[45]On India, see ibid., p. 130. Nayyar has suggested that, at least as far as India and Pakistan are concerned, the Eastern European countries are more likely to engage in resale than the USSR (p. 141, n. 79). On Afghanistan, see United Kingdom, Foreign and Com-monwealth Office, "Soviet Aid," p. 3.

[46]In addition to OECD reports, see J. Bhagwati, "The Tying of Aid," in *Foreign Aid,* J. Bhagwati and R. Eckhaus, ed. (London: Penguin, 1970), and "Untying of aid proves to be a slow process," *Ceres* 12 (May/June 1979).

TABLE 7-4
Tied Aid, Major OECD Donors, 1982–1983

Donor	% Total ODA Tied	% Total ODA Tied and Partially Tied	Bilateral ODA as % Total ODA	% Bilateral ODA Tied	% Bilateral ODA Tied and Partially Tied
United States	32	41	65	47	63
United Kingdom	41	42	55	75	76
France	46	54	85	54	63
West Germany	21	21	71	30	30
Japan	17	33	90	23	45
All DAC	30	37	69	44	54

Source: Organisation for Economic Co-operation and Development, *Twenty-Five Years of Development Co-Operation: A Review, 1985 Report* (Paris: OECD 1985), p. 299.

from the donor country. There is some evidence that the Soviet Union and Eastern European countries charge relatively high prices for the goods exported to aid recipients. For the Soviet Union, it has been asserted that "foreign trade prices were divided into four categories: the lowest were for transactions in hard currency, the next for barter operations and the highest for those linked with aid programmes."[47] It is difficult to compare the prices of manufactured goods across countries, but the Soviet Union appears to be charging its Cuban allies more for certain items than it charges other countries. "Although all other things are not necessarily equal, a sample of the prices paid by Cuba for Soviet products (fob) which appear comparable reads (with the average Soviet export price = 100): light cars 132, motorcycles 197, granulated urea 144, cement 121, window glass 171 (to the USA it was 60) and plywood 115."[48] For India, it has been suggested that the prices charged by the USSR on a wide range of goods but excluding machinery and transport equipment have tended to be lower than those charged by Western countries. There is a widespread belief in India that machinery and transport equipment from the Soviet Union and Eastern Europe have been of poorer quality than similar equipment available from the West and that India has been

[47] Bach, "A Note," pp. 274–75, n. 11.
[48] Ibid., p. 272.

required to pay a comparatively high price for these East-bloc imports. Deepak Nayyar, however, has argued that "Evidence in support of such a view is extremely hard to find, and wherever statements of this kind are made, they are rarely documented."[49]

A final point to be made about donor self-interest is that by seeking to fulfill their own political and economic objectives, donors have frequently used aid to support governments more concerned with maintaining themselves in power than in promoting development. These governments use aid to avoid making reforms essential for successful development but which might undermine their support by élite groups at home and abroad. Food aid, for example, has allowed governments either to prevent starvation without carrying out agrarian reform or to provide low-cost food to urban workers and other politically important groups. Budget support has enabled governments to keep public consumption at a high level without implementing tax reforms and without severely reducing the size of the public sector.[50] In these ways, aid can contribute to a status quo inimical to development.

THE INVESTMENT-CONSUMPTION DEBATE

Some analysts argue that the value of economic assistance is often reduced because only a portion of financial aid is invested; much of it is consumed. In the early days of economic assistance programs, most aid practitioners assumed that all financial aid would be invested. There were those, however, who saw from the beginning that this would not necessarily be the case. Ragnar Nurkse, for example, pointed out in 1953 that,

[49] Nayyar, "India's Trade," pp. 130–31.

[50] For example, in 1979, the Swedish International Development Authority (SIDA), a major donor to Bangladesh, reported that one effect of food aid has been to allow the government of Bangladesh "to continue with its policy of neglect of agriculture (and of land reform), a policy which has 'forced' the government to rely more and more heavily on imported food." Reported in "Bangladeshi aid: The new ruling class," *South*, March 1982, p. 47. Despite this and other criticisms of Bangladeshi government policy, SIDA has continued to increase its aid to Bangladesh. See Lars Bondestam, Staffan Lindberg and Stefan de Vylder, "Bra mål—dåligt bistånd" ("Good Objectives—Bad Aid"), *Rapport från SIDA*, no. 8 (1979): 34–36.

Numerous reports have shown that very little of the food aid provided to Bangladesh reaches the hungry majority in the rural areas. Canada is Bangladesh's largest aid donor. Two-thirds of the aid provided by Canada to Bangladesh in the 1970s consisted of food. A 1984 Canadian study estimated that only 15 percent of that food aid reached the poor. Most was sold by the government to members of the military, civil servants, and others in urban areas. See B. Cohen, "Pouring aid into a bottleneck," *South*, April 1984, p. 29. See also, Donald F. McHenry and Kai Bird, "Food Bungle in Bangladesh," *Foreign Policy* no. 27 (Summer 1977): 72–88, and Kai Bird and Sue Goldmark, "Food Aid vs. Development," *Worldview* 20 (January–February 1977): 38–41.

it is nearly always possible to some extent to substitute foreign funds for domestic saving so that the country's consumption is increased and little or no addition is made to the rate of accumulation. . . .

This applies to inter-governmental grants even more than to loans made by either private investors or governments to public authorities in underdeveloped countries. International grants can of course be used for capital formation in the same way as loans. In the case of loans there is generally some pressure to use them at least for specific productive purposes so that interest and amortization requirements can be met later on. . . . Grants can be used directly or indirectly for consumption without any subsequent inconvenience.

. . . Foreign aid will undoubtedly help to relieve the "dollar shortage", but will it relieve the shortage of capital? The problem of capital formation may remain completely unsolved.[51]

Since about 1970 the one-to-one relationship between aid and investment has increasingly been questioned. It is somewhat surprising that it took development economists so long to raise this challenge because, as Papanek has pointed out, the assumption that all aid will be invested does "not have any basis in traditional economic analysis. On the contrary, conventional wisdom would hold that any additional resources are used in part to increase consumption and only in part to augment investment. Analysis would normally focus on the respective portions. However, until recently, such analysis did not take place with respect to foreign resource inflows."[52] Although it is now acknowledged that all economic aid is not invested, it is difficult to evaluate how much is consumed and what effect the consumption of aid receipts has on development.

THE AID SAVINGS DEBATE

A number of critics of economic aid have argued that it has depressed the rate of saving in recipient countries. Many of the arguments and counterarguments on this point have been based on econometric analyses and suffer from the sorts of problems discussed in Chapter 4.[53] In addition, external factors such as variations in prices for Third World exports and in demand for Third World products in the industrialized countries or donor attitudes to economic aid will affect both domestic savings and the level of assistance received. As with all economic interactions, it is unlikely that one pattern applies to every country in a group as diverse as

[51] Nurkse, *Problems*, pp. 81–93.
[52] Papanek, "The Effect of Aid," pp. 934–35.
[53] See, for example, ibid., pp. 939–45, and Thomas E. Weisskopf, "The Impact of Foreign Capital on Domestic Savings in Underdeveloped Countries," *Journal of International Economics* 2 (February 1972): 26.

the one known as the Third World. Evidence of one type of relationship between the domestic savings rate and the inflow of economic assistance in one country at a particular moment in time does not necessarily explain the situation in other countries or even in the same country at a different period of time.

There is nonetheless some evidence that a number of Third World governments have failed to take the actions necessary to increase domestic savings rates because they knew that assistance from the more developed countries would be forthcoming. The clearest example of this strategy was provided by the Rhee government in South Korea in the 1950s which followed policies designed to encourage the United States to provide more economic aid that effectively reduced domestic savings.

These policies consisted of an overvalued exchange rate, relatively low tariffs on imports, no efforts to encourage exports, a deficit budget financed by borrowing from the Central Bank when taxes and aid-generated revenues were insufficient, Central Bank financing of commercial bank credit to the private sector, and low interest rates that assured excess demand for credit. Such policies inevitably produced an internal financial gap between government revenues and expenditures, and between financial savings and lending. They also insured an external financial gap between import demand and foreign exchange availabilities. A higher exchange rate would have curtailed import demand and probably increased savings. Higher taxes would have restrained consumption and added to savings. But the Rhee government insisted on holding to the low exchange, interest and tax rates so that the imbalances persisted. Their persistence was in turn cited as evidence of the need for more assistance at existing exchange rates to satisfy the excess demand for imports and the excess demand for internal finance.[54]

[54] David C. Cole and Princeton N. Lyman, *Korean Development: The Interplay of Politics and Economics* (Cambridge, Mass.: Harvard University Press, 1971), p. 170. See also Charles R. Frank, Jr., Kwang Suk Kim, and Larry E. Westphal, *South Korea* (New York: Columbia University Press for the National Bureau of Economic Research, 1975), p. 228, where it is argued that while foreign aid may have depressed domestic savings in Korea, "at the time, South Korea was desperately poor and needed the additional resources both for consumption and investment."
Papanek, "The Effect of Aid," p. 949, reported that, in addition to the South Korean case analysts have suggested that India and Pakistan neglected agricultural development, and therefore the savings which a rapidly growing agriculture could have provided, because they knew that shortfalls would be made good by United States surplus commodities; that opportunities for Cuban, Mexican and Central American investors were pre-empted by United States capital; and that negative savings rates in Liberia and extravagant expenditures leading to lower savings in Ghana were due to the ready availability of suppliers' credits.

WHEN these different shortcomings of economic aid are taken into account, there is cause to believe that, even if the availability of capital were the determining factor in the relative success of development programs, the contribution of foreign economic aid to growth and development has not been as great as its earliest supporters had anticipated. For one thing, a sizable share of economic aid has been directed toward Third World security sectors, not development projects. For another, development specialists have come to realize in the course of the post–World War II period that the availability of capital is a necessary but not sufficient element in the growth and development equation (see also Chapter 6 on this point). The efficient use of capital, the availability of skilled managers and workers, entrepreneurship, access to technology, and the existence of appropriate institutions are among the factors which must be added to that equation. Paul Streeten has commented that

> The contribution by the developed countries was seen too narrowly in terms of capital aid and technical assistance, instead of as the impact of all policies pursued by the rich countries, whether or not they were pursued with the express purpose of assisting development efforts. These would include science policies, the thrust of research and development expenditure, policies toward transnational companies, migration policy, monetary policy, regional policy, trade and employment policies, agricultural policy, as well as foreign policy and military alliances generally.[55]

SECURITY ASSISTANCE AND DEVELOPMENT

Providing assistance to the military establishments of foreign countries is not an invention of the modern world. It has been suggested, for example, that some 2,500 years ago, Mycenae obtained "a great quantity of gold" from Egypt in exchange for military aid which helped the Egyptians expel the Hyksos.[56] With the exception of eighteenth-century Europe, it is only in the twentieth century that military assistance offered to more than a handful of countries at a time has become an important element in international relations.

Current assistance to the security sector of Third World countries is of two main types: military assistance and security-related economic aid. Military assistance involves the transfer of military equipment and related services on concessional terms while security-related economic aid generally comprises budget or balance-of-payments support intended to

[55] Streeten, "Development Ideas," p. 47.
[56] National Archaeological Museum of Greece, *Catalogue*, Athens, p. 4.

reduce the financial burden of the recipient's security sector. The main forms that military assistance takes are: direct transfer of equipment, training (both in donor and recipient country), the provision of services (equipment maintenance, for example), the provision of operations and maintenance material, and credits on concessional terms for the purchase of equipment. Security-related economic support generally takes the form of economic and financial support and commodity assistance.

The main donors of security assistance in the post–World War II period have been the United States, the USSR, France, Great Britain, the Federal Republic of Germany, the German Democratic Republic, and China. A number of Third World countries, primarily capital-surplus oil exporters, have in recent years begun to provide security assistance to other developing countries; the most important of these are Saudi Arabia, Kuwait, Algeria, and Libya. Israel is an increasingly active supplier of weapons and military training to the Third World, but, according to available information, Israeli transactions are carried out on a cash basis. Whether they contain any concessional elements is not known. There are few developing countries that have not received some form of security assistance from one or another of these donors since the end of World War II, although individual donors have tended to concentrate their security assistance on particular countries in the same way as their economic assistance has been directed at selected countries. For the most part, security assistance is tied aid. The exceptions are grants provided by OPEC countries to enable recipients to purchase weapons in third countries and perhaps some economic and financial support grants.

The single largest donor of security assistance has been the United States. By 1983, the United States had provided some form of military assistance to about 95 of the nearly 120 Third World recipients of U.S. foreign assistance (economic plus military aid). Between 1946 and 1983, the United States had supplied some $78 billion in military grants and loans to Third World countries, two-thirds of which—nearly $53 billion—took the form of grants. Another $33 billion in ESF assistance, excluding PL-480 shipments, was made available during the same period. The precise division of ESF into loans and grants is not available, but the grant component is considerable.[57]

---

[57] The military assistance figures might be compared with U.S. economic assistance transfers. According to U.S. statistics, the U.S. government supplied Third World countries with a total of $100 billion in economic aid between 1946 and 1983, of this, about $58 billion took the form of grants. Recall that the $33 billion in ESF and an unspecified amount of PL-480 aid used for military budget support are included in this category, not in the military assistance accounts. Total security assistance thus ran to over $111 billion and economic aid to less than $67 billion, a ratio of about 2:1. All data from USAID, *US Overseas Loans and Grants*.

At the beginning of the U.S. Military Assistance Program (MAP), all equipment and services were transferred free-of-charge, and by far the largest amount went to the United States' European allies—for example, $3.5 billion of the $4 billion provided under MAP in 1951. The Foreign Military Sales (FMS) program was inaugurated in 1955 to make available credits for the purchase of U.S. military equipment and services. Throughout the 1950s and well into the 1960s most Third World recipients of U.S. military aid received grants. Beginning in the late 1960s and especially during the 1970s, however, "as many countries experienced relative economic stability and began to make major investments in development oriented programs, an effort was made to phase out grant military assistance and provide only FMS credits at Treasury rates. By 1980, grant MAP had been reduced to less than $200 million.[58]

There have been two kinds of FMS credits: direct loans and guaranteed loans. The former are made on-budget, the latter, off-budget. The conditions attached to them are roughly the same: interest rates equal to the cost of money to the U.S. government (plus two fees for the guaranteed loans) and a repayment period of twelve years upon delivery of the equipment with a one- or two-year grace period.[59] As discussed in Chapter 5, the Reagan administration began to increase the concessionality of FMS loans and to revive the MAP grant-aid program in the early 1980s, making U.S. weapons less expensive now for major U.S. clients than they were in the 1970s.

The Soviet Union has aided the security sector in some forty Third World countries. Between 1955 and 1982, the value of Soviet military assistance disbursed to noncommunist developing countries has been placed at $49 billion. These figures omit aid to North Korea, Vietnam, and Cuba; the sizable military transfers to these countries from the Soviet bloc have contained a significant grant element. Whether this figure is accurate and what proportion of these transfers has taken the form of

[58] "Statement of William Schneider, Jr., Under Secretary of State for Security Assistance, Science and Technology, Before the Senate Foreign Relations Committee," 26 September 1985, mimeograph, p. 5.

Stephanie Neuman has reported that "Between 1968–1972, 90 percent of US military assistance was concessional. Between 1978–1982, this percentage fell to less than 25 percent." Stephanie Neuman, "Offsets in the International Arms Market," p. 37, in *World Military Expenditures and Arms Transfers, 1985*, U.S. Arms Control and Disarmament Agency, Publication 123 (Washington, D.C.: ACDA, August 1985).

[59] U.S. Congress, House, Committee on Foreign Affairs, Subcommittee on Arms Control, International Security and Science, Report: *U.S. Military Sales and Assistance Programs: Laws, Regulations and Procedures*, Prepared by Congressional Research Service, Library of Congress, 99th Cong., 1st Sess. (Washington, D.C.: Government Printing Office, 23 July 1985), p. 53.

grants is difficult to ascertain. The USSR itself provides no information. Just as it is difficult to disentangle economic aid and trade, COMECON arms sales and aid are frequently considered to be one and the same thing. The major source of data—the U.S. Central Intelligence Agency— equates arms transfers with military assistance, and all those who write about Soviet military aid have adopted this practice.

Up to the early or mid-1970s, Soviet weapons were priced between one-quarter and one-half the list price of roughly comparable Western weapons. Discounts were frequently offered. Loans were made at low interest rates (2.5 to 3 percent) over long periods (twenty-five years with ten-year grace periods) and were repayable in commodities or soft currencies. Since then, terms have hardened for many recipients, and Soviet military aid has increasingly come to resemble purchases on commercial terms, especially for the oil-exporting countries. Repayment is required within ten years, grace periods of one or two years are given grudgingly, interest rates have increased to between 7 and 9 percent, and payment in hard currency is sometimes demanded. List prices have also been increased so that they are now close to those for comparable Western equipment.

Favored clients such as India and Ethiopia continue to be given easier terms. The Ethiopian government is said to be currently receiving weapons at a 50-percent discount, for example. Cuba and Vietnam have always received weapons free-of-charge from the East-bloc countries; Cuba reportedly obtained at least $400 million in military assistance in both 1981 and 1982 while Vietnam was said to have been granted $300 million of aid in both years. In addition to the outright grants to Cuba and Vietnam, Indonesia and Egypt have had credits converted to grants by their inability or unwillingness to repay Soviet and Eastern European suppliers. Until the early 1970s, the grant element in military assistance from COMECON countries may have been substantial given the degree of concessionality in many military sales and the fact that by 1970 transfers to Vietnam, Cuba, Indonesia, and Egypt accounted for well over half of all Soviet arms transfer to the Third World.[60] Nonetheless, the Soviet

[60] The value of grants to Cuba and Vietnam is from United Kingdom, Foreign and Commonwealth Office, "Soviet Aid," pp. 1–2. Other sources have placed military aid much higher. In 1984, "some western diplomats in Hanoi" were cited as estimating Soviet military aid to Vietnam at $1 billion per year, while "other western sources say the military aid is much greater—about $2 billion." John Spragens, Jr., "Vietnam and the Soviets: A Tighter Alliance," *Indochina Issues* no. 51 (November 1984): 2. The value of Soviet aid to non-COMECON countries is from United States Department of State, *Soviet and East European Aid to the Third-World, 1981* (Washington, D.C.: Department of State, February 1983), p. 4. East European military aid is placed at $5 billion for the same period. See also

Union and its Eastern European allies have provided considerably less military assistance than United States and its NATO allies, both in terms of geographic extent and volume.

Some security assistance is provided essentially for economic reasons. For example, the military assistance provided by the Federal Republic of Germany since the mid-1970s has been motivated at least in part by the desire to build links with countries interested in ordering equipment on a commercial basis from West German arms producers.[61] The movement away from grant assistance and the hardening of terms for credits which has characterized the military aid programs of most donor countries since the beginning of the 1970s—at least until the trend toward increased concessionality in U.S. military-related loans in the early 1980s— is an indication of the increasing importance of economic considerations in arms transfers. Nonetheless, most security assistance, particularly that provided in the 1950s and 1960s, has been motivated by politico-strategic concerns. The major security assistance donors, the United States and the USSR, have used this aid to strengthen their position vis-à-vis each other in the Third World.

Although there are problems involved in obtaining a precise valuation of security assistance for many donors, security-related aid has been a sig-

---

Roger E. Kanet, "Soviet Military Assistance to the Third World," pp. 48–50, in *Communist Nations' Military Assistance*, ed. John F. Copper and Daniel S. Papp (Boulder, Colo.: Westview, 1983); Stockholm International Peace Research Institute (SIPRI), *The Arms Trade with the Third World* (Stockholm: Almqvist & Wiksell, 1971), pp. 182–83; Orah Cooper and Carol Fogarty, "Soviet Economic and Military Aid to the Less Developed Countries, 1954–1978," p. 650, in Compendium: *Soviet Economy in a Time of Change*, U.S. Congress, Joint Economic Committee, Volume 2, 96th Cong., 1st Sess. (Washington, D.C.: Government Printing Office, 10 October 1979); and Joachim Krause, "Soviet Military Aid to the Third World," *Aussenpolitik* 34: 4 (1983): 395.

The amount of arms credits that the USSR was forced to write off as a result of Indonesia's inability to repay is not known precisely, but it can be estimated at $750–900 million (SIPRI, *The Arms Trade*, p. 460). The value of the weapons transferred to Egypt was considerably higher. A recent assessment of Egypt's military debt to the USSR estimated that between 1955 and 1973 (prior to the Yom Kippur War) Egypt had accumulated a military debt to the Soviet Union of $7.8 billion. Of this, $4.6 billion were said to be grants. Of the remaining $3.2 billion, an estimated $1.1 billion were repaid (by Egypt and other Arab states, notably Libya). It is thus possible that an additional $2.1 billion were, of necessity, written off by the USSR, but it is also possible that other Arab states also paid off some of these remaining credits. See Moshe Efrat, "The Defence Burden in Egypt During the Deepening of the Soviet Involvement in 1962–73," (Ph.D. diss., London, London School of Economics, May 1981), pp. 94–99. Many weapons supplied to Egypt by the USSR just before and during the 1973 War with Israel were purchased by other Arab countries. Third party payments for weapons are discussed in more detail in Chapter 3.

[61] *Wehrdienst*, no. 682/1978, 13 November 1978, p. 2.

nificant source of external capital resources for many countries. It is thus legitimate to question what the economic effects of this assistance have been for the recipients. When evaluating the economic effects of security assistance, its supporters often point out that the main justification for security assistance is its contribution to the security of both donor and recipient. If development is promoted by such aid, that is welcomed. The furtherance of development is not, however, a central objective of security assistance, especially its specifically military component. Some supporters of security aid also stress that economic development can be promoted most efficiently by investing directly in the civil sector, since the developmental spin-off from the security sector is small compared to the financial input. Security assistance is not, for example, intended to increase investment. Its impact in the industrial sector is thus indirect, based on the extent to which it stimulates demand for certain manufactures. Nonetheless, analysts who favor the provision of security assistance frequently argue that security assistance can have positive economic effects and that, at least in some cases, the positive effects outweigh the negative ones.[62] The attributes of security assistance most commonly cited as likely to strengthen the economies of Third World recipients are the way in which it provides development-promoting resources, creates demand for domestic products, and substitutes for domestic resources.

The Provision of Development-promoting Resources

Those who maintain that Third World armed forces can play a positive role in the development process have argued that the security sector can promote development by both contributing material resources and dual purpose infrastructure useful to both the military and civilians and assisting in manpower training. Military aid might play a similar role in the economy. A United States presidential commission, the Draper Committee, which studied the U.S. military assistance program at the end of the 1950s, concluded that primarily through manpower training and civic action programs military assistance could contribute to economic and social progress in the Third World.[63] (The contribution of military training to development is discussed in Chapter 8.)

---

[62] Charles Wolf, Jr., *Economic Impacts of Military Assistance*, P-4578 (Santa Monica, Calif.: Rand, February 1971), p. 7, and Hovey, *United States Military Assistance*, p. 124.

[63] *Volume II: Supplement to the Composite Report of The President's Committee To Study the United States Military Assistance Program*, (Washington, D.C.: 17 August 1959); hereafter, cited as *Draper Report*. Annex D, "Contributions of Military Resources to Economic and Social Progress," and Annex E, "Training and Education under the Assistance Programs," pp. 91–160.

The concept of civic action was particularly popular in the United States during the 1950s and 1960s. It had both an economic and a political orientation according to the U.S. Joint Chiefs of Staff who defined civic action as involving the use of "military forces on projects useful to the local populations at all levels in such fields as education, training, public works, agriculture, transportation, communications, health, sanitation, and others contributing to economic and social development, which would also serve to improve the standing of the military forces with the population."[64]

Critics of the development-promoting potential of security spending and military assistance have argued that the purpose of civic action programs has been primarily politico-military. There is much truth in this contention. The U.S. concept of civic action was developed in the 1950s against the background of domestic conflicts in a number of Southeast Asian countries where civic action was considered important in counterinsurgency programs. In the 1960s, U.S. military assistance programs increasingly urged civic action on Latin American armed forces. In some countries, notably Brazil, Chile, Argentina, and Paraguay, the army engineers had for many years been responsible for constructing and repairing public works and providing services (surveying, transportation, and so on) in rural areas. In other Latin American countries, this tradition was much weaker or nonexistent. The "public works programs" carried out by the Venezuelan military during the Gomez administration, for example, took the form of building roads to improve access to the many estates owned by the dictator. As in Asia, civic action in Latin America as conceived of by the U.S. government went hand-in-hand with counterinsurgency programs. The participation of the armed forces in civic action was also a means of justifying the continued existence of military establishments larger than would be warranted by the external threats faced by these countries. "It would meet the contention that large standing armies were a drain on the economy; it would make full use of idle hands and skills within the military organization."[65]

Despite the links between civic action and counterinsurgency, civic action programs have produced some infrastructure and services of poten-

---

[64] United States, Joint Chiefs of Staff, "Dictionary of United States Military Terms for Joint Usage," (Washington, D.C.: Joint Chiefs of Staff, 1 February 1964). See also Chapter 1 in this volume for a critical evaluation of the argument that the armed forces can promote development in the Third World.

[65] Willard F. Barber and C. Neale Ronning, *Internal Security and Military Power, Counterinsurgency and Civil Action in Latin America* (Columbus: Ohio State University Press, 1966), pp. 61–69, 141–78; quotation from p. 69.

tial use to the civil-sector economy. The Draper Report, for example, included a sizable list of civic action projects carried out during the 1950s in Latin America and Asia. Although some of these are of negligible value from the point of view of development, others would appear more useful. Questions have nonetheless been raised about the value of such projects to the civil economy. A mid-1960s survey of U.S. civic action programs in Latin America argued that projects carried out under these programs were generally not integrated into national development plans or coordinated at the national and local levels with civil-sector agencies. The survey also claimed that such projects tended to be oriented more toward the provision of welfare (occasional medical care, for example) than the development of infrastructure.[66]

Even where military programs have resulted in the creation of infrastructure which can be of use to civilians as well as to the armed forces, it is important to ask how much benefit civilians actually derive from them. For example, roads built by the Indian army in Nepal and Kashmir were categorized as civic action projects by the Draper Committee. One purpose of constructing these roads might have been to facilitate economic contacts between these regions and commercial centers in India and abroad, but the major objective was surely to improve access for the Indian armed forces to these strategically important border areas; such access is important not only in the event of war with China or Pakistan but also as a means of ensuring Indian government control over these areas. To the extent that the roads have increased economic contacts with the rest of the world, it is necessary to ask whether the poor majority in regions such as Kashmir and Nepal benefit from such contacts or whether, as has resulted from logging projects in Nepal, they are not increasingly forced to the margins of existence.[67]

The opportunity costs of dual purpose infrastructure must also be calculated. Bridges and roads, for example, that are to be used for military purposes must be able to bear heavier loads than those built solely for use by civilians. These special requirements mean that a road or bridge constructed to enable the armed forces to reach a strategically important region costs more than if built for normal civilian traffic. If the country must use its own resources to finance military infrastructure projects, the opportunity cost to the civil sector will be the cost of the dual purpose

[66] Ibid., pp. 224–25.

[67] On timber operations in Nepal, see Claire Sterling, "Nepal," *Atlantic*, October 1976, pp. 14–25. Concerning civic action programs in India and other countries in the 1950s, see *Draper Report*, Annex D, pp. 122–36.

road or bridge minus the cost of building the same structure only to meet civilian requirements.[68]

It is not enough to record that the armed forces have built a road or an air field or carried out geographical surveys which can in theory benefit the civil economy. Rather, it is necessary to evaluate the extent to which the civil sector actually benefits from the project, whether there is an opportunity cost attached to it, and whether the project improves the economic situation for all social groups or only serves to enrich élites at home and abroad. Although many civic action projects may have benefited the civilian economy to some degree, it is likely that most of these projects were devised to meet military and political, not economic, objectives; this has reduced their potential benefit to the civil sector.

Security-supporting economic assistance provided by the United States has also had the potential to contribute resources to the development effort. As explained above, security-supporting assistance during the 1950s and 1960s most commonly involved the sale of commodities provided by the U.S. government in the recipient country in order to generate revenue for the central government. By the mid-1980s, commodity assistance accounted for only about 20 percent of ESF. Recipient governments frequently used this income to support the defense sector. The commodities themselves, however, entered the civil economy and, depending on the use to which they were put, had the potential to promote civil-sector development.

Prior to 1972, it was legally possible to sell surplus agricultural goods from the United States under the PL-480 program for the same purpose. In 1966, the U.S. Congress amended the Food for Peace legislation so that from 1972 counterpart funds generated by PL-480 shipments had to be used for economic development, not to support military programs. In fact, as will be explained below, the U.S. government sought to circum-

---

[68] Peter Lock and Herbert Wulf, "Consequences of the Transfer of Military Technology on the Development Process," Paper prepared for the 27th Pugwash Symposium on Problems of Military Oriented Transfer of Technology in Developing Countries, Feldafing, 22–26 November 1976 (Hamburg: IFSH/Arbeitsgruppe Rüstung und Underentwicklung, 1976, mimeograph), p. 21.

It is sometimes argued that by using military conscripts to carry out construction in the security sector, the labor costs of infrastructure projects will be much lower than if civilians carried out the work commercially, thereby producing a saving to the government. Using military units for construction projects is not, however, always less expensive than employing commercial construction companies. The *Draper Report,* for example, explained that the Philippine Construction Corps, set up after World War II to build U.S. military facilities, operated only for two years because "it was found that the work could be done by civilian contractors at less cost than that required by the quasi-military organization" (p. 135).

vent this amendment and to use PL-480 shipments to support the defense budgets of particular countries even after 1972.

The developmental effects of these two forms of assistance are well illustrated by the experience of South Korea. Nearly 40 percent of the $6 billion in economic assistance provided by the United States to South Korea between 1946 and 1979 took the form of security-supporting assistance. (All forms of U.S. economic aid to South Korea have been negligible since the late 1970s.) As a rule of thumb, "From the end of the Korean war through the early 1960s, it was understood that US economic assistance would provide two-thirds of the ROK [Republic of Korea] defense budget."[69] The actual support received was even higher: in 1961, approximately 95 percent of the Korean defense budget was covered by U.S. economic assistance; by 1966, that proportion had dropped to 64 percent. Up to the mid-1960s, these funds were generated in part by selling fertilizer and petroleum products. The availability of these items helped promote farm production and industrial expansion. When South Korea developed the capacity to produce these commodities domestically, they ceased to be supplied under U.S. commodity assistance.[70]

The economic effect of PL-480 transfers of food was different. Nearly 35 percent of U.S. economic assistance to South Korea between 1946 and 1979 took the form of PL-480 shipments. Prior to 1971, 80 percent of the counterpart funds generated through the PL-480 program were used to support the South Korean security budget. In 1971, in order to obtain the agreement of the South Korean government to use its own resources to finance certain operations and maintenance expenditures previously funded by the United States under the military assistance program, the U.S. government promised to provide South Korea with $125 million worth of PL-480 shipments between 1971 and 1975. On the basis of economic criteria, South Korea should not have received these shipments, and their purpose was clearly to offset some 60 percent of the additional security expenditure the Korean government had agreed to fund from its own resources. The first $20 million worth of food shipped under this agreement arrived in 1971 and thus did not violate the amendment to the PL-480 legislation which only took effect in 1972; but the remaining

[69] U.S. Congress, House, Committee on International Relations, Subcommittee on International Organizations, Report: *Investigation of Korean-American Relations,* 95th Cong., 2nd Sess. (Washington, D.C.: Government Printing Office, 31 October 1978), p. 159.

[70] David C. Cole, "Foreign Assistance and Korean Development," pp. 190, 192, in *The Economic and Social Modernization of the Republic of Korea,* Edward S. Mason et al. (Cambridge, Mass.: Harvard University Press for Council on East Asian Studies, 1980).

$105 million worth of agricultural products shipped under this agreement undeniably did contravene that amendment.[71]

Although the PL-480 transfers accounted for the smallest share of U.S. security-related assistance to South Korea, their effect on the Korean economy was largely negative. The question of whether food aid acts as a disincentive to domestic food production in recipient countries has long been debated. Some analysts have argued that if recipient governments implement appropriate policies, the potential negative effects of food aid can be avoided. In some cases, it is clear that where governments fail to follow the correct policies food aid has hindered the development of the agricultural sector. This is what happened in South Korea.

The increase in farmers' incomes in the 1960's did not keep pace with that of urban workers. By the mid-1960's, AID noted that Korea's policy of purchasing some domestic food grains at below market prices allowed only minimal increases in farm incomes. This policy and the resulting slow growth of farm incomes was due both to the Government's efforts to reduce inflation and to the necessity of providing inexpensive staples to the low-paid urban workers.

By 1969, AID had come to view the disparity between agricultural and urban incomes as a serious economic and political problem:

"In 1963, farmers earned 16 percent more than urban workers, but by 1968 urban workers earned 38 percent more than farmers. . . . These wide disparities in income distribution and purchasing power seriously retard the national economy by (a) reducing farmers' means for expanding production and (b) reducing the capacity of the rural sector to purchase goods produced by urban populations. With farm population making up more than half the national total, and with 40 percent of that population at subsistence level, these efforts are of substantial economic magnitude."[72]

[71] U.S. Congress, House, *Investigation*, p. 204.

[72] Ibid., pp. 179–80. An Australian researcher has claimed that "By keeping a deliberately low ceiling on rice prices, in turn made possible by the availability of cheap American grain surpluses, the Government enforced a rapid decline in rural incomes, from 83 per cent (as compared to urban incomes) in 1966 to 53 per cent in 1968 and 59 per cent in 1970." Gavan McCormack, "The South Korean Phenomenon," *Australian Outlook* 32 (December 1978): 272. See also Cole, "Foreign Assistance," pp. 198, 204–5, and Dwight Perkins, "Income Distribution," pp. 425–29, in *The Economic and Social Modernization*, Mason et al.

On food aid, see, for example, S. J. Maxwell and Hans W. Singer, "Food Aid to Developing Countries: A Survey," *World Development* 7 (March 1979): 225–47. The positive aspects of food aid are stressed in Philip Griffin, "The Impact of Food Aid—Peru. A Case Study, *Food Policy* 4 (February 1979): 46–52 and J. S. Mann, "The Impact of Public Law 480 Imports on Prices and Domestic Supply of Cereals in India," *Journal of Farm Econom-*

Thus, PL-480 shipments were instrumental in enabling the South Korean government to keep prices for domestically produced grains low.

Stimulation of Local Demand

A second way in which security assistance can contribute to economic development is by stimulating demand from the armed forces of the recipient country for nonmilitary-specific goods and services that can be produced domestically or in other countries. (The role played by military industries in the development process is discussed in depth in Chapter 9.) These would include items such as clothing for the troops, office and medical equipment, and construction materials and services. Security assistance can fund purchases of nonlethal goods and services directly or act indirectly by increasing the resources available to the recipient government for security-related purchases.

It is extremely difficult to obtain a detailed picture of the goods and services purchased with the security assistance funds provided by most donors. It is known, for example, that the three major categories of security assistance provided by France to sub-Saharan Africa are training, technical assistance, and transfer of equipment and material. The latter category would appear to involve only the transfer of weapons. Thus, the potential for French security assistance to contribute to development by funding purchases from the domestic economies of recipient countries would only occur indirectly. By receiving training, technical assistance, and weapons free-of-charge, recipient governments might be able to spend more of their own resources on nonlethal goods and services, and some of these might even be produced domestically. British security assistance, on the other hand, has sometimes taken the form of budget support to help Third World governments meet the costs of their armed forces.[73] If these funds were used to purchase operating material and related services locally, they would increase aggregate demand within the domestic economy and benefit industries operating at less than full capacity.

For the United States it is possible to obtain somewhat more detailed information. The main components of U.S. security assistance are credits

---

ics 49 (February 1967): 131–46, and the negative aspects are emphasized in B. R. Shenoy, *PL 480 Aid and India's Food Problems* (New Delhi: East-West, 1974).

[73] On French security assistance see Jacques Guillemin, *Coopération et Intervention. La Politique Militaire de la France en Afrique Noire Francophone et à Madagascar* (Nice: Université de Nice, Institut du Droit de la Paix et du Dévelopment, 1979). On British security assistance see United Kingdom, *Civil Appropriations Accounts.*

for arms purchases, military assistance transfers of equipment and related services, training, and payments from the Economic Support Fund. Military assistance transfers are themselves divided into three categories: operating costs, investment, and supply operations. Supply operations include the costs involved with transferring material. Investment is expenditure on weapons, and operating covers outlays on nonlethal equipment. In the early years of the U.S. security-assistance program to Southeast Asia, "Many of the items and services furnished to the armed forces of aid recipients [were] not essentially different from those consumed by the civilian sector of the same economies (e.g., textiles, gasoline, food, and construction or other raw and semifinished materials)."[74]

If the items could not be produced in the recipient country, they would be provided under U.S. military assistance *from the United States*, even if they could be purchased in a neighboring Third World country. If the items could be produced in the recipient country, their purchase would not be funded through MAP but via the economic aid program. Until the mid- to late 1960s, economic assistance was seen, especially by the U.S. military, as a means of providing "the wherewithal for military assistance recipients to pay troops and purchase supplies. . . ."[75] In those cases where nonlethal items were provided by MAP, the assistance did not contribute to economic growth in either the recipient or any other developing country. Where local procurement was possible and facilitated by U.S. supporting assistance, it could be argued that security assistance had increased demand and thereby promoted development. In these cases, however, it is important to determine that the item procured was not already in short supply and that its purchase by the armed forces did not create shortages in the civil sector, perhaps requiring additional imports to meet civilian demand.

Once again the example of South Korea is instructive. Between 1950 and 1983, South Korea received $5.5 billion in U.S. military assistance program grants. Up to the end of the 1960s, most MAP funds were used for operations and maintenance expenditures while the Korean budget primarily financed salaries and related benefits for the troops. In the mid-1960s, as much as 80 percent of MAP grants was used to purchase items such as gasoline, other petroleum products, spare parts, and ammunition and to repair equipment. In about 1960, the U.S. government began to urge the Korean government to finance more of these operating costs through its own budget and to use a larger share of the MAP funds to

---

[74] Jordan, *Foreign Aid*, p. 145.
[75] Hovey, *United States Military Assistance*, p. 113. See also Jordan, *Foreign Aid*, p. 146.

procure weapons. The South Korean government resisted making these changes for as long as possible, fearing that its acquiescence would give the U.S. government the opportunity to cut the MAP grant. It has been suggested that the Korean government's persistence in using MAP funds to cover operations and maintenance expenditures harmed the economy. The Korean economy would have been stronger in the long run, it is argued, had the government stimulated the domestic production of certain of these nonlethal items rather than relying on imports for as long as it did.[76]

There is probably some truth in this criticism, but it cannot be said that the South Koreans failed to take advantage of all economic opportunities provided by U.S. security assistance. Korean firms in the private sector and Korean army units participated in the building of the many roads, bridges, and military facilities funded by U.S. assistance to South Korea. David Cole has suggested that this provided the basis for what subsequently became "a very large and efficient construction industry." An additional boost to this industry came from military construction jobs in South Vietnam funded by U.S. military assistance. According to Cole, orders from South Vietnam enabled the South Korean construction companies to expand and, simultaneously, offered "foreign experience on which they have capitalized successfully in recent years in the Middle East and elsewhere."[77]

South Korea was not the only developing country in Asia to benefit from the conflict in Indochina. Thailand, Singapore, the Philippines, Taiwan, and the British colony of Hong Kong also substantially increased their exports to South Vietnam during the 1960s in the wake of growing U.S. involvement there. It is difficult to determine how much of this business activity was due to security assistance expenditures and how much derived from other forms of U.S. spending associated with the war. It seems likely, however, that at least some portion of South Vietnam's imports of products such as iron and steel, cement, transport equipment, and finished structural products would have been financed through security assistance. In the mid-1960s, Vietnam's neighbors directed a large proportion (between 50 and 95 percent) of their exports of such goods to South Vietnam.[78]

---

[76] U.S. Congress, House, *Investigation*, pp. 173–74, and Hovey, *United States Military Assistance*, p. 28.

[77] Cole, "Foreign Assistance," pp. 183–84.

[78] Gavin Kennedy, *The Military in the Third World* (London: Duckworth, 1974), pp. 208–26.

It is clear that the opportunity exists for some types of security assistance to increase local demand which may, in turn, increase the growth potential of the economy. It seems likely, however, that the positive experiences of South Korea and the other beneficiaries of the war in Indochina are the exception, not the rule. Apart from U.S. security assistance to Israel and Egypt, the sums involved in security assistance programs are considerably smaller than those provided by the United States to South Korea and South Vietnam. The opportunity for most Third World countries to benefit economically from these programs is correspondingly smaller.

In addition, the amount of U.S. military assistance used for purchasing operating material has declined in recent years. At the end of the 1970s, for example, nonlethal equipment purchased with MAP funds accounted for between 3 and 6 percent of total outlays on the military assistance program.[79] It is important to recall that over the same period the emphasis in the U.S. military aid program shifted from MAP grants to credit financing under the Foreign Military Sale program; the recent increase in MAP expenditure may cause this proportion to rise once again. The volume and uses of security-supporting assistance have also changed over the years. Not only has it become a smaller component of total economic aid, but it has also increasingly been used to fund development projects, as opposed to budget support.

In the mid-1980s, approximately 50 percent of U.S. allocations under the Economic Support Fund took the form of balance-of-payments support, 20 percent was commodity aid, and 30 percent was used for long-term development aid (project aid). The proportions differ, of course, for individual countries. The fiscal year 1980 supporting assistance appropriation for Israel, for example, was to "be used to satisfy immediate balance of payments requirements and to provide for essential imported commodities." Israel's severe balance-of-payments crisis has, to a large extent, derived from its sizable expenditures in the security sector. In this case, security-supporting assistance would not contribute to growth through the increase in local demand, although it might be instrumental in preventing a collapse of the economy. A different use pattern has emerged in Jordan where two-thirds of the security-supporting assistance received in fiscal year 1980 from the United States was used to fund projects designed to improve food production, irrigation, water distribution, sewerage systems, basic health care, and education; one-third was allocated to budget support. As recently as FY 1975, some 75 percent of U.S. security-supporting assistance to Jordan had been designated as bud-

[79] *Congressional Presentation,* FY 1979, pp. 367–68.

get support.[80] Of course, like PL-480 shipments, security-supporting assistance need not be designated budget support to provide relief for the defense budget. By reducing expenses in one category, it enables the government to spend its resources in another category. It seems likely, however, that requiring security-supporting assistance to fund specific development-related projects rather than simply providing budget support increases the probability that development will be promoted.

Security Assistance as a Substitute
for Domestic Resources

It is frequently assumed that Third World governments faced with resource constraints will reduce expenditure on development programs in preference to cutting security spending. Some support for this notion has been provided by a 1984 study of thirty-seven developing countries carried out for the World Bank. This study found that governments are more likely to reduce both recurrent and capital expenditure on infrastructure and production than outlays for defense and administration.[81] Some analysts have suggested that inflows of security assistance can promote development by enabling governments to spend fewer of their own resources in the security sector and more on development.

For this to be true, other government revenues must be sufficient to finance recurrent and capital expenditure in the civil sector. Governments must also choose to spend domestic resources released from the security sector on development programs. Recall from the discussion in Chapter 5 that the simple availability of capital is not sufficient to ensure that growth and development will occur and that a number of Third

---

[80] See *Congressional Presentation*, FY 1980, pp. 115–21. On the Israeli economy, see, for example, J. Sachs, "Israel's Economic Disaster," *The New Republic*, 8 July 1985, pp. 21–23. With regard to Jordan, it is important to recall that it has received several million dollars each year since 1978 from Saudi Arabia and occasionally from other Arab states for not concluding a separate peace agreement with Israel. The oil wealthy Arab countries originally promised to donate $1.2 billion to Jordan annually. Reportedly only Saudi Arabia has fulfilled this pledge while others—notably Libya—have never transferred any of the promised sums. In 1983, Jordan was said to have received only $450 million. "Hussein hotar med fred" ("Hussein Threatens Peace"), *Dagens Nyheter*, 3 April 1986, p. 14.

[81] Norman Hicks and Anne Kubisch, "Cutting Government Expenditures in LDCs," *Finance & Development*, September 1984, pp. 38–39. Hicks and Kubisch caution that "Firm conclusion should not be drawn from this nonrandom and small sample. First, the data do not cover all public expenditures, and, second, individual country experiences clearly varied from the overall averages" (p. 38). As the example of Brazil cited in Chapter 8 indicates, expenditure in the security sector can be cut in favor of infrastructure investments, and both can increase simultaneously at the expense of other expenditure categories.

World governments have failed to collect as much revenue from domestic sources as they could. The tendency of Third World governments to consume, rather than invest, a very high proportion of available resources and the importance of what is being invested in have also been discussed. Taken together, these factors suggest that, while inflows of security assistance may well reduce the burden of the security sector for the state budget, it is by no means certain that the rate of development will increase. Developmental effects of security assistance vary from one country to another; this has not gone unnoticed by those who have made the substitutability argument.[82]

Security assistance can substitute for domestic resources in two ways. For some countries, a decline in security assistance is associated with a rise in the proportion of central government expenditure or gross product devoted to the security sector as a whole, suggesting that security assistance had replaced domestic resources in a variety of expenditure categories. This relationship characterized South Korea in the 1970s and Pakistan after the 1965 war with India when U.S. grant aid declined sharply for both. In addition to receiving large grants under the U.S. military assistance program (MAP), both countries had obtained considerable amounts of security-supporting assistance, used at least in part to finance the operating portions of their security budgets. PL-480 transfers provided additional resources for both countries while a high proportion of U.S. MAP grants to South Korea were used to finance operating costs. Thus, when U.S. security-related grants declined, all portions of the budgets of these two countries were affected. This same sort of across-the-board substitution may also have occurred in Colombia in some years during the 1945– 1961 period and in Bolivia and Uruguay between 1962 and 1970.[83]

For other countries, inflows of security assistance tend to be associated with lower capital outlays for security purposes. A 1965 study of U.S. security assistance stated that eight of the nine major Third World recipients of U.S. military aid were required to spend very little on the procurement of weapons since they received most of their arms free-of-charge

---

[82] Wolf, *Economic Impacts*, pp. 3–5.

[83] For Korean security spending, see Cole, "Foreign Assistance," p. 184. For Pakistani security spending, see Nicole Ball, *Third-World Security Expenditure: A Statistical Compendium*, C 10250-M5 (Stockholm: National Defence Research Institute, 1984), pp. 83–84. Security-assistance data from U.S. Department of Defense, *Foreign Military Sales*, and USAID, *US Overseas Loans and Grants*.

Information on Colombia, Uruguay, and Bolivia is found in Philippe C. Schmitter, "Foreign Military Assistance, National Military Spending and Military Rule in Latin America," p. 147, in *Military Rule in Latin America. Function, Consequences and Perspectives*, ed. Philippe C. Schmitter (Beverly Hills and London: Sage, 1973).

from the United States; these were Greece, Turkey, Iran, Pakistan, South Korea, the Philippines, Thailand, and Vietnam. The ninth country, India, chose to receive no military aid and to limit its purchases of weapons from the superpowers prior to 1962. About two-thirds of its military equipment had been obtained from Great Britain. After the 1962 conflict with China, India began to accept military assistance and its dependence on the Soviet Union as a source of arms increased significantly.[84] As discussed above, South Korea and Pakistan were able to substitute U.S. security assistance for both operating and capital expenditure. For Greece, Turkey, and Vietnam, it has not been possible to obtain disaggregated security expenditure to examine the security assistance–domestic spending relationship. For Iran and Thailand, no obvious patterns emerge from the available data.

For the Philippines, however, the link between large inflows of grants and low levels of security-related capital outlays in the domestic budget is clear. According to figures for actual outlays in the security sector provided in Philippine government documents, security-related outlays absorbed 0.3 to 1.6 percent of total security expenditure between 1951 and 1964. After 1965, capital expenditure increased somewhat, but it never reached more than 7.1 percent (the figure for 1966) of the security budget. Table 7-5 shows that for most of the period when security-related capital spending financed through the domestic budget was at its lowest, 1951 to 1964, the Philippine government received the equivalent of nearly one-third of domestic security expenditure in the form of MAP grants from the United States, much of which probably took the form of procurement.[85] The Philippine military budget does not include items acquired through foreign military grant aid, nor is there any reason to expect that it would do so since no real expenditure by the Philippine government is involved.

For many countries, the amount of security assistance received may be too small to affect their economies appreciably, even if substitution does

---

[84] The 1965 study is Hovey, *United States Military Assistance*, pp. 113–14. On arms supplies to India, see SIPRI, *The Arms Trade*, pp. 480–87. For many Third World countries, it is not possible to identify any consistent relationship between security assistance or its components and levels of domestic security expenditure.

[85] Data for Colombia show the same sort of trade-off for much of the 1960s. Between 1950 and 1969, capital outlays never accounted for more than 10 percent of total security spending, but between 1961 and 1967 their share was particularly low, 4 percent of the budget or less. U.S. military grants, however, supplied the equivalent of 11 percent of the security budget during these years. From 1970, capital costs came to account for a much larger share of total security expenditure. On both Colombia and the Philippines, see Ball, *Third-World*, pp. 89–92 and 201–3.

CHAPTER 7

TABLE 7-5

Philippines: Domestic Security Expenditure and U.S. Military Assistance
Grants, 1951–1976 (annual averages in million pesos)

Years	Security Budget (1)	US Military Aid[a] (2)	(2) / (1) (in percentages)
1951–1961	170	55	32
1962–1970	375	90	24
1971–1976	2,300	165	7

Source: Nicole Ball, *Third-World Security Expenditure: A Statistical Compendium,*
C 10250-M5 (Stockholm: National Defence Research Institute, 1984), pp. 89–91.
[a] U.S. Military Assistance Program grants only; does not include security supporting assistance or PL-480 shipments.

occur; for other countries, it has been suggested that security assistance
may produce negative effects. Charles Wolf has speculated, for example,
that if India and Pakistan had both received less, or even no, U.S. security
assistance during the 1960s, "competition for constrained resources
within those two countries would have been altered in such a way that
defense programs probably would have been smaller, development efforts
larger, and the countries' rates of economic growth probably higher." [86]

Wolf's argument appears based on the belief that security assistance
had enabled both countries to maintain military establishments larger
than those that could have been supported by domestic resources alone.
In his view, then, the withdrawal of external aid—from both sides simultaneously—would have necessitated a reduction in the size of their security forces and a decline in domestic outlays for security purposes, and
additional resources would have become available for investment in development programs. The reality for both countries was somewhat different. Security assistance from both the United States and the United Kingdom to India and Pakistan dropped sharply after 1967, although both
countries continued to receive economic development assistance. As already indicated, Pakistani domestic expenditure in the security sector increased considerably, from about 4 percent of gross product at the end of
the 1960s to, on average, 6.5 percent during the 1970s. Indian security
expenditure remained more or less stable around 3.5 percent of gross
product during the same period (Figures 7-1 and 7-2). To some degree,

[86] Wolf, *Economic Impacts,* p. 3.

284

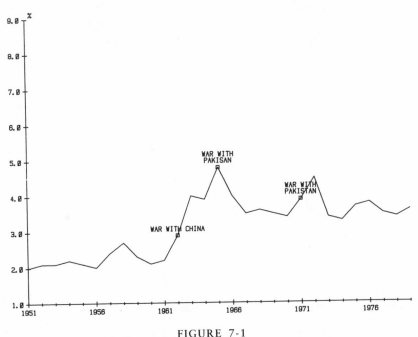

FIGURE 7-1

India: Security Expenditure as Percentage of GDP, 1951–1979

Source: Nicole Ball, *Third-World Security Expenditure: A Statistical Compendium,* C10250-M5 (Stockholm: National Defence Research Agency, 1984), p. 66.

this difference in share of gross product devoted to the security sector probably derived from the fact that India was purchasing weapons with Soviet credits on concessional terms. Equally important, some weapons acquired from the USSR were not accounted for in the defense budget and were paid for with goods exported to the USSR which were not included in official Indian trade statistics (see Chapter 3).

Yet, even if Pakistan had been able to reduce, rather than increase, the amount of domestic resources devoted to the security sector, it seems unlikely that development would have been promoted. The economic policy Ayub Khan's government (1958–1969) followed was designed to produce rapid growth but not to distribute the benefits of that growth to all groups within society. Wealth was highly concentrated. The main beneficiaries of the land reform program were the medium-sized farmers. In some cases, particularly in Sind, the government rewarded loyal civil ser-

285

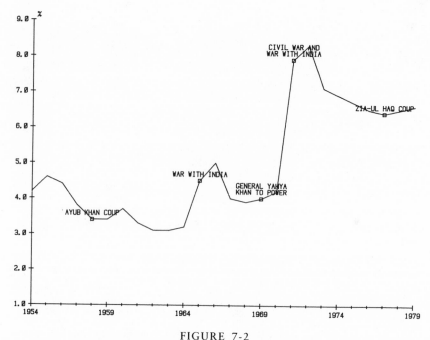

FIGURE 7-2

Pakistan: Security Expenditure as Percentage of GDP, 1954–1979

Source: Nicole Ball, *Third-World Security Expenditure: A Statistical Compendium,* C10250-M5 (Stockholm: National Defence Research Agency, 1984), p. 84.

vants and military officers with gifts of land.[87] The main beneficiaries of government investment in agriculture were the owners of the large- and medium-sized farms in just one of Pakistan's five provinces, the Punjab. Industry was initially concentrated in Karachi (in Sind). The government

[87] S. Javed Burki, *Agricultural Growth and Local Government in Punjab, Pakistan,* RLG no. 11 (Ithaca, N.Y.: Cornell University, Rural Development Committee, November 1974), pp. 62–63. Burki explained that, "The success of the agricultural sector in the seven Punjab districts was in large measure due to the creation of a system of local government that provided points of contact between the middle farmers and various government agencies. Sind's success was largely due to the grant of newly irrigated areas to the people who, because of their position, possessed excellent links with the administration" (p. 63). The Ayub Khan government sought to solve the problem of the poor in Punjab "like so many of its predecessors . . . by recruiting a very large proportion of the male labor force to a rapidly expanding armed forces. . . . Thus deprived of a significant portion of their work force, the rural areas of these districts continue to rely heavily upon remittances rather than on agricultural incomes. Land there continues to be poorly farmed" (pp. 63–64). See also, Edward Feit, *The Armed Bureaucrats* (Boston: Houghton Mifflin, 1973), pp. 81–82.

allowed some former landowners in the Punjab and Sind and a few Bengali businessmen to participate in the expansion of the industrial sector. Although industry grew quite rapidly during the 1960s, the number of people who benefited from its development was limited. In 1968, the members of the twenty-two wealthiest families in Pakistan controlled two-thirds of the country's industrial assets.

Income disparities between East and West Pakistan increased during the decade as the Bengali agricultural sector was squeezed to provide the foreign exchange necessary to finance the import of goods into West Pakistan.[88] This was an important contributing factor to the 1971 civil war. Conservative estimates indicate that 25 percent of the Pakistani population was living *below* the poverty line at the end of the 1960s; other estimates place that figure as high as 50 percent. It is true that U.S. security assistance supported the continuation of this inequitable system. An end to that assistance could not, however, in and of itself produce the changes necessary for broadly based development to occur. The problem of development in Pakistan has not only been one of resource constraints but also of serious structural imbalances which have perpetuated existing inequitable economic and social relations.

What can be said of the positive effects often ascribed to the substitution of security assistance for domestic resources? South Korea is a country that has received a large amount of capital in the form of foreign aid, a large share of which was designated specifically to relieve the government of a significant portion of the defense burden. In the 1950s and 1960s, the United States paid for two-thirds or more of the Korean security budget and provided all of the Korean armed forces' equipment free-of-charge.

In 1980, David Cole characterized the economic importance of U.S. foreign economic and military aid to South Korea:

> The massive inflow of foreign assistance before and during the Korean War was essential to the survival of South Korea as an independent country. Continuation of a high level of economic assistance for the decade after the war probably spelled the difference between some (1.5 percent per annum) and no growth in per capita income. Without this growth, the economic condition of the population would have remained desperate, political cohesion would have deteriorated, and the foundations for subsequent high growth would not have been forged. Thus, aid played a critical role for the two decades from the mid-1940s to the mid-1960s. Since then, it has added per-

[88] Khalid B. Sayeed, *Politics in Pakistan. The Nature and Direction of Change* (New York: Praeger, 1980), pp. 54–64. See also, Hassan Gardezi and Jamil Rashid, eds., *Pakistan—The Roots of Dictatorship: The Political Economy of a Praetorian State* (London: Zed Press, 1983).

haps 1 percent to the already high growth rate and therefore can be characterized as already inconsequential.[89]

At the same time, it should be recalled that Syngman Rhee's government used U.S. foreign aid as a means of avoiding certain reforms that would have improved the domestic savings rate and thereby reduced the need for such aid. U.S. aid thus seems to have been somewhat of a double-edged sword: it was necessary for the economic and military survival of South Korea in the 1950s, but because it financed such a large portion of the government budget certain economic reforms necessary to stimulate self-sustaining development could be avoided, at least for a while.

Probably the most important benefit derived from U.S. security assistance by the South Korean economy was the savings it allowed in foreign exchange. One of the most serious problems facing the Third World in the 1980s is that of indebtedness, and the security sector has undeniably contributed to this problem for many countries (see Chapter 5). As the financial terms under which weapons are transferred hardened during the 1970s, the security sector's share of Third World debt increased. For Western suppliers, the shift has essentially been from grants of equipment and related services to credit financing. For Soviet-bloc countries, the shift has primarily been from low-cost credit to more commercial terms. For Third World recipients of arms "aid," the effect has been fundamentally the same: More foreign exchange is necessary to support the security sector which has increased the chances that the armed forces will compete with investment for scarce foreign exchange resources.[90]

[89] Cole, "Foreign Assistance," pp. 203–4. On the various factors contributing to South Korea's rapid growth from 1965 onward, see also Larry E. Westphal, "The Republic of Korea's Experience with Export-Led Industrial Development," *World Development* 6 (March 1978): 374–76. On the contribution of aid to South Korea's economy, Westphal commented: "While Korea's successful development derives from its outward-looking strategy and the resulting process of export-led, labour-intensive industrialization, other factors have helped. The most obvious of these is the high level of foreign assistance, during the 1950s and early 1960s, which contributed to building the infrastructure for subsequent growth" (p. 375).

[90] For example, Raju G. C. Thomas, *The Defence of India* (Delhi: Macmillan Company of India, 1978), p. 134, has suggested that one of the more convincing arguments "on the adverse impact of defence spending on the [Indian] economy is found in its dependence on foreign exchange and the opportunity costs this represents for civilian projects."

Unlike economic aid, for which it can be argued that loans are preferable to grants since with the former there will be some pressure to invest in productive undertakings in order to generate funds needed for repayment, grants may be seen as preferable in the security sector. This would certainly be true if one could assume that grant aid would continue indefinitely. Loans acquired for the purchase of military equipment and services abroad are normally not designed to increase investment in the recipient's economy; therefore, they cannot

Prior to 1971, South Korea received all military assistance in the form of grants, and the grant component of security-supporting economic aid was probably very high. More than half of the PL-480 transfers were also grants. Although it was not until the mid-1970s that the U.S. Congress indicated a preference for FMS credit financing and cash sales rather than MAP grants for Third World recipients of U.S. military aid, the American government had in fact begun to provide a greater share of its military aid in the form of credits in the 1960s. South Korea, however, only received its first FMS loan, valued at $15 million, in 1971. At that point, Taiwan owed the U.S. government $167 million under the FMS program, Iran

---

be expected to generate the foreign exchange necessary for their repayment. The increasing use of offsets in arms sale agreements has changed this relationship somewhat.

> Offset agreements are customarily divided into two categories, direct and indirect offsets. Direct offsets involve compensation in related goods. They may permit the buyer to produce in-country certain components or subsystems of a military system being acquired, as a condition of sale. . . . Indirect offsets involve compensation in goods unrelated to the defense item being acquired, such as food, raw materials, manufactured goods, etc. The seller may agree, as a condition of sale, to purchase the buyer's products, materials, or services up to a certain currency amount, and usually over an extended period of time.

Neuman, "Offsets," p. 35. Indirect offsets are more likely to stimulate the civil economy than direct offsets and therefore are preferable from a developmental point of view. It is important to recognize, however, that some 80 percent of the offset agreements in which the United States has been involved have been concluded with NATO members and other industrialized allies. In the Third World primarily Egypt, Israel, the Philippines, Singapore, South Korea, and Turkey have benefited from offset arrangements with the United States. See Office of Management and Budget, *Impact of Offsets in Defence-Related Exports* (Washington, D.C.: Office of Management and Budget, December 1985), p. 117. See also, Office of Management and Budget, *Second Annual Report on the Impact of Offsets in Defense-Related Exports* (Washington, D.C.: Office of Management and Budget, December 1986), and United States, General Accounting Office, *Military Exports: Analysis of an Interagency Study on Trade Offsets*, NSIAD-86-99BR (Washington, D.C.: General Accounting Office, April 1986).

The Carlucci Commission, formed in February 1983 by President Reagan to survey U.S. economic and security assistance programs, argued in favor of increased concessionality of U.S. military assistance to reduce the security sector's contribution to Third World indebtedness. Some members of the commission, however, took the opposite position: "In the view of some members, concessional military aid can be justified only when a recipient nation faces a serious security threat and cannot meets it legitimate defense needs without concessional assistance. These members also argued that cost-of-money loans often have a desirable effect as they encourage recipient governments to think through more carefully the true economic cost of military spending." The Commission on Security and Economic Assistance, *A Report to the Secretary of State* (Washington, D.C., November 1983), p. 56; see also p. 51. As already discussed in Chapter 5, there is considerable merit in this latter position.

nearly $500 million, Saudi Arabia about $250 million, and Venezuela some $100 million.[91]

The situation was somewhat different for economic aid. In the mid-1960s the United States began to shift from grants to loans, and, of South Korea's other donors of economic aid, only Japan supplied some grant assistance. Thus, between 1965 and 1970, Korean indebtedness increased from $301.3 million to $2.5 billion. Export earnings grew rapidly during this period, however, and the Korean economy experienced no difficulty in servicing the debt through the end of the 1960s. By 1971, however, the U.S. AID mission in Seoul warned that the debt-service ratio had reached a "critical level." In 1965, only 6 percent of Korea's export earnings had been required to service the debt; in 1970 and 1971, that figure had reached 30 percent.[92]

If the South Korean government had had to purchase the items it received between 1950 and 1970 from the United States under MAP grants, South Korean indebtedness might well have been several billion dollars higher in 1970 than it actually was. Although it would have been impossible for the Korean government to have financed the entire $4 billion in security-related purchases received under MAP during those years, it could have paid for many of the items procured through MAP from the mid-1960s onward. In this case, South Korea would have been able to use less of its export earnings to finance economic growth, producing a slower rate of growth, lower export earnings, greater difficulty in meeting its debt payments, and so on.

The U.S. government sought to transfer some of the operating costs financed through MAP to the Korean government during the 1960s, although the U.S. armed forces were concerned that a drop in U.S. security assistance might mean less security expenditure on the part of the Korean

[91] United States, Department of Defense, *Foreign Military Sales*, 1978, pp. 7–10. Government credits are, of course, not the only source of funding for weapons purchased from the United States or any other supplier; the arms producers themselves may extend credits and money can be borrowed commercially. In addition, the United States has sometimes used the Export-Import Bank to finance purchases from U.S. arms manufacturers. See SIPRI, *The Arms Trade*, pp. 172–74.

Iran received a total of $620 million in loans for the purchase of military equipment and services from the Export-Import Bank between FY 1971 and 1974: $120 million (1971), $100 million (1972), $200 million (1973), $200 million (1974). There may have been subsequent loans for security-related purchases, but since the Bank's *Annual Report* ceased providing information on specific countries in 1975 it has become extremely difficult to ascertain the content of Ex-Im loans. See Ann Schulz, "Military Expenditures and Economic Performance in Iran, 1950–1980," (Worcester, Mass.: Clark University, 1981, mimeograph), p. 204.

[92] United States Congress, House, *Investigation*, pp. 170–71. Figures on indebtedness and debt-servicing ratio from Krueger, *The Developmental Role*, pp. 145, 147.

government because of resource constraints. The U.S. military wanted to forestall this outcome. By allowing some of its forces to participate in the war in Indochina in the late 1960s, the South Korean government succeeded in staving off the day when it would have to allocate more of its own resources to its security sector and begin purchasing weapons from the United States rather than receiving them as grants, but it could not prevent these changes indefinitely. While South Korea received some $2 billion in MAP grants between 1971 and 1984, it also accumulated an FMS debt of $1.9 billion—far in excess of the FMS debts incurred by any other Third World country with the exception of Israel, Egypt, and Turkey.[93]

It is clear that the United States significantly reduced the South Korean government's foreign exchange requirements from the late 1940s to about the mid-1970s. Since South Korea had no military debt in the mid-1960s when its economy began to expand rapidly, foreign exchange earnings and development loans could be concentrated on productive investments rather than on weapon procurement. Moreover, some two-thirds of the economic aid received by South Korea from the United States has been in the form of grants—a reflection of the U.S. desire to support the Korean security sector. The short- to medium-term effect of substituting U.S. security assistance for domestic resources would thus seem to have been positive for the Korean economy. Although few recipients of security assistance, either from the United States or other donors, have been able to make this sort of substitution on the same scale as the Korean government, even a small saving of foreign exchange in the security sector could be beneficial.

The long-term effect is less clear. Security assistance enables most countries to build up and maintain a larger and/or better equipped force than would have been possible using only domestic resources. This was certainly the case for South Korea up to the mid-1960s. It is also true for many of the small countries in West Africa such as Gabon, Cameroon, Burkina Faso, and Bénin which receive French military assistance. Gifts of equipment from France have enabled their armed forces to acquire weapons that they could not have afforded to purchase.[94] The gift of a weapon—say an aircraft—does save a country foreign exchange equivalent to the purchase price of the weapon; however, it also creates the expectation that the weapon will be replaced. The hardening of the terms on which military assistance is granted that began in the 1960s has meant that very few Third World governments can be certain replacements will be provided on concessional terms.

[93] Figures on value of MAP grants and FMS loans from Defense Security Assistance Agency, *Foreign Military Sales*, 1980, p. 39, and 1984, pp. 10–11, 58–59.
[94] Guillemin, *Coopération et Intervention*.

An additional consideration is that the purchase price of a weapon is far from being the only cost attached to that piece of equipment. Repair, maintenance, and other support costs routinely run to several times the original purchase price. An official of the U.S. Department of Defense's Security Assistance Agency pointed out in 1985 that "You end up spending five times the original cost on parts and modifications over a 10-to-20-year life span" for modern helicopters.[95] Training for use and maintenance of the equipment is another costly element for Third World countries. Over the long term, this can add considerably to the foreign exchange burden of military aid recipients. In some cases these additional costs can be covered by grant aid. This was the situation in South Korea for many years. It must also be the case for countries such as Israel, Egypt, Vietnam, and Cuba that receive all military assistance on a grant basis. For most countries, however, spare parts are sold on a cash basis, petroleum must be imported commercially, and so on. Iran had to pay thousands of foreign technicians to service its military equipment during the 1970s. Egypt reportedly paid the USSR hard currency for the personnel manning some of its Soviet-supplied weapon systems prior to the breakdown of relations between the two countries. (See also the discussion on the similarity of additional costs attached to weapon transfers from East and West in Chapter 1.)

Security assistance can substitute for domestic resources, but it cannot be assumed that the benefit to the recipient country will always be equivalent to the saving realized since there are various short- and long-term costs associated with this assistance. The degree to which domestic financing released from the security sector by security assistance promotes economic growth and development depends on the way in which the recipient government uses it. For example, since 1965 Taiwan and South Korea have, for the most part, seen that these funds have been used productively and efficiently; but Egypt appears to have benefited much less from the large inflows of security assistance received from the USSR, the United States, and a number of OPEC countries.[96]

PUTTING SECURITY ASSISTANCE IN CONTEXT

Access to capital is not the sole factor determining the success with which a Third World country develops its economy, but it is an important ele-

[95] Wayne Biddle, "The Big Business in Arms and Add-Ons," *New York Times*, 29 September 1985, p. E-5.

[96] On the problems confronting the Egyptian economy during the last two decades, see John Waterbury, *Egypt: Burdens of the Past. Options for the Future* (Bloomington: Indiana University Press for American Universities Field Staff, 1978), esp. Part III.

ment. To the extent that Third World development is constrained by a shortage of capital, particularly foreign exchange, the possibility exists that security assistance, like economic aid, can further the development process. It can do so by reducing the financial burden of the security sector, by providing infrastructure useful to the civil sector, and by transferring commodities required in the development process which are not available domestically and which cannot be imported, either at all or in sufficient quantity, due to a shortage of foreign exchange. Security assistance can also improve the efficiency with which capital is used by increasing domestic demand for locally produced, nonlethal goods consumed by the security sector.

The potential to assist development should not, however, be confused with a positive development outcome. Much depends on government policies. Certain security-related commodity transfers to South Korea (PL-480–financed food grains) hindered agricultural development while others (fertilizers) provided much-needed agricultural inputs and enabled scarce foreign exchange to be used for additional imports. PL-480 aid hampered development largely as a result of the South Korean government's desire to provide cheap food to industrial workers since the success of South Korea's industrial development program depended heavily on the ability to keep wages in the manufacturing sector at a very low level.

It can be argued that by failing to end PL-480 assistance once it became clear that U.S. food aid was allowing the South Korean government to maintain farm prices at an artificially low level and particularly by continuing to use food aid between 1971 and 1975, the U.S. government helped to create a situation in which U.S. food aid contributed to the rural-urban income gap and the other problems confronting South Korean agriculture after 1965. Although there may be merit in this argument, the point to be made here is simply that government policy determined the effect the food aid had, not some inherent characteristic of that aid itself.

The way in which resources are used is, of course, fundamental to the success of the development process in general. Thus, it seems unlikely that Pakistan, for example, would have managed to improve its development record even if substantial amounts of security assistance grants had been forthcoming since 1965. A relatively few individuals might have benefited from an infusion of additional resources through the security sector. Given the structure of the economy, however, very many more Pakistanis would have remained essentially untouched by whatever growth might have occurred, and this would have made it difficult to claim that development had been promoted.

It is also important to be able to differentiate between the long-term effects of security assistance and its short-term consequences. What may appear a favorable outcome in the short term may prove less advantageous as the years pass. Security assistance, particularly if available over a relatively long period of time, allows the armed forces to become accustomed to living beyond their means. If security assistance were provided indefinitely, that would not pose any problem in economic terms. The reality confronting most Third World countries since the mid-1960s, however, has been a decline in the grant element of security assistance. Because a reduction in the size of the armed forces is an extremely sensitive matter politically, a drop in the amount of security assistance available or a hardening of the terms on which such assistance is provided can imply a long-term increase in the defense burden of recipient countries. The rise in Pakistani security spending following the termination of most U.S. security assistance in 1965 can in part be attributed to this effect.

Finally, recall that the primary purpose of security assistance is to support the armed forces in the recipient country and to fulfill certain politico-military and economic objectives of the donor countries. While donors may express concern that the economies of developing countries could be damaged if those countries attempt to carry excessively heavy military burdens, it cannot be said that economic growth and development is an important objective for any donor of security assistance. Thus, security assistance has in certain cases furthered the development process; yet the beneficial effects obtained through security assistance are, in most cases, considerably less than the effects that could have been obtained had an equivalent amount of resources been devoted to the civil-sector economy. For most countries, the amount of security assistance received is probably too small to contribute significantly to the economy.

It is also important to ask whether security assistance contributes to the security of the recipient countries. A good case can be made that it in fact contributes to their insecurity, particularly for many major recipients. Security assistance has enabled them to engage in war (Indochina, Afghanistan, Central America, or the Horn of Africa) or to avoid having to make political concessions necessary to settle long-standing disputes (Middle East, Indian subcontinent, Korean peninsula). The negative implications of the continuation of these conflicts for the economies of the participant nations far outweigh whatever benefits security assistance might bring. Yet this issue is scarcely, if ever, touched upon either in the debates on the economic effects of security assistance or in the more general discussion of the effects of foreign aid.

8

• • • • • • • • • • • • • • • • • • •

MILITARY MANPOWER AND

HUMAN CAPITAL FORMATION

At independence, many countries in Asia and Africa experienced severe shortages of managerial, entrepreneurial, and technical personnel. This was a legacy of the colonial period when education systems tended to be oriented toward a small portion of the indigenous population. The purpose of colonial education was to train a few individuals to fill subordinate positions in colonial administration and commerce; it was not to provide a general education for a large number of people.

The more important a region was for the metropolitan economy, the more likely the colonial government was to invest in education. Differences thus arose between colonies (Tunisia versus Chad) and within colonies (northern versus southern Sudan). Training tended to be more widely available in the British colonies than in others, and a greater percentage of the population received formal training in Asia than in Africa. Throughout Africa, education expenditures were extremely low during the colonial period, and relatively few Africans received a European-style education. In French West Africa, for example, only 0.5 percent of the population attended school in 1938. Although the educational system was in general better developed in the British colonies (at least in part because of the activities of missionaries), differences existed there as well, with Nigeria, Uganda, and Ghana (Gold Coast) being particularly well endowed with educational facilities. As Table 8-1 shows, these differences were still evident on the eve of African independence in 1960.

In terms of élite education, the British were also more liberal. British-trained Africans, for example, were more likely to be given higher level positions than French-trained Africans, and larger numbers were educated. Prior to World War II in the French sub-Saharan colonies "some eight government schools had a virtual monopoly in training Africans to be doctors (medical assistants), teachers, pharmacists, middle-level administrators and lawyers. . . . Between 1918 and 1939 . . . the William Ponty School in Senegal graduated no more than 1,500 pupils for the whole of French West Africa, which then comprised a population of some

TABLE 8-1

School Enrollment, Selected Third World Countries, 1960

Country	Primary School Enrollment as % Age Group	Secondary School Enrollment as % Age Group
AFRICA		
Upper Volta	8	1
Mali	10	1
Chad	17	—
Tanzania	25	3
Sudan	25	3
Nigeria	36	4
Ghana	38	5
Ivory Coast	46	2
Morocco	47	5
Uganda	49	3
Tunisia	66	12
ASIA [a]		
Pakistan	30	11
Burma	56	10
India	61	20
Kampuchea	62	3
Indonesia	71	6
South Korea	94	27
Philippines	95	26
Malaysia	96	19
Singapore	111[b]	32
LATIN AMERICA		
Uruguay	111[b]	37
Venezuela	100	21
Brazil	95	11
Peru	83	15
Mexico	80	11
Honduras	67	8
Guatemala	45	7

Source: World Bank, *World Development Report 1984* (New York: Oxford University Press, 1984), pp. 266–67, Table 25. Education.

[a] Most of the Asian countries listed here had been independent for over a decade in 1960 which affects the comparability between Africa and Asia somewhat. Malaysia and Singapore, however, did not become independent until 1963.

[b] Children between the ages of 6 and 11 are included in the primary school age group. For countries with universal primary education, the enrollment ratio exceeds 100 percent when children younger than 6 or older than 11 attend primary school.

22,000,000.[1] Both the Belgians, who left the Congo virtually without trained manpower in 1960, and the Portuguese were even more delinquent in this respect.[2] But there were also differences among the various British colonies. There were, for example, far fewer opportunities for Africans to obtain high-level positions in the white settler colonies of East Africa than elsewhere. The Gold Coast had some sixty African lawyers in the 1920s whereas the first African lawyer was admitted to the bar in Kenya only in 1956.[3]

Although agriculture employed the vast majority of the people in the colonies, very little attempt was made to upgrade the agricultural technology available to them, with the exception of those engaged in cash cropping. Here again the British were most active, particularly in such favored colonies as Ghana. "It was not uncommon in British Africa for government to undertake special training of cash-crop producers. For example, in Ghana the government established in 1922 four Junior Trade Schools in hinterland areas (Kibi, Yondi, Mampong-Ashanti, and Asunantsi), which offered to ex-Standard III boys a four-year course in such fields as food farming, cash-crop agriculture, carpentry, masonry."[4] African producers of cash crops in the French colonies were not as well trained as their counterparts in British Africa.

There was thus an objective need for expanding and improving the educational systems in most of Asia and Africa at independence. The states in Latin America that had become independent during the nine-

[1] Martin Kilson, "The Emergent Elites of Black Africa, 1900 to 1960," p. 354, in *Colonialism in Africa, 1870–1960, Volume 2: The History and Politics of Colonialism 1914–1960*, ed. L. H. Gann and Peter Duignan (Cambridge: Cambridge University Press, 1970).

[2] In 1960, the Congo had some 30 university degree holders, about 3,000 clergymen trained up to seminary level, over 400 middle-ranking civil servants, and about 44,000 teachers. The vast majority of the teachers were "poorly educated primary-school teachers." There were also "84 secondary and post-secondary teachers, as well as 734 technical and agricultural teachers." Ibid., p. 390, n. 2. The World Bank has estimated the Congo's population at 14 million in 1960. World Bank, *World Tables, 1976* (Baltimore: Johns Hopkins University Press, 1976), p. 246.

[3] Kilson, "The Emergent Elites," p. 352.

[4] Ibid., p. 371, n. 2. In the white settler colonies of British East Africa, however, "European settlers, in conjunction with the colonial administration, deployed policies of land alienation (and the associated concept of 'African reserves'), discriminatory orientation of government research, credit and extension services, manipulations of prices and markets, and outright bans on African farming of certain crops, to develop and maintain the profitability of European farms. The 'African reserves' served as pools of wage labor to the European farms." Shankar N. Acharya, "Perspectives and Problems of Development in Low Income, Sub-Saharan Africa," pp. 5–6, in "Two Studies of Development in Sub-Saharan Africa," Shankar N. Acharya and Bruce Johnston, Staff Working Paper no. 300 (Washington, D.C.: World Bank, October 1978).

CHAPTER 8

teenth century had progressively expanded their educational systems, but, as Table 8-1 suggests, much remained to be done. Nonetheless, human capital formation did not receive the attention it deserved in many countries during the postwar period.

The development strategies pursued in much of the Third World during the first two decades after World War II—with their emphasis on capital accumulation, investment, and industrialization—conditioned the way in which Third World manpower requirements were perceived. Analysts anticipated that as the industrialization process proceeded, that is, as investment rates increased and levels of output grew, the modern sector would be able to provide a substantial number of jobs which, in turn, would facilitate a relatively orderly transfer of manpower from the agricultural to the industrial sector. Some analysts were so certain this transfer would occur that they argued it would be a waste of resources for developing countries to invest in human capital until industrialization was well under way. In 1962, Theodore Schulz summarized the arguments against investing in human capital:

(1) In Western Europe during the industrial revolution, large-scale investments were made in physical capital while human capital formation was essentially ignored. Yet, the industrial revolution succeeded in transforming the economies of Western Europe. Developing countries were thus advised to concentrate their scarce financial resources on increasing the supply of physical capital rather than splitting them between investment and manpower training.
(2) Third World economies had a limited need of skilled manpower since their agricultural sectors were so large and "backward," and it was believed that backward agriculture required no skilled workers.
(3) The fact that many educated men and women were unemployed in the Third World was taken as additional proof that human capital formation in the early stages of development was a "luxury" that most countries could ill afford.
(4) It was frequently pointed out that investment during the colonial period had primarily benefited infrastructure, the plantations and, to a lesser degree, industry. Expenditure on education in the colonies tended, as we have just seen, to be minimal. Nonetheless, growth did occur, and this was taken to indicate that, as independent countries, these same areas did not need to invest in human capital in the early stages of the industrialization process.[5]

[5]Theodore W. Schulz, "Investment in Human Capital in Poor Countries," pp. 3–6, in *Foreign Trade and Human Capital,* ed. Paul D. Zook (Dallas: Southern Methodist University Press, 1962).

There are a number of holes in these arguments. Schulz pointed out, for example, that

> poor countries entering upon industrialization are not employing the simple, primitive machinery and equipment of [the industrial revolution], and they are not adopting techniques of production of a century or two ago.
>
> . . . .
>
> The argument that a backward agriculture does not demand [advanced] skills is relevant only if a country is resigned to its lot. A modern agriculture can be had by each and all, but to develop such an agriculture requires a transformation from what the country has to a vast array of superior resources which entail many skills and much new knowledge on the part of those who farm. The so-called unemployed intellectuals and some of the returning students represent individuals who simply are not prepared to do the kind of skilled work that is required, either because of the education they have received or because of their preferences. Although foreign capital during earlier periods was seldom used to build and operate schools, it did bring with it competent personnel to run and manage the new plants and installations that were made possible by this capital.[6]

Schulz suggested that the Horvat formulation of the optimum rate of investment in which knowledge and skill were included as "a critical investment variable" was relevant to the situation in developing countries.[7]

Nevertheless, the emphasis remained on investment and industrialization with manpower issues relegated to the background for some years to come. By about the mid-1960s, however, many development experts realized that the industrial sector was not producing the number of jobs anticipated and that many Third World countries were faced with an employment crisis.

Although the industrial sector has expanded in most Third World countries over the last two or three decades, it has often failed to provide the amount of employment required by the economy. Contrary to expectations, unemployment levels in many countries have risen at the same time as output and the rate of investment have expanded. In 1972, the World Bank commented that "The limitations of modern industry as a means of absorbing the available manpower have become increasingly evident. The rate of growth in industrial employment tends to be only

[6] Ibid., pp. 4, 13–14.
[7] Ibid., p. 12. See B. Horvat, "The Optimum Rate of Investment," *Economic Journal* 68 (1958): 747–67.

about half that in industrial output."[8] To some degree, this problem has derived from the tendency to prefer capital-intensive technologies to more labor-intensive ones when setting up industries in the Third World. The reasons for this preference will be discussed in more detail in Chapter 9.

The severity of the unemployment problem is, however, not only due to the failure of the industrial sector to generate jobs. Third World populations have expanded extremely rapidly during the last thirty-five or forty years. Only in the last decade or so has any serious attempt been made to slow their rate of growth. Thus, a large number of new jobs must be created annually in most countries if the proportion of the labor force without work is simply to remain stable. In addition, too little attention has been paid to the rural sector. One consequence of this has been to make migration from the rural areas to the cities a problem of major proportions in most Third World countries, exacerbating an already serious urban unemployment situation.

Urban unemployment rates are also high because of the educated unemployed. In India in the 1960s, for example, there were reportedly 40,000 unemployed engineers. South Korea estimated that it had a surplus of engineers on the order of 55,000 in the 1970s. Korea also had a shortage of skilled technicians and craftsmen, which points up another very important aspect of the problem: the antitechnical bias of much Third World education. In a 1973 study of the role played by human resources in economic development, Frederick Harbison reported that secondary education in the Third World has tended to emphasize academic subjects at the expense of vocational training, much more so than in the industrialized countries.[9] People are thus often educated for jobs which

[8] This World Bank study ("Urbanization," Sector Working Paper, Washington, D.C.: 1972) is excerpted as "Urban Unemployment," pp. 207–13, in *Leading Issues in Economic Development*, ed. Gerald M. Meier, 3rd ed. (New York: Oxford University Press, 1976); quotation is found on page 208.

[9] The World Bank corroborated this finding in the late 1970s, suggesting that "The appropriate combination of academic and vocational training for the labor force is crucial during industrialization: in many developing countries the skills supplied by the educational system may not match the skills demanded by industry." At the same time, the Bank pointed out that some developing economies—for example, Saudi Arabia and Brazil—suffer from a lack of secondary school graduates. See World Bank, *World Development Report, 1979* (New York: Oxford University Press, August 1979), p. 53. See also Frederick H. Harbison, *Human Resources as the Wealth of Nations* (New York: Oxford University Press, 1973).

On India, see Paul Streeten, "Development Ideas in Historical Perspective," p. 40, in *Toward a New Strategy for Development. A Rothko Chapel Colloquium*, Albert O. Hirschman et al. (New York: Pergamon Press, 1979).

On Korea, see Labor Education and Research Institute, *Economic Development and Military Technical Manpower of Korea. A Study of Manpower Development in the Military in Korea* (Seoul: Korea University, 1976), pp. 365–66.

do not exist while manpower that could promote economic development is in short supply.

The unemployment problem is not, however, the core of the employment crisis facing the Third World today. The International Labour Office's World Employment Programme has demonstrated that the crucial point is not that people are unemployed, for the poor must work and often very long hours if they are to survive. Rather, the crux of the problem is that large numbers of people are neither employed productively nor paid adequately for their labor. ILO studies of individual countries have shown that the employment problem is, in reality, a problem of poverty and of inequality within and among nations.[10]

To deal with these basic problems and to use a country's labor force as efficiently as possible, it is necessary to recognize both that the quality of manpower is important (in the agricultural as well as the industrial sector) and that maximizing output should not be the only goal of development policy, particularly if output is maximized at the expense of the ability of large segments of the population to obtain meaningful, decently paid work. If governments are to deal at all successfully with their manpower problems and generate self-sustaining growth, they must formulate and implement employment policies which will "provide for the mobilization and allocation of domestic and foreign resources so as to achieve more labor-intensive output growth, investment in human capital, a more labor-intensive industrialization program, an agricultural program that is itself labor-absorbing and also contributory to industrialization, access to more appropriate technology, and the slowing down of population growth."[11]

THE ARMED FORCES AS
A SOURCE OF SKILLED MANPOWER

The earliest theorists of the potential role of the armed forces in the development process argued that one of the most important ways in which the military establishment could contribute to economic progress was through

---

[10] Streeten, "Development Ideas," p. 43. Portions of the ILO studies on Colombia and Kenya are presented in Meier, *Leading Issues*, pp. 193–200 and 214–21. For a critique of the Kenya study, see Colin Leys, "Interpreting African Underdevelopment: Reflections on the ILO Report on Employment, Incomes and Equality in Kenya," *African Affairs*, October 1973. Leys argues that the recommendations contained in the report would do nothing in the long run to eradicate the basic inequalities in Kenyan economic life which are at the root of the unemployment problem.

[11] "Policy Implications—Note," p. 245, in Meier, *Leading Issues*.

the formation of technical and administrative manpower. Morris Janowitz saw the armed forces as "a training ground for technical and administrative skills" while Marion Levy claimed that "Modern military men
are primarily administrators rather than fighters." [12] A report submitted
to the Draper Committee in 1959 argued in favor of "leadership training" for officers in armed forces receiving U.S. security assistance. Such
programs were motivated, it was suggested, not only because the effective
functioning of modern militaries depended on them but also for the roles
military men would play in civilian society.

The ranks of the officers corps in many less-developed countries
are a rich source of potential leaders for public administration, the
professions, politics, civic affairs and other non-military activities. In
many new countries a great proportion of the graduates of higher
educational institutions are in the armed forces. Here one usually
finds a high degree of discipline and national dedication, but only
sometimes a political sophistication in keeping with the demands of
the time. Furthermore, the free world must reckon with the possibility—indeed the probability—that in some cases the officer corps as a
unit may take the reins of government as the only alternative to domestic chaos and leftist coups. Both considerations point to the need
for a program for selection and preparation of promising officers for
eventual occupation of high level managerial posts in the civil life,
public and private. [13]

To this end, it was proposed that U.S. military and economic assistance
should provide the opportunity for Third World officers to receive training in such nonmilitary topics as psychology, political science, law, and
business administration in U.S. universities or military schools. Third
World governments were also to be encouraged to create educational facilities modeled after the U.S. National War College where military officers would be educated in "broad strategic, political and economic aspects of national life." It was proposed that U.S. Military Assistance
Advisory Groups (MAAG) could help establish such institutions to "in-

---

[12] Morris Janowitz, *The Military in the Political Development of New Nations* (Chicago
and London: Phoenix Books, 1964), p. 75, and Marion J. Levy, Jr., *Modernization and the
Structure of Societies: A Setting for International Affairs* (Princeton, N.J.: Princeton University Press, 1966), p. 605.

[13] Col. Richard G. Stilwell, "Annex E: Training and Education Under the Assistance Programs," in *Supplement to the Composite Report of the President's Committee to Study the
United States Military Assistance Program* (Washington, D.C.: 17 August 1959), p. 147;
hereafter cited as *Draper Report*, Vol. II.

sure, among other things, that the curricula deal realistically with concrete national problems."[14]

The acquisition of modern weapons was said to bring with it certain benefits in terms of technology transfer and technical training. Theorists argued that the possession of such weapons made military personnel both more aware of the technological gap between the industrialized and developing countries and more likely to act on this awareness than other societal groups. The training received by soldiers to enable them to use modern weapons and support equipment was said to provide them with just those "technical skills that are of particular value for economic development." Included here were "modern attitudes and aptitudes" (like working with machinery, using money, following instructions), reading and writing, training in trades such as plumbing, printing or metalworking, learning to drive and repair vehicles, as well as more advanced training in engineering and other sciences.[15]

This view of the ways in which the armed forces could contribute to human capital formation clearly reflected the development strategy prevalent in the 1950s and early 1960s which posited that development could be promoted most effectively by focusing resources on a relatively few key individuals said to be capable of using them most efficiently. Third World armed forces, especially their officer corps, were identified as just such a group of "modernizing élites." In the earliest strategies, development was also seen as very much of a technical task. The application of the correct amount of capital, skilled manpower, and modern technology was to produce economic growth which, in turn, would foster social and political development. The armed forces were believed to be particularly well suited to assist in or even lead this process because it implied a movement away from traditional life. Third World soldiers, it was argued, were being trained precisely to accept modern attitudes and practices. Other societal groups, such as the civil bureaucracy, had to "be more conscious of the need to accomodate their ambitions to existing condi-

---

[14] Ibid., pp. 147–48. It should be pointed out that despite recommendations of this type and despite the recognition by the U.S. Department of Defense that "inherent in training assistance are certain political, social, and economic benefits," the primary objective of U.S. military assistance training has always been building up the *military* capability of recipient armed forces. See Charles Windle and T. R. Vallance, "Optimizing Military Assistance Training," *World Politics* 15 (October 1962): 93.

[15] Lucien W. Pye, "Armies in the Process of Political Modernization," pp. 78–79, 82, in *The Role of the Military in Underdeveloped Countries,* John J. Johnson, ed. (Princeton, N.J.: Princeton University Press, 1962), and Emile Benoit, "Growth and Defense in Developing Countries," *Economic Development and Cultural Change* 26 (January 1978): p. 276.

tions."[16] For the earliest military-in-development theorists, then, rural areas in the Third World had nothing to contribute to the development process, and, of all the groups and institutions in Third World countries, only the military was seen to be firmly rooted in the urban sector.

The belief that military training could spill over into the civil sector was probably also encouraged by an incomplete understanding of the evolution of manpower in the armed forces and civil economy of the United States. In terms of broad occupational categories, considerable complementarity appears between these two sectors. Both experienced a decline in nonspecialized labor (combat soldiers and farming) and an increase in blue-collar and white-collar workers between 1860 and 1960. In addition, the level of skills required by blue-collar personnel in both sectors increased between the end of World War II and 1960 while for the white-collar groups administrative-clerical and professional-technical occupations increased most rapidly between 1920 and 1960. Once one examines the manpower requirements of the military and the civil sector in more detail, however, some very important differences between them become evident, militating against easy movement from the former to the latter.

The occupations employing the largest share of enlisted military men (that is, nonofficers) are those employing the smallest number of civilians and vice versa (Table 8-2). This fact in and of itself does not mean that military training has little or nothing to offer the civil sector, but there are other differences which further reduce the correspondence between "similar" jobs in the two sectors.

> Many of the "matchings" between enlisted and civilian occupations . . . involve occupations with a broad functional similarity in coverage, but where the skills and knowledge required may differ markedly because of differences in equipment, organization, and methods. For example, the military electronics technician, responsible for maintaining a missile-guidance control system, cannot be compared too well with the typical civilian radio or television repairman. Nor can a mechanic responsible for maintenance of an armored tank be equated with a civilian auto mechanic. Conversely, many civilian occupations—particularly in the skilled trades—demand a much higher degree of skill than is required of the typical enlisted man in counterpart occupations.[17]

[16] Pye, "Armies," p. 79.

[17] Harold Wool, *The Military Specialist: Skilled Manpower for the Armed Forces* (Baltimore: Johns Hopkins University Press, 1968), chap. 4: "Military and Civilian Occupational Structures: Similarities and Contrasts," pp. 55–56.

TABLE 8-2

Occupations Held by Enlisted Servicemen and Civilian Males
in the United States, 1960 (in percentages)

Occupation	Enlisted Men	Civilian Males
Uniquely military (ground combat)	13.4	—
Very high military frequency	38.0	1.3
of which: aircraft mechanics	10.6	0.3
electronics	7.2	0.4
medical and dental	4.6	0.4
shipboard machinery mechanics	4.3	<0.1
munitions and weapons mechanics	2.5	<0.1
Relatively high military frequency	29.0	9.6
of which: general administrative		
and clerical	7.1	2.9
supply clerks	6.8	1.2
food service	4.4	1.8
security	3.6	1.2
auto mechanics	3.2	1.5
Relatively high civilian frequency	7.6	14.4
of which: construction and utilities	3.2	7.5
motor transport operators	3.1	4.3
metal working	1.1	2.1
Very high civilian frequency	<0.1	20.6
of which: nonfarm laborers	<0.1	7.5
sales workers	<0.1	6.7
manufacturing workers	<0.1	6.4
Uniquely civilian (farm workers)	—	8.1

Source: Derived from Harold Wool, *The Military Specialist: Skilled Manpower for the Armed Forces* (Baltimore: Johns Hopkins University Press, 1968), p. 56, Table IV-2.

An additional consideration is the multiple nature of military jobs. All enlisted men are required to carry out a certain amount of nonoccupational tasks, some of which (guard duty, proficiency in using weapons) are common to all ranks. Although the amount of time spent on these sorts of jobs varies according to occupation and rank, no enlisted man is able to avoid spending some (and often a considerable amount of) time on these less skilled tasks.[18]

[18] Ibid., pp. 51–62. A study carried out at Ohio State University in the mid-1980s found "that only 12% of the men and 6% of the women in a sample group made any use of their

The point here is simply that if a country such as the United States, where military and civil-sector technology are at more or less the same level, cannot count on military training's applicability to the civil economy, then the opportunities for sectoral transfers in less-developed economies should not be overestimated.

Despite the availability of studies which question the transferability of military skills to the civil sector in industrialized countries and the many modifications which have occurred in thinking about the causes of under-development and the best means of promoting development, some analysts remain optimistic about the benefits of military training to the civil economy. Of course, some of the skills taught by the military can benefit the civil sector. Nonetheless, it is necessary to do more than simply repeat, as some researchers have done, the contention that military training can benefit the civil economy. It is also necessary to do more than "wonder," as Stephanie Neuman did in a 1978 *Orbis* article on Iran, "how . . . one would distinguish between the military and the civilian costs and benefits. What is the net balance over the long and short term? Furthermore, how are the skill levels related to the kinds of military technology Iran is importing? Does more sophisticated technology demand higher skills and, therefore, indirectly upgrade the educational level of the country, or does it draw away needed skilled manpower from the civilian sector?" [19]

Sufficient information is available for many countries, including Iran, to evaluate whether the civil economy is actually able to make use of manpower trained by the armed forces and what the economic implications of the kinds of training received in the military services really are.

---

military skills in civilian jobs. This was a 'surprising' finding and an 'apparent inconsistency', the researchers said, because 80% of the military occupational specialties ostensibly have civilian counterparts and because veterans cite 'training opportunities' more often than any other reason for their having enlisted." A large part of the problem can be traced to essential differences between military jobs and their civilian counterpart and the inadequacy of training received in the armed forces. See Toni Joseph, "Rude Awakening: Many Veterans Find Military Jobs no Road to Civilian Success," *The Wall Street Journal*, 9 October 1985.

[19] Stephanie Neuman, "Security, Military Expenditures and Socioeconomic Development: Reflections on Iran," *Orbis,* Fall 1978, p. 589. Other examples of an overly optimistic assessment of the effect of military training are found in Joungwon Alexander Kim, "Korean Kundaehwa: The Military as Modernizer," *Journal of Comparative Administration* 2 (November 1970): 358, and Changsoo Lee, "Civil-Military Relations and the Emergence of Civilary Bureaucrats in Korea," pp. 91–92, in *Modernization of Korea and the Impact of the West,* ed. Changsoo Lee (Los Angeles: East Asian Studies Center, University of Southern California, 1981).

The remainder of this chapter will look at how military training and human capital formation interact, both in general and in specific developing countries.

Some Basic Considerations

When evaluating the likely economic effect of military manpower training for the civil-sector economy, it is useful to know whether the armed forces obtain their manpower through conscription or are composed primarily of volunteers and what proportion of the economically active population is in the armed forces. The distinction between a conscript and a volunteer military is important because the turnover rate in the latter will tend to be lower than in a conscript force. As far as is known, paramilitary forces are staffed entirely by volunteers. This means that the civil economy will probably benefit less from skills acquired by members of a volunteer force since, on average, they are likely to remain in the military longer than conscripts. This is particularly true for countries where other job opportunities are limited. Figure 8-1 classifies ninety-nine Third World countries according to type of armed forces. Slightly more than 50 percent of the countries surveyed had volunteer forces with sub-Saharan Africa accounting for just over half of these.

It is important to know what proportion of the economically active population is in the armed forces because a low participation rate means that any benefits derived from military training will affect only a small segment of the economy. It has been possible to survey about one hundred developing countries and estimate the proportion of the population enlisted in the armed forces and the total security forces (armed forces plus paramilitary forces) around 1980. Appendix 4 provides the detailed results of this survey. Participation rates were calculated for both the armed forces and the total security forces as a proportion of (a) 15- to 44-year-old males, (b) 15- to 64-year-old males, and (c) total labor force (population between the ages of 15 and 64). It is frequently argued that 18- to 45-year-old males are the most economically productive group in Third World countries, but, given the way in which the available population data are presented, it has not been possible to obtain information for a broad spectrum of countries for exactly this age group. The 15- to 44-year-old group has thus been chosen as the closest approximation. Although males primarily serve in the armed forces and paramilitary groups, women are very much a part of the workforce in countries where, if one is as poor as most people are, then men, women, and children must work to ensure family survival. It was therefore decided to calculate the ratio of security personnel in the total labor force as well.

CONSCRIPT		VOLUNTEER	
Middle East [8]		**Middle East [4]**	
Iran	Syria	Bahrain	
Iraq	Turkey	Kuwait	
Israel[a]	Yemen, PDR	Oman	
Jordan	Yemen, AR	Saudi Arabia	
North Africa [4]		**North Africa [2]**	
Egypt		Algeria	
Libya		Sudan	
Morocco			
Tunisia			
Sub-Saharan Africa [9]		**Sub-Saharan Africa [28]**	
Benin[a]		Botswana	Mali
Burkina Faso		Burundi	Mauritania
Ethiopia		Cameroon	Mauritius[b]
Guinea		Central African	Mozambique
Madagascar		Republic	Nigeria
Malawi		Chad	Rwanda
Niger		Congo	Seychelles
Senegal		Gabon	Sierra Leone
Zimbabwe		Gabon[b]	Somalia
		Ghana	Tanzania
		Guinea-Bissau	Togo
		Ivory Coast	Uganda
		Kenya	Zambia
		Lesotho[b]	Zaire
		Liberia	
Asia [11]		**Asia [10]**	
Afghanistan	Korea, Rep.	Bangladesh	Nepal
Bhutan	Laos	Brunei	Pakistan
China, PR	Singapore	Burma	Philippines
China, Rep.	Thailand	India	Sri Lanka
Kampuchea	Vietnam	Indonesia[c]	
Korea, PDR		Malaysia	
Latin America [14]		**Latin America [9]**	
Argentina	Ecuador	Barbados[b]	Trinidad
Bolivia	El Salvador	Guyana	& Tobago
Brazil	Guatemala	Haiti	Uruguay
Chile	Nicaragua	Honduras[c]	
Colombia	Paraguay	Jamaica	
Cuba[a]	Peru	Mexico[d]	
Dominican	Venezuela	Panama	
Republic			
TOTAL = 46		TOTAL = 53	

FIGURE 8-1

Conscript and Volunteer Armed Forces

[a] Men and women liable for conscription.

[b] Police force only.

[c] Conscript system not utilized in peacetime as volunteers suffice to staff armed forces.

[d] Conscript system where many avoid service through bribery

TABLE 8-3
Security Forces as Percentage of Males in
15–44 and 15–64 Year Age Groups, 1980
(number of countries)

	<1.0%	1.0–5.0%	5.1–10.0%	10.1–15.0%	15.1–20.0%	>20.0%
Armed Forces n = 101						
15–44 years	33	50	14	2	1	1
15–64 years	43	43	12	2	1	0
Total Security n = 98						
15–44 years	22	51	18	5	0	2
15–64 years	32	48	15	2	1	0

Sources:

1. For demographic data: United Nations, Department of International Economic and Social Affairs, *Demographic Indicators of Countries: Estimates and Projections as Assessed in 1980*, ST/ESA/SER.A/82 (New York: United Nations, 1982).

2. For security force data: International Institute for Strategic Studies, *The Military Balance 1981/82* (London: IISS, 1982); *Annuaire de l'Afrique et du Moyen Orient 1980: Les Armées et la Défense* (Paris: Groupe Jeune Afrique, 1980); and *Defence & Foreign Affairs Handbook* (London: Copley, 1980).

Table 8-3 summarizes the data contained in Appendix 4 for males in the 15- to 44- and 15- to 64-year age groups. In a substantial number of countries, the security forces account for a rather small proportion of the economically active population, however defined. As a group, the Middle Eastern countries have the highest ratio of security personnel to economically active population. Central America and sub-Saharan Africa have the lowest ratios, although given the increased tensions in the former

Sources: International Institute for Strategic Studies, *The Military Balance, 1981/82* (London: IISS, 1982); *Defense & Foreign Affairs Handbook 1980* (London, Copley 1980); *Annuaire de l'Afrique et du Moyen-Orient 1980: Les Armées et la Défense* (Paris: Groupe Jeune Afrique, 1980); Robert C. Sellers, ed., *Armed Forces of the World, A Reference Handbook*, 3d ed. (New York: Praeger, 1971), and U.S. area handbooks for individual countries (Washington, D.C.: Government Printing Office).

region, it seems likely that its security force participation rate will have grown somewhat in the last few years.

Spillover from Military Training

TECHNICAL SKILLS

The early theorists of the role of the armed forces in development were not incorrect in hypothesizing that skills acquired while serving in the military could be of use when soldiers returned to civilian life. However, two types of problems have arisen in this theory's application. First, theory has often been confused with reality, and it has been assumed that because military training can benefit civil society, it always will. The second problem is typified by the quotation from the Neuman article cited above: Questions may be raised, but little effort is made to answer them in any detail.[20]

Different types of technical skills can be learned in the course of military training: basic ones such as driving vehicles, improved agricultural techniques, woodworking, plumbing, reading and writing, and more advanced ones such as operating and repairing sophisticated weapon systems, and electrical, chemical, and mechanical engineering. The military sector can also increase the skill level in an economy indirectly through the creation of domestic defense industries. (This will be discussed in the following chapter.) To evaluate the effect of this training on the civil economy, a series of questions must be answered for each country:

(1) Are the skills learned in the normal course of training?
(2) What skills are actually taught?
(3) Are the skills acquired transferred to the civil sector?
(4) Do the armed forces train more individuals than they can themselves employ or are they in competition with the civil sector for skilled manpower?

Only once these questions have been answered can the full repercussions of military technical training be known.

---

[20] David Whynes's discussion of military manpower combined both these problems. Whynes first supported his contention that the military and civil sectors do not compete for the same skilled manpower by briefly examining the case of one country, Ghana. As will be shown subsequently this conclusion does not apply to all developing countries. Whynes then compounded his error by simply repeating the theories set forward by Pye in "Armies" concerning the potential benefits to civil society of military training without offering any corroborating evidence whatsoever. As will be shown below, Pye's theories do not describe the situation in all developing countries. See David K. Whynes, *The Economics of Third World Military Expenditure* (London: Macmillan, 1979), pp. 61–63 and 67–69.

1. Are the skills learned in the normal course of training? The more advanced the skill, the more likely it will be taught in the normal course of training. A number of armed forces, however, offer vocational training courses to conscripts just prior to their release from active service. South Korea, for example, inaugurated its "Saemaul," or New Village program, in 1970. Under this program, all servicemen receive short-term vocational training just prior to their discharge. Men who have served in the army are given a course in farming techniques while men who have been in the navy learn fishing techniques. In Iran prior to the revolution, conscripts were given the opportunity to take three-month vocational training courses which, it was hoped, would assist them in finding jobs upon their release. Courses were offered for trades such as welding, carpentry, and plumbing. Similar training has been provided by the Indian army, and the People's Liberation Army (PLA) in China has recently begun a program to teach soldiers skills useful to the civil sector during their military service.

A number of points must be made here. First, these skills, judged to be useful to the broad mass of servicemen upon their reentry into the civil economy, are clearly not a part of regular military training. If they were, special prerelease courses would not be necessary. Whatever benefits might accrue from this training to the civil-sector economy cannot in all honesty be attributed to military training per se. It might be argued that attaching vocational training programs to military service makes it easier to reach those in need of them since one has, so to speak, a captive audience. This is true only insofar as all discharged servicemen are required to take such courses. In South Korea, they are; in prerevolutionary Iran, they were not. Official Iranian statistics indicate that only some 3 percent of the army received elementary vocational training each year.

Second, only a very small proportion of the population enters the armed forces in most Third World countries. Thus, even if all discharged servicemen were to receive vocational training, the benefit to the economy would not be large. In the case of Iran, some 2 percent of the economically active population received military training. Given that very few conscripts participated in the prerelease vocational programs, basic vocational training that could be ascribed to the Iranian military was practically infinitesimal. In India, the military participation rate is less than 1 percent. Clearly, if governments in countries such as these are serious about vocational training, they will invest in civil-sector programs with a chance of reaching a much larger proportion of the economically active men as well as women.

Finally, the usefulness of the training must be evaluated. South Korean researchers surveyed nearly 10,000 former servicemen in the mid-1970s and discovered that 34 percent had found the prerelease Saemaul pro-

311

gram of use in their work, although only 18 percent were actually using skills acquired through the Saemaul courses in their present jobs. Given the shortness of the training period, this was judged to be a "quite high" use rate.[21]

In China, there was clearly a need for vocational training for conscripts even before it was decided in 1984 to cut the size of the armed forces by one million men within a two-year period. Until recently, most soldiers received only infantry training and political education. As a result, "few enterprises would accept ex-soldiers because they didn't have the necessary production and management knowledge."[22] To overcome this problem, an attempt is being made to provide Chinese conscripts with skills required by society at large. These include architectural design, carpentry, bricklaying, plumbing, electrical work, agronomy, forestry, stockbreeding, economic management, mechanics, radio repair, transport, and food processing. Officially the Chinese claim that these training programs have greatly improved the marketability of exsoldiers and that small production units in rural areas are particularly keen to employ them. Just how accurate this portrayal of the situation is cannot at present be determined. It seems safe to conclude, however, that by helping to upgrade the quality of Chinese manpower in recent years these military vocational courses have made it more likely for former soldiers to find employment.

Skills similar to those taught in these prerelease programs can sometimes be learned through normal military service. Many Third World armed forces grow a portion of their own food. Some of the countries where servicemen farm are Tanzania, Mexico, India, Guyana, China, and Vietnam. In the latter, at least 20 percent of military consumption must come from the armed forces' own fields. Many South Koreans employed as drivers and mechanics in the civil sector received their first training in the military. People have also learned to read and write in the armed forces.[23]

[21] On Korea, see Labour Education and Research Institute, *Economic Development*, pp. 329–30. On Iran, see Ann Schulz, "Military Expenditures and Economic Performance in Iran 1950–1980" (Worcester, Mass.: Clark University, 1982, mimeograph), pp. 174–75. On India, see Emile Benoit, *Defense and Economic Growth in Developing Countries* (Lexington, Mass.: Lexington, 1973). In the case of India, the vocational training was available after the serviceman had left active duty.

[22] Wang Gangyi, "Science Studies Make Better Soldiers," *China Daily*, 1 March 1985. See also Zheng She, "Two-way Training in China's Army," *China Reconstructs*, November 1983, pp. 28–29, and "Soldiers Urged to Learn Skills," *Beijing Review*, 20 August 1984, p. 9. Numerous articles in the English-language *China Daily* in recent years discuss the demobilization of the one million soldiers and their integration into civilian society.

[23] According to the Draper Report, military literacy programs were in operation in the late 1950s in Brazil, Colombia, El Salvador, Guatemala, Jordan, Paraguay, Peru, Tunisia,

It is not sufficient merely to enumerate these examples, however; it is also important to put this on-the-job training into its correct context. While growing food may increase the agricultural skills of those soldiers involved, the problem of hunger in many Third World countries is not so much a product of inadequate skills as of the poverty of those who are hungry (making it difficult for them to earn enough money to purchase sufficient food) and of inequitable access to agricultural resources such as land, water, improved seeds, fertilizers, and tools.[24] A few soldiers learning improved farming techniques will not change these fundamental conditions. The number of recruits said by the Draper Report to have been taught to read and write in the late 1950s in Guatemala (2,500–3,000), Peru (15,000) and Turkey (120,000) accounted for 0.1, 0.1, and 0.4 percent, respectively, of the total population of these countries in 1960. Although becoming literate was no doubt important to the individuals concerned, military-financed literacy programs were obviously not the most rapid way of solving the literacy problem for these countries. In Guatemala, 70 percent of the adult population was estimated to be illiterate in 1960; in Peru, the figure was 40 percent; in Turkey, 60 percent.[25]

---

and Turkey. Other countries, for example Iran and Israel, have also taught the troops to read and write. It has been argued that in Israel literacy training was economically important during the years when large numbers of North African and Asian Jews emigrated to Israel. Once that wave of immigration came to an end and the Israeli economy became more developed, literacy training declined in importance. See Paul Rivlin, "The Burden of Israel's Defence," *Survival* 20: 4 (July–August 1978): 146–54. Another study maintained, however, that many Asian and African Jews conscripted into the Israeli armed forces left active duty fit only for unskilled labor. See J. C. Hurewitz, *Middle East Politics: The Military Dimension* (New York: Praeger, 1969), p. 432.

On the other literacy programs mentioned above, see Brig. Gen. Donald G. Shingler, "Annex D: Contributions of Military Resources to Economic and Social Progress," pp. 113, 131, in *Draper Report,* Vol. II. Shingler also reported that Brazilian military units "sponsor unit farms primarily to provide their own food, but appreciable surpluses are sold within the civil economy" (p. 123). It is neither known if this practice continues, nor if the countries listed as providing literacy training in the 1950s still do so today.

[24] For those interested in pursuing this point further, see the more than 3,000 references cited in Nicole Ball, *World Hunger: A Guide to the Economic and Political Dimensions* (Santa Barbara, Calif: ABC-Clio, 1981).

[25] Total population data from World Bank, *World Tables,* 2d ed. (Baltimore: Johns Hopkins University Press, 1980), pp. 90, 160, and 202, and literacy rates from pp. 457, 459. A survey carried out in Turkey in the early 1960s found that only 3 percent of the rural males who were literate had learned to read and write in the army. Frederick W. Frey, "Surveying Peasant Attitudes in Turkey," *The Public Opinion Quarterly* 27 (Fall 1963): 335–55, cited in Hurewitz, *Middle East Politics,* p. 431. It might be, of course, that upon release from the armed forces Turkish men congregate in cities or go abroad to work. This figure may therefore not reflect the true number of men who learned to read and write in the course of their military service.

2. What skills are actually taught? Just as all servicemen may not take part in prerelease vocational training programs, all soldiers are not given specialized technical training. The army is the largest of the military services in all countries, industrialized and developing alike. In the Third World, the ground forces tend to be very much larger than the air and naval forces. Most men serving in the army receive training in artillery, armored, infantry, and support activities; it is highly military specific, and relatively few receive more specialized technical training. This specialization is one reason why prerelease programs have been considered useful.

In South Korea, for example, nearly 50 percent of army personnel may be trained solely as combattants. Precise figures are hard to come by, but a survey of nearly 60,000 servicemen trained in 1968 indicated that by far the largest occupation was combattants (45 percent), followed by vehicles (13 percent), and administration (11 percent) (Table 8-4). Of those servicemen discharged from the armed forces each year, figures published in 1971 show that only about 20 percent can be considered "technically skilled manpower" (Table 8-5). While the army provides the bulk of the technical manpower released into the civil economy, the 30,500 men

TABLE 8-4

Distribution of Servicemen in South Korean Army According to
Military Occupational Areas, 1968

Combat (1)	Electronics (2)	Electricity (3)	Repairing (4)	Mechanics (5)	Vehicles (6)
45.2[a]	0.6	3.7	1.0	3.5	12.6

Administration (7)	Public Health (8)	Survey and Drawing (9)	Special (10)	Others
11.2	4.0	0.3	2.5	15.4

Source: Labor Education and Research Institute, *Economic Development and Military Technical Manpower of Korea. A Study of Manpower Development in the Military in Korea* (Seoul: Korea University, 1976), p. 294.

Note: The specialties included in each occupational area are found in Appendix 5; it is not known what the category "Others" includes.

[a] This estimate may be low. A 1972 study suggested that somewhat over 50 percent of all men serving in the army may belong to occupational area 1.

TABLE 8-5

Technically Skilled Manpower Released from South Korean
Armed Forces by Service

Total Discharged	Technically Skilled					
	Total	%	Army	Navy	Air Force	Marines
180,000–190,000	35,567	19–20	30,500	551	2,609	1,907

Source: Labor Education and Research Institute, *Economic Development and Military Technical Manpower of Korea. A Study of Manpower Development in the Military in Korea* (Seoul: Korea University, 1976), p. 321.

listed in Table 8-5 account for only 17 percent of the soldiers discharged from the army.

Prior to the overthrow of the shah in 1979, Iran was sometimes cited as a country in which military training should spill over into the civil economy as a consequence of the large influx of modern weapons during the 1970s which greatly expanded the need for technically advanced manpower in the armed forces. In the *Orbis* article cited above, Stephanie Neuman detailed the number of military personnel receiving technical training and commented that "its significance for the economic future of Iran must be considerable." [26] Recent research calls this conclusion into question and demonstrates the necessity to go beyond simple numbers and see what "technicians" are trained to do.

Much of the training received by Iranian military personnel was short-term instruction related to the operation of weapon systems. As such "the training did not produce engineers or even basic information about industrial equipment. Many of the skills learned by technicians were rudimentary, such as how to replace designated weapon's parts when defective. Under the assumption that much civilian skilled labor in highly mechanized or turn-key plants is similarly routine, workers' military experience would contribute only marginally to productivity through an enhanced familiarity with machinery." [27] In some cases, training consisted of "base-level maintenance," that is Iranian technicians were trained to identify what was wrong with a weapon by using automated testing equipment. They were not taught to repair the weapon, however, as this

[26] Neuman, "Security," pp. 588–89.
[27] Schulz, "Military Expenditures," p. 188.

315

function was carried out in the country from which the weapon had been purchased. To make matters worse, the training was costly. In 1975, for example, some 2,600 Iranians were trained under U.S. military programs at a cost of approximately $100,000 per individual. Fully 40 percent of this training was military/weapon-specific so that no civil-sector spinoff could be expected.[28]

3. Are the skills learned transferred to the civil sector? Some analysts of the relationship between the armed forces and human capital formation assume that all technical skills acquired in the armed forces transfer automatically to the civil economy.

Even today, the military is still one of the major sources supplying the technical manpower needed for industrial and economic development in Korea. According to a study, the number of servicemen discharged annually from the Korean Armed Forces are approximately 190,000. Of these, 25 percent are considered to be skilled or semiskilled craftsmen and technicians trained by the military. Assuming that the Korean economy has achieved an average annual growth of 7 percent since 1962, this indicates that these discharged servicemen have filled 30–40 percent of annual demand for technical manpower incurred by the development.[29]

Two questions should be considered here: Is the training applicable to the civil sector? And does the civil sector make the maximum use of skills learned in the course of military service? Clearly some military training can be used in the civil sector. In the case of Korea, many civil airline pilots, sailors in the merchant marine, airport mechanics and radiomen, and skilled workers in the electronics, automotive, shipbuilding, heavy construction, and civil engineering industries received their initial training in the armed forces.[30] At the same time, much training provided to Korean soldiers is of no benefit to the civil economy at all.

The Korean army contains some 85 percent of the total manpower

[28] Ibid., pp. 70, 183.
[29] Lee, "Civil-Military Relations," p. 91.
[30] Ibid., p. 91, and John P. Lovell, "The Military and Politics in Postwar Korea," p. 190, in *Korean Politics in Transition*, ed. Edward Reynolds Wright (Seattle and London: University of Washington Press, 1975).

Bruce Arlinghaus, *Military Development in Africa: The Political and Economic Risks of Arms Transfers* (Boulder and London: Westview Press, 1984), p. 77, has commented that "Armed forces of virtually all nations can expect to lose skilled personnel to expanding industries in need of already trained specialists. A good example of this in Africa has been the civilian airlines, which have drawn pilots and ground crew from the military, as the only source of trained African (rather than expatriate) manpower."

available to the South Korean armed forces. Nearly 85 percent of all army personnel are assigned to military occupational areas when they enlist or are conscripted (Table 8-4). These occupational areas are subdivided into 144 specialties of which 55 (or 40 percent) have no civil-sector counterpart whatsoever.[31] Although it is not known which 55 specialities are classified military specific, an examination of Appendix 5 suggests that a high proportion of the jobs in occupational areas 1 (combat) and 3 (electronics) might be included. It seems possible, therefore, that between 45 and 50 percent of all men serving in the South Korean army receive training that they cannot expect to use upon their return to civilian life (see Table 8-4).

Even where technical training that might be applicable in the civil sector has been received, the actual use is in some doubt according to South Korean researchers.

> The problem is that the military technical education is directed entirely to meet the needs of the military. Therefore, it attaches great importance to certain special fields only, and no attempt is being made to connect it with similar civilian enterprises. What is more, the content of this military technical education is limited to basic level. It is short time education which places emphasis on some practical skill and utilization of manpower. Theoretically it lacks any social nature. It must also be considered whether the present military technical education is suitable for the standard of technical skill in civilian enterprises.[32]

A similar situation obtained in the Iranian army during the 1970s. Approximately half the army was composed of conscripts. Their training consisted essentially of learning specialized military skills in the artillery, armored corps, infantry, and support services. Most skills acquired in the course of this training were not directly transferable to the civil sector although they might have served to make the conscripts generally more familiar with machinery and its repair and maintenance. In essence, however, the military training received by Iranian conscripts was oriented toward military purposes and was "not a direct substitute for civilian training programs."[33] As explained above, much of the more specialized

---

[31] Labor Education and Research Institute, *Economic Development*, p. 36. Another study reported that "about 70 out of 169 Military Occupational Specialties (MOS) can be utilized in the civilian sector." This implies that 60 percent of the MOS have no civil sector counterpart. See Jong-chun Baek, "The Role of the Republic of Korea Armed Forces in National Development: Past and Future," *The Journal of East Asian Affairs* 3: 2 (Fall/Winter 1983): 302. It has not been possible to reconcile these two rather different estimates.

[32] Ibid., pp. 328–29.

[33] Schulz, "Military Expenditures," pp. 175–76.

training received by Iranian military personnel was also weapon specific and nontransferable to the civil economy.

Very little information is available that would enable a detailed evaluation of the degree to which former servicemen use their military training once they have reentered civilian life. The South Korean Office of Veterans Administration surveyed nearly 2,500 enlisted men who had been discharged in 1968 found that 90.8 percent of the former servicemen were holding jobs entirely unrelated to the military occupational specialties in which they had been trained. A 1972 study obtained a figure of 93.1 percent. Even assuming that 50 percent of the exservicemen included in the two studies had been combat troops, these figures indicate an extremely low use-rate. More striking still was the finding of the 1972 study that 92.8 percent of the servicemen who had undergone specialty training at branch schools were employed outside the technical fields in which they had been trained in the military.[34]

The Korean case shows that while the potential may exist for transferring skills acquired in the course of military service to the civil-sector economy, there is nothing automatic about this transfer. In fact, Korean researchers have concluded that "it requires financial support from both civilian enterprises and the Government as a matter of policy." The Korean government realized in the mid-1960s that much military training useful to the civil sector was, in effect, being wasted and planned to set up prerelease programs for both enlisted men and officers designed to help servicemen make use of their military training in civilian life. A shortage of funds prevented the realization of this project. In the mid-1970s, the proposed plan was inaugurated on a pilot basis and, if successful, it would be expanded. In order to run a full-scale program, however, officials claimed that it would be necessary to obtain "financial contributions and support of facilities and personnel of civilian enterprises which will after all absorb the manpower to be discharged by the military."[35]

From even this brief discussion of the problems surrounding the trans-

[34] Labor Education and Research Institute, *Economic Development,* pp. 327–28. The fact that so few exservicemen were using their specialty training directly in the civil sector is not in and of itself an indication that that training was of no use to them. More detailed career surveys of former military personnel would be necessary to resolve this issue. It is also interesting to examine unemployment figures for exservicemen. The most recent survey available for Korea, carried out in 1967, showed that nearly 13 percent of all former soldiers were unemployed. Most of the unemployed had been trained as infantrymen (53.9 percent) or artillerymen (11.4 percent). Although some 2.3 million exservicemen were employed, nearly 65 percent were farmers (60 percent) or manual laborers (4.4 percent). Ibid., p. 323. The high proportion of farmers probably indicates why so many exservicemen found Saemaul training relevant to their work.
[35] Ibid., pp. 329–31.

fer of skills acquired during military service to the civil-sector economy in Korea, clearly the hope that discharged servicemen would supply between 30 and 40 percent of the 100,000 craftsmen and technicians estimated by the South Korean Ministry of Science and Technology to be needed annually up to 1986 was overly optimistic.[36] Large numbers of conscripts are trained in military-specific tasks, and few of those who receive more specialized technical training have to date automatically transferred their skills to the civil economy. If this is the case for a country such as South Korea with a large inventory of sophisticated weapons and a growing industrial sector, it is hard to imagine that the spillover from military training will be significantly greater for most other developing countries.

4. Do the armed forces train more individuals than they can themselves employ, or are they in competition with the civil sector for skilled manpower? It is not very helpful to the civil economy if the military trains technical specialists but does not release them for a large portion of their working lives. Figure 8-1 shows that approximately half the developing countries have conscript armed forces. The annual turnover rate in these is probably much higher, particularly in times of serious unemployment, than for volunteer armed forces. At the same time, conscripts are most likely to obtain the training least useful to the civil economy: instruction in combat techniques and in the operation and maintenance of specific weapons. Nonetheless, the South Korean example suggests that a not insignificant number of servicemen with skills needed by the civil economy can be released from conscript forces each year. In Iran, however, the situation during the 1970s was somewhat different.

The shah of Iran had always been interested in turning Iran into a regional power with a strong armed forces. Prior to the advent of the Nixon administration in 1969, the shah was not allowed to purchase all the weapons he wanted from the United States because many U.S. officials believed Iran was already spending too much on the armed forces to the detriment of economic development. The decision of the British government to withdraw its military forces east of Suez in the mid-1960s had caused the Johnson administration to begin to reevaluate this position. However, the enunciation of what has come to be known as the Nixon Doctrine in 1969 and the issuance of the so-called "blank check" of 1972 enabled the shah to attempt to realize this dream.[37] The Nixon Doctrine

---

[36] Ibid., pp. 321, 365–67.

[37] An excellent discussion of United States-Iranian relations from 1945 is found in Barry Rubin, *Paved with Good Intentions: The American Experience and Iran* (New York and Oxford: Oxford University Press, 1980).

said that in the future the United States would increasingly rely on the military forces of regional powers to maintain stability in strategically important areas in preference to committing its own troops. The success of this strategy implied, of course, that the United States would ensure that its clients were well armed. The 1972 "blank check" allowed the shah to purchase more or less whatever weapons he wanted from the United States.

Although some observers such as Stephanie Neuman have argued that this influx of sophisticated technology in the form of weapons and military support systems offered Iran a unique opportunity to upgrade its manpower and technological base through spinoff, the truth of the matter was that the Iranian military was forced not only to import foreign military technology, but it was also required to import foreign technical personnel to keep its weapons operational. Between 1950 and 1972 when such training ceased, 11,049 Iranians were trained under U.S. military assistance training programs; U.S. arms manufacturers trained perhaps an additional 11,000 Iranian military personnel under the Foreign Military Sales program between 1964 and 1977.[38]

It is difficult to obtain information on the exact numbers trained and just what was learned. Such details are important because it is potentially more useful to the civil economy to train an individual to maintain and repair a military vehicle, for example, than to operate an antiaircraft missile. One U.S. congressional report estimated that, in 1976, 61 percent of the Iranians in U.S. programs were trained in maintenance and communications/electronics. A second report for a private consulting firm estimated that by 1977 some 6,800 maintenance personnel, excluding operators, had been trained to service two of Iran's aircraft, the F-5E/F (1,500) and the F-4 (5,300). One-quarter of these men were classified as semiskilled specialists and half as expert technicians. As explained above, much of this training was weapon-specific and of limited value to the civil sector, and the actual qualifications of many Iranian technicians were not very high. If, however, the Iranians were to have been able to carry out all maintenance on all the aircraft in their inventory by themselves once their air force took delivery of the eighty F-14s the shah had ordered in 1976, another 7,000 trained technicians would have been required. And, of course, technicians were also needed to maintain other weapons the shah purchased in large numbers. Between 1975 and 1978, for example, Iran

---

[38] United States Department of Defense, Security Assistance Agency, *Foreign Military Sales, Foreign Military Construction Sales and Military Assistance Facts as of September 1981* (Washington, D.C.: Department of Defense, 1981), pp. 69–70, and Schulz, "Military Expenditures," p. 192.

took delivery of 287 Bell 214A helicopters and 39 Bell 214C helicopters.[39]

The result was that by 1978 some 9,000 U.S. citizens were working in Iran in military-related jobs. About 2,000 were working for the U.S. government as members of Technical Assistance Field Teams (TAFT) and Military Assistance Advisory Groups (MAAG); the remainder were working for arms manufacturers. The Grumman Aircraft Corporation alone employed 2,000 U.S. citizens "to run the F-14 support program and to promote sales and services of other Grumman products." It has been estimated that half of Iran's military purchases in the mid-1970s were software, including training, maintenance, and electronics engineering. Americans worked on military projects in Iran "as engineers, managers and planners. Many of the Iranian employees were unskilled laborers. Skilled workers from Korea, Pakistan and the Philippines maintained Iran's air force equipment."[40] Foreign personnel were also responsible for the technical training programs that existed in Iranian staff colleges and universities. These short-term courses were "entirely weapons related."

It was clearly going to take a long time before the military sector would supply technicians to the civil economy. The question arises, of course, of just how typical the Iranian experience was. Ann Schulz has argued that "Iran's case is illustrative for those countries that have a rapidly growing labor force, a shortage of technically-skilled workers, and a military establishment with both a sizable infantry and sophisticated weaponry."[41]

---

[39] United States, House of Representatives, Committee on International Relations, Hearings: *The Persian Gulf, 1975: The Continuing Debate on Arms Sales* (Washington, D.C.: Government Printing Office, 1975), p. 55, and Stephanie Neuman, *Unravelling the Triad: Arms Transfers, Indigenous Defense Production, and Dependency*, AD-A093, Sanders Associates, Inc., Nashua, N.H., Destruct Techniques Group (Washington, D.C.: Foreign Affairs Research Documentation Center, Department of State, 1979), p. 19.

See also U.S. Congress, Senate, Committee on Foreign Relations, *US Military Sales to Iran* (Washington, D.C.: Government Printing Office, 1976), pp. viii–xii, where it was stated quite bluntly, among other things, that

Iran is attempting to create an extremely modern military establishment in a country that lacks the technical, educational and industrial base to provide the necessary trained personnel and management capabilities to operate such an establishment effectively. Iran also lacks the experience in logistics and support operations and does not have the maintenance capabilities, the infrastructure (port facilities, roads, rail nets, etc.), and the construction capacity to implement its new programs independent of outside support.

Helicopter data from Stockholm International Peace Research Institute, *World Armaments and Disarmament, SIPRI Yearbook 1979* (London: Taylor & Francis, 1979), pp. 216–17.

[40] Schulz, "Military Expenditures," p. 72; see also pp. 179–83.

[41] Ibid., p. 174.

CHAPTER 8

Iran is far from the only country that has had to rely on foreign technicians to maintain or even operate sophisticated equipment, including equipment purchased from East-bloc countries.[42] Although this does not mean that Third World militaries have deficits in all skills and it has been shown that the potential does exist for releasing trained manpower into the economy, one must ask if in some countries the military sector does not compete with the civil sector for trained manpower. The claim that the military sector drains manpower from the civil sector is heard most frequently concerning military industries (see Chapter 9), but it is also relevant to this discussion. Bruce Arlinghous has commented:

> Both the military and civilian sectors in Africa are in desperate need of skilled labor. For the military, increases in the import of sophisticated weapons have fostered dependency upon the supplier for support personnel, both expatriates and local personnel trained overseas. But the demands of these systems for well-educated, capable personnel as technical trainees and the expense of training them have caused a situation where the military must draw on the small population of literate and educated people and take steps to hold on to them once trained.[43]

A U.S. congressional report from 1977, which examined U.S. arms sales policies to countries in the Middle East, concluded "Despite the oil wealth many of these states have, it is difficult for any of them, save perhaps Saudi Arabia, to have both guns and butter. Arms purchases mean that a greater and greater share of scarce skilled manpower and education programs must be geared to filling that sector."[44]

---

[42] The reliance of Saudi Arabia on foreign technicians is summarized in Helena Tuomi and Raimo Väyrynen, *Transnational Corporations, Armaments and Development. A Study of Transnational Military Production, International Transfer of Military Technology and Their Impact on Development*, Research Report no. 22 (Tampere, Finland: Tampere Peace Research Institute, 1980), pp. 249–51. See also Milton Leitenberg, "The Impact of the Worldwide Confrontation of the Great Powers: Aspects of Military Intervention and the Projection of Military Power," pp. 406–59, in *Armament—Development—Human Rights—Disarmament*, ed. G. Fischer (Brussels: Etablissements Bruyland pour la Faculté de Droit, Paris 5, 1985), and Arlinghaus, *Military Development*, pp. 64–82.
Arlinghaus points out that "the Ethiopians, Angolans, and Mozambicans are dependent upon Soviet, East German and Cuban pilots and maintenance personnel; foreigners, primarily French and Belgian, are considered vital to Zaire's forces; and, in Libya, 'if the Americans left, within six months, not one Chinook helicopter would be flying'" (p. 73).
[43] Arlinghaus, *Military Development*, p. 75.
[44] U.S. Congress, House, Committee on International Relations, Report: *United States Arms Policies in the Persian Gulf and Red Sea Areas: Past, Present and Future*, 95th Cong., 1st Sess. (Washington, D.C.: Government Printing Office, 1977), p. 15.

Given the shortages of technical personnel experienced by the Iranian armed forces in the 1970s, one would think that the military must have drawn skilled manpower from the civil sector, but it is not in fact clear that it did so. The Iranian security analyst, Shahram Chubin, has suggested that if the military sector had offered competitive salaries, it would have drained scarce technical manpower from the civil economy.[45] Although it is likely that there was at least some competition between the two sectors given the shah's intention of introducing advanced technology to both the military sector and civil industry simultaneously, it is impossible to determine the extent of that competition.

Similarly, with regard to education expenditures, it is clear that expensive military training programs did not always teach skills transferable to the civil economy. Had some portion of the funds devoted to military training been directed toward civil-sector manpower formation, there can be no doubt that a larger number of people could have acquired skills directly useful to the civil economy. But just how many fewer civilians received technical training because of the amount spent on military cannot be determined. The number of Iranians being trained under military programs, both technical and vocational, has been estimated at approximately 9,500 for 1975. The bulk of these (7,000) were the 3 percent of Iranian conscripts undergoing prerelease vocational training. This figure must be set against training for civilians; some 90,000 to 120,000 civilians were trained in Iranian schools and in-service training programs during the same year. In the mid-1970s, another 35,000 Iranian civilians were receiving scientific and technical training abroad, but at least half of those educated in other countries failed to return home.[46] Probably the best that can be said about the competition between the military and civil sectors for manpower and training is that both sectors were short of qualified personnel. Had the amount of money allocated to military training been reduced and the savings transferred to vocational and technical training for civilians, shortages in the civil sector would have become less severe, but they would by no means have disappeared.

It is frequently argued that increases in security expenditure, irrespective of the categories in which these occur, reduce the availability of public funds for education. This is assumed to effect human capital formation negatively and to slow the economic development rate. Available evidence on this issue is mixed. One study that compared military expen-

---

[45] Shahram Chubin, "Implications of the Military Buildup in Less Industrial States," in *Arms Transfers to the Third World: The Military Buildup in Less Industrial Countries* (Boulder, Colo: Westview, 1978). Cited in Schulz, "Military Expenditures," p. 184.

[46] Ibid., pp. 191–93.

ditures with public outlays on education for seventeen Latin American countries between 1948 and 1968 concluded that increases in the security budget did not appear to have occurred at the expense of spending on education. For both categories, changes in the level of spending appeared most closely linked with changes in government revenues and amount spent in the previous fiscal year. A more detailed examination of the situation in two of these countries suggests, however, that these sectors can at times compete with each other for government funding.

A study of patterns of government expenditure in Brazil between 1950 and 1967 concluded that trade-offs frequently occurred between military spending and social development (health, education, and welfare) outlays. Between 1950 and 1966, the share of defense in the total state budget increased while the share of social development declined. During the same period, however, spending on infrastructure development also appeared to grow at the expense of the social sector. The competition between these latter two categories was particularly evident in 1954–1955 and 1963–1966. In some years there also seemed to be trade-offs between infrastructure development and the defense budget. Since education was not dealt with separately in this study, it is impossible to judge precisely how these trade-offs affected human capital formation. It seems reasonable to assume, however, that since none of the "social development programs . . . appear to have been high on the agenda of any regime" during the period under consideration, higher spending in the Brazilian security sector was made possible in some years by reductions in the education budget.[47]

In Chile, the share of education in the central government budget increased by approximately 20 percent between 1952 and 1972 while the security sector's share declined by nearly 50 percent. In the early 1970s, education received a larger portion of the budget than the security sector (17.8 percent for education versus 13.9 percent for the security forces in 1972). These priorities changed dramatically following the 1973 coup d'état. The share of education stagnated, reaching 18 percent in 1979,

[47] The findings of the seventeen-country study are reported in Barry Ames and Ed Goff, "Education and Defense Expenditures in Latin America: 1948–1968," pp. 175–97, in *Comparative Public Policy: Issues, Theories, and Methods*, ed. Craig Liske, William Loehr, and John McCamant (New York: Halsted Press, 1975); see especially pages 179–81, 186. On Brazil see Margaret Daly Hayes, "Policy Consequences of Military Participation in Politics: An Analysis of Tradeoffs in Brazilian Federal Expenditures," pp. 21–52, in ibid.; see especially pages 32–33. It is, of course, not possible to argue that if the trade-off between the security and the education sectors in Brazil had been in the opposite direction, human capital formation would automatically have benefited. Higher expenditure on education might simply have meant higher salaries for bureaucrats and teachers, not more or better instruction.

while the security budget's share rose considerably to 32.9 percent in 1979. It is important to recall, however, that the entire state budget was 25 percent smaller in 1979 than it had been in 1973; this means that in absolute terms outlays on education had declined in preference to spending in the security sector.[48]

In some Third World countries a large amount of the responsibility for financing education rests with the private sector. In these cases, public outlays for education can be low, and security spending can rise without the two necessarily competing with each other. This has been the case in South Korea with its "vigorous system of high-quality private schools."[49] At the same time, South Korea has a surplus of engineers and a large shortage of technicians and craftsmen, indicating that the system is not entirely attuned to the needs of the economy. A reduction in security expenditure applied to vocational training programs would clearly help to right this imbalance, even if it cannot be claimed that it has been caused by the allocation of a large share of the South Korean state budget to the security sector.

ADMINISTRATIVE SKILLS

The earliest theorists of the military's role in the development process saw the armed forces as an important source of administrative manpower for Third World countries. It was claimed that the armed forces possessed organizational skills, a rational and efficient approach to problems, a coherence and a hierarchical structure that enabled them to cut through the chaos and disorganization said to characterize so much of civilian politics and government and to hinder development. That these particular attributes were highly valued by the theorists was at least in part a reflection of the tendency to view development as a technical problem, one that could easily be solved once the "correct" solutions were identified and properly implemented. The military's hierarchical structure, its discipline, and its organizational skills were precisely what was thought necessary to enforce the application of the "correct" solutions. Unfortunately, it was left to the imagination how these attributes would contribute to the identification of these correct solutions.

In addition, the academics who put forward these theories glossed over the fact that "discipline" and "organizational capacity" should not be confused with the ability to direct the development process. Even in the

[48] Carlos Portales and Augusto Varas, "The Role of Military Expenditure in the Development Process. Chile 1952–1973 and 1973–1980: Two Contrasting Cases," *Ibero Americana* 12: 1–2 (1983): 36, 48–49.

[49] Charles R. Frank, Jr., Kwang Suk Kim, and Larry E. Westphal, *South Korea* (New York: National Bureau of Economic Research, 1975), p. 242.

mid-1960s, there were those who understood that, although a military might be able to run its own affairs efficiently, it did not necessarily mean it could formulate and coordinate government policies in a similar manner. In 1964 Morris Janowitz commented:

> If a generalization is possible, it is that the wider the sphere of economic involvement, the less effectively is the military able to perform. As centers of technical training and a source of managerial personnel, and even as managers of specific installations, the military operates with reasonable effectiveness. But in tasks of managing wide sectors of the economy, or supplying central direction, it suffers from both the limitations inherent in the profession and sheer deficits of personnel resources.[50]

In view of the number of Third World countries that have been ruled by the military since the end of World War II, it is important to understand the strengths and weaknesses of military administrators. The distinction between officers as managers and officers as formulators of policy is well illustrated by the differences between the first period of military rule in Burma (1958–1960) and the second military government (which began in 1962 and continues today). During the first period, "the main thrust was modernization of administrative performance. Administrative talent was liberated from political interference, organizational slack taken up, and those bold programs of Pasabala which were of sufficient merit were carried out effectively. The concern was more with management and implementation than with planning."[51] Once the military sought to become involved with policy formulation in its second period of rule, it became evident that economic reform required more than firmness of purpose, as the economy stagnated and many reforms failed to produce the anticipated outcomes.[52]

Some analysts have suggested that the appointment of senior and retired officers to positions in the government bureaucracy and public corporations in itself indicates that military service equips officers for administrative positions in the civil sector. It is clear, however, that in many cases administrative capacity is only one quality that make officers attractive candidates for these jobs. For example, the prime minister of Korea

---

[50] Janowitz, *The Military*, p. 359.

[51] James F. Guyot, "Political Involution in Burma," *Journal of Comparative Administration* 2 (November 1970): 308. Pasabala, the acronym for the broadly based group which led Burma in the fight for independence and became the Burmese ruling party between 1948 and 1958, stands for Anti-Fascist Peoples' Freedom League.

[52] Ibid., p. 309, and Laurence D. Stifel, "Burmese Socialism: Economic Problems of the First Decade," *Pacific Affairs* 45 (Spring 1972): 60–74.

who was installed in May 1964, Chong Il-kwon, had been Army Chief of Staff during the Korean War and subsequently chairman of the Joint Chiefs of Staff before retiring from the army in 1959. He was said to have been particularly suitable for the prime ministership because of his "close ties with, and the confidence of, the military as well as national recognition for his role in the war, experience abroad including familiarity with the United States, strong but relatively quiet and uncontroversial administrative leadership, and loyalty to the president." [53]

What is more, it is clear that in South Korea, as well as in other countries, retired military officers have been appointed to official positions of one sort or another to keep them out of politics (that is, prevent them from conspiring against the government). The Park government was said to have made "a general effort . . . to avoid the internal frustrations among the military that had in 1961 erupted in political action" by appointing officers who retired from the armed forces to government positions. This does not mean that the officers were not good administrators; many have been. Cole and Lyman have argued that with the exception of some appointments to a number of the government-owned corporations, neither policies nor program objectives suffered from the presence of former military men in important administrative posts.[54] It does suggest, however, that administrative capability may not be the most important factor in determining whether an officer or a former officer is appointed to a government post.

One problem from which military officers frequently suffer is the lack of bargaining skills necessary to reach the political compromises essential to governing pluralistic societies. A survey carried out in the early 1980s of graduates of the (South) Korean Military Academy, for example, found that while officers ranked high in terms of characteristics such as honor, justice, responsibility, and anticommunism, they scored less well on management capability, flexibility, and adaptability.[55] When in power, military officers frequently attempt to deny the need for compromise and ex-

[53] David C. Cole and Princeton N. Lyman, *Korean Development: The Interplay of Politics and Economics* (Cambridge, Mass.: Harvard University Press, 1971), p. 45.

[54] Ibid., p. 47. This assessment was made at the beginning of the 1970s.

[55] Baek, "The Role," p. 315. A similar point has been made by a former Korean military officer, Do Young Chang, "The Republic of Korea Army and its Role in National Development" (Paper prepared for the Biennial International Conference of the Inter-University Seminar on Armed Forces and Society, Chicago, 18–20 October 1985, mimeograph), p. 9. Korean military officers who took part in government "often exhibited such professional traits as rigidity, self-righteousness, and attitudes of 'anti-introspection' and 'anti-politics' in exercising their leadership. They were, above all, lacking a sense of vision and a high purpose of democratic values and beliefs."

pect that once the government has decided the appropriate policy in any given area, it will be implemented without further discussion. Moreover, it is assumed that once implemented the policy will have the desired result. In the case of South Korea during the first two years following the 1961 coup by Park Chung Hee, the government believed ". . . that basic economic relationships could be quickly reordered by administrative fiat."[56] This proved to be wrong.

> By the time of the inauguration of the civilian government, however, it had become clear that many of the Military Government reforms had gone awry and that the tasks of national development were more complex than early prognostication had indicated. Inflation became a serious problem as government spending increased, and the currency reform of 1962 brought the economy to a near standstill. Scandals in the development of certain industries and of the stock market had not only hurt the economy, but confidence in the new leadership's intentions and ability as well. Efforts to help the rural population had also not had the desired results on agricultural production or income. As the new government, which took office at the end of 1963, began to focus on these problems, the need for professionalism at both the cabinet level and in the bureaucracy became clearer to the president.[57]

The need for an alliance between military rulers and civilian technicians and bureaucrats is a feature of government in most developing countries. Bureaucrats play an important role in policy formulation and implementation in state-dominated societies, and the bureaucracy was the best organized group at independence in many Third World countries. Despite what many early theorists believed, the armed forces in many newly independent developing countries were extremely weak organizationally, indeed practically nonexistent. This was especially true in Africa, where military officers from the former colonial powers tended to hold most of the staff positions in the nascent armed forces.

In former British Africa, the entire public sector was more modern at independence than the private sector, but within the public sector certain civil departments absorbed the most competent manpower. "The ablest

[56] Cole and Lyman, *Korean Development*, p. 39; see also p. 84.

[57] Ibid., p. 43. On the continued influence of military officers following the "civilianization" of the government, see ibid., pp. 39–41, and Lovell, "The Military and Politics," p. 188. The new, civilian government referred to here was essentially the same as the old, military one: The officers discarded their uniforms, declared themselves civilians, and held an election. Political power in South Korea continued to reside in the armed forces.

administrators were in the civil service. Careers in the army were generally looked down upon and did not attract talent." In former French Africa, the armed forces were "at best . . . on the same level" as the civil servants. In British Africa, just prior to independence in the late 1950s, administrators and other public employees such as doctors and engineers began to be seconded to the military. At the end of three years, they could chose to return to civilian life or remain in the armed services. In this manner Biafran leader Emeka Ojukwu came to join the Nigerian army. "Rather than being the depository of technical and managerial expertise in the country, the army had to borrow from the civilian bureaucracy." [58]

Although no military can govern entirely on its own—if for no other reason than its lack of sufficient manpower to staff all bureaucratic posts—some military governments are unable to follow the recommendations of their own advisers. This occurs at least in part because militaries are run on the basis of orders, and officers are not accustomed to functioning in an environment where policies are subject to critical appraisal by "subordinates." For example, in the case of the Velasco government in Peru (1968–1975), advisers were expected to support government policies uncritically rather than to make serious suggestions about either policy alternatives or the ways in which policies already implemented could be made more effective. Since the Velasco government wanted to institute some far-reaching reforms, this tendency to ignore its own advisers was particularly regrettable. [59]

In many countries, however, the military recognizes its limitations and relies heavily on civilian advisers, particularly in the economic sphere. In South Korea, for example, following their initial attempt to formulate economic policy, the armed forces

> retained the task of governance, while civil bureaucracy dominated the decision-making process in the technical areas of long-term development strategy. The creation of Economic Planning Board (EPB) is a case in point. The EPB has always been headed by civil technocrats with the rank of deputy prime minister. They have sweeping powers and responsibilities to establish not only overall plans for

[58] Uma O. Eleazu, "The Role of the Army in African Politics: A Reconsideration of Existing Theories and Practices," *The Journal of Developing Areas* 7 (January 1973): 265–86; see especially pp. 277–79. The relationship between the armed forces and civil servants in Nigeria is discussed in J. 'Bayo Adekanye, "The Role of Military Expenditure in the Development Process. Nigeria" (Ibadan: University of Ibadan, 1983, mimeograph), 3/6–3/12.

[59] José Encinas del Pando, "Economic, Military and Socio-Political Variables in Argentina, Chile and Peru (1950–1980): A Regional Analysis," (Lima: University of Lima, 1983, mimeograph), p. 138.

economic development but also for national budgeting, mobilization of resources and investment, and coordination with other ministries related to national economy and finance.[60]

Similarly in Nigeria during periods of military rule high-ranking civil servants have been rather important in initiating, formulating, and executing development policies. They have controlled such influential ministries as economic development and finance.[61] Other countries in which civilians have played an important role in recent years in economic planning during periods of military rule include Argentina, Chile, Brazil, Uruguay, Peru (after 1975 when Morales Bermúdez took over from Velasco), Turkey, Mauritania, Liberia, and Mali.

LIMITED SPINOFF

In general, one must conclude that the claims made for the armed forces as a source of technical and administrative training in Third World countries have been overly optimistic. Some skills required in the course of military training can be and have been used in the civil-sector economy. That military personnel are more competent than their civilian counterparts is, however, open to question.[62] As administrators, for example, military officers suffer from a number of shortcomings which limit their effectiveness. Ironically, these shortcomings are precisely those attributes identified by the earliest theorists as beneficial to the development process: a hierarchical structure and a rational approach to problems. In addition, military bureaucrats are just as likely as civilians to fall prey to corruption (see Chapter 1).

As a source of technical personnel, the military's usefulness is limited by several factors. Many armed forces are staffed by volunteers which restricts the number of men released into the civil economy each year. The fact that conscript forces discharge more men annually is not necessarily helpful because conscripts form the group most likely to receive the most military-specific training. Many vocational skills required by people

[60] Lee, "Civil-Military Relations," pp. 97–98. See also Cole and Lyman, *Korean Development*, pp. 43–47, 86–87.

[61] Adekanye, "The Role," p. 3/8.

[62] That they are considerably less competent is also not self-evident. Claude Welch, for example, has commented that "It is clear that the armed forces have not fulfilled the predictions of some social scientists, put forward during the early 1960's, that their organization, modernity and nationalism would make them the leaders of the modernization process in their countries. On the other hand, their performance as rulers in this regard has possibly not been worse than that which might have been achieved by the available civilian alternatives." Claude E. Welch, Jr., and Arthur K. Smith, *Military Role and Rule: Perspectives on Civil-Military Relations* (North Scituate, Mass.: Duxbury Press, 1974), p. 256.

in the Third World are not taught in the normal course of military training. Prerelease vocational training, offered by some militaries in recognition of this problem, often reaches only a relatively few recruits and a very small proportion of the workforce.

Many skills taught in the course of normal training are military/weapon-specific, and even in countries that have purchased large amounts of sophisticated military equipment only a small proportion of the armed forces can be defined as technically skilled. It is likely that in countries with smaller armed forces the potential spinoff in terms of technically skilled manpower is even less. A further problem is that, although skills that can be used in the civil sector may be learned in the course of military training, their transfer to the civil economy is far from automatic. Time and money are necessary to match the skills acquired by servicemen with available jobs in particular firms. In some cases, further training may be necessary.

Finally, far from training and releasing manpower into the civil sector, the military may itself experience shortages of skilled manpower. Particularly in countries where unemployment is high, skilled technicians may be encouraged to remain in the military for a large part of their working lives. The need for foreign technicians to operate and maintain the more sophisticated equipment in a country's arsenal places an additional burden on a country's resources since foreign technicians tend to be relatively expensive. Another drain on resources occurs when countries attempt to train sufficient national technicians to replace the foreigners.[63]

---

[63] Arlinghaus, *Military Development*, has noted some of the high costs

associated with civilian technicians. For example, US mobile training teams (MITs) are sent on extended temporary duty to train host-nation personnel in the country. Aside from per diem expenses, they receive no additional pay or benefits. Civilian technicians, however, receive sizable increases in pay, housing, and educational allowances and other benefits, which makes them cost significantly more. Not only are there cheaper alternative methods of securing technical aid, but the cost of one technician often represents the tuition for several host-nation students. And when the foreign technician leaves, that person's skills leave, too. . . .

The obvious solution therefore would be to train more African technicians and to use more military personnel in a country. But these options are constrained by two factors. African nations sending military personnel to the United States or elsewhere for training have to pay, usually in hard currency, the travel and living expenses of their personnel. As a result, many countries send very few personnel (even when they are on "scholarship" through grant-aid programs) and frequently have insufficient redundancy to compensate for course failures, illnesses, and so on. The second factor is that most African nations and arms suppliers are wary of too large a uniformed military presence in the region. Such a situation smacks of neocolonialism and provides a basis for fears of unwanted military involvement in local conflicts. (pp. 73–74)

Although the civil economy does undoubtedly benefit to some extent from military training, it is always less expensive and more efficient to train people directly for jobs in the civil sector. The purpose of military training should be to promote the effective functioning of a country's armed forces. The argument that military training can benefit the civil sector should never be used as an excuse for substituting military training for civil-sector training.

THE SECURITY SECTOR AND EMPLOYMENT

The employment problem confronting Third World countries today is only partially a function of insufficient skilled labor. As discussed at the beginning of this chapter, it is increasingly recognized that a main issue facing countries attempting to develop their economies is how to provide their citizens with remunerative, productive work. One way in which the security sector can help in this respect is by purchasing goods and services from the civil-sector economy, thereby increasing aggregate demand. (See the discussions on aggregate demand in Chapter 6 and on the economic stimulus provided by security assistance-funded purchases in Chapter 7.) In the case of Iran, for example, industries such as electronics, food, textiles, clothing, and furniture making have benefitted "tangentially" from purchases by the armed forces. A study on the Mexican military claimed that "scattering of the Armed Forces, throughout the country, allows for supply requirements to generate an aggregate demand around the military bases."[64] Recall, however, that there is nothing unique about security spending in this regard: All forms of public expenditure have the capacity to increase aggregate demand.

It has also been argued that because so much civil-sector industry in Third World countries is capital- rather than labor-intensive and there is such a surplus of unskilled and semiskilled manpower, the armed forces can reduce unemployment by providing work (as soldiers) for at least some of the men who would otherwise have been unemployed or underemployed.[65] The armed forces do fulfill this function in a number of countries. The armed forces of Indonesia and Honduras, for example, are legally conscript forces, but, due to a lack of alternative jobs, volunteers suffice to staff these forces. As a solution to the employment problem,

[64] Schulz, "Military Expenditures," p. 194, and Vincente Ernesto Perez Mendoza, "The Role of the Armed Forces in the Mexican Economy in the 1980's," Report no. NPS-54-81-006 (Master's thesis, Monterey, Calif., Naval Postgraduate School, June 1981), p. 41.

[65] Mendoza, "The Role," p. 41, and Whynes, The Economics, pp. 63–65.

however, military service—as either a conscript or a long-term volunteer—does not have more than a minimal role to play in most Third World countries.

In many instances, the capacity of the armed forces to absorb manpower is vastly outstripped by the number of new jobs that must be created annually if unemployment is to decline. In Mexico, for example, it was estimated in the early 1980s that 800,000 new jobs must be created each year. About 120,000 men in the armed forces are staffed by volunteers. While some people are discharged each year, the military clearly does not provide much help in terms of employment creation. Similarly in Brazil the military cannot hope to absorb more than a relatively small number of the one million new entrants to the job market each year.[66] The Brazilian armed forces have about 270,000 men, nearly half of which are conscripts. While conscription may temporarily solve the job problem for about 15 percent of each year's new crop of job-seekers, it offers little in terms of a long-term resolution for the employment problem.

Conscription in developing countries varies in length from one year to four or five years. Irrespective of how long a recruit serves, he (and, in some cases, she) must eventually return to civilian life. Conscripts often leave the armed forces without having acquired any marketable skill. But even if they do receive training which increases their value to the civil-sector economy, no benefit will be derived, either by individuals or the economy as a whole, if jobs are unavailable. The issue of creating jobs must still be faced.

In most countries, the armed forces account for a very small proportion of the labor force. This is true even for that portion of the labor force considered most productive, men between the ages of 18 and 45. Table 8-3 shows that in almost three-quarters of the approximately one hundred countries surveyed in Appendix 4, the security forces (armed forces plus paramilitary forces) absorbed 5 percent or less of the 15- to 44-age group. In nearly half these countries, the security forces absorbed less than 2 percent of the men aged 15 to 44.

The fact that only a small segment of the economically most productive population is diverted into the armed forces in so much of the Third World does not necessarily mean that the civil sector does not suffer in individual countries. Even 2 percent of the 15- to 44-year group could be significant if that 2 percent included a large proportion of the men with skills vitally needed by government and industry. However, this is proba-

[66] Mendoza, "The Role," p. 42, and Alan Riding, "Brazil's Hard Life with Austerity," *New York Times*, 12 August 1984.

bly not the case.[67] In many conscript armed forces, a large number of the recruits are illiterate and not highly skilled when they enter the military. In Iran during the 1970s, the illiteracy rate among conscripts was estimated at 50 percent. The countries most likely to experience a conflict between the security and the civil sectors in terms of manpower are those where a relatively high proportion of the economically active population serves in the armed forces.

In Singapore, for example, the economic cost of the armed forces is said to exceed the amount budgeted on them "because of loss to the workforce caused by national service and reserve training." At any one time, approximately 35,000 men are conscripted into the armed forces for periods of two to three years. Reserve training for officers continues up to the age of 50; for the lower ranks, up to the age of 40.[68] In 1980, some 42,000 men were serving in the armed forces; this accounted for 6.5 percent of the men aged 15 to 44 and 5.1 percent of the men aged 15 to 64. Paramilitary forces absorbed an additional 37,500 men; thus, approximately 12 percent of the 15- to 44-year-old men and nearly 10 percent of the 15- to 64-year-old men were withdrawn from the labor force during that year. As far as the Third World is concerned, however, Singapore is more the exception than the rule.

WHEN it comes to evaluating the role played by Third World armed forces in training manpower and creating employment, it is never enough to restrict oneself to gross figures. Knowing that so many hundreds or thousands of soldiers have received some kind of technical training does not indicate how useful this training is to the civil economy. Similarly, the size of the armed forces and the level of unemployment are an insufficient basis upon which to determine the capacity of the security sector to generate employment. There is no denying that the armed forces do provide training which is subsequently of use to the civil economy and that they do offer employment to some individuals. These positive effects should not, however, be exaggerated. It is always less expensive and more efficient to train men and women for civil-sector jobs and to invest directly in the civil economy than to count on what are in most cases marginal spillover effects from the military sector.

[67] An interesting exception is the Ivory Coast where the army recruits individuals who are as highly skilled as possible and then, after one or two years, discharges those with insufficient skills. Here it is a case of the civil sector providing training for the military.

[68] Patrick Smith and Philip Bowring, "Singapore Stresses Security as an Arm of Nation-Building," *Far Eastern Economic Review*, 13 January 1983, pp. 26, 28.

9

· · · · · · · · · · · · · · · · · · · ·

MILITARY-LED

INDUSTRIALIZATION

DEVELOPMENT AND INDUSTRIALIZATION

Development and industrialization have, to a large degree, been considered synonymous in the Third World. Whether a country has attempted to follow a capitalist or a socialist model of development, its objective has invariably been to increase the share of industrial output to levels comparable to those in Western industrialized countries—between 30 and 40 percent of gross product. The centrality assigned to industrialization has derived from two observations. First, demand for manufactured goods is considerably more responsive to changes in income than demand for food and other agricultural products; that is, the income inelasticity of demand for manufactures exceeds that for food and other agricultural products. Second, economists believe there are dynamic economies of scale in manufacturing. It has been argued that these two factors produce a faster rate of growth in the manufacturing sector, thereby increasing employment rates. The manufacturing sector can, in turn, raise productivity in the agricultural sector by absorbing underemployed labor and by providing improved inputs to increase the productivity of both land and labor. Outside the agricultural sector, the expansion of the manufacturing industry may increase productivity by intensifying the rate of technical change.[1]

Industrial Development Prior to Independence

The emphasis developing countries have placed on industrialization since the 1950s derives in no small measure from the experience of the colonial period. The major economic activities in the colonies—irrespective of

---

[1] These arguments have been summarized in Ajit Singh, "Third World Industrialization and the Structure of the World Economy," pp. 456–58, in *Microeconomic Analysis: Essays in Microeconomics and Economic Development,* ed. D. Currie, D. Peel, and W. Peters (London: Croom Helm, 1981).

which colonial power held sway—were trade, the production of cash crops for export, and mining. The emphasis on trade and the role assigned to the colonies as suppliers of raw materials and consumers of European-produced manufactures weakened, often fatally, those industries that had existed in many parts of Asia, Africa, and Latin America when contact was first made with Europeans. Perhaps the best known example of this phenomenon was the severe contraction of the Indian spinning and weaving industries occasioned by imports of British cloth and yarn.

> After the Napoleonic Wars the flow of machine-produced manufactures multiplied and petty-production everywhere suffered a severe setback. In 1822–23 cloth imports to the Bengal Presidency alone in India stood at a figure seven times that for 1813–14, while exports from the same area fell from 4,600,000 to 300,000 rupees. Spinners were affected there with a time-lag. In 1825–26, yarn imports were 81,000 rupees, but the next year the figure rose to 800,000 rupees. Those who survived this competition did so either due to market-imperfections—both geographical remoteness or switching to non-competing varieties—or by cutting into subsistence to sell cheap. Thus urban spinning and weaving were virtually wiped out while rural crafts though crippled often survived.[2]

This pattern, repeated throughout the European colonies, affected a variety of industries in addition to cloth making, for example the smelting and working of iron and pottery making.

Since the colonies were meant to supply raw materials for European industries, the expansion of manufacturing capacity within the colonies was not accorded high priority by colonial governments. In Africa, investment of all kinds was limited prior to the end of World War II, and trade was the focus of economic relations.[3] Even when investment in the

[2] Prabhat Patnaik, "On the Political Economy of Underdevelopment," *Economic and Political Weekly* 8: 4–6 (Annual Number 1973): 200–1.

Not only were indigenous industries seriously crippled, but the development of indigenous technical knowledge was stunted and even caused to regress "since people forgot even the simple techniques of their forefathers. The abandonment of traditional iron smelting in most parts of Africa is probably the most important instance of technological regression." Walter Rodney, *How Europe Underdeveloped Africa* (London: Bogle-L'Ouverture Publications, 1972), p. 114. Rodney also points out that where Africans asked for technical assistance from Europeans, beginning in about the seventeenth century, their requests were invariably ignored; see pp. 115–18.

[3] This was particularly the case in the French colonies. To the end of the colonial period, commercial companies dominated the economies of the French territories, whereas in other parts of Africa:

colonies increased following World War II, African industry received but a pittance. Between 1946 and 1954, less than 1 percent of the development funds allocated to Africa by the British Colonial Development and Welfare (CD&W) was invested in industry. The French development agency, FIDES (Fonds d'investissement et de développement économique et social des Territoires d'Outre-Mer), devoted less than 0.5 percent to industrialization between 1949 and 1953. Agriculture received small grants as well, despite the fact that it was the primary economic activity in Africa. Rather, a

high proportion of the "development" funds went into the colonies in the form of loans for ports, railways, electric power plants, water works, engineering workshops, warehouses, etc., which were necessary for more efficient exploitation in the long run. In the short run, such construction works provided outlets for European steel, concrete, electrical machinery and railroad rolling-stock. . . . Even the schools built under FIDES funds were of unnecessary high cost per

---

The monopolies which put their capital into agriculture and mining played the essential role; commerce was subordinate to production, and not the other way round as in the first colonial age.

West and Central Africa under French domination seem to have been an exception in this sense; here, as before, the economy was dominated by the commercial companies, and trade was fitted into the imperialist context. The legal monopoly of the older companies was replaced by a *de facto* monopoly of financial oligarchy. Here, too, it was exported capital that controlled the economy, but its chosen domain was the import and export trade, and not production. As a consequence, the volume of invested capital remained very small.

The traditional trade was integrated by imperialism. Political and military control guaranteed and consolidated the monopoly of the commercial companies and the level of their profits. The weakness of production, and consequently of sales resulting from insignificant investment in production, was compensated for by the rise of profit margins. Commerce extracted more than surplus produce; it took part of the produce required for natural growth, and reduced the producer to penury. This presented an obstacle to all forms of accumulation, or any kind of technical progress. Monopoly, mercantilism, parasitism, stagnation: these, in short, were the main features of French colonisation in tropical Africa.

Jean Suret-Canale, *French Colonialism in Tropical Africa, 1900–1945,* trans. Till Gottheiner (London: C. Hurst, 1971), pp. 159–60. See also Rodney, *How Europe Underdeveloped Africa,* p. 115.

French colonial investments were largely restricted to Morocco and Indochina. Industry, excluding mining, received about 10 percent of all private investment in French sub-Saharan Africa between 1900 and 1940. Suret-Canale cautions that "one should have no illusions about [investment in industry proper]; it was limited to the basic activities essential for the life of towns and ports and the provision of means of transport" (p. 165).

unit, because they had to be of the requisite standard to provide job outlets for white expatriates. Incidentally, loans were "tied" in such a way that the money had to be spent on buying materials manufactured in the relevant metropole.[4]

Despite the low level of investment, manufacturing industries were not entirely absent from the colonies. By the onset of World War II, India, for example, was self-sufficient in certain consumer goods such as textiles and sugar. There was also domestic production of items such as jute products, iron and steel, cement, and paper goods, and there was a small engineering sector. Although the Tata Iron and Steel Company, which began producing steel in 1912, "constitutes the single most important instance of pioneering by private enterprise in India during the twentieth century,"[5] much of the investment in colonial industry was made by Europeans who frequently received preferential treatment of the colonial authorities.

[4] Rodney, *How Europe Underdeveloped Africa*, pp. 233–34. For a description of investment in infrastructure and production in French Africa between 1945 and 1960, see Jean Suret-Canale, *Afrique Noire de la Colonisation aux Indépendances, 1945–1960* (Paris: Editions Sociales, 1972), pp. 167–303. The development of industries is discussed on pp. 262–303.

There were considerable differences between the degree of industrialization in British East Africa and in British West Africa. The share of manufacturing in colonial product in Nigeria in 1950 was 0.6 percent and in Ghana in 1954, 0.4 percent. In Kenya and Uganda in 1954 the figures were 8.9 percent and 7.2 percent, respectively. In part this difference can be explained by the size of the white settler population in the latter two colonies. The Europeans "possessed the necessary technical, managerial and entrepreneurial skills, the requisite contacts with home-based firms and the political leverage to influence the colonial administration to grant support and protection to industrial activities." In addition, the Ugandan administration's discrimination against Asian traders caused them to switch from trading cotton to cotton ginning and other industrial activities. See Shankar N. Acharya, "Perspectives and Problems of Development in Low Income, Sub-Saharan Africa," pp. 6–7, in "Two Studies of Development in Sub-Saharan Africa," Shankar N. Acharya and Bruce Johnston, Staff Working Paper no. 300 (Washington, D..C.: World Bank, October 1978).

[5] Amiya Kumar Bagchi, *Private Investment in India, 1900–1939* (Cambridge: Cambridge University Press, 1972), p. 291.

Regarding the establishment of manufacturing industries prior to World War II, see ibid.; Patnaik, "The Political Economy," p. 201; Suret-Canale, *Afrique Noire*, pp. 262–303; and Harold Butler, *Problems of Industry in the East with Special Reference to India, French India, Ceylon, Malaya and the Netherlands Antilles*, ILO Studies and Reports Series B. No. 29 (Geneva: ILO, 1938).

Although most of Latin America had become independent in the early nineteenth century, only Mexico and Argentina had attained "a significant degree of industrialisation before the First World War" (p. 105). This was in large part due to the dominance of European, primarily British, manufactures in the period following the termination of Spanish and Portuguese rule. The depression which began in 1929 provided the stimulus for an increased emphasis on import-substituting industrialization in those Latin American countries which had already begun to build up their manufacturing capacity.

In the usual accounts of the economic development of India, the scarcity of Indian entrepreneurial talent is also stressed. . . . It is rarely recognized that the free-trade policy of the Government of India favoured only certain types of entrepreneurial activity, such as foreign trade and production for exports, in which Europeans had a natural advantage. Before the convention was adopted around 1919 that Indian fiscal policy would largely be determined by the Government of India without interference from the British Parliament, most of India's trade and industry was geared towards foreign markets.[6]

Despite this, it is important not to lose sight of the fact that the interests of the colonial power and those of foreign capital were not always synonymous. In British India, for example, policies that discriminated against Indian manufacturers also discriminated against British firms located in the colony. For many years, especially prior to World War I, tariff, excise tax, and government procurement policies were designed to favor imports over domestically produced items, irrespective of whether the latter were manufactured in Indian- or European-owned firms.[7]

Limits on the size of colonial markets were also important in constraining the growth of the industrial sector in the Third World prior to in-

The sudden collapse of the capacity to import, the contraction of the export sector and the ensuing fall in export profits, the blocking of international channels of finance, all provoked by the 1929 crisis, profoundly altered the course of development of the Latin American economies, particularly those that had already begun to industrialise. The contraction of the export sector led to two types of reaction, depending on the degree of diversification attained by the economy concerned: (a) factors of production were shifted back into the pre-capitalist sector—subsistence agriculture and craft manufactures—as the money economy shrank; (b) the industrial sector geared to the home market was expanded in an effort to replace, wholly or in part, goods previously purchased abroad. (p. 117)

Celso Furtado, *Economic Development in Latin America*, trans. Suzette Macedo, 2d ed. (London: Cambridge University Press, 1976). The different stages of industrialization in Latin America are discussed in Part IV, pp. 100–30.

[6] Bagchi, *Private Investment*, p. 21; see also pp. 157–216.
[7] Ibid., pp. 420–23. Although Indian and European industrialists in India both suffered from policies implemented by the colonial government, Bagchi points out that

on the whole, [the European industrialists] were quite happy with the existing arrangements under which they had the major share of external trade, organized banking and finance, industries catering for the export markets, and industries depending primarily on government patronage. Protectionist policies might after all encourage the growth of indigenous Indian entrepreneurship and force the Europeans to compete with the Indians on somewhat more equal terms in the home market. The interests of Indian business or of Indian economic development inevitably received a low priority in the imperial scheme, and could be sacrificed in order to safeguard other interests in the preservation and smooth working of the system. (p. 423)

dependence. Markets were limited both because of the poverty of large segments of the population, also an important factor in Latin America after independence, and because colonial governments followed policies favoring imports.

Expansion of Industrial Sectors

Although there was some debate at the beginning of the 1950s about the wisdom of adopting the UN position that development strategies should focus on industrialization, by the end of the 1950s, the "industrialization first" approach was widely accepted. Those who argued in favor of this strategy essentially believed "Historical experience shows that a structural transformation mainly based on industry is a *sine qua non* of genuine development."[8] In view of the degree to which Third World economies had been dominated by European manufactures and the effort that the Europeans—notably the British and the French—had made to hinder the growth of manufacturing capacity in Asia, Africa, the Middle East, and Latin America, it is not surprising that high priority was accorded to industrialization throughout the Third World in the postwar period.

By the early 1980s, a number of developing countries had attained levels of industrial output equivalent to those of the industrialized countries, and many which had not yet reached the 30-percent mark did nonetheless manage to expand their industrial sectors significantly. Table 9-1 shows the growth of industry according to income group between 1960 and 1982, and Table 9-2 provides data on the expansion of industry in individual countries during the same period. This performance has led some analysts to be optimistic about the potential for further industrialization. Despite the global recession then underway, Ajit Singh commented in 1981 that

> third world countries are in principle in a better position to push ahead with industrialization than they were a couple of decades ago. A number of them now have the necessary infrastructure, a level of development of key industries, technical and scientific skills and, more importantly, the crucial framework for the further development of these skills, to be able to sustain much higher levels of industrial development. Although "technology" is still a handicap and will remain so for a long time, it is much less of a disadvantage, and the third world's absorptive capacity is very much higher, than even a decade ago.

[8] Arthur Ewing, "Some Recent Contributions to the Literature on Economic Development," *Journal of Modern African Studies* 4 (September 1966): 341.

TABLE 9-1

Industry and Manufacturing Subsector as Percentage of GDP, Income Groups,
1960–1982 (weighted averages)

Income Group[a]	Industry[b]			Manufacturing		
	1960	1979	1982	1960	1979	1982
LOW INCOME	26	36	32	13	13	14
China and India	28	41	35	—	—	—
Other low income	13	23	16	9	9	9
MIDDLE INCOME	30	38	38	21	24	20
Oil exporters	25	42	40	14	19	17
Oil importers	32	36	35	22	26	23
Lower middle income	22	—	35	15	—	17
Upper middle income	33	—	41	25	—	22
HIGH INCOME OIL EXPORTERS	—	75	74	—	5	4

Sources: For 1960 and 1982: World Bank, World Development Report, 1984 (New York: Oxford University Press, 1984), pp. 222–23; for 1979, World Bank, World Development Report, 1981 (New York: Oxford University Press, 1981), p. 138.
[a]There are slight differences in the composition of the groups between 1979 and 1982. In addition, the values provided for 1960 vary between the two sources in a few cases. The only significant differences are for industry in the low-income countries, where the 1981 report gives a figure of 17 percent, and manufacturing in the oil-exporting middle-income countries, where the 1981 report gives a figure of 17 percent.
[b]Industry includes mining, manufacturing, construction, electricity, water, and gas.

In general, the major constraint on future industrial development in the market economy countries of the third world is likely to be the rate of growth of demand, rather than the supply-side factors.[9]

Singh was also encouraged by the fact that between 1960 and 1975, developing countries had increased industrial employment by some 5 percent annually. This, he pointed out, was "considerably greater" than the rate of population increase. In addition, while industrial employment in the developed countries was declining even as production levels were rising, a 1-percent increase in industrial output was still producing a rate of growth for industrial employment of between 0.7 and 0.8 percent in the Third World.[10]

[9]Singh, "Third World Industrialisation," p. 483.
[10]Ibid., p. 463.

341

TABLE 9-2
Industry and Manufacturing Subsector as Percentage of GDP,
Thirty-two Developing Countries, 1960–1982

Country	Industry[a]			Manufacturing		
	1960	1979	1982	1960	1979	1982
LOW INCOME						
Africa						
Bénin	8	12	13	3	8	7
Burkina Faso	16	20	16	9	14	12
Kenya[b]	18	21	22	9	13	13
Rwanda	6	21	22[c]	1	15	16[c]
Tanzania	11	13	15	5	9	9
Togo	15	23	29	8	7	6
Uganda	12	7	4[c]	9	6	4[c]
Asia						
Bangladesh	7	13	14	5	8	7
Burma	12	14	13	8	10	9
India	20	27	26	14	18	16
Pakistan	16	24	25	12	16	17
Sri Lanka	20	31	27	15	21	15
LOWER MIDDLE INCOME						
Africa						
Morocco	26	32	31	16	17	16
Nigeria	11	45	39	5	5	6
Senegal	17	24	25	12	19	15
Zambia	63	41	36	4	16	19
Asia						
Indonesia[d]	14	33	39	8	9	13
Philippines	28	35	36	20	24	24
Thailand	19	28	28	13	19	19
Latin America						
Bolivia	25	29	27[c]	15	13	14[c]
Colombia	26	28	31	17	21	21
Costa Rica	20	26	27	14	19	20
Dominican Republic	23	26[e]	28[c]	17	16[e]	16[c]
El Salvador	19	22	20	15	15	15
Ecuador	20	37	40	16	19	12
Paraguay	20	24	26	17	16	16
UPPER MIDDLE INCOME						
Asia						
Korea, Republic of	20	39	39	14	27	28
Singapore	18	36	37	12	28	26

(TABLE 9-2 CONT.)

Country	Industry[a]			Manufacturing		
	1960	1979	1982	1960	1979	1982
UPPER MIDDLE INCOME						
Latin America						
Brazil	35	38	—	26	28	—
Chile	35	37[e]	34	21	24[e]	20
Mexico	29	38	38	19	29	21
Uruguay	28	37	33[c]	21	31	26[c]

Sources: For 1960 and 1982: World Bank, *World Development Report, 1984* (New York: Oxford University Press, 1984), pp. 222–23; for 1979: World Bank, *World Development Report, 1981* (New York: Oxford University Press, 1981), pp. 138–39.
[a] Industry includes mining, manufacturing, construction, electricity, water, and gas.
[b] In 1979, Kenya was classified as a middle-income country.
[c] Data from 1981.
[d] In 1979, Indonesia was classified as a low-income country.
[e] Data from 1978.

Despite the undeniable progress made by many Third World countries in expanding their industrial sectors, serious problems remain. Tables 9-1 and 9-2 show that much growth in Third World industrial sectors prior to 1982 occurred in the nonmanufacturing industries (mining, construction, and electricity, water, and gas). Indeed, as a group the upper middle-income countries have experienced a decline in the relative size of their manufacturing sectors. If one looks at sectoral growth rates, manufacturing grew more slowly than industry as a whole between 1970 and 1982 in the lower-income and lower middle-income countries while both grew at about the same rate in the upper middle-income countries.[11]

For individual countries, progress has also been uneven. Although some countries have succeeded in doubling or tripling the share of manufacturing in their gross domestic products, the value of manufacturing output has declined or stagnated in others. Furthermore, a number of countries owe the rapid expansion of their industrial sectors primarily to the growth of extractive industries. In Table 9-2 this would, for example, include Nigeria, Togo, Indonesia, Morocco, and Zambia. Additional evidence of the unevenness of manufacturing sector growth is provided by

[11] Sectoral growth rates from World Bank, *World Development Report, 1984* (New York: Oxford University Press, 1984), pp. 220–21.

UNIDO data on the share of world manufacturing value-added (MVA) accruing to individual countries. UNIDO has calculated that between 1962 and 1980, the share of all developing countries in world manufacturing value-added grew from 8.1 to 11.0 percent, or by just over 25 percent. Between 1973 and 1980, however, nearly three-quarters of the increase occurred in just ten countries while fourteen developing countries saw their share in MVA halved.[12] Since then, the world recession, coupled with high interest rates and an exceptionally strong U.S. dollar, has caused stagnation in or severely weakened the industrial sectors of many Third World countries. This can be seen by comparing the figures for 1979 with those for 1982 in Tables 9-1 and 9-2.

The effects of this situation on the economies of individual countries have in some cases been devastating. In large part, the economic difficulties facing the Third World in the mid-1980s derived from adverse international conditions over which the developing countries had little, if any, control. Nevertheless, the industrialization strategies pursued by many governments have also contributed to their current problems. The emphasis on industrial growth has in too many cases resulted in a stagnant agricultural sector (see Chapter 6). This has meant that scarce foreign exchange must be used to import food rather than industrial inputs, and the size of the domestic market for manufactures is artificially limited by primarily rural poverty. Although industrial employment may have grown at a respectable rate for the developing countries as a whole during the 1960s and the 1970s, unemployment and underemployment remain problems of considerable magnitude for most Third World countries. Many Third World industrial sectors are heavily dependent on imports—of machinery, know-how, components, raw materials, and intermediate goods—which makes them extremely vulnerable to shortfalls in the availability of foreign exchange.

Dependence on Foreign Technology

CAPITAL- VERSUS LABOR-INTENSIVE TECHNOLOGIES

The dependence on imported technology is of central importance because its ramifications are felt throughout the economy. One aspect of this dependence is that the industrial processes adopted in the Third World often require relatively more capital and relatively less labor than is optimum for most developing countries. Governments eager to modernize their economies as rapidly as possible have frequently followed

---

[12] For UNIDO data see Erich Andrlik, "Crisis and Industrialization," *Austria Today,* March 1984, p. 9.

policies that alter the relative costs of these two factors, making it more profitable for individual firms to adopt capital-intensive methods, even though it might be in the interests of society at large to employ more labor-intensive techniques. "Subsidized interest rates, allowances for accelerated depreciation, tax holidays, overvalued exchange rates, and facilities for duty-free imports of capital have enhanced the profitability of capital-intensive investments and often encouraged enterprises to economize on labor rather than on capital." [13]

Not only Third World governments, however, encourage the use of relatively capital-intensive industrial processes. The sellers of technology also provide what is most readily available and generally are unwilling to adapt processes and machinery to local conditions. Third World purchasers may lack the necessary expertise to choose between different technologies or to make the sorts of modifications to the processes or materials employed that would increase the labor content. It has also been suggested that plant managers in Third World countries "often consciously select labour-saving equipment . . . as a substitute for improved labour relations and for worker-training programmes." In addition, aid funds are frequently tied to the acquisition of equipment from the donor country; thus, even if technology better suited to the requirements of the recipient is available from a supplier in a third country, it cannot be purchased. [14]

Many development analysts take the position that "Where the scope for choice is quite broad . . . relatively labour-intensive techniques, rather than the current 'best-practice' techniques of the industrial economies, tend typically to be more appropriate for developing-country economies." [15] The use of relatively labor-intensive technologies is desirable from the point of view of maximizing employment, allocating foreign exchange in the optimal manner, and promoting technological mastery.

As explained in Chapter 8, industrial employment in the Third World has expanded much more slowly than industrial output. In the late 1960s,

---

[13] World Bank, *World Development Report 1979* (New York: Oxford University Press, 1979), p. 51. See also United Nations, Department of Economic and Social Affairs (UNDESA), "Appropriate Technology and Research for Industrial Development," ST/ECA/ 152 (New York: United Nations, 1972), p. 7, and Gerald M. Meier, ed., *Leading Issues in Economic Development*, 3rd ed. (New York: Oxford University Press, 1976), p. 654.

[14] UNDESA, *Appropriate Technology*, pp. 9–12.

[15] Carl Dahlman and Larry Westphal, "Technological Effort in Industrial Development: An Interpretative Survey of Recent Research," p. 110, in *The Economics of New Technology in Developing Countries*, ed. Frances Stewart and Jeffrey James (London and Colorado: Frances Pinter and Westview Press, 1982). See also A. F. Ewing, "Some Recent Contributions to the Literature on Economic Development," *Journal of Modern African Studies* 4: 3 (1966): 342.

TABLE 9-3

Labor Force by Sector, Thirty-two Developing Countries, 1960 and 1980
(in percentages)

Country	Agriculture		Industry		Services	
	1960	1980	1960	1980	1960	1980
LOW INCOME						
Africa						
Bénin	54	46	9	16	37	38
Burkina Faso	92	82	5	13	3	5
Kenya	86	78	5	10	9	12
Rwanda	95	91	1	2	4	7
Tanzania	89	83	4	6	7	11
Togo	80	67	8	15	12	18
Uganda	89	83	4	6	7	11
Asia						
Bangladesh	87	74	3	11	10	15
Burma	—	67	—	10	—	23
India	74	71	11	13	15	16
Pakistan	61	57	18	20	21	23
Sri Lanka	56	54	14	14	30	32
LOWER MIDDLE INCOME						
Africa						
Morocco	62	52	14	21	24	27
Nigeria	71	54	10	19	19	27
Senegal	84	77	5	10	11	13
Zambia	79	67	7	11	14	22
Asia						
Indonesia	75	58	8	12	17	30
Philippines	61	46	15	17	24	37
Thailand	84	76	4	9	12	15
Latin America						
Bolivia	61	50	18	24	21	26
Colombia	51	26	19	21	30	53
Costa Rica	51	29	19	23	30	48
Dominican Republic	67	49	12	18	21	33
El Salvador	62	50	17	22	21	28
Ecuador	57	52	19	17	24	31
Paraguay	56	49	19	19	25	32
UPPER MIDDLE INCOME						
Asia						
Korea, Republic of	66	34	9	29	25	37
Singapore	8	2	23	39	69	59

(TABLE 9-3 CONT.)

Country	Agriculture		Industry		Services	
	1960	1980	1960	1980	1960	1980
UPPER MIDDLE INCOME						
Latin America						
Brazil	52	30	15	24	33	46
Chile	30	19	20	19	50	62
Mexico	55	36	20	26	25	38
Uruguay	21	11	30	32	49	57

Source: World Bank, *World Development Report, 1984* (New York: Oxford University Press, 1984), pp. 258–59.

Note: These figures are based on projections made by the ILO and do not represent the actual division among sectors in 1980.

the ILO predicted that less than 10 percent of the approximately 226 million individuals entering the job market in developing countries in 1970 would be able to find employment in the urban-industrial sector. A decade later, the World Bank estimated that even if industrial employment in the very poorest countries (those with per capita incomes of $300 or less in 1977) were doubled, the industrial sector would still be able to employ only about one-third of the entrants to the labor force.[16] A comparison of the data in Tables 9-2 and 9-3 shows that, although industrial employment expanded significantly in some countries between 1960 and 1980, industrial workers still accounted for a rather small portion of the total labor force in many countries. Of the thirty-two countries listed in the tables, industrial output as a proportion of GDP exceeded estimated industrial employment as a proportion of the labor force at the end of the 1970s by a factor of at least 2 : 1 in Kenya, Rwanda, India, Sri Lanka, Nigeria, Senegal, Zambia, Indonesia, the Philippines, Thailand, and Ecuador.

Two additional points can be made about the information in Table 9-3. First, in the low-income countries and in many of the lower middle-income countries, agriculture continues to absorb a sizable portion of the labor force. Given the amount of underemployment in many Third World agricultural sectors, there is considerable scope for the creation of small-

[16] World Bank, *World Development Report, 1979*, p. 52, and UNDESA, *Appropriate Technology*, p. 9.

scale rural industries which would both absorb some of this excess manpower and provide the agricultural sector with goods that would improve its productivity and enhance the quality of rural life, hopefully stemming the tide of rural-urban migration.[17] Second, in most Latin American countries, the people released from the agricultural sector have been absorbed not so much by the industrial sector but by the service sector. In other words, they have become the urban unemployed, many of whom would also benefit from investment in small-scale industries and an emphasis on labor-using technologies.

IMPLICATIONS FOR AVAILABILITY OF FOREIGN EXCHANGE

Although the industrialization process may be set in motion to save foreign exchange by producing domestically what previously had to be imported or to earn foreign exchange by producing for export, the expansion of the industrial sector may cause substantial outflows of foreign exchange. It is clear that if foreign technology is to be acquired, some expenditure of foreign exchange must occur: to purchase machinery, licenses, patents, know-how, and even entire "turn-key" plants. The fact that transnational corporations control so much of this technology has, however, produced secondary costs which are said vastly to exceed the cost of acquiring the technology itself. The most important of these secondary costs include:

· overpricing of imports of intermediate products and equipment ("price mark-ups");
· profits on capitalization of know-how;
· a portion of repatriated profits of the wholly owned subsidiaries or joint ventures;
· price mark-up for technology included in the cost of imported capital goods and equipment. . . .

Illustrative data have recently been developed on the overpricing of imported inputs of intermediate products, equipment and spare parts.

The practice of including in transfer of technology agreements specific clauses limiting the purchase of such inputs to technology suppliers themselves, or to sources specifically designated for this

[17] On rural industrialization, see for example, Bepin Behari, *Rural Industrialization in India* (New Delhi: Vikas, 1976); Dwight Perkins et al., *Rural Small-Scale Industry in the People's Republic of China* (Berkeley: University of California Press, 1977); and Jon Sigurdson, *Rural Industrialization in China* (Cambridge, Mass.: Council on East Asian Studies, 1977).

purpose is very widespred. Such specific tie-in purchase clauses are not even necessary in the case of direct private investment. . . .

In a study prepared for UNCTAD III the Junta del Acuerdo de Cartagena showed that in the Colombia pharmaceutical industry the absolute amount of overpricing for foreign firms was equivalent to six times the royalties and 24 times the declared profits of those firms; for national firms in the same industry the absolute amount of overpricing did not exceed one fifth of declared profits. . . .

Similar evidence is available for other industries in the Andean Pact countries, e.g. electronics, rubber and chemicals. . . .

Apart from the limitation in transfer agreements concerning "tied" purchases, these agreements also contain various types of restrictions:

- total prohibition, partial limitation or geographical restraints on exports;
- guarantees against changes in taxes, tariffs and exchange rates affecting profits, royalties and remittances . . .[18]

The heavy dependence of industries in the Third World on imported raw materials, intermediate goods, and spare parts has already been cited as one cause of underutilized capacity. The need to purchase these inputs has also contributed to rising indebtedness in the Third World. While more equitable pricing policies on the part of the suppliers of technology would reduce the outflow of foreign exchange from the industrial sector, most developing countries also urgently need to reduce the import dependence of that sector. In essence, this is a call for increased import substitution. Writing of the most indebted countries in Latin America and the other newly industrialized countries, Ajit Singh has commented

As far as the problems of industrial adjustment in these countries are concerned, they have no choice in the short term but to greatly reduce their imports and to pursue vigorous import substitution policies so as to maintain as high a level of economic activity as possible. However, even in the medium to longer term, such countries as Brazil and Mexico will have to reduce the import intensity of their industrial production and lower their propensity to import industrial products if they are to go back to their previous trend rates of long-term growth.[19]

---

[18] Surendra J. Patel, "The Cost of Technological Dependence," *Ceres* no. 32 (March–April 1973): 18–19. See also World Bank, *World Development Report 1979*, p. 65.

[19] Ajit Singh, "The Interrupted Industrial Revolution of the Third World: Prospects and Policies for Resumption," *Industry and Development* no. 12 (1984): 62.

Restrictions imposed by the foreign suppliers of technology on the source of industrial inputs is not the only reason for import dependence in Third World industrial sectors. Transnational corporations have also purchased patents to eliminate competition from local enterpreneurs, have made excessive use of foreign personnel in their operations, and have discouraged the development of indigenous technical and R&D capabilities.[20] These activities not only raise the financial cost to Third World producers; they also undermine efforts to build up indigenous technological mastery and thus strike at the very heart of the industrialization process.

TECHNOLOGICAL MASTERY

Importation of industrial technology has been given high priority because developing economies are considered deficient in technical knowledge and skills, and it is assumed that by purchasing machinery and know-how from industrially more advanced countries, the desired knowledge and capabilities will be transferred to individuals and companies in the developing world. The ultimate objective is to build up an indigenous

[20]Dahlman and Westphal, "Technological Effort," p. 121, and Patel, "The Cost," p. 19.

The Malaysian government has recently complained, for example, that the high-technology industries it has encouraged to set up operations have failed to transfer technology or to stimulate the growth of local support industries. According to the Deputy Director of the electronics division of the Malaysian Industrial Development Authority, the foreign companies "import the plans, make the pieces and send the finished product back home. This is mainly an assembly operation, and the degree of integration in Malaysian industry is very shallow. Research and development facilities are not established here." Barbara Crosette, "Enthusiasm for High-Tech Industries is Waning in Malaysia," *International Herald Tribune*, 10 July 1985.

It has been evident for some years that developing countries are likely to encounter a number of problems when they act as subcontractors for multinational corporations. One is related to manpower training: "international sub-contracting operations in developing countries tend to be intensive in their use of unskilled or semi-skilled labour, but not intensive in their use of skilled labour or professional manpower." This limits the likelihood of technology transfer. A second problem is related to the degree to which subcontracting operations benefit the economy as a whole:

> Perhaps the most interesting and difficult question of all, is how important are the "spread" effects of international sub-contracting. Here the effects are likely to vary according to the technical type of subcontracting involved. On the whole, sub-contracting of single processes is likely to have the least "spread" effects: and certain operations of this type seem naturally to be of an enclave nature. For example, the assembly of semi-conductors in a developing country is rather unlikely to lead on to fabrication of the wafers, by direct backward linkage.

Michael Sharpston, "International Sub-Contracting," *Oxford Economic Papers* 27: 1 (1975): 100, 129.

technological base and reduce dependence on the industrialized world for both industrial products and technology. Surendra Patel has defined technological independence as "the ability to decide what technologies to import from abroad; under what terms and conditions to accept them; how to adjust and adapt them to national requirements, assimilate and diffuse them, derive the maximum benefits in terms of national skill formation; and determine the balance between imported and nationally developed technologies."[21] Attaining this independence is far from simple, however, because technology cannot

> be transferred wholesale and in working order. Capital goods can be transferred, but capital goods alone do not constitute a technology: they represent only that part of the technology which is embodied in hardware. . . . The remainder is comprised of disembodied technological knowledge and related social arrangements and although knowledge can be transferred, the ability to make effective use of it cannot. This ability can only be acquired through indigenous technological effort, leading to technological mastery through human capital formation.[22]

In short, a country cannot import a number of "turn-key" plants and expect that in the course of operating these plants mastery of the technology they embody will automatically be acquired. Rather, conscious efforts must be made by the recipient of technology to learn how and why plant and machinery function as they do. All too often, technology is imported without any transfer of technology occurring. Plants operate at less than optimum efficiency and with greater cost than necessary, and technology acquired through licenses and in the form of turn-key plants cannot be replicated because local technicians and engineers have not mastered the technology they are using. This failure to master imported technology occurs not only because transnational corporations are loathe to part with information but also because governments and firms in the Third World have not given sufficient priority to the training of manpower for these tasks.[23]

Dahlman and Westphal have identified four stages in the application of technological knowledge within industry. In ascending order of difficulty, these are:

(1) production engineering: ability to operate existing plants,

[21] Ibid., p. 16.
[22] Dahlman and Westphal, "Technological Effort," p. 106.
[23] Ibid., pp. 121–22, and Patel, "The Cost," p. 19.

(2) project execution: ability to create new production capacity,
(3) capital-goods manufacture: ability to reproduce technological knowledge embodied in physical facilities and equipment,
(4) research and development: ability to generate new technological knowledge.[24]

Economies do not pass in orderly fashion from mastery of production engineering to mastery of research and development. Different levels of competence are built up in different technologies. Even so, it is sometimes possible to identify the general position of a country on this scale. South Korea, for example, has been extremely successful in mastering production engineering—that is, it has been able to adapt a wide range of foreign technologies to Korean requirements. It has been less successful in replicating this technology and has only recently begun to build up a capital goods industry. By contrast, the capital goods industry in India is much stronger, and indigenous scientific effort, measured by the number of patents issued to Indian nationals, has increased significantly since 1950. Nonetheless, certain sectors of the Indian economy remain heavily dependent on foreign technology, particularly the chemical and pharmaceutical industries.[25]

The ability to adapt imported technologies to local conditions is crucial since such modifications may allow reduced production costs or render the product more suited to the requirements and preferences of the local market. Of course, not all technologies are amenable to such modifications, but it has been suggested that the importers of technology developed in the industrialized countries far too often tend to see the technology as an indivisible entity whereas, in reality, products and production processes consist of many elements. It is frequently possible, particularly in the case of consumer goods, to alter the way in which components are produced or the materials of which they are made and thereby increase the labor content of the item, reduce the foreign exchange costs, and/or increase the use of local raw materials.

An example is the manufacture of the crank case oil sump of engines. In the industrialized countries, the sump is usually manufactured by deep drawing, using heavy presses and expensive dies. At the scale of production prevailing in most developing countries, such heavy presses would not operate on a full-time basis and would thus be uneconomic. Moreover, the depreciation cost per unit produced would

[24]Dahlman and Westphal, "Technological Effort," pp. 106–07.
[25]On Korea, see ibid., pp. 129–30. On India, see Achin Vanaik, "II—Changing Pattern of India's Reliance," *Times of India*, 5 December 1980.

be excessive. By the welding of simple sheet metal components, such parts can be built up with substantial cost savings.[26]

In this manner developing countries progressively build up the capacity to produce more and more complex items with a minimum of dependence on foreign technology. Dahlman and Westphal, for example, have argued that "the increased mastery which results from experience with previously established technologies contributes to an economy's capacity to undertake independent technological efforts, including replication or adaption of foreign technologies as well as creation of new technologies."[27] Developing countries are understandably eager to expand their industrial and technological bases as rapidly as possible, and to seek shortcuts to technological independence. It should also be possible for them to progress more rapidly than the now-industrialized countries of Europe did during the industrial revolution because so much technology is currently available. Developing countries do not have to begin from the very beginning when introducing new technologies.

In terms of *absorbing* these technologies into their economies, however, developing countries must recognize that few shortcuts are available. The experience of the industrialized countries indicates that "the economic impact of replacing old technology by the new is generally less than the cumulative impact of gradual improvements made afterward."[28] One analyst has claimed that the single most important lesson to be learned from the Japanese experience with industrialization is "the cumulative importance of myriads of relatively simple improvements in technology which do not depart radically from tradition or require large units of new investment." Those developing countries that today have a relatively strong industrial base owe their success to having progressively created a manpower base with "the capability to make the right technological decisions at the right time and to implement them in an appropriate framework."[29]

[26] UNDESA, *Appropriate Technology*, pp. 14–15.

[27] Dahlman and Westphal, "Technological Effort," p. 116.

[28] Ibid.

[29] The first quotation is from William W. Lockwood, *The Economic Development of Japan: Growth and Structural Change, 1868–1938* (Princeton, N.J.: Princeton University Press, 1954), p. 198, cited in Keith Marsden, "Towards a Synthesis of Economic and Social Justice," *International Labour Review* 100 (November 1969): 406.

The second quotation is from Dahlman and Westphal, "Technological Effort," pp. 114–15. On South Korea, Dahlman and Westphal maintain that "Korea has effectively assimilated various elements of foreign technology, but without much direct foreign participation in its industrial sector. Assimilation was achieved through a succession of technological efforts over time, largely undertaken by domestic firms to extend their technological mastery and to accomplish minor technological changes" (p. 130).

CHAPTER 9

MILITARY INDUSTRIALIZATION

Third World countries seek to produce their own weapons for a combination of political, military, and economic reasons. A domestic weapons production capacity can be seen as an expression of national sovereignty, tangible evidence that a country intends to defend its independence. It is also believed to demonstrate that a country controls its own affairs and, because arms industries make use of some of the most sophisticated technology available, that the country is well along the path to modernization. In addition, a domestic weapon industry can ensure vital supplies of arms and ammunition in time of war, thereby reducing a country's dependence on foreign suppliers; it can enable a country to obtain weapons that it would otherwise have difficulty in procuring abroad; and it can be a useful element in promoting the foreign policy of the state. South Africa, for example, has expanded its defense-industrial sector because of United Nations embargos on the sale of weapons to Pretoria, and Israel has expanded its capacity to resupply troops during a conflict to minimize unwanted pressure from outside (i.e., the United States) to limit its military objectives in its periodic wars with its Arab neighbors.[30] Israel, Brazil, and China have all used arms transfers to gain political objectives in the Third World.[31]

Third World countries that set up domestic arms production facilities often have two economic objectives: to spur their industrialization pro-

[30] Robert E. Harkavy and Stephanie G. Neuman, "Israel," p. 198, in *Arms Production in Developing Countries: An Analysis of Decision Making*, ed. James Everett Katz (Lexington, Mass.: Lexington, 1984). The need for improved resupply capacity derived from the Israeli experience during the 1973 Middle East war when the United States slowed down its resupply operation to prevent Israel from destroying the Egyptian Third Army. U.S. policymakers feared that if Israel overran the Third Army and proceeded deeper into Egyptian territory, the Soviet Union might become actively involved in the conflict. Harkavy and Neuman exaggerate the seriousness of the situation in which the Israelis found themselves as a result of the United States slowdown, but there can be no doubt that this event led to decisions to increase the domestic resupply capacity.

Although it might be argued that Israel is not, strictly speaking, a developing country, it is often seen as a successful case of Third World military industrialization. It is included here as a sort of "upper limit" to the success that developing countries can hope to attain in the military-industrial sector. At the same time, recall that Israel is very much a special case, since such a large proportion of its security outlays of all kinds have been heavily subsidized by the U.S. government since 1973 (see Chapter 7).

[31] See for example, Steven E. Miller, "Arms and the Third World: Indigenous Weapons Production," PSIS Occasional Papers, no. 3 (Geneva: Graduate Institute of International Studies, December 1980), pp. 31–32, and Michael Moodie, *Sovereignty, Security and Arms,* The Washington Papers, Vol. 7, no. 67 (Beverly Hills and London: Sage, 1979), p. 25.

gram and to reduce the financial costs, particularly outlays of foreign exchange, associated with weapon procurement. The creation of military industries is said to promote the industrialization process by upgrading both technology and manpower and by making economies of scale possible in certain supplier industries. The expectation that foreign exchange can be saved by producing weapons domestically is based on the belief that the cost of importing licenses, know-how, raw materials, and components will be less than the purchase price of a complete weapon. Some savings might also occur because the cost of labor in Third World countries, even skilled labor and technical manpower, tends to be considerably less than in the industrialized countries.

The economic objectives will be of primary interest in this chapter. Before examining these, it may be of interest to examine briefly some reasons why arms producers in the industrialized countries transfer weapon technology. According to SIPRI, 85 percent of all production licenses for major weapons granted to Third World countries between 1950 and 1984 were sold by the United States, the United Kingdom, France, the Federal Republic of Germany, and the Soviet Union. Of the major suppliers, the USSR is the most restrictive, having granted only thirteen licenses for major weapons to two countries—India and North Korea. The United States has made thirty licenses for major weapons available to nine countries; half of these have gone to South Korea, ten, and Taiwan, five. As a group, the three West European countries have been most active, supplying some sixty licenses for major weapons to some fifteen countries.[32]

Arms producers have essentially four reasons for transferring technology to developing countries. Probably the most important is the desire to expand or protect their markets in the Third World. As explained earlier, weapon purchases are increasingly accompanied by offset agreements whereby all or part of the purchase price of the weaponry is offset by exports from the recipient country or by the production of some portion of the weapon in the recipient country (see Chapter 7, n. 91). A company unwilling to share at least some of its production technology may fail to make a sale.[33]

---

[32] Michael Brzoska and Thomas Ohlson, ed., *Arms Production in the Third World* (London: Taylor & Francis, for SIPRI, 1986), pp. 25–26. On license production, see also David J. Louscher and Michael D. Salomone, *Technology Transfer and U.S. Security Assistance: The Impact of Licensed Production* (Boulder, Colo.: Westview Press, 1987).

[33] Competition between suppliers of technology is often quite sharp as the proposals submitted by British Aerospace, Dornier and MBB—all European producers—to the Indian aircraft firm, Hindustan Aeronautics, in connection with its Light Combat Aircraft (LCA) project indicate.

CHAPTER 9

Another motive for the industrialized country producer may be to evade restrictions imposed by its own government on arms exports. Third World subsidiaries can often export to countries to which the parent company cannot. Having a subsidiary in a country such as Singapore which is extremely secretive about its entire defense-industrial sector is particularly desirable from this point of view. Setting up subsidiaries in the Third World also enables industrialized country arms producers to take advantage of the comparatively cheap labor and the weakness of labor unions in developing countries by having these subsidiaries produce the most labor intensive components. Finally, arms technology may be exported in order to help the supplier's government maintain political influence in particular Third World countries. Although this may be easiest to arrange when the company in question is nationalized, private firms have sometimes been prevailed upon to export technology for this purpose.[34]

Promoting Industrialization

Some analysts have argued that arms production can stimulate the industrialization process by purchasing inputs from domestic manufacturers and encouraging the introduction of new products, processes, and industries, by transferring technology, and by creating jobs and training manpower. Others have maintained that military industrialization entails serious economic costs by diverting financial, material, and human resources from the civil sectors of industry and that these costs "seem to preclude its development in all but the largest of the LDCs." Even in the larger arms-producing countries—such as China—and the more success-

---

MBB has offered to build an initial 200 LCAs for about US$4-billion, and to transfer the aluminium-lithium technology India will need to start local production. British Aerospace, which has perfected the use of carbon fibre in aircraft structures, has quoted US$3.5-billion for 200 aircraft, but will transfer knowhow only if India buys 200 pairs of wings made of carbon epoxy resin.

Dornier, already supplying India with a light transport aircraft, has offered the latest in navigation, avionics and control instrumentation technology.

Radhakrishna Rao, "India Raises its Sights," *South*, May 1985, p. 89.

[34] For example, Colt Industries has claimed that it was pressured by the United States government in 1969 to set up a factory in South Korea to produce the M-16 rifle under license. See United States Congress, House, Committee on International Relations, Subcommittee on International Organizations, Report: *Investigation of Korean-American Relations*, 95th Cong., 2nd Sess., 31 October 1978 (Washington, D.C.: Government Printing Office, 1978), pp. 76–78.

356

ful ones—such as Israel—the costs have not been insignificant.[35] No one, not even the most ardent supporter of defense industries, would deny that the industrialization process would be better served by investing directly in the civil sector. When it comes to making a calculation of the relative costs and benefits of defense industrialization, however, the political and military justifications weigh heavily in the balance, and even though the economic costs alone might seem quite high, governments are loathe to abandon their defense-industrial sectors.

LINKAGES WITH THE CIVIL SECTOR

In some developing countries, the desire to produce weapons domestically has led to governmental and military support for civil-sector industrialization. In some cases this backing has derived from the belief that a logical outgrowth of industrialization in the civil sector would be the establishment of military industries. This has been the position of the Chilean armed forces, for example, since the 1930s. In other cases, such as Taiwan over the last decade, a conscious effort has been made to create or strengthen the industrial base necessary to support defense industries.[36]

In other developing countries, the creation of a defense-industrial sector has been viewed as a way of encouraging industrialization in the civil sector. In Iran, the shah saw arms production as the leading edge which

[35] The quotation is from David K. Whynes, *The Economics of Third World Military Expenditure* (London: Macmillan, 1979), p. 49. On China, see Sydney Jammes, "China," pp. 257–77, in *The Structure of the Defense Industry: An International Survey*, ed. Nicole Ball and Milton Leitenberg (London: Croom Helm, 1983). On Israel, see Harkavy and Neuman, "Israel," p. 213; Paul Rivlin, "The Burden of Israel's Defence," *Survival* 20: 4 (July–August 1978): 146–54; and Jeffrey Sachs, "Israel's Economic Disaster," *The New Republic*, 8 July 1985, pp. 21–23.

[36] On Chile, see Carlos Portales and Augusto Varas, "The Role of Military Expenditure in the Development Process. Chile, 1952–1973 and 1973–1980: Two Contrasting Cases," *Ibero Americana* 12: 1–2 (1983): 29. On Taiwan, see A. J. Gregor, R. E. Harkavy, and S. G. Neuman, "Taiwan: Dependent 'Self-Reliance,'" pp. 237–39, in *Arms Production*, ed. Brzoska and Ohlson. They note that

As a consequence of the government's concern for the development of armaments-related industries, the electrical apparatus, precision instruments and machinery equipment industries have grown with remarkable rapidity. . . .

All of these developments support the effort to achieve some measure of arms production capability. The creation of basic steel, copper and aluminium industries, and the expansion of precision machinery and electronics industries, all serve the military needs of the nation. The expansion and sophistication of the shipbuilding industry is similarly calculated to supply some of the naval needs of Taiwan in the face of an international embargo. (p. 238)

would cause sophisticated technology to spread throughout the economy. The head of the Iranian military control bureau during the reign of the shah, General Katorijan, described domestic arms production as a precondition for industrialization.[37]

While defense industrialization may introduce new products, processes, and industries into developing economies, no Third World country can hope to support arms production of any magnitude if it does not already possess a reasonably strong, diversified industrial sector. As Michael Brzoska and Thomas Ohlson have pointed out, "One principle is particularly important here: that the arms industry is dependent on the state of technological know-how in the civilian industry. Neglecting this basic rule can be fatal, as evidenced by the enormous problems encountered by Argentina in the 1950s, by Egypt in the 1960s and by Peru in the early 1980s."[38] Very few Third World countries have sufficiently well developed industrial sectors to support significant defense production. Table 9-4 shows that India and Israel accounted for over half of Third World production of major weapons between 1950 and 1984 while just eight countries accounted for 95 percent.

To identify those countries capable of supporting arms industries, Herbert Wulf calculated the "arms production capacity" and "manpower base" at the end of the 1970s for thirty-four developing countries which produced at least some weapons domestically.

Since the United Nations system of International Standard Industrial Classification (ISIC) does not include a category "arms industry", an attempt has been made here to identify those sub-categories which are most relevant for arms production. These are ISIC no. 371, iron and steel; ISIC no. 372, non-ferrous metal; ISIC no. 381, metal products; ISIC no. 382, machinery (non-electrical); ISIC no. 383, electrical machinery; and ISIC no. 384, transportation equipment.

These six key industries, which will be called the "*relevant industries*" for arms production, are some of the most advanced industries in terms of their ability to incorporate new technologies and to apply research and development. Their output has been taken as the first indicator of arms production capacity. The second indicator, "man-

---

[37] Ann Schulz, "Military Expenditures and Economic Performance in Iran, 1950–1980," (Worcester, Mass.: Clark University, 1981, mimeograph), pp. 32, 76. See also, Ann Schulz, "Iran: An Enclave Arms Industry," p. 155, in *Arms Production,* ed. Brzoska and Ohlson.

[38] Brzoska and Ohlson, ed., *Arms Production,* p. 281. See also Michael Brzoska, "The Impact of Arms Production in the Third World," Working Papers 8 (Hamburg: IPW, Centre for the Study of Wars, Armaments and Development, February 1987).

TABLE 9-4

Third World Producers of Major Weapons, 1950–1984
(in percentages)

Country	%	Cumulative %
India	31	31
Israel	23	54
South Africa	9	63
Brazil	9	72
Taiwan	8	80
North Korea	6	86
Argentina	5	91
South Korea	4	95
Egypt	2	97
ASEAN countries[a]	2	99
Others[b]	1	100

Source: Michael Brzoska and Thomas Ohlson, ed., *Arms Production in the Third World* (London: Taylor & Francis, 1986), p. 10.
[a] Indonesia, Malaysia, Thailand, Philippines, Singapore
[b] Bangladesh, Burma, Chile, Colombia, Dominican Republic, Gabon, Madagascar, Mexico, Pakistan, Peru, Senegal, Sri Lanka

power base," consists of two sets of data: the employees or persons engaged in the "relevant industries" and the total number of scientists, engineers and technicians involved in R&D during the latest year for which data are available.[39]

Wulf concluded that the last nine countries on his list (those ranked below twenty-five) did not possess the minimum capacity needed to initiate arms production (Figure 9-1). Those ranked between fifteen (give or take a country or two) and twenty-five could not be expected to do more than assemble weapons. The first fifteen countries in Wulf's list should be capable of more extensive weapon production, and, with the exception of North Korea for which Wulf had no data, all the largest Third World

[39] Herbert Wulf, "Developing Countries," p. 325, in *The Structure,* ed. Ball and Leitenberg; emphasis in original. See also Herbert Wulf, "Arms Production in the Third World," pp. 339–41, in SIPRI, *World Armaments and Disarmament: SIPRI Yearbook, 1985* (London: Taylor & Francis, 1985), where Wulf updates his estimates of the arms production potential for twenty-seven developing countries. For the most part, the rankings do not vary appreciably between the two sources.

RANKING	COUNTRY	CAPACITY
1	India	
2	Brazil	
3	Yugoslavia	
4	South Africa	
5	Mexico	
		Diversified production
6	Argentina	
7	Taiwan	
8	South Korea	
9	Turkey	
10	Greece	
11	Iran	
12	Israel	
13	Portugal	
14	Egypt	
15	Hong Kong	
16	Chile	
17	Venezuela	
18	Philippines	
19	Colombia	
20	Thailand	
		Assembly
21	Algeria	
22	Singapore	
23	Indonesia	
24	Pakistan	
25	Peru	
26	Malaysia	
27	Nigeria	
28	Saudi Arabia	
29	Zimbabwe	
30	Morocco	
		Insufficient
31	Iraq	
32	Kenya	
33	Sri Lanka	
34	Syria	

FIGURE 9-1

Arms Production Capacity, 34 Developing Countries, Late 1970s

Source: Herbert Wulf, "Developing Countries," pp. 324–27, in *The Structure of the Defense Industry,* ed. Nicole Ball and Milton Leitenberg (London: Croom Helm, 1983).

producers of major weapons are ranked above fifteen. The People's Republic of China was not included in either the Brzoska-Ohlson or the Wulf studies. Egypt, which is in the process of building up its arms industry, and Turkey, which has ambitious arms production plans, are also among those theoretically capable of considerable domestic production. The Philippines, Indonesia, and Pakistan—all of which are planning to expand their defense industrial sectors significantly—are ranked between fifteen and twenty-five.

Wulf predicted that these latter countries will probably "experience economic and technical difficulties since their arms production programmes are not based on an adequate industrial base." Interestingly, he reached the same conclusion about Israel which, according to his calculations, is attempting to produce more sophisticated weapons than its industrial and manpower base suggests is possible.[40] Israel has managed to support its extensive arms industry thus far because of substantial economic and military aid received from the United States since 1973. Nonetheless, it is clear that Israel's entire military program is causing serious economic difficulties.

A more detailed examination of the industrial base of other countries ranked between one and fifteen on Wulf's list suggests that some of them may not be capable of supporting extensive arms production. As part of a study on the capacity of the Turkish economy to produce arms, Ron Ayres examined the same industrial sectors as Wulf at the subcategory level. Along with Gavin Kennedy, Ayres called these sectors "the potential defence capacity [PDC] industries."

In the three-digit manufacturing group Machinery (ISIC: 382) alone there are 64 six-digit sub-categories and 33 out of these 64 are not produced in Turkey, including steam turbines (ISIC: 382101), internal combustion engines (382108), gas turbines (382113), hydraulic turbines (382116), forging, stamping and die-casting machines (382307), grinding and sharpening machines (382310), metalforming machine tools (382331), rolling mills for rolling metals (382337) and electro-mechanical hand tools (382343). All of these six-digit subcategories could be required for defence production yet are not produced domestically in Turkey, and even those subcategories that are produced in Turkey are heavily dependent on imported parts and components.[41]

[40] Wulf, "Developing Countries," pp. 324–27.
[41] Ron Ayres, "Arms Production as a Form of Import-Substituting Industrialization: The Turkish Case," *World Development* 11: 9 (1983): 817. See also Ergin Yildziglu, "The Magician Who Lost His Touch," *South*, May 1985, p. 67.

According to Ayres, the main beneficiaries of any large-scale expansion of the Turkish defense industry would be foreign firms and technicians who would have to supply most of the necessary machinery, components, raw materials, and skills.

Iran was ranked eleventh on Wulf's list and therefore should have had a reasonable chance of surpassing simple assembly of weapons. The shah's government invested considerable sums in arms production and its supplier industries during the 1970s, but the military-industrial sector was poorly integrated into the domestic economy by the time the shah was removed from power. Almost all the inputs for the defense industries had to be imported. Although some supplier industries already existed and the Iranian government encouraged their expansion, demand from the military sector outstripped domestic supply in many cases. The Military Industries Organization was the largest single purchaser of machine tools in Iran; three-quarters of the metallurgical and metal-working equipment sold in Iran were imported. Military demand for plastics had to be met by imports as well because the domestic plastic industry manufactured primarily consumer goods.[42] Like Israel, Iran had, for a few years at least, enough foreign exchange to enable the necessary inputs to be purchased from abroad. Turkey, of course, has never had access to the amount of money, especially foreign exchange, necessary to implement its arms production plans as fully as some governments would have liked. Given the prevailing economic climate during the first half of the 1980s and the heavy import component of domestic arms industries, it seems unlikely that the shah, had he not been overthrown, could have continued his defense-industrial build-up at as rapid a place as planned throughout the 1980s.

Even in countries where the industrial structure is more developed than in Turkey and Iran, the links between the military and the civil sectors of industry may be minimal. David Whynes has suggested that only the largest developing countries can expect to benefit from the multiplier effects of defense industries. He considered India one of the few developing countries which could support a military industry and where civil-sector industry could supply inputs for the arms producers; yet even India has experienced difficulty in integrating its defense sector into the economy. "Backward linkages into other sectors of the economy have proved difficult to establish; invariably, demand is too small and specifications too difficult to meet."[43]

[42] Schulz, "Military Expenditures," pp. 73–74, and Schulz, "Iran," pp. 149–50.
[43] Chris Smith and Bruce George, MP, "The Defence of India," *Jane's Defence Weekly*, 2 March 1985, p. 370. See also, Peter Terhal, "Guns or Grain: Macro-Economic Costs of Indian Defence, 1960–1970," *Economic and Political Weekly*, 5 December 1981, p. 2000.

In 1966, for example, Indian military producers wanted to purchase some 350 million rupees worth of materials from civil-sector firms. Due to the limited capacity of these firms, orders were placed for only three-quarters of the desired material, and less than half the initial requirement was actually delivered. The inability of civil-sector industry to meet defense demand meant that Indian defense firms either had to import the necessary materials or produce them in-house. For instance, it was reported in the mid-1970s that Hindustan Aeronautics Ltd. (HAL) was producing approximately 70 to 80 percent of each aircraft in-house because subcontractors for many of the standard aircraft components did not exist in India. In countries with a well-developed network of subcontractors, the comparable figure is between 40 and 45 percent. The need to produce in-house has raised costs for HAL.[44] Most other companies in the defense public sector have had similar experiences.

In an attempt to resolve this problem, Indian defense producers have established their own subcontractors, but these firms tend to depend on the prime contractors for financing, technical assistance, and material.

> HAL has set up 23 Units at Bangalore, Hyderabad, Nasik and Koraput for development of ancillary industries. During 1979–80, HAL placed orders to the tune of Rs. 46.87 lakhs [approximately $500,000] on the above ancillary industries. The Company also renders technical guidance, supplies job tools and fixtures where necessary and also assists and guides the Units in setting up proper quality controls and inspection procedures etc. HAL is also bestowing its attention on establishing potential small scale industries for off-loading of jobs like manufacture of jigs, tools, fixtures, ground handling equipment, packing materials, etc. The value of orders raised on small scale industries during 1979–80 amounted to Rs. 85.69 lakhs [approximately $1 million].[45]

By 1980, Bharat Electronics Ltd. had fourteen ancillaries, and Bharat Earth Movers Ltd. had fifteen. Mazagon Dock Ltd., Goa Shipyards, and Bharat Dynamics Ltd. each had an unspecified number. To reduce the import of special metals required in weapon production, a major source of foreign exchange expenditures, the Indian government created a new defense public sector company, the Mishra Dhatu Nigam Ltd. (MIDHANI) in the 1970s. By 1981, MIDHANI had begun production,[46] but it is clear that

---

[44] Moodie, *Sovereignty*, p. 43.

[45] Government of India, Ministry of Defence, *Report, 1980–81* (New Delhi: Government of India, 1981), p. 52.

[46] Ibid., pp. 50, 52–53.

Indian defense producers will need to import a large amount of special metals for some years to come.

There are essentially two reasons for the lack of integration between the military and civil sectors of Indian industry. First, there is the difficulty in establishing backward linkages alluded to above. Because relatively small quantities of many inputs are required, domestic production becomes uneconomical if there is no civil-sector demand for the items. Due to the special nature of these inputs, civil sector demand is often too small to justify the investments that would be necessary to build up domestic production. Second, "the Indian political leadership is reluctant to open important parts of the economy to the private sector." This has severely reduced the ability of the Ministry of Defence to provide the incentives necessary to convince private industry to invest in the new production areas required by the defense-industrial sector. Were the government to reverse its policy and grant the private sector a more active role in those industries currently reserved for government ownership, a third obstacle would very likely arise: the lack of risk capital in the Indian private sector.[47]

Despite the lack of integration between military and civil-sector industry in the Third World, it has sometimes been possible to take advantage of military demand to create new industries that might not have been set up in the absence of military interest in their products. In Argentina, "by the end of the 30s, there were already military steel factories and other heavy industry plants. . . . Moreover, these enterprises were set forth as parts of an interlocking structure. For reasons of economies of scale, most of the production of these enterprises was planned for both civilian and military markets so that, in fact, military industries and industrial import substitution policies fed each other."[48] What frequently happens, however, is that a particular manufacturing capacity is created because of military demand, and the firms established subsequently expand into the civil sector. In South Korea, military demand was instrumental in setting up the textile and construction industries, in Israel, this tendency has been particularly marked, especially in the aircraft industry. Israeli Aircraft Industries has developed a number of civil aircraft, of which the Westwind Executive Jet has been quite successful on the export market. In addition, Israel Optics Ltd. and Elron (the latter originally producing

[47] Thomas W. Graham, "India," pp. 168–69, in *Arms Production in Developing Countries,* ed. Katz.

[48] José Encinas del Pando, "Economic, Military and Socio-Political Variables in Argentina, Chile and Peru (1950–1980). A Regional Analysis" (Lima: University of Lima: 1983, mimeograph) p. 32. See also V. Millán, "Argentina," p. 35, in *Arms Production,* ed. Brzoska and Ohlson.

military computers and weapon delivery systems) initially manufactured only military goods, but by the early 1980s half their output was sold in the civil sector.

Approximately half the output of India's nine defense public-sector companies is composed of goods for the civil market. Two companies, Bharat Earth Movers and Praga Tools, produce almost exclusively for the civil sector, in fact, the latter began as a civil company and was absorbed into the defense sector. Bharat Electronics increasingly produces electronic equipment and components that are purchased by both the non-military public sector and private industry. Mazagon Docks manufactures off-shore oil platforms and various nonmilitary vessels. Garden Reach also manufactures a wide range of products for the civil market: cranes, steel-plant equipment, material-handling and conveyor systems, pumps, diesel engines, generators, bailey bridges, deck machinery, and road rollers.[49]

JOB CREATION AND MANPOWER TRAINING

In the industrialized countries of the West, military production is frequently justified by the argument that it will create new jobs. In the Third World, where the expansion of the industrial sector is a goal of all governments, the job creation argument is also heard. In Israel, for example, an important rationale for the inauguration of the Kfir and Lavi aircraft programs was that they would "create thousands of jobs, and . . . serve as a brake on the brain drain of scientific and engineering talent." Overall, it has been estimated that between 10 and 15 percent of Israeli industrial workers are employed by the defense industry.[50]

In general, however, investing in arms production is not the most effective way of increasing employment. Like all capital-intensive processes, defense production employs relatively few people at a high cost per employee. In Israel, where there has been a labor shortage since the late 1960s, this might not be perceived as a serious problem, although obtain-

---

[49] Gerald Steinberg, "Israel," p. 297, in *The Structure*, ed. Ball and Leitenberg; Graham, "India," p. 159; and Government of India, *Report, 1980–81*, pp. 47–48.

[50] Proportion of industrial workers employed by defense industry based on Steinberg, "Israel," pp. 290–91; personal communication for Gerald Steinberg, 16 May 1985; Brzoska and Ohlson, ed., *Arms Production*, p. 22; and World Bank, *World Development Report, 1985* (New York: Oxford University Press, 1985), Tables 1 and 21.

The quotation is from Harkavy and Neuman, "Israel," p. 212. Harkavy and Neuman report that Israeli defense firms employ between one-third and one-half of the entire Israeli industrial labor force, but this estimate would seem much too high, unless it also includes indirect employment and is limited to the manufacturing sector. The "brain drain" argument was also made in Iran. See Schulz, "Iran," p. 155.

ing the necessary capital *has* caused difficulties. In many other major Third World arms-producing countries, and in those which aspire to increased domestic production, the annual growth in the labor force far outstrips the ability of the industrial sector to generate employment. In these countries, the creation of as many remunerative jobs as possible ought, therefore, to have priority.

It was pointed out earlier that products and production processes can sometimes be redesigned to increase their labor content. The scope of these kinds of modifications would seem extremely limited in weapon production. First, license agreements sometimes forbid the Third World producer to make any changes in the technology without the prior approval of the licensor.[51] Second, weapons have certain performance characteristics—durability, mobility, precision, and so on—which make it difficult to alter in any significant manner the way in which they are manufactured or the materials used in their construction. Companies acting as subcontractors to transnational arms producers would have no room for maneuver in this respect since their products would have to correspond exactly to the specifications of the major contractor.

More to the point in terms of Third World requirements is the upgrading of skills that arms production is believed to engender. Chapter 8 showed that although there is considerable unemployment in the Third World, among secondary school and university graduates as well as the unskilled, there are simultaneously shortages of trained technicians and other kinds of skilled manpower required by industry. Some analysts have therefore argued that if military industry enhances the skills of its employees, its developmental effect will be positive. It has been suggested, for example, that "the most important dimension in domestic arms production" may be that, in order to produce weapons, a government must "face up to the shortages in human resources. To meet its military ambitions it has to tackle some of the social barriers to development."[52]

Although there is every reason to expect that employment in the defense sector does enhance the skills possessed by some members of the workforce, it is important to put these gains into perspective. Precise figures for defense industry employment are hard to acquire, but it is nonetheless clear that for most Third World countries where arms are produced, the proportion of the industrial labor force employed by the defense sector is extremely small. Table 9–5 shows that only in Israel is a relatively large share of the industrial labor force employed in the arms

[51] Lt. Col. Gautam Sharma, "Defence Production in India," *IDSA Journal* 10: 4 (1978): 341.

[52] Gavin Kennedy, *The Military in the Third World* (London: Duckworth, 1974), p. 293.

TABLE 9-5
Share of Industrial Labor Force Employed in Arms Industry, early 1980s

Country	Employment in Arms Industry as Percentage of Industrial Employment	Estimated Direct Employment in Arms Industry
Israel	10.3	90,000
South Africa	2.0	100,000
Singapore	1.7	11,000
North Korea	1.5	55,000
Argentina	1.2	60,000
Egypt	1.0	75,000
India	0.5	280,000
Brazil	0.4	75,000
Pakistan	0.4	40,000
Indonesia	0.2	26,000
Peru	0.2	5,000
Thailand	0.2	5,000
Chile	0.2	3,000
Malaysia	0.2	3,000
South Korea	0.1	30,000
Philippines	0.1	5,000

Sources: Michael Brzoska and Thomas Ohlson, ed., *Arms Production in the Third World* (London: Taylor & Francis, 1986), p. 22; and World Bank, *World Development Report, 1985* (New York: Oxford University Press, 1985), Annex Tables 1 and 21.
Note: The data on which arms industry employment and total industrial employment have been based are frequently quite soft, and the figures presented in this table must be treated as estimates.

industry. For India, manufacturer of nearly one-third of the major weapons produced by Third World countries since 1950, and Brazil, the major Third World exporter of arms, the share is extremely small. Whatever benefits can be anticipated from defense employment, they will not be shared by more than a handful of those who work in the industrial sector in most Third World arms-producing countries.

It is also important to ask if the training received can be transferred to the civil sector. Studies of defense employees in the industrialized countries indicate that production workers are, in a sense, overtrained because of the much greater need for precision than in the civil sector. They quite simply work too slowly and with too much care for most nonmilitary production processes; this problem can fairly easily be overcome. But those who design weapons present a somewhat more difficult, although by no means insurmountable, problem. Accustomed to designing very complex equipment, they are also not particularly cost conscious. Similarly, managers, used to selling to the government, have poorly developed marketing skills.[53]

If the characteristics of many defense employees often do not fit well with the requirements of civil-sector industry in the industrialized countries, one must question their value to civil-sector industry in the Third World where the products and technologies used to manufacture them are likely to be quite different from those in the military sector. It is widely agreed that some sort of reeducation, ranging from on-the-job training to more formal courses, is necessary to transform defense employees in the industrialized countries into civil-sector employees; there is no reason to anticipate that similar retraining could be avoided for defense employees in the Third World. Thus, training received by defense-sector employees, costly to begin with, would have to be supplemented in many cases by some additional training to adapt defense workers to the civil environment. The severity of this problem would, however, vary from country to country and from sector to sector, depending on the items produced and the technology employed in both the military and the civil sectors.

It has also been suggested that demand from the defense sector for highly skilled workers may cause or exacerbate shortages in civil-sector industry while doing little to provide work for those most in need of it: the unskilled and semiskilled. "The reason for the low demand for unqualified personnel in arms production is the great complexity of weapons and the constant introduction of new types. Arms never mature and reach a significant stage of standardization in production; maturity and standardization in production, however, is a condition for the absorption of unskilled labor in the production process."[54]

[53] See, for example, Nicole Ball, "Converting Military Facilities: Shared Responsibilities and the Need for Planning," WEP 2-41/WP. 1 (Geneva: International Labour Office, October 1985, mimeograph), pp. 30–55.

[54] Herbert Wulf, "Dependent Militarism in the Periphery and Possible Alternative Concepts," p. 248, in *Arms Transfers in the Modern World*, ed. Stephanie G. Neuman and Robert F. Harkavy (New York: Praeger, 1979). This assessment may be less true for small arms which are produced in relatively large numbers, some assembly jobs in the electronic industry, and certain military vehicles and small aircraft which incorporates components used to manufacture similar equipment in the civil sector and are easily purchased on the international market. Examples of this latter category include Embraer's light transport aircraft, the Bandeirante, and armored vehicles and smaller military vehicles produced by Engesa and other Brazilian companies in the automotive industry. Not only does this equipment use many standard parts, but in some cases—notably with the Bandeirante—military and civilian versions have been manufactured.

‌ⁿ‌‌

‌‌‍‌‌‌

There is evidence from a number of countries that the military and civil sectors of industry have competed for skilled manpower. It has been reported, for example, that more R&D personnel are employed by the Indian defense sector than in private industry as a whole. A study of the Indian defense industrial sector in the 1960s concluded that the military and civil sectors were competing for scarce skilled labor. In Egypt, prior to the break with other Arab countries over the peace treaty with Israel, the Arab Organization for Industrialization was said to be developing its administrative base by taking "the best managerial talent from other industries." Since Egypt is pressing ahead with some of its defense production plans despite the withdrawal of financial support from Saudi Arabia, Qatar, and the United Arab Emirates, one can assume that skilled manpower continues to be acquired from the civil sector, although probably on a smaller scale than previously.[55]

Singapore is currently seeking to build up its capacity to produce high-technology goods, including arms. In the civil sector, one particular objective has been to enter the computer market. Although a training program is underway, it has been argued that "Singapore's labour pool of 1.2 million is too small to supply the number of skilled technicians needed by a sophisticated computer sector."[56] The same can probably be said of other high-technology sectors. In such an environment, the expansion of the defense industry can only reduce skilled manpower available to the civil sector, thereby jeopardizing important economic development programs.

Had the shah of Iran not been overthrown, the Iranian employment situation would have become highly competitive. The shah's industrialization program foresaw the creation of technologically sophisticated industries in both civil and military sectors. The military-industrial sector

---

[55] On India, see Peter Lock and Herbert Wulf, "Consequences of the Transfer of Military Technology on the Development Process," Paper prepared for the 27th Pugwash Symposium on Problems of Military-Oriented Transfer of Technology in Developing Countries, Feldafing, 22–26 November 1976 (Hamburg: IFSH, 1976, mimeograph), p. 26, and Terhal, "Guns or Grain," p. 1997. It is unclear to what extent this situation has persisted; Terhal's study covered only the period from 1960 to 1970. It is known that between 1950 and 1977, the number of scientists and technicians in India increased from 190,000 to 2.32 million. At the same time, doubts have been expressed "regarding the quality of much of the training and the available skills," and it seems likely that the defense sector would obtain a large share of the most qualified manpower. See Vaniak, "II-Changing Pattern of India's Reliance." See also Raju G. C. Thomas, *Indian Security Policy* (Princeton, N.J.: Princeton University Press, 1986), pp. 237–46.

On Egypt, see Moodie, *Sovereignty, Security and Arms*, p. 53.

[56] "Hi-Tech Vision of a Low-Growth Future," *Far Eastern Economic Review*, 14 March 1985, p. 69.

was, however, given priority. Had the expansion of the arms industry gone according to plan, it would have required tens of thousands of technicians and engineers. It has been estimated that the manpower requirements of the Iranian Aircraft Industries (IACI) alone—30,000 workers of which 3,250 were to be engineers and 6,000 technicians—would have exceeded the available supply of qualified scientific and technical personnel. Yet manpower planners did not include military manpower needs in their forecasts of the national job market. Because of the revolution, many of the shah's projects were never realized. Even so, by the time the shah was overthrown, one quarter of IACI's 3,000 employees were non-Iranians, and the foreigners held most of the skilled technical positions. If the shah's military industrialization program had continued, it would certainly have drained the civil sector of technical manpower and would simultaneously have been forced to rely even more heavily on foreign personnel.[57] (See also Chapter 8.)

Although many Third World arms producers are, like Iran, heavily dependent on foreign engineers and technical personnel from abroad and reduce their need for R&D personnel by acquiring foreign licenses, the military sector does absorb a sizable number of domestic engineers and technicians in many of the major arms-producing developing countries. This not only reduces the number of R&D personnel available to civil-sector industry, but it also increases the likelihood that nonmilitary R&D will tend toward high-technology products and processes. Third World economies need technical personnel who can both adapt foreign technology to the physical, social, and economic environments of the Third World and develop their own technologies with these same requirements in mind. This technology is not the sort normally spun off from the military-industrial sector, and the training that R&D personnel receive from the arms industries is not the kind that will encourage them to develop products in what will seem to be much more mundane technological fields.[58]

---

[57] Schulz, "Military Expenditures," pp. 72–73, 182–83, and Schulz, "Iran," pp. 153, 155.

[58] This does not mean that the military-industrial sector is incapable of designing and producing consumer goods and equipment required by civil-sector industry. Recent experience in China suggests that it can do so, if necessary. A major effort to take advantage of underutilized capacity in China's military industries began at the end of the 1970s. A decline in military procurement had left many Chinese arms producers with idle workers and machinery. A survey of defense industries in Yunnan province at the beginning of the 1980s discovered, for example, that "the labor productivity of all personnel was 38 percent lower in defense industries than in civilian industries. The productivity of metal-cutting machines was almost half of that of civilian counterparts. . . . And the profit that was realized from every 100 yuan of output was about 50 percent lower in defense compared to civil facto-

TECHNOLOGY TRANSFER

It has already been argued that the transfer of civil-sector technology from one society to another is a long-term process involving the step-by-step acquisition of technological mastery in many technical areas. Students of the military industrialization process have pointed out that arms production technology must also be mastered in stages. Different analysts have defined these stages in somewhat different ways, but all lists include the following essential elements: "The first step is the construction of repair and maintenance facilities for weapons already purchased from abroad. The assembly of knocked-down components comes next, normally followed by some kind of license production agreement. The aim, in most cases, is to proceed to local production of components using local raw materials and, eventually, to reach an indigenous design capability."[59]

Although it was always assumed that it would take time for Third World arms producers to build up the capacity necessary to produce weapons without relying on inputs of foreign technology, it is now suggested that the attainment of technological self-sufficiency may be impossible. Most analysts would agree that as long as Third World countries wish to replicate the weapons designed and produced in the industrialized countries, they will remain in a state of technological dependence. Military technology changes so fast in the latter, and its development requires both the expenditure of such large sums of money and the services

---

ries." See Richard J. Latham, "People's Republic of China: The Restructuring of Defense-Industrial Policies," p. 108, in *Arms Production in Developing Countries,* ed. Katz.

As a result of conditions such as these, a "new development strategy for military industries" was enunciated under which military firms were "to transform themselves into units serving both military and civil needs and establish links with each other and with civil enterprises." In 1980, the companies controlled by the Ministries of Nuclear Industry, Aviation, Ordnance and Space Industry sold 18 percent of their output to nonmilitary customers. By 1984, that figure had risen to 26 percent, and in 1985 it was calculated at about 40 percent. There are two other ministries in the Chinese defense-industrial structure: the Ministry of Electronics and the Ministry of the China State Shipbuilding Corporation. It is unclear how they have been affected by this policy. An extremely wide range of products is now reportedly manufactured, some of them incorporating relatively simply technology (electric fans, sewing machines, refrigerators) and others utilizing more advanced technology (chemicals, capital goods, communications equipment). See Latham, pp. 107–9, 111; "Premier on Military Industries," *China Daily,* 5 March 1986, p. 4; "Military Firms Make More Civilian Goods," *China Daily,* 21 November 1985; and "Shift in Defense Output Urged," *China Daily,* 23 November 1985.

[59] Thomas Ohlson, "Third World Arms Exporters—A New Facet of the Global Arms Race," *Bulletin of Peace Proposals* 13: 3 (1982): 214. See also Moodie, *Sovereignty,* pp. 46–47, and Miller, "Arms and the Third World," p. 7, for additional lists.

of so many engineers and other technical personnel that even the major European countries cannot produce the full complement of military equipment domestically.

In this respect, the experience of Israel is of interest. Israel's domestic industrial base is fairly well developed, and it has enjoyed the benefits of a highly educated and skilled labor force; in addition, Israel has received considerable financial assistance from the United States. As one result of this inflow of funds, Israel has been able to allocate much larger sums to military research and development than many developing countries with arms production ambitions could hope to spend. The United States, for example, essentially financed the R&D for Israel's latest aircraft project, the Lavi (which will not go into production), and for its main battle tank, the Merkava.

Israeli military industry is certainly capable of designing and producing sophisticated equipment. Yet, Israeli weapon production remains heavily dependent on foreign technology. Harkavy and Neuman report that "all modern Israeli indigenous major weapon systems contain at least one US component." For example, the Merkava uses a Teledyne engine and other U.S.-made components. Forty-five percent of the Kfir combat aircraft— the design of which is based on the French Mirage—must be imported from the United States, including the engine.[60]

The growth of what has been termed "add-up" and "add-on" engineering provides additional evidence that the last stage of domestic production—the indigenous design and manufacture of weapons—may not be attainable for many of the weapons Third World countries wish to produce. According to Michael Brzoska and Thomas Ohlson, add-on engineering "normally starts with a well-known and proven weapon, which is first imported and then produced under license, copied, or reverse-engineered. The designs are then studied, modified and adapted to specific local requirements, using available technology." The South African Impala-2 aircraft, the Israeli Nesher and Kfir aircraft, Shafrir missiles and Galil rifles, and the Egyptian Early Bird missile are all products of add-on engineering. Add-up engineering is more demanding: different components, taken from a variety of sources, are combined to form the desired weapon. Brazil has used this method to produce armored vehicles and aircraft, such as the Bandeirante, South Korea to produce howitzers and naval vessels, the Philippines to manufacture jeeps and trucks, and South

---

[60]Harkavy and Neuman, "Israel," pp. 195, 200, and Miller, "Arms and the Third World," p. 8. See also Gerald M. Steinberg, "Indigenous Arms Industries and Dependence: The Case of Israel," *Defense Analysis* 2 (December 1986): 291–305.

Africa to produce lightly armored (for example, the Eland) and nonarmored vehicles.[61]

SIPRI data show that older military technologies are easier for Third World arms producers to master,[62] and an examination of the military-industrial sector in developing countries indicates that arms producers are most successful when they gradually build up their competence over a period of years, when they have based their products on existing expertise frequently acquired in the civil sector, and when state-of-the-art technology has not been employed at too early a stage.

Brazil and South Africa have adopted this approach. In Brazil, the aircraft and motor vehicles industries, both military and civil, have been built up over a period of more than forty years. The main company in each sector—Empresa Brasileira de Aeronautica SA, Embraer, and Engenheiros Especializados SA, Engesa—have recently emerged as important suppliers to Third World armed forces. This success has been based on the production of "relatively simple, robust, and cheap light aircraft (at Embraer) and armoured vehicles (at Engesa) . . . using already existing and proven parts."[63]

Brazilian military vehicles use as many standard automobile and truck parts as possible. The Bandeirante, a twin-engine turboprop plane which

---

[61] The quotation is from Brzoska and Ohlson, *Arms Production*, p. 284; see also p. 24.
It is interesting to note that a certain amount of the technological mastery that has occurred in the defense-industrial sector has been accomplished by the "importation" of foreign technical personnel.

Design and production assistance by foreign emigrants played a major role in the early Argentine and Egyptian programmes; when they subsequently left these countries, local personnel were unable to continue production on their own. In these cases, most of the persons involved had been previously involved in the German World War II efforts. In the early 1970s many US engineers became unemployed when arms production was reduced; some of them participated in the South Korean and Taiwanese arms production programmes. South African arms production has from its inception profited from the immigration of foreign experts.

Ibid., pp. 284–85; see also p. 27; and R. Väyrynen and T. Ohlson, "Egypt: Arms Production in the Transnational Context," p. 107–8, 114–15, 117, in ibid.
At the end of 1987, it was reported that "The South African government has initiated a systematic campaign to attract engineers and technicians who worked on the Lavi [jet fighter] project." See Hirsh Goodman, "Pretoria Seeking to Lure Lavi Experts," *The Jerusalem Post*, 21 November 1987, p. 8.

[62] Brzoska and Ohlson, *Arms Production*, p. 24.

[63] Wulf, "Developing Countries," p. 339. See also Peter Lock, "Brazil: Arms for Export," pp. 79–104, in Brzoska and Ohlson, ed., *Arms Production*, and Andy Lee Ross, "Security and Self-Reliance: Military Dependence and Conventional Arms Production in Developing Countries" (Ph.D. diss., Cornell University, Ithaca, N.Y., 1984).

has proved popular on the export market, also comes in military and civil versions. Thus, economies of scale can be realized which would not be the case with more specialized weapons, for example fighter aircraft, which could neither be produced for the civil market nor draw on civil-sector expertise to the same degree as the simpler weapons. At the same time, it is important to recall that the Brazilian civil aircraft and automotive industries depend heavily on foreign technology; for example, many standard vehicle parts are either imported or produced in Brazil under license. It is thus by no means clear to what extent Brazilian technical personnel have actually mastered the technology included in the weapons they have designed.

The success that South Africa has had in building up its arms industry over the last twenty years has also been due to a concentration on comparatively simple weapons which use inputs already manufactured in the country. The limited demand for more complex weapons was initially met by producing under license. When the attempt was made to move from license to indigenous production, however, it became evident that the industrial base and available resources were insufficient to support the independent production of more sophisticated systems. Rather, the South African arms industry began to adapt foreign technology to its own requirements through add-on and add-up engineering. It has been most successful with add-on engineering, "concentrating," as Michael Brzoska has written, "on what it can do."[64]

India is one country that has attempted to follow a policy of limiting its dependence on foreign military technology as much as possible. The Indian defense industry has had varying degrees of success in indigenizing production. Certain weapons, such as small arms and military vehicles, are said to use only a minimal number of imported components; others, such as aircraft, have a much smaller indigenous content. The Indian aircraft industry has experienced certain problems in constructing its aircraft because it attempted to produce aircraft that are too sophisticated at too early a stage. Thomas Graham has argued that one success of the MIG production programs in India has been to encourage HAL to acquire technology in a more gradual and orderly fashion.

An important accomplishment of the MIG project was its positive impact on HAL's design and production strategy. Prior to this proj-

[64] Michael Brzoska, "South Africa: Evading the Embargo," p. 206, in *Arms Production,* ed. Brzoska and Ohlson. See also Michael Brzoska, "Shades of Grey: Ten Years of South African Arms Procurement in the Shadow of the Mandatory Arms Embargo," Working Papers 13, (Hamburg: IPW, Center for the Study of Wars, Armaments and Development, 1987).

ect Indian plans were extremely ambitious and great emphasis was placed on designing components indigenously. In the MIG project, HAL established a phased approach to the acceptance of foreign technology and, because of India's success in its various negotiations with the Soviet Union (1962, 1964, 1969, 1972, and 1976), HAL continually upgraded the technology it was acquiring. Since each of the three significantly different models of MIG-21 being built in India involves a 20 percent modification of the previous version, India has been able to build on its existing base while it obtains new technology.[65]

Although the establishment of a domestic capacity to produce arms is often justified in Third World countries by the technological spin-offs that can be expected from the military to the civil sector, present experience suggests that primarily the military sector benefits from know-how and other resources already available in civil-sector industry. The Brazilian and South African examples summarized here show this clearly, and it is also the case with Egypt and South Korea.[66] Different industrial branches are more or less amenable to technology transfer from the military to the civil sector. The Israeli and Indian experiences suggest that competence acquired in military electronics can be extended to civil-sector goods. Relatively few developing countries can be said, however, to have mastered military electronics to any significant extent.

In the case of military aircraft, spin-offs can be expected in the civil aviation sector, but even in industrialized countries it has been difficult to find spin-offs from aircraft production outside the aerospace sector. Discussing HAL's attempts to reduce its needs for imports, the Indian Ministry of Defense commented in the early 1980s that "The items to be indigenised cover a wide variety of materials and components which have to go through very rigid specifications and high standard of quality. Most of these materials are not used in general engineering/industry and are peculiar to the aircraft industry."[67]

A related problem is that even in the industrialized countries many technologies used to manufacture weapons are too sophisticated for the mass market. It is simply not profitable for civil-sector companies to produce goods incorporating many of the features of weapons (several back-up systems, for example) or to manufacture them by the same pro-

[65] Graham, "India," p. 172.
[66] Brzoska and Ohlson, ed., *Arms Production*, p. 288, and Katz, ed., *Arms Production in Developing Countries*, p. 9.
[67] Government of India, *Report, 1980–81*, p. 48.

CHAPTER 9

cesses as weapons.[68] In developing countries, the disparity between the needs of the mass market and the capabilities of the defense industry is, if anything, larger. The technology required to produce those goods most needed in the Third World can be acquired more readily by importing civil-sector technology than by importing military technology. Arguing that developing countries seeking to diversify and deepen their technological base should concentrate on technology developed specifically for the civil sector is by no means indicative of a desire to condemn Third World countries to technological inferiority; it is simply a recognition of the fact that military technology is an expensive source of technology, for industrialized and developing countries alike.

Military Industry and the Use of Foreign Exchange

Development of arms industries in the Third World is frequently justified by the foreign exchange savings assumed to flow from substituting domestic production for weapon imports. Herbert Wulf has suggested that it is extremely difficult for developing countries to reduce the import content of domestically produced weapons (even those characterized as "indigenous") below 30 percent. What is more, he has argued, attempts to increase the indigenous content of a weapon tends to lead to sharp rises in costs. This point is supported by Harkavy and Neuman who have commented that "domestic production for countries with small production lines and inadequate resources is more costly than off-the-shelf procurement from a country such as the United States."[69]

[68] Attempts by arms firms in the industrialized countries to produce goods for the mass market have frequently resulted in items which are technologically of very high quality but too costly to market. Even where the products have found buyers—for example, Boeing-Vertol and Rohr Corporation of California's ventures into land transport—projects have been characterized by technical surprises and excesses, as well as cost overruns. See Ball, "Converting Military Facilities," pp. 41–42.

It has been suggested that the proliferation of numerically controlled machine tools in the developed countries will help close the gap between military and civil technology, however, it is recognized that even these machines have their limits. They are most profitable when used to produce very high-quality goods. Both in terms of the goods most needed in developing countries and the high level of underutilized manpower in the Third World, it does not seem likely that such machinery will solve very many of the economic problems facing developing countries today. See *In Pursuit of Disarmament: Conversion from Military to Civil Production in Sweden, Volume 1A: Background, Facts and Analyses*, SOU 1984: 62 (Stockholm: Liber, 1984), pp. 138–39.

[69] Wulf, "Developing Countries," p. 330, and Harkavy and Neuman, "Israel," p. 213. See also Brzoska and Ohlson, ed., *Arms Production*, p. 288. It is often necessary to take the claims of Third World arms manufactures concerning the indigenous content of various weapon systems with a grain of salt. A former Indian military officer has commented that

Of concern here, however, is not total cost but outlays on imported goods and services. In the short- to medium-term, defense-related reports remain at a high level even after domestic production is inaugurated. The start-up costs of defense industries are considerable, and Third World companies cannot rely solely on domestic resources when inaugurating production. Licenses, patents, raw materials, components, subsystems, and the services of foreign technical personnel must be purchased if these companies are to function. Often, the domestic industries that provide inputs to the defense sector are themselves heavily dependent on imports. Some countries, such as India, have had a specific policy of reducing the import content of weapons to as close to zero as possible; others, for example Brazil and Singapore, have been more sanguine about their reliance on imports.[70] Equally important, domestic production does not eliminate the need to import weapons. Most Third World arms producers can only hope to produce a small range of weapons and will therefore continue to import those for which domestic production capacity does not exist. Even where a particular kind of weapon is produced locally, the armed forces may want to procure more than can be produced by domestic industry, requiring additional imports.

The question of whether domestic production reduces the total foreign exchange costs of the defense sector is difficult to answer satisfactorily

---

"indigenisation which is given in percentages of value or content is very often misleading, it being achieved by importing raw materials or components or both and the end-product bandied about as Indian." Sharma, "Defence Production," p. 340. See also Wulf, "Developing Countries," p. 337.

[70] In general, countries which have sought to limit foreign influence in their economies as a whole have also been particularly concerned to produce as much of their military equipment domestically as possible, using indigenous raw materials and R&D. Others such as Brazil and Singapore which have relied heavily on direct foreign investment to spur their economic growth have tended to be less concerned about substituting domestic for foreign resources and to welcome the participation of foreign arms producers in their defense-industrial sectors. For a comparison of import substitution in the defense industry and internationally integrated arms production, see Wulf, "Developing Countries," pp. 328–39. On the involvement of foreign firms in the defense sector in the Third World, see Helena Tuomi and Raimo Väyrynen, *Transnational Corporations, Armaments and Development: A Study of Transnational Military Technology and Their Impact on Development*, Research Reports, no. 22 (Tampere, Finland: Tampere Peace Research Institute, 1980), chaps. 4–6, and the individual chapters in Brzoska and Ohlson, ed., *Arms Production*, and Katz, ed., *Arms Production in Developing Countries*.

Finally, Lock and Wulf have pointed out that according to the U.S. government, even in countries such as Taiwan, South Korea, and the Philippines, all of which had a certain industrial base when arms production was initiated, the import costs of inaugurating the production of M16 rifles have ranged between 53 and "well over 80" percent of total costs for the first five years or so. Lock and Wulf, "Consequences," p. 17.

due to the lack of data. Defense industry imports generally cannot be distinguished from other imports for the industrial sector, and defense budgets do not reflect these costs. Based on the experience of India, Thomas Graham has suggested that developing countries cannot expect to realize foreign exchange savings for at least the first twenty years of domestic arms production. The Indian experience also demonstrates quite clearly that such savings are realized most rapidly in the fields of small arms, ammunition, and military vehicles.[71] The more sophisticated the weapon and the more electronics and special materials it incorporates, the more likely it is that the import content and foreign exchange expenditures will remain high. For example, in 1975 the average import content of Indian military aircraft was estimated at 68 percent. Although HAL has constantly strived to reduce the import content of the aircraft it produces, much remains to be done in the fields of air frames, aeroengines, and avionics.[72]

Different HAL projects have had different degrees of success in terms of saving foreign exchange. Analysts have calculated that the foreign exchange cost of producing the MIG-21 aircraft in India was roughly the same as or may even have exceeded the cost of importing finished aircraft directly from the Soviet Union. The light jet fighter Gnat Mk 1, developed together with two British firms, Folland and Bristol-Siddeley, in the late 1950s was a different story.

Initial production began in 1962. This plane proved to be effective against more sophisticated aircraft during the 1965 war with Pakistan. As a result additional orders were placed in 1966. Two hundred fourteen planes have been produced, which has allowed HAL to achieve economies of scale. The foreign-exchange ratio of imported parts and materials to cost of a completed model was positive, unlike many HAL projects. By 1971, 60 percent of the engine and 85 percent of the air-frame were indigenously produced. Most of the jigs and tools used to produce parts for the plane were manufactured in India and considerable knowledge was acquired as problems were successfully overcome.[73]

Low import content of a particular weapon is not an automatic guarantee that considerable foreign exchange savings will occur. For one

[71] Graham, "India," pp. 167–68, 173–74.
[72] Michael Brzoska, Peter Lock, Ralf Peters, Miarianne Reichel, and Herbert Wulf, "Transnational Transfer of Arms Production Technology" (Hamburg: Study Group on Armaments and Underdevelopment, IFSH, c. 1980, mimeograph), p. 62, and Government of India, *Report 1980–81,* p. 48.
[73] Graham, "India," p. 171.

thing, the items which still must be imported are likely to be the most technologically sophisticated ones—engines, special metals, electronics—and thus expensive. Special metals have been such a source of outflow of foreign exchange for the Indian defense sector that it has now created its own firm to produce these items—Mishra Dhatu Nigam (MIDHANI). The foreign exchange costs of setting up this facility must have been considerable, and it is likely that Indian imports of such metals will remain an important item on the import bill as MIDHANI builds up its production capacity. Another problem is that the domestic production of a large part of a weapon may be achieved at the expense of quantity. For example, the Indian shipyard, Mazagon Docks, has produced several domestically designed frigates, claimed to have a high indigenous content. However, because Mazagon Docks has concentrated its efforts on indigenization, it has produced fewer vessels than required by the Indian Navy; the import of frigates as well as other kinds of naval vessels has thus continued.[74]

The problem of producing sufficient numbers of weapons to meet domestic demand has confronted all Third World arms producers. Although fewer weapons may need to be imported once the domestic defense industry increases its production capacity, foreign exchange outlays for off-the-shelf weapons have not been inconsiderable, even for a country like Israel which possesses a diversified arms industry. The weapons which are, for one reason or another, not produced domestically tend to be those that are more complex and difficult to manufacture and thus come with a substantial price tag. The fact that domestic production frequently does not meet demand has led some Third World military officers to prefer imported weapons to indigenously produced ones. In addition, Third World armed forces often seek weapons incorporating technology which is as advanced as possible. Because defense industries in the developing countries remain dependent for new technology on the arms producers of the industrialized countries, particularly those in the West, they are unable to introduce innovations, assuming their technical capability, until well after these have been developed abroad. But technological progress in the field of armaments moves very quickly. Weapons produced in the Third World are frequently technically obsolete by the time they are delivered to the armed forces. Of course, this does not make them unusable, for example, the success of India's Gnat against more sophisticated Pakistani-flown aircraft in 1965 was noted above.

Even defense officials in a country as committed to domestic production as Israel sometimes question the value of indigenous production.

[74] Ibid., pp. 175–77. On claims regarding indigenous content, see note 69 above.

They point out that more advanced weapons can be procured more rapidly and often at less cost through direct imports. The Israeli Air Force, in particular, has preferred the purchase of advanced weapons from the United States to domestic production. In India, it is reported that "a tradition has emerged within the armed forces which eschews indigenous military technology, except when pragmatism is demanded."[75]

In addition to increasing the indigenous content of weapons produced domestically, foreign exchange costs can be reduced by trading foreign technology for commodities produced in the developing country and by exporting weapons. India has succeeded in reducing the foreign exchange costs of domestic arms production significantly by trading manufactures and other commodities for Soviet aviation technology. The Soviet Union has also allowed India to pay in rupees. This has enabled HAL to expand its capacity without worrying about obtaining foreign exchange to pay for its imported technology. These barter arrangements have the additional advantage of freeing foreign exchange for use by other companies in India's defense-industrial sector. India is thus able to purchase much more foreign technology than one might think given the amount of foreign exchange consumed by the defense sector.[76]

Questions have been raised about the economics of such barter arrangements. It was pointed out in Chapter 7 that some manufactured goods and other commodities exported by India to COMECON countries in payment for imports from the East bloc may have been reexported in order to earn hard currency. To the extent that this occurs, India is losing valuable foreign exchange income through these barter agreements with the USSR.[77]

Most Third World producers have sought to export weapons in order to recoup some of the foreign exchange costs involved in domestic arms production. Exports are also important in reducing the total costs of

[75] Smith and George, "The Defence of India," p. 365. See also Steinberg, "Israel," p. 303, and Harkavy and Neuman, "Israel," pp. 212–13.

[76] Graham, "India," p. 173. Graham points out that this may have had at least one negative effect.

Since the foreign-exchange requirements have appeared moderate at any particular period of time, there has been little incentive for Indian economic planners to critically review HAL's operations. This lack of financial criticism outside the Ministry of Defense has given HAL the opportunity to develop an infrastructure without the normal cyclical variation in funding that has affected many other Indian industries. It is not clear whether this had resulted in significant inefficiencies and underutilization of capacity, as suggested by some. (p. 173)

[77] Raju G. C. Thomas, *The Defence of India: A Budgetary Perspective of Strategy and Politics* (Delhi: Macmillan Company of India, 1978), pp. 134–35.

manufacturing weapons because they allow lengthened production runs. This spreads development and production costs over a greater number of weapons and reduces the unit cost. Both Brazil and Israel have strongly promoted their weapons on the world market in recent years, and both have succeeded in selling sizable amounts of military equipment. Other developing countries may export a smaller number of weapons but may be no less dependent on exports for that. Singapore's Sheng-Li Holding Company, which accounts for a large share of that country's arms production, reportedly exported half its output in 1981.[78]

Although their dependence on foreign technology may require Third World arms producers to sell as much as they can abroad, it paradoxically often limits their ability to do so. Just as transfer-of-technology agreements in the civil sector between transnational corporations and Third World firms may contain restrictions on the amount or geographic destination of Third World products, industrialized country governments may restrict the countries to which arms incorporating technology developed within their boundaries can be sold.[79] The U.S. government, for example, reserves the right to approve the sale of any weapon built with U.S. components or subsystems irrespective of where that weapon is manufactured (third-party transfers). This means that the Israelis, for example, cannot export weapons such as the Kfir and the Merkava without U.S. approval because both have U.S. engines and other U.S.-made components. A few Kfir aircraft have been sold to Latin American countries, but the Merkava had not been sold to any foreign country by 1985. The bulk of Israeli arms exports have consisted of Gabriel and Shafrir missiles, Soltam mortars, ammunition, projectiles, and bombs. Although these have

[78] The position of Industria de Material Belico do Brasil (Imbel) on exports is well known: "We will sell to the left, to the right, to the center, up above and down below. If the government authorizes it, we'll do it." Quoted in Tuomi and Väyrynen, *Transnational Corporations*, p. 155.

As far as Israel is concerned, it has been argued that military-related exports were extremely important in holding unemployment at about 4 percent in the early 1980s when exports from the civil sector declined by 30 percent. Nathan Schacher, "Kraftig bantning hotar försvaret" ("Sharp Reduction Threatened for the Military,") *Dagens Nyheter*, 13 August 1983. See also Harkavy and Neuman, "Israel," pp. 211–12.

On Singapore, see Thomas Ohlson, "The ASEAN Countries: Low-Cost Latecomers," p. 68, in *Arms Production*, ed. Brzoska and Ohlson.

[79] United Nations Conference on Trade and Development, "Major Issues Arising from the Transfer of Technology to Developing Countries," TD/B/AC.11/10/Rev. 2, 1975, pp. 18–21, discusses some of the restrictions on civil sector exports imposed by transnational corporations.

In the arms sector, these limitations may occur for economic reasons which generally leads to agreements dividing up the market or for political reasons which may shut off a portion of the market. See the discussion on India below.

brought in a good deal of money, it is clear that the inability to export the more expensive major weapons has cost Israel much needed foreign exchange income.[80]

India has faced restrictions from both West and East. For example, a license agreement with the British firm Vickers restricted the amount of spare parts for tanks that could be exported by India. It was thus able to meet only part of the demand from Jordan for these items. The licensing agreement with the Soviet Union for production of the MIG-21 prevents India from exporting spare parts for this aircraft to countries not approved by Moscow. Thomas Graham has argued that this, in effect, shuts India out of the large market for MIG spares because countries wanting to import these spares are either closely allied with the USSR and would therefore obtain the spares directly from Moscow, or, like Egypt, at political loggerheads with the USSR and would not be seen by the Soviet Union as acceptable clients. India has not exported a significant amount of military equipment to date, partly becaue of such restrictions, partly because its own export policy has been restrictive, and partly because Indian weapons do not seem to have been attractive to potential buyers. So far, most of the foreign exchange earned by the Indian defense-industrial sector has come from the sale of nonlethal equipment and services: ship repair, earth-moving equipment, railroad coaches and spare parts, civil-sector electronics.[81]

ATTAINING THE GOALS OF
MILITARY INDUSTRIALIZATION

From the foregoing discussion clearly it is extremely difficult for developing countries to attain the two main economic objectives of domestic

[80]Harkavy and Neuman, "Israel," pp. 208–9; Steinberg, "Israel," pp. 300–2; and David Lennon, "Defence Planners in a Dilemma," *Financial Times,* 27 March 1983.

[81]Thomas Graham, "India's Military Industrial Research Complex" (Paper prepared for the Panel on Impact of Defense Industries on Economies of Industrializing Countries, International Studies Association, Cincinnati, Ohio, 25 March 1982), pp. 30–31; Graham, "India," pp. 177–78; and Government of India, *Report, 1980–81,* pp. 51–52.

In 1983 it was reported that "The Indian cabinet recently took a policy decision to promote arms exports, particularly to countries in the Third World, in an effort to establish or increase India's influence in these countries while at the same time improving its own trade balance. Items to be exported include small arms, mortars, light artillery, jeeps and other military vehicles, defense electronics, and helicopters." "India Seeks European Weapons and Collaboration," *International Defense Review* no. 12 (1983): 1701.

According to Michael Brzoska, it is clear that the Indian government does want to export at least some military equipment, but since the 1983 statement appears to exclude the export of tanks, fixed-wing aircraft, and warships it seems to be following a somewhat restricted export policy. Personal communication, 5 May 1986.

arms production: the promotion of industrialization and the reduction of foreign exchange outlays in the defense sector. For domestic arms production even to be contemplated, a certain industrial/manpower base must already be in place. Most developing countries do not have a sufficiently diversified industrial sector, enough qualified manpower, the necessary production equipment, or adequate supplies of special raw materials to support a military-industrial sector of any size. Because of this weak industrial base, design and production capability must be purchased from abroad, and this frequently entails substantial outlays of scarce foreign exchange. Having established arms production facilities, Third World countries often find that these cannot be operated at full capacity, further increasing costs.

An additional problem is the relative lack of linkage between the civil and military-industrial sectors. The civil sector either cannot produce the necessary inputs in large enough quantity, cannot produce items of sufficient quality, or simply cannot produce the required items at all. This means that Third World arms producers either must manufacture these components themselves or must rely on imports. In-house production invariably raises the cost of weapons while imports make additional demands on scarce foreign exchange resources.

The military sector does, of course, provide jobs, but, because of the capital intensity of the arms production process, it will provide fewer jobs per unit of investment than many other industries. Recall this point of particular concern for developing countries: "Where the scope for choice is quite broad . . . relatively labour-intensive techniques, rather than the current 'best-practice' techniques of the industrial economies, tend typically to be more appropriate. . . ."[82] Moreover, the jobs created are for skilled workers, engineers, and technicians; they are not for the ordinary worker in the Third World whose industrial skill level tends to be fairly low. Although some workers will have their skills upgraded by employment in the military-industrial sector, they will account for only a very small proportion of the industrial labor force in most Third World countries and an insignificant share of the total labor force. The skills acquired by these individuals will, in some cases, not be directly transferrable to the civil sector. Military industrialization does not provide the answer to either the problem of unemployment/underemployment or that of human-capital formation in the Third World.

There is, in fact, good reason to fear that the implications of training manpower to design and produce weapons may be a decline in the supply of technically qualified labor in the civil sector. This is a serious problem

[82] Dahlman and Westphal, "Technological Effort," p. 110.

because the ability to diversify and deepen the technological base of developing countries depends on the existence of technical personnel capable of absorbing technology from abroad and of innovating. The absorption of a large share of a country's technical manpower by the military sector can only retard the development of technological mastery in the civil sector. In the short- to medium- term, demand for technical personnel within the military sector will be high, and it unlikely that many skilled workers or technicians trained by the arms producers will move into the civil sector, particularly if salaries are higher in the defense industries. In the longer term, the familiarity of technical personnel in the military sector with high technology products and production processes is likely to bias industrial development toward expensive, labor-saving techniques and products that do not correspond to the needs of most people in the Third World.

The following UN evaluation of the technology requirements of developing countries is no less valid now than when it was written in 1974:

> Most developing countries are heavily dependent on technologies for industrialization available in the industrialized countries. Research efforts in the developing countries to develop technologies more suited to their requirements need to be strengthened. A primary aim of technological innovation in these countries should be to make available at the lowest possible cost the basic necessities of life for the mass of the people, utilizing to the fullest extent the resources of manpower and materials available in them.[83]

A large portion of the goods produced in Third World countries today are either destined for export, primarily to the industrialized countries, or oriented toward the domestic middle and upper classes who, in most developing countries, still account for a rather limited share of the total population. Although industrial output may have expanded in many countries, quite rapidly in some, poverty has remained the lot of a significant number of people living in the Third World. This is largely due to the relative neglect of small-scale enterprises and small farmers and landless peasants.[84]

When industries are created to meet military needs, these problems are exacerbated. Large sums of money are invested in developing expertise in technologies of little relevance to the material needs of most people in the

---

[83] United Nations, Committee on Planning, Department of Economic and Social Affairs, *Industrialization for New Development Needs* (New York: United Nations, 1974), summarized in *Leading Issues in Economic Development*, ed. Gerald Meier, 3rd ed. (New York: Oxford University Press, 1976), p. 670.

[84] Keith Griffin, "Economic Development in a Changing World," *World Development* 9 (March 1982): 224.

Third World. Scarce foreign exchange, which could be used to expand the productive capacity of the civil sector and to meet some of the unfulfilled needs of the poorest numbers of society, is used for the same end. Far from reducing the foreign exchange requirements of the defense sector, domestic production of arms may actually increase them, particularly in the short- to medium term.

In an effort to recoup as much of these outflows of foreign exchange as possible, many Third World arms producers have strongly promoted weapon exports, and the number of eager sellers on the international arms market can only be expected to grow as more countries increase their arms production capacity. From a purely national economic point of view, this is of course a rational solution, at least in the short term. Eventually, however, more competition among suppliers can be anticipated. In addition, from an international economic point of view, one must ask how many exporters of arms the world can support and what effect an even greater trade in weapons will have on the economies of developing nations.

Equally serious, from a politico-military point of view, it is important to consider what effect an expansion of the international trade in weapons will have on global and regional peace and security. Most analysts agree that the expansion of Third World arms production capacity bodes ill for arms control and can only hinder attempts to resolve conflicts in a peaceful manner.[85] The Third World is replete with examples of how conflicts—both internal and external in nature—have undermined economic growth and seriously worsened the prospects for development. Thus, while the promotion of weapon exports may help individual countries overcome some of their immediate foreign exchange and balance-of-payments constraints, there is every reason to believe that the long-term economic and security effects of such a policy will be detrimental.

---

[85] See, for example, Andrew Ross, *Arms Production in Developing Countries: The Continuing Proliferation of Conventional Weapons*, N-1615-AF (Santa Monica, Calif.: Rand, October 1981), pp. 29–30; Miller, *Arms and the Third World*, pp. 35, 40–41; and Brzoska and Ohlson, ed., *Arms Production*, pp. 289–90.

10

. . . .

THE DEVELOPMENTAL ROLE OF

SECURITY EXPENDITURE

Very few development analysts have shown more than passing interest in the relationship between security expenditure and economic growth and development in the Third World. Although this apparent lack of concern for outlays which absorbed more than 15 percent of central government expenditure in about 40 percent of the developing countries between 1973 and 1983 may be politically expedient, it is counterproductive for the theory and, more important, the practice of economic development[1] (Figure 10–1). In the introduction it was shown that expenditure on the armed forces is but one of a number of factors that can contribute to the failure to generate self-sustaining economic growth; in some countries its importance is negligible or nonexistent. This cannot lead to the conclusion, however, that security expenditure can be disregarded as a source of maldevelopment in the Third World. On the contrary, expenditure in the security sector has hindered economic growth and distorted development in many parts of Asia, Africa, Latin America, and the Middle East.

A central theme of this book has been the difficulties associated with generalizing about the role played by security expenditure in the development process. Chapter 1 examined some of the theories that have been expounded over the years to explain the relationship between security expenditure and economic growth and development. Many of these theories are characterized by their failure to incorporate crucial facts. This problem has particularly afflicted those who have argued in favor of a positive developmental role for security expenditure, but it has not been absent from the theoretical constructs of those who see primarily negative consequences flowing from expenditure in the security sector. To a large

---

[1] Of the ninety-nine countries in Asia, Africa, Latin America, the Caribbean, and the Middle East shown in Figure 10-1 forty-one spent on average over 15 percent of their central government expenditure (CGE) on the military in 1973 to 1983. If expenditure on paramilitary forces were included, this figure would certainly be higher.

0 - 5%		5 - 10%	
Barbados	Mexico	Algeria	Liberia
Botswana	Niger	Bangladesh	Malawi
Brazil	Panama	Cameroon	Nepal
Costa Rica	Papua New	Colombia	Senegal
Fiji	Guinea	Cyprus	Swaziland
Gabon	Sierra Leone	Dominican	Togo
Gambia	Sri Lanka	Republic	Tunisia
Ivory Coast	Trinidad &	Ghana	Venezuela
Jamaica	Tobago	Guinea Bissau	Zaire
Lesotho		Guyana	
Mauritius		Haiti	
	[18]		[19]

10 - 15%		15 - 20%	
Argentina	Kenya	Bolivia	Morocco
Bahrain	Madagascar	Burkina Faso	Paraguay
Burundi	Malaysia	Ecuador	Philippines
Central	Nicaragua	India	Somalia
African Rep.	Nigeria	Kuwait	Thailand
Chile	Qatar	Lebanon	Zimbabwe
Congo	Rwanda	Mali	
El Salvador	South Africa	Mauritania	
Guatemala	Sudan		
Honduras			
Indonesia			
	[21]		[14]

20 - 25%		25+%	
Afghanistan	Turkey	China, PR	Saudi Arabia
Burma	Uganda	Egypt	Korea, Rep.
Chad		Iran	Syria
Ethiopia		Iraq	Taiwan
Libya		Israel	United Arab
Mozambique		Jordan	Emirates
Korea, PDR		Oman	Yemen, PDR
Singapore		Pakistan	Yemen, AR
		Peru	Zambia
	[10]		[17]

FIGURE 10-1

Average Share of Military Expenditure in Central Government
Expenditure, 99 Developing Countries, 1973–1983

Source: United States Arms Control and Disarmament Agency, *World Military Expenditures and Arms Transfers* (Washington, D.C.: ACDA, August 1985).

extent, this gap between theory and fact has arisen because of the ideological blinders worn by both proponents and opponents of security expenditure which enable them to disregard evidence that does not fit the desired pattern.

Yet even if this problem of excessive selectivity could be overcome, the possibility of ever creating an all-embracing theory of the relationship between security expenditure and economic growth and development must be judged small. Despite certain structural similarities, the considerable variations in the ways in which Third World economies actually function and in their potential for development, as well as differences in the size and nature of the security outlays of individual countries, greatly reduce the likelihood that one pattern could be discovered to describe the situation in all developing countries at all times. This volume has accordingly sought to assist the reader in identifying those areas in which security expenditure is most likely to interact with economic growth and development and to indicate the kinds of questions that should be asked to determine the nature of the interaction.

A serious problem confronting all analyses of the relation of security expenditure to growth and development is the weakness of much of the available data on security expenditure. Data validity and reliability can be improved to some extent by additional research. On the whole, however, problems with accuracy are likely to persist into the foreseeable future because of the tendency of most governments to provide as little information as possible on all security-related issues. The weakness of these data have particular relevance for econometric analyses where the quality of the conclusions depends heavily on the accuracy of the data employed; moreover, such analyses cannot incorporate the multiplicity of nonquantifiable factors, especially political relationships and policy decisions, so important in evaluating how well governments succeed in promoting development.

Despite the difficulty in obtaining accurate security expenditure data, available evidence does suggest that expenditure in the security sector is more likely to hinder than to promote economic growth and development in the Third World. Although the disadvantages of allocating human, financial, and material resources to the security sector tend to outweigh the advantages, it is important to recognize both positive and negative outcomes. This point is frequently not sufficiently appreciated by opponents of security spending. It is also important when evaluating the economic effects of security expenditure to avoid equating "can" with "will": that a particular outcome *can* occur is no guarantee that it *will* do so. Rather, experience indicates that considerable variation must be anticipated in the developmental effects of security expenditure, both positive and negative, among countries and over time.

The potential positive effects of security expenditure discussed in Chapters 5 through 9 were:

· improvement of the government's tax-collection effort,
· expansion of aggregate demand,
· creation of dual-purpose infrastructure,
· substitution of security assistance for domestic financing, increasing the resources available to the civil sector,
· stimulation of certain industrial sectors, and
· limited manpower training.

The potential negative effects identified included:

· curtailment of some kinds of public investment,
· reduction of expenditure in the social sector (for instance, education and health),
· contribution to trade imbalances,
· reduction of foreign exchange available to the civil sector,
· increase in indebtedness,
· aggravation of inflationary tendencies,
· exacerbation of biases against rural development,
· transfer of inappropriate technology,
· use of economic aid to support the security sector,
· withdrawal of technically skilled manpower from the civil sector, and
· distortion of the R&D effort.

Although taken as a group, the potential negative effects would seem to carry more economic weight than the potential positive effects, it is next to impossible to make general statements about the likelihood of any of these being experienced by individual countries. In the case of aggregate demand, for example, it was shown in Chapter 6 that benefits are most likely to be felt where excess capacity exists. Increased demand from the security sector may not, however, enable that excess capacity to be employed since output may be restricted by factors unrelated to the level of demand, such as a lack of foreign exchange to purchase production inputs from abroad. Alternatively, increased demand may stimulate production in one sector but be rendered ineffective by bottlenecks in other sectors. Similarly, the size of a country's security budget and the level of its military-related imports are no guides to the magnitude of its military-related debt. Some countries spend a considerable share of their national budget in the security sector and import a large quantity of weapons and related equipment but have adequate supplies of foreign exchange to finance these purchases without resort to borrowing. Others barter weapons for goods produced domestically. Still others receive large parts of their military-related purchases free-of-charge from their major power patrons. To reach an understanding of the effects of security expenditure on the economies of Third World countries thus requires considerable knowledge of each country's economy and the composition of its security expenditure.

One negative effect of security expenditure which has not been discussed in depth in this volume but which has serious implications for economic growth and development in the Third World is political: the strengthening of the armed forces at the expense of civilian groups within society. The political role of the armed forces and its effects on economic growth and development deserves extensive treatment, and it cannot adequately be summarized in a few paragraphs. Nonetheless, some of these effects will be discussed briefly here.

In many parts of the Third World, economic systems function primarily to benefit a relatively limited number of people, and political systems are frequently manipulated to guarantee continued élite dominance. The general public often has little or no opportunity to influence the policy-making process or to participate fully in the economic system. These domestic inequalities, along with an international economic system not designed to operate in the interests of Third World countries, are at the root of underdevelopment.

It has been argued that "There is now agreement across a wide political spectrum that the central development problems for most LDCs are internal . . . that the real solution of the development problem lies in the capacity of each of the developing countries to mobilize its resources and energies."[2] The experience of most Third World countries over the last thirty years strongly suggests that the domination of the economic and political systems by a small proportion of the population is not the best way of mobilizing "resources and energies" for self-sustaining socioeconomic development. Rather, it has proved to be an open invitation for the few—distinguished by characteristics such as class, ethnicity, religion, occupation—to exploit the many. (Most Latin American countries, of course, offer a 150-year example of this point.) The inability or un-

[2] Geoffrey Barraclough, "The Struggle for the Third World," *New York Review of Books*, 9 November 1979, p. 53. The first quotation cited by Barraclough is part of a statement by Carlos Diaz-Alejandro in Albert Fishlow, Carlos Diaz-Alejandro, Richard B. Fagen, and Roger D. Hansen, *Rich and Poor Nations in the World Economy* (New York: McGraw Hill, 1978), p. 156. The second is from "Towards a New International Order: An Appraisal of Prospects," Report on the Joint Meeting of the Club of Rome and of the International Ocean Institute, Algiers, 25–28 October 1976 (Algiers: 1977), p. 21.

willingness of many governments to deal with the primary causes of underdevelopment has led them to arm themselves against their own people as well as against potential external enemies. By relying on the armed forces to remain in power or by producing political and economic conditions that provide the military with the justification for intervention, many governments have facilitated the entry of the armed forces into the political arena.

If economic development that meets the needs of all social groups is to take place, there must be, among other things, a relatively equitable distribution of resources and a political system that both allows all groups to articulate their demands and is capable of producing workable compromises between competing interests. The greater the political power of the armed forces, the less likely it is that these requirements will be met. Most Third World armed forces have not supported the growth of participatory forms of government or the implementation of development strategies designed to promote the well-being of the poorer segments of the population. Rather, they have become important both as mediators between different élite groups (wealthy landowners, industrialists, transnational corporations, politicians, bureaucrats, communist parties) and as guarantors of élite-dominated political and economic systems. The armed forces have helped to perpetuate these systems primarily because they believe that they stand to gain more, both personally and professionally, from them than they would from more participatory systems.

By helping to maintain a system in which the state is seen as a source of wealth to be tapped by a privileged minority of the population, the armed forces seriously complicate the task of implementing structural changes necessary for the attainment of self-sustaining growth and the improvement of the lives of the poorest groups in society. This is not, however, the only way in which politically active military institutions can hinder development. It was shown in Chapter 2 that although military governments frequently raise security expenditure upon taking power, they are often unable to sustain these higher levels for more than a year or two. For the Third World as a whole, there is no clearly identifiable tendency on the part of military governments to spend more in the security sector than civilian governments. What may occur, however, and certainly has occurred in individual cases, is that a politically active military may drive up the level of security expenditure in civilian regimes as the civilians attempt to guarantee the loyalty of the armed forces, or segments of it, by increasing security-related outlays. Similarly, the greater the political strength of the armed forces, the more likely the government would be to act on military requests for the establishment or expansion of a domestic arms production capability and for the procurement of military equipment from abroad. It may also be that governments dominated by the armed forces will engage in conflict against external or domestic opponents more readily than those dominated by civilians. All of this would increase the likelihood that the negative effects of security expenditure described in Chapters 5 through 9 would be felt.

Just as security expenditure is not the sole, or even often the major, cause of many of the economic ills currently confronting the Third World, it is far from being the primary source of military authoritarianism. The heritage of authoritarian, bureaucratic rule from the colonial period, the failure of many civilian politicians in the Third World to develop a truly national consciousness, and their tendency to manipulate the political system to derive maximum benefits for the groups with which they are associated are far more important than the effects of spending a large share of the national budget in the security sector. Nonetheless, the reduction in security expenditure would clearly reduce the burden of the security sector on the economy and thereby mitigate the impact of whatever negative effects might have been generated by the security budget. It would also signal the armed forces that their economic and political roles are to be more limited in the future than they have been in the past.

The problem then becomes one of determining how significant and permanent reductions in security assistance can be achieved in individual developing countries. A government can, of course, unilaterally declare its economic situation so precarious that austerity measures are necessary, and the armed forces must accept its share of the cuts. Such a policy is likely to succeed only in the short term if no attempts are made to alter the environment in which decisions about security expenditure are made. The most frequently discussed means of reducing security-related outlays of Third World countries are reductions in the arms trade and regional conflict resolution. In the absence of supplier control—extremely difficult to achieve even in isolated instances and nearly impossible to effectuate across-the-board—it is unlikely that reductions in the arms trade will occur as long as interstate conflicts remain unresolved. The resolution of outstanding conflicts would have the dual benefit of removing some justification for security expenditure and reducing the opportunities for foreign military intervention which frequently exacerbates local and regional conflicts.[3]

[3] Upon assuming office in July 1985, the Peruvian President Alan Garcia Pérez made the following proposal:

I proclaim the need for a regional agreement to reduce expenditure on armaments and freeze the acquisition thereof, in conformity with the spirit of the Declaration of Ayacucho signed in 1974, believing, as in the case of indebtedness, that it is essential

It is not clear, however, how much of an effect conflict resolution would have on the allocation of resources to the security sector in the Third World. The widely held assumptions that high levels of military expenditure are primarily caused by externally generated or supported conflicts and that military expenditure in Third World countries consists mainly of weapon procurement were shown in Chapters 2 and 3 frequently to be at odds with the facts. It is true that those countries which allocate the greatest amount of resources to their security sectors tend to be those engaged in active war or in a long-standing conflict that periodically erupts into war. It is equally true, however, that fewer interstate wars would not necessarily reduce the incentive to maintain security forces. It was explained in Chapter 2 that the internal security role of the armed forces is considerable throughout the Third World and, in many cases, is their primary function. The examination of the available data on the composition of security expenditure supports the notion of the primacy of the internal political role. Even allowing for significant underreporting of procurement expenditures, most Third World countries appear to spend a very high proportion of their security budgets on operating costs, particularly salaries and emoluments for the troops. These two factors suggest that it will be difficult to produce large reductions in the level of Third World security expenditure simply by imposing limitations on the arms trade and by encouraging the resolution of inter-

---

to proceed from words and good intentions to action and example. In keeping with this principle, I hereby announce to the peoples of the world our decision to reduce substantially all purchases of war material, beginning with a cut in the number of Mirage aircraft we are at present negotiating to purchase.

"Letter Dated 7 August 1985, Addressed to the President of the Conference on Disarmament from the Acting Chargé d'Affaires of the Delegation of Peru, Transmitting the Proposal on Regional Disarmament Formulated by the Constitutional President of Peru, Dr. Alan García Pérez, in his Inaugural Message on Taking Office on 28 July 1985," CD/631 (New York: United Nations, 7 August 1985).

On 29 July, a number of Latin American heads of government who had attended the García inauguration signed a "Declaration of Lima" in which they state that a reduction in military expenditure and the application of resources to the creation of confidence building measures was considered "positive and convenient." See "Peru at a Final Crossroads," *FAS Public Interest Report* 39 (April 1986): 4.

The Peruvian decision to reduce its military outlays was probably primarily motivated by its economic crisis, including a heavy debt burden. According to U.S. Arms Control and Disarmament Agency, *World Military Expenditures, 1985*. Peruvian military expenditure averaged 25.9 percent of total central government expenditure between 1973 and 1983, by far the highest level of security expenditure in South America. It also owes a not inconsiderable proportion of its debt to military purchases (see Chapter 5).

state conflicts. This does not mean that such activities are not in themselves desirable and may not lead to somewhat smaller security budgets. But unless domestic inequalities can also be greatly reduced and strong domestic political systems controlled by civilians and responsive to the needs of all groups within society are established, sustained reductions in Third World security expenditure are unlikely.

APPENDIXES

APPENDIX 1
Preponderance of Operating Costs in Third World Security Budgets,[a] 1951–1979
(in percentage of total security expenditure)

Country	1951	1952	1953	1954	1955	1956	1957	1958	1959	1960	1961	1962	1963	1964
ASIA														
India[b]														
Operating Costs[c]	93.5	94.6	93.4	93.8	91.0	90.3	89.5	88.8	85.9	84.6	84.9[d]	83.4[d]	81.1[d]	79.7[d]
Personnel Costs	45.4	45.4	44.6	44.8	45.9	42.8	37.2	36.4	38.4	38.6	42.0[d]	32.3[d]	25.6[d]	27.4[d]
Iran[e, f]														
Operating Costs[c]														87.0
Malaysia[b]														
Operating Costs[c]													75.8	75.6
Personnel Costs													49.1	45.7
Pakistan[e]														
Operating Costs[c]	53.6	66.1	77.0	79.0	79.1	83.9	90.9	89.4	86.5	86.1	87.8	91.9	94.6	92.5
Philippines[b]														
Operating Costs[c]	99.7	99.4	99.3	99.6	99.6	99.1	99.1	96.2	98.3	94.6	99.3	99.2	98.4	99.0
Personnel Costs	62.7	61.3	74.4	59.8	80.8	78.5	75.9	68.5	79.4	72.6	72.4	70.2	76.1	83.9
Sri Lanka[e]														
Operating Costs[c]	76.5	63.5	84.3	63.9	72.6	73.5	77.0	77.9	73.0	77.5	88.8	94.7	92.9	93.2
Personnel Costs	50.1	41.8	56.8	44.2	47.6	46.9	47.2	43.6	43.5	48.1	59.8	72.8	69.0	68.9

(APPENDIX 1 CONT.)

Country	1965	1966	1967	1968	1969	1970	1971	1972	1973	1974	1975	1976	1977	1978	1979
ASIA															
India[b]															
Operating Costs[c]	82.3[d]	80.6[d]	80.3[d]	81.4[d]	80.4[d]	79.8[d]	80.5[d]	82.1[d]	81.6[d]	81.8[d]	82.3[d]	80.8[d]	80.6[d]	82.4[d]	81.6[d]
Personnel Costs	38.5[d]	33.7[d]	—	—	—	—	—	—	—	—	—	—	—	—	—
Iran[c,f]															
Operating Costs[c]	82.4	79.0	56.8	62.4	55.6	48.1	42.9	42.5	25.7	20.9	29.6	30.6	—	—	—
Malaysia[b]															
Operating Costs[c]	80.3	70.3	76.5	77.9	77.7	76.1	80.7	79.4	88.6	81.7	84.3	73.1	75.2	—	—
Personnel Costs	46.6	41.9	47.2	49.0	48.7	43.5	47.8	53.0	53.7	46.8	44.3	47.0	51.4	—	—
Pakistan[e]															
Operating Costs[c]	g	g	g	g	g	g	g	g	g	g	g	g	g	g	g
Philippines[b]															
Operating Costs[c]	99.6	99.5	98.9	97.7	97.4	98.3	98.0	96.9	93.4	96.8	90.8	90.2	91.9	—	—
Personnel Costs	82.2	80.1	72.4	68.8	69.3	69.2	67.0	56.0	55.7	60.7	38.5	49.4	43.5	—	—
Sri Lanka[e]															
Operating Costs[c]	95.1	84.2	86.7	91.8	92.3	85.2	75.2	84.7	93.9	93.1	84.9	92.2	90.9	—	—
Personnel Costs	72.0	68.2	65.4	66.4	66.5	60.9	50.6	58.2	64.7	65.7	55.8	59.2	60.5	—	—

(APPENDIX 1 CONT.)

Country	1951	1952	1953	1954	1955	1956	1957	1958	1959	1960	1961	1962	1963	1964
AFRICA														
Ghana[e]														
Operating Costs[c]									91.9	68.1	59.5	71.6	88.0	60.6
Liberia[h]														
Operating Costs[c]					98.6	95.8	95.6	99.3	97.9	98.5	—	97.9	—	—
Personnel Costs					50.3	58.4	49.9	50.9	57.1	55.6	—	39.6	—	—
Malagasy Republic[h]														
Operating Costs[c]											97.0	98.2	97.7	96.5
Personnel Costs[c]											72.2	64.2	74.1	67.8
Morocco[i]														
Operating Costs[c]						90.7	82.9	60.5	70.3	90.0	91.2	93.6	94.6	—
Nigeria[b]														
Operating Costs[c]										91.6	79.8	59.2	57.9	59.5
Sierra Leone[b]														
Operating Costs[c]											97.6[m]	97.6[m]	93.6[m]	93.7[m]

(APPENDIX 1 CONT.)

Country	1965	1966	1967	1968	1969	1970	1971	1972	1973	1974	1975	1976	1977	1978	1979
AFRICA															
Ghana[e]															
Operating Costs[c]	60.5	80.8	91.1	91.4	91.1	82.9	80.7	82.0	82.0	74.7	70.2	75.1	78.4	71.3	—
Liberia[h]															
Operating Costs[c]	94.3	99.7	87.5	95.4	—	—	89.5	—	—	—	92.1	91.8	95.1	95.1	91.9
Personnel Costs	52.9	57.1	48.5	56.6	—	—	47.8	—	—	—	79.1	77.3	45.3	42.1	72.0
Malagasy Republic[h]															
Operating Costs[c]	97.5	97.9	95.0	95.4	97.3	99.1	98.6	98.2	96.8	95.4	98.1	85.2	96.1	91.9	84.7
Personnel Costs	72.9	71.7	71.5	71.1	73.4	74.5	69.9	72.2	72.4	64.4	67.9	55.2	67.5	57.5	54.3
Morocco[i]															
Operating Costs[c]	—	96.9[j]	96.4[j]	96.0[j]	99.5[j]	97.3[j]	—	—	81.5[j]	—	71.3[j]	58.8[j]	54.4[j]	66.5[j]	67.5[j]
Nigeria[b]															
Operating Costs[c]	55.3	59.8	39.7	56.9	68.2	78.7	85.6	88.4	81.3	67.0	66.4	59.1	55.5	48.0[k]	46.2[k]
Sierra Leone[b]															
Operating Costs[c]	94.1	96.1[h]	92.8[h]	93.7	92.6	92.6[e]	95.7	96.9[m]	96.2[m]	95.9[m]	96.5[e]	82.7[h]	—	—	—

Country	1951	1952	1953	1954	1955	1956	1957	1958	1959	1960	1961	1962	1963	1964
LATIN AMERICA														
Argentina[b]														
Operating Costs[c]	67.4	73.5	64.2	64.0	66.4	77.1	77.4	84.8	84.3	82.5	82.4	84.0	87.2	88.5
Brazil[h]														
Operating Costs[c]														
Personnel Costs														
Chile[b]														
Operating Costs[c]	g	g	g	g	g	g	g	g	g	g	94.4	96.6	96.2	96.9
Colombia[i]														
Operating Costs[c]	95.8	84.6	93.2	87.8	74.0	77.3	80.5	93.3	94.9	93.2	97.4	98.6	98.7	96.4
Guyana[b]														
Operating Costs[c]														
Personnel Costs														
Nicaragua[h]														
Operating Costs[c]						74.5	76.9	85.5	94.0	94.6	95.6	95.8	95.8	96.3
Trinidad & Tobago[b]														
Operating Costs[c]												94.6	92.9	85.2
Personnel Costs												80.9	77.3	70.6
Venezuela[h]														
Operating Costs[c]											93.2	96.1	95.9	—
Personnel Costs											66.3	68.5	67.2	—

Country	1965	1966	1967	1968	1969	1970	1971	1972	1973	1974	1975	1976	1977	1978	1979
LATIN AMERICA															
Argentina[b]															
Operating Costs[c]	87.8	89.4	84.4	83.4	83.3	84.3	78.9	76.1	82.1	80.7	67.8	65.1	56.0	65.3	67.5[e]
Brazil[h]															
Operating Costs[c]							83.7	87.0	83.1	78.2	84.3	83.5	84.1	83.7	85.0
Personnel Costs							70.7	75.7	73.5	62.3	65.4	60.9	61.7	61.7	68.3
Chile[b]															
Operating Costs[c]	96.8	97.2	97.4	97.7	97.6	98.9	98.5	96.0	94.2	88.6	92.3	95.4	96.9	96.9	95.7
Colombia[i]															
Operating Costs[c]	97.8	96.5	97.4	91.2	93.3	85.6	51.9	72.8	81.0	—	—	—	—	—	—
Guyana[b]															
Operating Costs[c]		85.1	85.5	91.6	97.9	97.6	96.2	97.3	92.6	91.2	81.2	76.4	86.6	98.2[h]	97.4[h]
Personnel Costs		64.7	64.3	65.8	64.5	60.8	65.1	65.6	63.2	61.6	43.8	g	g	g	g
Nicaragua[h]															
Operating Costs[c]	96.3	96.7	93.5	94.7	96.1	—	—	96.6	97.8	89.8	92.3	99.1	—	99.2	100.0
Trinidad & Tobago[b]															
Operating Costs[c]	90.4	96.3	98.7	97.3	98.1	89.9[h]	90.2[h]	98.4	95.4	—	—	—	—	—	—
Personnel Costs	74.4	79.9	83.5	82.9	84.1	74.8[h]	76.5[h]	78.6	74.4	—	—	—	—	—	—
Venezuela[h]															
Operating Costs[c]	94.7	92.5	89.0	89.6	—	92.2	94.0	81.7	—	—	—	—	—	—	—
Personnel Costs	64.9	61.3	62.1	63.1	—	63.1	69.9	61.8	—	—	—	—	—	—	—

(APPENDIX 1 CONT.)

a Security expenditure includes outlays on police/paramilitary forces.
b Based on actual expenditure.
c Operating costs are composed of personnel costs and operations and maintenance costs.
d These values are slightly underestimated because it was impossible to disaggregate police/paramilitary outlays.
e Based on a combination of actual and estimated expenditure.
f Outlays on the Ministry of Defense only.
g No disaggregation of data possible.
h Based on estimated expenditure.
i Based on approved estimates.
j These estimates are less reliable than those for other years.
k Based on provisional expenditure.
m Recurrent expenditure only; no development budget available.

Source: Derived from country budgets collected by the author. Data for security expenditure in current local currencies disaggregated according to operating, capital, and research and development costs for military forces, police/paramilitary forces, and military industry are available in Nicole Ball, *Third-World Security Expenditure. A Statistical Compendium,* FOA Report C10250-M5 (Stockholm: National Defense Research Institute, 1984).

APPENDIX 2
Definitions of Military Expenditure

INTERNATIONAL MONETARY FUND

In IMF publications, the category defense " . . . covers all expenditure, whether by defense or other departments for the maintenance of military forces, including the purchase of military supplies and equipment (including the stockpiling of finished items but not the industrial raw materials required for their production), military construction, recruiting, training, equiping, moving, feeding, clothing and housing members of the armed forces, and providing remuneration, medical care, and other services for them. Also included are capital expenditures for the provision of quarters to families of military personnel, outlays on military schools, and research and development serving clearly and foremost the purpose of defense. Military forces also include paramilitary organizations such as gendarmerie, constabulary, security forces, border and customs guards, and other trained, equipped and available for use as military personnel. Also falling under this category are expenditure for purposes of strengthening the public services to meet wartime emergencies, training civil defense personnel and acquiring materials and equipment for these purposes. Included also are expenditure for foreign military aid and contributions to international organizations and alliances.

This category excludes expenditure for nonmilitary purposes though incurred by a ministry or department of defense, and any payments or services provided to war veterans and retired military personnel." *Source:* International Monetary Fund, "Manual on Government Finance Statistics," draft.

UNITED STATES ARMS CONTROL AND DISARMAMENT AGENCY

"Data on NATO country military expenditures were obtained from NATO publications and are based on NATO definitions. In summary, (a) civilian-type expenditures of each NATO defense ministry are excluded but military-type expenditures of other ministries are included; (b) grant military assistance is included in the expenditures of the donor country; and (c) purchases of military equipment for credit are included at the time the debt is incurred, not at the time of payment."

403

"For other non-communist countries, data are generally the expenditures of the ministry of defense. When these are known to include the costs of internal security, an attempt is made to remove these expenditures. . . ."

"In some of these cases (as indicated in the footnotes of Table I), it is believed that a better estimate of total military expenditures is obtained by summing the value of arms imports shown in Table II (as converted to local currency by current exchange rates) with nominal military expenditures. . . ."

"Particular problems arise in estimating the military expenditures of communist countries due to the exceptional scarcity and ambiguity of released information. As in the past eight editions of this publication, data on Soviet military expenditures are based upon Central Intelligence Agency (CIA) estimates of what it would cost in the United States in dollars to develop, procure, staff and operate a military force similar to that of the Soviet Union. . . ." *Source:* U.S. Arms Control and Disarmament Agency, *World Military Expenditures and Arms Transfers,* Publication 123 (Washington, D.C.: ACDA, August 1985), pp. 139–40.

STOCKHOLM INTERNATIONAL PEACE RESEARCH INSTITUTE

"The NATO definition of military expenditure is used as a guideline throughout. Where possible, the following items are *included:* all current and capital expenditure on the armed forces and in the running of defence departments and other government agencies engaged in defence projects; the cost of paramilitary forces and police when judged to be trained and equipped for military operations; military R & D, tests and evaluation costs; costs of retirement pensions of service personnel, including pensions of civilian employees. Military aid is included in the budget of the donor country. *Excluded:* civil defense, interest on war debts and some types of veterans' payments." *Source:* Stockholm International Peace Research Institute, *World Armaments and Disarmament, SIPRI YEARBOOK 1985* (London: Taylor & Francis, 1985), p. 285.

APPENDIX 3
Major Empirical Studies of the Growth- Military Expenditure Relationship

Study	Time Period	Countries	Main Hypotheses/Purpose
A. Benoit	1950–1965	44 LDCs	Defense burden and rate of growth of civilian national product are inversely correlated: higher defense burden associated with lower rates of growth.
B. Whynes	1972–1977	91 countries of which 59 LDCs	Test the validity of Benoit's findings.
C. Faini, Arnez, and Taylor (MIT group)	1952–1970	48 LDC 15 DCs 6 Not Classified (Spain, Greece, Portugal, South Africa, Yugoslavia, Israel)	Test the validity of Benoit's findings.

Sources:

Emile Benoit, *Defense and Economic Growth in Developing Countries* (Lexington, Mass.: Lexington, 1973).

David Whynes, *The Economics of Third World Military Expenditure* (London: MacMillan, 1979).

Riccardo Faini, Patricia Arnez, and Lance Taylor, "Defense Spending, Economic Structure and Growth: Evidence Among Countries and Over Time" (Cambridge, Mass.: MIT, October 1980, mimeograph).

Variables Tested	Conclusions (LDCs Only)
A. 1. Defense burden: milex as % civilian GDP. 2. Civilian GDP: GDP minus milex. 3. Growth rate: percentage increase in GDP. 4. Bilateral economic aid: government-to-government economic aid, *no* military aid. 5. Rate of investment: gross capital formation as % GDP.	1. Strong positive correlation between defense burden and growth rate for simple correlation. 2. Influence of aid and investment may have been more important on growth. 3. Nonetheless, there *could* be a significant positive causal link between defense burden and growth. 4. Unable to establish whether net effects positive or negative; believe, however, that on balance net effects positive.
B. 1. Annual defense expenditure growth rate. 2. Defense expenditure as % GDP (1977 only). 3. Annual growth rate of per capita income. 4. Per capita income (1977 only).	1. Strong correlation between growth of defense expenditure and growth of per capita income (.496 for LDCs). 2. Positive (but not very strong) relationship between defense burden (variable 2) and per capita income. 3. It is likely that higher defense expenditure leads to higher growth *and* vice versa. Depends on situation.
C. 1. Growth of GDP. 2. Growth of exports. 3. Growth of population. 4. Growth of defense burden (milex as % GDP). 5. Growth of capital inflows. 6. Growth of capital stock.	1. Milex has clear negative effect on growth rate. 2. Export expansion improves growth rate. 3. Population growth (outside Africa) promotes growth. 4. Capital inflows promote Latin American growth but hinder it in other LDCs.
1. Defense burden. 2. Investment as % GDP. 3. Imports as % GDP. 4. Industry as % GDP. 5. Agriculture as % GDP. 6. Tax receipts as % GDP.	Rising defense burden implies 1. Decline in investment/GDP. 2. Very small decline in imports/GDP. 3. Increase in industry/GDP. 4. Decline in agriculture/GDP. 5. Strong increase in tax receipts/GDP. When data for India alone run: 1. Fairly strong *positive* relation between defense burden and investment/GDP. 2. Significant *negative* relation between defense burden and agriculture/GDP. 3. Negative but not significant relation between defense burden and growth of civilian GDP and total GDP.

Study	Time Period	Countries	Main Hypotheses/Purpose
D. Deger and Smith (University of London group)	1965–1973	50 LDCs	Test hypothesis that military expenditure can promote economic growth in LDCs by increasing savings ratio.
E. Lim	1965–1973	54 LDCs (including Greece)	Test the validity of Benoit's findings.
F. Frederiksen and Looney	1950–1965	Benoit's 44 LDCs	1. Negative relation between defense burden and growth for poorer LDCs because they must choose between defense and investment. 2. Positive relation between defense burden and growth for richer LDCs as they do not have to choose.
G. Brzoska and Wulf	1966–1975	92 LDCs	Test the validity of Benoit's findings for a later period.
H. Ravenhill	1960–1973	33 African LDCs	None explicitly stated.

Sources:

Saadet Deger and Ron Smith, "Military Expenditure and Growth in Less Developed Countries," *The Journal of Conflict Resolution* 27 (June 1983): 335–53.

David Lim, "Another Look at Growth and Defense in Less Developed Countries," *Economic Development and Cultural Change* 31 (January 1983): 377–84.

P. C. Frederiksen and Robert E. Looney, "Defense Expenditures and Economic Growth in Developing Countries," *Armed Forces and Society* 9 (Summer 1983): 633–45.

Michael Brzoska and Herbert Wulf, "Rejoinder to Benoit's 'Growth and Defense in Developing Countries': Misleading Results and Questionable Methods" (Hamburg: IFSH-Arbeitsgruppe Rüstung und Unterentwicklung, c. 1980, mimeograph).

John Ravenhill, "Comparing Régime Performance in Africa: The Limitations of Cross-National Aggregate Analysis," *Journal of Modern African Studies* 18: 1 (1980): 99–126.

Variables Tested	Conclusions (LDCs Only)
D. 1. Average annual increase in GDP. 2. Savings as % national income. 3. Military burden: milex as % GDP.	1. The indirect effect of military burden on growth via savings is negative.
E. 1. Incremental capital-output ratio. 2. Military expenditure as % GDP. 3. Military expenditure as % CGE. 4. Deficit on current account/gross national savings ratio.	1. Military expenditure in Africa and Western hemisphere LCDs adversely affects growth but no adverse effect for Asia or Mid-East/South European LDCs. 2. For a given investment ratio made possible by a surplus of the sum of domestic and foreign capital over defense expenditure, a higher productivity of capital tends to produce a higher rate of growth.
F. 1. Defense burden: milex as % GDP. 2. Capital formation as % GDP. 3. Receipts of bilateral aid as % GDP. 4. Real growth of GDP minus real growth of defense expenditures.	1. Defense expenditure in relatively resource unconstrained countries competes less for scarce resources. 2. For the resource constrained countries defense expenditure siphons funds from investment and leads to slower growth.
G. 1. Growth rate of civilian GDP. 2. Defense burden: milex as % GDP.	1. No very clear relationship between variables evident from simple regression analysis for entire sample. 2. Significant *positive* relationship for OPEC plus Oman group of countries. 3. Significant *negative* correlation for most seriously affected countries and all countries minus OPEC.

H. 1. Rate of growth of milex.
2. Level of milex as % GNP.
3. Level of development (GNP in 1960).
4. Level of GNP.
5. Level of gross domestic investment.
6. Constant export.
	1. Significant *negative* relation between level of development and rate of growth of milex.
	2. *Negative* but not significant relation between milex as % GDP and
	  a. GNP
	  b. gross domestic investment
	  c. constant exports.

APPENDIX 4
Security Forces as a Proportion of Economically Active Population in the Third World, 1980

Country and Region	Security Forces[a] (thousands)			15–44 Year Old Males			Population in 15–64 Year Old Group					
	Armed Forces	Para-military Forces	Total	Thousands[b]	Armed Forces as %	Total Security as %	Males (thousands[b])	Armed Forces as %	Total Security as %	Males and Females (thousands[b])	Armed Forces as %	Total Security as %
MIDDLE EAST												
Iran	195.0	75.0	270.0	8,072	2.4	3.3	9,939	2.0	2.7	19,646	1.0	1.4
Iraq	252.5	79.8	332.3	2,753	9.2	12.1	3,382	7.5	9.8	6,657	3.8	5.0
Israel	172.0	4.5	176.5	847	20.3	20.8	1,141	15.1	15.5	2,295	7.5	7.7
Jordan	67.5	11.0	78.5	680	9.9	11.5	830	8.1	9.5	1,615	4.2	4.9
Kuwait	12.4	18.0	30.4	320	3.9	9.5	394	3.1	7.7	704	1.8	4.3
Lebanon	20.3	7.5	27.8	530	3.8	5.2	708	2.9	3.9	1,468	1.4	1.9
Oman	14.5	3.3	17.8	187	7.8	9.5	235	6.2	7.6	463	3.1	3.8
Qatar	9.7	0.0	9.7	99	9.8	9.8	120	8.1	8.1	157	6.2	6.2
Saudi Arabia	51.7	36.5	88.2	2,193	2.4	4.0	2,665	1.9	3.3	4,765	1.1	1.9
Syria	222.5	9.8	232.3	1,819	12.2	12.8	2,266	9.8	10.3	4,427	5.0	5.2
Turkey	569.0	120.0	689.0	10,134	5.6	6.8	13,112	4.6	5.5	25,716	2.3	2.8
United Arab Emirates	43.0	—	—	326	13.2	—	379	11.3	—	489	8.8	—
Yemen, PDR	24.3	15.0	39.3	361	6.7	10.9	460	5.3	8.5	953	2.5	4.1
Yemen, AR	32.1	20.0	52.1	954	3.4	5.5	1,310	2.5	4.0	2,963	1.1	1.8
NORTH AFRICA												
Algeria	101.0	10.0	111.0	3,653	2.8	3.0	4,520	2.2	2.5	9,292	1.1	1.2
Egypt	367.0	139.0	506.0	9,503	3.9	5.3	12,011	3.1	4.2	23,807	1.5	2.1
Libya	55.0	5.0	60.0	667	8.2	9.0	833	6.6	7.2	1,521	3.6	3.9
Morocco	120.0	30.0	150.0	4,048	3.0	3.7	5,091	2.4	2.9	10,340	1.2	1.5
Sudan	71.0	3.5	74.5	3,945	1.8	1.9	4,926	1.4	1.5	9,734	0.7	0.8
Tunisia	28.6	8.5	37.1	1,338	2.1	2.8	1,740	1.6	2.1	3,483	0.8	1.1

Country and Region	Security Forces[a] (thousands)			15–44 Year Old Males			Population in 15–64 Year Old Group					
	Armed Forces	Para-military Forces	Total	Thou-sands[b]	Armed Forces as %	Total Security as %	Males (thou-sands[b])	Armed Forces as %	Total Security as %	Males and Females (thou-sands[b])	Armed Forces as %	Total Security as %
SUB-SAHARAN AFRICA												
Angola	33.0	9.0	42.0	1,448	2.2	2.9	1,837	1.8	2.3	3,757	0.9	1.1
Bénin	3.1	1.1	4.2	708	0.5	0.6	882	0.4	0.5	1,803	0.2	0.2
Botswana	2.0	1.3	3.3	140	1.4	2.4	162	1.2	2.0	384	0.5	0.9
Burkina Faso	3.8	0.9	4.7	1,427	0.3	0.3	1,795	0.2	0.3	3,632	0.1	0.1
Burundi	6.0	1.5	7.5	898	0.7	0.8	1,134	0.5	0.7	2,324	0.3	0.3
Cameroon	7.3	5.0	13.3	1,723	0.4	0.8	2,241	0.3	0.6	2,590	0.2	0.3
Cape Verde	3.0	0.0	3.0	78	3.8	3.8	96	3.1	3.1	117	2.6	2.6
Central African Republic	2.4	3.0	5.4	463	0.5	1.2	595	0.4	0.9	1,243	0.2	0.4
Chad	3.2	6.0	9.2	927	0.3	1.0	1,192	0.3	0.8	2,434	0.1	0.4
Congo, Republic of	9.6	3.9	13.5	314	3.1	4.3	401	2.4	3.4	819	1.2	1.6
Ethiopia	230.0	169.0	399.0	6,593	3.5	6.1	8,192	2.8	4.9	16,471	1.4	2.4
Gabon	1.9	2.8	4.7	120	1.6	3.9	166	1.1	2.8	335	0.6	1.4
Gambia	0.0	0.7	0.7	125	0.6	0.6	156	0.0	0.4	318	0.0	0.2
Ghana	15.3	5.0	20.3	2,337	0.7	0.9	2,905	0.5	0.7	5,916	0.3	0.3
Guinea	9.9	9.2	19.1	1,039	1.0	1.8	1,321	0.7	1.4	2,670	0.4	0.7
Guinea-Bissau	6.2	5.0	11.2	121	5.1	9.3	163	3.8	6.9	326	1.9	3.4
Ivory Coast	6.0	5.5	11.5	1,847	0.3	0.6	2,289	0.3	0.5	4,291	0.1	0.3
Kenya	14.7	8.0	22.7	3,039	0.5	0.7	3,757	0.4	0.6	7,644	0.2	0.3
Lesotho	0.0	4.5	4.5	280	0.0	1.6	364	0.0	1.2	734	0.0	0.6
Liberia	5.4	1.7	7.1	395	1.4	1.8	484	1.1	1.5	974	0.6	0.7
Madagascar	20.9	6.0	26.9	1,788	1.2	1.5	2,265	0.9	1.2	4,642	0.5	0.6
Malawi	5.0	0.6	5.6	1,220	0.4	0.5	1,502	0.3	0.4	3,072	0.2	0.2
Mali	4.9	5.0	9.9	1,409	0.3	0.7	1,762	0.3	0.6	3,602	0.1	0.3

(APPENDIX 4 CONT.)

Country and Region	Security Forces[a] (thousands)			15–44 Year Old Males			Population in 15–64 Year Old Group					
	Armed Forces	Para-military Forces	Total	Thou-sands[b]	Armed Forces as %	Total Security as %	Males (thou-sands[b])	Armed Forces as %	Total Security as %	Males and Females (thou-sands[b])	Armed Forces as %	Total Security as %
SUB-SAHARAN AFRICA												
Mauritania	9.8	1.5	11.3	333	2.9	3.4	413	2.4	2.7	838	1.2	1.3
Mauritius	0.0	0.4	0.4	232	0.0	0.2	291	0.0	0.1	586	0.0	0.1
Mozambique	26.7	2.0	28.7	2,120	1.3	1.4	2,707	1.0	1.1	5,543	0.5	0.6
Niger	2.2	2.1	4.3	1,076	0.2	0.4	1,334	0.2	0.3	2,702	0.1	0.2
Nigeria	156.0	0.0	156.0	15,413	1.0	1.0	18,995	0.8	0.8	38,663	0.4	0.4
Rwanda	5.1	1.2	6.3	953	0.5	0.7	1,187	0.4	0.5	2,428	0.2	0.3
Senegal	9.6	2.3	11.9	1,169	0.8	1.0	1,471	0.7	0.8	2,976	0.3	0.4
Sierra Leone	2.7	0.8	3.5	453	0.6	0.8	894	0.3	0.4	1,834	0.1	0.2
Somalia	62.6	9.5	72.1	834	7.5	8.6	1,061	5.9	6.8	2,465	2.5	2.9
Swaziland	0.3	1.0	1.3	113	0.3	1.2	140	0.2	0.9	288	0.1	0.5
Tanzania	44.8	1.4	46.2	3,575	1.3	1.3	4,499	1.0	1.0	9,142	0.5	0.5
Togo	3.5	1.5	5.0	532	0.7	0.9	663	0.5	0.8	1,355	0.3	0.4
Uganda	7.5	2.5	10.0	2,677	0.3	0.4	3,360	0.2	0.3	6,822	0.1	0.1
Zaire	22.1	35.0	57.1	5,863	0.4	1.0	7,222	0.3	0.8	14,873	0.1	0.4
Zambia	15.5	1.2	16.7	1,158	1.3	1.4	1,436	1.1	1.2	2,901	0.5	0.6
Zimbabwe	34.0	10.0	44.0	1,476	2.3	3.0	1,822	1.9	2.4	3,697	0.9	1.2

(APPENDIX 4 CONT.)

Country and Region	Security Forces[a] (thousands)			15–44 Year Old Males			Population in 15–64 Year Old Group					
	Armed Forces	Para-military Forces	Total	Thousands[b]	Armed Forces as %	Total Security as %	Males (thousands[b])	Armed Forces as %	Total Security as %	Males and Females (thousands[b])	Armed Forces as %	Total Security as %
ASIA												
Afghanistan	43.0	30.0	73.0	3,478	1.2	2.1	4,480	1.0	1.6	8,385	0.5	0.9
Bangladesh	77.0	66.0	143.0	18,857	0.4	0.8	23,526	0.3	0.6	45,535	0.2	0.3
Burma	179.0	73.0	252.0	7,339	2.4	3.4	10,112	1.8	2.5	19,418	0.9	1.3
China, PR	4,700.0	12,000.0	16,700.0	235,808	2.0	7.1	311,656	1.5	5.4	604,958	0.8	2.8
India	1,104.0	300.0	1,404.0	157,809	0.7	0.9	201,763	0.5	0.7	389,378	0.3	0.4
Indonesia	273.0	82.0	355.0	32,875	0.8	1.1	42,132	0.6	0.8	85,242	0.3	0.4
Kampuchea	20.0	0.0	20.0	1,653	1.2	1.2	2,047	1.0	1.0	4,097	0.5	0.5
Korea, DPR	782.0	38.0	820.0	3,959	19.8	20.7	5,483	14.3	15.0	10,078	7.8	8.1
Korea, Republic of	601.6	—	—	9,604	6.3	—	12,397	4.9	—	23,911	2.5	—
Laos	55.7	0.0	55.7	814	6.8	6.8	1,027	5.4	5.4	2,036	2.7	2.7
Malaysia	102.0	90.0	192.0	3,207	3.2	6.0	3,962	2.6	4.8	7,900	1.3	2.4
Pakistan	450.6	109.1	559.7	18,832	2.4	3.0	23,456	1.9	2.6	45,299	1.0	1.2
Papua New Guinea	3.5	0.0	3.5	600	0.6	0.6	899	0.4	0.4	1,715	0.2	0.2
Philippines	112.8	110.5	223.3	11,189	1.0	2.0	13,723	0.8	1.6	27,219	0.4	0.8
Singapore	42.0	37.5	79.5	649	6.5	12.2	829	5.1	9.6	1,618	2.6	4.9
Sri Lanka	14.8	23.0	37.8	3,479	0.4	1.1	4,545	0.3	0.8	8,810	0.2	0.4
Thailand	238.1	43.5	281.6	10,655	2.2	2.6	13,137	1.8	2.1	26,236	0.9	1.1
Vietnam	1,029.0	70.0	1,099.0	11,690	8.8	9.4	14,129	7.3	7.8	29,366	3.5	3.7

(APPENDIX 4 CONT.)

Country and Region	Security Forces[a] (thousands)			15–44 Year Old Males			Population in 15–64 Year Old Group					
	Armed Forces	Para-military Forces	Total	Thousands[b]	Armed Forces as %	Total Security as %	Males (thousands[b])	Armed Forces as %	Total Security as %	Males and Females (thousands[b])	Armed Forces as %	Total Security as %
LATIN AMERICA												
Central America												
Costa Rica	0.0	2.5	2.5	530	0.0	0.5	650	0.0	0.4	1,294	0.0	0.2
El Salvador	9.8	7.0	16.8	997	1.0	1.7	1,238	0.8	1.4	2,465	0.4	0.7
Guatemala	15.0	3.0	18.0	1,572	1.0	1.1	1,936	0.8	0.9	3,854	0.4	0.5
Honduras	11.2	3.0	14.2	736	1.5	1.9	917	1.2	1.5	1,825	0.6	0.8
Mexico	119.5	0.0	119.5	13,466	0.9	0.9	18,103	0.7	0.7	36,170	0.3	0.3
Nicaragua	6.7	8.0	14.7	558	1.2	2.6	664	1.0	2.2	1,354	0.5	1.1
Panama	4.8	—	—	430	1.1	—	544	0.9	—	1,062	0.5	—
South America												
Argentina	185.5	43.0	228.5	5,960	3.1	3.8	8,607	2.2	2.7	17,133	1.1	1.3
Bolivia	26.6	5.0	31.6	1,144	2.3	2.8	1,495	1.8	2.1	2,967	0.9	1.1
Brazil	272.6	185.0	457.6	27,615	1.0	1.7	34,945	0.8	1.3	69,448	0.4	0.7
Chile	92.0	27.0	119.0	3,655	2.5	3.3	3,409	2.7	3.5	6,884	1.3	1.7
Colombia	70.0	50.0	120.0	5,971	1.2	2.0	7,371	0.9	1.6	14,719	0.5	0.8
Ecuador	38.8	5.8	44.6	1,675	2.3	2.7	2,086	1.9	2.1	4,173	0.9	1.1
Guyana	7.0	5.0	12.0	200	3.5	6.0	248	2.8	4.8	494	1.4	2.4
Paraguay	16.0	4.0	20.0	684	2.3	2.9	845	1.9	2.4	1,706	0.9	1.2
Peru	130.0	25.0	155.0	3,824	3.4	4.1	4,794	2.7	3.2	9,580	1.4	1.6
Uruguay	29.7	1.5	31.2	596	5.0	5.2	903	3.3	3.5	1,828	1.6	1.7
Venezuela	40.8	20.0	60.8	3,946	1.0	1.5	4,295	0.9	1.4	8,601	0.5	0.7

(APPENDIX 4 CONT.)

Country and Region	Security Forces[a] (thousands)			15–44 Year Old Males			Population in 15–64 Year Old Group					
								Males (thousands)			Males and Females (thousands)	
	Armed Forces	Para-military Forces	Total	Thou-sands[b]	Armed Forces as %	Total Security as %	Males (thou-sands[b])	Armed Forces as %	Total Security as %	Males and Females (thou-sands[b])	Armed Forces as %	Total Security as %
Caribbean												
Barbados	0.0	0.7	0.7	62	0.0	1.1	77	0.0	0.9	163	0.0	0.4
Cuba	227.0	18.0	245.0	2,284	9.9	10.7	3,035	7.4	8.1	5,974	3.8	4.1
Dominican Republic	23.0	10.0	33.0	1,295	1.8	2.5	1,573	1.5	2.1	3,116	0.7	1.1
Haiti	7.5	14.9	22.4	1,189	0.6	1.9	1,490	0.5	1.5	3,072	0.2	0.7
Jamaica	4.0	8.2	12.2	433	0.9	2.8	563	0.7	2.2	1,168	0.3	1.1
Trinidad & Tobago	1.3	0.0	1.3	292	0.4	0.4	373	0.3	0.3	729	0.2	0.2

Sources:

1. For demographic data: United Nations, Department of International Economic and Social Affairs, *Demographic Indicators of Countries: Estimates and Projections as Assessed in 1980*, ST/ESA/SER.A/82 (New York: 1982).

2. For security force data: International Institute for Strategic Studies, *The Military Balance 1981/82* (London: IISS, 1982); *Annuaire de l'Afrique et du Moyen Orient 1980: Les Armées et la Défense* (Paris: Groupe Jeune Afrique, 1980); *Defense & Foreign Affairs Handbook* (London: Copley, 1980).

Note: The demographic data used here are projections based on estimates of population size and age structure and may not accurately reflect the 1980 situation in particular countries. Similarly, variations exist in estimates of the size of the armed forces and, especially, the paramilitary forces of some countries. The ratios present here should therefore be considered approximate, rather than precise, indications of the amount of manpower absorbed by the security sector.

[a] Data for 1980 or thereabouts; an attempt has been made to exclude paramilitary groups not permanently mobilized.
[b] Estimates for 1980.

Military Occupational Specialties of the South Korean Army

Occupational Area	Entry Groups	Specialties	Managing Branch
1 Combat	10 Infantry	100 Rifles	Infantry
		103 Infantry Operation Training Men	Infantry
		104 Machine Guns	Infantry
		105 Trench Mortars	Infantry
		106 Unrecoiling Guns	Infantry
		107 Anti-aircraft Fire	Infantry
	11 Engineer	110 Field Operation Engineer	Engineer
		115 Construction Engineer	Engineer
	12 Armor	120 Tank Operation	Armor
		121 Tank Maintenance Men	Armor
		122 Tankgun Maintenance Men	Armor
		125 Tank Signal Maintenance Men	Armor
	13 Field Artillery	130 Fieldguns	Artillery
		133 Fieldgun Operation Intelligence	Artillery
	14 Artillery Skill	141 Pyrotechnics	Artillery
		142 Sound and Flash	Artillery
		144 Artillery Survey	Artillery
	15 Anti-air Artillery	150 Anti-air Guns	Artillery
		155 Anti-air Operation Intelligence	Artillery
	17 Operation of Air Defense Missile	174 Operation of Hawk	Artillery
		176 Operation of Hawk Firing	Artillery
		177 Operation of Nike	Artillery
		179 Nike Firing Control	Artillery
	18 Operation of Air Defense Radar	181 Operation of Air Defense Radar	Artillery
		186 Distributive Installation of Air Defense Firearms	Artillery

Occupational Area	Entry Groups	Specialties	Managing Branch
2 Electronics	22 Air Defense Electronics Maintenance	221 Equipping Hawk Missile	Artillery
		222 Equipping Hawk Electronics	Artillery
		223 Equipping Hawk Fire Regulator	Artillery
		226 Equipping Nike Electronics	Artillery
		227 Equipping Nike Firing Regulator	Artillery
	25 Air Defense Missile Electronic Inducing Equipment maintenance	250 Repair of Electronic Firing Regulator	Ordnance
		251 Repair of Hawk Radar	Ordnance
		252 Repairing Hawk Capturing Radar	Ordnance
		253 Repair of Hawk Chasing Radar	Ordnance
		255 Repair of Nike Firing Regulator	Ordnance
		256 Repair of Nike Capturing Radar	Ordnance
		257 Repair of Nike Chasing Radar	Ordnance
		258 Repair of Nike Inducing Equipment	Ordnance
	28 Electronic Communication Maintenance and Repair	280 Repair of Wireless and Measuring Equipments	Communications
		283 Operation of Transmitter and Carriers	Communications
		285 Repair of Carriers	Communications
		286 Repair of Radars	Communications
		287 Operation of Microwave	Communications
		288 Repair of Microwave	Communications
		289 Repair of Air Defense Listening Equipment	Communications
3 Electricity	30 Repair of Electric Equipment	300 Electricians	Engineer
		301 Operation and Repair of Generators	Engineer
		304 Air Defense Supporting Engineer	Engineer
	36 Repair of Wire Communications	360 Light Installment	Engineer
		361 Heavy Installment	Engineer
		362 Repair of Wire	Engineer

Occupational Area	Entry Groups	Specialties	Managing Branch
		364 Repair of Electric Typewriters	Engineer
4 Repairing	40 Repair of Iron Equipment	401 Welding & R I Equipment	Weapons
		402 Mechanics	Weapons
	42 Repair of Arms	420 Repair of Guns	Weapons
		421 Repair of Field Guns	Weapons
		423 Repair of Turret Guns	Weapons
	43 Machine Repair	432 Repair of Movie Projectors	Communications
		433 Repair of Chemical Equipment	Chemistry
		434 Repair of Machinery	Weapons
		434 Repair of Medical Equipment	Medical Affairs
	44 Logistic Repair	441 Repairs of Clothing and Machinery	Logistics
		442 Repair of Boots and Machinery	Logistics
		443 Repair of Office Machinery	Logistics
		444 Packing and Repair of Parachutes	Logistics
		447 Laundry and Repair of Washing Machines	Logistics
5 Mechanics	50 Construction	501 Carpentry	Engineer
		503 Fire Fighting	Engineer
		504 Water Supply	Engineer
		505 Heating and Refrigerator	Engineer
		506 Plumbing	Engineer
	51 CBR	501 CBR War	Chemistry
		513 CBR Operation Control	Chemistry
	52 Logistical	524 Graves Registration Logistics	Chemistry
		525 Management of Oils	Logistics
	53 Operation of Harbors	531 Operation of Winches	Transportation
		533 Operation of Landingcraft	Transportation
	54 Ammunition	540 Management of Ammunition	Weapons
		542 Repair and Examination of Ammunition	Weapons
		543 Disposition of Ammunition	Weapons

Occupational Area	Entry Groups	Specialties	Managing Branch
6 Vehicles	60 Operation of Engineering Heavy Equipment	601 Operation of Air Compressor	Engineer
		602 Operation of Cranes	Engineer
		603 Tractor Driving	Engineer
		604 Operation of Graders	Engineer
		605 Operation of Smashers	Engineer
		606 Operation of Road Paver	Engineer
		608 Equipment of Engineering Heavy Machines	Engineer
	61 Vehicle Transportation	610 Vehicle Operation	Transportation
		611 Operation of Goods Handling Equipment	Logistics
		618 Equipping Vehicles	Engineer
	62 Repair of Heavy Engineering Equipment	621 Repair of Diesel Engines	Engineer
		622 Repair of Engineering Heavy Equipment	Engineer
	63 Vehicle Repairs	630 Repair of Vehicles	Ordnance
		633 Repair of Tramcars	Ordnance
	66 Repair of Aircrafts	660 Rigging of Aircrafts	Air Transportation
		661 Repair of Aircrafts	Air Transportation
7 Administration	70 General Administration	700 Clerk	Adjutant
		702 Korean Typing	Adjutant
		703 English Typing	Adjutant
		709 Personnel Administration	Adjutant
	71 Communication Administration	711 Telephone Exchange	Communications
		712 Wiretelephone	Communications
		713 Wireless Telegraphy	Communications
		715 Wire & Wireless Typing	Communications
	72 Transportation Administration	721 Management of Transportation Movement	Transportation
		722 Checking and Receiving Freights	Transportation

Occupational Area	Entry Groups	Specialties	Managing Branch
	73 Accounting Administration	730 Accounting Business	Accounting
	74 Legal Administration	740 Judicial Business	Judicial Affairs
	75 Political Information Administration	750 Political Information	Political Information
	76 Logistics Administration	760 Unit Logistics 761 Construction Unit Supplies	Logistics Infantry Munitions
	78 Religious Administration	780 Religions	Chaplain
8 Public Health	80 General Health	801 Barbers 802 Cooking 803 Relief Men	Medical Affairs Logistics Infantry Relief
	81 Medical Affairs 82 Medical Laboratory	810 General Medical Affairs 821 Medical Laboratory 823 X-Ray 824 Pharmacy	Medical Affairs Medical Affairs Medical Affairs Medical Affairs
9 Survey and Drawing	91 Drawing & Survey	911 Survey 913 Drawing	Engineer Engineer
	92 Photography	920 Photographer 921 Recording & Projection	Communications Communications
	93 Printing	930 Book-binding 935 Offset Printing 939 Typeprinting	Adjutant Adjutant Adjutant
0 Special	00 No Skill 01 Military Bands	001 Skill-less Men 010 Signal Bugler 011 Military Band Men	Adjutant Adjutant Adjutant
	05 Military Police 06	050 Military Police 051 Criminal Investigation	Military Police Military Police

Occupational Area	Entry Groups	Specialties	Managing Branch
	Information	060 Battle Information	Infantry Information
		063 Military Information	Infantry Information
	07 Communications Information	070 Cryptograph	Communications
		072 Special Communication Information	Infantry Information
		073 Operation of Secret Code Instruments	Infantry Information
	08 Special Information	081 Intelligence	Infantry Information
		082 Counter-Intelligence	Infantry Information

Source: Labor Education and Research Institute, *Economic Development and Military Technical Manpower of Korea. A Study of Manpower Development in the Military in Korea* (Seoul: Korea University, 1976), pp. 288–92.

420

INDEX

absorptive capacity, xxvi, 106n, 227–36

Aden, 72

Afghanistan: arms transfers to, 110; economic conditions in, 180; Soviet economic aid, 253n, 260–61; Soviet intervention in, 43, 69, 72, 74; Soviet security assistance, 28, 294

Africa: composition of security expenditure, 108n; determinants of security expenditure, 40, 51, 294; economic assistance, 258n, 337; economic conditions in, 176, 182, 184, 231, 239; heritage of colonialism, 228, 229n, 295–97, 328–29, 336–37, 338n, 340; industrial development in, 336–37, 338n, 340, 342, 346; labor-force statistics, 346; military participation rates, 307, 309, 409–11; military training, 307, 308, 331n; political role of armed forces, 16; security assistance, 53, 196, 277, 294, 331n; security expenditure-growth nexus, 127. *See also individual countries*

aggregate demand, role in security expenditure-growth nexus, xxvi, 213–18, 277–81, 293, 332, 389

agricultural development. *See* rural development

Algeria, 75, 360; arms transfers to, xix, 110; determinants of security expenditure, 68; economic conditions in, 179; security assistance, 118; security expenditure-growth nexus, 132n; Soviet economic assistance, 253, 256n

Angola, 27, 73, 179, 254, 322n

Argentina, 78, 338n; arms transfers to, 36; composition of security expenditure, 108n, 109; determinants of security expenditure, 34, 36, 41, 57, 66n, 82; Falklands/Malvinas war, 81; military industry, 358, 359, 360, 364, 367, 373n; political role of the armed forces, 41, 81–82, 330; security expenditure data,

35, 400–401; security expenditure-growth nexus, 124, 132n, 142, 147, 151, 168, 227, 272, 364, 367; UN reporting mechanism, 99

armed forces: civilian control over, 26–27; economic role, 3n, 10–15, 18–31 passim, 132, 141n, 170–72, 227, 233–35, 326, 328, 329–30; political role, xxii–xxiii, xxiv, 3–31 passim, 40–50, 81–82, 213, 226–27, 231–35, 326–30, 390–92; social composition of, 13, 18n. *See also* participation

Arms Control and Disarmament Agency (ACDA), 403–4; arms transfer data, 109, 186, 189; Benoit study, 18n, 124, 130, 134–46, 153–56, 204–5, 215, 238n, 405–8; security expenditure data, xvii, xviii, 4, 47, 85–96 passim, 127–28, 387

arms production. *See* industrial development; military industry; military technology

arms races, 37, 75

arms transfers, 108, 117, 137; and appropriate technology, 79, 82–83; barter agreements, xxi–xxii, 28, 29n, 120–21, 137, 185, 186, 390; confused with security expenditure, 107, 111; contribution to indebtedness, xvii, 172, 185–86, 194–203; data incompleteness, 109–22, 186, 189; economic consequences of, 19–20, 28–30, 76, 106n, 111, 172, 187–203, 204n, 291–92; effects of limits on, 392, 393–94; embargos, 77; regional concentration, 109–10, 196; social and political aspects, 20, 21, 29–30, 194n. *See also individual countries;* offsets

Asia, 108, 243; composition of security expenditure, 273; determinants of security expenditure, 41n, 70; economic assistance, 250; economic conditions in, 176, 182, 183, 239; heritage of colonialism,

expenditure-growth nexus, 132 n, 142, 144, 151, 168, 282, 283 n, 312; UN reporting mechanism, 99; U.S. security assistance, 55, 144, 282, 283 n
colonialism: effect on security expenditure, 69–72; and human capital, 295–98, 339; and industrial development, 335–40; and political development, 228–30, 232, 392; role of force, 18, 19
Comoros, 180
Congo-Brazzaville, 72, 180
corruption: in Burkina Faso, 152 n; in Ghana, 10, 12; in India, 235; in Indonesia, 48, 62–64, 113; in Mexico, 26; in Nigeria, 50; as obstacle to development, xvi, 156, 213, 228, 231–36; as rationale for coups d'état, 11–12, 50, 152 n; in Republic of Korea, 12–13, 235; role of armed forces, 11–13, 16, 62, 81, 113, 232–36, 330; in Thailand, 16, 62–63, 233–36; in Zaire, 235 n
Costa Rica, xxiii; security expenditure-growth nexus, 132 n, 142, 168
coups d'état, 5, 103, 123 n; in Brazil, 21, 65; in Burkina Faso, 152 n; in Burma, 43; in Chile, 21, 65, 74, 78; in the Dominican Republic, 21; economic objectives, 11–12, 21, 25, 43, 66; effect on security expenditure, 64–67, 73–74; in Egypt, 21; in Ghana, 3, 9–10, 12, 25, 66, 67; in Guatemala, 21, 27; in Indonesia, 79; in Kampuchea, 74; in Liberia, 58, 66; in Nigeria, 50, 58, 60; in Peru, 21, 170; political objectives, 21, 24, 27; role of corporate grievances, 12, 25–27, 46; role of ethnicity, 25, 43; in Thailand, 24; in Uganda, 21, 46, 74; in Venezuela, 25–26
Cuba, 42, 72, 322 n; arms transfers to, 110; economic conditions, 180, 265 n; Soviet economic assistance, 254–56, 260, 262; Soviet security assistance, 268–69, 292. See also intervention
Cyprus, 98, 99
Czechoslovakia, arms transfers from, 120, 138

debt, xvi, 174, 178, 181–84, 201–3, 241, 257, 349; contribution of security sector, xvii, 117, 119, 185–86, 194–203, 288, 290, 389. See also individual countries

Deger, Saadet, 127, 131 n, 146 n, 147, 156–57, 205 n
Denmark, 99, 100
disarmament, and development, 97, 102, 104
Djibouti, 72
Dominican Republic, 72, 180; military industry, 359; security expenditure-growth nexus, 132 n, 142, 168. See also coups d'état

East Germany. See German Democratic Republic
economic assistance, 6, 166, 194, 239; from Comecon countries, 253–57, 260–63; consumption vs. investment, 263–64; economic objectives, 246, 251–53, 257–63; from France, 248–49, 252–53, 259, 261, 337; from Great Britain, 248–49, 252–53, 261, 337; impact on growth, 141, 244–45, 259, 276, 288 n; influence on savings rate, 264–66; from Japan, 248–49, 252–53, 261–62, 290; official development assistance (ODA), 245–46, 248–49, 261, 262; from People's Republic of China, 254–55; political objectives, 246, 253, 257–63; role in security expenditure-growth nexus, 135–47 passim, 155–56, 209, 278, 389; from Soviet Union, 253–57, 260–63; tied aid, 253, 261–62, 345; from U.S., 239, 243, 246–53, 261, 267 n, 276, 278, 290, 291; from West Germany, 248–49, 252–53, 261. See also security assistance; trade
economic development, xxiv, 5–7, 165–66, 239, 303; developed country interest in, 239, 258, 263; élite commitment to, 153, 156, 229–36, 259, 263, 282, 292, 293, 298, 390–92; export-oriented strategies, xvi, 14, 19–20, 192–93, 215 n, 220, 222, 225 n, 226 n, 241–42, 257, 259 n, 288 n, 384; objectives of, xv, 5; role of armed forces, 18–19, 26–27, 30, 226 n, 231, 302–3, 391; role of capital, xv, 6, 147, 156, 212, 214, 239–40, 266, 281–82, 292–93, 303, 364; role of direct foreign investment, 242–43, 257; role of export

nology, 355. *See also* economic assistance; intervention; security assistance

Greece, 360; composition of security expenditure, 282–83; economic assistance, 250; security expenditure-growth nexus, 132 n, 140, 142, 144, 200, 282–83; U.S. security assistance, 144, 199–200, 250, 282–83

Grenada, 72, 180

Guatemala, 72, 296; agricultural development, 219 n; security expenditure-growth nexus, 132 n, 142, 151, 168, 208, 312 n, 313. *See also* coups d'état; rural development

Guinea, 132 n, 260

Guinea-Bissau, 180

Guyana, xxiii, 180, 312; composition of security expenditure, 108 n, 400–401; security expenditure data, 91–92, 95–96, 400–401

Haiti, 168

Honduras, 180, 296; security expenditure-growth nexus, 132 n, 142, 168, 332; U.S. security assistance, 198

Hong Kong, 225, 243, 279, 360

human capital: administrative/managerial, xv, xvi, 164, 228, 295, 301, 302, 325–30; colonial heritage, 295–97, 298, 339; competition between civil and military sectors, 310 n, 319–25, 331, 333–34, 368–70, 383–84; developmental requirements, 163–66, 222, 225 n, 228, 239, 245, 298–301, 345, 347–48, 353; employment issues, xvi, 156, 301, 332–34, 347–48, 381; military participation rates, 307–10, 409–14; professional, 295, 297, 298, 300, 350 n; role of security sector, xvii, xxii, xxvi, 122, 146, 148, 162, 238, 259, 301–34, 365–70, 381, 383, 389; technical, 295, 300, 301–307, 310–325, 330–31, 350 n. *See also individual countries;* military training

imports. *See* trade

India, 33, 282; arms transfers from, 382; arms transfers to, xxi, 29, 77, 79, 110, 120, 189; composition of security expenditure, 55, 109, 396–97; determinants

of security expenditure, 37–39, 55–57, 71, 205, 284–85, 294; development expenditure, 102 n, 284; development policies, 265 n; economic conditions in, 183, 215–16, 241, 336, 338–39, 347, 352; heritage of colonialism, 336, 338–39; human capital formation, 296, 300, 311–12, 339, 367, 369; military industry, 62, 189, 355, 356 n, 357–69 passim, 374–82 passim; security assistance, 269, 283–84, 294; security expenditure data, xxi, xxii, 38, 56, 102–3, 111, 120–21, 128, 189, 396–97; security expenditure-growth nexus, 124, 132 n, 142, 149, 151, 154–55, 168, 173, 185, 189, 205–6, 208, 214–16, 273, 284, 288 n, 311–12, 362, 264, 265, 267, 269; Soviet economic assistance, 253, 256 n, 260–63. *See also* corruption; Sino-Indian war

Indonesia, 296; arms transfers to, 79, 114; determinants of security expenditure, 40, 43, 48, 58, 63–64; economic assistance, 253; economic conditions in, 179, 343, 347; economic role of the armed forces, 112–14; military industry, 359, 360, 361, 367; off-budget financing of security sector, 64, 101, 111–14, 119, 122, 128; political role of armed forces, 40, 43, 48, 112–13; security assistance, 144, 199, 250, 269–70; security expenditure-growth nexus, 119, 132 n, 142, 168, 332, 367; UN reporting mechanism, 99–101. *See also* corruption; coups d'état

industrial development, 340–44, 343–44, 384; as base for military production, 14–15, 227, 321 n, 357–64, 369–70, 373–75, 383; colonial heritage, 335–40; consumer goods, 222–25, 227; excess capacity, 184–85, 205 n, 213–14, 216, 226 n, 349, 389; industrialization-first strategies, xvi, 6, 15–16, 219–21, 340, 344, 384; influence of security sector, xvii, 106, 146, 148, 193, 205 n, 217–18, 227, 271; and job creation, 298–300, 335, 341, 342, 344, 345–48; producer goods, 222–25, 227; role in development, xvi, xvii, 6, 7, 218–19, 299, 335–53; use of capital-intensive

savings (*continued*)
  expenditure-growth nexus, 147, 156,
    163–66
security assistance, xxvi, 6–7, 104; definition of, 266–67; donor economic objectives, 251–52, 270; donor political
  objectives; 27, 198, 251–52, 270, 272,
  274, 302; from East Germany, 267; Economic Support Fund and predecessors,
  118, 237, 247–52, 267, 274–75, 278,
  280–82; from France, 54, 75, 196, 267,
  277, 291; grants, xxi, 14, 38, 53–54,
  59, 74–75, 108, 117–19, 136–37, 193,
  196–200, 251–52, 266–70, 277–91
  passim, 294, 390; from Great Britain,
  53, 75, 196, 267, 277, 284; and increased security expenditure, xx, 75–76,
  117–18, 137, 197–98, 283–85, 294;
  loans, xxi, 54, 74–76, 117, 118–19,
  137, 195–200, 267–70, 277–78, 280,
  288–89, 291; as offset to domestic expenditure, 53–54, 108–9, 136–37,
  140, 155, 198, 209, 238, 271, 275,
  281–92, 389; from OPEC countries, 75,
  118–19, 196, 237, 267, 281n, 292;
  from People's Republic of China, 267;
  PL-480, 237, 250, 252, 267, 274–77,
  281, 289, 293; role in development debate, 237–38; role in security expenditure-growth nexus, 136–37, 144–45,
  193–94, 196–210, 209, 238, 271–94,
  302, 332; as source of capital, 271,
  280–92 passim; from the Soviet Union,
  27–28, 75, 117, 137, 145, 196, 267–
  70, 288, 292; from the United States,
  38, 42, 53–54, 75, 117–18, 136–37,
  144, 195, 197–201, 237–38, 246–52,
  267–68, 270–93 passim, 302, 320–21,
  361, 372; from West Germany, 267, 270
security expenditure, xxi, 281; civil-sector
  trade-offs, 324–25; composition of, 29,
  36, 46, 54–55, 57–58, 80, 86, 91–111
  passim, 115–17, 140, 190–92, 211,
  216–17, 282–83, 393, 396–402; constraints on, 42–43, 47–50, 65–68, 78;
  data reliability, xxvi, 4, 85–97, 103–4,
  111–22, 127–29, 388; definition of,
  85–86, 94, 403–4; and job creation,
  332–34; as percent central government
  expenditure (CGE), xxi, xxii, 35, 51–52,
  129n, 282, 387; as percent GDP/GNP,

xxi, xxii, 31, 51–52, 129n; 147, 169,
  282; proposals for reductions in, 97,
  104, 392, 393n; and the provision of security, xxvi, 60, 79–83, 122, 294; regional distribution of, xviii, xix, xx, xxi,
  35, 102–3; role of intelligence agencies,
  87–89; sources of data, 85–97, 106–7;
  statistics, xvii, xviii, xix, xx, xxv, 4, 35,
  39, 47, 49, 53, 67, 93, 96, 150, 169,
  190, 197, 284, 285, 286, 387, 396–
  402; UN reporting mechanism, 97–106.
  See also coups d'état; economic growth,
  individual countries; security expenditure determinants; statistical analyses
security expenditure determinants, xx,
  xxv; bureaucratic factors, 32–33, 57–
  60, 66, 79, 393; corporate factors,
  32–33, 58–64, 66, 78–79, 393; domestic political factors, 54–57, 60–61,
  65–66, 78, 82n, 226, 391; external conflict, 32–40, 70, 73, 77–79, 109–10,
  154, 196, 226, 294, 392–94; internal
  security, 32–33, 40–50, 70, 72–73,
  226, 393; regime type, 64–68, 226,
  391; role of external powers, 32–33,
  68–77, 282–94, 392
Senegal, 99, 149, 347, 359
Seychelles, 179; UN reporting mechanism,
  98, 99
Sierra Leone, 149, 168, 180, 229n,
  398–99
Singapore: arms transfers from, 381; arms
  transfers to, 289n; determinants of security expenditure, 33; economic development, 225, 226n, 243, 296, 334;
  military industry, 356, 359, 360, 367,
  369, 377, 381; security expenditure-
  growth nexus, 132n, 279, 367, 369
Sino-Indian war, 39, 56, 154–55, 205,
  215
Smith, Ron, 127, 131–32, 146n, 147,
  156–57, 205n, 214n
Somalia: arms transfers to, 29; determinants of security expenditure, 70; economic conditions in, 179; intervention
  in, 72, 74; security expenditure-growth
  nexus, 132n
South Africa: arms transfers to, xix; civil
  war, 83; military industry, 354, 359,
  360, 367, 372–73, 374, 375; security
  expenditure-growth nexus, 132n, 142,